境外资本市场重要法律文献译丛 ⑦
欧洲卷

欧盟金融监管体制改革法规汇编

（中英文对照本）

Laws on Reforms to the Supervisory
Structure of the Financial Sector within the European Union

中国证券监督管理委员会　组织编译

法律出版社
LAW PRESS · CHINA

《境外资本市场重要法律文献译丛》

编 委 会

《欧盟金融监管体制改革法规汇编》

致　　谢

深圳证券交易所对本书的出版给予了大力支持！

译者说明

2007~2008 年全球金融危机暴露了欧盟对金融体系的宏观审慎监管和微观审慎监管存在着诸多问题。在宏观审慎监管方面，在欧盟层面上没有一个机构对宏观审慎风险包括源于宏观经济失衡产生的风险进行恰当的分析，微观和宏观审慎分析相互割裂，对金融机构之间的依赖性和关联性认识不足，在金融危机蓄积和发生过程中监管当局缺乏恰当的纠正行动和监管合作。[1] 在微观审慎监管方面，在现有的监管模式下东道国和母国利益不平衡导致了在金融监管尤其是跨境危机管理上各国有不同的积极性和主动性，成员国不同的监管规则和监管实践在一定程度上促使了金融机构产生竞争扭曲和监管套利的风险，成员国监管机构之间监管合作和信息交流不够充分以及分割又不一致的金融监管给跨境金融机构带来了过多的成本和管理负担。[2] 为此，2009 年 9 月欧盟委员会提出了欧盟金融监管体制改革的一系列立法建议，主要内容是设立两个新的机构：一是欧洲系统性风险委员会（European Systemic Risk Board）；二是欧洲金融监管机构体系（European System of Financial Supervisors），分别负责宏观审慎监管和微观审慎监管。欧洲系统性风险委员会负责监管和评估来自宏观经济发展和金融系统内部发展对金融稳定产生的潜在威胁。欧洲金融监管机构体系由成员国金融监管机构和新设的欧洲金融监管机构组成，欧洲金融监管机构由欧洲银行业管理局（European Banking Authority）、欧洲保险与职业养老金管理局（European Insurance and Occupational Pensions Authority）和欧洲证券与市场管理局（European Securities and Markets Authority）组成，它们分别从原先的欧洲银行业监管机构委员会、欧洲保险与职业养老金监管机构委员会和欧洲证券监管机构委员会转变而来。

2010 年 11 月，欧洲议会和欧盟理事会通过相关法律，对欧盟委员会的建议作出了正式的立法确认。这些法令包括：2010 年 11 月 24 日通过的《欧洲议会与欧盟理事会关于欧盟对金融系统的宏观审慎监控以及设立欧洲系统性风险委员会的第 1092/2010 号（欧盟）条例》（以下简称第 1092 号条例）、2010 年 11 月 17 日通过的《欧盟理事会关于赋予欧洲中央银行有关欧洲系统性风险委员会运行方面的特定职责的

1 欧共体委员会：《影响评估报告》，SEC（2009）1234，2009 年 9 月 23 日，第 6 页。

2 同上，第 4 页。

第 1096/2010 号(欧盟)条例》(以下简称第 1096 号条例)、2010 年 11 月 24 日通过的《欧洲议会与欧盟理事会设立欧洲监管机构欧洲银行业管理局并修正第 716/2009/EC 号决定和废止欧盟委员会第 2009/78/EC 号决定的第 1093/2010 号(欧盟)条例》(以下简称第 1093 号条例)、2010 年 11 月 24 日通过的《欧洲议会与欧盟理事会设立欧洲监管机构欧洲保险与职业养老金管理局并修正第 716/2009/EC 号决定和废止欧盟委员会第 2009/79/EC 号决定的第 1094/2010 号(欧盟)条例》(以下简称第 1094 号条例)、2010 年 11 月 24 日通过的《欧洲议会与欧盟理事会设立欧洲监管机构欧洲证券与市场管理局并修正第 716/2009/EC 号决定和废止欧盟委员会第 2009/77/EC 号决定的第 1095/2010 号(欧盟)条例》(以下简称第 1095 号条例)、2010 年 11 月 24 日通过的《欧洲议会与欧盟理事会修正关于欧洲银行业管理局、欧洲保险与职业养老金管理局、欧洲证券与市场管理局等欧洲监管机构权力的第 98/26/EC 号指令、第 2002/87/EC 号指令、第 2003/6/EC 号指令、第 2003/41/EC 号指令、第 2003/71/EC 号指令、第 2004/39/EC 号指令、第 2004/109/EC 号指令、第 2005/60/EC 号指令、第 2006/48/EC 号指令、第 2006/49/EC 号指令和第 2009/65/EC 号指令的第 2010/78/EU 号指令》(以下简称第 2010/78/EU 号指令)。

第 1092 号条例正式设立了独立的欧洲系统性风险委员会,负责对整个欧盟金融系统的宏观审慎监控。欧洲系统性风险委员会的主要职责包括收集和分析信息、识别系统性风险、对重大系统性风险发布预警并提出相应的行动建议、监控对预警和建议所作出的跟进行动、在宏观审慎监管方面与欧洲金融监管机构和国际机构特别是国际货币基金组织、金融稳定委员会以及第三国相关机构予以协调等。从这些法定职责看,立法并没有授予欧洲系统性风险委员会可对成员国采取具有约束力措施的权力。这一方面是考虑到,欧洲系统性风险委员会的法定职责已足够广泛和敏感,再授予其可采取强制性措施的权力可能会过多干预成员国的政策制定;另一方面是考虑到,欧洲系统性风险委员会是一个有声誉的机构,可通过高层次的构成成员的道义权威影响政策制定者和监管机构的行为。但是,尽管欧洲系统性风险委员会对所识别的风险提出的行动建议不具有法定的强制性,收到建议的一方不采取该建议的,必须提供充分的理由,欧洲系统性风险委员会同时会将该情况通知各相关的欧洲监管机构和欧盟理事会。

鉴于欧洲中央银行在宏观审慎问题上的专业知识,第 1096 号条例赋予欧洲中央银行有关欧洲系统性风险委员会运行方面的特定职责,期望欧洲中央银行能为欧盟金融系统的有效宏观审慎监控作出重大贡献。为此,立法要求欧洲中央银行承担欧洲系统性风险委员会秘书处的工作,保障后者的运行有足够的人力和财力资源,向后者提供分析、统计、行政和后勤的支持。

依据第 1093 号条例、第 1094 号条例和第 1095 号条例,欧盟分别设立了欧洲监管机构欧洲银行业管理局、欧洲监管机构欧洲保险与职业养老金管理局和欧洲监管机构欧洲证券与市场管理局(以下统称欧洲金融监管机构)。除了对各监管机构所涉的具体领域作出了特别规定外,这三个条例在结构和内容上基本相同。新设的三个欧洲金融监管机构是具有法人地位的欧盟机构，在各个成员国内享有该成员国国内法律授予法人的民事能力。

在三个条例出台之前，原有的欧洲银行业监管机构委员会、欧洲保险与职业养老金监管机构委员会和欧洲证券监管机构委员会并无实质性的监管权力，只有咨询功能，发布不具有约束力的指引和建议。成员国监管机构对跨境机构的监管虽然可在监管团内进行合作，但一旦出现分歧，欧盟层面没有任何机制予以协调和解决。许多技术性规则由成员国自行制定，各国规则差别甚大；即使通过欧盟立法予以协调，但各成员国在具体适用时常常做法不一。为了消除欧盟金融监管分割又不一致的现状，上述三个条例赋予了新设的欧洲金融监管机构下列职责：起草适用于全欧盟的监管性技术标准和实施性技术标准草案，促进欧盟法律的统一和有效的实施并解决不同成员国监管机构之间的分歧，推动各成员国监管机构之间的职责委托，与欧洲系统性风险委员会紧密合作，组织和开展同行审评，对市场变化进行监控、分析，促进对存款人、投资者、保单持有人等的保护，促进监管团能统一、有效地行使职能，监控、评估和计量系统性风险，制定和协调实施金融机构的恢复和清盘计划。另外，欧洲证券与市场管理局享有直接监管信用评级机构的权力。

上述三个条例并没有改变欧洲金融监管体制的现行格局，即成员国监管机构仍然承担着对金融业的日常监管工作，新的欧洲金融监管机构对成员国监管机构和金融机构并没有直接的监管权。但是，法律规定了例外情形。在出现法定的紧急情况时，欧洲金融监管机构对所涉成员国的监管机构可作出个别决定，要求后者采取必要的行动；如后者未能在规定的时间内采取行动，欧洲金融监管机构可对金融机构作出个别决定，要求其采取必要的行动包括停办业务。对于成员国监管机构未能实施或者疑似以违法方式实施欧盟相关立法或者监管性技术标准和实施性技术标准的，欧洲金融监管机构可自行或者经相关监管机构、欧洲议会、欧盟理事会、欧盟委员会或银行业利益相关者小组的请求对涉嫌违反或不适用欧盟法律的情况进行调查，并在启动调查后向所涉监管机构提出建议，提出后者需采取的行动。所涉监管机构如在规定期限内仍未遵守欧盟法律的，欧盟委员会可发出正式意见，要求所涉监管机构采取必要的行动。如所涉监管机构未在欧盟委员会正式意见所规定的期限内遵守该正式意见，欧洲金融监管机构在符合法定条件下可直接针对金融机构作出个别决定，要求其采取必要的行动以履行其在欧盟法律中的义务。对于不同成员国监管机构之间就跨境监管事宜发生争议的，欧洲金融监管机构有责任予以协调。欧洲金融监管机构按照法定程序就争议作出的决定，对所涉成员国的监管机构具有法定的约束效力。某成员国监管机构未能遵守欧洲金融监管机构决定的，后者可以直接对金融机构作出个别决定，要求其采取必要的行动包括停办业务。

由于新设了上述三个欧洲金融监管机构以及对这些机构的职责作出了新的立法安排，有必要修改相关的欧盟法律。第 2010/78/EU 号指令就是对原有的欧盟指令涉及这三个监管机构有关的事项作出修改。因而，它并没有规定新的内容，只是依据第 1093 号条例、第 1094 号条例和第 1095 号条例就三个监管机构的职责范围、权力等对相关欧盟指令作出了增补、删节、修正。

尽管上述欧盟立法仍然秉承着欧盟立法的辅助性原则，并没有创设具有实质监管权力的欧盟统一金融监管机构，但已经显示出欧盟努力走向金融监管统一化的端倪。这是因为欧盟立法者认为当今金融市场已经变成全欧洲性和全球性的，而不仅仅局限于成员国一国内部，因而对它们的监管也必须是全欧洲性和全球性的。这种立法的基本理念将会深刻影响欧盟金融立法和金融监管的未来走向。从第 1093 号条例、第 1094 号条例和第 1095 号条例看，三个欧洲金融监管机构虽然未被授予对成员国或者金融机构直接的监管权，但在个别特殊情形下（如发生紧急情况或者成员国以违法的方式实施欧盟立法或者监管性和实施性技术标准），它们有权对成员国和金融机构作出决定。对于属于全欧盟性质的机构，立法认为成员国监管机构不可能对其所有活动有全面的了解，应由欧盟统一监管。目前这样的机构虽然只限于信用评级机构，但上述条例为欧盟对类似性质机构实施统一监管预留了进一步立法的空间。

上海财经大学　周仲飞

总译校：

沈四宝，毕业于北京大学法律系，获硕士和学士学位。1981 年赴美国哥伦比亚大学法学院深造，兼备深厚的中西方法学理论基础，尤其在国际商法领域有较高造诣。现任对外经济贸易大学法学院教授、博士研究生导师，上海大学法学院院长，担任教育部社会科学委员会法学部委员、中国国际经济法学研究会会长、中国仲裁法研究会副会长、上海大学仲裁与 ADR 研究院院长，最高人民法院专家咨询员。2006 年获教育部颁发的“国家级教学名师奖”，享受国务院政府特殊津贴。

审校人员：

周仲飞，上海财经大学副校长，法学教授。兼任中国国际经济法学研究会副会长，国际金融法专业委员会主任。毕业于伦敦大学玛丽皇后学院，获法学博士学位。多年从事金融法和国际金融法教学与研究，出版《银行法原理》、《银行法研究》等著作，在《法学研究》等刊物发表论文多篇，主持国家社科课题、教育部重大课题、亚洲开发银行课题。

楼建波，北京大学法学院教授、博士研究生导师。毕业于北京大学，获法学学士学位、硕士学位，英国伦敦大学哲学博士（法律）。中国法学会商法学研究会理事，曾任英国剑桥大学中国商法讲师，负责审校欧盟第 2010/78/EU 号指令以及第 1092/2010 号、第 1093/2010 号、第 1094/2010 号、第 1095/2010 号和第 1096/2010 号条例。

张昕，伦敦大学法学博士，伦敦大学法律硕士（银行与金融法方向），厦门大学国际经济法法学硕士与法学学士，具有中国律师与英格兰及威尔士事务律师资格。曾就职于厦门群贤律师事务所、中国建设银行深圳市分行及英国年利达律师事务所，现就职于北京市环球律师事务所。负责审校欧盟第 2010/78/EU 号指令以及第 1092/2010 号、第 1093/2010 号、第 1094/2010 号、第 1095/2010 号和第 1096/2010 号条例。

翻译人员：

瞿乃明，法国巴黎高等翻译学校翻译学硕士、法国巴黎第九大学国际企业管理硕士、台湾大学经济学学士，北京优笔客翻译中心总经理。主要翻译作品有《欧盟金融工具市场指令》、《中国证监会 2011 年年报》、《美国商品交易法》、《美国证券交易委员会自身组织与通用规章》、《欧盟另类投资基金管理人指令》和《美国多德—弗兰克华尔街改革与消费者保护法》等。

程宇凡，首都经贸大学法律学士，现任某美国律师事务所专职法律翻译。主要翻译作品有《美国证券交易委员会自身组织与通用规章》、《欧盟另类投资基金管理人指令》和《美国多德—弗兰克华尔街改革与消费者保护法》等。

区欣，波兰什切青大学伊拉斯谟世界（Erasmus Mundus）硕士课程班学习欧盟法，中山大学西方哲学硕士，北京优笔客翻译中心专职译者。主要翻译作品有《欧盟证券监管法规汇编》和《美国多德—弗兰克华尔街改革与个人消费者保护法》等。

总　　序

中国资本市场是适应我国经济体制改革和对外开放的形势要求逐步建立发展起来的。为了有效借鉴境外成熟市场的制度经验，中国资本市场从成立伊始，就特别注重按照“立足国情，为我所用”的原则，不断学习、消化和吸收境外成熟市场的运行规则和监管制度。目前，中国资本市场现行有效的法律、法规、规章、规范性文件共521件，加上大量的交易所和协会的自律规则，基本形成了我国资本市场的法律制度规范体系。这些制度规范构建起一整套与国际通行原则基本相符的法律框架、交易规则和监管体系，有效维护了市场秩序，保证了市场功能和作用的发挥，保护了投资者的合法权益。

经过20余年的改革发展，我国资本市场进入了创新发展的新阶段。立足于服务实体经济发展的大局需要，重点解决资本市场自身结构不平衡、服务实体经济能力不足、为居民提供投资理财产品相对匮乏等突出现实问题，资本市场现有的以股票公开发行并在交易所上市交易为主的境内市场体系，将逐步发展成为一个公募与私募并重、股票与债券平衡、场内与场外协调发展的资本市场体系。与此相适应，需要进一步发展壮大财富管理行业，立足于功能监管的制度定位，统一资产管理行为规则，放松行政管制，增强创新活力。实现这样的改革目标，需要我们更加重视学习境外成熟市场的制度经验，充分借鉴境外市场有关私募发行、债权融资、资产管理、期货及衍生品等方面的法律制度，在尊重市场规律的前提下，大胆进行制度和机制创新，确保我们的各项制度适应和满足市场改革的实际需要。

坚持对外开放是中国资本市场改革和发展的一贯方针。在经济全球化深入发展的时代背景下，适应我国经济结构调整和经济方式转变和“逐步实现人民币资本项目可兑换”的金融对外开放的总体要求，中国资本市场必须以更加积极的态度参与全球经济竞争，提高在全球范围内配置资源，服务实体经济发展的能力。不论是支持境内企业到境外发行融资，鼓励境内机构和个人到境外进行证券投资，还是畅通境外企业到境内发行融资渠道，平等保护境外机构和个人到境内进行证券投资，都需要在立足国情的前提下，实现制度衔接互通，消除制度壁垒。特别重要的是，市场竞争首先是制度规则的竞争，增强我国资本市场的国际竞争力，一方面要确保我国市场通过制度规则体现法治环境吸引力，另一方面还要增强我国在涉及资本市场对外开放的国际规则的制定中的话语权,增强我国在国际监管合作和跨境执法合作中的主动权。

同时,我们也注意到,2008 年国际金融危机发生后,境外资本市场对监管体制、机制做了较为重大的调整,提出了不少新的监管要求,出台了不少新的法律文件。例如,美国制定了具有金融综合监管性质的《多德—弗兰克华尔街改革与消费者保护法》,英国则将原来集证券、银行、保险于一身的《2000 年金融服务与市场法》修改成《2010 年金融服务法》。对于境外相关法律制度的动态发展,需要及时掌握情况,借鉴有益经验,为进一步完善我国资本市场的基础性制度建设提供参考。

经过长期的努力,中国资本市场的制度借鉴和引进已经越过了概念化、碎片状的发展阶段,进入全面、系统、精细化的更高阶段。由于种种原因,对境外资本市场法律制度的介绍,无论是在法学界、法律界,还是在证券期货行业内,一直以来都存在及时性不够、系统性不足、权威性不强的情况。特别是翻译介绍的质量不高、精品不多,这在客观上影响了对境外经验的学习和借鉴。

为了适应资本市场学习借鉴境外制度经验的形势要求,中国证监会精选了境外资本市场国家和地区的重要法律文献,包括境外主要资本市场的重要法律、监管部门的监管规则、经典的司法判例、最新的资本市场立法成果以及相关法学理论权威著作等,组织翻译出版了这套《境外资本市场重要法律文献译丛》。译丛的翻译出版工作,在系统单位、部门和关心市场发展的专家学者的共同努力下,紧紧抓住保质量、出精品的关键环节,建立了"竞标择优确定翻译人员、知名专家评审保证翻译质量、适当报酬和学术声誉结合激励"的工作机制,落实"精选译题、精细翻译、精心审校、精致出版"的工作要求,是中国证监会打造国人了解国际资本市场法律制度权威平台的有益尝试。为此,愿以本文向参与丛书翻译、审校的国际金融、法律方面的专家和学者表示感谢,并与大家共勉,共同为建设起一个权利公平、机会公平、规则公平的资本市场而努力。

中国证监会

2013 年 2 月

序

当今世界，经济全球化、政治多极化、信息网络化正在深刻地影响着世界历史的进程。经济全球化，作为正在改变全球社会面貌的基础，其核心内容就是通过各国国内市场和国际市场的逐步统一来使世界生产要素进行全球化的优化配置。而这种统一和配置是通过市场背后的法律规范的逐步统一来实施的，因此国际经济全球化带给各国法律领域的重要任务就是要求各国法律的日益趋同化。所谓趋同化，是指各国在维护其核心利益的前提下，尽量与更能反映经济发展规律的公约、国际惯例或更发达的国家和地区的较先进的法律逐步保持一致的过程。因此，了解和熟悉国际经济法和各发达国家的法律及其法律规范，成了深度介入经济全球化的我国法学界必须承担的历史任务。

由我参与校对的《欧盟金融监管体制改革法规汇编》是欧盟数十年来的金融实践经验的总结，也是整合欧洲金融工具市场的尝试。从一定意义上来说，它们又是与美国激烈竞争的产物。因此，无论从哪个角度讲，该书的出版对我国金融业的法制建设都将产生较大的启迪作用。

至于欧盟通过的《欧盟金融监管体制改革法规》在实际中的效用，只能通过其实施的结果来检验。但是，这一系列的法案生不逢时，它们出台之际正值由华尔街次贷危机引发的金融海啸之时，它们出台不久，欧洲金融市场如醉汉一样无力控制自己，金融危机在欧盟内部四处蔓延，欧盟重要国家的机构信用评级出现了普遍性下调。由此可见，再好的法律规范在猛烈的经济衰退面前，也只能望洋兴叹。

20 世纪 60 年代中期，我考入北京大学法律系，从那之后就进入了法律圈而不可自拔。屈指一算，竟要接近半个世纪了。我一直对公司法和证券法情有独钟：早在 80 年代初就翻译出版了“美国标准公司法”；1984 年又出版了全国第一部较全面系统介绍西方国家公司法的“西方国家公司法原理”；90 年代初，又参与了全国股份制实践，以后又参加了我国公司法的起草和修订。在公司法领域多年的教学科研和实践告诉我一个真理，即“法律的真谛是实践”：法律规定得再全面、再完善，如果没有实践，它们仍然是没有经过检验也没有效用的一堆废纸；只有通过实践，才能使其产生效用和不断发展。我相信，现在翻译出版的一系列“法案”，通过实践的检验，一定会对我国金融立法产生较大影响。

此译本是经过多位学者、专家和教授共同辛苦劳动的结晶，作为终审者，我只是对已经栽培成功的一朵鲜花进行了微不足道的修饰而已，它的成功出版必定要归功于为此作出无私劳动的各位同人，尤其是年轻有为的国际金融法专家周仲飞教授！

同时，我还要特别感谢我的助手程华儿法学博士为此做出的努力！

沈四宝

2013年7月

CONTENTS

目　录

DIRECTIVE 2010/78/EU OF THE EUROPEAN PARLIAMENT AND OF THE COUNCIL

欧洲议会与欧盟理事会第 2010/78/EU 号指令

DIRECTIVE 2010/78/EU OF THE EUROPEAN PARLIAMENT AND OF THE COUNCIL

of 24 November 2010

amending Directives 98/26/EC, 2002/87/EC, 2003/6/EC, 2003/41/EC, 2003/71/EC, 2004/39/EC, 2004/109/EC, 2005/60/EC, 2006/48/EC, 2006/49/EC and 2009/65/EC in respect of the powers of the European Supervisory Authority (European Banking Authority), the European Supervisory Authority (European Insurance and Occupational Pensions Authority) and the European Supervisory Authority (European Securities and Markets Authority)(Text with EEA relevance)

THE EUROPEAN PARLIAMENT AND THE COUNCIL OF THE EUROPEAN UNION,

Having regard to the Treaty on the Functioning of the European Union, and in particular Article 50, Article 53(1) and Articles 62 and 114 thereof,

Having regard to the proposal from the European Commission,

Having regard to the opinion of the European Central Bank[1],

Having regard to the opinion of the European Economic and Social Committee[2],

Acting in accordance with the ordinary legislative procedure[3],

Whereas:

(1) The financial crisis in 2007 and 2008 exposed important shortcomings in financial supervision, both in particular cases and in relation to the financial system as a whole. Nationally based supervisory models have lagged behind financial globalisation and the integrated and interconnected reality of European financial markets, in which many financial institutions operate across borders. The crisis exposed shortcomings in the areas of cooperation, coordination, consistent application of Union law and trust between national competent authorities.

---

1 Opinion of 18 March 2010(OJ C 87, 1. 4. 2010, p. 1).

2 Opinion of 18 March 2010(not yet published in the Official Journal).

3 Position of the European Parliament of 22 September 2010(not yet published in the Official Journal) and decision of the Council of 17 November 2010.

欧洲议会与欧盟理事会第2010/78/EU号指令

[本指令于2010年11月24日通过
修正关于欧洲监管机构(欧洲银行业管理局、欧洲保险与职业养老金管理局、
欧洲证券与市场管理局等)权力的第98/26/EC号指令、第2002/87/EC号指令、
第2003/6/EC号指令、第2003/41/EC号指令、第2003/71/EC号指令、第2004/39/EC号指令、
第2004/109/EC号指令、第2005/60/EC号指令、第2006/48/EC号指令、
第2006/49/EC号指令和第2009/65/EC号指令](欧洲经济区适用文本)

欧洲议会和欧盟理事会,

根据《欧洲联盟运行条约》,特别是其中的第50条、第53条第1款、第62条和第114条,

根据欧盟委员会的提案,

根据欧洲中央银行的意见[1],

根据欧洲经济与社会委员会的意见[2],

依照正常的立法程序[3],

鉴于下列情形,通过本指令:

(1)2007年和2008年的金融危机暴露出金融监管的重要缺陷,不论就特殊事例而言抑或就金融系统整体而言。局限于国家这一层级的监管模式已落后于金融全球化的步伐,亦无法适应众多金融机构已实现跨境运营的欧洲金融市场在一体化和相互关联方面的现实态势。危机暴露出的问题体现在国家级主管部门之间的合作与协调不够、欧盟法律适用一致性的缺乏及相互信任的不足这几个方面。

---

1 2010年3月18日的意见(2010年4月1日《欧盟公报》C 87,第1页)。

2 2010年3月18日的意见(尚未在《欧盟公报》公布)。

3 2010年9月22日欧洲议会立场(尚未在《欧盟公报》公布)以及2010年11月17日欧盟理事会决定。

(2) In several resolutions before and during the financial crisis, the European Parliament has called for a move towards more integrated European supervision, in order to ensure a true level playing field for all actors at Union level and reflect the increasing integration of financial markets in the Union (in its resolutions of 13 April 2000 on the Commission communication on implementing the framework for financial markets: Action Plan, of 21 November 2002 on prudential supervision rules in the European Union, of 11 July 2007 on financial services policy(2005 to 2010) White Paper, of 23 September 2008 with recommendations to the Commission on hedge funds and private equity, and of 9 October 2008 with recommendations to the Commission on Lamfalussy follow-up: future structure of supervision, and in its positions of 22 April 2009 on the amended proposal for a directive of the European Parliament and of the Council on the taking-up and pursuit of the business of Insurance and Reinsurance(Solvency Ⅱ) and of 23 April 2009 on the proposal for a regulation of the European Parliament and of the Council on Credit Rating Agencies).

(3) In November 2008, the Commission mandated a High-Level Group chaired by Jacques de Larosière to make recommendations on how to strengthen European supervisory arrangements with a view to better protecting the citizen and rebuilding trust in the financial system. In its final report presented on 25 February 2009(the 'de Larosière Report'), the High-Level Group recommended that the supervisory framework be strengthened to reduce the risk and severity of future financial crises. It recommended far-reaching reforms to the supervisory structure of the financial sector within the Union. The de Larosière Report also recommended that a European System of Financial Supervisors(ESFS) be created, comprising three European Supervisory Authorities (ESA)-one for each of the banking, the securities and the insurance and occupational pensions sectors-and a European Systemic Risk Council.

(4) In its Communication of 4 March 2009 entitled 'Driving European Recovery', the Commission proposed to put forward draft legislation creating the ESFS and in its Communication of 27 May 2009 entitled 'European Financial Supervision', it provided more details of the possible architecture of that new supervisory framework.

(5) In its conclusions following its meeting on 18 and 19 June 2009, the European Council recommended that a European System of Financial Supervisors, comprising three new ESA, be established. The system should be aimed at upgrading the quality and consistency of national supervision, strengthening oversight of cross-border groups, establishing a

(2)欧洲议会在金融危机发生前及其持续期间通过数项决议呼吁进一步整合欧洲的金融监管，以便确保能在欧盟这一层级为所有市场主体提供真正公平的竞争环境,并反映欧盟金融市场不断一体化的现实[参见欧洲议会2000年4月13日关于欧盟委员会通报《落实金融市场框架:行动计划》的决议、2002年11月21日关于欧盟审慎监管规则的决议、2007年7月11日关于《2005年至2010年金融服务政策白皮书》的决议、2008年9月23日关于对冲基金和私募股权的决议（含向欧盟委员会提出的建议)、2008年10月9日关于《莱姆法路西的后续行动:未来监管结构》的决议(含向欧盟委员会提出的建议)、2009年4月22日对《欧洲议会与欧盟理事会关于开办和经营保险与再保险业务的指令》(保险偿付能力标准Ⅱ)修正稿提案所持立场以及2009年4月23日对《欧洲议会与欧盟理事会关于信用评级机构的条例》提案所持立场]。

(3)2008年11月,欧盟委员会委托一个由雅克·德·拉罗西埃领导的高级工作组,就如何加强欧洲监管安排以更好地保护公众利益并重建公众对金融系统的信任提出建议。在其于2009年2月25日提交的最终报告(《德·拉罗西埃报告》)中,高级工作组建强化监管框架以降低未来出现金融危机的风险及其严重程度,并建议对欧盟金融行业的监管结构实行意义深远的改革。该小组还建议成立欧洲金融监管机构体系(ESFS)[1],该体系应由银行、证券以及保险与职业养老金三大金融行业的欧洲监管机构(ESA)组成,并建议创设一个欧洲系统性风险理事会。[2]

(4)在2009年3月4日名为《推动欧洲复苏》的通报中,欧盟委员会提议起草相关立法草案以创建欧洲金融监管体系,并在2009年5月27日名为《欧洲金融监管》的通报中提供了该新监管框架可能之架构的更多细节。

(5)在2009年6月18日和19日的会后结论中,欧洲理事会建议设立一个由三个新的

1 “ESFS”在正文中有时为“European System of Financial Supervision”,有时为“European system of financial supervision”(除了 European 之外,其他词语以小写形式出现)简称,有时作 European System of Financial Supervisors 的简称,疑为笔误,即使在同一条例的不同段落中(如两个紧邻的段落)也出现了不统一的情况,或者,在不同条例的类似段落中出现不统一的情况。译者将“European System of Financial Supervision”译为欧洲金融监管体系,将“European System of Financial Supervisors”译为欧洲金融监管机构体系,仅以缩写方式出现时,根据上文采用的译法相应处理,但是由于有的条例中,“Supervision”和“Supervisors”并存,只能尽量统一。——译者注

2 英文表述疑误,与第 1093/2010 号(欧盟)条例、第 1094/2010 号(欧盟)条例、第 1095/2010 号(欧盟)条例中的类似表述比较:“The group also concluded that a European System of Financial Supervisors should be created, comprising three European Supervisory Authorities, one for the banking sector, one for the securities sector and one for the insurance and occupational pensions sector, and recommended the creation of a European Systemic Risk Council.”, 在 “a European Systemic Risk Council”之前少了“and recommended the creation of”,已在译文中补正。——译者注

European single rulebook applicable to all financial institutions in the internal market. It emphasised that the ESA should also have supervisory powers for credit rating agencies and invited the Commission to prepare concrete proposals on how the ESFS could play a strong role in crisis situations.

(6) On 23 September 2009, the Commission adopted proposals for three regulations establishing the ESFS including the creation of the three ESA.

(7) In order for the ESFS to work effectively, changes to legal acts of the Union in the field of operation of the three ESA are necessary. Such changes concern the definition of the scope of certain powers of the ESA, the integration of certain powers established in legal acts of the Union, and amendments to ensure a smooth and effective functioning of the ESA in the context of the ESFS.

(8) The establishment of the three ESA should be accompanied by the development of a single rulebook to ensure consistent harmonisation and uniform application and thus contribute to a more effective functioning of the internal market.

(9) The regulations establishing the ESFS provide that, in the areas specifically set out in the relevant legislation, the ESA may develop draft technical standards, to be submitted to the Commission for adoption in accordance with Articles 290 and 291 of the Treaty on the Functioning of the European Union (TFEU) by means of delegated or implementing acts. This Directive should identify a first set of such areas and should be without prejudice to adding further areas in the future.

(10) The relevant legislation should define those areas where the ESA are empowered to develop draft technical standards and how they should be adopted. The relevant legislation should lay down the elements, conditions and specifications as detailed in Article 290 TFEU in the case of delegated acts.

(11) The identification of areas for technical standards should strike an appropriate balance between building a single set of harmonised rules and avoiding unduly complicated regulation and enforcement. The only areas selected should be those in which consistent technical rules will contribute significantly and effectively to the achievement of the objectives of the relevant legislation, while ensuring that policy decisions are taken by the European Parliament, the Council and the Commission in accordance with their usual procedures.

(12) Matters subject to technical standards should be genuinely technical, where their development requires the expertise of supervisory experts. The technical standards adopted as delegated acts should further develop, specify and determine the conditions for consistent harmonisation of the rules included in basic instruments adopted by the European Parliament and the Council, supplementing or amending certain non-essential

欧洲监管机构组成的欧洲金融监管机构体系。该体系旨在改善国家级监管工作的质量和一致性、加强对跨境集团的监控、建立适用于欧盟内部市场所有金融机构的欧洲单一规则手册。欧洲理事会还强调了欧洲监管机构对信用评级机构的监管权，并要求欧盟委员会针对欧洲金融监管机构体系在危机情况下如何发挥强有力作用制定具体的提案。

(6)2009年9月23日，欧盟委员会通过了三项旨在建立欧洲金融监管体系(包括创建三个欧洲监管机构)的条例的提案。

(7)为使欧洲金融监管体系有效运行，有必要对规制上述三个欧洲监管机构运作的欧盟立法进行修改。修改应涉及三个欧洲监管机构某些权力范围的界定、欧盟立法中确立的某些权力的整合，并为确保该等欧洲监管机构在欧洲金融监管体系中平稳有效的运行作出必要的调整。

(8)设立上述三个欧洲监管机构的同时，应制定单一规则手册以确保规则的一致协调和统一适用，从而促进欧盟内部市场更加有效地运行。

(9)设立欧洲金融监管体系的条例规定，在相关立法具体列明的领域中，欧洲监管机构可起草技术标准草案，呈报欧盟委员会根据《欧洲联盟运行条约》(TFEU)第290条和第291条以授权立法或实施性立法的形式通过。本指令将初步列出此类领域，但该等列举并不妨碍以后根据需要而增加其他的领域。

(10)相关立法应对欧洲监管机构有权起草技术标准草案的领域以及通过该等草案的方式作出界定。技术标准以授权立法的形式通过的，相关立法应当就《欧洲联盟运行条约》第290条详述的要素、条件和规范作出规定。

(11)确定欧洲监管机构有权起草技术标准草案的领域时，应尽力建立单一的协调一致的规则，同时也应避免过于复杂的监管和执法程序，力求实现两者之间的平衡。只有当一致的技术规则对于实现相关立法目的能起显著有效作用，并且不影响欧洲议会、欧盟理事会以及欧盟委员会的政策制定权时，才可作出在所涉领域制定技术规则的选择。

(12)受技术标准约束的事项其性质应当属于真正的技术性问题，并且制定技术标准时应有来自监管机构具备专门知识的专家参与。欧洲议会和欧盟理事会通过的基本法律文件所含规则应在何等条件下进行统一协调，以授权立法形式通过的技术标准应对此作出进一步阐述、说明和确定，以补充或修正框架立法中的某些非基本要素。以实施性立法形式通过的技术标准则应确立具有法律约束力的欧盟文件统一适

elements of the legislative act. The technical standards adopted as implementing acts should set conditions for the uniform application of legally binding Union acts. Technical standards should not involve policy choices.

(13) In the case of regulatory technical standards it is appropriate to introduce the procedure provided for in Articles 10 to 14 of Regulation (EU) No 1093/2010 of the European Parliament and of the Council of 24 November 2010 establishing a European Supervisory Authority (European Banking Authority)[1], of Regulation (EU) No 1094/2010 of the European Parliament and of the Council of 24 November 2010 establishing a European Supervisory Authority (European Insurance and Occupational Pensions Authority)[2] and of Regulation (EU) No 1095/2010 of the European Parliament and of the Council of 24 November 2010 establishing a European Supervisory Authority (European Securities and Markets Authority)[3], respectively. Implementing technical standards should be adopted in accordance with the procedure provided for in Article 15 of Regulation (EU) No 1093/2010, of Regulation (EU) No 1094/2010 and of Regulation (EU) No 1095/2010, respectively. The European Council endorsed the four-level 'Lamfalussy' approach to make the regulatory process for Union financial legislation more efficient and transparent. The Commission is empowered to adopt level-2 measures in many areas, and a large number of level-2 Commission regulations and directives are in force. In cases where the regulatory technical standards are designed to further develop, specify or determine the conditions of application of such level-2 measures, they should be adopted only once the relevant level-2 measures have been adopted and should be compatible with that level-2 measure.

(14) Binding technical standards contribute to a single rulebook for financial services legislation as endorsed by the European Council in its conclusions of June 2009. To the extent that certain requirements in Union legislative acts are not fully harmonised, and in accordance with the precautionary principle on supervision, binding technical standards developing, specifying or determining the conditions of application for those requirements should not prevent Member States from requiring additional information or imposing more stringent requirements. Technical standards should therefore allow Member States to do so in specific areas, when those legislative acts provide for such discretion.

1 See page 12 of this Official Journal.

2 See page 48 of this Official Journal.

3 See page 84 of this Official Journal.

用的条件。技术标准不得涉及政策选择。[1]

（13）就监管性技术标准而言，有必要出台下列各项条例第10条至第14条规定的程序：《欧洲议会与欧盟理事会设立欧洲监管机构欧洲银行业管理局的第1093/2010号（欧盟）条例》[2]（2010年11月24日）、《欧洲议会与欧盟理事会设立欧洲监管机构欧洲保险与职业养老金管理局的第1094/2010号（欧盟）条例》[3]（2010年11月24日）以及《欧洲议会与欧盟理事会设立欧洲监管机构欧洲证券与市场管理局的第1095/2010号（欧盟）条例》[4]（2010年11月24日）。应依照第1093/2010号（欧盟）条例、第1094/2010号（欧盟）条例以及第1095/2010号（欧盟）条例第15条规定的程序制定实施性技术标准。欧洲理事会已经同意并支持"莱姆法路西"四级立法程序，以保证欧盟金融领域立法的监管程序更高的效率和透明度。在许多领域，欧盟委员会都有权通过第二级的细则，大量属于第二级细则的欧盟委员会条例和指令已经生效。监管性技术标准旨在进一步阐述、说明或确定第二级细则的适用条件的，在相关的第二级细则通过后该等技术标准才能获得通过，并且技术标准应与第二级细则保持一致。

（14）正如欧洲理事会2009年6月的结论中所认可的，有法律约束力的技术标准有助于推动金融服务立法的单一规则手册的形成。在欧盟框架立法中的某些要求尚未达到完全协调一致的情形下，根据监管的预防性原则，具有法律约束力的技术标准即使阐述、说明或确定了该等要求的适用条件，也不得妨碍各成员国要求提供额外的信息或施加更为严格的要求。因此，当该等框架立法规定了该等自由裁量权时，技术标准应允许各成员国在特定的领域要求提供额外的信息或施加更为严格的要求。

---

1 《里斯本条约》区分了框架立法和非框架立法，框架立法包括指令、条例和决定。条例通过后即可对所有成员国强制执行，而指令则为成员国指定一个目标，要求各成员国在规定期限内按其自行选择的方式来实现该目标，因此指令首先要转化为成员国国内法。非框架立法包括授权立法、实施性立法、建议和意见等。为便于欧盟立法在欧盟范围内的统一适用，欧盟委员会被授予根据欧洲监管机构起草的监管性技术标准和实施性技术标准草案分别通过授权立法和实施性立法的权力。授权立法对框架立法的非基本要素进行补充和修正，其中主要针对一些敏感问题，如就金融服务条例以及是否在机场使用人体扫描仪此类问题作出更详细具体的规定，实施性立法则为欧盟立法的统一适用设定条件，其处理的问题相对较为常规，例如如何实施欧盟共同农业政策、欧盟项目的资金和授予资金和补助等。——译者注

2 请见本《欧盟公报》，第12页。

3 请见本《欧盟公报》，第48页。

4 请见本《欧盟公报》，第84页。

(15) As set out in the regulations establishing the ESFS, before submitting the technical standards to the Commission, the ESA should, where appropriate, conduct open public consultations relating thereto and analyse the potential related costs and benefits.

(16) It should be possible for technical standards to provide for transitional measures subject to adequate deadlines, if the costs of immediate implementation would be excessive compared to the benefits involved.

(17) The regulations establishing the ESFS provide for a mechanism to settle disagreements between national competent authorities. Where a competent authority disagrees with the procedure or content of an action or inaction by another competent authority in areas specified in legal acts of the Union in accordance with Regulation (EU) No 1093/2010, Regulation (EU) No 1094/2010 and Regulation (EU) No 1095/2010, where the relevant legislation requires cooperation, coordination or joint decision-making by national competent authorities from more than one Member State, the ESA, at the request of one of the competent authorities concerned, should be able to assist the authorities in reaching an agreement within the time limit set by the ESA which should take into account any relevant time limits in the relevant legislation, and the urgency and complexity of the disagreement. In the event that such disagreement persists, the ESA should be able to settle the matter.

(18) The regulations establishing the ESA require that the cases where the mechanism to settle disagreements between national competent authorities may be applied are to be specified in the sectoral legislation. This Directive should identify a first set of such cases and should be without prejudice to adding further cases in the future. This Directive should not prevent the ESA from acting in accordance with other powers or fulfilling tasks specified in their establishing regulations, including non-binding mediation and contributing to the consistent, efficient and effective application of legal acts of the Union. Moreover, in those areas where some form of non-binding mediation is already established in the relevant legal act, or where there are time limits for joint decisions to be taken by one or more national competent authorities, amendments are needed to ensure clarity and minimum disruption of the process for reaching a joint decision, but also that where necessary, the ESA should be able to resolve disagreements. The binding procedure for the settlement of disagreements is designed to solve situations where national competent authorities cannot resolve, among themselves, procedural or substantive issues relating to compliance with legal acts of the Union.

(19) This Directive should therefore identify situations in which a procedural or a substantive issue of compliance with Union law needs to be resolved and the national competent authorities are not able to resolve the matter on their own. In such a situation, one of the national competent authorities concerned should be able to raise the issue with

(15)根据设立欧洲金融监管体系的相关条例规定,在向欧盟委员会呈报技术标准前,欧洲监管机构在可能的情形下应就技术标准公开征求公众意见,并对潜在的相关成本和收益进行分析。

(16)立即实施技术标准的成本相对于其所能带来的收益而言过高的,可制定过渡规定,但应给出适当的实施期限。

(17)设立欧洲金融监管体系的条例确立了解决各国家级主管部门之间分歧的机制。根据第1093/2010号(欧盟)条例、第1094/2010号(欧盟)条例以及第1095/2010号(欧盟)条例,某主管部门对另一主管部门在欧盟立法指定领域采取行动或不采取行动依据的程序或相关内容有异议,且相关立法要求多个成员国的国家级主管部门合作、协作或共同决策的,经其中一个所涉主管部门请求,欧洲监管机构应能协助各主管部门在其所设定的时限内达成一致,欧洲监管机构在设定该时限时应考虑到相关立法规定的任何相关时限以及该项分歧的紧迫和复杂程度。时限过后仍然存在分歧的,欧洲监管机构应能对该问题作出决断。

(18)设立欧洲监管机构的条例要求行业立法具体说明在何等情形下可以利用国家级主管部门间的分歧解决机制。本指令应初步列出此类情形,并且不影响未来增加其他情形。本指令不应妨碍欧洲监管机构行使各个机构的设立条例所授予的其他权力或履行该等条例所赋予的职责,包括进行无法律约束力的调解以及推动欧盟立法一致的且兼具效率和成效的适用。此外,在相关立法已经建立某种形式的无法律约束力调解机制的领域,或在已对一个或多个国家级主管部门的共同决策程序设定了时限的领域,相关立法需要作出修正,以确保达成共同决策的程序明确清晰并且尽可能不受干扰;但是在必要时,欧洲监管机构应有能力解决分歧。设置具有约束力的解决分歧程序的目的是在各国家级主管部门无法解决彼此之间发生的与遵守欧盟立法有关的程序性或实体性问题时,提供一种解决方式。

(19)因此,本指令应指明在何等情形下需要解决关于欧盟法律是否得到遵守的程序性或实体性问题,该等问题应当是各国家级主管部门无法自行解决的,并且在该等情形下,任何一个所涉国家级主管部门都应能向所涉欧洲监管机构提出有关问题,该欧洲监管机构则应根据其自身的设立条例以及本指令处理。所涉欧洲监管机构应

the European Supervisory Authority concerned. That European Supervisory Authority should act in accordance with its establishing regulation and with this Directive. The European Supervisory Authority concerned should be able to require the competent authorities concerned to take specific action or to refrain from action in order to settle the matter and to ensure compliance with Union law, with binding effects on the competent authorities concerned. In cases where the relevant legal act of the Union confers discretion on Member States, decisions taken by a European Supervisory Authority should not replace the exercise of discretion by the competent authorities in compliance with Union law.

(20) Directive 2006/48/EC of the European Parliament and of the Council of 14 June 2006 relating to the taking up and pursuit of the business of credit institutions[1] provides for mediation or joint decisions as regards the determination of significant branches for the purposes of supervisory college membership, model validation and group risk assessment. In all of those areas, amendments should clearly state that in the event of disagreement during a specified time period, the European Supervisory Authority (European Banking Authority) may resolve the disagreement using the process outlined in Regulation (EU) No 1093/2010. That approach makes it clear that, while the European Supervisory Authority (European Banking Authority) should not replace the exercise of discretion by the competent authorities in compliance with Union law, it should be possible for disagreements to be resolved and cooperation to be strengthened before a final decision is taken or issued to an institution.

(21) In order to ensure a smooth transition of the current tasks of the Committee of European Banking Supervisors, the Committee of European Insurance and Occupational Pensions Supervisors and the Committee of European Securities Regulators to the new ESA, references to those Committees should be replaced in the relevant legislation with references to the European Supervisory Authority (European Banking Authority), the European Supervisory Authority (European Insurance and Occupational Pensions Authority) and the European Supervisory Authority (European Securities and Markets Authority), respectively.

(22) In order to give full effect to the new framework provided for in the TFEU, it is necessary to adapt and replace the implementing powers designed under Article 202 of the Treaty establishing the European Community (EC Treaty) with the appropriate provisions in accordance with Articles 290 and 291 TFEU. That review should be finalised within 3 years from the entry into force of the Treaty of Lisbon and the remaining powers conferred under Article 202 EC Treaty should cease to apply on that date.

1 OJ L 177, 30. 6. 2006, p. 1.

有权通过要求所涉主管部门采取特定行动或不采取行动的方式解决有关事宜并确保欧盟法律得到遵守，此等要求应对所涉主管部门具有约束力。对于欧盟相关立法授予成员国自由裁量权的情形，欧洲监管机构作出的决定不应取代成员国主管部门依欧盟法律行使自由裁量权。

（20）《欧洲议会与欧盟理事会关于开办和经营信贷机构业务的第2006/48/EC号指令》[1]（2006年6月14日）规定，在涉及监管团成员资格、模型验证以及集团风险评估时，可以采取调解或共同决策的方式判定哪些分支机构属于重要的分支机构。上述各领域的法律修正应明文规定，在分歧持续的一定期限内，欧洲监管机构欧洲银行业管理局可以根据第1093/2010号（欧盟）条例所列程序解决分歧。该等程序清楚表明，虽然欧洲监管机构欧洲银行业管理局的介入不应取代国家级主管部门依欧盟法律行使自由裁量权，但在国家级主管部门作出或向任一机构颁布最终决定之前，应当提供解决分歧并促进合作的机会。

（21）为确保欧洲银行业监管机构委员会、欧洲保险与职业养老金监管机构委员会以及欧洲证券监管机构委员会的现有职能顺利转移给新欧洲监管机构，相关立法提及上述委员会时应分别将其表述为欧洲监管机构欧洲银行业管理局、欧洲监管机构欧洲保险与职业养老金管理局以及欧洲监管机构欧洲证券与市场管理局。

（22）为使《欧洲联盟运行条约》确立的新框架全面生效，有必要根据《欧洲联盟运行条约》第290条和第291条的规定，对《欧洲共同体条约》（《欧共体条约》）第202条设定的实施权进行调整并替之以适当的规定。该项审评工作应于《里斯本条约》生效后3年内完成，《欧共体条约》第202条授予的其他权力应自该期限届满后停止适用。

1 2006年6月30日《欧盟公报》L 177，第1页。

(23) The alignment of committee procedures to the TFEU and, in particular, to Articles 290 and 291 thereof, should be effected on a case-by-case basis. In order to take account of the technical developments in the financial markets and to specify the requirements laid down in the directives amended by this Directive, the Commission should be empowered to adopt delegated acts in accordance with Article 290 TFEU.

(24) The European Parliament and the Council should have 3 months from the date of notification to object to a delegated act. At the initiative of the European Parliament or the Council, it should be possible to prolong that period by 3 months in regard to significant areas of concern. It should also be possible for the European Parliament and the Council to inform the other institutions of their intention not to raise objections. Such early approval of delegated acts is particularly appropriate when deadlines need to be met, for example where there are timetables in the basic act for the Commission to adopt delegated acts.

(25) In the Declaration (No 39) on Article 290 TFEU, annexed to the Final Act of the Intergovernmental Conference which adopted the Treaty of Lisbon, the Conference took note of the Commission's intention to continue to consult experts appointed by the Member States in the preparation of draft delegated acts in the financial services area, in accordance with its established practice.

(26) The new supervisory architecture established by the ESFS will require national competent authorities to cooperate closely with the ESA. Amendments to the relevant legislation should ensure there are no legal obstacles to the information sharing obligations included in the regulations establishing the ESA.

(27) Information transmitted to or exchanged between competent authorities and the ESA or the ESRB should be covered by the obligation of professional secrecy, to which the persons employed or formerly employed by the competent authorities receiving the information are subject.

(28) The regulations establishing the ESA provide that they may develop contacts with supervisory authorities from third countries and assist in preparing equivalence decisions pertaining to supervisory regimes in third countries. Directive 2004/39/EC of the European Parliament and of the Council of 21 April 2004 on markets in financial instruments[1] and Directive 2006/48/EC should be amended to allow the ESA to establish cooperation agreements with third countries and exchange information where those third countries can provide guarantees that professional secrecy will be protected.

(29) Having a single consolidated list or register for each category of financial institution in the Union, which is currently the duty of each national competent authority,

1 OJ L 145, 30. 4. 2004, p. 1.

(23)根据《欧洲联盟运行条约》(尤其是第290条和第291条)的规定调整委员会程序的工作应视具体情况逐项完成。为反映金融市场的技术发展动态并具体说明经本指令修正的其他指令设定的要求,欧盟委员会应当有权根据《欧洲联盟运行条约》第290条的规定通过授权立法。

(24)欧洲议会和欧盟理事会应当可以在通知之日起3个月内对授权立法提出异议。对涉及重大问题的授权立法,经欧洲议会或欧盟理事会请求,该期限可延长3个月。同时,欧洲议会和欧盟理事会也应有权通报其他机构其无意就有关事项提出异议。此类对授权立法的提前批准尤其适用于有时间限制的情形,如基本立法要求欧盟委员会在规定的时间表内通过授权立法的情形。

(25)在通过《里斯本条约》的政府间会议《最后决议》的附录中,一项关于《欧洲联盟运行条约》第290条的声明(第39号)表明:会议注意到,在起草金融服务领域的授权立法草案时,欧盟委员会有意按其既定惯例继续公开征求各成员国指定专家的意见。

(26)欧洲金融监管体系所建立的新监管架构将要求各国家级主管部门与欧洲监管机构紧密合作。对相关立法的修正应确保不会对设立欧洲监管机构的该等条例规定的信息共享义务造成法律障碍。

(27)在主管部门与欧洲监管机构或欧洲系统性风险委员会(ESRB)之间传递或交换的信息应在职业保密义务覆盖范围内,接收信息的主管部门的前任或现任雇员应受职业保密义务约束。

(28)设立欧洲监管机构的条例规定,欧洲监管机构可与第三国监管机构建立联系,并在与第三国监管体制有关的等效性决定起草过程中提供协助。应对《欧洲议会与欧盟理事会关于金融工具市场的第2004/39/EC 号指令》[1](2004年4月21日)以及第2006/48/EC 号指令进行修正,使其允许欧洲监管机构与第三国签订合作协议并在第三国保证职业秘密受到保护的情形下与之交换信息。

(29)编制欧盟各类金融机构合并名册或注册档案将有助于提高透明度并能更好满足单一金融市场的要求,而此项工作目前由各国家级主管部门负责。欧洲监管机构

1 2004年4月30日《欧盟公报》L 145,第1页。

will improve transparency and is more appropriate in the context of the single financial market. The ESA should be given the task of establishing, publishing and regularly updating registers and lists of financial actors within the Union. This concerns the list of authorisations of credit institutions granted by national competent authorities, the register of all investment firms and the list of regulated markets under Directive 2004/39/EC. Similarly, the European Supervisory Authority(European Securities and Markets Authority) should be given the task of establishing, publishing and regularly updating the list of approved prospectuses and the certificates of approval under Directive 2003/71/EC of the European Parliament and of the Council of 4 November 2003 on the prospectus to be published when securities are offered to the public or admitted to trading[1].

(30) In those areas where the ESA are under an obligation to develop draft technical standards, those draft technical standards should be submitted to the Commission within 3 years of the creation of the ESA unless another deadline is established by the relevant legislative act.

(31) The tasks of the European Supervisory Authority (European Securities and Markets Authority) in relation to Directive 98/26/EC of the European Parliament and of the Council of 19 May 1998 on settlement finality in payment and securities settlement systems[2] should be without prejudice to the competence of the European System of Central Banks to promote the smooth operation of payment systems, in line with the fourth indent of Article 127(2) TFEU.

(32) The technical standards to be drafted by the European Supervisory Authority (European Insurance and Occupational Pensions Authority) in accordance with this Directive and in relation to Directive 2003/41/EC of the European Parliament and of the Council of 3 June 2003 on the activities and supervision of institutions for occupational retirement provision[3] should be without prejudice to the competences of Member States with regard to prudential requirements on such institutions as provided for in Directive 2003/41/EC.

(33) Under Article 13 (5) of Directive 2003/71/EC, the competent authority of the home Member State may transfer the approval of a prospectus to the competent authority of another Member State, subject to the agreement of that competent authority. Article 28 (4) of Regulation (EU) No 1095/2010 requires that such delegation agreements be notified to the European Supervisory Authority (European Securities and Markets Authority) at least 1 month before they are put into effect. However, given the experience in transfer of

1 OJ L 345, 31. 12. 2003, p. 64.
2 OJ L 166, 11. 6. 1998, p. 45.
3 OJ L 235, 23. 9. 2003, p. 10.

应被赋予建立、公布并定期更新欧盟内金融市场主体的注册档案和名册的职能，其中包括各国家级主管部门核准的信贷机构名册、包含了所有投资公司的注册档案以及第2004/39/EC号指令下的受监管市场名册。同样，欧洲监管机构欧洲证券与市场管理局应被赋予下列职责，即负责建立、公布并定期更新《欧洲议会与欧盟理事会关于向公众发行证券或证券获准交易时所应公布的招募说明书的第2003/71/EC号指令》[1]（2003年11月4日）中的获批招募说明书和批准证书清单。

（30）欧洲监管机构应在其建立后3年内将其负责起草的技术标准草案呈报欧盟委员会，相关框架立法对期限另有规定的除外。

（31）欧洲监管机构（欧洲证券与市场管理局）涉及《欧洲议会与欧盟理事会关于支付系统和证券结算系统的结算终结性的第98/26/EC号指令》[2]（1998年5月19日）的工作，不应影响《欧洲联盟运行条约》第127条第2款第4目授予欧洲中央银行体系的促进支付系统顺畅运作的职权。

（32）欧洲监管机构（欧洲保险与职业养老金管理局）按照本指令起草的涉及《欧洲议会与欧盟理事会关于职业退休金管理机构的活动和监管的第2003/41/EC号指令》[3]（2003年6月3日）的技术标准草案，不应影响第2003/41/EC号指令规定的各机构对职业退休金管理机构施加审慎要求的职权。

（33）按照第2003/71/EC号指令第13条第5款，母国主管部门可将招募说明书的审批权委托给另一成员国的主管部门，但须经该成员国的主管部门同意。第1095/2010号（欧盟）条例第28条第4款要求至少应在生效之前1个月通知欧洲监管机构（欧洲证券与市场管理局）该等委托协议。第2003/71/EC号指令对审批权的委托规定了更短的通知期限，鉴于根据该指令进行审批权委托的实际经验，不宜适用第1095/2010号（欧盟）条例第28条第4款。

---

1 2003 年 12 月 31 日《欧盟公报》L 345，第 64 页。

2 1998 年 6 月 11 日《欧盟公报》L 166，第 45 页。

3 2003 年 9 月 23 日《欧盟公报》L 235，第 10 页。

approval under Directive 2003/71/EC, which provides for shorter deadlines, it is appropriate not to apply Article 28(4) of Regulation (EU) No 1095/2010 to that situation.

(34) There is currently no need for the ESA to develop draft technical standards on the existing requirements that the persons who effectively direct the business of investment firms, credit institutions, UCITS and their management companies be of sufficiently good repute and sufficiently experienced so as to ensure their sound and prudent management. However, given the importance of those requirements, the ESA should give priority to identifying best practices in guidelines and to ensuring the convergence of supervisory and prudential processes towards those best practices. They should similarly identify best practices and ensure convergence with respect to prudential requirements relative to the head office of those bodies.

(35) The European single rulebook, applicable to all financial institutions in the internal market, should ensure adequate harmonisation of criteria and methodology to be applicable by the competent authorities to assess the risk of credit institutions. More particularly, the purpose of developing draft technical standards in relation to the Internal Ratings Based approach, the Advanced Measurement Approach and the internal model for market risk approach, as provided for by this Directive, should be to ensure the quality and robustness of such approaches, as well as the consistency of their review by the competent authorities. Those technical standards should allow the competent authorities to permit financial institutions to develop different approaches based on their experience and specificities, in accordance with the requirements laid down in Directive 2006/48/EC and Directive 2006/49/EC of the European Parliament and of the Council of 14 June 2006 on the capital adequacy of investment firms and credit institutions[1] and subject to the requirements of the relevant technical standards.

(36) Since the objectives of this Directive, namely improving the functioning of the internal market by means of ensuring a high, effective and consistent level of prudential regulation and supervision, protecting depositors, investors and beneficiaries and thereby businesses and consumers, protecting the integrity, efficiency and orderly functioning of financial markets, maintaining the stability and sustainability of the financial system, preserving the real economy, safeguarding public finances and strengthening international supervisory coordination, cannot be sufficiently achieved by the Member States and can, therefore, by reason of their scale, be better achieved at Union level, the Union may adopt measures, in accordance with the principle of subsidiarity as set out in Article 5 of the Treaty on European Union. In accordance with the principle of proportionality, as set out

1 OJ L 177, 30. 6. 2006, p. 201.

(34)对于实际领导投资公司、信贷机构、可转让证券集合投资计划(UCITS)及其管理公司业务的主体而言,欧洲监管机构目前不必针对该等主体适用的现行要求——为确保上述主体的稳健和审慎管理其应具备足够良好的声誉和足够丰富的经验——起草技术性标准草案。但是鉴于该等要求的重要性,欧洲监管机构应以指引的方式确定最佳实践并确保监管和审慎程序与最佳实践的趋同,以此作为其工作重点。同样,欧洲监管机构应就上述各机构总部的审慎要求确定最佳实践并确保审慎要求与最佳实践的趋同。

(35)适用于欧盟内部市场所有金融机构的欧洲单一规则手册应确保主管部门评估信贷机构风险时所采用的标准和方法彼此充分协调。特别是,正如本指令所规定的,起草关于内部评级法、高级计量法以及市场风险内部模型法的技术标准草案时,应当确保该等方法的质量和稳健性以及主管部门对其进行审评时的一致性。该等技术标准应使主管部门能够允许金融机构依照第2006/48/EC号指令和《欧洲议会与欧盟理事会关于投资公司和信贷机构资本充足性的第2006/49/EC号指令》[1](2006年6月14日)并在遵守相关技术标准要求的前提下,根据各自的经验和具体状况制定不同的风险计量方法。

(36)本指令的目标在于确保高水平、有效和一致的审慎规制和监管以改善欧盟内部市场的运行,保护存款人、投资者和受益人进而保护企业和消费者,维护金融市场的诚信度、效率和有序运行,维持金融系统的稳定和可持续性,保护实体经济,保障公共财政以及加强国际监管协调;上述目的单靠成员国自身无法完全实现,但基于此等目的触及的范围,在欧盟层面上能够得到更好的实现,因此欧盟可根据《欧洲联盟条约》第5条规定的辅助性原则制定相关细则。根据《欧洲联盟条约》第5条规定的比例原则,本指令仅作出实现上述目标所必要的规定。

1 2006年6月30日《欧盟公报》L 177,第201页。

in that Article, this Directive does not go beyond what is necessary in order to achieve those objectives.

(37) The Commission should, by 1 January 2014, report to the European Parliament and to the Council on the submission by the ESA of the draft technical standards provided for in this Directive and present any appropriate proposals.

(38) Directive 98/26/EC of the European Parliament and of the Council of 19 May 1998 on settlement finality in payment and securities settlement systems[1], Directive 2002/87/EC of the European Parliament and of the Council of 16 December 2002 on the supplementary supervision of credit institutions, insurance undertakings and investment firms in a financial conglomerate[2], Directive 2003/6/EC of the European Parliament and of the Council of 28 January 2003 on insider dealing and market manipulation (market abuse)[3], Directive 2003/41/EC, Directive 2003/71/EC, Directive 2004/39/EC, Directive 2004/109/EC of the European Parliament and of the Council of 15 December 2004 on the harmonisation of transparency requirements in relation to information about issuers whose securities are admitted to trading on a regulated market[4], Directive 2005/60/EC of the European Parliament and of the Council of 26 October 2005 on the prevention of the use of the financial system for the purpose of money laundering and terrorist financing[5], Directive 2006/48/EC, Directive 2006/49/EC and Directive 2009/65/EC of the European Parliament and of the Council of 13 July 2009 on the coordination of laws, regulations and administrative provisions relating to undertakings for collective investment in transferable securities (UCITS)[6] should therefore be amended accordingly.

HAVE ADOPTED THIS DIRECTIVE:

Article 1 Amendments to Directive 98/26/EC

Directive 98/26/EC is hereby amended as follows:

(1) Article 6(3) is replaced by the following:

'3. The Member State referred to in paragraph 2 shall immediately notify the European Systemic Risk Board, other Member States and the European Supervisory Authority (European Securities and Markets Authority)(hereinafter "ESMA"), established by Regulation (EU) No 1095/2010 of the European Parliament and of the Council (*).

(*) OJ L 331, 15. 12. 2010, p. 84. '.

1 OJ L 166, 11. 6. 1998, p. 45.
2 OJ L 35, 11. 2. 2003, p. 1.
3 OJ L 96, 12. 4. 2003, p. 16.
4 OJ L 390, 31. 12. 2004, p. 38.
5 OJ L 309, 25. 11. 2005, p. 15.
6 OJ L 302, 17. 11. 2009, p. 32.

(37)欧盟委员会应在2014年1月1日之前就欧洲监管机构向其提交本指令规定的技术标准草案事宜向欧洲议会和欧盟理事会提出报告,并提出相关的提案。

(38)因此,应对下列指令作出相应修正:《欧洲议会与欧盟理事会关于支付系统和证券结算系统的结算终结性的第98/26/EC号指令》[1](1998年5月19日)、《欧洲议会与欧盟理事会关于对金融集团下属信贷机构、保险公司以及投资公司实施补充监管的第2002/87/EC号指令》[2](2002年12月16日)、《欧洲议会与欧盟理事会关于内幕交易和市场操纵(市场滥用)的第2003/6/EC号指令》[3](2003年1月28日)、第2003/41/EC号指令、第2003/71/EC号指令、第2004/39/EC号指令、《欧洲议会与欧盟理事会关于协调证券获准在受监管市场交易的发行人的信息透明度要求的第2004/109/EC号指令》[4](2004年12月15日)、《欧洲议会与欧盟理事会关于防范利用金融系统从事洗钱和恐怖分子融资的第2005/60/EC号指令》[5](2005年10月26日)、第2006/48/EC号指令、第2006/49/EC号指令以及《欧洲议会与欧盟理事会协调关于可转让证券集合投资计划(UCITS)的法律、法规和规章的第2009/65/EC号指令》[6](2009年7月13日)。

兹通过本指令如下:

第1条 对第98/26/EC号指令的修正

特此对第98/26/EC号指令修正如下:

(1)第6条第3款替以下列内容:

“3.第2款所述成员国应立即通知欧洲系统性风险委员会、其他成员国以及依据《欧洲议会与欧盟理事会第1095/2010号(欧盟)条例》*设立的欧洲监管机构(欧洲证券与市场管理局)(以下简称欧洲证券与市场管理局,英文简称ESMA)。

*《欧盟公报》L 331,2010年12月15日,第84页。”

1 1998年6月11日《欧盟公报》L 166,第45页。
2 2003年2月11日《欧盟公报》L 35,第1页。
3 2003年4月12日《欧盟公报》L 96,第16页。
4 2004年12月31日《欧盟公报》L 390,第38页。
5 2005年11月25日《欧盟公报》L 309,第15页。
6 2009年11月17日《欧盟公报》L 302,第32页。

(2) In Article 10(1) the first subparagraph is replaced by the following:

'1. Member States shall specify the systems, and the respective system operators, which are to be included in the scope of this Directive and shall notify them to ESMA and inform it of the authorities chosen in accordance with Article 6(2). ESMA shall publish that information on its website. '.

(3) The following Article is inserted:'

'*Article 10a*

1. The competent authorities shall cooperate with ESMA for the purposes of this Directive, in accordance with Regulation (EU) No 1095/2010.

2. The competent authorities shall provide, without delay, ESMA with all the information necessary to carry out its duties, in accordance with Article 35 of Regulation (EU) No 1095/2010. '.

Article 2 Amendments to Directive 2002/87/EC

Directive 2002/87/EC is hereby amended as follows:

(1) Article 4 is amended as follows:

(a) paragraph 2 is replaced by the following:

'2. The coordinator appointed in accordance with Article 10 shall inform the parent undertaking at the head of a group or, in the absence of a parent undertaking, the regulated entity with the largest balance sheet total in the most important financial sector in a group, that the group has been identified as a financial conglomerate and of the appointment of the coordinator.

The coordinator shall also inform the competent authorities which have authorised regulated entities in the group and the competent authorities of the Member State in which the mixed financial holding company has its head office, and the Joint Committee of the European Supervisory Authorities (ESA) established by Articles 54 of Regulation (EU) No 1093/2010 of the European Parliament and of the Council of 24 November 2010 establishing a European Supervisory Authority (European Banking Authority) (*), of Regulation (EU) No 1094/2010 of the European Parliament and of the Council of 24 November 2010 establishing a European Supervisory Authority (European Insurance and Occupational Pensions Authority) (**) and of Regulation (EU) No 1095/2010 of the European Parliament and of the Council of 24 November 2010 establishing a European Supervisory Authority (European Securities and Markets Authority) (***) (hereinafter "the Joint Committee"), respectively.

(*) OJ L 331, 15. 12. 2010, p. 12.

(**) OJ L 331, 15. 12. 2010, p. 48.

(***) OJ L 331, 15. 12. 2010, p. 84. ';

(b) the following paragraph is added:

(2)第10条第1款第1项替换为下列内容:

"1.成员国应具体说明将被纳入本指令范围内的各个系统以及相应的系统运营者,通知欧洲证券与市场管理局该等信息,并应通知欧洲证券与市场管理局其根据第6条第2款的规定所选择的机构。欧洲证券与市场管理局应在其网站上公布该等信息。"

(3)增加下列条款:

"第10a条

1.主管部门应根据第1095/2010号(欧盟)条例的规定,为本指令之目的与欧洲证券与市场管理局合作。

2.主管部门应根据第1095/2010号(欧盟)条例第35条的规定,立即向欧洲证券与市场管理局提供其履行职责所必要的一切信息。"

第2条　对第2002/87/EC号指令的修正

特此对第2002/87/EC号指令修正如下:

(1)第4条修正如下:

(a)第2款替换为下列内容:

"2.根据第10条任命的协调单位应将某集团被认定为金融集团以及其自身被任命为协调单位之事实通知该集团母公司;如不存在母公司,则应通知该集团中属于最重要的金融行业里资产负债表总额最高的受监管实体。

同时,协调单位应通知对集团内受监管实体作出核准的主管部门和混合金融控股公司总部所在的成员国主管部门,以及依据《欧洲议会与欧盟理事会设立欧洲监管机构(欧洲银行业管理局)第1093/2010号(欧盟)条例》*(2010年11月24日)、《欧洲议会与欧盟理事会设立欧洲监管机构(欧洲保险与职业养老金管理局)第1094/2010号(欧盟)条例》**(2010年11月24日)、《欧洲议会与欧盟理事会设立欧洲监管机构(欧洲证券与市场管理局)第1095/2010号(欧盟)条例》***(2010年11月24日)第54条所设立的欧洲监管机构(ESA)联合委员会(以下简称联合委员会)。

*《欧盟公报》L 331,2010年12月15日,第12页。

**《欧盟公报》L 331,2010年12月15日,第48页。

***《欧盟公报》L 331,2010年12月15日,第84页。"

(b)增加下列内容:

'3. The Joint Committee shall publish on its website and keep up-to-date the list of identified financial conglomerates. That information shall be available by hyperlink on each of the European Supervisory Authority's websites. '.

(2) In Article 9(2), the following point is added:

'(d) arrangements in place to contribute to and develop, if required, adequate recovery and resolution arrangements and plans. Such arrangements shall be updated regularly. '.

(3) The title of Section 3 is replaced by the following:

'MEASURES TO FACILITATE SUPPLEMENTARY SUPERVISION AND POWERS OF THE JOINT COMMITTEE'.

(4) The following Article is inserted in Section 3:

'*Article 9a*

Role of the Joint Committee

The Joint Committee shall, in accordance with Article 56 of Regulation (EU) No 1093/2010, of Regulation (EU) No 1094/2010 and of Regulation (EU) No 1095/2010 respectively, ensure coherent cross-sectoral and cross-border supervision and compliance with Union legislation. '.

(5) Article 10(1) is replaced by the following:

'1. In order to ensure adequate supplementary supervision of the regulated entities in a financial conglomerate, a single coordinator, responsible for coordination and exercise of supplementary supervision, shall be appointed from among the competent authorities of the Member States concerned, including those of the Member State in which the mixed financial holding company has its head office. The identity of the coordinator shall be published on the Joint Committee's website. '.

(6) In Article 11(1), the second subparagraph is replaced by the following:

'In order to facilitate and establish supplementary supervision on a broad legal basis, the coordinator, and the other relevant competent authorities, and, where necessary, the other competent authorities concerned, shall have coordination arrangements in place. The coordination arrangements may entrust additional tasks to the coordinator and may specify the procedures for the decision-making process among the relevant competent authorities as referred to in Articles 3 and 4, Article 5(4), Article 6, Article 12(2) and Articles 16 and 18, and for cooperation with other competent authorities.

In accordance with Article 8 and the procedure set out in Article 56 of Regulation (EU) No 1093/2010, of Regulation (EU) No 1094/2010 and of Regulation (EU) No 1095/2010 respectively, the ESA, through the Joint Committee, shall develop guidelines aimed at the convergence of supervisory practices with regard to the consistency of supervisory coordination arrangements in accordance with Article 131a of Directive 2006/

“3.联合委员会应在其网站上公布并持续更新已明确认定的金融集团的名册。该等信息应可通过各欧洲监管机构网站上的超链接获得。”

(2)第9条第2款增加下列内容：
“(d)设置一定的安排，以(在需要时)促成和制定充分的恢复和清盘安排与计划。该等安排应定期更新。”

(3)第3节的标题替换为：
“有利于补充监管的措施以及联合委员会的权力”。

(4)在第3节中增加下列条款：
“第9a条
联合委员会的作用
根据第1093/2010号(欧盟)条例、第1094/2010号(欧盟)条例以及第1095/2010号(欧盟)条例第56条的规定，联合委员会应确保一致的跨业和跨境监管，并确保欧盟立法能得到遵守。”

(5)第10条第1款替换为下列内容：
“1.为确保对金融集团下属的受监管实体实施充分的补充监管，应从所涉成员国的主管部门，包括混合金融控股公司总部所在成员国的主管部门当中指定一个协调单位，负责协调和补充监管的实施。协调单位的身份信息应在联合委员会的网站上公布。”

(6)第11条第1款第2项替换为下列内容：
“为能在广泛的法律基础上促进和建立补充监管，协调单位和其他相关主管部门以及(如有必要)其他所涉主管部门应落实协调安排。协调安排可委托协调单位承担额外的工作，也可以就第3条和第4条、第5条第4款、第6条、第12条第2款以及第16条和第18条所述相关主管部门的决策方式以及与其他主管部门的合作制定程序。

欧洲监管机构应按照第8条以及第1093/2010号(欧盟)条例、第1094/2010号(欧盟)条例和第1095/2010号(欧盟)条例第56条规定的程序，通过联合委员会制定指引，以促进监管实践的趋同，从而保证依照第2006/48/EC号指令第131a条以及第2009/138/EC号指令第248条第4款建立的监管协调安排的一致性。”

48/EC and Article 248(4) of Directive 2009/138/EC. '.

(7) In Article 12(1), the third subparagraph is replaced by the following:

'The competent authorities may also exchange with the following authorities such information as may be needed for the performance of their respective tasks, regarding regulated entities in a financial conglomerate, in line with the provisions laid down in the sectoral rules: central banks, the European System of Central Banks, the European Central Bank and the European Systemic Risk Board in accordance with Article 15 of Regulation (EU) No 1092/2010 of the European Parliament and of the Council of 24 November 2010 on European Union macro-prudential oversight of the financial system and establishing a European Systemic Risk Board (*).

(*) OJ L 331, 15. 12. 2010, p. 1. '.

(8) The following Article is inserted:

'*Article 12a*

Cooperation and exchange of information with the Joint Committee

1. The competent authorities shall cooperate with the Joint Committee for the purposes of this Directive, in accordance with Regulation (EU) No 1093/2010, Regulation (EU) No 1094/2010, and Regulation (EU) No 1095/2010.

2. The competent authorities shall without delay provide the Joint Committee with all information necessary to carry out its duties in accordance with Article 35 of Regulation (EU) No 1093/2010, of Regulation (EU) No 1094/2010, and of Regulation (EU) No 1095/2010 respectively. '.

(9) Article 14(1) is replaced by the following:

'1. Member States shall ensure that there are no legal impediments within their jurisdiction preventing the natural and legal persons included within the scope of supplementary supervision, whether or not a regulated entity, from exchanging with each other any information which would be relevant for the purposes of supplementary supervision and from exchanging information in accordance with this Directive and with the ESA in accordance with Article 35 of Regulation (EU) No 1093/2010, of Regulation (EU) No 1094/2010 and of Regulation (EU) No 1095/2010 respectively, where necessary through the Joint Committee. '.

(10) The second paragraph of Article 16 is replaced by the following:

'Without prejudice to Article 17(2), Member States may determine what measures may be taken by the competent authorities with respect to mixed financial holding companies. In accordance with Articles 16 and 56 of Regulation (EU) No 1093/2010, of Regulation (EU) No 1094/2010 and of Regulation (EU) No 1095/2010 respectively, the ESA, through the Joint Committee, may develop guidelines for measures in relation to mixed financial

（7）第12条第1款第3项替换为下列内容：

“根据《欧洲议会与欧盟理事会关于欧盟对金融系统的宏观审慎监控以及设立欧洲系统性风险委员会的第1092/2010号（欧盟）条例》*（2010年11月24日）第15条的规定，主管部门也可依照行业规则与下列机构交换为履行其各自工作所必要的有关金融集团下属受监管实体的信息：成员国中央银行、欧洲中央银行体系、欧洲中央银行以及欧洲系统性风险委员会。

*《欧盟公报》L 331，2010年12月15日，第1页。”

（8）增加下列条款：

“第12a条

与联合委员会合作以及交换信息

1.主管部门应根据第1093/2010号（欧盟）条例、第1094/2010号（欧盟）条例以及第1095/2010号（欧盟）条例的规定，为本指令之目的与联合委员会合作。

2.根据第1093/2010号（欧盟）条例、第1094/2010号（欧盟）条例以及第1095/2010号（欧盟）条例第35条的规定，主管部门应立即向联合委员会提供履行其职责所必要的一切信息。”

（9）第14条第1款替换为下列内容：

“1.各成员国应确保在其辖区内不存在任何法律障碍，妨碍补充监管范围内的自然人和法人（不论是否属于受监管实体）互相交换补充监管的相关信息，妨碍其根据本指令互相交换信息，或妨碍其根据第1093/2010号（欧盟）条例、第1094/2010号（欧盟）条例以及第1095/2010号（欧盟）条例第35条的规定与欧洲监管机构交换信息（以及在必要情形下通过联合委员会与欧洲监管机构交换信息）。”

（10）第16条第2项替换为下列内容：

“在不影响第17条第2款的情形下，各成员国可决定主管部门可以对混合金融控股公司采取的措施。根据第1093/2010号（欧盟）条例、第1094/2010号（欧盟）条例，以及第1095/2010号（欧盟）条例第16条和第56条的规定，欧洲监管机构可以通过联合委员会就可对混合金融控股公司采取的措施制定指引。”

holding companies. '.

(11) Article 18 is amended as follows:

(a) paragraph 1 is replaced by the following:

'1. Without prejudice to the sectoral rules, where Article 5(3) applies, the competent authorities shall verify whether the regulated entities, the parent undertaking of which has its head office in a third country are subject to supervision by that third country's competent authority, which is equivalent to that provided for by this Directive on the supplementary supervision of regulated entities referred to in Article 5(2). The verification shall be carried out by the competent authority which would be the coordinator if the criteria set out in Article 10(2) were to apply, on the request of the parent undertaking or of any of the regulated entities authorised in the Union or on its own initiative.

That competent authority shall consult the other relevant competent authorities, and shall make every effort to comply with any applicable guidelines prepared through the Joint Committee in accordance with Articles 16 and 56 of Regulation (EU) No 1093/2010, of Regulation (EU) No 1094/2010 and of Regulation (EU) No 1095/2010 respectively. ';

(b) the following paragraph is inserted:

'1a. Where a competent authority disagrees with the decision taken by another relevant competent authority under paragraph 1, Article 19 of Regulation (EU) No 1093/2010, of Regulation (EU) No 1094/2010 and of Regulation (EU) No 1095/2010 respectively shall apply. '.

(12) Article 19(2) is replaced by the following:

'2. Without prejudice to Article 218(1) and (2) of the Treaty on the Functioning of the European Union(TFEU), the Commission shall, with the assistance of the Joint Committee, the European Banking Committee, the European Insurance and Occupational Pensions Committee and the Financial Conglomerates Committee, examine the outcome of the negotiations referred to in paragraph 1 and the resulting situation. '.

(13) In Article 20(1), the following subparagraph is added:

'Those measures shall not include the subject matter of the power delegated and conferred on the Commission with regard to the items listed in Article 21a. '.

(14) Article 21 is amended as follows:

(a) paragraph 4 is replaced by the following:

'4. The ESA, through the Joint Committee, may provide general guidelines as to whether the supplementary supervision arrangements of competent authorities in third countries are likely to achieve the objectives of the supplementary supervision as defined in this Directive, in relation to the regulated entities in a financial conglomerate, the head of which has its head office in a third country. The Joint Committee shall keep any such

（11）第18条修正如下：

（a）第1款替换为下列内容：

“1.在不影响行业规则的情形下，如适用第5条第3款，则主管部门应核查，母公司总部设在第三国的受监管实体所受到的第三国主管部门监管是否与本指令规定的对第5条第2款所述受监管实体实施的补充监管等效。如果第10条第2款所规定的标准适用，应由作为协调单位的主管部门实施该等核查。经母公司或在欧盟获得核准的任何受监管实体请求，作为协调单位的主管部门应进行核查，此外，该主管部门亦可主动进行核查。

该主管部门应咨询其他相关主管部门意见，并应尽力遵守欧洲监管机构根据第1093/2010号（欧盟）条例、第1094/2010号（欧盟）条例以及第1095/2010号（欧盟）条例第16条和第56条的规定通过联合委员会编制的任何适用的指引。”

（b）增加下列条款：

“1a.如某主管部门不同意另一相关主管部门根据第1款作出的决定，则应适用第1093/2010号（欧盟）条例、第1094/2010号（欧盟）条例以及第1095/2010号（欧盟）条例的第19条。”

（12）第19条第2款修改为：

“2.在不影响《欧洲联盟运行条约》（TFEU）第281条第1款及第2款的情形下，欧盟委员会应在联合委员会、欧洲银行业委员会、欧洲保险与职业养老金委员会以及金融集团委员会的协助下，审查第1款所述谈判结果以及该结果所导致的情形。”

（13）在第20条第1款中增加：

“该等措施不应包括就第21a条所列事项而委托并授予欧盟委员会权力的内容。”

（14）对第21条修正如下：

（a）第4款替换为下列内容：

“4.欧洲监管机构可通过联合委员会提供一般性指引，据以认定第三国主管部门的补充监管安排是否有可能达到本指令所界定的对总部设在第三国的金融集团下属的受监管实体实施补充监管的目标。联合委员会应定期对上述指引进行审评，并考量该等主管部门所实施的补充监管发生的任何变化。”

guidelines under review and take into account any changes to the supplementary supervision carried out by such competent authorities. '.

(b) paragraph 5 is replaced by the following:

'5. By 1 December 2011 the Commission shall review Article 20 and present any appropriate legislative proposals in order to allow the full application of delegated acts under Article 290 TFEU and implementing acts under Article 291 TFEU in respect of this Directive . Without prejudice to implementing measures already adopted, the powers conferred on the Commission in Article 21 to adopt implementing measures that remain after the entry into force of the Lisbon Treaty, shall cease to apply on 1 December 2012. '.

(15) The following Article is inserted:

'*Article 21a*

Technical standards

1. In order to ensure consistent harmonisation of this Directive, the ESA, in accordance with Article 56 of Regulation (EU) No 1093/2010, of Regulation (EU) No 1094/2010, and of Regulation (EU) No 1095/2010 respectively may develop draft regulatory technical standards with regard to:

(a) Article 2(11) in order to specify the application of Article 17 of Council Directive 78/660/EEC in the context of this Directive;

(b) Article 2(17) in order to establish procedures or specify criteria for the determination of "relevant competent authorities";

(c) Article 3(5) in order to specify the alternative parameters for the identification of a financial conglomerate.

Power is delegated to the Commission to adopt the regulatory technical standards referred to in the first subparagraph in accordance with the procedure laid down in Articles 10 to 14 of Regulation (EU) No 1093/2010, of Regulation (EU) No 1094/2010, and of Regulation (EU) No 1095/2010 respectively.

2. In order to ensure uniform conditions of application of this Directive, the ESA, in accordance with Articles 56 of Regulation (EU) No 1093/2010, of Regulation (EU) No 1094/2010, and of Regulation (EU) No 1095/2010 respectively may develop draft implementing technical standards with regard to:

(a) Article 6(2) in order to ensure uniform conditions of application of the calculation methods listed in Annex I part II, but without prejudice to Article 6(4);

(b) Article 7(2) in order to ensure uniform conditions of application of the procedures for including the items within the scope of the definition of "risk concentrations" in the supervisory overview referred to in the second subparagraph of Article 7(2);

(c) Article 8(2) in order to ensure uniform conditions of application of the procedures

(b)第5款替换为下列内容：

“5.欧盟委员会应于2011年12月1日前对第20条进行审评并提交任何适当的立法提案以促使《欧洲联盟运行条约》第290条中的授权立法以及《欧洲联盟运行条约》第291条中的实施性立法就本指令而言能全面适用。在不影响已经制定的实施细则的情形下，第21条授予欧盟委员会制定实施细则且在《里斯本条约》生效后仍然有效的权力应于2012年12月1日停止适用。”

(15)增加下列条款：

“第21a条

技术标准

1.为确保本指令的一致协调，根据第1093/2010号(欧盟)条例、第1094/2010号(欧盟)条例以及第1095/2010号(欧盟)条例第56条的规定，欧洲监管机构可就下列条款起草监管性技术标准草案：

(a)第2条第11款，以具体说明欧洲经济共同体理事会第78/660/EEC 号指令第17条在本指令背景下的适用；

(b)第2条第17款，以制定或具体说明据以判定“相关主管部门”的程序和标准；

(c)第3条第5款，以具体说明认定金融集团的替代性指标。

经委托授权，欧盟委员会有权根据第1093/2010号(欧盟)条例、第1094/2010号(欧盟)条例以及第1095/2010号(欧盟)条例第10条至第14条规定的程序通过第1项所述监管性技术标准。

2.为确保本指令适用条件的统一，根据第1093/2010号(欧盟)条例、第1094/2010号(欧盟)条例以及第1095/2010号(欧盟)条例第56条的规定，欧洲监管机构可为下列条款起草实施性技术标准草案：

(a)第6条第2款，旨在确保附录一第二部分所列的计算方法具有统一的适用条件，但不得影响第6条第4款；

(b)第7条第2款，旨在确保将“风险集中”定义涵盖的项目纳入第7条第2款第2项所述监管评估中的程序具有统一的适用条件；

(c)第8条第2款，旨在确保将“集团内部交易”定义涵盖的项目纳入第8条第2款第3

for including the items within the scope of the definition of "intra group transactions" in the supervisory overview referred to in the third subparagraph of Article 8(2).

Power is conferred on the Commission to adopt the implementing technical standards referred to in the first subparagraph in accordance with Article 15 of Regulation (EU) No 1093/2010, of Regulation (EU) No 1094/2010, and of Regulation (EU) No 1095/2010 respectively. '.

Article 3 Amendments to Directive 2003/6/EC

Directive 2003/6/EC is hereby amended as follows:

(1) In Article 1(5) the following subparagraphs are added:

'The European Supervisory Authority (European Securities and Markets Authority) (hereinafter "ESMA"), established by Regulation (EU) No 1095/2010 of the European Parliament and of the Council (*) may develop draft implementing technical standards to ensure uniform conditions of application of the acts adopted by the Commission in accordance with this Article in relation to accepted market practices.

Power is conferred on the Commission to adopt the implementing technical standards referred to in the second subparagraph in accordance with Article 15 of Regulation (EU) No 1095/2010.

(*) OJ L 331, 15. 12. 2010, p. 84. '.

(2) In Article 6, the following paragraph is added:

'11. ESMA may develop draft implementing technical standards to ensure uniform conditions of application of the acts adopted by the Commission in accordance with the sixth indent of the first subparagraph of paragraph 10.

Power is conferred on the Commission to adopt the implementing technical standards referred to in the first subparagraph in accordance with Article 15 of Regulation (EU) No 1095/2010. '.

(3) Article 8 is amended as follows:

(a) the existing text is numbered as paragraph 1.

(b) the following paragraph is added:

'2. ESMA may develop draft implementing technical standards to ensure uniform conditions of application of acts adopted by the Commission in accordance with paragraph 1.

Power is conferred on the Commission to adopt the implementing technical standards referred to in the first subparagraph in accordance with Article 15 of Regulation (EU) No 1095/2010. '.

(4) In Article 14 the following paragraph is added:

'5. Member States shall provide ESMA annually with aggregated information regarding all administrative measures and sanctions imposed in accordance with

项所述监管评估中的程序具有统一的适用条件。

兹授予欧盟委员会依照第1093/2010号(欧盟)条例、第1094/2010号(欧盟)条例以及第1095/2010号(欧盟)条例第15条的规定通过第1项所述实施性技术标准的权力。”

第3条　对第2003/6/EC号指令的修正

特此对第2003/6/EC号指令修正如下:

(1)第1条第5款增加下列内容:

“为确保欧盟委员会根据本条制定的关于认可的市场实践的立法具有统一的适用条件,依据欧洲议会与欧盟理事会第1095/2010号(欧盟)条例*设立的欧洲监管机构欧洲证券与市场管理局(以下简称欧洲证券与市场管理局,英文简称ESMA)可起草实施性技术标准草案。

兹授予欧盟委员会依照第1095/2010号(欧盟)条例第15条的规定通过第2项所述实施性技术标准的权力。

*《欧盟公报》L 331,2010年12月15日,第84页。”

(2)第6条增加下列内容:

“11.为确保欧盟委员会按照第10款第1项第6目通过的立法具有统一的适用条件,欧洲证券与市场管理局可起草实施性技术标准草案。

兹授予欧盟委员会依照第1095/2010号(欧盟)条例第15条的规定通过第1项所述实施性技术标准的权力。”

(3)对第8条修正如下:

(a)将现有文字重新编号,改为第1款。

(b)增加下列内容:

“2.为确保欧盟委员会依照第1款通过的立法具有统一的适用条件,欧洲证券与市场管理局可起草实施性技术标准草案。

兹授予欧盟委员会依照第1095/2010号(欧盟)条例第15条的规定通过第1项所述实施性技术标准的权力。”

(4)第14条增加下列内容:

“5.各成员国应每年向欧洲证券与市场管理局提供根据第1款和第2款实施的所有行政措施与处罚方面的汇总信息。

paragraphs 1 and 2.

Where the competent authority has disclosed an administrative measure or a sanction to the public, it shall contemporaneously report that fact to ESMA.

Where a published sanction relates to an investment firm authorised in accordance with Directive 2004/39/EC, ESMA shall add a reference to the published sanction in the register of investment firms established under Article 5(3) of Directive 2004/39/EC. '.

(5) The following Article is inserted:

'*Article 15a*

1. The competent authorities shall cooperate with ESMA for the purposes of this Directive, in accordance with Regulation (EU) No 1095/2010.

2. The competent authorities shall, without delay, provide ESMA with all information necessary to carry out its duties, in accordance with Article 35 of Regulation (EU) No 1095/2010. '.

(6) Article 16 is amended as follows:

(a) in paragraph 2, the fourth subparagraph is replaced by the following:

'Without prejudice to Article 258 of the Treaty on the Functioning of the European Union (TFEU), a competent authority whose request for information is not acted upon within a reasonable time or whose request for information is rejected may refer that rejection or absence of action within a reasonable timeframe to ESMA. In the situations referred to in the first sentence, ESMA may act in accordance with Article 19 of Regulation (EU) No 1095/2010, without prejudice to the possibilities for refusing to act on a request for information provided for in the second subparagraph of this paragraph and to the possibility of ESMA acting in accordance with Article 17 of Regulation (EU) No 1095/2010. ';

(b) in paragraph 4, the fifth subparagraph is replaced by the following:

'Without prejudice to Article 258 TFEU, a competent authority whose application to open an inquiry or whose request for authorisation for its officials to accompany those of the other Member State's competent authority is not acted upon within a reasonable time or is rejected may refer that rejection or absence of action within a reasonable timeframe to ESMA. In the situations referred to in the first sentence, ESMA may act in accordance with Article 19 of Regulation (EU) No 1095/2010, without prejudice to the possibilities for refusing to act on a request for information provided in the fourth subparagraph of this paragraph and to the possibility of ESMA acting in accordance with Article 17 of Regulation (EU) No 1095/2010. ';

(c) paragraph 5 is replaced by the following:

'5. In order to ensure uniform conditions of application of paragraphs 2 and 4, ESMA may develop draft implementing technical standards on the procedures and forms

主管部门向公众披露某项行政措施或处罚后，应同时向欧洲证券与市场管理局报告。

公布的处罚涉及根据第2004/39/EC号指令获得核准的投资公司的，欧洲证券与市场管理局应当在根据第2004/39/EC号指令第5条第3款建立的投资公司注册档案中记录此项处罚。”

(5)增加下列条款：

“第15a条

1.主管部门应根据第1095/2010号(欧盟)条例的规定，为本指令之目的与欧洲证券与市场管理局合作。

2.主管部门应根据第1095/2010号(欧盟)条例第35条的规定，立即向欧洲证券与市场管理局提供履行其职责所必要的一切信息。”

(6)对第16条修正如下：

(a)第2款第4项替换为下列内容：

“在不影响《欧洲联盟运行条约》(TFEU)第258条的情形下，主管部门提出的信息请求未在合理的时间内落实或者请求被拒的，该主管部门可在合理的期限内将该等情况移交欧洲证券与市场管理局处理。在第一句所述情形下，欧洲证券与市场管理局可依照第1095/2010号(欧盟)条例第19条行事，但不影响被请求主管部门依本款第2项拒绝信息请求的权利，也不影响欧洲证券与市场管理局依照第1095/2010号(欧盟)条例第17条的规定行事的权利；”

(b)第4款第5项替换为下列内容：

“在不影响《欧洲联盟运行条约》第258条的情形下，主管部门提出的启动调查的申请或允许其官员陪同其他成员国主管部门官员的请求未在合理的时间内落实或被拒绝的，该主管部门可在合理期限内将该等情况移交欧洲证券与市场管理局处理。在第一句所述情况下，欧洲证券与市场管理局可依照第1095/2010号(欧盟)条例第19条的规定行事，但不影响被请求主管部门依本款第4项拒绝信息请求的权利，也不影响欧洲证券与市场管理局依照第1095/2010号(欧盟)条例第17条的规定行事的权利；”

(c)第5款替换为下列内容：

“5.为确保第2款和第4款具有统一的适用条件，欧洲证券与市场管理局可就本条所述信息交换和跨境检查的程序和形式起草实施性技术标准草案。

for exchange of information and for cross-border inspections as referred to in this Article.

Power is conferred on the Commission to adopt the implementing technical standards referred to in the first subparagraph in accordance with Article 15 of Regulation (EU) No 1095/2010. '.

(7) The following Article is inserted:

'*Article 17a*

By 1 December 2011 the Commission shall review Articles 1, 6, 8, 14, and 16 and present any appropriate legislative proposals in order to allow the full application of the delegated acts under Article 290 TFEU and implementing acts under Article 291 TFEU in respect of this Directive. Without prejudice to implementing measures already adopted, the powers conferred on the Commission in Article 17 to adopt implementing measures that remain after the entry into force of the Lisbon Treaty shall cease to apply on 1 December 2012. '.

Article 4 Amendments to Directive 2003/41/EC

Directive 2003/41/EC is hereby amended as follows:

(1) Article 9 is amended as follows:

(a) in paragraph 1, point (a) is replaced by the following:

'(a) the institution is registered in a national register by the competent authority or authorised; in the case of cross-border activities referred to in Article 20, the register shall also indicate the Member States in which the institution is operating; that information shall be communicated to the European Supervisory Authority (European Insurance and Occupational Pensions Authority)(hereinafter "EIOPA"), established by Regulation (EU) No 1094/2010 of the European Parliament and of the Council (*) which shall publish it on its website;

(*) OJ L 331, 15. 12. 2010, p. 48. ';

(b) paragraph 5 is replaced by the following:

'5. In the case of cross-border activity as referred to in Article 20, the conditions of operation of the institution shall be subject to a prior authorisation by the competent authorities of the home Member State. When giving such authorisation, Member States shall immediately inform EIOPA. '.

(2) Article 13 is amended as follows:

(a) the existing text is numbered as paragraph 1;

(b) the following paragraph is added:

'2. EIOPA may develop draft implementing technical standards on the forms and formats for the documents listed in paragraph 1(c)(i) to (vi).

Power is conferred on the Commission to adopt the implementing technical standards referred to in the first subparagraph in accordance with Article 15 of Regulation (EU) No

兹授予欧盟委员会依照第1095/2010号(欧盟)条例第15条的规定通过第1项所述实施性技术标准的权力。”

(7)增加下列条款:

“第17a条

欧盟委员会应于2011年12月1日前对第1条、第6条、第8条、第14条和第16条进行审评并提交任何适当的立法提案,以促使《欧洲联盟运行条约》第290条中的授权立法以及《欧洲联盟运行条约》第291条中的实施性立法就本指令而言得以全面适用。在不影响已经制定的实施细则的情形下,第17条授予欧盟委员会制定实施细则且在《里斯本条约》生效后仍然有效的权力应于2012年12月1日停止适用。”

第4条　对第2003/41/EC号指令的修正

特此对第2003/41/EC号指令修正如下:

(1)第9条修正如下:

(a)第1款第a目替换为下列内容:

“(a)该机构经主管部门在国家注册档案中登记或获得核准;对于第20条所述的跨境活动,注册档案还应指明机构营业地所在的成员国;应通知依据《欧洲议会与欧盟理事会第1094/2010号(欧盟)条例》*设立的欧洲监管机构(欧洲保险与职业养老金管理局)(英文简称EIOPA)该等信息并在后者网站上公布;

*《欧盟公报》L 331,2010年12月15日,第48页。”

(b)第5款替换为下列内容:

“5.在从事第20条所述跨境活动的情形下,从事该活动的机构的运作条件应事先获得母国主管部门核准。各成员国应在授予核准后立即通知欧洲保险与职业养老金管理局。”

(2)对第13条修正如下:

(a)将现有文字重新编号,改为第1款;

(b)增加下列条款:

“2.欧洲保险与职业养老金管理局可起草实施性技术标准草案,具体说明第1款第c项第i目至第vi目所列文件的形式和格式。

兹授予欧盟委员会依照第1094/2010号(欧盟)条例第15条的规定通过第1项所述实施性技术标准的权力。”

1094/2010. '.

(3) In Article 14(4), the second subparagraph is replaced by the following:

'Any decision to prohibit the activities of an institution shall contain detailed reasons and be notified to the institution in question. It shall also be notified to EIOPA. '.

(4) In Article 15(6), the first subparagraph is replaced by the following:

'6. With a view to further harmonisation of the rules regarding the calculation of technical provisions which may be justified-in particular the interest rates and other assumptions influencing the level of technical provisions-the Commission, drawing on advice from EIOPA, shall, every 2 years or at the request of a Member State, issue a report on the situation concerning the development in cross-border activities. '.

(5) In Article 20, the following paragraph is added:

'11. Member States shall report to EIOPA their national provisions of prudential nature relevant to the field of occupational pension schemes, which are not covered by the reference to national social and labour law in paragraph 1.

Member States shall update that information on a regular basis and at least every 2 years and EIOPA shall make that information available on its website.

In order to ensure uniform conditions of application of this paragraph, EIOPA shall develop draft implementing technical standards on the procedures to be followed and formats and templates to be used by the competent authorities when transmitting and updating the relevant information to EIOPA. EIOPA shall submit those draft implementing technical standards to the Commission by 1 January 2014.

Power is conferred on the Commission to adopt the implementing technical standards referred to in the third subparagraph in accordance with Article 15 of Regulation (EU) No 1094/2010. '.

(6) Article 21 is amended as follows:

(a) the title is replaced by the following:

'Cooperation between Member States, EIOPA and the Commission';

(b) the following paragraph is inserted:

'2a. The competent authorities shall cooperate with EIOPA for the purposes of this Directive, in accordance with Regulation (EU) No 1094/2010.

The competent authorities shall without delay provide EIOPA with all information necessary to carry out its duties under this Directive and under Regulation (EU) No 1094/2010, in accordance with Article 35 of that Regulation. ';

(c) paragraph 3 is replaced by the following:

'3. Each Member State shall inform the Commission and EIOPA of any major difficulties to which the application of this Directive gives rise.

The Commission, EIOPA and the competent authorities of the Member States

(3)第14条第4款第2项替换为下列内容：

“禁止某机构活动的任何决定均应包含具体的理由并应通知所涉机构，同时应通知欧洲保险与职业养老金管理局。”

(4)第15条第6款第1项替换为下列内容：

“6.为进一步协调或有理由存在的技术准备金的各种计算规则——特别是利率以及影响技术准备金水平的其他假设——根据欧洲保险与职业养老金管理局的建议，欧盟委员会应每2年或经成员国请求发布关于跨境活动发展动态的报告。”

(5)第20条增加下列内容：

“11.各成员国应向欧洲保险与职业养老金管理局报告其国内制定的有关职业养老金计划的审慎规定，该等规定不属于第1款所述成员国国内的社会保障和劳动法覆盖的范围。

各成员国应定期更新该等信息，至少每2年1次，欧洲保险与职业养老金管理局应在其网站上公布该等信息。

为确保本款具有统一的适用条件，欧洲保险与职业养老金管理局应起草实施性技术标准草案，具体说明主管部门向欧洲保险与职业养老金管理局发送和更新相关信息应遵循的程序，以及应使用的格式和模板。欧洲保险与职业养老金管理局应于2014年1月1日前将该等实施性技术标准草案提交欧盟委员会。

兹授予欧盟委员会依照第1094/2010号(欧盟)条例第15条的规定通过第3项所述实施性技术标准的权力。”

(6)对第21条修正如下：

(a)标题替换为：

“各成员国、欧洲保险与职业养老金管理局和欧盟委员会之间的合作”；

(b)增加下列内容：

“2a.主管部门应根据第1094/2010号(欧盟)条例的规定，为本指令之目的与欧洲保险与职业养老金管理局合作。

主管部门应根据第1094/2010号(欧盟)条例第35条的规定，立即向欧洲保险与职业养老金管理局提供其按本指令以及该条例履行职责所必要的一切信息。”

(c)第3款替换为下列内容：

“3.因适用本指令而造成任何重大困难的，各成员国应通报欧盟委员会和欧洲保险与职业养老金管理局。

欧盟委员会、欧洲保险与职业养老金管理局以及所涉成员国的主管部门应尽快

concerned shall examine such difficulties as quickly as possible in order to find an appropriate solution. '.

Article 5 Amendments to Directive 2003/71/EC

Directive 2003/71/EC is hereby amended as follows:

(1) In Article 4, paragraph 3 is replaced by the following:

'3. In order to ensure consistent harmonisation of this Directive, the European Supervisory Authority (European Securities and Markets Authority) (hereinafter "ESMA") established by Regulation (EU) No 1095/2010 of the European Parliament and of the Council (*) may develop draft regulatory technical standards to specify the exemptions concerning the points (a) to (e) of paragraph 1 and points (a) to (h) of paragraph 2.

Power is delegated to the Commission to adopt the regulatory technical standards referred to in the first subparagraph in accordance with the procedure laid down in Articles 10 to 14 of Regulation (EU) No 1095/2010.

(*) OJ L 331, 15. 12. 2010, p. 84. ';

(2) In Article 5(2), the following subparagraphs are added:

'In order to ensure uniform conditions of application of this Directive and of the delegated acts adopted by the Commission in accordance with paragraph 5, ESMA shall develop draft implementing technical standards in order to ensure uniform conditions of application of the delegated acts adopted by the Commission in accordance with paragraph 5 in relation to a uniform template for the presentation of the summary and to allow investors to compare the security concerned with other relevant products.

Power is conferred on the Commission to adopt the implementing technical standards referred to in the first subparagraph in accordance with Article 15 of Regulation (EU) No 1095/2010. '.

(3) In Article 7, the following paragraph is added:

'4. ESMA may develop draft implementing technical standards in order to ensure uniform conditions of application of the delegated acts adopted by the Commission in accordance with paragraph 1.

Power is conferred on the Commission to adopt the implementing technical standards referred to in the first subparagraph in accordance with Article 15 of Regulation (EU) No 1095/2010. '.

(4) In Article 8, the following paragraph is added:

'5. ESMA may develop draft implementing technical standards to ensure uniform conditions of application of the delegated acts adopted by the Commission in accordance with paragraph 4.

Power is conferred on the Commission to adopt the implementing technical standards referred to in the first subparagraph in accordance with Article 15 of Regulation (EU) No

对上述困难进行审查,找出适当的解决方案。”

第5条　对第2003/71/EC号指令的修正

特此对第2003/71/EC号指令修正如下:

(1)第4条第3款替换为下列内容:

“3.为确保本指令的一致协调,依据《欧洲议会与欧盟理事会第1095/2010号(欧盟)条例》*设立的欧洲监管机构(欧洲证券与市场管理局)(以下简称欧洲证券与市场管理局,英文简称ESMA)可起草监管性技术标准草案,具体说明对第1款第a目至第e目以及第2款第a目至第h目的豁免。

经委托授权,欧盟委员会有权根据第1095/2010号(欧盟)条例第10条至第14条规定的程序通过第1项所述监管性技术标准。

*《欧盟公报》L 331,2010年12月15日,第84页。”

(2)第5条第2款增加下列内容:

“为确保本指令以及欧盟委员会根据第5款通过的授权立法具有统一的适用条件,欧洲证券与市场管理局应起草实施性技术标准草案,以便欧盟委员会按照第5款通过的关于摘要列报统一模板的授权立法具有统一的适用条件,并使投资者得以将所涉证券与其他相关产品进行比较。

兹授予欧盟委员会依照第1095/2010号(欧盟)条例第15条的规定通过第1项所述实施性技术标准的权力。”

(3)第7条增加下列内容:

“4.为确保欧盟委员会根据第1款通过的授权立法具有统一的适用条件,欧洲证券与市场管理局可起草实施性技术标准草案。

兹授予欧盟委员会依照第1095/2010号(欧盟)条例第15条的规定通过第1项所述实施性技术标准的权力。”

(4)第8条增加下列内容:

“5.为确保欧盟委员会根据第4款通过的授权立法具有统一的适用条件,欧洲证券与市场管理局可起草实施性技术标准草案。

兹授予欧盟委员会依照第1095/2010号(欧盟)条例第15条的规定通过第1项所述实施性技术标准的权力。”

1095/2010. '.

(5) Article 13 is amended as follows:

(a) in paragraph 2, the following subparagraph is added:

'The competent authority shall notify ESMA of the approval of the prospectus and any supplement thereto at the same time as that approval is notified to the issuer, the offeror or the person asking for admission to trading on a regulated market, as the case may be. The competent authorities shall at the same time provide ESMA with a copy of the prospectus and any supplement thereto. ';

(b) paragraph 5 is replaced by the following:

'5. The competent authority of the home Member State may transfer the approval of a prospectus to the competent authority of another Member State, subject to prior notification to ESMA and the agreement of the competent authority. Such a transfer shall be notified to the issuer, the offeror or the person asking for admission to trading on a regulated market within three working days from the date of the decision taken by the competent authority of the home Member State. The time limit referred to in paragraph 2 shall apply from that date. Article 28(4) of Regulation(EU) No 1095/2010 shall not apply to the transfer of the approval of the prospectus in accordance with this paragraph.

In order to ensure uniform conditions of application of this Directive and to facilitate communication between the competent authorities and between the competent authorities and ESMA, ESMA may develop draft implementing technical standards to establish standard forms, templates and procedures for the notifications provided for in this paragraph.

Power is conferred on the Commission to adopt the implementing technical standards referred to in the second subparagraph in accordance with Article 15 of Regulation (EU) No 1095/2010. '.

(6) Article 14 is amended as follows:

(a) paragraph 1 is replaced by the following:

'1. Once approved, the prospectus shall be filed with the competent authority of the home Member State, shall be accessible to ESMA through the competent authority and shall be made available to the public by the issuer, the offeror or the person asking for admission to trading on a regulated market as soon as practicable and, in any event, at a reasonable time in advance of, and at the latest at the beginning of, the offer to the public or the admission to trading of the securities involved. In addition, in the case of an initial public offer of a class of shares not already admitted to trading on a regulated market that is to be admitted to trading for the first time, the prospectus shall be available at least six working days before the end of the offer. ';

(5)对第13条修正如下：

(a)第2款增加下列内容：

“通知发行人、要约人或请求使其证券获准在受监管市场交易的人(视具体情况而定)其招募说明书及其任何补充说明获得批准的同时，主管部门还应通知欧洲证券与市场管理局该项批准。主管部门还应同时向欧洲证券与市场管理局提供一份招募说明书及其任何补充说明；”

(b)第5款替换为下列内容：

“5.母国主管部门可将招募说明书的审批权委托给另一成员国的主管部门，但须事先通知欧洲证券与市场管理局并经该另一成员国主管部门的同意。母国主管部门作出该等委托决定之日起3个工作日内，须通知发行人、要约人或请求使其证券获准在受监管市场交易的人。第2款所述的时限应从该日起算。第1095/2010号(欧盟)条例第28条第4款不应适用于依照本款进行的招募说明书审批权的委托。

为确保本指令具有统一的适用条件，促进各主管部门之间以及主管部门和欧洲证券与市场管理局之间的沟通，欧洲证券与市场管理局可起草实施性技术标准草案，就本款规定的通知制定标准的格式、模板和程序。

兹授予欧盟委员会依照第1095/2010号(欧盟)条例第15条的规定通过第2项所述实施性技术标准的权力。”

(6)对第14条修正如下：

(a)第1款替换为下列内容：

“1.招募说明书一旦获得批准即应提交母国主管部门。欧洲证券与市场管理局可通过主管部门查阅招募说明书。发行人、要约人或请求使其证券获准在受监管市场交易的人应尽快向公众公布招募说明书。在任何情形下，提交和公布时间均应在所涉证券向公众发行或获准交易之前的一段合理时间内，并且最迟应在所涉证券开始向公众发行或获准交易之时。此外，涉及未曾获准在受监管市场交易的某一类别股票的首次公开发行的，应在发行结束前至少6个工作日公布该招募说明书；”

(b) the following paragraph is inserted:

'4a. ESMA shall publish on its website the list of prospectuses approved in accordance with Article 13, including, if applicable, a hyperlink to the prospectus published on the website of the competent authority of the home Member State, or on the website of the issuer, or on the website of the regulated market. The published list shall be kept up-to-date and each item shall remain on the website for a period of at least 12 months. '.

(7) In Article 16, the following paragraph is added:

'3. In order to ensure consistent harmonisation, to specify the requirements laid down in this Article and to take account of technical developments on financial markets, ESMA shall develop draft regulatory technical standards to specify situations where a significant new factor, material mistake or inaccuracy relating to the information included in the prospectus requires a supplement to the prospectus to be published. ESMA shall submit those draft regulatory technical standards to the Commission by 1 January 2014.

Power is delegated to the Commission to adopt the regulatory technical standards referred to in the first subparagraph in accordance with the procedure laid down in Articles 10 to 14 of Regulation (EU) No 1095/2010. '.

(8) Article 17 is amended as follows:

(a) paragraph 1 is replaced by the following:

'1. Without prejudice to Article 23, where an offer to the public or admission to trading on a regulated market is provided for in one or more Member States, or in a Member State other than the home Member State, the prospectus approved by the home Member State and any supplements thereto shall be valid for the public offer or the admission to trading in any number of host Member States, provided that ESMA and the competent authority of each host Member State are notified in accordance with Article 18. Competent authorities of host Member States shall not undertake any approval or administrative procedures relating to prospectuses. ';

(b) paragraph 2 is replaced by the following:

'2. If significant new factors, material mistakes or inaccuracies come to light after approval of the prospectus, as referred to in Article 16, the competent authority of the home Member State shall require the publication of a supplement to be approved in accordance with Article 13(1). ESMA and the competent authority of the host Member State may inform the competent authority of the home Member State of the need for new information. '.

(9) In Article 18, the following paragraphs are added:

'3. The competent authority of the home Member State shall notify ESMA of the certificate of approval of the prospectus at the same time as it is notified to the competent

(b)增加下列内容:

"4a.欧洲证券与市场管理局应在其网站上公布根据第13条获得批准的招募说明书的清单,包括(如适用)能链接到在母国主管部门、发行人或者受监管市场的网站上公布的招募说明书的超链接。所公布的清单应持续更新,并且每个项目均应在网站上保留至少12个月。"

(7)第16条增加下列内容:

"3.为确保一致协调、具体说明本条所列之要求并反映金融市场的技术发展动态,欧洲证券与市场管理局应起草监管性技术标准草案,以列明由于招募说明书信息出现重大的新要素、实质错误或误差而需公布招募说明书补充说明的情况。欧洲证券与市场管理局应于2014年1月1日前将该等监管性技术标准草案呈报给欧盟委员会。

经委托授权,欧盟委员会有权根据第1095/2010号(欧盟)条例第10条至第14条规定的程序通过第1项所述监管性技术标准。"

(8)对第17条修正如下:

(a)第1款替换为下列内容:

"1.在不影响第23条的情形下,准备在一个或多个成员国或在一个非母国的成员国向公众发行或获准在受监管市场交易证券的,经母国批准的招募说明书及其任何补充说明对在各个东道国公开发行或获准交易证券均应有效;前提是欧洲证券与市场管理局以及每个东道国主管部门均按第18条的规定收到通知。对于该等招募说明书,东道国主管部门不应施加任何审批或行政程序。"

(b)第2款替换为下列内容:

"2.如果如第16条所述的,招募说明书获得批准后出现重大的新要素、实质错误或者误差,则母国主管部门应要求公布应按第13条第1款获得批准的招募说明书补充说明。欧洲证券与市场管理局和东道国主管部门可通知母国主管部门该等应要求提供新信息的情况。"

(9)第18条增加下列内容:

"3.母国主管部门应在向东道国主管部门通知招募说明书批准证书的同时通知欧洲证券与市场管理局。

authority of the host Member State.

ESMA and the competent authority of the host Member State shall publish on their websites the list of certificates of approval of prospectuses and any supplements thereto, which are notified in accordance with this Article, including, if applicable, a hyperlink to those documents published on the website of the competent authority of the home Member State, on the website of the issuer, or on the website of the regulated market. The published list shall be kept up-to-date and each item shall remain on the websites for a period of at least 12 months.

4. In order to ensure uniform conditions of application of this Directive and to take account of technical developments on financial markets, ESMA may develop draft implementing technical standards to establish standard forms, templates and procedures for the notification of the certificate of approval, the copy of the prospectus, the supplement of the prospectus and the translation of the summary.

Power is conferred on the Commission to adopt the implementing technical standards referred to in the first subparagraph in accordance with Article 15 of Regulation (EU) No 1095/2010. '.

(10) Article 21 is amended as follows:

(a) the following paragraphs are inserted:

'1a. The competent authorities shall cooperate with ESMA for the purposes of this Directive, in accordance with Regulation (EU) No 1095/2010.

1b. The competent authorities shall without delay provide ESMA with all information necessary to carry out its duties, in accordance with Article 35 of Regulation (EU) No 1095/2010. ';

(b) in paragraph 2, the third subparagraph is replaced by the following:

'The Member States shall inform the Commission, ESMA and the competent authorities of other Member States of any arrangements entered into with regard to delegation of tasks, including the precise conditions regulating such delegation. ';

(c) in paragraph 4, the following subparagraph is added:

'In accordance with Article 21 of Regulation (EU) No 1095/2010, ESMA shall be entitled to participate in on-site inspections referred to in point (d) where they are carried out jointly by two or more competent authorities. '.

(11) Article 22 is amended as follows:

(a) in paragraph 2, the following subparagraph is added:

'The competent authorities may refer to ESMA situations where a request for cooperation, in particular to exchange information, has been rejected or has not been acted upon within a reasonable time. Without prejudice to Article 258 of the Treaty on the Functioning of the European Union (TFEU), ESMA may, in the situations referred to

欧洲证券与市场管理局以及东道国主管部门应在其网站上公布已依本条作出相应通知的招募说明书的批准证书清单以及对其所作的任何补充说明的清单，包括（如适用）一个能够链接到母国主管部门网站、发行人网站以及受监管市场网站上的该等文件的超链接。所公布的清单应持续更新，并且每个项目均应在网站上保留至少12个月。

4.为确保本指令具有统一的适用条件以及反映金融市场的技术发展动态，欧洲证券与市场管理局可起草实施性技术标准草案，就批准证书的通知、招募说明书的复本和补充说明以及摘要的翻译制定标准的格式、模板和程序。

兹授予欧盟委员会依照第1095/2010号（欧盟）条例第15条的规定通过第1项所述实施性技术标准的权力。”

（10）对第21款修正如下：

（a）增加下款：

“1a.主管部门应根据第1095/2010号（欧盟）条例的规定，为本指令之目的与欧洲证券与市场管理局合作。

“1b.主管部门应根据第1095/2010号（欧盟）条例第35条的规定，立即向欧洲证券与市场管理局提供其履行职责所必要的一切信息。”

（b）第2款第3项替换为下列内容：

“各成员国应通知欧盟委员会、欧洲证券与市场管理局以及其他成员国的主管部门任何有关职责委托的安排，包括规范该等委托的确切条件。”

（c）第4款增加下列内容：

“根据第1095/2010号（欧盟）条例第21条的规定，在有2个或以上主管部门共同参与的情形下，欧洲证券与市场管理局应有权参与第d目所述的现场检查。”

（11）对第22条修正如下：

（a）第2款增加下列内容：

“主管部门提出的合作请求（特别是信息交换请求）被拒绝或未在合理的时间内落实的，该主管部门可将该等情况移交欧洲证券与市场管理局处理。在不影响《欧洲联盟运行条约》（TFEU）第258条的情形下，欧洲证券与市场管理局可在第一句所述情况下，依照第1095/2010号（欧盟）条例第19条授予的权力行事。”

in the first sentence, act in accordance with the power conferred on it under Article 19 of Regulation (EU) No 1095/2010. ';

(b) paragraph 3 is replaced by the following:

'3. Paragraph 1 shall not prevent the competent authorities from exchanging confidential information or from transmitting confidential information to ESMA or the European Systemic Risk Board (hereinafter the "ESRB"), subject to constraints relating to firm-specific information and effects on third countries as provided for in Regulation (EU) No 1095/2010 and Regulation (EU) No 1092/2010 of the European Parliament and of the Council of 24 November 2010 on European Union macro-prudential oversight of the financial system and establishing a European Systemic Risk Board (*) respectively. Information exchanged between competent authorities and ESMA or the ESRB shall be covered by the obligation of professional secrecy, to which the persons employed or formerly employed by the competent authorities receiving the information are subject.

(*) OJ L331, 15. 12. 2010, p. 1. ';

(c) The following paragraph is added:

'4. In order to ensure consistent harmonisation of this Article and to take account of technical developments on financial markets, ESMA shall develop draft regulatory technical standards to specify the information required in paragraph 2.

Power is delegated to the Commission to adopt the regulatory technical standards referred to in the first subparagraph in accordance with Articles 10 to 14 of Regulation (EU) No 1095/2010.

In order to ensure uniform conditions of application of paragraph 2, and to take account of technical developments on financial markets, ESMA may develop draft implementing technical standards to establish standard forms, templates and procedures for the cooperation and exchange of information between competent authorities.

Power is conferred on the Commission to adopt the implementing technical standards referred to in the third subparagraph in accordance with Article 15 ofRegulation (EU) No 1095/2010. '.

(12) Article 23 is replaced by the following:

'*Article 23*

Precautionary measures

1. Where the competent authority of the host Member State finds that irregularities have been committed by the issuer or by the financial institutions in charge of the public offer or that the issuer has breached its obligations by reason of the fact that securities are admitted to trading on a regulated market, it shall refer those findings to the competent authority of the home Member State and to ESMA.

2. If, despite the measures taken by the competent authority of the home Member

(b)第3款替换为下列内容:

"3.第1095/2010号(欧盟)条例以及《欧洲议会与欧盟理事会关于欧盟对金融系统的宏观审慎监控以及设立欧洲系统性风险委员会的第1092/2010号(欧盟)条例》*(2010年11月24日)就具体企业的信息以及对第三国产生的影响规定了各种限制。在遵守该等限制的情形下,第1款不得妨碍各主管部门交换保密信息或将保密信息发送给欧洲证券与市场管理局或欧洲系统性风险委员会(英文简称ESRB)。主管部门和欧洲证券与市场管理局或欧洲系统性风险委员会之间交换的信息应在职业保密义务覆盖范围内,接收信息的主管部门的前任或现任雇员应受职业保密义务约束。

*《欧盟公报》L 331,2010年12月15日,第1页。"

(c)增加下列内容:

"4.为确保本条规定一致协调以及反映金融市场的技术发展动态,欧洲证券与市场管理局应起草监管性技术标准草案,具体说明第2款所要求的信息。

经委托授权,欧盟委员会有权根据第1095/2010号(欧盟)条例第10条至第14条的规定通过第1项所述监管性技术标准。

为确保第2款具有统一的适用条件以及反映金融市场的技术发展动态,欧洲证券与市场管理局可起草实施性技术标准草案,就主管部门之间的合作和信息交换制定标准的格式、模板和程序。

兹授予欧盟委员会依照第1095/2010号(欧盟)条例第15条的规定通过第3项所述实施性技术标准的权力。"

(12)第23条替换为下列内容:

"第23条

预防性措施

1.如认定发行人或负责公开发行的金融机构有违法违规行为,或发行人由于证券获准在受监管市场交易的事实而违反了其义务,东道国主管部门应将其认定结果移交母国主管部门和欧洲证券与市场管理局处理。

2.尽管母国主管部门已采取措施,或由于事实证明采取的措施不充分,发行人或

State or because such measures prove inadequate, the issuer or the financial institution in charge of the public offer persists in breaching the relevant legal or regulatory provisions, the competent authority of the host Member State, after informing the competent authority of the home Member State and ESMA, shall take all appropriate measures in order to protect investors and shall inform the Commission and ESMA thereof at the earliest opportunity. '.

Article 6 Amendments to Directive 2004/39/EC

Directive 2004/39/EC is hereby amended as follows:

(1) Article 5(3) is replaced by the following:

'3. Member States shall register all investment firms. The register shall be publicly accessible and shall contain information on the services or activities for which the investment firm is authorised. It shall be updated on a regular basis. Every authorisation shall be notified to the European Supervisory Authority (European Securities and Markets Authority) (hereinafter "ESMA"), established by Regulation (EU) No 1095/2010 of the European Parliament and of the Council(*).

(*) OJ L 331, 15. 12. 2010, p. 84. '.

ESMA shall establish a list of all investment firms in the Union. The list shall contain information on the services or activities for which the investment firm is authorised and it shall be updated on a regular basis. ESMA shall publish and keep up-to-date that list on its website.

Where a competent authority has withdrawn an authorisation in accordance with Article 8(b) to (d), that withdrawal shall be published on the list for a period of 5 years.

(2) In Article 7, the following paragraph is added:

'4. In order to ensure consistent harmonisation of this Article and of Article 9(2) to (4), Article 10(1) and (2), ESMA may develop draft regulatory technical standards to specify:

(a) the information to be provided to the competent authorities under Article 7(2) including the programme of operations;

(b) the requirements applicable to the management of investment firms under Article 9(4) and the information for the notifications under Article 9(2);

(c) the requirements applicable to shareholders and members with qualifying holdings, as well as obstacles which may prevent effective exercise of the supervisory functions of the competent authority, under Article 10(1) and (2).

Power is delegated to the Commission to adopt the regulatory technical standards referred to in the first subparagraph in accordance with Articles 10 to 14 of Regulation (EU) No 1095/2010.

In order to ensure uniform conditions of application of Article 7(2) and Article 9(2),

负责公开发行的金融机构继续违反相关法律规章的，则东道国主管部门应在通知母国主管部门和欧洲证券与市场管理局后采取保护投资者所需的一切适当措施，并尽早将情况告知欧盟委员会和欧洲证券与市场管理局。”

第6条　对第2004/39/EC号指令的修正

特此对第2004/39/EC号指令修正如下：

（1）第5条第3款替换为下列内容：

“3.各成员国应对所有投资公司进行注册。注册档案应可供公众查阅并应包含与核准投资公司提供的服务或开展的活动有关的信息。注册档案应定期更新。应通知依据《欧洲议会与欧盟理事会第1095/2010号（欧盟）条例》*设立的欧洲监管机构（欧洲证券与市场管理局）（以下简称欧洲证券与市场管理局，英文简称ESMA）授予的每项核准。

*《欧盟公报》L 331，2010年12月15日，第84页。”

欧洲证券与市场管理局应制定一份包含了欧盟内所有投资公司的名册。名册应包含与核准投资公司开展的服务或活动有关的信息并应定期更新。欧洲证券与市场管理局应在其网站上公布该名册，并持续更新。

主管部门已经根据第8条第b款至第d款撤销了某项核准的，该项撤销应在名册上公布，且公布时间应长达5年。

（2）第7条增加下列内容：

“4.为确保本条和第9条第2款至第4款、第10条第1款和第2款的一致协调，欧洲证券与市场管理局可起草监管性技术标准草案，具体说明：

（a）按照第7条第2款应提供给主管部门的信息（包括运营计划）；

（b）第9条第4款中适用于投资公司管理层的规定以及第9条第2款要求通知的信息；

（c）第10条第1款和第2款所述适用于拥有重大持股数额的股东和成员的规定以及可能妨碍主管部门有效行使监管职能的障碍。

经委托授权，欧盟委员会有权根据第1095/2010号（欧盟）条例第10条至第14条的规定通过第1项所述监管性技术标准。

为确保第7条第2款和第9条第2款具有统一的适用条件，欧洲证券与市场管理局

ESMA may develop draft implementing technical standards to determine standard forms, templates and procedures for the notification or provision of information provided for in those Articles.

Power is conferred on the Commission to adopt the implementing technical standards referred to in the third subparagraph in accordance with Article 15 of Regulation (EU) No 1095/2010. '.

(3) In Article 8 the following paragraph is added:

'Every withdrawal of authorisation shall be notified to ESMA. '.

(4) In Article 10a, the following paragraph is added:

'8. In order to ensure consistent harmonisation of this Article, ESMA shall develop draft regulatory technical standards to establish an exhaustive list of information, referred to in paragraph 4, to be included by proposed acquirers in their notification, without prejudice to paragraph 2.

ESMA shall submit those draft regulatory technical standards to the Commission by 1 January 2014.

Power is delegated to the Commission to adopt the regulatory technical standards referred to in the first subparagraph in accordance with Articles 10 to 14 of Regulation (EU) No 1095/2010.

In order to ensure uniform conditions of application of Articles 10, 10a and 10b, ESMA shall develop draft implementing technical standards to determine standard forms, templates and procedures for the modalities of the consultation process between the relevant competent authorities as referred to in Article 10(4).

ESMA shall submit those draft implementing technical standards to the Commission by 1 January 2014.

Power is conferred on the Commission to adopt the implementing technical standards referred to in the fourth subparagraph in accordance with Article 15 of Regulation (EU) No 1095/2010. '.

(5) Article 15 is amended as follows

(a) paragraph 1 is replaced by the following:

'1. Member States shall inform the Commission and ESMA of any general difficulties which their investment firms encounter in establishing themselves or providing investment services and/or performing investment activities in any third country. '

(b) paragraph 2 is replaced by the following:

'2. Whenever it appears to the Commission, on the basis of information submitted to it under paragraph 1, that a third country does not grant Union investment firms effective market access comparable to that granted by the Union to investment firms from that third country, the Commission, taking into account guidance issued by ESMA, shall submit

可起草实施性技术标准草案，就该等条款规定的通知或信息提供制定标准的格式、模板和程序。

兹授予欧盟委员会依照第1095/2010号（欧盟）条例第15条的规定通过第3项所述实施性技术标准的权力。”

（3）第8条增加下列内容：

“应通知欧洲证券与市场管理局被撤销的每一项核准。”

（4）第10a条增加下列内容：

“8.在不影响第2款的情形下，为确保本条款一致协调，欧洲证券与市场管理局应起草监管性技术标准草案，制定一份第4款所述的应提供的信息的详尽清单。拟议收购方须将该等信息纳入其通知中。

欧洲证券与市场管理局应于2014年1月1日前将该等监管性技术标准草案呈报给欧盟委员会。

经委托授权，欧盟委员会有权根据第1095/2010号（欧盟）条例第10条至第14条的规定通过第1项所述监管性技术标准。

为确保第10条、第10a条和第10b条具有统一的适用条件，欧洲证券与市场管理局应起草实施性技术标准草案，就第10条第4款所述相关主管部门之间的磋商程序开展的方式制定标准的格式、模板和程序。

欧洲证券与市场管理局应于2014年1月1日之前将该等实施性技术标准草案呈报给欧盟委员会。

兹授予欧盟委员会依照第1095/2010号（欧盟）条例第15条的规定通过第4项所述实施性技术标准的权力。”

（5）对第15条修正如下：

（a）第1款替换为下列内容：

“1.如投资公司在任何第三国设立机构或提供投资服务和/或进行投资活动时遭遇普遍性困难，则其所属成员国应通知欧盟委员会和欧洲证券与市场管理局。”

（b）第2款替换为下列内容：

“2.基于按第1款呈报的信息，欧盟委员会初步判断，与欧盟给予来自某第三国投资公司的实际市场准入相比，该第三国并未同等对待来自欧盟的投资公司的，欧盟委员会应参照欧洲证券与市场管理局发布的指引，向欧盟理事会提议授予欧盟委员会适当的委托以与第三国进行谈判，为欧盟的投资公司争取具有可比性的竞争机会。欧

proposals to the Council for an appropriate mandate for negotiation with a view to obtaining comparable competitive opportunities for Union investment firms. The Council shall act by qualified majority.

The European Parliament shall be immediately and fully informed at all stages of the procedure in accordance with Article 217 of the Treaty on the Functioning of the European Union (TFEU).

ESMA shall assist the Commission for the purposes of this Article. '.

(6) In Article 16(2), the following subparagraph is added:

'ESMA may develop guidelines regarding the monitoring methods referred to in this paragraph. '.

(7) In Article 19(6), the first indent is replaced by the following:

'the services referred to in the introductory part relate to shares admitted to trading on a regulated market or in an equivalent third-country market, money market instruments, bonds or other forms of securitised debt (excluding those bonds or securitised debt that embed a derivative), UCITS and other non-complex financial instruments. A third-country market shall be considered as equivalent to a regulated market if it complies with equivalent requirements to those established under Title Ⅲ. The Commission and ESMA shall publish on their websites a list of those markets that are to be considered as equivalent. That list shall be updated periodically. ESMA shall assist the Commission in the assessment of third-country markets. '.

(8) In Article 23(3), the first subparagraph is replaced by the following:

'3. Member States that decide to allow investment firms to appoint tied agents shall establish a public register. Tied agents shall be registered in the public register in the Member State where they are established. ESMA shall publish on its website references or hyperlinks to the public registers established under this Article by the Member States that decide to allow investment firms to appoint tied agents. '.

(9) Article 25 is amended as follows:

(a) paragraph 1 is replaced by the following:

'1. Without prejudice to the allocation of responsibilities for enforcing the provisions of Directive 2003/6/EC of the European Parliament and of the Council of 28 January 2003 on insider dealing and market manipulation (market abuse) (*), Member States coordinated by ESMA in accordance with Article 31 of Regulation (EU) No 1095/2010 shall ensure that appropriate measures are in place to enable the competent authority to monitor the activities of investment firms to ensure that they act honestly, fairly and professionally and in a manner which promotes the integrity of the market.

(*) OJ L 96, 12. 4. 2003, p. 16. ';

(b) paragraph 2 is replaced by the following:

盟理事会应按特定多数的决策规则行事。

应当依照《欧洲联盟运行条约》(TFEU)第217条的规定,即时并全面地向欧洲议会通知上述程序所有环节。

欧洲证券与市场管理局应为本条之目的协助欧盟委员会。”

(6)第16条第2款增加下列内容:

“欧洲证券与市场管理局可就本款所述的监控方法制定指引。”

(7)第19条第6款第1目替换为下列内容:

“导言所述的服务是指与下列各项有关的服务:获准在受监管市场或具有等效性的第三国市场交易的股票、货币市场工具、债券或其他形式的证券化债务(不包括嵌入衍生品的债券或证券化债务)、可转让证券集合投资计划以及其他非复杂金融工具。第三国市场遵循了与第三编制定的要求具有等效性的要求的,应被视为与受监管市场具有等效性的市场。欧盟委员会和欧洲证券与市场管理局应在其网站上公布一份名册,列明可被视为具有等效性的市场的第三国市场。该名册应定期更新。欧洲证券与市场管理局应协助欧盟委员会对第三国市场进行评估。”

(8)第23条第3款第1项替换为下列内容:

“3.成员国决定允许投资公司指定固定代理人的,应建立公开注册档案。固定代理人应在其设立地所在成员国的公开注册档案中注册登记。欧洲证券与市场管理局应在其网站上公布允许投资公司指定固定代理人的成员国按本条规定建立的公开注册档案的名称或超链接。”

(9)对第25条修正如下:

(a)第1款替换为下列内容:

“1.在不影响《欧洲议会与欧盟理事会关于内幕交易和市场操纵(市场滥用)第2003/6/EC号指令》*(2003年1月28日)条款执行的职责分工的情形下,成员国应在欧洲证券与市场管理局依照第1095/2010号(欧盟)条例第31条的协调下,确保落实适当的措施,使主管部门能够监控投资公司的活动,保障投资公司以诚实、公平、专业和提升市场诚信度的方式行事。

*《欧盟公报》L 96,2003年4月12日,第16页。”

(b)第2款替换为下列内容:

'2. Member States shall require investment firms to keep at the disposal of the competent authority, for at least 5 years, the relevant data relating to all transactions in financial instruments which they have carried out, whether on own account or on behalf of a client. In the case of transactions carried out on behalf of clients, the records shall contain all the information and details of the identity of the client, and the information required under Directive 2005/60/EC.

ESMA may request access to that information in accordance with the procedure and under the conditions set out in Article 35 of Regulation (EU) No 1095/2010. '.

(10) Article 27(2) is replaced by the following:

'2. The competent authority of the most relevant market in terms of liquidity as defined in Article 25 for each share shall determine at least annually, on the basis of the arithmetic average value of the orders executed in the market in respect of that share, the class of shares to which it belongs. That information shall be made public to all market participants and transmitted to ESMA, which shall publish it on its website. '.

(11) Article 31 is amended as follows:

(a) in paragraph 2, the second subparagraph is replaced by the following:

'In cases where the investment firm intends to use tied agents, the competent authority of the home Member State of the investment firm shall, at the request of the competent authority of the host Member State and within a reasonable time, communicate the identity of the tied agents that the investment firm intends to use in that Member State. The host Member State may make public such information. ESMA may request access to that information in accordance with the procedure and under the conditions set out in Article 35 of Regulation (EU) No 1095/2010. '.

(b) the following paragraph is added:

'7. In order to ensure consistent harmonisation of this Article, ESMA may develop draft regulatory technical standards to specify the information to be notified in accordance with paragraphs 2, 4 and 6.

Power is delegated to the Commission to adopt the regulatory technical standards referred to in the first subparagraph in accordance with Articles 10 to 14 of Regulation (EU) No 1095/2010.

In order to ensure uniform conditions of application of this Article, ESMA may develop draft implementing technical standards to establish standard forms, templates and procedures for the transmission of information in accordance with paragraphs 3, 4 and 6.

Power is conferred on the Commission to adopt the implementing technical standards referred to in the third subparagraph in accordance with Article 15 of Regulation (EU) No 1095/2010. '.

(12) In Article 32, the following paragraph is added:

“2.各成员国应当要求投资公司将其进行的所有金融工具交易(不论是自营交易还是代理客户进行的交易)的相关数据至少保留5年,以备主管部门查阅。代理客户进行的交易记录应包括客户所有的身份信息和详情,并包括第2005/60/EC 号指令所要求的信息。

欧洲证券与市场管理局可依照第1095/2010号(欧盟)条例第35条规定的程序和条件提出查阅该等信息的请求。”

(10)第27条第2款替换为下列内容:

“2.根据第25条定义的流动性,某一市场属于特定个股的最密切相关市场的,该市场的主管部门应至少每年1次,根据该市场执行的该个股所有交易指令之算术平均值判断该股票应当划归哪一类别。该等信息应向所有市场参与者公布并发送给欧洲证券与市场管理局,由欧洲证券与市场管理局在其网站上公布。”

(11)对第31条修正如下:

(a)第2款第2项替换为下列内容:

“投资公司拟使用固定代理人的,经东道国主管部门提出要求,投资公司母国主管部门应当在合理的期限内告知东道国该投资公司拟在东道国聘用的固定代理人的身份信息。东道国可公开该等信息。欧洲证券与市场管理局可依照第1095/2010号(欧盟)条例第35条规定的程序和条件提出查阅该等信息的请求。”

(b)增加下列内容:

“7.为确保本条规定的一致协调,欧洲证券与市场管理局可起草监管性技术标准草案,具体说明根据第2款、第4款和第6款应通知的信息。

经委托授权,欧盟委员会有权根据第1095/2010号(欧盟)条例第10条至第14条的规定通过第1项所述监管性技术标准。

为确保本条规定具有统一的适用条件,欧洲证券与市场管理局可起草实施性技术标准草案,就依照第3款、第4款和第6款进行的信息发送制定标准的格式、模板和程序。

兹授予欧盟委员会依照第1095/2010号(欧盟)条例第15条的规定通过第3项所述实施性技术标准的权力。”

(12)第32条增加下列内容:

'10. In order to ensure consistent harmonisation of this Article, ESMA may develop draft regulatory technical standards to specify the information to be notified in accordance with paragraphs 2, 4 and 9.

Power is delegated to the Commission to adopt the regulatory technical standards referred to in the first subparagraph in accordance with Articles 10 to 14 of Regulation (EU) No 1095/2010.

In order to ensure uniform conditions of application of this Article, ESMA may develop draft implementing technical standards to establish standard forms, templates and procedures for the transmission of information in accordance with paragraphs 3 and 9.

Power is conferred on the Commission to adopt the implementing technical standards referred to in the third subparagraph in accordance with Article 15 of Regulation (EU) No 1095/2010. '.

(13) In Article 36, the following paragraph is added:

'6. ESMA shall be notified of any withdrawal of authorisation. '.

(14) Article 41(2) is replaced by the following:

'2. A competent authority which requests the suspension or removal of a financial instrument from trading on one or more regulated markets shall immediately make public its decision and inform ESMA and the competent authorities of the other Member States. Save where it is likely to cause significant damage to the investors' interests or the orderly functioning of the internal market, the competent authorities of the other Member States shall request the suspension or removal of that financial instrument from trading on the regulated markets and MTFs that operate under their supervision. '.

(15) In Article 42(6), the second subparagraph is replaced by the following:

'The regulated market shall communicate to the competent authority of its home Member State the Member State in which it intends to provide such arrangements. The competent authority of the home Member State shall communicate that information to the Member State in which the regulated market intends to provide such arrangements within 1 month. ESMA may request access to that information in accordance with the procedure and under the conditions set out in Article 35 of Regulation (EU) No 1095/2010. '.

(16) Article 47 is replaced by the following:

'*Article 47*

List of regulated markets

Each Member State shall draw up a list of the regulated markets for which it is the home Member State and shall forward that list to the other Member States and ESMA. A similar communication shall be effected in respect of each change to that list. ESMA shall publish and keep up-to-date a list of all regulated markets on its website. '.

(17) Article 48 is amended as follows:

“10.为确保本条规定的一致协调，欧洲证券与市场管理局可起草监管性技术标准草案，具体说明根据第2款、第4款和第9款应通知的信息。

经委托授权，欧盟委员会有权根据第1095/2010号(欧盟)条例第10条至第14条的规定通过第1项所述监管性技术标准。

为确保本条规定具有统一的适用条件，欧洲证券与市场管理局可起草实施性技术标准草案，就依照第3款和第9款进行的信息发送制定标准的格式、模板和程序。

兹授予欧盟委员会依照第1095/2010号(欧盟)条例第15条的规定通过第3项所述实施性技术标准的权力。”

(13)第36条增加下列内容：

“6.应通知欧洲证券与市场管理局被撤销的每一项核准。”

(14)第41条第2款替换为下列内容：

“2.当某主管部门要求将获准在一个或多个受监管市场交易的金融工具停牌或摘牌时，应当立刻公开该决定并通知欧洲证券与市场管理局和其他成员国的主管部门。其他成员国的主管部门应当要求所涉金融工具在受其监管的受监管市场和多边交易设施上停牌或摘牌；但是，可能会对投资者利益或市场有序运行造成重大损害的除外。”

(15)第42条第6款第2项替换为下列内容：

“受监管市场应当向母国主管部门告知拟前往哪个成员国提供该等安排。母国主管部门应在接到告知后1个月内将该等信息提供给该等拟议目的国。欧洲证券与市场管理局可依照第1095/2010号(欧盟)条例第35条规定的程序和条件提出查阅该等信息的请求。”

(16)第47条替换为下列内容：

“第47条

受监管市场名册

各成员国应当编制以其为母国的受监管市场的名册，并应当将此名册转发给其他成员国和欧洲证券与市场管理局。名册出现任何一项变更的，相关成员国均应履行类似的通知程序。欧洲证券与市场管理局应在其网站上公布包含了所有受监管市场的名册，并持续更新。”

(17)对第48条修正如下：

(a) paragraph 1 is replaced by the following:

'1. Each Member State shall designate the competent authorities which are to carry out each of the duties provided for in this Directive. Member States shall inform the Commission, ESMA and the competent authorities of other Member States of the identity of the competent authorities responsible for enforcement of each of those duties, and of any division of those duties. ';

(b) in paragraph 2, the third subparagraph is replaced by the following:

'Member States shall inform the Commission, ESMA and the competent authorities of other Member States of any arrangements entered into with regard to delegation of tasks, including the precise conditions regulating such delegation. ';

(c) paragraph 3 is replaced by the following:

'3. ESMA shall publish and keep up-to-date a list of the competent authorities referred to in paragraphs 1 and 2 on its website. '.

(18) In Article 51, the following paragraphs are added:

'4. Member States shall provide ESMA annually with aggregated information about all administrative measures and sanctions imposed in accordance with paragraphs 1 and 2.

5. Where the competent authority has disclosed an administrative measure or sanction to the public, it shall, contemporaneously, report that fact to ESMA.

6. Where a published sanction relates to an investment firm authorised in accordance with this Directive, ESMA shall add a reference to the published sanction in the register of investment firms established under Article 5(3). '.

(19) In Article 53, the following paragraph is added:

'3. The competent authorities shall notify ESMA of the complaint and redress procedures referred to in paragraph 1 which are available under its jurisdictions.

ESMA shall publish and keep up-to-date a list of all extra-judicial mechanisms on its website. '.

(20) The Title of Chapter II is replaced by the following:

'Cooperation between the competent authorities of the Member States and with ESMA'.

(21) Article 56 is amended as follows:

(a) in paragraph 1, the third subparagraph is replaced by the following:

'In order to facilitate and accelerate cooperation, and more particularly exchange of information, Member States shall designate a single competent authority as a contact point for the purposes of this Directive. Member States shall communicate to the Commission, ESMA and to the other Member States the names of the authorities which are designated to receive requests for exchange of information or cooperation pursuant to this paragraph. ESMA shall publish and keep up-to-date a list of those authorities on its website. ';

(a)第1款替换为下列内容:

"1.各成员国应当指定负责履行本指令中各项职责的主管部门。成员国在确定负责执行各项职责的主管部门以及该等职责的细化分工后,应相应通知欧盟委员会、欧洲证券与市场管理局及其他成员国的主管部门。"

(b)第2款第3项替换为下列内容:

"成员国应当将与工作委托有关的任何安排,包括规范工作委托的确切条件通知欧盟委员会、欧洲证券与市场管理局以及其他成员国的主管部门。"

(c)第3款替换为下列内容:

"3.欧洲证券与市场管理局应在其网站上公布第1款和第2款所述主管部门的名册,并持续更新。"

(18)第51条增加下列内容:

"4.成员国应每年向欧洲证券与市场管理局提供关于根据第1款和第2款施加的所有行政措施和行政处罚的汇总信息。

5.主管部门向公众披露某项行政措施或行政处罚的同时,也应向欧洲证券与市场管理局报告。

6. 受罚主体是按本指令获得核准的投资公司的,欧洲证券与市场管理局应在依照第5条第3款所建立的投资公司注册档案中加入有关公布的该项处罚的记录。"

(19)第53条增加下列内容:

"3.主管部门应向欧洲证券与市场管理局通知第1款所述其辖区内适用的投诉和整改程序。

欧洲证券与市场管理局应在其网站上公开所有司法外机制的清单,并持续更新。"

(20)第二章标题替换为:

"各成员国主管部门之间以及与欧洲证券与市场管理局之间的合作"

(21)第56条修正如下:

(a)第1款第3项替换为下列内容:

"为推动并加速合作,尤其为促进信息交换,各成员国应当各自指定一个单一的主管部门作为本指令中的联络方。成员国应当向欧盟委员会、欧洲证券与市场管理局以及其他成员国告知根据本款要求指定的负责接收信息交换或合作请求的部门。欧洲证券与市场管理局应在其网站上公布该等主管部门的名册,并持续更新;"

(b) paragraph 4 is replaced by the following:

'4. Where a competent authority has good reasons to suspect that acts contrary to the provisions of this Directive, carried out by entities not subject to its supervision, are being or have been carried out on the territory of another Member State, it shall notify the competent authority of the other Member State and ESMA in as specific a manner as possible. The notified competent authority shall take appropriate action. It shall inform the notifying competent authority and ESMA of the outcome of the action and, to the extent possible, of significant interim developments. This paragraph shall be without prejudice to the competence of the notifying competent authority. ';

(c) the following paragraph is added:

'6. In order to ensure uniform conditions of application of this Article, ESMA may develop draft implementing technical standards to establish standard forms, templates and procedures for the cooperation arrangements referred to in paragraph 2.

Power is conferred on the Commission to adopt the implementing technical standards referred to in the first subparagraph in accordance with Article 15 of Regulation (EU) No 1095/2010. '.

(22) Article 57 is amended as follows:

(a) the existing text is renumbered as paragraph 1.

(b) the following paragraphs are added:

'2. With the objective of converging supervisory practices, ESMA shall be able to participate in the activities of the colleges of supervisors, including on-site verifications or investigations, carried out jointly by two or more competent authorities in accordance with Article 21 of Regulation (EU) No 1095/2010.

3. In order to ensure consistent harmonisation of paragraph 1, ESMA may develop draft regulatory technical standards to specify the information to be exchanged between competent authorities when cooperating in supervisory activities, on-the-spot-verifications, and investigations.

Power is delegated to the Commission to adopt the regulatory technical standards referred to in the first subparagraph in accordance with Articles 10 to 14 of Regulation. (EU) No 1095/2010.

In order to ensure uniform conditions of application of paragraph 1, ESMA may develop draft implementing technical standards to establish standard forms, templates and procedures for competent authorities to cooperate in supervisory activities, on -site verifications, and investigations.

Power is conferred on the Commission to adopt the implementing technical standards referred to in the third subparagraph in accordance with Article 15 of Regulation (EU) No 1095/2010. '.

(b)第4款替换为下列内容：

“4.主管部门有充分的理由怀疑其监管范围之外的实体正在或已经在另一成员国境内从事违反本指令的活动的，应当以尽可能具体的方式通知该成员国的主管部门以及欧洲证券与市场管理局。收到通知的主管部门应当采取适当的行动，并应将其行动的结果通知向其转发信息的主管部门以及欧洲证券与市场管理局，在可能的范围内还应通知其行动的重要阶段性进展。本款规定并不影响转发信息的主管部门自身的职权范围。”

(c)增加下列内容：

“6.为确保本条规定具有统一的适用条件，欧洲证券与市场管理局可起草实施性技术标准草案，就第2款所述合作安排制定标准的格式、模板和程序。

兹授予欧盟委员会依照第1095/2010号(欧盟)条例第15条的规定通过第1项所述实施性技术标准的权力。”

(22)第57条修正如下：

(a)将现有文字重新编号，改为第1款。

(b)增加下列内容：

“2.根据第1095/2010号(欧盟)条例第21条的规定，为实现监管实践的趋同，欧洲证券与市场管理局应能参与监管团的活动，包括参与2个或多个主管部门进行的现场核查或调查。

3.为确保第1款的一致协调，欧洲证券与市场管理局可起草监管性技术标准草案，具体说明主管部门合作开展监管活动、现场核查以及调查时需要交换的信息。

经委托授权，欧盟委员会有权根据第1095/2010号(欧盟)条例第10条至第14条的规定通过第1项所述监管性技术标准。

为确保第1款具有统一的适用条件，欧洲证券与市场管理局可起草实施性技术标准草案，就主管部门在监管活动、现场核查以及调查中的合作制定标准的格式、模板和程序。

兹授予欧盟委员会依照第1095/2010号(欧盟)条例第15条的规定通过第3项所述实施性技术标准的权力。”

(23) Article 58 is amended as follows:

(a) paragraph 4 is replaced by the following:

'4. In order to ensure uniform conditions of application of paragraphs 1 and 2, ESMA may develop draft implementing technical standards to establish standard forms, templates and procedures for the exchange of information.

Power is conferred on the Commission to adopt the implementing technical standards referred to in the first subparagraph in accordance with Article 15 of Regulation (EU) No 1095/2010. ';

(b) paragraph 5 is replaced by the following:

'5. Neither this Article nor Articles 54 or 63 shall prevent a competent authority from transmitting to ESMA, the European Systemic Risk Board (hereinafter the "ESRB"), central banks, the European System of Central Banks and the European Central Bank, in their capacity as monetary authorities, and, where appropriate, to other public authorities responsible for overseeing payment and settlement systems, confidential information intended for the performance of their tasks; likewise such authorities or bodies shall not be prevented from communicating to the competent authorities such information as they may need for the purpose of performing their functions provided for in this Directive. '.

(24) The following Article is inserted:

'*Article 58a*

Binding mediation

The competent authorities may refer to ESMA situations where a request relating to one of the following has been rejected or has not been acted upon within a reasonable time:

(a) to carry out a supervisory activity, an on-the-spot verification, or an investigation, as provided for in Article 57; or

(b) to exchange information as provided for in Article 58.

In the situations referred to in the first paragraph, ESMA may act in accordance with Article 19 of Regulation (EU) No 1095/2010, without prejudice to the possibilities for refusing to act on a request for information foreseen in Article 59a and to the possibility of ESMA acting in accordance with Article 17 of Regulation (EU) No 1095/2010. '.

(25) Article 59, the second paragraph is replaced by the following:

'In the case of such a refusal, the competent authority shall notify the requesting competent authority and ESMA accordingly, providing as detailed information as possible. '.

(26) In Article 60, the following paragraph is added:

'4. In order to ensure uniform conditions of application of paragraphs 1 and 2, ESMA may develop draft implementing technical standards to establish standard forms, templates and procedures for the consultation of other competent authorities prior to

(23)第58款修正如下:

(a)第4款替换为下列内容:

“4.为确保第1款和第2款具有统一的适用条件,欧洲证券与市场管理局可起草实施性技术标准草案,就信息交换制定标准的格式、模板和程序。

兹授予欧盟委员会依照第1095/2010号(欧盟)条例第15条的规定通过第1项所述实施性技术标准的权力。”

(b)第5款替换为下列内容:

“5.本条、第54条和第63条均不妨碍主管部门向下列部门或机构发送供其各自履行工作必要的保密信息:欧洲证券与市场管理局、欧洲系统性风险委员会(英文简称ESRB)、中央银行、欧洲中央银行体系及欧洲中央银行等货币管理当局,以及(如适当)负责监控支付系统和结算系统的其他公共机构。同样地,本条、第54条和第63条不影响上述部门或机构向主管部门告知为履行本指令规定的职能所必要的相关信息。”

(24)增加下列条款:

“第58a条

具有约束力的调解

主管部门提出的有关下列任何一方面的请求未在合理的时间内落实或者请求被拒的,该主管部门可将该等情况移交欧洲证券与市场管理局处理:

(a)按第57条规定开展监管活动、现场核查或调查;或

(b)按第58条规定交换信息。

在第1款所述的情形下,欧洲证券与市场管理局可依照第1095/2010号(欧盟)条例第19条行事,但不影响被请求主管部门拒绝第59a条规定之信息请求的权利,也不影响欧洲证券与市场管理局依照第1095/2010号(欧盟)条例第17条的规定行事的权利。”

(25)第59条第2款替换为下列内容:

“主管部门拒绝合作请求的,应当相应通知提出该等请求的主管部门以及欧洲证券与市场管理局,并在拒绝通知中提供尽可能详细的信息。”

(26)第60条增加下列内容:

“4.为确保第1款和第2款具有统一的适用条件,欧洲证券与市场管理局可起草实施性技术标准草案,就授予核准前咨询其他主管部门意见的程序制定标准的格式、模板和程序。

granting an authorisation.

Power is conferred on the Commission to adopt the implementing technical standards referred to in the first subparagraph in accordance with Article 15 of Regulation (EU) No 1095/2010. '.

(27) Article 62 is amended as follows:

(a) in paragraph 1, the second subparagraph is replaced by the following:

'If, despite the measures taken by the competent authority of the home Member State or because such measures prove inadequate, the investment firm persists in acting in a manner that is clearly prejudicial to the interests of host Member State investors or the orderly functioning of markets, the following shall apply:

(a) after informing the competent authority of the home Member State, the competent authority of the host Member State shall take all the appropriate measures needed in order to protect investors and the proper functioning of the markets, which shall include the possibility of preventing offending investment firms from initiating any further transactions within their territories. The Commission and ESMA shall be informed of such measures without delay;

(b) in addition, the competent authority of the host Member State may refer the matter to ESMA, which may act in accordance with the powers conferred on it under Article 19 of Regulation (EU) No 1095/2010. ';

(b) in paragraph 2, the third subparagraph is replaced by the following:

'If, despite the measures taken by the host Member State, the investment firm persists in breaching the legal or regulatory provisions referred to in the first subparagraph in force in the host Member State, the following shall apply:

(a) after informing the competent authority of the home Member State, the competent authority of the host Member State shall take all the appropriate measures needed in order to protect investors and the proper functioning of the markets. The Commission and ESMA shall be informed of such measures without delay;

(b) in addition, the competent authority of the host Member State may refer the matter to ESMA, which may act in accordance with the powers conferred on it under Article 19 of Regulation (EU) No 1095/2010. ';

(c) in paragraph 3, the second subparagraph is replaced by the following:

'If, despite the measures taken by the competent authority of the home Member State or because such measures prove inadequate, that regulated market or the MTF persists in acting in a manner that is clearly prejudicial to the interests of host Member State investors or the orderly functioning of markets, the following shall apply:

(a) after informing the competent authority of the home Member State, the competent authority of the host Member State shall take all the appropriate measures needed in order

兹授予欧盟委员会依照第1095/2010号(欧盟)条例第15条的规定通过第1项所述实施性技术标准的权力。”

(27)第62条修正如下:

(a)第1款第2项修改为:

“尽管母国主管部门已采取措施,或由于事实证明采取的措施不充分,投资公司继续以明显有损东道国投资者利益或妨碍市场有序运行的方式行事的,应适用下列规定:

(a)通知母国主管部门后,东道国主管部门应当采取保护投资者和市场有序运行所需的一切措施,包括可以阻止违法违规的投资公司在其境内启动任何其他交易。东道国主管部门应当立即通知欧盟委员会和欧洲证券与市场管理局其所采取的措施;

(b)此外,东道国主管部门可将该等事宜移交欧洲证券与市场管理局,欧洲证券与市场管理局可依照第1095/2010号(欧盟)条例第19条所授予的权力处理。”

(b)第2款第3项替换为下列内容:

“虽然东道国已采取措施,但投资公司仍继续违反第1项所述的东道国现行法律规章的,应适用下列规定:

(a)通报母国主管部门后,东道国主管部门应当采取保护投资者和市场有序运行所需的一切措施。东道国主管部门应当立即通知欧盟委员会和欧洲证券与市场管理局其所采取的措施;

(b)此外,东道国主管部门可将该等事宜移交欧洲证券与市场管理局,欧洲证券与市场管理局可依照第1095/2010号(欧盟)条例第19条所授予的权力处理。”

(c)第3款第2项替换为下列内容:

“尽管母国主管部门已采取措施,或由于事实证明采取的措施不充分,上述受监管市场或多边交易设施仍然以明显有损东道国投资者利益或妨碍市场有序运行的方式行事的,应适用下列规定:

(a)通报母国主管部门后,东道国主管部门应当采取保护投资者和市场有序运行所需的一切措施,包括可以阻止上述受监管市场或多边交易设施将其建立的安排提

to protect investors and the proper functioning of the markets, which shall include the possibility of preventing that regulated market or the MTF from making their arrangements available to remote members or participants established in the host Member State. The Commission and ESMA shall be informed of such measures without delay;

(b) in addition, the competent authority of the host Member State may refer the matter to ESMA, which may act in accordance with the powers conferred on it under Article 19 of Regulation (EU) No 1095/2010. '.

(28) The following Article is inserted:

'*Article 62a*

Cooperation and exchange of information with ESMA

1. The competent authorities shall cooperate with ESMA for the purposes of this Directive, in accordance with Regulation (EU) No 1095/2010.

2. The competent authorities shall, without delay, provide ESMA with all information necessary to carry out its duties under this Directive and in accordance with Article 35 of Regulation (EU) No 1095/2010. '.

(29) Article 63(1) is replaced by the following:

'1. Member States and in accordance with Article 33 of Regulation (EU) No 1095/2010, ESMA may conclude cooperation agreements providing for the exchange of information with the competent authorities of third countries only if the information disclosed is subject to guarantees of professional secrecy at least equivalent to those required under Article 54. Such exchange of information must be intended for the performance of the tasks of those competent authorities.

Member States and ESMA may transfer personal data to a third country in accordance with Chapter Ⅳ of Directive 95/46/EC.

Member States and ESMA may also conclude cooperation agreements providing for the exchange of information with third country authorities, bodies and natural or legal persons responsible for one or more of the following:

(a) the supervision of credit institutions, other financial institutions, insurance undertakings and the supervision of financial markets;

(b) the liquidation and bankruptcy of investment firms and other similar procedures;

(c) the carrying out of statutory audits of the accounts of investment firms and other financial institutions, credit institutions and insurance undertakings, in the performance of their supervisory functions, or which administer compensation schemes, in the performance of their functions;

(d) oversight of the bodies involved in the liquidation and bankruptcy of investment firms and other similar procedures;

(e) oversight of persons charged with carrying out statutory audits of the accounts

供给在该东道国设立的远程会员或参与者使用。东道国主管部门应当立即通知欧盟委员会和欧洲证券与市场管理局其所采取的措施；

(b)此外，东道国主管部门可将该事宜移交欧洲证券与市场管理局，欧洲证券与市场管理局可依照第1095/2010号(欧盟)条例第19条所授予的权力处理。"

(28)增加下列条款：

"第62a条

与欧洲证券与市场管理局合作和交换信息

1.主管部门应根据第1095/2010号(欧盟)条例的规定，为本指令之目的与欧洲证券与市场管理局合作。

2. 主管部门应立即向欧洲证券与市场管理局提供其为履行本指令以及第1095/2010号(欧盟)条例第35条中的职责所必要的一切信息。"

(29)第63条第1款替换为下列内容：

"1.仅当披露的信息的职业保密保证至少与第54条的要求具有等效性时，各成员国以及欧洲证券与市场管理局[根据第1095/2010号(欧盟)条例第33条的规定]方可与第三国主管部门缔结信息交换合作协议。上述信息交换应以履行该等主管部门的工作为目的。

各成员国和欧洲证券与市场管理局可以根据第95/46/EC号指令第四章的规定将个人数据传输给第三国。

各成员国和欧洲证券与市场管理局也可缔结合作协议，据以和负责下列一项或多项工作的第三国政府部门、机构以及自然人或法人交换信息：

(a)信贷机构、其他金融机构、保险公司和金融市场的监管；

(b)投资公司的清算和破产及其他类似程序；

(c)履行监管职能过程中对投资公司及其他金融机构、信贷机构和保险企业开展的法定审计，或履行职能过程中对补偿计划的管理；

(d)对参与投资公司清算和破产和其他类似程序的机构的监督；

(e)对承担保险企业、信贷机构、投资公司和其他金融机构账目法定审计工作的主

of insurance undertakings, credit institutions, investment firms and other financial institutions.

The cooperation agreements referred to in the third subparagraph may be concluded only where the information disclosed is subject to guarantees of professional secrecy at least equivalent to those required under Article 54. Such exchange of information shall be intended for the performance of the tasks of those authorities or bodies or natural or legal persons. '.

(30) The following Article is inserted

'*Article 64a*

Sunset clause

By 1 December 2011 the Commission shall review Articles 2, 4, 10b, 13, 15, 18, 19, 21, 22, 24 and 25, Articles 27 to 30, and Articles 40, 44, 45, 56 and 58 and present any appropriate legislative proposal in order to allow the full application of the delegated acts under Article 290 TFEU and implementing acts under Article 291 TFEU in respect of this Directive. Without prejudice to implementing measures already adopted, the powers conferred on the Commission in Article 64 to adopt implementing measures that remain after the entry into force of the Lisbon Treaty on 1 December 2009 shall cease to apply on 1 December 2012. '.

Article 7 Amendments to Directive 2004/109/EC

Directive 2004/109/EC is hereby amended as follows:

(1) Article 2(3) is amended as follows:

(a) the first subparagraph is replaced by the following:

'3. In order to take account of technical developments on financial markets, to specify the requirements and to ensure the uniform application of paragraph 1, the Commission shall adopt, in accordance with Article 27(2a), (2b) and (2c), and subject to the conditions of Articles 27a and 27b, measures concerning the definitions set out in paragraph 1. '.

(b) the third subparagraph is replaced by the following:

'The measures referred to in points (a) and (b) of the second subparagraph shall be laid down by means of delegated acts in accordance with Article 27(2a), (2b) and (2c), and subject to the conditions of Articles 27a and 27b. '.

(2) Article 5(6) is amended as follows:

(a) the first subparagraph is replaced by the following:

'6. The Commission shall adopt, in accordance with Article 27(2) or Article 27(2a), (2b) and (2c), in order to take account of technical developments on financial markets, measures to specify the requirements and ensure the uniform application of paragraphs 1 to 5 of this Article. ';

体的监督。

仅当披露的信息的职业保密保证至少与第54条的要求具有等效性的情形下，方可缔结第3项所述的合作协议。该等信息交换必须以履行该等部门或机构或自然人或法人的工作为目的。”

(30)增加下列条款：

“第64a条

日落条款

欧盟委员会应于2011年12月1日前对第2条、第4条、第10b条、第13条、第15条、第18条、第19条、第21条、第22条、第24条、第25条、第27条至第30条、第40条、第44条、第45条、第56条以及第58条进行审评，并提出任何适当的立法提案以使《欧洲联盟运行条约》(TFEU)第290条中的授权立法以及《欧洲联盟运行条约》第291条中的实施性立法就本指令而言全面适用。在不影响已经制定的实施细则的情形下，第64条授予欧盟委员会制定实施细则且在2009年12月1日《里斯本条约》生效后仍然有效的权力应于2012年12月1日停止适用。”

第7条　对第2004/109/EC号指令的修正

特此对第2004/109/EC号指令修正如下：

(1)第2条第3款修正如下：

(a)第1项替换为下列内容：

“3.为反映金融市场的技术发展动态并说明第1款的要求及确保第1款的统一适用，欧盟委员会应依照第27条第2a款、第2b款和第2c款的规定并遵守第27a条和第27b条所列条件，针对第1款中的定义制定相关细则。”

(b)第3项替换为下列内容：

“第2项第a目和第b目所述细则应按照第27条第2a款、第2b款和第2c款的规定并遵守第27a条和第27b条的条件，以授权立法的形式制定。”

(2)第5条第6款修正如下：

(a)第1项替换为下列内容：

“6.为反映金融市场的技术发展动态，欧盟委员会应依照第27条第2款或第27条第2a款、第2b款和第2c款制定相关细则，说明本条第1款至第5款的要求并确保本条第1款至第5款统一适用。”

(b) the third subparagraph is replaced by the following:

'The measures referred to in point (a) shall be adopted in accordance with the regulatory procedure referred to in Article 27(2). The measures referred to in points (b) and (c) shall be laid down by means of delegated acts in accordance with Article 27(2a), (2b) and (2c), and subject to the conditions of Articles 27a and 27b. ';

(c) the fourth subparagraph is replaced by the following:

'Where appropriate, the Commission may also adapt the five-year period referred to in paragraph 1 by means of a delegated act in accordance with Article 27(2a), (2b) and (2c), and subject to the conditions of Articles 27a and 27b. '.

(3) Article 9(7) is amended as follows:

(a) the first subparagraph is replaced by the following:

'7. The Commission shall adopt, by means of delegated acts in accordance with Article 27(2a),(2b) and(2c), and subject to the conditions of Articles 27a and 27b, measures in order to take account of technical developments on financial markets and to specify the requirements laid down in paragraphs 2, 4 and 5. '.

(b) the second subparagraph is replaced by the following:

'The Commission shall specify, by means of delegated acts in accordance with Article 27(2a), (2b) and (2c), and subject to the conditions of Articles 27a and 27b, the maximum length of the "short settlement cycle" referred to in paragraph 4 of this Article, as well as the appropriate control mechanisms by the competent authority of the home Member State. '.

(4) Article 12 is amended as follows:

(a) in paragraph 8:

(i) in the first subparagraph, the introductory part is replaced by the following:

'8. In order to take account of technical developments on financial markets and to specify the requirements laid down in paragraphs 1, 2, 4, 5 and 6 of this Article, the Commission shall adopt, in accordance with Article 27(2a), (2b) and (2c), and subject to the conditions of Articles 27a and 27b, measures:';

(ii) point (a) is deleted;

(iii) the second subparagraph is deleted;

(b) the following paragraph is added:

'9. In order to ensure the uniform conditions of application of this Article and to take account of technical developments on financial markets, the European Supervisory Authority(European Securities and Markets Authority)(hereinafter "ESMA"), established by Regulation (EU) No 1095/2010 of the European Parliament and of the Council (*) may develop draft implementing technical standards to establish standard forms, templates and procedures to be used when notifying the required information to the issuer under

（b）第3项替换为下列内容：

“第a目所述细则应依照第27条第2款所述监管程序予以制定。第b目和第c目所述细则应依照第27条第2a款、第2b款和第2c款的规定并遵守第27a条和第27b条的条件，以授权立法的形式制定。”

（c）第4项替换为下列内容：

“欧盟委员会也可依照第27条第2a款、第2b款和第2c款的规定并遵守第27a条和第27b条的条件，在适当时以授权立法的形式调整第1款所述的5年期限。”

（3）第9条第7款修正如下：

（a）第1项替换为下列内容：

“7.欧盟委员会应依照第27条第2a款、第2b款和第2c款的规定并遵守第27a条和第27b条的条件，以授权立法的形式制定相关细则，以反映金融市场的技术发展动态并说明第2款、第4款以及第5款所列之要求。”

（b）第2项替换为下列内容：

“欧盟委员会应依照第27条第2a款、第2b款和第2c款的规定并遵守第27a条和第27b条的条件，通过授权立法具体说明本条第4款中‘短结算周期’的最长期限以及母国主管部门的适当控制机制。”

（4）第12条修正如下：

（a）在第8款中：

（i）第1项中的导言替换为下列内容：

“8.为反映金融市场的技术发展动态并说明本条第1款、第2款、第4款、第5款以及第6款所列之要求，欧盟委员会应依照第27条第2a款、第2b款和第2c款的规定并遵守第27a条和第27b条的条件，制定相关细则：”

（ii）删除第a目；

（iii）删除第2项。

（b）加入下列内容：

“9.为确保本条规定具有统一的适用条件并反映金融市场的技术发展动态，依据《欧洲议会与欧盟理事会第1095/2010号（欧盟）条例》*设立的欧洲监管机构（欧洲证券与市场管理局）（以下简称欧洲证券与市场管理局，英文简称ESMA）可起草实施性技术标准草案，就通知发行人其应提交的信息或根据第19条第3款提交信息所需遵循的格式、模板和程序制定标准。

paragraph 1 of this Article or when filing information under Article 19(3).

Power is conferred on the Commission to adopt the implementing technical standards referred to in the first subparagraph in accordance with Article 15 of Regulation (EU) No 1095/2010.

(*) OJ L 331, 15. 12. 2010, p. 84. '.

(5) Article 13 is amended as follows:

(a) in paragraph 2:

(i) the first subparagraph is replaced by the following:

'2. The Commission shall adopt, by means of delegated acts in accordance with Article 27(2a), (2b) and (2c), and subject to the conditions of Articles 27a and 27b, measures in order to take account of technical developments on financial markets and to specify the requirements laid down in paragraph 1. It shall in particular determine:';

(ii) point (c) is replaced by the following:

'(c) the contents of the notification to be made;';

(iii) the second subparagraph is deleted;

(b) the following paragraph is added:

'3. In order to ensure uniform conditions of application of paragraph 1 of this Article and to take account of technical developments on financial markets, ESMA may develop draft implementing technical standards to establish standard forms, templates and procedures to be used when notifying the required information to the issuer under paragraph 1 of this Article or when filing information under Article 19(3).

Power is conferred on the Commission to adopt the implementing technical standards referred to in the first subparagraph in accordance with Article 15 of Regulation (EU) No 1095/2010. '.

(6) Article 14(2) is replaced by the following:

'2. The Commission shall adopt, by means of delegated acts in accordance with Article 27(2a),(2b) and (2c), and subject to the conditions of Articles 27a and 27b, measures in order to take account of technical developments on financial markets and to specify the requirements laid down in paragraph 1. '.

(7) Article 17(4) is replaced by the following:

'4. The Commission shall adopt, by means of delegated acts in accordance with Article 27(2a),(2b) and(2c), and subject to the conditions of Articles 27a and 27b, measures in order to take account of technical developments on financial markets, to take account of developments in information and communication technology and to specify the requirements laid down in paragraphs 1, 2 and 3. The Commission shall, in particular, specify the types of financial institution through which a shareholder may exercise the financial rights provided for in paragraph 2(c). '.

兹授予欧盟委员会依照第1095/2010号(欧盟)条例第15条的规定通过第1项所述实施性技术标准的权力。

*《欧盟公报》L 331,2010年12月15日,第84页。"

(5)第13条修正如下:

(a)在第2款中:

(i)第1项替换为下列内容:

"2.为反映金融市场的技术发展动态并说明第1款所列之要求,欧盟委员会应依照第27条第2a款、第2b款和第2c款的规定并遵守第27a条和第27b条的条件,以授权立法的形式制定相关细则。欧盟委员会尤其应确定:"

(ii)第c目替换为下列内容:

"(c)需要通知的内容;"

(iii)删除第2项;

(b)增加下列内容:

"3.为确保本条第1款具有统一的适用条件以及反映金融市场的技术发展动态,欧洲证券与市场管理局可起草实施性技术标准草案,就根据第1款通知发行人其应提交的信息或根据第19条第3款提交信息所需遵循的格式、模板和程序制定标准。

兹授予欧盟委员会依照第1095/2010号(欧盟)条例第15条的规定通过第1项所述实施性技术标准的权力。"

(6)第14条第2款替换为下列内容:

"2.欧盟委员会应依照第27条第2a款、第2b款和第2c款的规定并遵守第27a条和第27b条的条件,以授权立法的形式制定相关细则,以反映金融市场的技术发展动态并说明第1款所列之要求。"

(7)第17条第4款替换为下列内容:

"4.欧盟委员会应依照第27条第2a款、第2b款和第2c款的规定并遵守第27a条和第27b条的条件,以授权立法的形式制定相关细则,以反映金融市场的技术发展动态和信息通信技术的发展动态,并说明第1款、第2款和第3款所列之要求。欧盟委员会应特别规定股东可通过哪些类型金融机构行使第2款第c项规定之财务权利。"

(8) Article 18(5) is replaced by the following:

'5. The Commission shall adopt, by means of delegated acts in accordance with Article 27(2a),(2b) and(2c), and subject to the conditions of Articles 27a and 27b, measures in order to take account of technical developments on financial markets, to take account of developments in information and communication technology and to specify the requirements laid down in paragraphs 1 to 4. The Commission shall, in particular, specify the types of financial institution through which a debt security holder may exercise the financial rights provided for in paragraph 2(c). '.

(9) Article 19(4) is replaced by the following:

'4. The Commission shall adopt, by means of delegated acts in accordance with Article 27(2a),(2b) and(2c), and subject to the conditions of Articles 27a and 27b, measures in order to specify the requirements laid down in paragraphs 1, 2 and 3.

The Commission shall, in particular, specify the procedure in accordance with which an issuer, a holder of shares or other financial instruments, or a person or entity referred to in Article 10, is to file information with the competent authority of the home Member State under paragraph 1 or 3, respectively, in order to enable filing by electronic means in the home Member State. '.

(10) Article 21(4) is replaced by the following:

'4. The Commission shall adopt, by means of delegated acts in accordance with Article 27 (2a),(2b) and (2c), and subject to the conditions of Articles 27a and 27b, measures to take account of technical developments on financial markets, to take account of developments in information and communication technology and to specify the requirements laid down in paragraphs 1, 2 and 3.

The Commission shall, in particular, specify:

(a) minimum standards for the dissemination of regulated information, as referred to in paragraph 1;

(b) minimum standards for the central storage mechanism as referred to in paragraph 2.

The Commission may also specify and update a list of media for the dissemination of information to the public. '.

(11) In Article 22, the first subparagraph of paragraph 1 is replaced by the following:

'1. ESMA shall draw up guidelines, in accordance with Article 16 of Regulation (EU) No 1095/2010, with a view to further facilitating public access to information to be disclosed under Directive 2003/6/EC, Directive 2003/71/EC and under this Directive. '.

(12) Article 23 is amended as follows:

(a) paragraph 1 is replaced by the following:

(8)第18条第5款替换为下列内容:

“5.欧盟委员会应依照第27条第2a款、第2b款和第2c款的规定并遵守第27a条和第27b条的条件,以授权立法的形式制定相关细则,以反映金融市场的技术发展动态和信息通信技术的发展动态,并说明第1款至第4款所列之要求。欧盟委员会应特别规定债务证券持有人可通过哪些类型金融机构行使第2款第c项规定之财务权利。”

(9)第19条第4款替换为下列内容:

“4.欧盟委员会应依照第27条第2a款、第2b款和第2c款的规定并遵守第27a条和第27b条的条件,以授权立法的形式制定相关细则来说明第1款、第2款和第3款所列之要求。

欧盟委员会应特别规定发行人、股票或其他金融工具持有人或第10条所述的个人或实体分别按第1款或第3款向母国主管部门提交信息时所应遵循的程序,以实现在母国以电子方式提交信息。”

(10)第21条第4款替换为下列内容:

“4.欧盟委员会应依照第27条第2a款、第2b款和第2c款的规定并遵守第27a条和第27b条的条件,以授权立法的形式制定相关细则,以反映金融市场的技术发展动态和信息通信技术的发展动态,并说明第1款、第2款和第3款所列之要求。

欧盟委员会应特别规定:

(a)第1款所述的受监管信息传播的最低标准;

(b)第2款所述的中央存储机制的最低标准。

欧盟委员会也可制定一份向公众传播信息用的媒体名册,并予以更新。”

(11)第22条第1款第1项替换为下列内容:

“1.根据第1095/2010号(欧盟)条例第16条的规定,欧洲证券与市场管理局应起草指引,为公众查阅按照第2003/6/EC号指令、第2003/71/EC号指令以及本指令予以披露的信息提供进一步便利。”

(12)第23条修正如下:

(a)第1款替换为下列内容:

'1. Where the registered office of an issuer is situated in a third country, the competent authority of the home Member State may exempt that issuer from requirements under Articles 4 to 7, Article 12(6) and Articles 14 to 18, provided that the law of the third country in question lays down equivalent requirements or such an issuer complies with requirements of the law of a third country that the competent authority of the home Member State considers as equivalent.

The competent authority shall then inform ESMA of the exemption granted.'.

(b) paragraph 4 is replaced by the following:

'4. In order to ensure the uniform conditions of application of paragraph 1, the Commission shall adopt, in accordance with the procedure referred to in Article 27(2), implementing measures:

(i) setting up a mechanism ensuring the establishment of equivalence of information required under this Directive, including financial statements and information, required under the law, regulations or administrative provisions of a third country;

(ii) stating that, by reason of its domestic law, regulations, administrative provisions, or of the practices or procedures based on the international standards set by international organisations, the third country where the issuer is registered ensures the equivalence of the information requirements provided for in this Directive.

In the context of point (ii) of the first subparagraph, the Commission shall also adopt, by means of delegated acts in accordance with Article 27(2a),(2b) and (2c), and subject to the conditions of Articles 27a and 27b, measures concerning the assessment of standards relevant to the issuers of more than one country.

The Commission shall, in accordance with the procedure referred to in Article 27(2), take the necessary decisions on the equivalence of accounting standards which are used by third-country issuers under the conditions set out in Article 30(3). If the Commission decides that the accounting standards of a third country are not equivalent, it may allow the issuers concerned to continue using such accounting standards during an appropriate transitional period.

In the context of the third subparagraph, the Commission shall also adopt, by means of delegated acts in accordance with Article 27(2a), (2b) and (2c), and subject to the conditions of Articles 27a and 27b, measures aimed at establishing general equivalence criteria regarding accounting standards relevant to issuers of more than one country.'.

(c) paragraph 5 is replaced by the following:

'5. In order to specify the requirements laid down in paragraph 2, the Commission may adopt, by means of delegated acts in accordance with Article 27(2a), (2b) and (2c), and subject to the conditions of Articles 27a and 27b, measures defining the type of information disclosed in a third country that is of importance to the public in the Union.'.

“1.发行人注册地位于第三国的，母国主管部门可豁免第4条至第7条、第12条第6款以及第14条至第18条的要求，前提是所涉第三国的法律所规定的要求与上述要求具有等效性，或该发行人遵守了母国主管部门认为与上述要求具有等效性的第三国法律要求。

主管部门应通知欧洲证券与市场管理局其所核准的豁免。”

(b)第4款替换为下列内容：

“4.为确保第1款具有统一的适用条件，欧盟委员会应依照第27条第2款规定的程序制定实施细则，以便：

(i)设立一项机制，据以确定相关信息(包括第三国法律、法规和规章所要求的财务报表和财务信息)与本指令要求提供的信息具有等效性；

(ii)作出如下声明：发行人注册地所在的第三国依据其国内法律、法规、规章或基于国际组织采用的国际标准制定的国内实践或程序，能够确保其信息要求与本指令所规定的信息要求具有等效性。

在第1项第ii目所述的情形下，欧盟委员会还应依照第27条第2a款、第2b款和第2c款的规定并遵守第27a条和第27b条的条件，以授权立法的形式制定相关细则，以评估适用于在多个国家发行证券的发行人的各种标准。

欧盟委员会应按照第27条第2款所述程序，就第三国发行人按第30条第3款的条件采用的会计标准是否具有等效性作出必要的决定。欧盟委员会在认定第三国的会计准则不具有等效性时，可以允许所涉发行人在适当的过渡期限内继续使用上述标准。

在第3项所述情形下，欧盟委员会还应依照第27条第2a款、第2b款和第2c款的规定并遵守第27a条和第27b条的条件，以授权立法的形式制定相关细则，就在多个国家发行证券的发行人适用的各种会计准则制定总体等效性标准。”

(c)第5款替换为下列内容：

“5.为说明第2款所列之要求，欧盟委员会可依照第27条第2a款、第2b款和第2c款的规定并遵守第27a条和第27b条的条件，以授权立法的形式制定相关细则，就第三国披露的对欧盟公众具有重要性的信息类型进行界定。”

(d) in paragraph 7, the second subparagraph is replaced by the following:

'The Commission shall also adopt, by means of delegated acts in accordance with Article 27(2a),(2b) and(2c), and subject to the conditions of Articles 27a and 27b, measures aimed at establishing general equivalence criteria for the purpose of the first subparagraph. '.

(e) the following paragraph is added:

'8. ESMA shall assist the Commission in carrying out its tasks under this Article in accordance with Article 33 of Regulation (EU) No 1095/2010. '.

(13) Article 24 is amended as follows:

(a) in paragraph 1, the first subparagraph is replaced by the following:

'1. Each Member State shall designate the central authority referred to in Article 21 (1) of Directive 2003/71/EC as the central competent administrative authority responsible for carrying out the obligations provided for in this Directive and for ensuring that the provisions adopted pursuant to this Directive are applied. Member States shall inform the Commission and ESMA accordingly. '.

(b) paragraph 3 is replaced by the following:

'3. Member States shall inform the Commission, ESMA in accordance with Article 28(4) of Regulation(EU) No 1095/2010, and competent authorities of other Member States of any arrangements entered into with regard to the delegation of tasks, including the precise conditions for regulating the delegations. '.

(14) Article 25 is amended as follows:

(a) the following paragraphs are inserted:

'2a. The competent authorities may refer to ESMA situations where a request for cooperation has been rejected or has not been acted upon within a reasonable time. Without prejudice to the Article 258 of the Treaty on the Functioning of the European Union (TFEU), ESMA may, in situations referred to in the first sentence, act in accordance with the powers conferred on it under Article 19 of Regulation(EU) No 1095/2010.

2b. The competent authorities shall cooperate with ESMA for the purposes of this Directive, in accordance with Regulation (EU) No 1095/2010.

2c. The competent authorities shall without delay provide ESMA with all information necessary to carry out its duties under this Directive and under Regulation (EU) No 1095/2010, in accordance with Article 35 of that Regulation. ';

(b) in paragraph 3, the first sentence is replaced by the following:

'3. Paragraph 1 shall not prevent the competent authorities from exchanging confidential information with, or from transmitting information to, other competent authorities, ESMA and the European Systemic Risk Board (ESRB) established by

(d)第7款第2项替换为下列内容:

"欧盟委员会还应依照第27条第2a款、第2b款和第2c款的规定并遵守第27a条和第27b条的条件,以授权立法的形式制定相关细则,就第1项之目的制定总体等效性标准。"

(e)增加下列内容:

"8.欧洲证券与市场管理局应根据第1095/2010号(欧盟)条例第33条的规定,协助欧盟委员会履行其在本条规定中的工作。"

(13)第24条修正如下:

(a)第1款第1项替换为下列内容:

"1.各成员国应指定第2003/71/EC号指令第21条第1款所述的中央机构作为中央行政主管部门,负责履行本指令规定的义务,并确保按本指令通过的规定得以适用。成员国应相应通知欧盟委员会和欧洲证券与市场管理局。"

(b)第3款替换为下列内容:

"3.成员国应根据第1095/2010号(欧盟)条例第28条第4款通知欧盟委员会和欧洲证券与市场管理局以及其他成员国的主管部门与工作委托有关的任何安排,包括规范该等委托的确切条件。"

(14)第25条修正如下:

(a)增加下款:

"2a.主管部门提出的合作请求被拒绝或未在合理的时间内落实的,该主管部门可将该等情况移交欧洲证券与市场管理局,在不影响《欧洲联盟运行条约》(TFEU)第258条的情形下,欧洲证券与市场管理局可在第一句所述情况下依照第1095/2010号(欧盟)条例第19条授予的权力处理。

"2b.主管部门应根据第1095/2010号(欧盟)条例的规定,为本指令之目的与欧洲证券与市场管理局合作。

"2c.主管部门应根据第1095/2010号(欧盟)条例第35条的规定,立即向欧洲证券与市场管理局提供其为履行本指令及上述条例中的职责所必要的一切信息。"

(b)第3款第一句替换为下列内容:

"3.第1款不妨碍主管部门与其他主管部门、欧洲证券与市场管理局以及依据《欧洲议会与欧盟理事会关于欧盟对金融系统的宏观审慎监控以及设立欧洲系统性风险委员会的第1092/2010号(欧盟)条例》*(2010年11月24日)设立的欧洲系统性风险委员

Regulation (EU) No 1092/2010 of the European Parliament and of the Council of 24 November 2010 on European Union macro-prudential oversight of the financial system and establishing a European Systemic Risk Board (*).

(*) OJ L 331, 15. 12. 2010, p. 1. ';

(c) paragraph 4 is replaced by the following:

'4. Member States and ESMA in accordance with Article 33 of Regulation (EU) No 1095/2010, may conclude cooperation agreements providing for the exchange of information with the competent authorities or bodies of third countries enabled by their respective legislation to carry out any tasks under this Directive in accordance with Article 24. Member States shall notify ESMA when they conclude cooperation agreements. Such an exchange of information is subject to guarantees of professional secrecy at least equivalent to those referred to in this Article. Such an exchange of information shall be intended for the performance of the supervisory task of the authorities or bodies mentioned. Where the information originates in another Member State, it shall not be disclosed without the express agreement of the competent authorities which disclosed it and, where appropriate, solely for the purposes for which those authorities gave their agreement. '.

(15) Article 26 is replaced by the following:

'*Article 26*

Precautionary measures

1. Where the competent authority of a host Member State finds that the issuer or the holder of shares or other financial instruments, or the person or entity referred to in Article 10, has committed irregularities or infringed its obligations, it shall refer its findings to the competent authority of the home Member State and to ESMA.

2. If, despite the measures taken by the competent authority of the home Member State, or because such measures prove inadequate, the issuer or the security holder persists in infringing the relevant legal or regulatory provisions, the competent authority of the host Member State shall, after informing the competent authority of the home Member State, take, in accordance with Article 3(2), all the appropriate measures in order to protect investors, informing the Commission and ESMA thereof at the earliest opportunity. '.

(16) The title of Chapter VI is replaced by the following:

'DELEGATED ACTS AND IMPLEMENTING MEASURES'.

(17) Article 27 is amended as follows:

(a) paragraph 2a is replaced by the following:

'2a. The power to adopt the delegated acts referred to in Article 2(3), Article 5(6), Article 9(7), Article 12(8), Article 13(2), Article 14(2), Article 17(4), Article 18(5), Article 19(4), Article 21(4), Article 23(4), Article 23(5) and Article 23(7) shall be

会(ESRB)交换保密信息或向其发送信息。

*《欧盟公报》L 331,2010年12月15日,第1页。”

(c)第4款替换为下列内容:

“4.根据第1095/2010号(欧盟)条例第33条,成员国和欧洲证券与市场管理局可缔结合作协议,就主管部门或第三国机构依照第24条在其各自立法下为履行本指令任何工作而交换信息作出规定。成员国缔结合作协议时应通知欧洲证券与市场管理局。上述信息交换需要作出的职业保密保证至少应与本条所述职业保密保证具有等效性。该等信息交换必须以履行上述部门或机构的监管工作为目的。对于来源于另一成员国的信息,唯有经披露该等信息的主管部门明确同意方能予以披露,且仅能在适当时就该等部门同意之目的披露。”

(15)第26条替换为下列内容:

“第26条

预防性措施

1.如认定发行人或股票或其他金融工具持有人或第10条所述的个人或实体有违法违规行为或违反其义务,东道国主管部门应将其认定结果移交母国主管部门和欧洲证券与市场管理局处理。

2.尽管母国主管部门已采取措施,或由于事实证明采取的措施不充分,发行人或证券持有人继续违反相关法律规章的,则东道国主管部门应在通知母国主管部门后按照第3条第2款之规定采取保护投资者所需的一切适当措施,并尽早将情况告知欧盟委员会和欧洲证券与市场管理局。”

(16)第六章标题替换为:

“授权立法和实施细则”。

(17)第27条修正如下:

(a)第2a款替换为下列内容:

“2a.自2011年1月4日起,应授予欧盟委员会第2条第3款、第5条第6款、第9条第7款、第12条第8款、第13条第2款、第14条第2款、第17条第4款、第18条第5款、第19条第4款、第21条第4款、第23条第4款、第23条第5款以及第23条第7款所述通过授权立法的

conferred on the Commission for a period of 4 years from 4 January 2011. The Commission shall draw up a report in respect of delegated power at the latest 6 months before the end of the four-year period. The delegation of power shall be automatically extended for periods of an identical duration, unless the European Parliament or the Council revokes it in accordance with Article 27a. '.

(b) the following paragraphs are inserted:

'2b. As soon as it adopts a delegated act, the Commission shall notify it simultaneously to the European Parliament and to the Council.

2c. The power to adopt delegated acts is conferred on the Commission subject to the conditions laid down in Articles 27a and 27b. '.

(18) The following Articles are inserted:

'*Article 27a*

Revocation of the delegation

1. The delegation of power referred to in Article 2(3), Article 5(6), Article 9(7), Article 12(8), Article 13(2), Article 14(2), Article 17(4), Article 18(5), Article 19(4), Article 21(4), Article 23(4), Article 23(5) and Article 23(7) may be revoked at any time by the European Parliament or by the Council.

2. The institution which has commenced an internal procedure for deciding whether to revoke a delegation of power shall endeavour to inform the other institution and the Commission within a reasonable time before the final decision is taken, indicating the delegated power which could be subject to revocation.

3. The decision of revocation shall put an end to the delegation of the power specified in that decision. It shall take effect immediately or at a later date specified therein. It shall not affect the validity of the delegated acts already in force. It shall be published in the Official Journal of the European Union.

Article 27b

Objections to delegated acts

1. The European Parliament or the Council may object to a delegated act within a period of 3 months from the date of notification. At the initiative of the European Parliament or the Council that period shall be extended by 3 months.

2. If, on the expiry of the period referred to in paragraph 1, neither the European Parliament nor the Council has objected to the delegated act, it shall be published in the Official Journal of the European Union and shall enter into force on the date stated therein.

The delegated act may be published in the Official Journal of the European Union and enter into force before the expiry of that period if the European Parliament and the Council have both informed the Commission of their intention not to raise objections.

权力，权力有效期为4年。欧盟委员会最迟应在4年期限届满前6个月(含)，就被委托的权力起草一份报告。除非欧洲议会或欧盟理事会依照第27a条撤销委托授权，否则委托授权的期限届满后应自动展延，每次展延的期限与原期限相同。”

(b)增加下款：

“2b.欧盟委员会应在通过授权立法后立即同时通知欧洲议会和欧盟理事会。

“2c.在遵守第27a条和第27b条规定的条件的前提下，授予欧盟委员会通过授权立法的权力。”

(18)增加如下条款：

“第27a条

撤销委托授权

1.欧洲议会或欧盟理事会可以随时撤销第2条第3款、第5条第6款、第9条第7款、第12条第8款、第13条第2款、第14条第2款、第17条第4款、第18条第5款、第19条第4款、第21条第4款、第23条第4款、第23条第5款以及第23条第7款所述的委托授权。

2.欧洲议会或欧盟理事会已经启动决定是否撤销某项委托授权的内部程序的，应当尽力在作出最终决定前的合理时间内通知彼此以及欧盟委员会，指明可能被撤销的委托授权。

3.撤销决定将使其列明的委托授权效力终止。撤销决定应立即生效，或在决定中规定的较晚日期生效。撤销决定不影响已生效的监管性技术标准的效力。撤销决定应在《欧盟公报》公布。

第27b条

对授权立法提出异议

1.欧洲议会或欧盟理事会可在通知之日起3个月期限内对授权立法提出异议。经欧洲议会或欧盟理事会主动要求，该期限可延长3个月。

2.在第1款所述期限届满前，欧洲议会及欧盟理事会均未对相关授权立法提出异议的，该授权立法应在《欧盟公报》公布，并自其规定的生效日期起生效。

在第1款所述期限届满前，欧洲议会和欧盟理事会均已通知欧盟委员会其无意提出异议的，授权立法可提前在《欧盟公报》公布并生效。

3. If either the European Parliament or the Council objects to a delegated act within the period referred to in paragraph 1, it shall not enter into force. In accordance with Article 296 TFEU, the institution which objects shall state the reasons for objecting to the delegated act. '.

Article 8 Amendments to Directive 2005/60/EC

Directive 2005/60/EC is hereby amended as follows:

(1) Article 11(4) is replaced by the following:

'4. The Member States shall inform each other, the European Supervisory Authority (European Banking Authority) (hereinafter "EBA"), established by Regulation (EU) No 1093/2010 of the European Parliament and of the Council (*), the European Supervisory Authority (European Insurance and Occupational Pensions Authority) (hereinafter "EIOPA"), established by Regulation (EU) No 1094/2010 of the European Parliament and of the Council (**), and the European Supervisory Authority (European Securities and Markets Authority) (hereinafter "ESMA"), established by Regulation (EU) No 1095/2010 of the European Parliament and of the Council (***) (collectively, the "ESA") to the extent relevant for the purposes of this Directive and in accordance with the relevant provisions of Regulation (EU) No 1093/2010, of Regulation (EU) No 1094/2010 and of Regulation (EU) No 1095/2010, and the Commission of cases where they consider that a third country meets the conditions laid down in paragraphs 1 or 2 or in other situations which meet the technical criteria established in accordance with Article 40(1)(b).

(*) OJ L 331, 15. 12. 2010, p. 12.

(**) OJ L 331, 15. 12. 2010, p. 48.

(***) OJ L 331, 15. 12. 2010, p. 84. '

(2) Article 16(2) is replaced by the following:

'2. The Member States shall inform each other, the ESA to the extent relevant for the purposes of this Directive and in accordance with the relevant provisions of Regulation (EU) No 1093/2010, of Regulation (EU) No 1094/2010, and of Regulation (EU) No 1095/2010, and the Commission of cases where they consider that a third country meets the conditions laid down in paragraph 1(b). '.

(3) Article 28(7) is replaced by the following:

'7. The Member States shall inform each other, the ESA to the extent relevant for the purposes of this Directive and in accordance with the relevant provisions of Regulation (EU) No 1093/2010, of Regulation (EU) No 1094/2010, and of Regulation (EU) No 1095/2010 and the Commission of cases where they consider that a third country meets the conditions laid down in paragraphs 3, 4 or 5. '.

(4) Article 31 is amended as follows:

3.欧洲议会或欧盟理事会任一方在第1款所述期限内对授权立法提出异议的，授权立法不得生效。根据《欧洲联盟运行条约》第296条的规定，对授权立法提出异议的机构应说明异议理由。”

第8条　对第2005/60/EC号指令的修正

特此对第2005/60/EC号指令修正如下：

（1）第11条第4款修正如下：

“4.如果成员国认为第三国符合第1款或第2款的条件，或在其他情况下符合依照第40条第1款第b项所制定的技术标准，则各成员国应互相通知上述情况，并应根据第1093/2010号（欧盟）条例*、第1094/2010号（欧盟）条例**以及第1095/2010号（欧盟）条例***的有关规定在与本指令具有相关性时通知依据欧洲议会与欧盟理事会第1093/2010号（欧盟）条例设立的欧洲监管机构（欧洲银行业管理局）（以下简称欧洲银行业管理局，英文简称EBA）、依据欧洲议会与欧盟理事会第1094/2010号（欧盟）条例设立的欧洲监管机构（欧洲保险与职业养老金管理局）（以下简称欧洲保险与职业养老金管理局，英文简称EIOPA）、依据欧洲议会与欧盟理事会第1095/2010号（欧盟）条例设立的欧洲监管机构（欧洲证券与市场管理局）（以下简称欧洲证券与市场管理局，英文简称ESMA）（以下统称欧洲监管机构，英文简称ESA），同时通知欧盟委员会。

*《欧盟公报》L 331，2010年12月15日，第12页。

**《欧盟公报》L 331，2010年12月15日，第48页。

***《欧盟公报》L 331，2010年12月15日，第84页。”

（2）第16条第2款替换为下列内容：

“2.如果成员国认为第三国符合第1款第b项的条件，则各成员国应互相通知上述情况，并应根据第1093/2010号（欧盟）条例、第1094/2010号（欧盟）条例，以及第1095/2010号（欧盟）条例的有关规定在与本指令具有相关性时通知欧洲监管机构，同时通知欧盟委员会。”

（3）第28条第7款替换为下列内容：

“7.如果成员国认为第三国符合第3款、第4款或第5款的条件，则各成员国应互相通知上述情况，并应根据第1093/2010号（欧盟）条例、第1094/2010号（欧盟）条例，以及第1095/2010号（欧盟）条例的有关规定在与本指令具有相关性时通知欧洲监管机构，同时通知欧盟委员会。”

（4）第31条修正如下：

(a) paragraph 2 is replaced by the following:

'2. The Member States, the ESA to the extent relevant for the purposes of this Directive and in accordance with the relevant provisions of Regulation (EU) No 1093/2010, of Regulation (EU) No 1094/2010, and of Regulation (EU) No 1095/2010 and the Commission shall inform each other of cases where the legislation of the third country does not permit application of the measures required under the first subparagraph of paragraph 1 and coordinated action could be taken to pursue a solution. ';

(b) the following paragraph is added:

'4. In order to ensure consistent harmonisation of this Article and to take account of technical developments in the fight against money laundering and terrorist financing, the ESA taking into account the existing framework and cooperating, as appropriate, with other relevant Union bodies in that field, may develop draft regulatory technical standards in accordance with Article 56 of Regulation (EU) No 1093/2010, of Regulation (EU) No 1094/2010, and of Regulation (EU) No 1095/2010 respectively to specify the type of additional measures referred to in paragraph 3 of this Article and the minimum action to be taken by credit and financial institutions where the legislation of the third country does not permit application of the measures required under the first subparagraph of paragraph 1 of this Article.

Power is delegated to the Commission to adopt the regulatory technical standards referred to in the first subparagraph in accordance with Articles 10 to 14 of Regulation (EU) No 1093/2010. '.

(5) In Article 34, the following paragraph is added:

'3. In order to ensure consistent harmonisation and to take account of technical developments in the fight against money laundering and terrorist financing, the ESA, taking into account the existing framework and cooperating, as appropriate, with other relevant Union bodies in that field, may develop draft regulatory technical standards in accordance with Article 56 of Regulation (EU) No 1093/2010, of Regulation (EU) No 1094/2010 and of Regulation (EU) No 1095/2010 respectively, to specify the minimum content of the communication referred to in paragraph 2.

Power is delegated to the Commission to adopt the regulatory technical standards referred to in the first subparagraph in accordance with Articles 10 to 14 of Regulation (EU) No 1093/2010. '.

(6) The following Article is inserted:

'*Article 37a*

1. The competent authorities shall cooperate with the ESA for the purposes of this Directive, in accordance with Regulation (EU) No 1093/2010, Regulation (EU) No 1094/2010, and Regulation (EU) No 1095/2010, respectively.

(a)第2款替换为下列内容：

“2.第三国的立法不允许适用第1款第1项所规定的措施并且可以采取协调行动来解决问题的，各成员国、欧洲监管机构[只有与本指令具有相关性才需通知欧洲监管机构，且该等通知应根据第1093/2010号(欧盟)条例、第1094/2010号(欧盟)条例，以及第1095/2010号(欧盟)条例执行]以及欧盟委员会应互相通知上述情况。”

(b)增加下列内容：

“4.为确保本条规定的一致协调和反映在打击洗钱和恐怖分子融资的斗争中的技术发展动态，欧洲监管机构可基于现有的框架并与该领域其他相关联盟机构进行适当合作，依照第1093/2010号(欧盟)条例、第1094/2010号(欧盟)条例以及第1095/2010号(欧盟)条例各自第56条的规定起草监管性技术标准草案，规定本条第3款所述额外措施的类型以及第三国立法不允许适用本条第1款第1项所规定的措施的情形下信贷机构和金融机构所应采取的最低限度的行动。

经委托授权，欧盟委员会有权根据第1093/2010(欧盟)条例第10条至第14条的规定通过第1项所述监管性技术标准。”

(5)在第34条中增加下列规定：

“3.为确保一致协调和反映在打击洗钱和恐怖分子融资的斗争中的技术发展动态，欧洲监管机构可基于现有的框架并与该领域其他相关联盟机构进行适当合作，依照第1093/2010号(欧盟)条例、第1094/2010号(欧盟)条例，以及第1095/2010号(欧盟)条例各自第56条的规定起草监管性技术标准草案，规定第2款所述的通知至少应包括的内容。

经委托授权，欧盟委员会有权根据第1093/2010(欧盟)条例第10条至第14条的规定通过第1项所述监管性技术标准。”

(6)增加下列条款：

“第37a条

1.主管部门应根据第1093/2010号(欧盟)条例、第1094/2010号(欧盟)条例以及第1095/2010号(欧盟)条例的规定，为本指令之目的与欧洲监管机构合作。

2. The competent authorities shall provide the ESA with all information necessary to carry out their duties under this Directive and under Regulation (EU) No 1093/2010, Regulation (EU) No 1094/2010 and Regulation (EU) No 1095/2010, respectively. '.

(7) The title of Chapter Ⅵ is replaced by the following:

'DELEGATED ACTS AND IMPLEMENTING MEASURES'

(8) Article 40 is amended as follows:

(a) in paragraph 1:

(i) in the first subparagraph, the introductory part is replaced by the following:

'1. In order to take account of technical developments in the fight against money laundering and terrorist financing and to specify the requirements laid down in this Directive, the Commission may, adopt the following measures:';

(ii) the second subparagraph is replaced by the following:

'The measures shall be adopted by means of delegated acts in accordance with Article 41(2a), (2b) and (2c), and subject to the conditions of Articles 41a and 41b. ';

(b) in paragraph 3, the second subparagraph is replaced by the following:

'The measures shall be adopted by means of delegated acts in accordance with Article 41(2a), (2b) and (2c), and subject to the conditions of Articles 41a and 41b. '.

(9) Article 41 is amended as follows:

(a) in paragraph 2, the first subparagraph is replaced by the following:

'2. Where reference is made to this paragraph, Articles 5 and 7 of Decision 1999/468/EC shall apply, having regard to Article 8 thereof and provided that the measures adopted in accordance with that procedure do not modify the essential provisions of this Directive. ';

(b) paragraph 2a is replaced by the following:

'2a. The power to adopt delegated acts referred to in Article 40 shall be conferred on the Commission for a period of 4 years from 4 January 2011. The Commission shall draw up a report in respect of the delegated power at the latest 6 months before the end of the four-year period. The delegation of power shall be automatically extended for periods of an identical duration, unless the European Parliament or the Council revokes it in accordance with Article 41a. ';

(c) the following paragraphs are inserted:

'2b. As soon as it adopts a delegated act, the Commission shall notify it simultaneously to the European Parliament and to the Council.

2c. The power to adopt delegated acts is conferred on the Commission subject to the conditions laid down in Articles 41a and 41b. ';

(d) paragraph 3 is deleted.

(10) The following Articles are inserted:

2.主管部门应为各欧洲监管机构提供其为履行本指令以及分别在第1093/2010号(欧盟)条例、第1094/2010号(欧盟)条例以及第1095/2010号(欧盟)条例中的职责所必要的一切信息。”

(7)第六章标题替换为:

“授权立法和实施细则”。

(8)第40条修正如下:

(a)在第1款中:

(i)第1项的导言替换为下列内容:

“1.为反映在打击洗钱和恐怖分子融资的斗争中的技术发展动态并详细说明本指令列出的要求,欧盟委员会可通过下列措施:”

(ii)第2项替换为下列内容:

“应依照第41条第2a款、第2b款和第2c款的规定并遵守第41a条和第41b条的条件,以授权立法的形式制定相关细则。”

(b)第3款第2项替换为下列内容:

“应依照第41条第2a款、第2b款和第2c款的规定并遵守第41a条和第41b条的条件,以授权立法的形式制定相关细则。”

(9)第41条修正如下:

(a)第2款第1项替换为下列内容:

“2.涉及第1999/468/EC号决定第8条的规定的,引用本款内容时应适用该决定的第5条和第7条,但是根据该项程序所制定的细则不会改变本指令的基本规定;”

(b)第2a款替换为下列内容:

“2a.自2011年1月4日起,授予欧盟委员会第40条所述通过授权立法的权力,该权力有效期为4年。欧盟委员会最迟应在4年期限届满前6个月(含)就被委托的权力起草一份报告。除非欧洲议会或欧盟理事会依照第41a条撤销委托授权,否则委托授权的期限届满后应自动展延,每次展延的期限与原期限相同。”

(c)增加下列条款:

“2b.欧盟委员会应在通过授权立法后立即同时通知欧洲议会和欧盟理事会。

2c.在遵守第41a条和第41b条规定的条件的前提下,授予欧盟委员会通过授权立法的权力。”

(d)删除第3款。

(10)增加下列条款:

'*Article 41a*

Revocation of the delegation

1. The delegation of power referred to in Article 40 may be revoked at any time by the European Parliament or by the Council.

2. The institution which has commenced an internal procedure for deciding whether to revoke a delegation of power shall endeavour to inform the other institution and the Commission within a reasonable time before the final decision is taken, indicating the delegated power which could be subject to revocation.

3. The decision of revocation shall put an end to the delegation of the power specified in that decision. It shall take effect immediately or on a later date specified therein. It shall not affect the validity of the delegated acts already in force. It shall be published in the Official Journal of the European Union.

Article 41b

Objections to delegated acts

1. The European Parliament or the Council may object to a delegated act within a period of 3 months from the date of notification. At the initiative of the European Parliament or the Council that period shall be extended by 3 months.

2. If, on the expiry of the period referred to in paragraph 1, neither the European Parliament nor the Council has objected to the delegated act, it shall be published in the Official Journal of the European Union and shall enter into force on the date stated therein.

The delegated act may be published in the Official Journal of the European Union and enter into force before the expiry of that period if the European Parliament and the Council have both informed the Commission of their intention not to raise objections.

3. If either the European Parliament or the Council objects to a delegated act within the period referred to in paragraph 1, it shall not enter into force. In accordance with Article 296 TFEU, the institution which objects shall state the reasons for objecting to the delegated act. '.

Article 9 Amendments to Directive 2006/48/EC

Directive 2006/48/EC is hereby amended as follows:

(1) Article 6 is amended as follows:

(a) the existing paragraph is replaced by the following:

'1. Member States shall require credit institutions to obtain authorisation before commencing their activities. Without prejudice to Articles 7 to 12, they shall lay down the requirements for such authorisation and notify the Commission and the European Supervisory Authority (European Banking Authority) established by Regulation (EU) No 1093/2010 of the European Parliament and of the Council(*)(hereinafter "EBA")

"第41a条

撤销委托授权

1.欧洲议会或欧盟理事会可以随时撤销第40条所述的委托授权。

2.欧洲议会或欧盟理事会已经启动决定是否撤销某项委托授权的内部程序的,应当尽力在作出最终决定前的合理时间内通知彼此以及欧盟委员会,指明可能被撤销的委托授权。

3.撤销决定将使其列明的委托授权效力终止。撤销决定应立即生效,或在决定中规定的较晚日期生效。撤销决定不影响已生效的监管性技术标准的效力。撤销决定应在《欧盟公报》公布。

第41b条

对授权立法的异议

1.欧洲议会或欧盟理事会可在通知之日起3个月期限内对授权立法提出异议,经欧洲议会或欧盟理事会主动要求,该期限可延长3个月。

2.在第1款所述期限届满前,欧洲议会和欧盟理事会均未对相关授权立法提出异议的,该授权立法应在《欧盟公报》公布,并应在其规定的生效日期生效。

在第1款所述期限届满前,欧洲议会和欧盟理事会无意提出异议的,在告知欧盟委员会其上述意向后,授权立法可提前在《欧盟公报》公布并生效。

3.欧洲议会或欧盟理事会任一方在第1款所述期限内对授权立法提出异议的,授权立法不得生效。根据《欧洲联盟运行条约》第296条的规定,对授权立法提出异议的机构应说明异议理由。"

第9条　对第2006/48/EC号指令的修正

特此对第2006/48/EC号指令修正如下:

(1)第6条修正如下:

(a)现行条款替换为下列内容:

"1.各成员国应要求信贷机构在经营活动开始之前先获得核准。在不影响第7条至第12条的规定的情形下,各成员国应制定获得上述核准所应符合的要求并通知欧盟委员会以及依据欧洲议会与欧盟理事会第1093/2010号(欧盟)条例*设立的欧洲监管机构(欧洲银行业管理局)(以下简称欧洲银行业管理局,英文简称EBA)该等要求。

thereof.

(*) OJ L 331, 15. 12. 2010, p. 12. ';

(b) the following paragraphs are added:

'2. In order to ensure consistent harmonisation of this Article, EBA may develop draft regulatory technical standards:

(a) on the information to be provided to the competent authorities in the application for the authorisation of credit institutions, including the programme of operations provided for in Article 7;

(b) specifying the conditions to comply with the requirement set out in Article 8;

(c) specifying the requirements applicable to shareholders and members with qualifying holdings, as well as to specify obstacles which may prevent effective exercise of the supervisory functions of the competent authority, as provided for in Article 12.

Power is delegated to the Commission to adopt the regulatory technical standards referred to in points (a),(b) and (c) of the first subparagraph in accordance with the procedure laid down in Articles 10 to 14 of Regulation (EU) No 1093/2010.

3. In order to ensure uniform conditions of application of this Article, EBA may develop draft implementing technical standards on standard forms, templates and procedures for such provision of information;

Power is conferred on the Commission to adopt the implementing technical standards referred to in the first subparagraph in accordance with Article 15 of Regulation (EU) No 1093/2010. '.

(2) In Article 9(2), point b is replaced by the following:

'(b) the Member States concerned shall notify the Commission and EBA of their reasons for exercising that option; and'.

(3) Article 14 is replaced by the following:

'*Article 14*

Every authorisation shall be notified to EBA.

The name of each credit institution to which authorisation has been granted shall be entered in a list. EBA shall publish and keep that list up-to-date on its website. '.

(4) Article 17(2) is replaced by the following:

'2. Withdrawal of authorisation shall be notified to the Commission and EBA and shall be reasoned. The persons concerned shall be notified of those reasons. '.

(5) In Article 19, the following paragraph is added:

'9. In order to ensure consistent harmonisation of this Article, EBA may develop draft regulatory technical standards to establish an exhaustive list of information, referred to in Article 19a(4), to be included by proposed acquirers in their notification, without prejudice to paragraph 3 of this Article.

*《欧盟公报》L 331，2010年12月15日，第12页。”

(b)增加下列条款：

“2.为确保本条规定的一致协调，欧洲银行业管理局可制定监管性技术标准草案，具体说明：

(a)信贷机构申请核准时应向主管部门提供的信息(包括第7条规定的运营计划)；

(b)为符合第8条所列要求所应具备的条件；

(c)第12条所述适用于有重大持股数额的股东和成员的规定，并说明可能妨碍主管部门有效行使监管职能的障碍。

经委托授权，欧盟委员会有权根据第1093/2010号(欧盟)条例第10条至第14条规定的程序通过第1项第a目、第b目和第c目所述监管性技术标准。

3.为确保本条规定具有统一的适用条件，欧洲银行业管理局可起草实施性技术标准草案，就上述信息提供制定标准格式、模板和程序；

兹授予欧盟委员会依照第1093/2010号(欧盟)条例第15条的规定通过第1项所述实施性技术标准的权力。”

(2)第9条第2款第b目替换为下列内容：

“(b)所涉成员国应通知欧盟委员会和欧洲银行业管理局其作出该项选择的理由；及”

(3)第14条替换为下列内容：

“第14条

应通知欧洲银行业管理局授予的每项核准。

应将获得核准的每一家信贷机构的名称录入一份名册。欧洲银行业管理局应在其网站上公布该名册，并持续更新。”

(4)第17条第2款替换为下列内容：

“2.撤销核准必须具有充分的理由，除通知欧盟委员会和欧洲银行业管理局撤销之事实外，还应告知所涉人员撤销核准的理由。”

(5)第19条增加下列内容：

“9.在不违背本条第3款的情形下，为确保本条规定的一致协调，欧洲银行业管理局可起草监管性技术标准草案，制定一份第19a条第4款所述的应提供的信息的详尽清单。拟议收购方须将该等信息纳入其通知中。

Power is delegated to the Commission to adopt the regulatory technical standards referred to in the first subparagraph in accordance with Articles 10 to 14 of Regulation (EU) No 1093/2010.

In order to ensure uniform conditions of application of this Directive, EBA may develop draft implementing technical standards to establish common procedures, forms and templates for the consultation process between the relevant competent authorities as referred to in Article 19b.

Power is conferred on the Commission to adopt the implementing technical standards referred to in the third subparagraph in accordance with Article 15 of Regulation (EU) No 1093/2010. '.

(6) In Article 22, the following paragraph is added:

'3. In order to specify the requirements laid down in this Article and to ensure the convergence of supervisory practices, EBA may develop draft regulatory technical standards to specify the arrangements, processes and mechanisms referred to in paragraph 1, in accordance with the principles of proportionality and comprehensiveness set out in paragraph 2.

Power is delegated to the Commission to adopt the regulatory technical standards referred to in the first subparagraph in accordance with the procedure laid down in Articles 10 to 14 of Regulation (EU) No 1093/2010. '.

(7) In Article 25, the following paragraph is added:

'5. In order to ensure consistent harmonisation of this Article, EBA shall develop draft regulatory technical standards to specify the information to be notified in accordance with this Article.

In order to ensure uniform conditions of application of this Article, EBA shall develop draft implementing technical standards to establish standard forms, templates and procedures for such notification.

EBA shall submit those draft technical standards to the Commission by 1 January 2014.

Power is delegated to the Commission to adopt the regulatory technical standards referred to in the first subparagraph in accordance with the procedure laid down in Articles 10 to 14 of Regulation (EU) No 1093/2010.

Power is also conferred on the Commission to adopt the implementing technical standards referred to in the second subparagraph in accordance with Article 15 of Regulation (EU) No 1093/2010. '.

(8) In Article 26, the following paragraph is added:

'5. In order to ensure consistent harmonisation of this Article, EBA shall develop draft regulatory technical standards to specify the information to be notified in accordance

经委托授权，欧盟委员会有权根据第1093/2010号(欧盟)条例第10条至第14条的规定通过第1项所述监管性技术标准。

为确保本指令具有统一的适用条件，欧洲银行业管理局可起草实施性技术标准草案，就第19b条所述相关主管部门之间的磋商程序制定通用的程序、格式和模板。

兹授予欧盟委员会依照第1093/2010号(欧盟)条例第15条的规定通过第3项所述实施性技术标准的权力。”

(6)第22条增加下列内容：

“3.根据第2款所规定的比例原则和全面性原则，为说明本条所规定的要求并确保监管实践的趋同，欧洲银行业管理局可起草监管性技术标准草案，具体说明第1款所述的安排、程序和机制。

经委托授权，欧盟委员会有权根据第1093/2010号(欧盟)条例第10条至第14条规定的程序通过第1项所述监管性技术标准。”

(7)第25条增加下列内容：

“5.为确保本条规定的一致协调，欧洲银行业管理局应起草监管性技术标准草案，具体说明根据本条应通知的信息。

为确保本条规定具有统一的适用条件，欧洲银行业管理局应起草实施性技术标准草案，就上述通知制定标准的格式、模板和程序。

欧洲银行业管理局应于2014年1月前将该等技术标准草案呈报欧盟委员会。

经委托授权，欧盟委员会有权根据第1093/2010号(欧盟)条例第10条至第14条规定的程序通过第1项所述监管性技术标准。

欧盟委员会也被授予根据第1093/2010号(欧盟)条例第15条的规定通过第2项所述实施性技术标准的权力。”

(8)第26条增加下列内容：

“5.为确保本条规定的一致协调，欧洲银行业管理局应起草监管性技术标准草案，具体说明根据本条应通知的信息。

with this Article.

In order to ensure uniform conditions of application of this Article, EBA shall develop draft implementing technical standards to establish standard forms, templates and procedures for such notification.

EBA shall submit those draft technical standards to the Commission by 1 January 2014.

Power is delegated to the Commission to adopt the regulatory technical standards referred to in the first subparagraph in accordance with the procedure laid down in Articles 10 to 14 of Regulation (EU) No 1093/2010.

Power is also conferred on the Commission to adopt the implementing technical standards referred to in the second subparagraph in accordance with Article 15 of Regulation (EU) No 1093/2010. '.

(9) In Article 28, the following paragraph is added:

'4. In order to ensure consistent harmonisation of this Article, EBA shall develop draft regulatory technical standards to specify the information to be notified in accordance with this Article.

In order to ensure uniform conditions of application of this Article, EBA shall develop draft implementing technical standards to establish standard forms, templates and procedures for such notification.

EBA shall submit those draft technical standards to the Commission by 1 January 2014.

Power is delegated to the Commission to adopt the regulatory technical standards referred to in the first subparagraph in accordance with Articles 10 to 14 of Regulation (EU) No 1093/2010.

Power is also conferred on the Commission to adopt the implementing technical standards referred to in the second subparagraph in accordance with Article 15 of Regulation (EU) No 1093/2010. '.

(10) In Article 33, the first paragraph is replaced by the following:

'Before following the procedure provided for in Article 30, the competent authorities of the host Member State may, in emergencies, take any precautionary measures necessary to protect the interests of depositors, investors and others to whom services are provided. The Commission, EBA and the competent authorities of the other Member States concerned shall be informed of such measures at the earliest opportunity. '.

(11) Article 36 is replaced by the following:

'*Article 36*

The Member States shall inform the Commission and EBA of the number and type of cases in which there has been a refusal pursuant to Article 25 and Article 26(1), (2)

为确保本条规定具有统一的适用条件，欧洲银行业管理局应起草实施性技术标准草案，就上述通知制定标准的格式、模板和程序。

欧洲银行业管理局应于2014年1月前将该等技术标准草案呈报给欧盟委员会。

经委托授权，欧盟委员会有权根据第1093/2010号（欧盟）条例第10条至第14条规定的程序通过第1项所述监管性技术标准。

欧盟委员会也被授予根据第1093/2010号（欧盟）条例第15条的规定通过第2项所述实施性技术标准的权力。”

（9）第28条增加下列内容：

“4.为确保本条规定的一致协调，欧洲银行业管理局应起草监管性技术标准草案，具体说明根据本条应通知的信息。

为确保本条规定具有统一的适用条件，欧洲银行业管理局应起草实施性技术标准草案，就上述通知制定标准的格式、模板和程序。

欧洲银行业管理局应于2014年1月前将该等技术标准草案呈报欧盟委员会。

经委托授权，欧盟委员会有权根据第1093/2010号（欧盟）条例第10条至第14条的规定通过第1项所述监管性技术标准。

欧盟委员会也被授予根据第1093/2010号（欧盟）条例第15条的规定通过第2项所述实施性技术标准的权力。”

（10）第33条第1款替换为下列内容：

“在履行第30条规定的程序之前，东道国主管部门可在紧急情况下采取必要的预防性措施保护存款人、投资者以及其他服务对象的利益。东道国主管部门应尽早通知欧盟委员会、欧洲银行业管理局以及其他所涉成员国的主管部门上述措施。”

（11）第36条替换为下列内容：

“第36条

在发生第25条以及第26条第1款、第2款和第3款的拒绝履行的情形下，或在按照第30条第3款采取了相应措施的情形下，成员国应通知欧盟委员会和欧洲银行业管理

and (3) or in which measures have been taken in accordance with Article 30(3). '.

(12) Article 38(2) is replaced by the following:

'2. The competent authorities shall notify the Commission, EBA and the European Banking Committee of all authorisations for branches granted to credit institutions having their head office in a third country. '.

(13) In Article 39 is amended as follows:

(a) in paragraph 2, the following point is added:

'(c) that EBA is able to obtain the information from the competent authorities of the Member States received from national authorities of third countries in accordance with Article 35 of Regulation (EU) No 1093/2010. ';

(b) the following paragraph is added:

'4. EBA shall assist the Commission for the purposes of this Article in accordance with Article 33 of Regulation (EU) No 1093/2010. '.

(14) In Article 42, the following paragraphs are added:

'The competent authorities may refer to EBA situations where a request for collaboration, in particular to exchange information, has been rejected or has not been acted upon within a reasonable time. Without prejudice to Article 258 of the Treaty on the Functioning of the European Union (TFEU), EBA may, in situations referred to in the first sentence, act in accordance with the powers conferred on it under Article 19 of Regulation (EU) No 1093/2010.

In order to ensure consistent harmonisation of this Article, EBA shall develop draft regulatory technical standards to specify the information contained in this Article.

In order to ensure uniform conditions of application of this Article, EBA shall develop draft implementing technical standards to establish standard forms, templates and procedures for the information sharing requirements which are likely to facilitate the monitoring of credit institutions.

EBA shall submit those draft technical standards to the Commission by 1 January 2014.

Power is delegated to the Commission to adopt the regulatory technical standards referred to in the third paragraph in accordance with the procedure laid down in Articles 10 to 14 of Regulation (EU) No 1093/2010.

Power is also conferred on the Commission to adopt the implementing technical standards referred to in the fourth paragraph in accordance with Article 15 of Regulation (EU) No 1093/2010. '.

(15) Article 42a is amended as follows:

(a) in paragraph 1, the following subparagraph is inserted after the fourth subparagraph:

局上述情况出现的次数和类型。”

（12）第38条第2款替换为下列内容：

“2.主管部门应向欧盟委员会、欧洲银行业管理局以及欧洲银行业委员会通知针对总部在第三国的信贷机构开设分支机构的申请所授予的一切核准。”

（13）第39条修正如下：

（a）在第2款中增加下目：

“（c）欧洲银行业管理局能根据第1093/2010号（欧盟）条例第35条从成员国主管部门获得后者从第三国国家级监管机构接收的信息。”

（b）增加下列内容：

“4.欧洲银行业管理局应根据第1093/2010号（欧盟）条例第33条的规定，为本条规定之目的协助欧盟委员会。”

（14）第42条增加下列内容：

“主管部门提出的合作请求（特别是信息交换请求）被拒绝或未在合理的时间内落实的，该主管部门可将该等情况移交欧洲银行业管理局，在不影响《欧洲联盟运行条约》（TFEU）第258条的情形下，欧洲银行业管理局可在第一句所述情况下依照第1093/2010号（欧盟）条例第19条授予的权力处理。

为确保本条规定的一致协调，欧洲银行业管理局应起草监管性技术标准草案，具体说明本条规定所包含的信息。

为确保本条规定具有统一的适用条件，欧洲银行业管理局应起草实施性技术标准草案，就可能有利于信贷机构监控的信息共享要求制定标准的格式、模板和程序。

欧洲银行业管理局应于2014年1月1日前将该等技术标准草案呈报给欧盟委员会。

经委托授权，欧盟委员会有权根据第1093/2010号（欧盟）条例第10条至第14条规定的程序通过第3项所述监管性技术标准。

欧盟委员会也被授予根据第1093/2010号（欧盟）条例第15条的规定通过第4项所述实施性技术标准的权力。”

（15）第42a条修正如下：

（a）在第1款第4项后增加下项内容：

'If, at the end of the initial two-month period any of the competent authorities concerned has referred the matter to EBA in accordance with Article 19 of Regulation (EU) No 1093/2010, the competent authorities of the host Member State shall defer their decision and await the decision that EBA may take in accordance with Article 19(3) of that Regulation. The competent authorities of the host Member State shall take their decision in conformity with that of EBA. The two-month period shall be deemed to be the "conciliation phase" within the meaning of Article 19 of that Regulation. EBA shall take its decision within 1 month. The matter shall not be referred to EBA after the end of the initial two month period or after a joint decision has been reached. ';

(b) in paragraph 3, the following subparagraphs are added:

'In order to ensure consistent harmonisation of this Article, EBA may develop draft regulatory technical standards in order to specify general conditions for the functioning of colleges of supervisors.

Power is delegated to the Commission to adopt the regulatory technical standards referred to in the fourth subparagraph in accordance with the procedure laid down in Articles 10 to 14 of Regulation (EU) No 1093/2010.

In order to ensure uniform conditions of application of this Article, EBA may develop draft implementing technical standards in order to determine the operational functioning of colleges of supervisors.

Power is conferred on the Commission to adopt the implementing technical standards referred to in the sixth subparagraph in accordance with Article 15 of Regulation (EU) No 1093/2010. '.

(16) Article 42b is amended as follows:

(a) paragraph 1 is replaced by the following:

'1. In the exercise of their duties, the competent authorities shall take into account the convergence in respect of supervisory tools and supervisory practices in the application of the laws, regulations and administrative requirements adopted pursuant to this Directive. For that purpose, Member States shall ensure that:

(a) the competent authorities participate in the activities of EBA;

(b) the competent authorities follow the guidelines and recommendations of EBA and state the reasons if they do not do so;

(c) national mandates conferred on the competent authorities do not inhibit the performance of their duties as members of EBA or under this Directive. ';

(b) paragraph 2 is deleted.

(17) Article 44(2) is replaced by the following:

'2. Paragraph 1 shall not prevent the competent authorities of the various Member States from exchanging information or transmitting information to EBA in accordance with

“2个月的初始期限届满时，任何所涉主管部门已经依照第1093/2010号（欧盟）条例第19条规定将该事宜移交欧洲银行业管理局处理的，东道国主管部门应延迟其决定，以等待欧洲银行业管理局可能根据该条例第19条第3款规定作出的决定，并且最终应作出与欧洲银行业管理局决定相符的决定。2个月的期限应被视为该条例第19条所定义的调解期。欧洲银行业管理局应在1个月内作出决定。2个月的初始期限届满后或共同决定作出后，即不再有权将该事宜移交欧洲银行业管理局处理。”

（b）第3款增加下列内容：

“为确保本条规定的一致协调，欧洲银行业管理局可起草监管性技术标准草案，规定监管团运作的一般条件。

经委托授权，欧盟委员会有权根据第1093/2010号（欧盟）条例第10条至第14条规定的程序通过第4项所述监管性技术标准。

为确保本条规定具有统一的适用条件，欧洲银行业管理局可起草实施性技术标准草案，以确定监管团具体的运作方式。

欧盟委员会被授予根据第1093/2010号（欧盟）条例第15条的规定通过第6项所述实施性技术标准的权力。”

（16）第42b条修正如下：

（a）第1款替换为下列内容：

“1.主管部门在履行职责过程中，应考虑到涉及根据本指令通过的法律、法规和规章适用的监管工具和监管实践趋同。为此，各成员国应确保：

（a）主管部门参与欧洲银行业管理局的活动；

（b）主管部门遵循欧洲银行业管理局的指引和建议，不遵循的须说明理由；

（c）成员国授予主管部门的任务不限制其履行作为欧洲银行业管理局成员的职责或在本指令中的职责。”

（b）删除第2款。

（17）第44条第2款替换为下列内容：

“2.第1款不妨碍各成员国主管部门根据本指令、其他适用于信贷机构的指令以及第1093/2010号（欧盟）条例第31条和第35条的规定与欧洲银行业管理局交换信息或向

this Directive, with other Directives applicable to credit institutions, and with Articles 31 and 35 of Regulation (EU) No 1093/2010. That information shall be subject to the conditions relating to professional secrecy set out in paragraph 1'.

(18) Article 46 is replaced by the following:

'*Article 46*

In accordance with Article 33 of Regulation (EU) No 1093/2010, Member States and EBA may conclude cooperation agreements, providing for exchanges of information, with the competent authorities of third countries or with authorities or bodies of third countries as defined in Article 47 and Article 48(1) of this Directive only if the information disclosed is subject to guarantees of professional secrecy at least equivalent to those referred to in Article 44(1) of this Directive. Such exchange of information shall be for the purpose of performing the supervisory tasks of those authorities or bodies.

Where the information originates in another Member State, it shall not be disclosed without the express agreement of theauthorities which have disclosed it and, where appropriate, solely for the purposes for which those authorities gave theiragreement. '.

(19) Article 49 is amended as follows:

(a) the first paragraph is replaced by the following:

'This Section shall not prevent a competent authority from transmitting information to the following for the purposes of their tasks:

(a) central banks of the European System of the Central Banks and other bodies with a similar function in their capacity as monetary authorities when the information is relevant for the exercise of their respective statutory tasks, including the conduct of monetary policy and related liquidity provision, oversight of payments, clearing and settlement systems, and the safeguarding of stability of the financial system;

(b) where appropriate, other public authorities responsible for overseeing payment systems;

(c) the European Systemic Risk Board (hereinafter the "ESRB"), where that information is relevant for the exercise of its statutory tasks under Regulation (EU) No 1092/2010 of the European Parliament and of the Council of 24 November 2010 on European Union macro-prudential oversight of the financial system and establishing a European Systemic Risk Board (*).

This Section shall not prevent the authorities or bodies referred to in the first subparagraph from communicating to the competent authorities such information as they may need for the purposes of Article 45.

(*) OJ L 331, 15. 12. 2010, p. 1. ';

(b) the fourth paragraph is replaced by the following:

'In an emergency situation as referred to in Article 130(1), Member States shall allow

欧洲银行业管理局发送信息。交换和发送上述信息时应遵守第1款规定的关于职业保密的条件。”

(18)第46条替换为下列内容：

“第46条

根据第1093/2010号(欧盟)条例第33条的规定,仅当披露的信息的职业保密保证至少与本指令第44条第1款所述职业保密保证具有等效性时,各成员国以及欧洲银行业管理局方可与第三国主管部门或如本指令第47条和第48条第1款所定义的第三国部门或机构缔结信息交换合作协议。上述信息交换应以履行该等部门或机构的监管工作为目的。

对于来源于另一成员国的信息,唯有经披露信息的主管部门明确同意方能予以披露,且仅能在适当时就该等部门同意之目的披露。”

(19)第49条修正如下：

(a)第1款替换为下列内容：

“本节不妨碍主管部门为下列主体履行工作之目的向其发送信息：

(a)欧洲中央银行体系内各家中央银行以及其他作为货币管理当局具有类似职能的机构,前提是信息与其各自法定职责的履行(包括货币政策的实施以及与此相关的流动性供应,支付、清算和证券结算系统的监控以及对金融系统稳定的维护)相关;

(b)负责监控支付系统的其他公共机构(如适当);

(c)欧洲系统性风险委员会(英文简称ESRB),前提是信息与其在《欧洲议会与欧盟理事会关于欧盟对金融系统的宏观审慎监控以及设立欧洲系统性风险委员会的第1092/2010号(欧盟)条例》*(2010年11月24日)中的法定职责的履行相关。

本节不得妨碍第1项所述的部门或机构向主管部门提供就第45条而言其所需之信息。

*《欧盟公报》L 331,2010年12月15日,第1页。”

(b)第4款替换为下列内容：

“在第130条第1款所述的紧急情况下,成员国应允许主管部门立即向欧洲中央银

the competent authorities to communicate, without delay, information to the central banks in the European System of the Central Banks where that information is relevant for the exercise of their statutory tasks, including the conduct of monetary policy and related liquidity provision, the oversight of payments, clearing and securities settlement systems, and the safeguarding stability of the financial system, and to the ESRB under Regulation (EU) No 1092/2010, where such information is relevant for the exercise of its statutory tasks.'

(20) Article 63a is amended as follows:

(a) paragraph 4 is replaced by the following:

'4. The provisions governing the instrument shall provide for principal, unpaid interest or dividend to be such as to absorb losses and to not hinder the recapitalisation of the credit institution through appropriate mechanisms, as developed by EBA under paragraph 6';

(b) paragraph 6 is replaced by the following:

'6. In order to ensure consistent harmonisation and to ensure the convergence of supervisory practices, EBA shall develop draft regulatory technical standards to specify the requirements applicable to the instruments referred to in paragraph 1 of this Article. EBA shall submit those draft regulatory technical standards to the Commission by 1 January 2014.

Power is delegated to the Commission to adopt the regulatory technical standards referred to in the first subparagraph in accordance with the procedure laid down in Articles 10 to 14 of Regulation (EU) No 1093/2010.

EBA shall also issue guidelines in relation to instruments referred to in point (a) of the first paragraph of Article 57.

EBA shall monitor the application of those guidelines.'.

(21) In Article 74(2), the second subparagraph is replaced by the following:

'In order to ensure uniform conditions of application of this Directive, for the communication of those calculations by credit institutions, the competent authorities shall apply, from 31 December 2012, uniform formats, frequencies and dates of reporting. In order to ensure uniform conditions of application of this Directive, EBA shall develop draft implementing technical standards to introduce, within the Union, uniform formats (with associated instructions), frequencies and dates of reporting before 1 January 2012. The reporting formats shall be proportionate to the nature, scale and complexity of the credit institutions' activities.

In order to ensure uniform conditions of application of this Directive, EBA shall also develop draft implementing technical standards regarding IT solutions to be applied for such reporting.

行体系内的各家中央银行通知与其法定职责的履行(包括货币政策的实施以及与此相关的流动性供应,支付、清算和证券结算系统的监控以及对金融系统稳定的维护)相关的信息,如果上述信息与欧洲系统性风险委员会法定职责的履行相关,还应按第1092/2010号(欧盟)条例的规定通知欧洲系统性风险委员会。”

(20)第63a条修正如下:

(a)第4款替换为下列内容:

“4.规制金融工具的条款应规定,本金、未付利息或股息应足以吸收损失并且不妨碍通过欧洲银行业管理局依照第6款所建立的适当机制对信贷机构进行再注资。”

(b)第6款替换为下列内容:

“6.为确保一致协调并确保各国监管实践的趋同,欧洲银行业管理局应起草监管性技术标准草案,具体说明适用于本条第1项所述工具的要求。欧洲银行业管理局应于2014年1月1日前将该等监管性技术标准草案呈报给欧盟委员会。

经委托授权,欧盟委员会有权根据第1093/2010号(欧盟)条例第10条至第14条规定的程序通过第1项所述监管性技术标准。

欧洲银行业管理局也应针对第57条第1款第a目所述的工具发布指引。

欧洲银行业管理局应对该等指引的适用进行监控。”

(21)第74条第2款第2项替换为下列内容:

“为确保本指令具有统一的适用条件,从2012年12月31日起,主管部门应就信贷机构采用的与该等计算有关的信息提供适用统一的报告格式、频率和日期。为确保本指令具有统一的适用条件,欧洲银行业管理局应起草实施性技术标准草案,以期于2012年1月1日前在欧盟范围内开始实施统一的报告格式(连同相关的说明)、频率和日期。报告格式应与信贷机构活动的性质、规模及复杂性成比例。

为确保本指令具有统一的适用条件,欧洲银行业管理局还应针对适用于上述报告的IT解决方案起草实施性技术标准草案。

Power is conferred on the Commission to adopt the implementing technical standards referred to in the second and third subparagraphs in accordance with Article 15 of Regulation (EU) No 1093/2010. '.

(22) In Article 81(2) the following subparagraphs are added:

'In order to ensure consistent harmonisation of this Article, EBA, in consultation with the European Supervisory Authority (European Securities and Markets Authority) (hereinafter "ESMA"), established by Regulation (EU) No 1095/2010 of the European Parliament and of the Council (*), shall develop draft regulatory technical standards to specify the assessment methodology relating to credit assessments. EBA shall submit those draft regulatory technical standards to the Commission by 1 January 2014.

Power is delegated to the Commission to adopt the regulatory technical standards referred to in the second subparagraph in accordance with the procedure laid down in Articles 10 to 14 of Regulation (EU) No 1093/2010.

(*) OJ L 331, 15. 12. 2010, p. 84. '.

(23) In Article 84(2), the following subparagraphs are added:

'In order to ensure consistent harmonisation of this Article, EBA may develop draft regulatory technical standards to specify the assessment methodology under which the competent authorities permit credit institutions to use the IRB approach.

Power is delegated to the Commission to adopt the regulatory technical standards referred to in point (a) of the first subparagraph in accordance with the procedure laid down in Articles 10 to 14 of Regulation (EU) No 1093/2010. '.

(24) In Article 97(2), the following subparagraphs are added:

'In order to ensure consistent harmonisation of this Article, EBA, in consultation with ESMA, shall develop draft regulatory technical standards to specify the assessment methodology relating to credit assessments. EBA shall submit those draft regulatory technical standards to the Commission by 1 January 2014.

Power is delegated to the Commission to adopt the regulatory technical standards referred to in the second subparagraph in accordance with the procedure laid down in Articles 10 to 14 of Regulation (EU) No 1093/2010. '.

(25) In Article 105(1), the following subparagraphs are added:

'In order to ensure consistent harmonisation of this Article, EBA may develop draft regulatory technical standards to specify the assessment methodology under which the competent authorities permit credit institutions to use Advanced Measurement Approaches.

Power is delegated to the Commission to adopt the regulatory technical standards referred to in the second subparagraph in accordance with the procedure laid down in Articles 10 to 14 of Regulation (EU) No 1093/2010. '.

兹授予欧盟委员会依照第1093/2010号(欧盟)条例第15条的规定通过第2项和第3项所述实施性技术标准的权力。"

(22)第81条第2款增加下列内容:

"为确保本条规定的一致协调,欧洲银行业管理局与依据《欧洲议会与欧盟理事会第1095/2010号(欧盟)条例》*设立的欧洲监管机构(欧洲证券与市场管理局)(以下简称欧洲证券与市场管理局,英文简称ESMA)磋商后,应起草监管性技术标准草案,具体说明信用评估的方法。欧洲银行业管理局应于2014年1月1日前将该监管性技术标准草案呈报欧盟委员会。

经委托授权,欧盟委员会有权根据第1093/2010号(欧盟)条例第10条至第14条规定的程序通过第2项所述监管性技术标准。

*《欧盟公报》L 331,2010年12月15日,第84页。"

(23)第84条第2款增加下列内容:

"为确保本条规定的一致协调,欧洲银行业管理局可起草监管性技术标准草案,具体说明采用何等评估方法能使主管部门允许信贷机构使用内部评级法。

经委托授权,欧盟委员会有权根据第1093/2010号(欧盟)条例第10条至第14条规定的程序通过第1项第a目所述监管性技术标准。"

(24)第97条第2款增加下列内容:

"为确保本条规定的一致协调,欧洲银行业管理局与欧洲证券与市场管理局磋商后,应起草监管性技术标准草案,具体说明信用评估的方法。欧洲银行业管理局应于2014年1月1日前将该等监管性技术标准草案呈报欧盟委员会。

经委托授权,欧盟委员会有权根据第1093/2010号(欧盟)条例第10条至第14条规定的程序通过第2项所述监管性技术标准。"

(25)第105条第1款增加下列内容:

"为确保本条规定的一致协调,欧洲银行业管理局可起草监管性技术标准草案,具体说明采用何等评估方法能使主管部门允许信贷机构使用高级计量法。

经委托授权,欧盟委员会有权根据第1093/2010号(欧盟)条例第10条至第14条规定的程序通过第2项所述监管性技术标准。"

(26) In Article 106(2), the second subparagraph is replaced by the following:

'In order to ensure consistent harmonisation of this paragraph, EBA shall develop draft regulatory technical standards in order to specify the exemptions in points (c) and (d) as well as to specify the conditions used to determine the existence of a group of connected clients, as stated in paragraph 3. EBA shall submit those draft regulatory technical standards to the Commission by 1 January 2014.

Power is delegated to the Commission to adopt the regulatory technical standards referred to the second subparagraph in accordance with the procedure laid down in Articles 10 to 14 of Regulation (EU) No 1093/2010. '.

(27) Article 110(2) is replaced by the following:

'2. Member States shall provide that reporting shall be carried out at least twice a year. The competent authorities shall apply, from 31 December 2012, uniform formats, frequencies and dates of reporting. In order to ensure uniform conditions of application of this Directive, EBA shall develop draft implementing technical standards to introduce, within the Union, uniform formats (with associated instructions), frequencies and dates of reporting before 1 January 2012. The reporting formats shall be proportionate to the nature, scale and complexity of the credit institutions' activities.

In order to ensure uniform conditions of application of this Directive, EBA shall also develop draft implementing technical standards regarding IT solutions to be applied for such reporting.

Power is conferred on the Commission to adopt the implementing technical standards referred to in the first and second subparagraphs in accordance with the procedure laid down in Article 15 of Regulation (EU) No 1093/2010. '.

(28) In Article 111(1), the fourth subparagraph is replaced by the following:

'Member States may set a lower limit than EUR 150 million and shall inform EBA and the Commission thereof. '.

(29) Article 122a(10) is replaced by the following:

'10. EBA shall report to the Commission annually on the compliance with this Article by the competent authorities.

In order to ensure consistent harmonisation of this Article, EBA shall develop draft regulatory technical standards for the convergence of supervisory practices with regard to this Article, including the measures taken in case of breach of the due diligence and risk management obligations. EBA shall submit those draft regulatory technical standards to the Commission by 1 January 2014.

Power is delegated to the Commission to adopt the regulatory technical standards referred to in the second subparagraph in accordance with the procedure laid down in Articles 10 to 14 of Regulation (EU) No 1093/2010. '.

(26)第106条第2款第2项替换为下列内容:

"为确保本款的一致协调,欧洲银行业管理局应起草监管性技术标准草案,具体说明第c目和第d目的豁免情形,以及用于确定是否存在第3款所述关联客户的条件。欧洲银行业管理局应于2014年1月1日前将该等监管性技术标准草案呈报欧盟委员会。

经委托授权,欧盟委员会有权根据第1093/2010号(欧盟)条例第10条至第14条规定的程序通过第2项所述监管性技术标准。"

(27)第110条第2款替换为下列内容:

"2.各成员国应规定每年至少进行2次报告。主管部门应从2012年12月31日起采用统一的报告格式、频率和日期。为确保本指令具有统一的适用条件,欧洲银行业管理局应起草实施性技术标准草案,以期于2012年1月1日前在欧盟范围内开始实施统一的报告格式(连同相关的说明)、频率和日期。报告格式应与信贷机构活动的性质、规模和复杂性成比例。

为确保本指令具有统一的适用条件,欧洲银行业管理局还应针对上述报告所采用的IT解决方案起草实施性技术标准草案。

兹授予欧盟委员会依照第1093/2010号(欧盟)条例第15条规定的程序通过第1项和第2项所述实施性技术标准的权力。"

(28)第111条第1款第4项替换为下列内容:

"成员国可设定一个低于1.5亿欧元的上限,并应通知欧洲银行业管理局及欧盟委员会该上限。"

(29)第122a条第10款替换为下列内容:

"10.欧洲银行业管理局应每年向欧盟委员会报告主管部门遵守本条规定的情况。

为确保本条规定的一致协调,欧洲银行业管理局应针对本条的监管实践的趋同起草监管性技术标准草案,包括在发生违反尽职义务和风险管理义务的情况时所采取的措施。欧洲银行业管理局应于2014年1月1日前将该等监管性技术标准草案呈报欧盟委员会。

经委托授权,欧盟委员会有权根据第1093/2010号(欧盟)条例第10条至第14条规定的程序通过第2项所述监管性技术标准。"

(30) In Article 124, the following paragraph is added:

'6. In order to ensure consistent harmonisation of this Article, EBA may develop draft regulatory technical standards to specify this Article and a common risk assessment procedure and methodology.

Power is delegated to the Commission to adopt the regulatory technical standards referred to in the first subparagraph in accordance with the procedure laid down in Articles 10 to 14 of Regulation (EU) No 1093/2010. '.

(31) Article 126(4) is replaced by the following.

'4. The competent authorities shall notify the Commission and EBA of any agreement falling within paragraph 3. '.

(32) Article 129 is amended as follows:

(a) in paragraph 1, the following subparagraph is inserted after the first subparagraph:

'Where the consolidating supervisor fails to carry out the tasks referred to in the first subparagraph or where the competent authorities do not cooperate with the consolidating supervisor to the extent required in carrying out the tasks in the first subparagraph, any of the competent authorities concerned may refer the matter to EBA, which may act in accordance with Article 19 of Regulation (EU) No 1093/2010. ';

(b) in paragraph 2, the following is added to the fifth subparagraph:

'If, at the end of the six month period, any of the competent authorities concerned has referred the matter to EBA in accordance with Article 19 of Regulation (EU) No 1093/2010, the consolidating supervisor shall defer its decision and await any decision that EBA may take in accordance with Article 19(3) of that Regulation on its decision, and shall take its decision in conformity with the decision of EBA. The six-month period shall be deemed the conciliation period within the meaning of that Regulation. EBA shall take its decision within 1 month. The matter shall not be referred to EBA after the end of the six month period or after a joint decision has been reached. ';

(c) in paragraph 2, the following subparagraphs are added:

'EBA may develop draft implementing technical standards to ensure uniform conditions of application of the joint decision process referred to in this paragraph, with regard to the applications for permissions referred to in Article 84(1), Article 87(9) and Article 105 and in Annex Ⅲ part 6, with a view to facilitating joint decisions.

Power is conferred on the Commission to adopt the implementing technical standards referred to in the sixth and the seventh subparagraphs in accordance with the procedure laid down in Article 15 of Regulation (EU) No 1093/2010. ';

(d) paragraph 3 is amended as follows:

(i) in the third subparagraph, the term 'Committee of European Banking

(30)第124条增加下列内容:

"6.为确保本条规定的一致协调,欧洲银行业管理局可起草监管性技术标准草案,具体说明本条规定以及通用的风险评估程序和方法。

经委托授权,欧盟委员会有权根据第1093/2010号(欧盟)条例第10条至第14条规定的程序通过第1项所述监管性技术标准。"

(31)第126条第4款替换为下列内容:

"4.主管部门应通知欧盟委员会及欧洲银行业管理局第3款规定范围内的任何协议。"

(32)第129条修正如下:

(a)在第1款第1项后增加下列内容:

"并表监管机构无法履行第1项所述的工作,或者主管部门未向并表监管机构提供其履行第1项工作所需的合作的,任何所涉主管部门均可将该事宜移交欧洲银行业管理局,由欧洲银行业管理局依照第1093/2010号(欧盟)条例第19条处理。"

(b)在第2款第5项中加入下列内容:

"6个月期限届满时,任何所涉主管部门已经依照第1093/2010号(欧盟)条例第19条将该事宜移交欧洲银行业管理局处理的,并表监管机构应延迟其决定,以等待欧洲银行业管理局可能根据该条例第19条第3款规定作出的决定,并且最终应作出与欧洲银行业管理局决定相符的决定。6个月的期限应被视为该条例所定义的调解期。欧洲银行业管理局应在1个月内作出决定。6个月的调解期届满后或共同决定作出后,即不再有权将该事宜移交欧洲银行业管理局处理。"

(c)第2款增加下列内容:

"欧洲银行业管理局可针对第84条第1款、第87条第9款以及第105条所述的以及附录三第6部分所述的许可申请起草实施性技术标准草案,确保本款所述共同决策程序具有统一的适用条件,以便于作出共同决定。

兹授予欧盟委员会依照第1093/2010号(欧盟)条例第15条规定的程序通过第6项和第7项所述实施性技术标准的权力。"

(d)第3款修正如下:

(i)第3项中,"欧洲银行业监管机构委员会"一词替换为"欧洲银行业管理局";

Supervisors' is replaced by 'EBA';

(ii) the fourth subparagraph is replaced by the following:

'In the absence of such a joint decision between the competent authorities within 4 months, a decision on the application of Articles 123 and 124 and Article 136(2) shall be taken on a consolidated basis by the consolidating supervisor after duly considering the risk assessment of subsidiaries performed by relevant competent authorities. If, at the end of the four month period, any of the competent authorities concerned has referred the matter to EBA in accordance with Article 19 of Regulation (EU) No 1093/2010, the consolidating supervisor shall defer its decision and await any decision that EBA may take in accordance with Article 19 (3) of that Regulation, and shall take its decision in conformity with the decision of EBA. The four month period shall be deemed the conciliation period within the meaning of the Regulation. EBA shall take its decision within 1 month. The matter shall not be referred to EBA after the end of the four month period or after a joint decision has been reached.';

(iii) the fifth subparagraph is replaced by the following:

'The decision on the application of Articles 123 and 124 and Article 136(2) shall be taken by the respective competent authorities responsible for supervision of subsidiaries of a Union parent credit institution or a Union parent financial holding company on an individual or sub-consolidated basis after duly considering the views and reservations expressed by the consolidating supervisor. If, at the end of the four-month period, any of the competent authorities concerned has referred the matter to EBA in accordance with Article 19 of Regulation (EU) No 1093/2010, the competent authorities shall defer their decision and await any decision that EBA shall take in accordance with Article 19(3) of that Regulation, and shall take its decision in conformity with the decision of EBA. The four month period shall be deemed the conciliation period within the meaning of that Regulation. EBA shall take its decision within 1 month. The matter shall not be referred to EBA after the end of the four-month period or after a joint decision has been reached.';

(iv) the seventh subparagraph is replaced by the following:

'Where EBA has been consulted, all the competent authorities shall consider its advice, and explain any significant deviation therefrom.';

(v) the tenth subparagraph is replaced by the following:

'EBA may develop draft implementing technical standards to ensure uniform conditions of application of the joint decision process referred to in this paragraph, with regard to the application of Articles 123 and 124 and Article 136(2) with a view to facilitating joint decisions.

Power is conferred on the Commission to adopt the implementing technical standards

(ii)第4项替换为下列内容：

“主管部门在4个月内未作出共同决定的，并表监管机构应在充分考虑相关主管部门对子公司所作的风险评估后，在并表基础上作出是否适用第123条和第124条以及第136条第2款规定的决定。4个月期限届满时，任何所涉主管部门已经依照第1093/2010号(欧盟)条例第19条的规定将该事宜移交欧洲银行业管理局处理的，并表监管机构应延迟其决定，以等待欧洲银行业管理局可能根据该条例第19条第3款作出的决定，并且最终应作出与欧洲银行业管理局决定相符的决定。4个月的期限应被视为该条例所定义的调解期。欧洲银行业管理局应在1个月内作出决定。4个月的调解期届满后或共同决定作出后，即不再有权将该事宜移交欧洲银行业管理局处理。”

(iii)第5项替换为下列内容：

“信贷机构或金融控股公司的子公司，若其母公司设于欧盟的，对该等子公司实施单独监管或者次并表监管的各个主管部门充分考虑并表监管机构所表达的观点和保留意见后，应对第123条和第124条以及第136条第2款的适用作出决定。4个月期限届满时，任何所涉主管部门已经依照第1093/2010号(欧盟)条例第19条将该事宜移交欧洲银行业管理局处理的，主管部门应延迟其决定，以等待欧洲银行业管理局可能根据该条例第19条第3款规定作出的决定，并且最终应作出与欧洲银行业管理局决定相符的决定。4个月的期限应被视为该条例所定义的调解期。欧洲银行业管理局应在1个月内作出决定。4个月的调解期届满后或共同决定作出后，即不再有权将该事宜移交欧洲银行业管理局处理。”

(iv)第7项替换为下列内容：

“每一主管部门在咨询欧洲银行业管理局意见后均应考虑其建议，并对严重偏离其建议的情形予以解释。”

(v)第10项替换为下列内容：

“欧洲银行业管理局可针对第123条、第124条以及第136条第2款的适用起草实施性技术标准草案，确保本款所述共同决策程序具有统一的适用条件，以便于作出共同决定。

兹授予欧盟委员会依照第1093/2010号(欧盟)条例第15条规定的程序通过第10项

referred to in the tenth subparagraph in accordance with the procedure laid down in Article 15 of Regulation (EU) No 1093/2010. '.

(33) In Article 130(1), the first and second subparagraphs are replaced by the following:

'1. Where an emergency situation, including a situation as defined in Article 18 of Regulation (EU) No 1093/2010 or a situation of adverse developments in markets, arises, which potentially jeopardises the market liquidity and the stability of the financial system in any of the Member State where entities of a group have been authorised or where significant branches referred to in Article 42a are established, the consolidating supervisor shall, subject to Chapter 1, Section 2, alert as soon as is practicable, EBA, ESRB and the authorities referred to in the fourth subparagraph of Article 49 and in Article 50 and shall communicate all information essential for the pursuance of their tasks. Those obligations shall apply to all competent authorities under Articles 125 and 126 and to the competent authority identified under Article 129(1).

If the authority referred to in the fourth paragraph of Article 49 becomes aware of a situation described in the first subparagraph, it shall alert as soon as is practicable the competent authorities referred to in Articles 125 and 126, and EBA. '.

(34) In Article 131, the third paragraph is replaced by the following:

'The competent authorities responsible for authorising the subsidiary of a parent undertaking which is a credit institution may, by bilateral agreement, in accordance with Article 28 of Regulation (EU) No 1093/2010, delegate their responsibility for supervision to the competent authorities which authorised and supervise the parent undertaking so that they assume responsibility for supervising the subsidiary in accordance with this Directive. EBA shall be kept informed of the existence and content of such agreements. It shall forward such information to the competent authorities of the other Member States and to the European Banking Committee. '.

(35) Article 131a is amended as follows:

(a) paragraph 1 is replaced by the following:

'1. The consolidating supervisor shall establish colleges of supervisors to facilitate the exercise of the tasks referred to in Article 129 and Article 130(1) and subject to the confidentiality requirements of paragraph 2 of this Article and compatibility with Union law, ensure appropriate coordination and cooperation with relevant third-country competent authorities where appropriate.

EBA shall contribute to promoting and monitoring the efficient, effective and consistent functioning of colleges of supervisors referred to in this Article in accordance with Article 21 of Regulation (EU) No 1093/2010. To that end, EBA shall participate as it deems appropriate and shall be considered as a competent authority for that purpose.

所述实施性技术标准的权力。”

(33)第130条第1款第1项和第2项替换为下列内容:

“1.对于某集团下属实体获准在其境内经营或者在其境内设立第42a条所述重要分支机构的成员国而言,出现可能会危害该成员国市场流动性以及金融系统稳定的紧急情况[包括第1093/2010号(欧盟)条例第18条所界定的情形]或市场不利变化时,在符合第一章第2节规定的前提下,并表监管机构应尽早向欧洲银行业管理局、欧洲系统性风险委员会以及第49条第4项和第50条所述部门发出预警,并应向其提供对履行其工作而言至关重要的一切信息。该等义务应适用于第125条和第126条中的所有主管部门以及依照第129条第1款所认定的主管部门。

第49条第4款所述的部门一旦知悉第一项所述的情况,在可行的情形下应尽早向第125条和第126条所述主管部门以及欧洲银行业管理局发出预警。”

(34)第131条第3款替换为下列内容:

“负责授予信贷机构(亦即母公司)下属子公司核准的主管部门,可根据第1093/2010号(欧盟)条例第28条的规定,通过双边协议将其监管责任委托给授予该母公司核准并对其进行监管的其他主管部门,以便后者按照本指令承担监管该等子公司的责任。应通知欧洲银行业管理局该等协议的内容和存在,欧洲银行业管理局应将该等信息转发给其他成员国的主管部门以及欧洲银行业委员会。”

(35)第131a条修正如下:

(a)第1款替换为下列内容:

“1.并表监管机构应设立监管团,以便履行第129条和第130条第1款所述的工作,在遵守本条第2款的保密要求并且与欧盟法律相容的前提下,在适当的情况下应确保与相关的第三国主管部门之间适当的协调和合作。

根据第1093/2010号(欧盟)条例第21条的规定,欧洲银行业管理局应致力于促进和监控本条所述的监管团高效率、高成效和协调一致的运作。为此,欧洲银行业管理局应以其认为适当的方式参与监管团工作并就此被视为主管部门。

Colleges of supervisors shall provide a framework for the consolidating Supervisor, EBA and the other competent authorities concerned to carry out the following tasks:

(a) exchanging information among themselves and with EBA in accordance with Article 21 of Regulation (EU) No 1093/2010;

(b) agreeing on voluntary entrustment of tasks and voluntary delegation of responsibilities where appropriate;

(c) determining supervisory examination programmes based on a risk assessment of the group in accordance with Article 124;

(d) increasing the efficiency of supervision by removing unnecessary duplication of supervisory requirements, including in relation to the information requests referred to in Article 130(2) and Article 132(2);

(e) consistently applying the prudential requirements under this Directive across all entities within a banking group without prejudice to the options and discretions available in Union legislation;

(f) applying Article 129(1)(c) taking into account the work of other forums that may be established in that area.

The competent authorities participating in the colleges of supervisors and EBA shall cooperate closely. The confidentiality requirements under Chapter 1, Section 2 shall not prevent the competent authorities from exchanging confidential information within colleges of supervisors. The establishment and functioning of colleges of supervisors shall not affect the rights and responsibilities of the competent authorities under this Directive. ';

(b) in paragraph 2:

(i) the second subparagraph is replaced by the following:

'In order to ensure consistent harmonisation of this Article, EBA may develop draft regulatory technical standards in order to specify general conditions of functioning of the colleges of supervisors.

Power is delegated to the Commission to adopt the regulatory technical standards referred to in the second subparagraph in accordance with the procedure laid down in Articles 10 to 14 of Regulation (EU) No 1093/2010.

In order to ensure uniform conditions of application of this Article, EBA may develop draft implementing technical standards in order to determine the operational functioning of the colleges of supervisors.

Power is conferred on the Commission to adopt the implementing technical standards referred to in the fourth subparagraph in accordance with the procedure laid down in Article 15 of Regulation (EU) No 1093/2010. ';

(ii) the sixth subparagraph is replaced by the following:

'The consolidating supervisor, subject to the confidentiality requirements under

监管团应为并表监管机构、欧洲银行业管理局以及其他所涉主管部门提供履行下列工作的框架：

(a)互相交换信息，并根据第1093/2010号(欧盟)条例第21条的规定与欧洲银行业管理局交换信息；

(b)在适当的情况下，自愿接受工作的委派以及责任的委托；

(c)依照第124条，基于对集团的风险评估确定监管检查计划；

(d)通过删除不必要的、重复的监管要求(包括针对第130条第2款和第132条第2款所述的信息请求)的方式提高监管效率；

(e)在不影响欧盟立法中适用的选择权和自由裁量权的情形下，对同一个银行业集团下属所有实体协调一致地适用本指令中的审慎要求；

(f)在考虑到可能在该领域设立的其他监管团的工作的同时，适用第129条第1款第c项。

参加监管团的主管部门和欧洲银行业管理局应紧密合作。第一章第2节的保密要求不妨碍主管部门在监管团内交换保密信息。监管团的设立和运作不得对主管部门在本指令中的权利和责任产生影响。”

(b)在第2款中：

(i)第2项替换为下列内容：

“为确保本条规定的一致协调，欧洲银行业管理局可起草监管性技术标准草案，具体说明监管团的一般运作条件。

经委托授权，欧盟委员会有权根据第1093/2010号(欧盟)条例第10条至第14条规定的程序通过第2项所述监管性技术标准。

为确保本条规定具有统一的适用条件，欧洲银行业管理局可起草实施性技术标准草案，以确定监管团具体的运作方式。

兹授予欧盟委员会依照第1093/2010号(欧盟)条例第15条规定的程序通过第4项所述实施性技术标准的权力。”

(ii)第6项替换为下列内容：

“并表监管机构在遵守第一章第2节的保密要求的前提下，应通知欧洲银行业管

Chapter 1, Section 2, shall inform EBA of the activities of the college of supervisors, including in emergency situations, and communicate to EBA all information that is of particular relevance for the purposes of supervisory convergence. '.

(36) Article 132(1) is amended as follows:

(a) the following subparagraphs are inserted after the first subparagraph:

'The competent authorities shall cooperate with EBA for the purposes of this Directive, in accordance with Regulation (EU) No 1093/2010.

The competent authorities shall provide EBA with all information necessary to carry out its duties under this Directive and under Regulation (EU) No 1093/2010, in accordance with Article 35 of that Regulation. ';

(b) the following subparagraphs are added:

'The competent authorities may refer to EBA situations where:

(a) a competent authority has not communicated essential information, or

(b) a request for cooperation, in particular to exchange relevant information, has been rejected or has not been acted upon within a reasonable time.

Without prejudice to Article 258 TFEU, EBA may, in situations referred to in the seventh subparagraph, act in accordance with the powers conferred on it under Article 19 of Regulation (EU) No 1093/2010. '.

(37) In Article 140, paragraph 3 is replaced by the following:

'3. The competent authorities responsible for supervision on a consolidated basis shall establish lists of the financial holding companies referred to in Article 71(2). Those lists shall be communicated to the competent authorities of the other Member States, to EBA and to the Commission. '.

(38) Article 143 is amended as follows:

(a) paragraph (2) is amended as follows:

(i) the following sentence is added at the end of the first subparagraph:

'EBA shall assist the Commission and the European Banking Committee in carrying out those tasks, including as to whether such guidance should be updated. ';

(ii) the second subparagraph is replaced by the following:

'The competent authority carrying out the verification referred to in the first subparagraph of paragraph 1 shall take into account any such guidance. For that purpose, the competent authority shall consult EBA before adopting a decision. '.

(b) in paragraph 3, the fourth subparagraph is replaced by the following:

'The supervisory techniques shall be designed to achieve the objectives of consolidated supervision as defined in this Chapter and shall be notified to the other competent authorities involved, EBA and the Commission. '.

(39) In Article 144, the following paragraphs are added:

理局监管团的活动，包括在紧急情况下作出的活动，并应通知欧洲银行业管理局所有与监管趋同高度相关的信息。”

（36）第132条第1款修正如下：

（a）在第1项后增加下项内容：

“主管部门应根据第1093/2010号（欧盟）条例的规定，为本指令之目的与欧洲银行业管理局合作。

主管部门应根据第1093/2010号（欧盟）条例第35条的规定，向欧洲银行业管理局提供履行其在本指令以及该条例中的职责所必要的一切信息。”

（b）增加下列内容：

“主管部门可将下列情况移交欧洲银行业管理局处理：

（a）某主管部门没有提供至关重要的信息，或

（b）合作请求（特别是交换相关信息的请求）未在合理的时间内落实或被拒绝。

在不影响《欧洲联盟运行条约》第258条的情形下，欧洲银行业管理局可在第7项所述情况下依照第1093/2010号（欧盟）条例第19条授予的权力行事。”

（37）第140条第3款替换为下列内容：

“3.负责以并表方式进行监管的主管部门应建立第71条第2款所述金融控股公司名册，并将该等名册提供给其他成员国的主管部门、欧洲银行业管理局以及欧盟委员会。”

（38）第143条修正如下：

（a）第2款修正如下：

（i）在第1项结尾增加下列内容：

“欧洲银行业管理局应协助欧盟委员会和欧洲银行业委员会履行该等工作，包括就是否应该更新上述指引提供协助。”

（ii）第2项替换为下列内容：

“开展第1款第1项所述核查的主管部门应将任何上述指引纳入考虑。为此，该主管部门应在作出决定之前咨询欧洲银行业管理局的意见。”

（b）第3款第4项替换为下列内容：

“应通知所涉的其他主管部门、欧洲银行业管理局以及欧盟委员会旨在实现本章界定的并表监管目的之监管技术。”

（39）第144条增加下列内容：

'In order to ensure uniform conditions of application of this Article, EBA shall develop draft implementing technical standards to determine the format, structure, contents list and annual publication date of the disclosures provided for in this Article. EBA shall submit those draft implementing technical standards to the Commission by 1 January 2014.

Power is conferred on the Commission to adopt the implementing technical standards referred to in the third paragraph in accordance with Article 15 of Regulation (EU) No 1093/2010.'.

(40) In Article 150, the following paragraph is added:

'3. EBA shall develop draft implementing technical standards to ensure uniform conditions of application of this Directive with respect to the conditions of application of:

(a) points 15 to 17 of Annex V;

(b) point 23(l) of Annex V as regards the criteria to determine the appropriate ratios between fixed and the variable component of the total remuneration and of point 23(o)(ii) of Annex V as regards specifying the classes of instruments that satisfy the conditions laid down in that point.

(c) Part 2 of Annex VI as regards the quantitative factors referred to in point 12, the qualitative factors referred to in point 13 and the benchmark referred to in point 14;

EBA shall submit those draft implementing technical standards to the Commission by 1 January 2014.

Power is conferred on the Commission to adopt the implementing technical standards referred to in the first subparagraph in accordance with the procedure laid down in Article 15 of Regulation (EU) No 1093/2010.'.

(41) Article 156 is amended as follows:

(a) the term 'Committee of European Banking Supervisors' is replaced by 'EBA';

(b) the first subparagraph is replaced by the following:

'The Commission, in cooperation with EBA and the Member States, and taking into account the contribution of the European Central Bank, shall periodically monitor whether this Directive, together with Directive 2006/49/EC, has significant effects on the economic cycle and, in the light of that examination, shall consider whether any remedial measures are justified.'.

Article 10 Amendments to Directive 2006/49/EC

Directive 2006/49/EC is hereby amended as follows:

(1) In Article 18, the following paragraph is added:

'5. The European Supervisory Authority (European Banking Authority) (hereinafter "EBA") established by Regulation (EU) No 1093/2010 of the European Parliament and of the Council(*), may develop draft regulatory technical standards to specify the assessment

"为确保本条规定具有统一的适用条件,欧洲银行业管理局应起草实施性技术标准草案,以确定本条所规定的披露的格式、结构、内容列表以及每年的公布日期。欧洲银行业管理局应于2014年1月1日前将该等实施性技术标准草案呈报欧盟委员会。

兹授予欧盟委员会依照第1093/2010号(欧盟)条例第15条的规定通过第3项所述实施性技术标准的权力。"

(40)第150条增加下列内容:

"3.为确保本指令具有统一的适用条件,欧洲银行业管理局应就下列各项的适用条件起草实施性技术标准草案:

(a)附录五第15条至第17条;

(b)附录五第23条第l款(关于确定总报酬固定部分和可变部分适当比例的标准),以及附录五第23条第o款第ii项(关于满足该项所列条件之工具类别的具体说明);

(c)附录六第二部分(关于第12条所述的定量因素、第13目所述的定性因素以及第14目所述的基准);

欧洲银行业管理局应于2014年1月1日之前将该等实施性技术标准草案呈报欧盟委员会。

兹授予欧盟委员会依照第1093/2010号(欧盟)条例第15条的规定通过第1项所述实施性技术标准的权力。"

(41)第156条修正如下:

(a)将"欧洲银行业监管机构委员会"一词替换为"欧洲银行业管理局";

(b)第1项替换为下列内容:

"欧盟委员会应与欧洲银行业管理局以及各成员国合作,在考虑到欧洲中央银行发挥的作用的前提下,定期监控本指令连同第2006/49/EC号指令是否对经济周期产生重大影响,并根据该项评估结果考虑是否应采取任何补救措施。"

第10条　对第2006/49/EC号指令的修正

特此对第2006/49/EC号指令修正如下:

(1)在第18条中增加下列内容:

"5.依据《欧洲议会与欧盟理事会第1093/2010号(欧盟)条例》*设立的欧洲监管机构(欧洲银行业管理局)(以下简称欧洲银行业管理局,英文简称EBA)可起草监管性技术标准草案,具体说明采用何等评估方法能使主管部门允许信贷机构使用内部模型

methodology under which competent authorities permit institutions to use internal models for the purposes of calculating capital requirements under this Directive.

Power is delegated to the Commission to adopt the regulatory technical standards referred to in the first subparagraph in accordance with the procedure laid down in Articles 10 to 14 of Regulation (EU) No 1093/2010.

(*) OJ L 331, 15. 12. 2010, p. 12. '.

(2) In Article 22(1), the following subparagraph is added:

'Where the competent authorities waive the application of capital requirements on a consolidated basis provided for in this Article, they shall notify the Commission and EBA. '.

(3) Article 32(1) is amended as follows:

(a) the second subparagraph is replaced by the following:

'The competent authorities shall notify EBA, the Council and the Commission of those procedures. ';

(b) the following subparagraph is added:

'EBA shall issue guidelines in relation to the procedures referred to in this paragraph. '.

(4) Article 36(1) is replaced by the following:

'1. Member States shall designate the authorities which are competent to carry out the duties provided for in this Directive. They shall inform EBA and the Commission thereof, indicating any division of duties. '.

(5) In Article 38(1), the following subparagraphs are added:

'The competent authorities shall cooperate with EBA for the purposes of this Directive, in accordance with Regulation (EU) No 1093/2010.

The competent authorities shall without delay provide EBA with all information necessary to carry out its duties under this Directive and under Regulation (EU) No 1093/2010, in accordance with Article 35 of that Regulation. '.

Article 11 Amendments to Directive 2009/65/EC

Directive 2009/65/EC is hereby amended as follows:

(1) In Article 5, the following paragraph is added:

'8. In order to ensure consistent harmonisation of this Article the European Supervisory Authority(European Securities and Markets Authority)(hereinafter "ESMA"), established by Regulation (EU) No 1095/2010 of the European Parliament and of the Council (*) may develop draft regulatory technical standards to specify the information to be provided to the competent authorities in the application for authorisation of a UCITS.

Power is delegated to the Commission to adopt the regulatory technical standards referred to in the first subparagraph in accordance with the procedure laid down in

法计算本指令中的资本要求。

经委托授权,欧盟委员会有权根据第1093/2010号(欧盟)条例第10条至第14条规定的程序通过第1项所述监管性技术标准。

*《欧盟公报》L 331,2010年12月15日,第12页。"

(2)在第22条第1款中增加下列内容:

"主管部门豁免本条规定的并表适用资本要求的,应通知欧盟委员会和欧洲银行业管理局。"

(3)第32条第1款修正如下:

(a)第2项替换为下列内容:

"主管部门应通知欧洲银行业管理局、欧盟理事会以及欧盟委员会该等程序。"

(b)增加下列内容:

"欧洲银行业管理局应就本款所述程序颁布指引。"

(4)第36条第1款替换为下列内容:

"1.各成员国应当指定负责履行本指令中各项职责的主管部门,通知欧洲银行业管理局和欧盟委员会该等指定结果并说明具体的职责分工。"

(5)第38条第1款增加下列内容:

"主管部门应根据第1093/2010号(欧盟)条例的规定,为本指令之目的与欧洲银行业管理局合作。

主管部门应根据第1093/2010号(欧盟)条例第35条的规定,立即向欧洲银行业管理局提供为履行其在本指令以及该条例中的职责所必要的一切信息。"

第11条　对第2009/65/EC号指令的修正

特此对第2009/65/EC号指令修正如下:

(1)第5条增加下列内容:

"8.为确保本条规定的一致协调,依据《欧洲议会与欧盟理事会第1095/2010号(欧盟)条例》*设立的欧洲监管机构(欧洲证券与市场管理局)(以下简称欧洲证券与市场管理局,英文简称ESMA)可起草监管性技术标准草案,具体说明申请可转让证券集合投资计划核准时应向主管部门提供的信息。

经委托授权,欧盟委员会有权根据第1095/2010号(欧盟)条例第10条至第14条规定的程序通过第1项所述监管性技术标准。

Articles 10 to 14 of Regulation (EU) No 1095/2010.

(*) OJ L 331, 15. 12. 2010, p. 84. '.

(2) In Article 6(1) the following subparagraph is added:

'ESMA shall be notified of every authorisation granted and shall publish and keep up-to-date a list of authorised management companies on its website. '.

(3) In Article 7, the following paragraph is added:

'6. In order to ensure consistent harmonisation of this Article, ESMA may develop draft regulatory technical standards to specify:

(a) the information to be provided to the competent authorities in the application for the authorisation of the management company, including the programme of activity;

(b) the requirements applicable to the management company under paragraph 2 and the information for the notification provided for in paragraph 3;

(c) the requirements applicable to shareholders and members with qualifying holdings, as well as obstacles which may prevent effective exercise of the supervisory functions of the competent authority, as provided for in Article 8(1) of this Directive and in Article 10(1) and (2) of Directive 2004/39/EC, in accordance with Article 11 of this Directive.

Power is delegated to the Commission to adopt the regulatory technical standards referred to in the first subparagraph in accordance with Articles 10 to 14 of Regulation (EU) No 1095/2010.

In order to ensure uniform conditions of application of this Article, ESMA may develop draft implementing technical standards to determine standard forms, templates and procedures for the notification or provision of information provided for in points (a) and (b) of the first subparagraph.

Power is conferred on the Commission to adopt the implementing technical standards referred to in the third subparagraph in accordance with Article 15 of Regulation (EU) No 1095/2010. '.

(4) Article 9(2) is replaced by the following:

'2. Member States shall inform ESMA and the Commission of any general difficulties which UCITS encounter in marketing their units in any third country.

The Commission shall examine such difficulties as quickly as possible in order to find an appropriate solution. ESMA shall assist it in discharging that task. '.

(5) In Article 11, the following paragraph is added:

'3. In order to ensure consistent harmonisation of this Directive, ESMA may develop draft regulatory technical standards to establish an exhaustive list of information, as provided for in this Article, with reference to Article 10b(4) of Directive 2004/39/EC, to be included by proposed acquirers in their notification, without prejudice to Article 10a

*《欧盟公报》L 331,2010年12月15日,第84页。”

（2）第6条第1款增加下列内容：

“应通知欧洲证券与市场管理局被授予的每一项核准,在其网站上公布获得核准的管理公司的名册,并持续更新。”

（3）第7条增加下列内容：

“6.为确保本条规定的一致协调,欧洲证券与市场管理局可起草监管性技术标准草案,具体说明：

（a）管理公司在申请核准时应提供给主管部门的信息（包括运营计划）;

（b）第2款中适用于管理公司的规定以及第3款要求通知的信息;

（c）本指令第11条、本指令第8条第1款和第2004/39/EC号指令第10条第1款和第2款所述适用于拥有重大持股数额的股东和成员的规定以及可能妨碍主管部门有效行使监管职能的障碍。

经委托授权,欧盟委员会有权根据第1095/2010号（欧盟）条例第10条至第14条的规定通过第1项所述监管性技术标准。

为确保本条规定具有统一的适用条件,欧洲证券与市场管理局可起草实施性技术标准草案,就第1项第a目和第b目所规定的通知或信息提供制定标准的格式、模板和程序。

兹授予欧盟委员会根据第1095/2010号（欧盟）条例第15条的规定通过第3项所述实施性技术标准的权力。”

（4）第9条第2款替换为下列内容：

“2.可转让证券集合投资计划在任何第三国营销其投资单位时遭遇任何普遍性困难的,成员国应通知欧洲证券与市场管理局以及欧盟委员会。

欧盟委员会应尽快对上述困难进行审查,找出适当的解决方案。欧洲证券与市场管理局应协助其完成该项工作。”

（5）第11条增加下列内容：

“3.为确保本指令一致协调,在不影响第2004/39/EC号指令第10a条第2款的情形下,欧洲证券与市场管理局可起草监管性技术标准草案,参照该指令第10b条第4款,按本条规定制定一份应提供的信息的详尽清单。拟议收购方须将该等信息纳入其通知中。

(2) of that Directive.

Power is delegated to the Commission to adopt the regulatory technical standards referred to in the first subparagraph in accordance with Articles 10 to 14 of Regulation (EU) No 1095/2010.

In order to ensure uniform conditions of application of this Article, ESMA may develop draft implementing technical standards to establish standard forms, templates and procedures for the modalities of the consultation process between the relevant competent authorities, as provided for in this Article, with reference to Article 10(4) of Directive 2004/39/EC.

Power is conferred to the Commission to adopt the implementing technical standards referred to in the third subparagraph in accordance with Article 15 of Regulation (EU) No 1095/2010. '.

(6) Article 12 is amended as follows:

(a) paragraph 3 is amended as follows:

(i) the first subparagraph is replaced by the following:

'3. Without prejudice to Article 116, the Commission shall adopt, by means of delegated acts in accordance with Article 112(2),(3) and (4), and subject to the conditions of Articles 112a and 112b, measures specifying the procedures and arrangements as referred to under point (a) of the second subparagraph of paragraph 1 and the structures and organisational requirements to minimise conflicts of interests as referred to under point (b) of the second subparagraph of paragraph 1. ';

(ii) the second subparagraph is deleted.

(b) the following paragraph is added:

'4. In order to ensure uniform conditions of application of this Article, ESMA may develop draft implementing technical standards to determine the conditions of applications of the delegated acts adopted by the Commission regarding the procedures, arrangements, structures and organisational requirements referred to in paragraph 3.

Power is conferred on the Commission to adopt the implementing technical standards referred to in the first subparagraph in accordance with Article 15 of Regulation (EU) No 1095/2010. '.

(7) Article 14 is amended as follows:

(a) paragraph 2 is amended as follows:

(i) in the first subparagraph, the introductory part is replaced by the following:

'2. Without prejudice to Article 116, the Commission shall adopt, by means of delegated acts in accordance with Article 112(2),(3) and (4), and subject to the conditions of Articles 112a and 112b, measures with a view to ensuring that the management company complies with the duties set out in paragraph 1, in particular to:';

经委托授权，盟委员会有权根据第1095/2010号（欧盟）条例第10条至第14条的规定通过第1项所述监管性技术标准。

为确保本条规定具有统一的适用条件，欧洲证券与市场管理局可起草实施性技术标准草案，参照第2004/39/EC号指令第10条第4款，就本条所述相关主管部门之间磋商程序开展的方式制定标准的格式、模板和程序。

兹授予欧盟委员会依照第1095/2010号（欧盟）条例第15条的规定通过第3项所述实施性技术标准的权力。”

（6）第12条修正如下：

（a）第3款修正如下：

（i）第1项替换为下列内容：

“3.在不影响第116条的情形下，欧盟委员会应依照第112条第2款、第3款和第4款的规定并遵守第112（a）条和第112（b）条的条件，以授权立法的形式制定相关细则，具体说明第1款第2项第a目所述的程序和安排以及第1款第2项第b目所述旨在使利益冲突最小化的结构和组织要求。”

（ii）删除第2项。

（b）增加下列内容：

“4.为确保本条规定具有统一的适用条件，欧洲证券与市场管理局可起草实施性技术标准草案，以确定第3款中欧盟委员会针对程序、安排、结构和组织要求通过的授权立法的适用条件。

兹授予欧盟委员会依照第1095/2010号（欧盟）条例第15条的规定通过第1项所述实施性技术标准的权力。”

（7）第14条修正如下：

（a）第2款修正如下：

（i）第1项的导言替换为下列内容：

“2.在不影响第116条的情形下，欧盟委员会应依照第112条第2款、第3款和第4款的规定并遵守第112a条和第112b条的条件，以授权立法的形式制定相关细则，以确保管理公司履行第1款所列的职责，特别是：”

(ii) the second subparagraph is deleted.

(b) the following paragraph is added:

'3. In order to ensure uniform conditions of application of this Article, ESMA may develop draft implementing technical standards to determine the delegated acts adopted by the Commission regarding the criteria, principles and steps referred to in paragraph 2.

Power is conferred on the Commission to adopt the implementing technical standards referred to in the first subparagraph in accordance with Article 15 of Regulation (EU) No 1095/2010.'.

(8) In Article 17, the following paragraph is added:

'10. In order to ensure consistent harmonisation of this Article ESMA may develop draft regulatory technical standards to specify the information to be notified in accordance with paragraphs 1, 2, 3, 8 and 9.

Power is delegated to the Commission to adopt the regulatory technical standards referred to in the first subparagraph in accordance with Articles 10 to 14 of Regulation (EU) No 1095/2010.

In order to ensure uniform conditions of application of this Article, ESMA may develop draft implementing technical standards to establish standard forms, templates and procedures for the transmission of information in accordance with paragraphs 3 and 9.

Power is conferred on the Commission to adopt the implementing technical standards referred to in the third subparagraph in accordance with Article 15 of Regulation (EU) No 1095/2010.'.

(9) In Article 18, the following paragraph is added:

'5. In order to ensure consistent harmonisation of this Article ESMA may develop draft regulatory technical standards to specify the information to be notified in accordance with paragraphs 1, 2 and 4.

Power is delegated to the Commission to adopt the regulatory technical standards referred to in the first subparagraph in accordance with Articles 10 to 14 of Regulation (EU) No 1095/2010.

In order to ensure uniform conditions of application of this Article, ESMA may develop draft implementing technical standards to establish standard forms, templates and procedures for the transmission of information in accordance with paragraphs 2 and 4.

Power is conferred on the Commission to adopt the implementing technical standards referred to in the third subparagraph in accordance with Article 15 of Regulation (EU) No 1095/2010.'.

(10) In Article 20, the following paragraph is added:

'5. In order to ensure consistent harmonisation of this Article, ESMA may develop draft regulatory technical standards to determine the information to be provided to the

(ii)删除第2项。

(b)增加下列内容:

“3.为确保本条规定具有统一的适用条件,欧洲证券与市场管理局可起草实施性技术标准草案,以具体说明欧盟委员会就第2款所述的标准、原则和步骤通过的授权立法的适用条件。

兹授予欧盟委员会依照第1095/2010号(欧盟)条例第15条的规定通过第1项所述实施性技术标准的权力。”

(8)第17条增加下列内容:

“10.为确保本条规定的一致协调,欧洲证券与市场管理局可起草监管性技术标准草案,具体说明根据第1款、第2款、第3款、第8款和第9款应通知的信息。

经委托授权,欧盟委员会有权根据第1095/2010号(欧盟)条例第10条至第14条的规定通过第1项所述监管性技术标准。

为确保本条规定具有统一的适用条件,欧洲证券与市场管理局可起草实施性技术标准草案,就依照第3款和第9款进行的信息发送制定标准的格式、模板和程序。

兹授予欧盟委员会依照第1095/2010号(欧盟)条例第15条的规定通过第3项所述实施性技术标准的权力。”

(9)第18条增加下列内容:

“5.为确保本条规定的一致协调,欧洲证券与市场管理局可起草监管性技术标准草案,具体说明根据第1款、第2款和第4款应通知的信息。

经委托授权,欧盟委员会有权根据第1095/2010号(欧盟)条例第10条至第14条的规定通过第1项所述监管性技术标准。

为确保本条规定具有统一的适用条件,欧洲证券与市场管理局可起草实施性技术标准草案,就依照第2款和第4款进行的信息发送制定标准的格式、模板和程序。

兹授予欧盟委员会依照第1095/2010号(欧盟)条例第15条的规定通过第3项所述实施性技术标准的权力。”

(10)第20条增加下列内容:

“5.为确保本条规定的一致协调,欧洲证券与市场管理局可起草监管性技术标准草案,具体说明申请管理在其他成员国设立的可转让证券集合投资计划时应向主管部门提供的信息。

competent authorities in the application for managing a UCITS established in another Member State.

The Commission may adopt the regulatory technical standards referred to in the first subparagraph in accordance with the procedure laid down in Articles 10 to 14 of Regulation (EU) No 1095/2010.

In order to ensure uniform conditions of application of this Article, ESMA may develop draft implementing technical standards to establish standard forms, templates and procedures for such provision of information.

Power is conferred on the Commission to adopt the implementing technical standards referred to in the third subparagraph in accordance with Article 15 of Regulation (EU) No 1095/2010. '.

(11) Article 21 is amended as follows:

(a) paragraph 5 is replaced by the following:

'5. If, despite the measures taken by the competent authorities of the management company's home Member State or because such measures prove to be inadequate or are not available in the Member State in question, the management company continues to refuse to provide the information requested by the management company's host Member State pursuant to paragraph 2, or persists in breaching the legal or regulatory provisions, referred to in the same paragraph, in force in the management company's host Member State, the competent authorities of the management company's host Member State may take either of the following actions:

(a) after informing the competent authorities of the management company's home Member State, take appropriate measures, including under Articles 98 and 99, to prevent or penalise further irregularities and, in so far as necessary, to prevent that management company from initiating any further transaction within its territory. Member States shall ensure that within their territories it is possible to serve the legal documents necessary for those measures on management companies. Where the service provided within the management company's host Member State is the management of a UCITS, the management company's host Member State may require the management company to cease managing that UCITS; or

(b) where they consider that the competent authority of the management company's home Member State has not acted adequately, refer the matter to ESMA, which may act in accordance with the powers conferred on it under Article 19 of Regulation (EU) No 1095/2010. ';

(b) in paragraph 7, the first and second subparagraphs are replaced by the following:

'7. Before following the procedure laid down in paragraphs 3, 4 or 5, the competent authorities of the management company's host Member State may, in emergencies, take

经委托授权，欧盟委员会有权根据第1095/2010号（欧盟）条例第10条至第14条的规定通过第1项所述监管性技术标准。

为确保本条规定具有统一的适用条件，欧洲证券与市场管理局可起草实施性技术标准草案，就上述信息提供制定标准的格式、模板和程序。

兹授予欧盟委员会依照第1095/2010号（欧盟）条例第15条的规定通过第3项所述实施性技术标准的权力。”

（11）第21条修正如下：

（a）第5款替换为下列内容：

“5.尽管管理公司的母国主管部门已采取措施，或由于事实证明采取的措施不充分或不适用于所涉成员国，管理公司仍然拒绝提供管理公司东道国根据第2款所要求的信息，或继续违反同一款所指的管理公司东道国现行有效的法律规章的，则管理公司东道国的主管部门可采取下列任何一项行动：

（a）在通知管理公司的母国主管部门之后采取适当的措施，包括第98条和第99条中的措施，以防范进一步不法行为或对之进行处罚，并在必要时阻止管理公司在其境内启动任何其他交易。成员国应确保对该等管理公司采取措施所必要的法律文件能在其境内送达。如果管理公司在东道国提供的服务是可转让证券集合投资计划管理，则管理公司的东道国可要求管理公司停止管理其所管理的可转让证券集合投资计划；或

（b）如其认为管理公司的母国主管部门未采取充分的行动，则可将该事宜移交欧洲证券与市场管理局，欧洲证券与市场管理局可依其在第1095/2010号（欧盟）条例第19条中的权力处理。”

（b）第7款第1项和第2项替换为下列内容：

“7.在履行第3款、第4款或第5款规定的程序之前，管理公司的东道国主管部门可在紧急情况下采取必要的预防性措施保护投资者以及其他服务对象的利益。应尽早

any precautionary measures necessary to protect the interests of investors and others for whom services are provided. The Commission, ESMA, and the competent authorities of the other Member States concerned shall be informed of such measures at the earliest opportunity.

After consulting the competent authorities of the Member States concerned, the Commission may decide that the Member State in question must amend or abolish those measures, without prejudice to power of ESMA under Article 17 of Regulation (EU) No 1095/2010. ';

(c) in paragraph 9, the first subparagraph is replaced by the following:

'9. Member States shall inform ESMA and the Commission of the number and type of cases in which they refuse authorisation under Article 17 or an application under Article 20 and of any measures taken in accordance with paragraph 5 of this Article. '.

(12) Article 23(6) is amended as follows:

(a) the first subparagraph is replaced by the following:

'6. The Commission may adopt, by means of delegated acts in accordance with Article 112(2), (3) and (4), and subject to the conditions of Articles 112a and 112b, measures in relation to the measures to be taken by a depositary in order to fulfil its duties regarding a UCITS managed by a management company established in another Member State, including the particulars that need to be included in the standard agreement to be used by the depositary and the management company in accordance with paragraph 5. ';

(b) the second subparagraph is deleted.

(13) In Article 29, the following paragraphs are added:

'5. In order to ensure consistent harmonisation of this Directive, ESMA may develop draft regulatory technical standards to specify:

(a) the information to be provided to the competent authorities in the application for the authorisation of the investment company, including the programme of operations; and

(b) the obstacles which may prevent effective exercise of the supervisory functions of the competent authority under paragraph 1(c).

Power is delegated to the Commission to adopt the regulatory technical standards referred to in the first subparagraph in accordance with Articles 10 to 14 of Regulation (EU) No 1095/2010.

6. In order to ensure uniform conditions of application of this Article, ESMA may develop draft implementing technical standards to establish standard forms, templates and procedures for the provision of information referred to in point (a) of the first subparagraph of paragraph 5.

Power is conferred on the Commission to adopt the implementing technical standards

通知欧盟委员会、欧洲证券与市场管理局以及其他所涉成员国的主管部门上述措施。

在不影响欧洲证券与市场管理局在第1095/2010号(欧盟)条例第17条中的权力的情形下,咨询相关成员国主管部门意见后,欧盟委员会可决定所涉成员国必须对该等措施予以修正或废止。”

(c)第9款第1项替换为下列内容:

“9.成员国拒绝授予第17条中的核准或拒绝批准第20条中的申请的,应通知欧洲证券与市场管理局和欧盟委员会拒绝的次数和类型以及依照本条第5款采取的任何措施。”

(12)第23条第6款修正如下:

(a)第1项替换为下列内容:

“6.欧盟委员会可依照第112条第2款、第3款和第4款的规定并遵守第112a条和第112b条的条件,就存管机构为履行与设立于其他成员国的管理公司管理的可转让证券集合投资计划有关的职责所应采取之措施,以授权立法的形式制定相关细则(包括需要纳入存管机构和管理公司根据第5款使用的标准协议中的具体内容)。”

(b)删除第2项。

(13)第29条增加下列内容:

“5.为确保本指令的一致协调,欧洲证券与市场管理局可制定监管性技术标准草案,具体说明:

(a)投资公司申请核准时应向主管部门提供的信息(包括运营计划);及

(b)可能妨碍主管部门有效行使其在第1款第c项中的监管职能的障碍。

经委托授权,欧盟委员会有权根据第1095/2010号(欧盟)条例第10条至第14条的规定通过第1项所述监管性技术标准。

6.为确保本条规定具有统一的适用条件,欧洲证券与市场管理局可起草实施性技术标准草案,就第5款第1项第a目所述信息提供制定标准的格式、模板和程序。

兹授予欧盟委员会根据第1095/2010号(欧盟)条例第15条的规定通过第1项所述实施性技术标准的权力。”

referred to in the first subparagraph in accordance with Article 15 of Regulation (EU) No 1095/2010. '.

(14) Article 32(6) is replaced by the following:

'6. Member States shall inform ESMA and the Commission of the identities of the investment companies benefiting from the derogations provided for in paragraphs 4 and 5. '.

(15) Article 33(6) is amended as follows:

(a) the first subparagraph is replaced by the following:

'6. The Commission may adopt, by means of delegated acts in accordance with Article 112(2), (3) and (4), and subject to the conditions of Articles 112a and 112b, mea sures in relation to the measures to be taken by a depositary in order to fulfil its duties regarding a UCITS managed by a management company established in another Member State, including the particulars that need to be included in the standard agreement to be used by the depositary and the management company in accordance with paragraph 5. ';

(b) the second subparagraph is deleted.

(16) Article 43 is amended as follows:

(a) in paragraph 5:

(i) the first subparagraph is replaced by the following:

'5. The Commission may adopt, by means of delegated acts in accordance with Article 112(2), (3) and (4), and subject to the conditions of Articles 112a and 112b, measures specifying the detailed content, format and method by which to provide the information referred to in paragraphs 1 and 3. ';

(ii) the second subparagraph is deleted.

(b) the following paragraph is added:

'6. In order to ensure uniform conditions of application of this Article, ESMA may develop draft implementing technical standards to determine the conditions of applications of the delegated acts adopted by the Commission regarding the content, format and method by which the information referred to in paragraphs 1 and 3 of this Article is to be provided.

Power is conferred on the Commission to adopt the implementing technical standards referred to in the first subparagraph in accordance with Article 15 of Regulation (EU) No 1095/2010. '.

(17) In Article 50, the following paragraph is added:

'4. In order to ensure consistent harmonisation of this Article ESMA may develop draft regulatory technical standards to specify the provisions concerning the categories of assets in which UCITS can invest in accordance with this Article and with delegated acts adopted by the Commission which relate to such provisions.

（14）第32条第6款替换为下列内容：

“6.成员国应通知欧洲证券与市场管理局和欧盟委员会享受第4款和第5款例外待遇的投资公司的身份信息。”

（15）第33条第6款修正如下：

（a）第1项替换为下列内容：

“6.欧盟委员会可依照第112条第2款、第3款和第4款的规定并遵守第112a条和第112b条的条件，就存管机构为履行其与设立于其他成员国的管理公司管理的可转让证券集合投资计划有关的职责所应采取之措施，以授权立法的形式制定相关细则（包括需要纳入存管机构和管理公司根据第5款使用的标准协议中的具体内容）。”

（b）删除第2项。

（16）第43条修正如下：

（a）在第5款中：

（i）第1项替换为下列内容：

“5.欧盟委员会可依照第112条第2款、第3款和第4款的规定并遵守第112a条和第112b条的条件，以授权立法的形式制定相关细则，具体说明提供第1款和第3款所指信息时应包含的具体内容、符合的格式以及遵循的方法。”

（ii）删除第2项。

（b）增加下列内容：

“6.为确保本条规定具有统一的适用条件，欧洲证券与市场管理局可起草实施性技术标准草案，以确定欧盟委员会就本条第1款和第3款所述信息提供的内容、格式以及方法所通过的授权立法的适用条件。

兹授予欧盟委员会根据第1095/2010号（欧盟）条例第15条的规定通过第1项所述实施性技术标准的权力。”

（17）第50条增加下列内容：

“4.为确保本条规定的一致协调，欧洲证券与市场管理局可起草监管性技术标准草案，具体说明可转让证券集合投资计划可以投资的资产类别的相关条款，且可转让证券集合投资计划必须依照本条规定以及欧盟委员会针对该等条款所通过的授权立法进行该等投资。

Power is delegated to the Commission to adopt the regulatory technical standards referred to in the first subparagraph in accordance with Articles 10 to 14 of Regulation (EU) No 1095/2010. '.

(18) Article 51 is amended as follows:

(a) in paragraph 1, the following subparagraph is added:

'Competent authorities shall ensure that all information received under the third paragraph aggregated in respect of all the management or investment companies they supervise is accessible to ESMA in accordance with Article 35 of the Regulation (EU) No 1095/2010, and the European Systemic Risk Board (the "ESRB") established by Regulation (EU) No 1092/2010 of the European Parliament and of the Council of 24 November 2010 on European Union macro-prudential oversight of the financial system and establishing a European Systemic Risk Board (*) in accordance with Article 15 of that Regulation for the purpose of monitoring systemic risks at Union level.

(*) OJ L 331, 15. 12. 2010, p. 1. ';

(b) paragraph 4 is replaced by the following:

'4. Without prejudice to Article 116, the Commission shall adopt, by means of delegated acts in accordance with Article 112(2),(3) and(4), and subject to the conditions of Articles 112a and 112b, measures specifying the following:

(a) criteria for assessing the adequacy of the risk management process employed by the management company in accordance with the first subparagraph of paragraph 1;

(b) detailed rules regarding the accurate and independent assessment of the value of OTC derivatives; and

(c) detailed rules regarding the content of and procedure to be followed for communicating the information referred to in the third subparagraph of paragraph 1 to the competent authorities of the management company's home Member State. ';

(c) the following paragraph is added:

'5. In order to ensure uniform conditions of application of this Article, ESMA may develop draft implementing technical standards to determine the conditions of application of the delegated acts adopted by the Commission regarding the criteria and rules referred to in paragraph 4.

Power is conferred on the Commission to adopt the implementing technical standards referred to in the first subparagraph in accordance with Article 15 of Regulation (EU) No 1095/2010. '.

(19) In Article 52(4), the third subparagraph is replaced by the following:

'Member States shall send to ESMA and to the Commission a list of the categories of bonds referred to in the first subparagraph together with the categories of issuers authorised, in accordance with the laws and supervisory arrangements mentioned in that

经委托授权，欧盟委员会有权根据第1095/2010号（欧盟）条例第10条至第14条的规定通过第1项所述监管性技术标准。”

（18）第51条修正如下：

（a）第1款增加下列内容：

“为在欧盟层面监控系统性风险，主管部门应确保下列机构可以根据相关规定查阅主管部门依照第3款接收到的其监管的所有管理或投资公司的所有汇总信息：欧洲证券与市场管理局，根据第1095/2010号（欧盟）条例第35条的规定执行；依据《欧洲议会与欧盟理事会关于欧盟对金融系统的宏观审慎监控以及设立欧洲系统性风险委员会的第1092/2010号（欧盟）条例》*（2010年11月24日）设立的欧洲系统性风险委员会（英文简称ESRB），根据该条例第15条的规定执行。

*《欧盟公报》L 331，2010年12月15日，第1页。”

（b）第4款替换为下列内容：

“4.在不影响第116条的情形下，欧盟委员会可依照第112条第2款、第3款和第4款的规定并遵守第112a条和第112b条的条件，以授权立法的形式制定相关细则，具体说明下列各项：

（a）评估管理公司依照第1款第1项使用的风险管理程序的充分性的标准；

（b）对场外交易衍生品的价值进行准确独立评估的详细规则；及

（c）关于向管理公司的母国主管部门通知第1款第3项所述信息时应包含的内容和应遵循的程序的详细规则。”

（c）增加下列内容：

“5.为确保本条规定具有统一的适用条件，欧洲证券与市场管理局可起草实施性技术标准草案，具体说明欧盟委员会就第4项所述的标准和规则通过的授权立法的适用条件。

兹授予欧盟委员会根据第1095/2010号（欧盟）条例第15条的规定通过第1项所述实施性技术标准的权力。”

（19）第52条第4款第3项替换为下列内容：

“成员国应向欧洲证券与市场管理局和欧盟委员会发送一份关于第1项所述债券类别的清单以及根据该项提及的法律和监管安排获准按本条所列标准发行债券的发行人类别的清单。该等清单还应随附一份通知，说明所提供担保的状态。欧盟委员会

subparagraph, to issue bonds complying with the criteria set out in this Article. A notice specifying the status of the guarantees offered shall be attached to those lists. The Commission and ESMA shall immediately forward that information to the other Member States together with any comments they consider appropriate and shall make the information available to the public on their website. Such communications may be the subject of exchanges of views within the European Securities Committee referred to in Article 112(1).'.

(20) Article 60 is amended as follows:

(a) in paragraph 6:

(i) in the first subparagraph, the introductory part is replaced by the following:

'6. The Commission may adopt, by means of delegated acts in accordance with Article 112(2), (3) and (4), and subject to the conditions of Articles 112a and 112b, measures specifying:';

(ii) the second subparagraph is deleted;

(b) the following paragraph is added:

'7. In order to ensure uniform conditions of application of this Article, ESMA may develop draft implementing technical standards to determine the conditions of application of the delegated acts adopted by the Commission regarding the agreement, measures and procedures referred to in paragraph 6.

Power is conferred on the Commission to adopt the implementing technical standards referred to in the first subparagraph in accordance with the Article 15 of Regulation (EU) No 1095/2010.'.

(21) Article 61 is amended as follows:

(a) paragraph 3 is replaced by the following:

'3. The Commission may adopt, by means of delegated acts in accordance with Article 112(2), (3) and (4), and subject to the conditions of Articles 112a and 112b, measures further specifying the following:

(a) the particulars that need to be included in the agreement referred to in paragraph 1; and

(b) the types of irregularities referred to in paragraph 2 which are deemed to have a negative impact on the feeder UCITS.'.

(b) the following paragraph is added:

'4. In order to ensure uniform conditions of application of this Article, ESMA may develop draft implementing technical standards to determine the conditions of application of the delegated acts adopted by the Commission regarding the agreement, measures and types of irregularities referred to in paragraph 3.

Power is conferred on the Commission to adopt the implementing technical standards

和欧洲证券与市场管理局应立即将该等信息连同其认为适当的任何评论转发给其他成员国,并应在其网站上向公众公开该等信息。上述通知的信息可作为第112条第1款所述的欧洲证券委员会内部意见交流的主题。”

(20)第60条修正如下:

(a)在第6款中:

(i)第1项的导言替换为下列内容:

“6.欧盟委员会可依照第112条第2款、第3款和第4款的规定并遵守第112a条和第112b条的条件,以授权立法的形式制定相关细则,具体说明:”

(ii)删除第2项;

(b)增加下列内容:

“7.为确保本条规定具有统一的适用条件,欧洲证券与市场管理局可起草实施性技术标准草案,具体说明欧盟委员会就第6款所述协议、措施和程序所通过的授权立法的适用条件。

兹授予欧盟委员会依照第1095/2010号(欧盟)条例第15条的规定通过第1项所述实施性技术标准的权力。”

(21)第61条修正如下:

(a)第3款替换为下列内容:

“3.欧盟委员会可依照第112条第2款、第3款和第4款的规定并遵守第112a条和第112b条的条件,以授权立法的形式制定相关细则,进一步具体说明:

(a)第1款所述协议所需包含的具体内容;及

(b)第2款中被视为对可转让证券集合投资计划联接基金具有负面影响的不法行为的类型。”

(b)增加下列内容:

“4.为确保本条规定具有统一的适用条件,欧洲证券与市场管理局可起草实施性技术标准草案,具体说明欧盟委员会就第3款所述协议、措施以及不法行为的类型所通过的授权立法的适用条件。

兹授予欧盟委员会依照第1095/2010号(欧盟)条例第15条的规定通过第1项所述

referred to in the first subparagraph in accordance with Article 15 of Regulation (EU) No 1095/2010. '.

(22) Article 62(4) is replaced by the following:

'4. The Commission may adopt, by means of delegated acts in accordance with Article 112(2), (3) and (4), and subject to the conditions of Articles 112a and 112b, measures specifying the content of the agreement referred to in the first subparagraph of paragraph 1. '.

(23) Article 64 is amended as follows:

(a) paragraph 4 is replaced by the following:

'4. The Commission may adopt, by means of delegated acts in accordance with Article 112(2), (3) and (4), and subject to the conditions of Articles 112a and 112b, measures specifying:

(a) the format and the manner in which to provide the information referred to in paragraph 1; or

(b) in the event that the feeder UCITS transfers all or parts of its assets to the master UCITS in exchange for units, the procedure for valuing and auditing such a contribution in kind and the role of the depositary of the feeder UCITS in that process. '.

(b) the following paragraph is added:

'5. In order to ensure uniform conditions of application in which the information is provided, ESMA may develop draft implementing technical standards to determine the conditions of application of the delegated acts adopted by the Commission regarding the format and the manner of the information provided and procedure referred to in paragraph 4.

Power is conferred on the Commission to adopt the implementing technical standards referred to in the first subparagraph in accordance with Article 15 of Regulation (EU) No 1095/2010. '.

(24) In Article 69, the following paragraph is added:

'5. In order to ensure consistent harmonisation of this Article, ESMA may develop draft regulatory technical standards to specify the provisions concerning the content of the prospectus, the annual report and the half-yearly report as laid down in Annex I, and the format of those documents.

Power is delegated to the Commission to adopt the regulatory technical standards referred to in the first subparagraph in accordance with Articles 10 to 14 of Regulation (EU) No 1095/2010. '.

(25) In Article 75, paragraph 4 is replaced by the following:

'4. The Commission may adopt, by means of delegated acts in accordance with Article 112(2), (3) and (4), and subject to the conditions of Articles 112a and 112b, measures which define the specific conditions which need to be met when providing the

实施性技术标准的权力。”

(22)第62条第4款替换为下列内容：

“4.欧盟委员会可依照第112条第2款、第3款和第4款的规定并遵守第112a条和第112b条的条件，以授权立法的形式制定相关细则，具体说明第1款第1项所指协议的内容。”

(23)第64条修正如下：

(a)第4款替换为下列内容：

“4.欧盟委员会可依照第112条第2款、第3款和第4款的规定并遵守第112a条和第112b条的条件，以授权立法的形式制定相关细则，具体说明：

(a)提供第1款所述信息应使用的格式和方法；或

(b)如果可转让证券集合投资计划联接基金将其所有或部分资产转让给可转让证券集合投资计划目标基金以换取投资单位，则说明该项实物出资的估值和审计程序以及可转让证券集合投资计划联接基金的存管机构在该程序中的作用。”

(b)增加下列内容：

“5.为确保信息的提供具有统一的适用条件，欧洲证券与市场管理局可起草实施性技术标准草案，以确定欧盟委员会就第4款所述之信息提供格式和方法以及程序所通过的授权立法的适用条件。

兹授予欧盟委员会依照第1095/2010号(欧盟)条例第15条的规定通过第1项所述实施性技术标准的权力。”

(24)第69条增加下列内容：

“5.为确保本条规定的一致协调，欧洲证券与市场管理局可起草监管性技术标准草案，具体说明附录一所规定的招募说明书、年度报告以及半年报告的内容的相关条款以及该等文件的格式。

经委托授权，欧盟委员会有权根据第1095/2010号(欧盟)条例第10条至第14条的规定通过第1项所述监管性技术标准。”

(25)第75条第4款替换为下列内容：

“4.欧盟委员会可依照第112条第2款、第3款和第4款的规定并遵守第112a条和第112b条的条件，以授权立法的形式制定相关细则，界定通过非纸质耐久媒介或不构成耐久媒介的网站提供招募说明书时所应符合的具体条件。”

prospectus in a durable medium other than paper or by means of a website which does not constitute a durable medium. '.

(26) Article 78 is amended as follows:

(a) paragraph 7 is replaced by the following:

'7. The Commission shall adopt, by means of delegated acts in accordance with Article 112(2), (3) and (4), and subject to the conditions of Articles 112a and 112b, measures which define the following:

(a) the detailed and exhaustive content of the key investor information to be provided to investors as referred to in paragraphs 2, 3 and 4;

(b) the detailed and exhaustive content of the key investor information to be provided to investors in the following specific cases:

(i) for UCITS having different investment compartments, the key investor information to be provided to investors subscribing to a specific investment compartment, including how to pass from one investment compartment into another and the costs related thereto,

(ii) for UCITS offering different share classes, the key investor information to be provided to investors subscribing to a specific share class,

(iii) for fund of funds structures, the key investor information to be provided to investors subscribing to a UCITS, which invests itself in other UCITS or other collective investment undertakings referred to in Article 50(1)(e),

(iv) for master-feeder structures, the key investor information to be provided to investors subscribing to a feeder UCITS,

(v) for structured, capital protected and other comparable UCITS, the key investor information to be provided to investors in relation to the special characteristics of such UCITS; and

(c) the specific details of the format and presentation of the key investor information to be provided to investors as referred to in paragraph 5. ';

(b) the following paragraph is added:

'8. In order to ensure uniform conditions of application of this Article, ESMA may develop draft implementing technical standards to determine the conditions of application of the delegated acts adopted by the Commission in accordance with paragraph 7 regarding the information referred to in paragraph 3.

Power is conferred on the Commission to adopt the implementing technical standards referred to in the first subparagraph in accordance with Article 15 of Regulation (EU) No 1095/2010. '.

(27) Article 81(2) is replaced by the following:

'2. The Commission may adopt, by means of delegated acts in accordance with Article 112(2), (3) and (4), and subject to the conditions of Articles 112a and 112b,

（26）第78条修正如下：

（a）第7款替换为下列内容：

“7.欧盟委员会应依照第112条第2款、第3款和第4款的规定并遵守第112a条和第112b条的条件，以授权立法的形式制定相关细则，对下列事项予以界定：

（a）第2款、第3款以及第4款所述之应向投资者提供的主要投资者信息的具体详尽内容；

（b）在下列特殊情形下，应向投资者提供的主要投资者信息的具体详尽内容：

（i）设有不同投资单元的可转让证券集合投资计划：应向认购某一特定投资单元的投资者提供主要投资者信息（包括如何从一个投资单元转到另一个投资单元以及相关的费用信息）；

（ii）提供不同类别投资份额的可转让证券集合投资计划：应向认购某一特定类别份额的投资者提供主要投资者信息；

（iii）组合基金结构：应向认购将自身资金投资到其他可转让证券集合投资计划或第50条第1款第e项所述其他集合投资计划的可转让证券集合投资计划的投资者提供主要投资者信息；

（iv）目标基金—联接基金结构：应向认购可转让证券集合投资计划联接基金的投资者提供主要投资者信息；

（v）结构性、保本及其他类似的可转让证券集合投资计划：应向投资者提供与该可转让证券集合投资计划的特征有关的主要投资者信息；及

（c）第5款所述的应向投资者提供的主要投资者信息的格式和列报方式的具体细节。”

（b）增加下列内容：

“8.为确保本条规定具有统一的适用条件，欧洲证券与市场管理局可起草实施性技术标准草案，以确定欧盟委员会根据第7款就第3款所述信息通过的授权立法的适用条件。

兹授予欧盟委员会依照第1095/2010号（欧盟）条例第15条的规定通过第1项所述实施性技术标准的权力。”

（27）第81条第2款替换为下列内容：

“2.欧盟委员会可依照第112条第2款、第3款和第4款的规定并遵守第112a条和第112b条的条件，以授权立法的形式制定相关细则，界定通过非纸质耐久媒介或不构成

measures which define the specific conditions which need to be met when providing key investor information in a durable medium other than on paper or by means of a website which does not constitute a durable medium. '.

(28) In Article 83, the following paragraph is added:

'3. In order to ensure consistent harmonisation of this Article, ESMA may develop draft regulatory technical standards to specify the requirements of this Article relating to borrowing.

Power is delegated to the Commission to adopt the regulatory technical standards referred to in the first subparagraph in accordance with Articles 10 to 14 of Regulation (EU) No 1095/2010. '.

(29) In Article 84, the following paragraph is added:

'4. In order to ensure consistent harmonisation of this Article, ESMA may develop draft regulatory technical standards to specify the conditions which need to be met by the UCITS after the adoption of the temporary suspension of the re-purchase or redemption of the units of the UCITS as referred to in paragraph 2(a), once the suspension has been decided.

Power is delegated to the Commission to adopt the regulatory technical standards referred to in the first subparagraph in accordance with Articles 10 to 14 of Regulation (EU) No 1095/2010. '.

(30) Article 95 is replaced by the following:

'*Article 95*

1. The Commission may adopt, by means of delegated acts in accordance with Article 112(2), (3) and (4), and subject to the conditions of Articles 112a and 112b, measures specifying:

(a) the scope of the information referred to in Article 91(3);

(b) the facilitation of access for the competent authorities of the UCITS host Member States to the information or documents referred to in Article 93(1),(2) and(3) in accordance with Article 93(7).

2. In order to ensure uniform conditions of application of Article 93, ESMA may develop draft implementing technical standards to determine:

(a) the form and contents of a standard model notification letter to be used by a UCITS for the purpose of notification referred to in Article 93(1), including an indication as to which documents the translations refer to;

(b) the form and contents of a standard model attestation to be used by competent authorities of Member States referred to in Article 93(3);

(c) the procedure for the exchange of information and the use of electronic communication between competent authorities for the purpose of notification under

耐久媒介的网站提供主要投资者信息时所应符合的具体条件。”

(28)第83条增加下列内容:

“3.为确保本条规定的一致协调,欧洲证券与市场管理局可起草监管性技术标准草案,对本条关于借款的要求予以说明。

经委托授权,欧盟委员会有权根据第1095/2010号(欧盟)条例第10条至第14条的规定通过第1项所述监管性技术标准。”

(29)第84条增加下列内容:

“4.为确保本条规定的一致协调,欧洲证券与市场管理局可起草监管性技术标准草案,具体说明一旦可转让证券集合投资计划按照第2款第a项作出了暂停回购或赎回投资单位的决定,可转让证券集合投资计划在回购或赎回暂停后所应满足的条件。

经委托授权,欧盟委员会有权根据第1095/2010号(欧盟)条例第10条至第14条的规定通过第1项所述监管性技术标准。”

(30)第95条替换为下列内容:

“第95条

1.欧盟委员会可依照第112条第2款、第3款和第4款的规定并遵守第112a条和第112b条的条件,以授权立法的形式制定相关细则,具体说明:

(a)第91条第3款所述信息的范围;

(b)依照第93条第7款为可转让证券集合投资计划的东道国主管部门查阅第93条第1款、第2款和第3款所述信息或文件所提供的便利。

2.为确保第93条具有统一的适用条件,欧洲证券与市场管理局可起草实施性技术标准草案,以确定:

(a)可转让证券集合投资计划作出第93条第1款所述的通知时所应使用的标准通知信函范本的格式和内容,其中包括对每份翻译文本对应的源文件的标注;

(b)第93条第3款中成员国主管部门所使用的标准证明范本的格式和内容;

(c)主管部门为第93条的通知之目的进行信息交流以及电子通信使用的程序。

Article 93.

Power is conferred on the Commission to adopt the implementing technical standards referred to in the first subparagraph in accordance with Article 15 of Regulation (EU) No 1095/2010. '.

(31) Article 97(1) is replaced by the following:

'1. Member States shall designate the competent authorities which are to carry out the duties provided for in this Directive. They shall inform ESMA and the Commission thereof, indicating any division of duties. '.

(32) Article 101 is amended as follows:

(a) the following paragraph is inserted:

'2a. The competent authorities shall cooperate with ESMA for the purposes of this Directive, in accordance with Regulation (EU) No 1095/2010.

The competent authorities shall without delay provide ESMA with all information necessary to carry out its duties, in accordance with Article 35 of Regulation (EU) No 1095/2010. ';

(b) paragraphs 8 and 9 are replaced by the following:

'8. The competent authorities may refer to ESMA situations where a request:

(a) to exchange information as provided for in Article 109 has been rejected or has not been acted upon within a reasonable time;

(b) to carry out an investigation or on-the-spot verification as provided for in Article 110 has been rejected or has not been acted upon within a reasonable time; or

(c) for authorisation for its officials to accompany those of the competent authority of the other Member State has been rejected or has not been acted upon within a reasonable time.

Without prejudice to Article 258 of the Treaty of on the Functioning of the European Union (TFEU), ESMA may, in situations referred to in the first subparagraph, act in accordance with the powers conferred on it under Article 19 of Regulation (EU) No 1095/2010, without prejudice to the possibilities for refusing to act on a request for information or for an investigation provided for in paragraph 6 of this Article and to the ability of ESMA to act in accordance with Article 17 of that Regulation in those cases.

9. In order to ensure uniform conditions of application of this Article, ESMA may develop draft implementing technical standards to establish common procedures for competent authorities to cooperate in on-the-spot verifications and investigations as referred to in paragraphs 4 and 5.

Power is conferred on the Commission to adopt the implementing technical standards referred to in the first subparagraph in accordance with Article 15 of Regulation (EU) No 1095/2010. '.

兹授予欧盟委员会依照第1095/2010号(欧盟)条例第15条的规定通过第1项所述实施性技术标准的权力。”

(31)第97条第1款替换为下列内容:

“1.各成员国应当指定负责履行本指令中各项职责的主管部门,通知欧洲银行业管理局和欧盟委员会该等指定结果并说明具体的职责分工。”

(32)第101条修正如下:

(a)插入下列内容:

“2a.主管部门应根据第1095/2010号(欧盟)条例的规定,为本指令之目的与欧洲证券与市场管理局合作。

主管部门应根据第1095/2010号(欧盟)条例第35条的规定,立即向欧洲证券与市场管理局提供其履行职责所必要的一切信息。”

(b)第8款和第9款替换为下列内容:

“8.主管部门可将下列情况移交欧洲证券与市场管理局处理:

(a)第109条的信息交换请求被拒绝或未在合理的时间内落实;

(b)第110条的调查或现场核查请求被拒绝或未在合理时间内落实;或

(c)允许其官员陪同其他成员国主管部门的官员的请求被拒绝或未在合理时间内落实。

在不影响《欧洲联盟运行条约》(TFEU)第258条的情形下,欧洲证券与市场管理局可在第1项所述情况下依照第1095/2010号(欧盟)条例第19条授予的权力行事,但不影响被请求主管部门依第6款规定拒绝信息或调查请求的权利,也不影响欧洲证券与市场管理局在该等情况下依照该条例第17条的规定行事的权利。

9.为确保本条规定具有统一的适用条件,欧洲证券与市场管理局可起草实施性技术标准草案,就主管部门在第4款和第5款所述的现场核查和调查中的合作制定通用的程序。

兹授予欧盟委员会依照第1095/2010号(欧盟)条例第15条的规定通过第1项所述实施性技术标准的权力。”

(33) Article 102 is amended as follows:

(a) in paragraph 2, the first subparagraph is replaced by the following:

'2. Paragraph 1 shall not prevent the competent authorities of the Member States from exchanging information in accordance with this Directive or other Union legislation applicable to UCITS or to undertakings contributing towards their business activity or from transmitting it to ESMA in accordance with Regulation (EU) No 1095/2010 or the ESRB. That information shall be subject to the conditions of professional secrecy laid down in paragraph 1. ';

(b) in paragraph 5, the following point is added:

'(d) ESMA, the European Supervisory Authority (European Banking Authority) established by Regulation (EU) No 1093/2010 of the European Parliament and of the Council (*), the European Supervisory Authority (European Insurance and Occupational Pensions Authority) established by Regulation (EU) No 1094/2010 of the European Parliament and of the Council (**) and the ESRB.

(*) OJ L 331, 15. 12. 2010, p. 12.

(**) OJ L 331, 15. 12. 2010, p. 48. '.

(34) Article 103 is amended as follows:

(a) paragraph 3 is replaced by the following:

'3. Member States shall communicate to ESMA, to the Commission and to the other Member States the names of the authorities which may receive information pursuant to paragraph 1. ';

(b) paragraph 7 is replaced by the following:

'7. Member States shall communicate to ESMA, to the Commission and to the other Member States the names of the authorities or bodies which may receive information pursuant to paragraph 4. '.

(35) Article 105 is replaced by the following:

'*Article 105*

In order to ensure uniform conditions of application of the provisions in this Directive concerning the exchange of information, ESMA may develop draft implementing technical standards to determine the conditions of application with regard to the procedures for exchange of information between competent authorities and between the competent authorities and ESMA.

Power is conferred on the Commission to adopt the implementing technical standards referred to in the first subparagraph in accordance with Article 15 of Regulation (EU) No 1095/2010. '.

(36) Article 108(5) is amended as follows:

(a) point (b) of the first subparagraph is replaced by the following:

(33)第102条修正如下：

(a)第2款第1项替换为下列内容：

“2.第1款不妨碍各成员国主管部门依照本指令或依照适用于可转让证券集合投资计划或其他有助于其业务活动的计划的欧盟立法互相交换信息，亦不妨碍其依据第1095/2010号(欧盟)条例向欧洲证券与市场管理局或向欧洲系统性风险委员会发送信息。该等信息应符合第1款所规定的职业保密条件。”

(b)第5款增加下列内容：

“(d)欧洲证券与市场管理局、依据《欧洲议会与欧盟理事会第1093/2010号(欧盟)条例》*设立的欧洲监管机构(欧洲银行业管理局)、依据《欧洲议会与欧盟理事会第1094/2010号(欧盟)条例》**设立的欧洲监管机构(欧洲保险与职业养老金管理局)以及欧洲系统性风险委员会。

*《欧盟公报》L 331，2010年12月15日，第12页。

**《欧盟公报》L 331，2010年12月15日，第48页。”

(34)第103条修正如下：

(a)第3款替换为下列内容：

“3.成员国应向欧洲证券与市场管理局、欧盟委员会以及其他成员国告知可以根据第1款接收信息的部门的名称。”

(b)第7款替换为下列内容：

“7.成员国应向欧洲证券与市场管理局、欧盟委员会以及其他成员国告知可以根据第4款接收信息的部门或机构的名称。”

(35)第105条替换为下列内容：

“第105条

为确保本指令有关信息交换的条款具有统一的适用条件，欧洲证券与市场管理局可起草实施性技术标准草案，具体说明主管部门之间以及主管部门和欧洲证券与市场管理局之间交换信息的程序的适用条件。

兹授予欧盟委员会依照第1095/2010号(欧盟)条例第15条的规定通过第1项所述实施性技术标准的权力。”

(36)第108条第5款修正如下：

(a)第1项第b目替换为下列内容：

'(b) if necessary, refer the matter to ESMA, which may act in accordance with the powers conferred on it under Article 19 of Regulation (EU) No 1095/2010.';

(b) the second subparagraph is replaced by the following:

'The Commission and ESMA shall be informed without delay of any measure taken pursuant to point (a) of the first subparagraph.'.

(37) The title of chapter XIII is replaced by the following:

'DELEGATED ACTS AND POWERS OF EXECUTION'

(38) Article 111 is replaced by the following:

'*Article 111*

The Commission may adopt technical amendments to this Directive in the following areas:

(a) clarification of the definitions in order to ensure consistent harmonisation and uniform application of this Directive throughout the Union; or

(b) alignment of terminology and the framing of definitions in accordance with subsequent acts on UCITS and related matters.

The measures referred to in the first subparagraph shall be adopted by means of delegated acts in accordance with Article 112(2),(3) and(4), and subject to the conditions of Articles 112a and 112b.'.

(39) Article 112 is replaced by the following:

'*Article 112*

1. The Commission shall be assisted by the European Securities Committee established by Commission Decision 2001/528/EC.

2. The power to adopt the delegated acts referred to in Articles 12, 14, 23, 33, 43, 51, 60, 61, 62, 64, 75, 78, 81, 95 and 111 shall be conferred on the Commission for a period of 4 years from 4 January 2011. The Commission shall draw up a report in respect of delegated powers at the latest 6 months before the end of the four-year period. The delegation of power shall be automatically extended for periods of an identical duration, unless the European Parliament or the Council revokes them in accordance with Article 112a.

3. As soon as it adopts a delegated act, the Commission shall notify the European Parliament and the Council thereof simultaneously.

4. The power to adopt delegated acts is conferred on the Commission subject to the conditions laid down in Articles 112a and 112b.'.

(40) The following Articles are inserted:

'*Article 112a*

Revocation of the delegation

1. The delegation of power referred to in Articles 12, 14, 23, 33, 43, 51, 60, 61, 62,

“(b)如有必要,将该事宜移交欧洲证券与市场管理局,由欧洲证券与市场管理局依其在第1095/2010号(欧盟)条例第19条中的权力处理。”

(b)第2项替换为下列内容:

“应立即通知欧盟委员会和欧洲证券与市场管理局根据第1项第a目采取的任何措施。”

(37)第八章的标题替换为:

“授权立法和执法权”。

(38)第111条替换为下列内容:

“第111条

欧盟委员会可通过对本指令所作的下列方面的技术性修正:

(a)对定义进行澄清,确保本指令在整个欧盟范围的一致协调和统一适用;或

(b)根据有关可转让证券集合投资计划以及相关事宜的后续法案对术语进行统一并对定义进行界定。

第1项中的细则应依照第112条第2款、第3款和第4款,在满足第112a条和第112b条条件的前提下,以授权立法的形式制定。”

(39)第112条替换为下列内容:

“第112条

1.依据欧盟委员会第2001/528/EC号决定设立的欧洲证券委员会应协助欧盟委员会工作。

2.自2011年1月4日起,应授予欧盟委员会通过第12条、第14条、第23条、第33条、第43条、第51条、第60条、第61条、第62条、第64条、第75条、第78条、第81条、第95条以及第111条所述授权立法的权力,权力有效期为4年。欧盟委员会应最晚在4年期限届满前6个月,就被委托的权力起草一份报告。除非欧洲议会或欧盟理事会依照第112a条撤销委托授权,否则委托授权的期限届满后应自动展延,每次展延的期限与原期限相同。

3.欧盟委员会应在通过授权立法后立即同时通知欧洲议会和欧盟理事会。

4.在遵守第112a条和第112b条规定的条件的前提下,授予欧盟委员会通过授权立法的权力。”

(40)增加下列条款:

“第112a条

撤销委托授权

1.欧洲议会或欧盟理事会可以随时撤销第12条、第14条、第23条、第33条、第43条、

64, 75, 78, 81, 95 and 111 may be revoked at any time by the European Parliament or by the Council.

2. The institution which has commenced an internal procedure for deciding whether to revoke a delegation of power shall endeavour to inform the other institution and the Commission within a reasonable time before the final decision is taken, indicating the delegated power which could be subject to revocation.

3. The decision of revocation shall put an end to the delegation of the power specified in that decision. It shall take effect immediately or at a later date specified therein. It shall not affect the validity of the delegated acts already in force. It shall be published in the Official Journal of the European Union.

Article 112b

Objections to delegated acts

1. The European Parliament or the Council may object to a delegated act within a period of 3 months from the date of notification. At the initiative of the European Parliament or the Council that period may be extended by 3 months.

2. If, on the expiry of the period referred to in paragraph 1, neither the European Parliament nor the Council has objected to the delegated act, it shall be published in the Official Journal of the European Union and shall enter into force on the date stated therein.

The delegated act may be published in the Official Journal of the European Union and enter into force before the expiry of that period if the European Parliament and the Council have both informed the Commission of their intention not to raise objections.

3. If either the European Parliament or the Council objects to a delegated act within the period referred to in paragraph 1, it shall not enter into force. In accordance with Article 296 TFEU, the institution which objects shall state the reasons for objecting to the delegated act. '.

Article 12 Review

The Commission shall, by 1 January 2014, submit to the European Parliament and to the Council a report specifying whether the ESA have submitted the draft regulatory technical standards and the draft implementing technical standards provided for in this Directive, whether the submission is mandatory or optional, with any appropriate proposals.

Article 13 Transposition

1. Member States shall bring into force the laws, regulations and administrative provisions necessary to comply with Article 1(1) and (2), Article 2(1)(a), Article 2(2), (5), (7) and (9), Article 2(11)(b), Article 3(4), Article 3(6)(a) and (b), Article 4 (1)(a), Article 4(3), Article 5(5)(a), the first subparagraph of Article 5(5)(b), Article

第51条、第60条、第61条、第62条、第64条、第75条、第78条、第81条、第95条以及第111条所述的委托授权。

2.欧洲议会或欧盟理事会已经启动决定是否撤销某项委托授权的内部程序的，应当尽力在作出最终决定前的合理时间内通知彼此以及欧盟委员会，指明可能被撤销的委托授权。

3.撤销决定将使其列明的委托授权效力终止。撤销决定应立即生效，或在决定中规定的较晚日期生效。撤销决定不影响已生效的监管性技术标准的效力。撤销决定应在《欧盟公报》公布。

第112b条

对授权立法的异议

1.欧洲议会或欧盟理事会可在通知之日起3个月期限内对相关授权立法提出异议，经欧洲议会或欧盟理事会主动要求，该期限可延长3个月。

2.在第1款所述期限届满前，欧洲议会和欧盟理事会均未对相关授权立法提出异议的，该授权立法应在《欧盟公报》公布，并应在其规定的生效日期生效。

在第1款所述期限届满前，欧洲议会和欧盟理事会均已通知欧盟委员会其无意提出异议的，授权立法可提前在《欧盟公报》公布并生效。

3.欧洲议会或欧盟理事会任一方在第1款所述期限内对授权立法提出异议的，授权立法不得生效。根据《欧洲联盟运行条约》第296条的规定，对授权立法提出异议的机构应说明异议理由。”

第12条　审评

欧盟委员会应于2014年1月1日前向欧洲议会以及欧盟理事会提交一份报告，说明欧洲监管机构是否呈报了本指令所规定的监管性技术标准草案和实施性技术标准草案（无论报告的呈报是强制性还是选择性的）以及任何适当的提案。

第13条　转化

1.各成员国应于2011年12月31日前实施必要的法律、法规和规章，以使本指令第1条第1款和第2款、第2条第1款第a项、第2条第2款、第5款、第7款和第9款、第2条第11款第b项、第3条第4款、第3条第6款第a项和第b项、第4条第1款第a项、第4条第3款、第5条第5款第a项、第5条第5款第b项第1项、第5条第6款、第8款、第9款（与第2003/71/EC号指

5(6), (8), (9) (in relation to Article 18(3) of Directive 2003/71/EC), Article 5(10), Article 5(11)(a) and (b), Article 5(12), Article 6(1) (in relation to the first subparagraph of Article 5(3) of Directive 2004/39/EC), Article 6(3), Article 6(5)(a), Article 6(10), (13), (14) and (16), Article 6(17)(a) and (b), Article 6(18) and (19) (in relation to the first subparagraph of Article 53(3) of Directive 2004/39/EC), Article 6(21)(a) and (b), Article 6(23)(b), Article 6(24), (25) and (27), Article 7(12)(a), Article 7(13), (14) (15) and (16), Article 9(1)(a), Article 9(2), (3), (4), (10), (11), (12), (15), (16), (17), (18), (20), (29) and (32), Article 9(33)(a) and (b), Article 9(33)(d) (ii) to (iv), Article 9(34)and (35), Article 9(36)(b)(ii), Article 9(37)(b), Article 9 (38)and (39), Article 10(2), Article 10(3)(a), Article 10(4), Article 11(2), (4), (11), (14), (19) and (31), Article 11(32)(b) in regard to Article 101(8) of Directive 2009/65/EC, and Article 11(33), (34) and (36) of this Directive, by 31 December 2011. They shall forthwith communicate to the Commission the text of those provisions and a correlation table between those provisions and this Directive.

When Member States adopt those measures, they shall contain a reference to this Directive or shall be accompanied by such reference on the occasion of their official publication. The methods of making such reference shall be laid down by Member States.

2. Member States shall communicate to the Commission the text of the main provisions of national law which they adopt in the field covered by this Directive.

Article 14 Entry into force

This Directive shall enter into force on the 20th day following its publication in the Official Journal of the European Union.

Article 15 Addressees

This Directive is addressed to the Member States.

Done at Strasbourg, 24 November 2010.

For the European Parliament	For the Council
The President	The President
J. BUZEK	O. CHASTEL

令第18条第3款有关)、第5条第10款、第5条第11款第a项和第b项、第5条第12款、第6条第1款(与第2004/39/EC 号指令第5条第3款第1项有关)、第6条第3款、第6条第5款第a项、第6条第10款、第13款、第14款和第16款、第6条第17款第a项和第b项、第6条第18款和第19款(与第2004/39/EC 号指令第53条第3款第1项有关)、第6条第21款第a项和第b项、第6条第23款第b项、第6条第24款、第25款和第27款、第7条第12款第a项、第7条第13款、第14款、第15款和第16款、第9条第1款第a项、第9条第2款、第3款、第4款、第10款、第11款、第12款、第15款、第16款、第17款、第18款、第20款、第29款和第32款、第9条第33款第a项和第b项、第9条第33款第d项第ii目至第iv目、第9条第34款和第35款、第9条第36款第b项第ii目、第9条第37款第b项、第9条第38款和第39款、第10条第2款、第10条第3款第a项、第10条第4款、第11条第2款、第4款、第11款、第14款、第19款和第31款、(关于第2009/65/EC号指令第101条第8款的)第11条第32款第b项以及第11条第33款、第34款以及第36款得到遵守。成员国应在该期限后立即向欧盟委员会通知该等条款的文本以及一份该等条款与本指令的关联对照表。

成员国制定该等法律、法规和规章时,应在其中对本指令予以援引,或在官方正式公布该等法律、法规和规章时予以援引。援引的具体方式,由成员国决定。

2.各成员国应向欧盟委员会提供其在本指令所覆盖的领域内制定的本国法律的主要条款的文本。

第14条　生效

本指令应于《欧盟公报》公布,公布后20日生效。

第15条　对象

本指令对象为各成员国。

2010年11月24日于斯特拉斯堡通过。

欧洲议会议长　　　　欧盟理事会主席

J.布泽克　　　　O.查斯特尔

REGULATION (EU) NO 1092/2010 OF THE EUROPEAN PARLIAMENT AND OF THE COUNCIL

欧洲议会与欧盟理事会 第 1092/2010 号(欧盟)条例

REGULATION (EU) NO 1092/2010 OF THE EUROPEAN PARLIAMENT AND OF THE COUNCIL

of 24 November 2010

on European Union macro-prudential oversight of the financial system and establishing a European Systemic Risk Board

THE EUROPEAN PARLIAMENT AND THE COUNCIL OF THE EUROPEAN UNION,

Having regard to the Treaty on the Functioning of the European Union, and in particular Article 114 thereof,

Having regard to the proposal from the European Commission,

Having regard to the opinion of the European Central Bank[1],

Having regard to the opinion of the European Economic and Social Committee[2],

Acting in accordance with the ordinary legislative procedure[3],

Whereas:

(1) Financial stability is a precondition for the real economy to provide jobs, credit and growth. The financial crisis has revealed important shortcomings in financial supervision, which has failed to anticipate adverse macro-prudential developments and to prevent the accumulation of excessive risks within the financial system.

(2) The European Parliament called repeatedly for the reinforcement of a true level playing field for all actors at the level of Union while pointing out significant failures in the Union's supervision of ever more integrated financial markets (in its resolutions of 13

1 OJ C 270, 11. 11. 2009, p. 1.

2 Opinion of 22 January 2010 (not yet published in the Official Journal).

3 Position of the European Parliament of 22 September 2010 (not yet published in the Official Journal) and decision of the Council of 17 November 2010.

欧洲议会与欧盟理事会
第1092/2010号(欧盟)条例

(本条例于2010年11月24日通过,关于欧盟对金融系统的
宏观审慎监控以及设立欧洲系统性风险委员会)

欧洲议会和欧盟理事会,

根据《欧洲联盟运行条约》,特别是其中的第114条,

根据欧盟委员会的提议,
根据欧洲中央银行的意见[1],
根据欧洲经济与社会委员会的意见[2],
依照正常的立法程序[3],
鉴于下列情形,通过本条例:

(1)金融稳定是实体经济提供就业岗位、信用和增长的前提条件。金融危机反映出金融监管的若干重要缺陷——既无法预见不利的宏观审慎变化,也无法避免金融系统内过度的风险累积。

(2)在日益一体化的金融市场监管方面,欧洲议会反复呼吁在欧盟这一层级为所有市场主体提供真正公平的竞争环境[请参见:欧洲议会2000年4月13日关于欧盟委

1 2009年11月11日《欧盟公报》C 270,第1页。
2 2010年1月22日的意见(尚未在《欧盟公报》公布)。
3 2010年9月22日欧洲议会立场(尚未在《欧盟公报》公布)以及2010年11月17日欧盟理事会决定。

April 2000 on the Commission communication on implementing the framework for financial markets: Action Plan[1], of 21 November 2002 on prudential supervision rules in the European Union[2], of 11 July 2007 on financial services policy (2005 to 2010) White Paper[3], of 23 September 2008 with recommendations to the Commission on hedge funds and private equity[4] and of 9 October 2008 with recommendations to the Commission on Lamfalussy follow-up: future structure of supervision[5], and in its positions of 22 April 2009 on the amended proposal for a directive of the European Parliament and of the Council on the taking-up and pursuit of the business of Insurance and Reinsurance (Solvency II)[6] and of 23 April 2009 on the proposal for a regulation of the European Parliament and of the Council on Credit Rating Agencies[7]).

(3) In November 2008, the Commission mandated a High-Level Group chaired by Jacques de Larosière to make recommendations on how to strengthen European supervisory arrangements with a view to better protecting the citizen and rebuilding trust in the financial system.

(4) In its final report presented on 25 February 2009 (the 'de Larosière Report'), the High-Level Group recommended, inter alia, the establishment of a Union level body charged with overseeing risk in the financial system as a whole.

(5) In its Communication of 4 March 2009 entitled 'Driving European Recovery', the Commission welcomed and broadly supported the recommendations of the de Larosière Report. At its meeting of 19 and 20 March 2009, the European Council agreed on the need to improve the regulation and supervision of financial institutions within the Union and to use the de Larosière Report as a basis for action.

(6) In its Communication of 27 May 2009 entitled 'European Financial Supervision', the Commission suggested a series of reforms to the current arrangements for safeguarding financial stability at the Union level, in particular including the creation of a European Systemic Risk Board (ESRB) responsible for macro-prudential oversight. The Council on 9 June 2009 and the European Council at its meeting of 18 and 19 June 2009 supported the Commission's suggestions and welcomed its intention to put forward legislative proposals for the new framework to be in place in the course of 2010. In line with the views of the Commission, the Council concluded, inter alia, that the European Central Bank (ECB) 'should provide analytical, statistical, administrative and logistical support

1 OJ C 40, 7. 2. 2001, p. 453.
2 OJ C 25 E, 29. 1. 2004, p. 394.
3 OJ C 175 E, 10. 7. 2008, p. 392.
4 OJ C 8 E, 14. 1. 2010, p. 26.
5 OJ C 9 E, 15. 1. 2010, p. 48.
6 OJ C 184 E, 8. 7. 2010, p. 214.
7 OJ C 184 E, 8. 7. 2010, p. 292.

员会通报《落实金融市场框架:行动计划》的决议[1],2002年11月21日关于欧盟审慎监管规则的决议[2],2007年7月11日关于《2005年至2010年金融服务政策白皮书》的决议[3],2008年9月23日关于对冲基金和私募股权的决议(含向欧盟委员会提出的建议)[4],2008年10月9日关于《莱姆法路西的后续行动:未来监管结构》的决议(含向欧盟委员会提出的建议)[5],2009年4月22日对《欧洲议会与欧盟理事会关于开办和经营保险与再保险业务的指令》(保险偿付能力标准II)的修正稿提案所持立场[6]以及2009年4月23日对《欧洲议会以及欧盟理事会关于信用评级机构的条例》提案所持立场[7]]。

(3)2008年11月,欧盟委员会委托一个由雅克·德·拉罗西埃先生领导的高级工作组,就如何加强欧洲监管安排以更好地保护公众利益并重建公众对金融系统的信任提出建议。

(4)在其于2009年2月25日提交的最终报告(《德·拉罗西埃报告》)中,高级工作组特别建议设立一个欧盟层级的机构,负责监管整个金融体系的风险。

(5)在2009年3月4日名为《推动欧洲复苏》的通报中,欧盟委员会欣然接受并支持《德·拉罗西埃报告》提出的建议。欧洲理事会在其2009年3月19日和20日的会议中同意,有必要改善对欧盟金融机构的规制和监管并以《德·拉罗西埃报告》作为行动的基础。

(6)在2009年5月27日名为《欧洲金融监管》的通报中,欧盟委员会建议对目前欧盟层级保证金融稳定的安排进行一系列的改革,尤其包括设立一个负责宏观审慎监控的欧洲系统性风险委员会(ESRB)。欧盟理事会和欧洲理事会分别在2009年6月9日以及2009年6月18日和19日的会议中,对欧盟委员会的建议表示支持,并欢迎其为2010年中落实的新框架提出立法提案。欧盟理事会特别提出,根据欧盟委员会的观点,欧洲中央银行(ECB)"同样应利用成员国中央银行和监管机构的技术性建议,为欧洲系统性风险委员会提供分析、统计、行政和后勤支持"。欧洲中央银行向欧洲系统性风险委员会提供的支持以及欧洲系统性风险委员会被赋予的职责,均不得影响欧洲中央银行

1 2001年2月7日《欧盟公报》C 40,第453页。
2 2004年1月29日《欧盟公报》C 25 E,第394页。
3 2008年7月10日《欧盟公报》C 175 E,第392页。
4 2010年1月14日《欧盟公报》C 8 E,第26页。
5 2010年1月15日《欧盟公报》C 9 E,第48页。
6 2010年7月8日《欧盟公报》C 184 E,第214页。
7 2010年7月8日《欧盟公报》C 184 E,第292页。

to the ESRB, also drawing on technical advice from national central banks and supervisors'. The support provided by the ECB to the ESRB, as well as the tasks assigned to the ESRB, should be without prejudice to the principle of the independence of the ECB in the performance of its tasks pursuant to the Treaty on the Functioning of the European Union (TFEU).

(7) Given the integration of international financial markets and the contagion risk of financial crises, there is a need for a strong commitment on the part of the Union at the global level. The ESRB should draw expertise from a high-level scientific committee and take on all the global responsibilities required in order to ensure that the voice of the Union is heard on issues relating to financial stability, in particular by cooperating closely with the International Monetary Fund(IMF) and the Financial Stability Board (FSB), which are expected to provide early warnings of macro-prudential risks at the global level, and the partners of the Group of Twenty (G-20).

(8) The ESRB should contribute, inter alia, towards implementing the recommendations of the IMF, the FSB and the Bank for International Settlements (BIS) to the G-20.

(9) The report of the IMF, the BIS and the FSB, of 28 October 2009, presented to the G-20 Finance Ministers and Central Bank Governors, entitled 'Guidance to Assess the Systemic Importance of Financial Institutions, Markets and Instruments: Initial Considerations' also states that the assessment of systemic risk is likely to vary depending on the economic environment. It will also be conditioned by the financial infrastructure and crisis management arrangements and the capacity to deal with failures when they occur. Financial institutions may be systemically important for local, national or international financial systems and economies. The key criteria helping to identify the systemic importance of markets and institutions are size (the volume of financial services provided by the individual component of the financial system), substitutability (the extent to which other components of the system can provide the same services in the event of failure) and interconnectedness (linkages with other components of the system). An assessment based on those three criteria should be supplemented by a reference to financial vulnerabilities and the capacity of the institutional framework to deal with financial failures and should consider a wide range of additional factors such as, inter alia, the complexity of specific structures and business models, the degree of financial autonomy, intensity and scope of supervision, transparency of financial arrangements and linkages that may affect the overall risk of institutions.

(10) The ESRB's task should be to monitor and assess systemic risk in normal times for the purpose of mitigating the exposure of the system to the risk of failure of systemic components and enhancing the financial system's resilience to shocks. In that

履行其在《欧洲联盟运行条约》(TFEU)中的职责时的独立性原则。

(7)鉴于国际金融市场的一体化以及金融危机的传播风险,需要欧盟在全球层面上作出强有力的承诺。欧洲系统性风险委员会应从高水平的科学委员会中吸取专长,并承担其应承担的全球责任,特别是应通过与国际货币基金组织(IMF)和金融稳定委员会 (FSB)——两者预期能为全球范围的宏观审慎危机提供早期预警——以及二十国集团(G-20)合作伙伴之间紧密合作,确保欧盟就金融稳定相关事宜所发表的意见受到相应的关注。

(8)欧洲系统性风险委员会应致力于贯彻落实国际货币基金组织、金融稳定委员会以及国际清算银行(BIS)向二十国集团提出的建议。

(9)国际货币基金组织、国际清算银行和金融稳定委员会于2009年10月28日向二十国集团财政部长和中央银行行长递交的题为《金融机构、市场和工具之系统性重要性的评估指引:初步意见》的报告同样指出,在不同的经济环境下,系统性风险评估结果可能会出现各种差异,同时,系统性风险评估结果也为金融基础设施和危机管理安排以及处理各种金融失败的能力所制约。金融机构对于本地、国内或国际金融系统和经济体均可能具有系统重要性。识别市场和机构的系统重要性的关键标准是规模(金融系统个别组成部分提供金融服务的数量)、可替代性(系统中的个别组成部分濒临倒闭时,其他组成部分能在多大程度上提供同样服务)以及相互关联性(与系统其他组成部分的关联)。基于上述三个标准作评估时,还应考虑金融方面的薄弱环节以及机构制度处理金融失败的能力,并考虑各种各样的额外因素,特别是如特殊结构和经营模式的复杂性、财务自主权的程度、监管的力度和范围、财务安排的透明度以及可能会对机构整体风险产生影响的关联情况。

(10)欧洲系统性风险委员会的职责应当是监控和评估正常时期的系统性风险,以缓释系统因系统组成部分濒临倒闭所遭受的风险,并加强金融系统受到冲击时的抗冲击能力。就此而言,欧洲系统性风险委员会应致力于确保金融稳定和减少内部市

respect, the ESRB should contribute to ensuring financial stability and mitigating the negative impacts on the internal market and the real economy. In order to accomplish its objectives, the ESRB should analyse all the relevant information.

(11) The present arrangements of the Union place too little emphasis on macro-prudential oversight and on interlinkages between developments in the broader macroeconomic environment and the financial system. Responsibility for macro-prudential analysis remains fragmented, and is conducted by various authorities at different levels with no mechanism to ensure that macro-prudential risks are adequately identified and that warnings and recommendations are issued clearly, followed up and translated into action. A proper functioning of Union and global financial systems and the mitigation of threats thereto require enhanced consistency between macro- and micro-prudential supervision.

(12) A newly designed system of macro-prudential oversight requires credible and high-profile leadership. Therefore, given its key role and its international and internal credibility, and in the spirit of the recommendations of the de Larosière Report, the President of the ECB should be the Chair of the ESRB for a first term of 5 years following the entry into force of this Regulation. In addition, the accountability requirements should be increased and the ESRB bodies should be able to draw on a wide range of experience, backgrounds and opinions.

(13) The de Larosière Report also states that macro-prudential oversight is not meaningful unless it can somehow impact on supervision at the micro level whilst micro-prudential supervision cannot effectively safeguard financial stability without adequately taking account of macro-level developments.

(14) A European System of Financial Supervision (ESFS) should be established, bringing together the actors of financial supervision at national level and at the level of the Union, to act as a network. Pursuant to the principle of sincere cooperation in accordance with Article 4(3) of the Treaty on European Union, the parties to the ESFS should cooperate with trust and full mutual respect, in particular to ensure that appropriate and reliable information flows between them. At the level of the Union, the network should comprise the ESRB and three micro-supervisory authorities: the European Supervisory Authority (European Banking Authority), established by Regulation (EU) No 1093/2010 of the European Parliament and of the Council[1], the European Supervisory Authority (European Insurance and Occupational Pensions Authority), established by Regulation (EU) No 1094/2010 of the European Parliament and of the Council[2], and the

1 See page 12 of this Official Journal.

2 See page 48 of this Official Journal.

场和实体经济所受到的负面影响。欧洲系统性风险委员会应对所有相关的信息进行分析以实现其目的。

(11)欧盟现有安排过于轻视宏观审慎监控以及广义宏观经济环境与金融系统两者发展之间的关联。宏观审慎分析的责任仍然是分散的,由各层级的不同部门负责完成,并无任何机制确保宏观审慎风险得到充分的识别,亦无任何机制确保预警和建议能够明确发布并予以跟进和付诸行动。为了欧盟和全球金融系统的稳健运行并缓释其所面临的威胁,需要增强宏观和微观审慎监管之间的一致性。

(12)新设计的宏观审慎监控系统要求可信和突出的领导才能。因此,鉴于其所将发挥的关键作用及其在国内外的信誉,本着《德·拉罗西埃报告》建议的精神,欧洲中央银行行长应在本条例生效后担任欧洲系统性风险委员会主席,任期5年。此外,应对欧洲系统性风险委员会提出更高的问责要求,其下属机构也应有能力在其工作中利用和吸收各种经验、背景和意见。

(13)《德·拉罗西埃报告》同时表明,宏观审慎监控在满足下列前提下才有意义:宏观审慎监控应能在某种程度上对微观层面的监管发挥影响。而微观审慎监管也只有在充分考虑宏观层面变化的情形下才能有效地保障金融稳定。

(14)应设立一个欧洲金融监管体系(ESFS),以其作为一个网络,汇集国家层级和欧盟层级的金融监管机构。根据《欧洲联盟条约》第4条第3款的精诚合作原则,欧洲金融监管体系的各方应在合作过程中相互信任和充分尊重,以特别确保各方能够彼此交流适当和可靠的信息。在欧盟层级,该网络应包括欧洲系统性风险委员会和三个微观监管机构:依据《欧洲议会与欧盟理事会第1093/2010号(欧盟)条例》[1] 设立的欧洲监管机构(欧洲银行业管理局)、依据《欧洲议会与欧盟理事会第1094/2010号(欧盟)条例》[2] 设立的欧洲监管机构(欧洲保险与职业养老金管理局)以及依据《欧洲议会与欧

1 请见本《欧盟公报》,第 12 页。
2 请见本《欧盟公报》,第 48 页。

European Supervisory Authority (European Securities and Markets Authority), established by Regulation (EU) No 1095/2010 of the European Parliament and of the Council[1] (hereinafter collectively referred to as the 'ESAs').

(15) The Union needs a specific body responsible for macro-prudential oversight across its financial system, which would identify risks to financial stability and, where necessary, issue risk warnings and recommendations for action to address such risks. Consequently, the ESRB should be established as a new independent body, covering all financial sectors as well as guarantee schemes. The ESRB should be responsible for conducting macro-prudential oversight at the level of the Union and should have no legal personality.

(16) The ESRB should comprise a General Board, a Steering Committee, a Secretariat, an Advisory Scientific Committee and an Advisory Technical Committee. The composition of the Advisory Scientific Committee should take into account adequate rules of conflict of interests adopted by the General Board. The establishment of the Advisory Technical Committee should take into account existing structures with a view to avoiding any duplication.

(17) The ESRB should issue warnings and, where it deems necessary, recommendations either of a general or a specific nature, which should be addressed in particular to the Union as a whole or to one or more Member States, or to one or more of the ESAs, or to one or more of the national supervisory authorities with a specified timeline for the relevant policy response.

(18) The ESRB should elaborate a colour code in order to allow interested parties better to assess the nature of the risk.

(19) In order to increase their influence and legitimacy, such warnings and recommendations should also be transmitted, subject to strict rules of confidentiality, to the Council and the Commission and, where addressed to one or more national supervisory authorities, to the ESAs. The deliberations of the Council should be prepared by the Economic and Financial Committee (EFC) in accordance with its role as defined in the TFEU. In order to prepare the Council's discussions and provide it with timely policy advice, the ESRB should inform the EFC regularly and should send the texts of any warnings and recommendations as soon as they have been adopted.

(20) The ESRB should also monitor compliance with its warnings and recommendations, based on reports from addressees, in order to ensure that its warnings and recommendations are effectively followed. Addressees of recommendations should act on them and provide an adequate justification in case of inaction ('act or explain'

1 See page 84 of this Official Journal.

盟理事会第1095/2010号(欧盟)条例》[1] 设立的欧洲监管机构(欧洲证券与市场管理局)(以下统称欧洲监管机构)。

(15)欧盟需要有专门的机构负责整个金融系统的宏观审慎监控,识别金融稳定的风险并在必要时发布风险预警以及针对该等风险的行动建议。为此,欧洲系统性风险委员会应作为一个新的独立机构设立,其职权管辖范围覆盖所有的金融行业以及担保计划。欧洲系统性风险委员会应负责在欧盟层级开展宏观审慎监控,并且不应具有法人性质。

(16)欧洲系统性风险委员会应由总委员会、指导委员会、秘书处、科学咨询委员会以及技术咨询委员会组成。科学咨询委员会的构成应将总委员会制定的适当的利益冲突规则纳入考虑。技术咨询委员会的设立则应将现有的结构纳入考虑,以避免任何重复。

(17)欧洲系统性风险委员会应发布预警,并在其认为必要时针对整个欧盟或针对一个或多个成员国、一个或多个欧洲监管机构或一个或多个国家级监管机构提出一般或特别建议,要求其在指定的时间段内作出相关的政策回应。

(18)欧洲系统性风险委员会应制定一套颜色代码,让利益相关方能够更好地评估风险的性质。

(19)为增强其影响力与合法性,上述预警和建议应按照严格的保密规则传达给欧盟理事会和欧盟委员会,如果是针对一个或多个国家级监管机构的预警和建议,则还须发送给各欧洲监管机构。经济与金融委员会(EFC)应根据《欧洲联盟运行条约》中所规定的职责准备欧盟理事会的审议工作。为了对欧盟理事会的审议作出准备并向其提供及时的政策建议,欧洲系统性风险委员会应定期向经济与金融委员会提供相关信息并在其制定完预警和建议后立即向经济与金融委员会发送该等预警或建议的文本。

(20)同时,欧洲系统性风险委员会应基于被预警方和被建议方发来的报告,监控其遵循预警和建议的情况,以确保预警和建议得到有效的跟进。被建议方应就建议采取行动,不采取行动的,应提供充分的理由(行动或解释机制)。欧洲系统性风险委员会认为回应不当的,应按照严格的保密规则通知该等被预警方或被建议方和欧盟理

1 请见本《欧盟公报》,第84页。

mechanism). If the ESRB considers that the reaction is inadequate, it should inform, subject to strict confidentiality rules, the addressees, the Council and, where appropriate, the European Supervisory Authority concerned.

(21) The ESRB should decide, on a case-by-case basis and after having informed the Council sufficiently in advance so that it is able to react, whether a recommendation should be kept confidential or made public, bearing in mind that public disclosure can help to foster compliance with the recommendations in certain circumstances.

(22) If the ESRB detects a risk which could seriously jeopardise the orderly functioning and integrity of financial markets or the stability of the whole or part of the Union's financial system, it should promptly inform the Council of the situation. If the ESRB determines that an emergency situation may arise, it should contact the Council and provide an assessment of the situation. The Council should then assess the need to adopt a decision addressed to the ESAs determining the existence of an emergency situation. During that process, due protection of confidentiality is of the outmost importance.

(23) The ESRB should report to the European Parliament and the Council at least annually, and more frequently in the event of widespread financial distress. Where appropriate, the European Parliament and the Council should be able to invite the ESRB to examine specific issues related to financial stability.

(24) The ECB and the national central banks should have a leading role in macro-prudential oversight because of their expertise and their existing responsibilities in the area of financial stability. National supervisors should be involved in providing their specific expertise. The participation of micro-prudential supervisors in the work of the ESRB is essential to ensure that the assessment of macro-prudential risk is based on complete and accurate information about developments in the financial system. Accordingly, the chairpersons of the ESAs should be members with voting rights. One representative of the competent national supervisory authorities of each Member State should attend meetings of the General Board, without voting rights. In a spirit of openness, 15 independent persons should provide the ESRB with external expertise through the Advisory Scientific Committee.

(25) The participation of a Member of the Commission in the ESRB will help to establish a link with the macroeconomic and financial surveillance of the Union, while the presence of the President of the EFC will reflect the role of Member States' ministries responsible for finance and the Council in safeguarding financial stability and performing economic and financial oversight.

(26) It is essential that the members of the ESRB perform their duties impartially and consider only the financial stability of the Union as a whole. Where consensus cannot be reached, voting on warnings and recommendations within the ESRB should not be

事会,并在适当时通知相关的欧洲监管机构。

(21)提前向欧盟理事会作出充分通知以便其能作出反应之后,欧洲系统性风险委员会应根据具体情形决定是否应对某项建议保密或应予公布,但须谨记,在某些情形下,公开披露有助于促使被建议方遵循建议。

(22)欧洲系统性风险委员会发现某项风险,而该项风险可能会严重损害到金融市场的有序运行和诚信度或者整个或部分欧盟金融系统的稳定的,应立即通知欧盟理事会该等状况。欧洲系统性风险委员会判定可能会出现紧急情况的,应与欧盟理事会联系并提供对该状况的评估。欧盟理事会应评估是否有必要向欧洲监管机构发布关于存在紧急情况的决定。在上述过程中,谨遵保密原则是最为重要的。

(23)欧洲系统性风险委员会每年应至少向欧洲议会和欧盟理事会报告1次,在金融系统出现大范围困境的情形下,报告应更频繁地进行。在适当时,欧洲议会和欧盟理事会应能要求欧洲系统性风险委员会对与金融稳定有关的特定事宜进行审查。

(24)鉴于欧洲中央银行和成员国中央银行在金融稳定方面的专长和现有职责,这两个机构应在宏观审慎监控中承担领导作用;国家级监管机构则提供其特定的专长,以此方式参与宏观审慎监控。为确保宏观审慎风险的评估能在关于金融系统变化的完整准确信息基础上开展,让微观审慎监管机构参与欧洲系统性风险委员会的工作至关重要。为此,各个相关的欧洲监管机构主席应当是欧洲系统性风险委员会有表决权的委员。各成员国国家级主管部门则应有1名代表列席总委员会的会议,但无表决权。本着开放的精神,应有15名独立的个人通过科学咨询委员会向欧洲系统性风险委员会提供外部专业支持。

(25)欧盟委员会委员参与欧洲系统性风险委员会,将有助于与欧盟的宏观经济监控和金融监控之间的衔接,而经济与金融委员会主席的参与则反映了各成员国财政部长以及欧盟理事会在保护金融稳定和开展经济和金融监控中的作用。

(26)欧洲系统性风险委员会委员公正地履行其职责并仅以欧盟整体的金融稳定为考虑是至关重要的。在无法达成一致的情形下,欧洲系统性风险委员会就预警和建议作出的表决不应加权计算票数,并且作为规则,一般应以简单多数票通过决定。

weighted and decisions should, as a rule, be taken by simple majority.

(27) The interconnectedness of financial institutions and markets implies that the monitoring and assessment of potential systemic risks should be based on a broad set of relevant macroeconomic and micro-financial data and indicators. Those systemic risks include risks of disruption to financial services caused by a significant impairment of all or parts of the Union's financial system that have the potential to have serious negative consequences for the internal market and the real economy. Any type of financial institution and intermediary, market, infrastructure and instrument has the potential to be systemically significant. The ESRB should therefore have access to all the information necessary to perform its duties while preserving the confidentiality of that information as required.

(28) The measures for the collection of information set out in this Regulation are necessary for the performance of the tasks of the ESRB and should be without prejudice to the legal framework of the European Statistical System in the field of statistics. This Regulation should therefore be without prejudice to Regulation (EC) No 223/2009 of the European Parliament and of the Council of 11 March 2009 on European statistics[1] and to Council Regulation (EC) No 2533/98 of 23 November 1998 concerning the collection of statistical information by the European Central Bank[2].

(29) Market participants can provide valuable input to the understanding of the evolutions affecting the financial system. Where appropriate, the ESRB should therefore consult private sector stakeholders, including financial sector representatives, consumer associations, user groups in the financial services area established by the Commission or by Union legislation, and give them a fair opportunity to make observations.

(30) The establishment of the ESRB should contribute directly to achieving the objectives of the internal market. The Union macro-prudential oversight of the financial system is an integral part of the overall new supervisory arrangements in the Union as the macro-prudential aspect is closely linked to the micro-prudential supervisory tasks attributed to the ESAs. Only with arrangements in place that properly acknowledge the interdependence of micro-and macro-prudential risks can all stakeholders have sufficient confidence to engage in cross-border financial activities. The ESRB should monitor and assess risks to financial stability arising from developments that can impact on a sectoral level or at the level of the financial system as a whole. By addressing such risks, the ESRB should contribute directly to an integrated Union supervisory structure necessary to promote timely and consistent policy responses among the Member States, thus preventing

1 OJ L 87, 31. 3. 2009, p. 164.

2 OJ L 318, 27. 11. 1998, p. 8.

(27)金融机构和市场的相互关联意味着对潜在系统性风险的监控和评估应以一系列广泛的相关宏观经济和微观金融数据和指标为基础。该等系统性风险包括由整个或部分欧盟金融系统遭受的重大损害所造成的金融服务扰乱风险,并且该等风险可能会对内部市场和实体经济造成严重消极后果。任何类型的金融机构和中介机构、市场、基础设施和工具均可能具有系统重要性。因此,欧洲系统性风险委员会应可查阅履行其职责所必要的一切信息,同时按要求对该等信息予以保密。

(28)本条例所规定的信息收集措施为欧洲系统性风险委员会履行职责所必要的,不得在统计领域中违背欧洲统计系统的法律框架。因此,本条例不得违背《欧洲议会与欧盟理事会关于欧洲统计的第223/2009号(欧共体)条例》[1](2009年3月11日)以及《欧盟理事会关于欧洲中央银行统计信息收集工作的第2533/98号(欧共体)条例》[2](1998年11月23日)。

(29)市场参与者能够对理解金融系统的发展提供有价值的信息。因此,适当时,在由欧盟委员会或欧盟立法所确立的金融服务领域里,欧洲系统性风险委员会应征求私营部门利益相关者的意见,包括金融行业代表、消费者协会、用户小组等在内,并给予其发表意见的公平机会。

(30)欧洲系统性风险委员会的设立应旨在直接促进内部市场目标的实现。由于宏观审慎监控与欧洲监管机构所承担的微观审慎监管职责紧密关联,欧盟对金融系统的宏观审慎监控是欧盟整个新的监管安排不可或缺的一部分。唯有具备正确承认微观和宏观审慎风险之间相互依赖性的安排时,各利益相关者才能有足够的信心参与跨境金融活动。欧洲系统性风险委员会应监控和评估由于可能对各行业或金融系统整体造成冲击的变化所造成的金融稳定风险。通过应对上述风险,欧洲系统性风险委员会应能对具有整合性的欧盟监管结构的建立直接产生助益。对于推动成员国之间及时和一致的政策回应,此等具有整合性的监管结构诚属必要,可避免出现各种分歧的模式并改善内部市场的运行。

1 2009年3月31日《欧盟公报》L 87,第164页。
2 1998年11月27日《欧盟公报》L 318,第8页。

diverging approaches and improving the functioning of the internal market.

(31) The Court of Justice in its judgment of 2 May 2006 in Case C-217/04 (United Kingdom of Great Britain and Northern Ireland v. European Parliament and Council of the European Union) held that 'nothing in the wording of Article 95 EC [now Article 114 TFEU] implies that the addressees of the measures adopted by the Community legislature on the basis of that provision can only be the individual Member States. The legislature may deem it necessary to provide for the establishment of a Community body responsible for contributing to the implementation of a process of harmonisation in situations where, in order to facilitate the uniform implementation and application of acts based on that provision, the adoption of non-binding supporting and framework measures seems appropriate'[1]. The ESRB should contribute to the financial stability necessary for further financial integration in the internal market by monitoring systemic risks and issuing warnings and recommendations where appropriate. Those tasks are closely linked to the objectives of the Union legislation concerning the internal market for financial services. The ESRB should therefore be established on the basis of Article 114 TFEU.

(32) As suggested in the de Larosière Report, a step-by-step approach is necessary and the European Parliament and the Council should conduct a full review of the ESFS, the ESRB and the ESAs by 17 December 2013.

(33) Since the objective of this Regulation, namely an effective macro-prudential oversight of the Union financial system, cannot be sufficiently achieved by the Member States because of the integration of the Union financial markets, and can therefore be better achieved at the Union level, the Union may adopt measures in accordance with the principle of subsidiarity, as set out in Article 5 of the Treaty on European Union. In accordance with the principle of proportionality, as set out in that Article, this Regulation does not go beyond what is necessary to achieve that objective,

HAVE ADOPTED THIS REGULATION:

CHAPTER I GENERAL PROVISIONS

Article1 Establishment

1. A European Systemic Risk Board (ESRB) is established. It shall have its seat in Frankfurt am Main.

2. The ESRB shall be part of the European System of Financial Supervision (ESFS),

1 European Court Reports 2006 Page I-03771, para 44.

（31）欧盟法院在其2006年5月2日对第C-217/04号案件（大不列颠及北爱尔兰联合王国诉欧洲议会及欧盟理事会）的判决中表明："《欧洲共同体条约》第95条（现《欧洲联盟运行条约》第114条）的措辞并未暗示欧共体立法机构基于该条款通过的措施只能适用于具体成员国。为促进基于《欧洲共同体条约》第95条的立法能得到统一实施和适用，应制定无法律约束力的辅助性和框架性措施时，立法机构可以认为有必要颁布设立该等欧共体机构的规定，由该机构负责推动协调程序的落实"[1]。欧洲系统性风险委员会应通过监控系统性风险并在适当时发布预警和建议，致力于为内部市场进一步的金融一体化所必不可少的金融稳定。该等职责与欧盟金融服务内部市场立法的宗旨紧密关联。因此，欧洲系统性风险委员会应建立在《欧洲联盟运行条约》第114条的基础上。

（32）依《德·拉罗西埃报告》的建议，有必要采用分步走的模式，并且欧洲议会和欧盟理事会应在2013年12月17日前对欧洲金融监管体系、欧洲系统性风险委员会以及欧洲监管机构进行全面的审评。

（33）由于欧盟金融市场的一体化，本条例对欧盟金融系统有效地进行宏观审慎监控的目的单靠成员国自身无法完全实现，但基于此等目的触及的范围，能在欧盟层面上得到更好的实现，因此，欧盟可根据《欧洲联盟条约》第5条规定的辅助性原则制定相关细则。根据《欧洲联盟条约》第5条规定的比例原则，本条例仅作出实现上述目标的必要规定。

兹通过本指令如下：

第一章　总　　则

第1条　设立

1.本条例设立欧洲系统性风险委员会（ESRB），其总部位于美因河畔的法兰克福。

2.欧洲系统性风险委员会应为欧洲金融监管体系（ESFS）的一部分，其目的是确保

---

1 《2006年欧洲法院报告》第44款，第I-03771页。

the purpose of which is to ensure the supervision of the Union's financial system.

3. The ESFS shall comprise:

(a) the ESRB;

(b) the European Supervisory Authority (European Banking Authority) established by Regulation (EU) No 1093/2010;

(c) the European Supervisory Authority (European Insurance and Occupational Pensions Authority) established by Regulation (EU) No 1094/2010;

(d) the European Supervisory Authority (European Securities and Markets Authority) established by Regulation (EU) No 1095/2010;

(e) the Joint Committee of the European Supervisory Authorities (Joint Committee) provided for by Article 54 of Regulation (EU) No 1093/2010, of Regulation (EU) No 1094/2010 and of Regulation (EU) No 1095/2010;

(f) the competent or supervisory authorities in the Member States as specified in the Union acts referred to in Article 1(2) of Regulation(EU) No 1093/2010, of Regulation (EU) No 1094/2010 and of Regulation (EU) No 1095/2010.

4. Pursuant to the principle of sincere cooperation in accordance with Article 4(3) of the Treaty on European Union, the parties to the ESFS shall cooperate with trust and full mutual respect, in particular to ensure that appropriate and reliable information flows between them.

Article 2 Definitions

For the purpose of this Regulation, the following definitions shall apply:

(a) 'financial institution' means any undertaking that falls within the scope of the legislation referred to in Article 1(2) of Regulation(EU) No 1093/2010, of Regulation (EU) No 1094/2010 and of Regulation (EU) No 1095/2010, as well as any other undertaking or entity in the Union whose main business is of a similar nature;

(b) 'financial system' means all financial institutions, markets, products and market infrastructures;

(c) 'systemic risk' means a risk of disruption in the financial system with the potential to have serious negative consequences for the internal market and the real economy. All types of financial intermediaries, markets and infrastructure may be potentially systemically important to some degree.

Article 3 Mission, objectives and tasks

1. The ESRB shall be responsible for the macro-prudential oversight of the financial system within the Union in order to contribute to the prevention or mitigation of systemic risks to financial stability in the Union that arise from developments within the financial system and taking into account macroeconomic developments, so as to avoid periods of widespread financial distress. It shall contribute to the smooth functioning of the internal

对欧盟金融系统的监管。

3.欧洲金融监管体系由下列机构组成：

(a)欧洲系统性风险委员会；

(b)依据第1093/2010号(欧盟)条例设立的欧洲监管机构(欧洲银行业管理局)；

(c)依据第1094/2010号(欧盟)条例设立的欧洲监管机构(欧洲保险与职业养老金管理局)；

(d)依据第1095/2010号(欧盟)条例设立的欧洲监管机构(欧洲证券与市场管理局)；

(e)第1093/2010号(欧盟)条例、第1094/2010号(欧盟)条例以及第1095/2010号(欧盟)条例的第54条所规定的欧洲监管机构联合委员会(以下简称联合委员会)；

(f)第1093/2010号(欧盟)条例、第1094/2010号(欧盟)条例以及第1095/2010号(欧盟)条例的第1条第2款所述欧盟立法所规定的成员国主管部门或监管机构。

4.根据《欧洲联盟条约》第4条第3款所指的精诚合作原则，欧洲金融监管体系各方应在合作过程中相互信任和充分尊重，以特别确保各方能够彼此交流适当和可靠的信息。

第2条　定义

在本条例中适用下列定义：

(a)“金融机构”一词，系指属于第1093/2010号(欧盟)条例、第1094/2010号(欧盟)条例以及第1095/2010号(欧盟)条例的第1条第2款所述范围内的任何企业，以及主营业务具有类似性质的任何其他欧盟企业或实体；

(b)“金融系统”一词，系指所有金融机构、市场、产品和市场基础设施；

(c)“系统性风险”一词，系指金融系统发生扰乱并可能会对内部市场和实体经济造成严重消极后果的风险。所有类型的金融中介机构、市场和基础设施均可能存在某程度上的系统重要性。

第3条　使命、宗旨和职责

1.欧洲系统性风险委员会应负责对欧盟金融系统的宏观审慎监控，致力于预防或缓释欧盟金融稳定面临的由金融系统内的变化造成的系统性风险，并对宏观经济的发展予以考量，以期避免金融系统出现大范围的困境。欧洲系统性风险委员会应致力于促进内部市场的平稳运行，从而确保金融行业持续促进经济增长。

market and thereby ensure a sustainable contribution of the financial sector to economic growth.

2. For the purposes of paragraph 1, the ESRB shall carry out the following tasks:

(a) determining and/or collecting and analysing all the relevant and necessary information, for the purposes of achieving the objectives described in paragraph 1;

(b) identifying and prioritising systemic risks;

(c) issuing warnings where such systemic risks are deemed to be significant and, where appropriate, making those warnings public;

(d) issuing recommendations for remedial action in response to the risks identified and, where appropriate, making those recommendations public;

(e) when the ESRB determines that an emergency situation may arise pursuant to Article 18 of Regulation (EU) No 1093/2010, of Regulation (EU) No 1094/2010 and of Regulation (EU) No 1095/2010 issuing a confidential warning addressed to the Council and providing the Council with an assessment of the situation, in order to enable the Council to assess the need to adopt a decision addressed to the ESAs determining the existence of an emergency situation;

(f) monitoring the follow-up to warnings and recommendations;

(g) cooperating closely with all the other parties to the ESFS; where appropriate, providing the ESAs with the information on systemic risks required for the performance of their tasks; and, in particular, in collaboration with the ESAs, developing a common set of quantitative and qualitative indicators (risk dashboard) to identify and measure systemic risk;

(h) participating, where appropriate, in the Joint Committee;

(i) coordinating its actions with those of international financial organisations, particularly the IMF and the FSB as well as the relevant bodies in third countries on matters related to macro-prudential oversight;

(j) carrying out other related tasks as specified in Union legislation.

CHAPTER Ⅱ ORGANISATION

Article 4 Structure

1. The ESRB shall have a General Board, a Steering Committee, a Secretariat, an Advisory Scientific Committee and an Advisory Technical Committee.

2. The General Board shall take the decisions necessary to ensure the performance of the tasks entrusted to the ESRB, pursuant to Article 3(2).

2.为第1款之目的,欧洲系统性风险委员会应履行下列职责:

(a)确定和/或收集并分析所有相关和必要的信息,以实现第1款所述目的;

(b)识别并优先处理系统性风险;

(c)当上述系统性风险被视为重大风险时发出预警,并在适当时公布该预警;

(d)为回应其所识别的风险,发出补救行动建议,并在适当时公布该等建议;

(e)欧洲系统性风险委员会判定可能会出现第1093/2010号(欧盟)条例、第1094/2010号(欧盟)条例以及第1095/2010号(欧盟)条例第18条规定的紧急情况的,应向欧盟理事会发布保密的预警,并向欧盟理事会提供对该状况的评估结果,以便欧盟理事会能够评估是否有必要向欧洲监管机构作出关于存在紧急情况的决定;

(f)对预警和建议的跟进行动予以监控;

(g)与欧洲金融监管体系其他各方紧密合作;在适当时向欧洲监管机构提供履行其职责所必要的关于系统性风险的信息;尤其应与各欧洲监管机构合作,制定用以识别和计量系统性风险的一组通用的定量和定性指标(风险监控表);

(h)在适当时参加联合委员会;

(i)就与宏观审慎监控相关的事宜,与国际金融组织,特别是国际货币基金组织和金融稳定委员会以及第三国的相关机构协调行动;

(j)履行欧盟立法所规定的其他相关职责。

第二章 组织结构

第4条 结构

1.欧洲系统性风险委员会设有总委员会,指导委员会,秘书处,科学咨询委员会以及技术咨询委员会。

2.总委员会应作出必要的决策,以确保根据第3条第2款委托给欧洲系统性风险委员会的职责得到履行。

3. The Steering Committee shall assist in the decision-making process of the ESRB by preparing the meetings of the General Board, reviewing the documents to be discussed and monitoring the progress of the ESRB's ongoing work.

4. The Secretariat shall be responsible for the day-to-day business of the ESRB. It shall provide high-quality analytical, statistical, administrative and logistical support to the ESRB under the direction of the Chair and the Steering Committee in accordance with Council Regulation (EU) No 1096/2010[1]. It shall also draw on technical advice from the ESAs, national central banks and national supervisors.

5. The Advisory Scientific Committee and the Advisory Technical Committee referred to in Articles 12 and 13 shall provide advice and assistance on issues relevant to the work of the ESRB.

Article 5 Chair and Vice-Chairs of the ESRB

1. The ESRB shall be chaired by the President of the ECB for a term of 5 years following the entry into force of this Regulation. For the subsequent terms, the Chair of the ESRB shall be designated in accordance with the modalities determined on the basis of the review provided for in Article 20.

2. The first Vice-Chair shall be elected by and from the members of the General Council of the ECB for a term of 5 years, with regard to the need for a balanced representation of Member States overall and between those whose currency is the euro and those whose currency is not the euro. The first Vice-Chair may be re-elected once.

3. The second Vice-Chair shall be the Chair of the Joint Committee as appointed pursuant to Article 55(3) of Regulation (EU) No 1093/2010, of Regulation (EU) No 1094/2010 and of Regulation (EU) No 1095/2010.

4. The Chair and the Vice-Chairs shall present to the European Parliament, during a public hearing, how they intend to discharge their duties under this Regulation.

5. The Chair shall preside at the meetings of the General Board and the Steering Committee.

6. The Vice-Chairs, in order of precedence, shall preside at the General Board and/or the Steering Committee when the Chair is unable to participate in a meeting.

7. If the term of office of a member of the General Council of the ECB elected as first Vice-Chair ends before the completion of the five-year term or if for any reason the first Vice-Chair is unable to discharge his duties, a new first Vice-Chair shall be elected in accordance with paragraph 2.

8. The Chair shall represent the ESRB externally.

1 See page 162 of this Official Journal.

3.指导委员会应通过筹备总委员会的会议、审评待讨论的文件以及监控欧洲系统性风险委员会当前工作的进度,协助欧洲系统性风险委员会作出决策。

4.秘书处应负责欧洲系统性风险委员会的日常业务。根据欧盟理事会第1096/2010号(欧盟)条例[1],秘书处应在主席和指导委员会的指导下,向欧洲系统性风险委员会提供高水平的分析、统计、行政和后勤支持。秘书处还应听取来自各欧洲监管机构、成员国中央银行和国家级监管机构的技术性建议。

5.第12条和第13条所述的科学咨询委员会和技术咨询委员会应就欧洲系统性风险委员会工作的相关事宜提供建议和协助。

第5条　欧洲系统性风险委员会的主席和副主席

1.欧洲系统性风险委员会的主席应由欧洲中央银行行长担任,任期为5年,自本条例生效后开始。继任主席应按照依第20条作出的审评结果所确定的方式指定。

2.委员会第一副主席应由欧洲中央银行总理事会在其理事中推选,任期5年,应顾及委员会应均衡地代表不同成员国以及欧元国与非欧元国的需要。第一副主席可连选连任1次。

3.第二副主席应为根据第1093/2010号(欧盟)条例、第1094/2010号(欧盟)条例以及第1095/2010号(欧盟)条例第55条第3款任命的联合委员会主席。

4.主席和副主席均应在公开听证中向欧洲议会陈述其将如何履行本条例中的职责。

5.总委员会和指导委员会的会议应由主席主持。

6.在主席无法出席会议的情形下,由第一副主席主持;第一副主席也不能出席的,由第二副主席主持总委员会及/或指导委员会的会议。

7.当选为第一副主席的欧洲中央银行总理事会理事的任期在第一副主席5年任期内结束,或第一副主席由于任何其他原因无法履行职责的,应根据第2款选出新的第一副主席。

8.主席对外代表欧洲系统性风险委员会。

1 请见本《欧盟公报》,第162页。

Article 6 General Board

1. Members of the General Board with voting rights shall comprise:

(a) the President and the Vice-President of the ECB;

(b) the Governors of the national central banks;

(c) a Member of the Commission;

(d) the Chairperson of the European Supervisory Authority (European Banking Authority);

(e) the Chairperson of the European Supervisory Authority (European Insurance and Occupational Pensions Authority);

(f) the Chairperson of the European Supervisory Authority (European Securities and Markets Authority);

(g) the Chair and the two Vice-Chairs of the Advisory Scientific Committee;

(h) the Chair of the Advisory Technical Committee.

2. Members of the General Board without voting rights shall comprise:

(a) one high-level representative per Member State of the competent national supervisory authorities, in accordance with paragraph 3;

(b) the President of the Economic and Financial Committee (EFC).

3. With regard to the representation of the national supervisory authorities under paragraph 2(a), the respective high-level representatives shall rotate depending on the item discussed, unless the national supervisory authorities of a particular Member State have agreed on a common representative.

4. The General Board shall establish rules of procedure for the ESRB.

Article 7 Impartiality

1. When participating in the activities of the General Board and of the Steering Committee or when conducting any other activity relating to the ESRB, the members of the ESRB shall perform their duties impartially and solely in the interest of the Union as a whole. They shall not seek nor take instructions from the Member States, the Union institutions or any other public or private body.

2. No member of the General Board (whether voting or non-voting) shall have a function in the financial industry.

3. Neither the Member States, the Union institutions nor any other public or private body shall seek to influence the members of the ESRB in the performance of the tasks set out in Article 3(2).

Article 8 Professional secrecy

1. Members of the General Board and any other persons who work or who have worked for or in connection with the ESRB (including the relevant staff of central banks, the Advisory Scientific Committee, the Advisory Technical Committee, the ESAs and the

第6条　总委员会

1.总委员会有表决权的委员由下列人员组成：

(a)欧洲中央银行的行长和副行长；

(b)成员国中央银行行长；

(c)欧盟委员会的1名委员；

(d)欧洲监管机构(欧洲银行业管理局)主席；

(e)欧洲监管机构(欧洲保险与职业养老金管理局)主席；

(f)欧洲监管机构(欧洲证券与市场管理局)主席；

(g)科学咨询委员会的主席以及2名副主席；

(h)技术咨询委员会的主席。

2.总委员会中无表决权的委员应包括：

(a)根据第3款，各成员国1名来自国家级主管部门的高级别代表；

(b)经济与金融委员会(EFC)的主席。

3.就第2条第a款中的国家级监管机构代表而言，各国家级监管机构的高级别代表应根据所讨论的议题轮流参加总委员会，某成员国的各个相关国家级监管机构一致同意以某位共同代表作为其全体代表的除外。

4.总委员会应为欧洲系统性风险委员会制定程序规则。

第7条　公正性

1.欧洲系统性风险委员会的委员在参与总委员会以及指导委员会的活动或开展任何其他与欧洲系统性风险委员会有关的活动时，应公正地并仅为欧盟整体利益履行其职责，不得寻求或听从成员国、欧盟机构或任何其他公共和私人机构的指示。

2.总委员会的任何委员(不论是否有表决权)均不得在金融业内任职。

3.成员国、欧盟机构或任何其他公共或私人机构均不得试图影响欧洲系统性风险委员会的委员履行第3条第2款所规定的职责。

第8条　职业保密

1.总委员会的委员以及欧洲系统性风险委员会的任何现任或前任工作人员或任何工作内容与欧洲系统性风险委员会相关或曾经相关的人(包括成员国中央银行、科学咨询委员会、技术咨询委员会、各欧洲监管机构以及各成员国国家级主管部门的相

Member States' competent national supervisory authorities) shall not disclose information that is subject to professional secrecy, even after their duties have ceased.

2. Information received by members of the ESRB shall be used only in the course of their duties and in performing the tasks set out in Article 3(2).

3. Without prejudice to Article 16 and the application of criminal law, no confidential information received by the persons referred to in paragraph 1 whilst performing their duties shall be divulged to any person or authority whatsoever, except in summary or aggregate form, such that individual financial institutions cannot be identified.

4. The ESRB shall, together with the ESAs, agree on and establish specific confidentiality procedures in order to safeguard information regarding individual financial institutions and information from which individual financial institutions can be identified.

Article 9 Meetings of the General Board

1. Ordinary plenary meetings of the General Board shall be convened by the Chair of the ESRB and shall take place at least four times a year. Extraordinary meetings may be convened at the initiative of the Chair of the ESRB or at the request of at least one third of the members of the General Board with voting rights.

2 Each member shall be present in person at the meetings of the General Board and shall not be represented.

3. By way of derogation from paragraph 2, a member who is prevented from attending the meetings for a period of at least 3 months may appoint an alternate. That member may also be replaced by a person who has been formally appointed under the rules governing the institution concerned for the substitution of representatives on a temporary basis.

4. Where appropriate, high-level representatives from international financial organisations carrying out activities directly related to the tasks of the ESRB set out in Article 3(2) may be invited to attend the meetings of the General Board.

5. Participation in the work of the ESRB may be open to high-level representatives of the relevant authorities from third countries, in particular from EEA countries, strictly limited to issues of particular relevance to those countries. Arrangements may be made by the ESRB specifying, in particular, the nature, scope and procedural aspects of the involvement of those third countries in the work of the ESRB. Such arrangements may provide for representation, on an ad-hoc basis, as an observer, on the General Board and should concern only items of relevance to those countries, excluding any case where the situation of individual financial institutions or Member States may be discussed.

6. The proceedings of the meetings shall be confidential.

Article 10 Voting modalities of the General Board

1. Each member of the General Board with a voting right shall have one vote.

2. Without prejudice to the voting procedures set out in Article 18(1), the General Board

关工作人员）在任职期间以及任职结束后均不得披露受限于职业保密的信息。

2.欧洲系统性风险委员会委员接收到的信息应仅在其任职期间履行第3条第2款所规定的职责时使用。

3.在不影响第16条以及刑法适用的情形下，第1款所述人员在履行职责时接收到的任何保密信息均不得泄露给任何个人或部门，但是，以无法识别具体金融机构的摘要或汇总形式披露的除外。

4.欧洲系统性风险委员会应与欧洲监管机构约定并建立具体的保密程序，以保护关于具体金融机构的信息以及从中可识别具体金融机构的信息。

第9条　总委员会会议

1.总委员会的全体例会由欧洲系统性风险委员会的主席召集，每年应至少召开4次。临时会议可由欧洲系统性风险委员会的主席主动召集或经总委员会中1/3以上具有表决权的委员的请求召集。

2.各委员均应亲自出席总委员会的会议，不得由他人代为出席。

3.作为第2款的例外，至少3个月不能参加会议的委员可指定1名替补人员。该委员也可由根据所涉机构适用的临时代表替补规则正式指定的人员替代。

4.国际金融组织中的高级别代表如其活动与第3条第2款所规定的欧洲系统性风险委员会职责直接相关，可在适当时被邀请参加总委员会的会议。

5.来自第三国尤其是欧洲经济区国家的相关部门高级别代表可参与欧洲系统性风险委员会的工作，但其参与范围应严格限于与本国相关的事宜。欧洲系统性风险委员会可以制定相关安排，特别规定该等第三国参与欧洲系统性风险委员会工作的性质、范围及程序，该等安排可包括临时派代表作为观察员出席总委员会，但应仅涉及与该等国家相关的事项，讨论议题涉及某个金融机构或成员国状况的应予排除。

6.会议议程应予保密。

第10条　总委员会的表决方式

1.总委员会有表决权的每名委员均各有一票投票权。

2.在不影响第18条第1款规定的表决程序的情形下，总委员会应按有表决权的与

shall act by a simple majority of members present with voting rights. In the event of a tie, the Chair of the ESRB shall have the casting vote.

3. By derogation from paragraph 2, a majority of two-thirds of the votes cast shall be required to adopt a recommendation or to make a warning or recommendation public.

4. A quorum of two-thirds of the members with voting rights shall be required for any vote to be taken by the General Board. If the quorum is not met, the Chair of the ESRB may convene an extraordinary meeting at which decisions may be taken with a quorum of one-third. The rules of procedure referred to in Article 6(4) shall provide for adequate notice for convening an extraordinary meeting.

Article 11 Steering Committee

1. The Steering Committee shall be composed of:

(a) the Chair and first Vice-Chair of the ESRB;

(b) the Vice-President of the ECB;

(c) four other members of the General Board who are also members of the General Council of the ECB, with regard to the need for a balanced representation of Member States overall and between those whose currency is the euro and those whose currency is not the euro. They shall be elected by and from among the members of the General Board who are also members of the General Council of the ECB, for a period of 3 years;

(d) a Member of the Commission;

(e) the Chairperson of the European Supervisory Authority (European Banking Authority);

(f) the Chairperson of the European Supervisory Authority (European Insurance and Occupational Pensions Authority);

(g) the Chairperson of the European Supervisory Authority (European Securities and Markets Authority);

(h) the President of the EFC;

(i) the Chair of the Advisory Scientific Committee; and

(j) the Chair of the Advisory Technical Committee.

Any vacancy for an elected member of the Steering Committee shall be filled by the election of a new member by the General Board.

2. Meetings of the Steering Committee shall be convened by the Chair of the ESRB at least quarterly, before each meeting of the General Board. The Chair of the ESRB may also convene ad-hoc meetings.

Article 12 Advisory Scientific Committee

1. The Advisory Scientific Committee shall be composed of the Chair of the Advisory Technical Committee and 15 experts representing a wide range of skills and experiences proposed by the Steering Committee and approved by the General Board for a four-year,

会委员的简单多数规则行事。票数相同时,欧洲系统性风险委员会主席的投票具有决定性。

3.作为第2款的例外,要通过建议或公布预警或建议,须获得2/3的大多数赞成票。

4.总委员会任何表决的法定人数均为具有表决权的委员总数的2/3。如未达到法定人数,则欧洲系统性风险委员会主席可召集临时会议,临时会议通过决定所需的法定人数为有表决权委员总数的1/3。第6条第4款所述的程序规则应就召集临时会议时如何进行充分的通知作出规定。

第11条　指导委员会

1.指导委员会应由下列人员组成:

(a)欧洲系统性风险委员会的主席和第一副主席;

(b)欧洲中央银行副行长;

(c)总委员会委员中同时担任欧洲中央银行总理事会理事的4名其他成员,应顾及总委员会应均衡地代表不同成员国以及欧元成员国和非欧元成员国的需要,由总委员会委员中同时担任欧洲中央银行总理事会理事的委员在彼此中推选,任期为3年;

(d)欧盟委员会的1名委员;

(e)欧洲监管机构(欧洲银行业管理局)主席;

(f)欧洲监管机构(欧洲保险与职业养老金管理局)主席;

(g)欧洲监管机构(欧洲证券与市场管理局)主席;

(h)经济与金融委员会主席;

(i)科学咨询委员会主席;及

(j)技术咨询委员会主席。

指导委员会的委员出现任何空缺时,应由总委员会选出1名新委员填补。

2.欧洲系统性风险委员会主席应至少每个季度召集1次指导委员会会议,并在总委员会每次召开会议之前召集。欧洲系统性风险委员会主席还可召集临时会议。

第12条　科学咨询委员会

1.科学咨询委员会应由技术咨询委员会主席以及来自各专业领域的15名专家组成,该等专家由指导委员会提名并经总委员会批准,任期4年,可续任。候选人不得为欧洲监管机构的成员,并应根据其总体技能和其在学术领域或其他行业(尤其是中小

renewable mandate. The nominees shall not be members of the ESAs and shall be chosen on the basis of their general competence and their diverse experience in academic fields or other sectors, in particular in small and medium-sized enterprises or trade-unions, or as providers or consumers of financial services.

2. The Chair and the two Vice-Chairs of the Advisory Scientific Committee shall be appointed by the General Board following a proposal from the Chair of the ESRB and they shall each have a high level of relevant expertise and knowledge, for example by virtue of their academic background in the sectors of banking, securities markets, or insurance and occupational pensions. The chairmanship of the Advisory Scientific Committee should rotate between those three persons.

3. The Advisory Scientific Committee shall provide advice and assistance to the ESRB in accordance with Article 4(5), at the request of the Chair of the ESRB.

4. The ESRB Secretariat shall support the work of the Advisory Scientific Committee and the head of the Secretariat shall participate in its meetings.

5. Where appropriate, the Advisory Scientific Committee shall organise consultations at an early stage with stakeholders such as market participants, consumer bodies and academic experts, in an open and transparent manner, while taking into account the requirement of confidentiality.

6. The Advisory Scientific Committee shall be provided with all necessary means in order to successfully complete its tasks.

Article 13 Advisory Technical Committee

1. The Advisory Technical Committee shall be composed of:

(a) a representative of each national central bank and a representative of the ECB;

(b) one representative per Member State of the competent national supervisory authorities, in accordance with the second subparagraph;

(c) a representative of the European Supervisory Authority (European Banking Authority);

(d) a representative of the European Supervisory Authority (European Insurance and Occupational Pensions Authority);

(e) a representative of the European Supervisory Authority (European Securities and Markets Authority);

(f) two representatives of the Commission;

(g) a representative of the EFC; and

(h) a representative of the Advisory Scientific Committee.

The supervisory authorities of each Member State shall choose one representative in the Advisory Technical Committee. With regard to the representation of national supervisory authorities under point (b) of the first subparagraph, the respective representatives shall

企业或行业工会)或作为金融服务提供商或消费者的各种经验选出。

2.科学咨询委员会的主席和2名副主席应由总委员会根据欧洲系统性风险委员会主席的提议任命,并且均应具备高水平的相关特长和专业知识(如银行业、证券市场或保险和职业养老金等行业的学术背景)。科学咨询委员会的主席职责应由这3人轮流担任。

3.经欧洲系统性风险委员会主席请求,科学咨询委员会应按第4条第5款为欧洲系统性风险委员会提供建议和协助。

4.欧洲系统性风险委员会的秘书处应支持科学咨询委员会的工作,并且秘书长应参加其会议。

5.科学咨询委员会适当时并在符合保密性要求的前提下,应在早期以公开、透明的方式组织由市场参与者、消费者团体、学术专家等利益相关者参加的意见征询活动。

6.应为科学咨询委员会提供顺利完成其职责所必要的各种条件。

第13条　技术咨询委员会

1.技术咨询委员会应由下列人员组成:

(a)各成员国中央银行的1名代表以及欧洲中央银行的1名代表;

(b)根据第2项,各成员国1名来自国家级主管部门的代表;

(c)欧洲监管机构(欧洲银行业管理局)1名代表;

(d)欧洲监管机构(欧洲保险与职业养老金管理局)1名代表;

(e)欧洲监管机构(欧洲证券与市场管理局)1名代表;

(f)欧盟委员会2名代表;

(g)经济与金融委员会1名代表;及

(h)科学咨询委员会1名代表。

各成员国的监管机构应各选出1名代表参加技术咨询委员会。就第1项第b目中的国家级监管机构代表而言,各国家级监管机构的代表应根据所讨论的议题轮流参加技术咨询委员会,某成员国的各个相关国家级监管机构一致同意以某位共同代表作

rotate depending on the item discussed, unless the national supervisory authorities of a particular Member State have agreed on a common representative.

2. The Chair of the Advisory Technical Committee shall be appointed by the General Board following a proposal from the Chair of the ESRB.

3. The Advisory Technical Committee shall provide advice and assistance to the ESRB in accordance with Article 4(5) at the request of the Chair of the ESRB.

4. The ESRB Secretariat shall support the work of the Advisory Technical Committee and the head of the Secretariat shall participate in its meetings.

5. The Advisory Technical Committee shall be provided with all necessary means in order to successfully complete its tasks.

Article 14 Other sources of advice

In performing the tasks set out in Article 3(2), the ESRB shall, where appropriate, seek the views of relevant private sector stakeholders.

CHAPTER Ⅲ TASKS

Article 15 Collection and exchange of information

1. The ESRB shall provide the ESAs with the information on risks necessary for the achievement of their tasks.

2. The ESAs, the European System of Central Banks (ESCB), the Commission, the national supervisory authorities and national statistics authorities shall cooperate closely with the ESRB and shall provide it with all the information necessary for the fulfilment of its tasks in accordance with Union legislation.

3. Subject to Article 36(2) of Regulation (EU) No 1093/2010, of Regulation (EU) No 1094/2010 and of Regulation (EU) No 1095/2010, the ESRB may request information from the ESAs, as a rule in summary or aggregate form such that individual financial institutions cannot be identified.

4. Before requesting information in accordance with this Article, the ESRB shall first take account of the existing statistics produced, disseminated and developed by the European Statistical System and the ESCB.

5. If the requested information is not available or is not made available in a timely manner, the ESRB may request the information from the ESCB, the national supervisory authorities or the national statistics authorities. If the information remains unavailable, the ESRB may request it from the Member State concerned, without prejudice to the prerogatives conferred, respectively, on the Council, the Commission (Eurostat), the ECB,

为其全体代表的除外。

2.技术咨询委员会的主席应由总委员会根据欧洲系统性风险委员会主席的提名任命。

3.根据第4条第5款,经欧洲系统性风险委员会主席请求,技术咨询委员会应为欧洲系统性风险委员会提供建议和协助。

4.欧洲系统性风险委员会秘书处应支持技术咨询委员会的工作,秘书长应参加技术咨询委员会的会议。

5.应为技术咨询委员会提供顺利完成其职责所必要的各种条件。

第14条　其他意见来源

在适当时,欧洲系统性风险委员会履行第3条第2款规定的职责时应咨询相关私营部门利益相关者的意见。

第三章　职　　责

第15条　信息的收集与交流信息

1.欧洲系统性风险委员会应向各欧洲监管机构提供履行其职责所必要的风险信息。

2.根据欧盟立法,各欧洲监管机构、欧洲中央银行体系(ESCB)、欧盟委员会、国家级监管机构以及国家级统计机构应与欧洲系统性风险委员会紧密合作,并向后者提供其履行职责所必要的一切信息。

3.在遵守第1093/2010号(欧盟)条例、第1094/2010号(欧盟)条例以及第1095/2010号(欧盟)条例第36条第2款的前提下,欧洲系统性风险委员会可请求各欧洲监管机构以不透露具体金融机构信息的摘要或汇总形式向其提供相关信息。

4.在根据本条提出信息请求前,欧洲系统性风险委员会应先考虑欧洲统计系统和欧洲中央银行体系已经制作、传播并开发的现有统计数据。

5.未能获得或未能及时获得请求的信息的,欧洲系统性风险委员会可请求欧洲中央银行体系、国家级监管机构或国家级统计机构提供信息。仍然无法获得信息的,欧洲系统性风险委员会可向所涉成员国提出信息请求,但不得影响在统计和数据收集领域分别授予欧盟理事会、欧盟委员会(欧洲统计局)、欧洲中央银行、欧元体系以及欧洲中央银行体系的特殊权利。

the Eurosystem and the ESCB in the field of statistics and data collection.

6. If the ESRB requests information that is not in summary or aggregate form, the reasoned request shall explain why data on the respective individual financial institution is deemed to be systemically relevant, and necessary, considering the prevailing market situation.

7. Before each request for information which is not in summary or aggregate form, the ESRB shall duly consult the relevant European Supervisory Authority in order to ensure that the request is justified and proportionate. If the relevant European Supervisory Authority does not consider the request to be justified and proportionate, it shall, without delay, send the request back to the ESRB and ask for additional justification. After the ESRB has provided the relevant European Supervisory Authority with such additional justification, the requested information shall be transmitted to the ESRB by the addressees of the request, provided that they have legal access to the relevant information.

Article 16 Warnings and recommendations

1. When significant risks to the achievement of the objective in Article 3(1) are identified, the ESRB shall provide warnings and, where appropriate, issue recommendations for remedial action, including, where appropriate, for legislative initiatives.

2. Warnings or recommendations issued by the ESRB in accordance with Article 3 (2)(c) and (d) may be of either a general or a specific nature and shall be addressed in particular to the Union as a whole or to one or more Member States, or to one or more of the ESAs, or to one or more of the national supervisory authorities. If a warning or a recommendation is addressed to one or more of the national supervisory authorities, the Member State(s) concerned shall also be informed thereof. Recommendations shall include a specified timeline for the policy response. Recommendations may also be addressed to the Commission in respect of the relevant Union legislation.

3. At the same time as they are transmitted to the addressees in accordance with paragraph 2, the warnings or recommendations shall be transmitted, in accordance with strict rules of confidentiality, to the Council and the Commission and, where addressed to one or more national supervisory authorities, to the ESAs.

4. In order to enhance the awareness of risks in the economy of the Union and to prioritise such risks, the ESRB, in close cooperation with the other parties to the ESFS, shall elaborate a colour-coded system corresponding to situations of different risk levels.

Once the criteria for such classification have been elaborated, the ESRB's warnings and recommendations shall indicate, on a case-by-case basis, and where appropriate, to which category the risk belongs.

Article 17 Follow-up of the ESRB recommendations

1. If a recommendation referred to in Article 3(2)(d) is addressed to the Commission,

6.欧洲系统性风险委员会所请求的信息不属于摘要或汇总信息的，应在信息请求中解释，为何在现有市场状况下，其将所请求的具体金融机构的数据视为具有系统相关性和必要性。

7.在每次提出并非摘要或汇总形式的信息请求前，欧洲系统性风险委员会应适当咨询相关的欧洲监管机构意见，以确保该请求是合理并成比例的。相关的欧洲监管机构认为该请求是不合理、不成比例的，应立即将该请求发还欧洲系统性风险委员会并要求提供补充理由。欧洲系统性风险委员会向相关欧洲监管机构提供补充的理由后，在被请求方自身能合法获得相关信息的前提下，信息被请求方应将所请求的信息发送给欧洲系统性风险委员会。

第16条　预警和建议

1.若发现存在损及第3条第1款的目标的重大风险，欧洲系统性风险委员会应提供预警并在适当时提出补救行动建议，包括在适当时提出立法倡议。

2.欧洲系统性风险委员会可根据第3条第2款第c项和第d项发布一般或特别预警或建议，既可以针对整个欧盟，也可以针对一个或多个成员国，或一个或多个欧洲监管机构或一个或多个国家级监管机构。针对一个或多个国家级监管机构发布预警或建议的，还应告知所涉成员国相关情况。建议中应包含作出政策回应的具体时间表。欧洲系统性风险委员会也可向欧盟委员会提出与欧盟立法有关的建议。

3.根据第2款将预警或建议发送给被预警方或被建议方的同时，应按照严格的保密规则将其发送给欧盟理事会和欧盟委员会。针对一个或多个国家级监管机构的预警或建议，还应同时发送给各欧洲监管机构。

4.为强化欧盟经济风险意识并优先处理该等风险，欧洲系统性风险委员会应与欧洲金融监管体系的其他各方紧密合作，建立与各种风险等级相对应的颜色代码系统。

制定上述分类标准之后，欧洲系统性风险委员会的预警和建议应根据具体情况并在适当时说明风险所属类别。

第17条　对欧洲系统性风险委员会建议的跟进

1.第3条第2款第d项所述建议以欧盟委员会、一个或多个成员国、一个或多个欧洲

to one or more Member States, to one or more ESAs, or to one or more national supervisory authorities, the addressees shall communicate to the ESRB and to the Council the actions undertaken in response to the recommendation and shall provide adequate justification for any inaction. Where relevant, the ESRB shall, subject to strict rules of confidentiality, inform the ESAs without delay of the answers received.

2. If the ESRB decides that its recommendation has not been followed or that the addressees have failed to provide adequate justification for their inaction, it shall, subject to strict rules of confidentiality, inform the addressees, the Council and, where relevant, the European Supervisory Authority concerned.

3. If the ESRB has made a decision under paragraph 2 on a recommendation that has been made public following the procedure set out in Article 18(1), the European Parliament may invite the Chair of the ESRB to present that decision and the addressees may request to participate in an exchange of views.

Article 18 Public warnings and recommendations

1. The General Board shall decide on a case-by-case basis, after having informed the Council sufficiently in advance so that it is able to react, whether a warning or a recommendation should be made public. Notwithstanding Article 10(3), a quorum of two-thirds shall always apply to decisions taken by the General Board under this paragraph.

2. If the General Board decides to make a warning or recommendation public, it shall inform the addressees in advance.

3. The addressees of warnings and recommendations made public by the ESRB shall also be provided with the right of making public their views and reasoning in response thereto.

4. Where the General Board decides not to make a warning or a recommendation public, the addressees and, where appropriate, the Council and the ESAs shall take all the measures necessary for the protection of their confidential nature.

CHAPTER Ⅳ FINAL PROVISIONS

Article 19 Accountability and reporting obligations

1. At least annually and more frequently in the event of widespread financial distress, the Chair of the ESRB shall be invited to an annual hearing in the European Parliament, marking the publication of the ESRB's annual report to the European Parliament and the Council. That hearing shall be conducted separately from the monetary

监管机构或一个或多个国家级监管机构为对象的，被建议方应向欧洲系统性风险委员会以及欧盟理事会通知其所采取的行动，作为回应；不采取行动的，应提供充分的理由。适当时，欧洲系统性风险委员会应在遵守严格的保密规则的前提下，立即将收到的答复通知各欧洲监管机构。

2.欧洲系统性风险委员会认定其建议未得到跟进，或被建议方无法提供充分的理由解释为何不采取行动的，应在遵守严格的保密规则的前提下通知被建议方和欧盟理事会，适当时，还应通知所涉的欧洲监管机构。

3.对于遵循第18条第1款规定的程序所公布的建议，欧洲系统性风险委员会作出了第2款中的决定的，欧洲议会可以要求欧洲系统性风险委员会主席向其递交该项决定，而被建议方可以请求参与意见交流。

第18条　公开的预警和建议

1.在提前充分通知欧盟理事会以便其能作出反应之后，总委员会应根据具体情况决定是否应公布某项预警或建议。尽管有第10条第3款的规定，总委员会依照本款所作的决定应总是适用2/3法定人数的规定。

2.总委员会决定公布预警或建议的，应提前通知被预警方或被建议方。

3.欧洲系统性风险委员会所公布的预警和建议所针对的被预警方和被建议方有权公开其面对预警和建议的观点和论述。

4.总委员会决定不公布预警或建议的，被预警方或被建议方以及在适当时欧盟理事会以及各欧洲监管机构应采取所有必要的措施对其进行保密。

第四章　最终条款

第19条　问责机制和报告义务

1.欧洲系统性风险委员会主席应至少每年1次获邀参与欧洲议会的年度听证，向欧洲议会和欧盟理事会公布欧洲系统性风险委员会的年度报告，在金融系统出现大范围困境的情形下，应更频繁地受邀参与欧洲议会的听证。该等听证应在欧洲议会和欧洲中央银行行长就货币事宜的对话之外单独进行。

dialogue between the European Parliament and the President of the ECB.

2. The annual report referred to in paragraph 1 shall contain the information that the General Board decides to make public in accordance with Article 18. The annual report shall be made available to the public.

3. The ESRB shall also examine specific issues at the invitation of the European Parliament, the Council or the Commission.

4. The European Parliament may request the Chair of the ESRB to attend a hearing of the competent Committees of the European Parliament.

5. The Chair of the ESRB shall hold confidential oral discussions at least twice a year and more often if deemed appropriate, behind closed doors with the Chair and Vice-Chairs of the Economic and Monetary Affairs Committee of the European Parliament on the ongoing activity of the ESRB. An agreement shall be concluded between the European Parliament and the ESRB on the detailed modalities of organising those meetings, with a view to ensuring full confidentiality in accordance with Article 8. The ESRB shall provide a copy of that agreement to the Council.

Article 20 Review

By 17 December 2013, the European Parliament and the Council shall examine this Regulation on the basis of a report from the Commission and, after having received an opinion from the ECB and the ESAs, shall determine whether the mission and organisation of the ESRB need to be reviewed.

They shall, in particular, review the modalities for the designation or election of the Chair of the ESRB.

Article 21 Entry into force

This Regulation shall enter into force on the day following its publication in the Official Journal of the European Union.

This Regulation shall be binding in its entirety and directly applicable in all Member States.

Done at Strasbourg, 24 November 2010.

For the European Parliament
The President
J. BUZEK

For the Council
The President
O. CHASTEL

2.第1款所述的年度报告应包含总委员会根据第18条决定公布的信息。年度报告应向公众公开。

3.欧洲系统性风险委员会还应经欧洲议会、欧盟理事会或欧盟委员会的要求对某些特定问题进行审查。

4.欧洲议会可请求欧洲系统性风险委员会的主席参与欧洲议会相关委员会的听证会。

5.欧洲系统性风险委员会的主席每年至少参与欧洲议会经济与货币事务委员会主席和副主席就欧洲系统性风险委员会开展中的活动举行的2次保密关门口头讨论会,并在其认为适当的情形下应更频繁地参与。欧洲议会和欧洲系统性风险委员会应就组织该等会议的具体形式达成一致协议,以确保符合第8条的全面保密要求。欧洲系统性风险委员会应向欧盟理事会提供该协议的复本。

第20条 审评

2013年12月17日前,欧洲议会和欧盟理事会应根据从欧盟委员会收到的报告对本条例进行审查,并应在收到欧洲中央银行和欧洲监管机构的意见之后决定是否有必要审评欧洲系统性风险委员会的使命和组织结构。

欧洲议会和欧盟理事会尤其应审评欧洲系统性风险委员会主席的指定或推选形式。

第21条 生效

本条例应于《欧盟公报》公布,公布的次日生效。

本条例所有内容对各成员国均具有约束力,并直接适用于所有成员国。

2010年11月24日于斯特拉斯堡通过。

欧洲议会议长　　　　欧盟理事会主席

J.布泽克　　　　O.查斯特尔

REGULATION (EU) NO 1093/2010 OF THE EUROPEAN PARLIAMENT AND OF THE COUNCIL

欧洲议会与欧盟理事会第 1093/2010 号(欧盟)条例

REGULATION (EU) NO 1093/2010 OF THE EUROPEAN PARLIAMENT AND OF THE COUNCIL

of 24 November 2010 establishing a European Supervisory Authority (European Banking Authority), amending Decision No 716/2009/EC and repealing Commission Decision 2009/78/EC

THE EUROPEAN PARLIAMENT AND THE COUNCIL OF THE EUROPEAN UNION,

Having regard to the Treaty on the Functioning of the European Union, and in particular Article 114 thereof,

Having regard to the proposal from the European Commission,

Having regard to the opinion of the European Central Bank [1],

Having regard to the opinion of the European Economic and Social Committee [2],

Acting in accordance with the ordinary legislative procedure [3],

Whereas:

(1) The financial crisis in 2007 and 2008 exposed important shortcomings in financial supervision, both in particular cases and in relation to the financial system as a whole. Nationally based supervisory models have lagged behind financial globalisation and the integrated and interconnected reality of European financial markets, in which many financial institutions operate across borders. The crisis exposed shortcomings in the areas of cooperation, coordination, consistent application of Union law and trust between national supervisors.

(2) Before and during the financial crisis, the European Parliament has called for a

1 OJ C 13, 20. 1. 2010, p. 1.

2 Opinion of 22 January 2010 (not yet published in the Official Journal).

3 Position of the European Parliament of 22 September 2010 (not yet published in the Official Journal) and decision of the Council of17 November 2010.

欧洲议会与欧盟理事会
第 1093/2010 号(欧盟)条例

[本条例于 2010 年 11 月 24 日通过,设立欧洲监管机构(欧洲银行业管理局)并修正第 716/2009/EC 号决定和废止欧盟委员会第 2009/78/EC 号决定]

欧洲议会和欧盟理事会,

根据《欧洲联盟运行条约》,特别是其中的第114条,

根据欧盟委员会的提议,

根据欧洲中央银行的意见[1],

根据欧洲经济与社会委员会的意见[2],

依照正常的立法程序[3],

鉴于下列情形,通过本条例:

(1)2007年和2008年的金融危机暴露出金融监管的重要缺陷,不论就特殊事例而言抑或就金融系统整体而言。局限于国家这一层级的监管模式已落后于金融全球化的步伐,亦无法适应众多金融机构已实现跨境运营的欧洲金融市场在一体化和相互关联方面的现实态势。危机暴露出的问题体现在国家级监管机构之间的合作与协调不够、欧盟法律适用一致性的缺乏及相互信任的不足这几个方面。

(2)欧洲议会在其于金融危机发生前及其持续期间,呼吁进一步整合欧洲的金融

1 2010年1月20日《欧盟公报》C 13,第1页。

2 2010年1月22日的意见(尚未在《欧盟公报》公布)。

3 2010年9月22日欧洲议会立场(尚未在《欧盟公报》公布)以及2010年11月17日欧盟理事会决定。

move towards more integrated European supervision in order to ensure a true level playing field for all actors at the level of the Union and to reflect the increasing integration of financial markets in the Union (in its resolutions of 13 April 2000 on the Commission communication on implementing the framework for financial markets: Action Plan [1], of 21 November 2002 on prudential supervision rules in the European Union [2], of 11 July 2007 on financial services policy (2005 to 2010) White Paper [3], of 23 September 2008 with recommendations to the Commission on hedge funds and private equity [4] and of 9 October 2008 with recommendations to the Commission on Lamfalussy follow-up: future structure of supervision [5], and in its positions of 22 April 2009 on the amended proposal for a directive of the European Parliament and of the Council on the taking-up and pursuit of the business of Insurance and Reinsurance (Solvency II) [6] and of 23 April 2009 on the proposal for a regulation of the European Parliament and of the Council on Credit Rating Agencies [7]).

(3) In November 2008, the Commission mandated a High-Level Group chaired by Jacques de Larosière to make recommendations on how to strengthen European supervisory arrangements with a view to better protecting the citizen and rebuilding trust in the financial system. In its final report presented on 25 February 2009 (the 'de Larosière Report'), the High-Level Group recommended that the supervisory framework be strengthened to reduce the risk and severity of future financial crises. It recommended reforms to the structure of supervision of the financial sector in the Union. The group also concluded that a European System of Financial Supervisors should be created, comprising three European Supervisory Authorities, one for the banking sector, one for the securities sector and one for the insurance and occupational pensions sector, and recommended the creation of a European Systemic Risk Council. The report represented the reforms the experts considered were needed and on which work had to begin immediately.

(4) In its Communication of 4 March 2009 entitled 'Driving European Recovery', the Commission proposed to put forward draft legislation creating a European system of financial supervision and a European systemic risk board. In its Communication of 27 May 2009 entitled 'European Financial Supervision', it provided more detail about the possible architecture of such a new supervisory framework reflecting the main thrust of the

1 OJ C 40, 7. 2. 2001, p. 453.
2 OJ C 25 E, 29. 1. 2004, p. 394.
3 OJ C 175 E, 10. 7. 2008, p. 392.
4 OJ C 8 E, 14. 1. 2010, p. 26.
5 OJ C 9 E, 15. 1. 2010, p. 48.
6 OJ C 184 E, 8. 7. 2010, p. 214.
7 OJ C 184 E, 8. 7. 2010, p. 292.

监管,以便确保能在欧盟这一层级为所有市场主体提供真正公平的竞争环境,并反映欧盟金融市场不断一体化的现实[请参见:欧洲议会2000年4月13日关于欧盟委员会通报《落实金融市场框架:行动计划》的决议[1]、2002年11月21日关于欧盟审慎监管规则的决议[2]、2007年7月11日关于《2005年至2010年金融服务政策白皮书》的决议[3]、2008年9月23日关于对冲基金和私募股权的决议(含向欧盟委员会提出的建议)[4]、2008年10月9日关于《莱姆法路西的后续行动:未来监管结构》的决议(含向欧盟委员会提出的建议)[5]、2009年4月22日对《欧洲议会与欧盟理事会关于开办和经营保险与再保险业务的指令》(保险偿付能力标准Ⅱ)的修正稿提案所持立场[6]以及2009年4月23日对《欧洲议会与欧盟理事会关于信用评级机构的条例》的提案所持立场[7]]。

(3)2008年11月,欧盟委员会委托一个高级工作组在雅克·德·拉罗西埃的领导下,就如何加强欧洲监管安排以更好保护公众利益并重建公众对金融系统的信任提出建议。在其于2009年2月25日提交的最终报告(《德·拉罗西埃报告》)中,高级工作组建议强化监管框架以降低未来出现金融危机的风险及其严重程度,并建议对欧盟金融行业的监管结构进行改革,该小组还得出了应成立欧洲金融监管机构体系的结论,欧洲金融监管机构体系应由银行、证券以及保险与职业养老金三大金融行业的欧洲监管机构组成,并建议创设一个欧洲系统性风险理事会。此份报告阐述了专家们认为需要进行的改革以及必须立刻开展的工作。

(4)在2009年3月4日名为《推动欧洲复苏》的通报中,欧盟委员会提议起草相关立法草案以创建欧洲金融监管体系和欧洲系统性风险委员会,并在其2009年5月27日名为《欧洲金融监管》的通报中提供了该新监管框架可能之架构的更多细节,体现了《德·拉罗西埃报告》的要旨。

1 2001年2月7日《欧盟公报》C 40,第453页。
2 2004年1月29日《欧盟公报》C 25 E,第394页。
3 2008年7月10日《欧盟公报》C 175 E,第392页。
4 2010年1月14日《欧盟公报》C 8 E,第26页。
5 2010年1月15日《欧盟公报》C 9 E,第48页。
6 2010年7月8日《欧盟公报》C 184 E,第214页。
7 2010年7月8日《欧盟公报》C 184 E,第292页。

de Larosière Report.

(5) The European Council, in its conclusions of 19 June 2009, confirmed that a European System of Financial Supervisors, comprising three new European Supervisory Authorities, should be established. The system should be aimed at upgrading the quality and consistency of national supervision, strengthening oversight of cross-border groups and establishing a European single rulebook applicable to all financial institutions in the internal market. It emphasised that the European Supervisory Authorities should also have supervisory powers in relation to credit rating agencies and invited the Commission to prepare concrete proposals on how the European System of Financial Supervisors could play a strong role in crisis situations, while stressing that decisions taken by the European Supervisory Authorities should not impinge on the fiscal responsibilities of Member States.

(6) On 17 June 2010, the European Council agreed that 'Member States should introduce systems of levies and taxes on financial institutions to ensure fair burden-sharing and to set incentives to contain systemic risk. Such levies or taxes should be part of a credible resolution framework. Further work is urgently required on their main features and issues of level playing field and cumulative impacts of various regulatory measures should be carefully assessed'.

(7) The financial and economic crisis has created real and serious risks to the stability of the financial system and the functioning of the internal market. Restoring and maintaining a stable and reliable financial system is an absolute prerequisite to preserving trust and coherence in the internal market, and thereby to preserve and improve the conditions for the establishment of a fully integrated and functioning internal market in the field of financial services. Moreover, deeper and more integrated financial markets offer better opportunities for financing and risk diversification, and thus help to improve the capacity of the economies to absorb shocks.

(8) The Union has reached the limits of what can be done with the present status of the Committees of European Supervisors. The Union cannot remain in a situation where there is no mechanism to ensure that national supervisors arrive at the best possible supervisory decisions for cross-border financial institutions; where there is insufficient cooperation and information exchange between national supervisors; where joint action by national authorities requires complicated arrangements to take account of the patchwork of regulatory and supervisory requirements; where national solutions are most often the only feasible option in responding to problems at the level of the Union, and where different interpretations of the same legal text exist. The European System of Financial Supervision (hereinafter 'the ESFS') should be designed to overcome those deficiencies and provide a system that is in line with the objective of a stable and single Union financial market for

(5)欧洲理事会在其2009年6月19日的结论中确认,应当建立一个由三个新的欧洲监管机构组成的欧洲金融监管机构体系。该体系应旨在改善国家级监管工作的质量和一致性、加强对跨境集团的监控、建立适用于欧盟内部市场所有金融机构的欧洲单一规则手册。欧洲理事会还强调了欧洲监管机构对信用评级机构的监管权,并要求欧盟委员会针对欧洲金融监管机构体系在危机情况下如何发挥强有力作用制定具体的提案,但同时也强调欧洲监管机构作出的决策不应影响成员国的财政责任。

(6)2010年6月17日,欧洲理事会同意:"成员国应实行对金融机构的计征费和税费制度,以确保公平的责任分担、激励金融机构遏制系统性风险。该等计征费或税费应作为一个可信的清盘框架的一部分。欧盟迫切需要就上述制度的主要特征开展进一步工作,同时应对公平竞争问题和各种监管措施累加造成的影响作审慎评估。"

(7)金融与经济危机对金融系统稳定以及内部市场运行带来了切实而严重的风险。恢复与维持一个稳定可靠的金融系统,无疑是维持公众对内部市场的信任和内部市场自身凝聚力的先决条件,建立一个完全一体化和全面运行的金融服务内部市场所需条件也因而能得到维持和改善。此外,更为深化和一体化的金融市场为融资和风险分散提供了更好的机会,从而有助于提高各经济体化解冲击的能力。

(8)以欧洲监管机构委员会现有的身份和状态,欧盟已穷尽各种可能。欧盟不能面对下列困境坐视不管:欧盟缺乏一套能确保国家级监管机构对跨境金融机构作出尽可能最佳的监管决定的机制;国家级监管机构之间缺乏足够的合作和信息交流;鉴于各国规制和监管要求的差异,国家级监管机构需要复杂的安排才能作出共同行动;目前为止,应对欧盟层级问题最常见且唯一可行的解决方案往往只是国家层级的解决方案;不同成员国对同一法律文本存在各种不同的解释。欧洲金融监管体系(英文简称ESFS)应旨在克服该等不足,并建立符合"稳定和单一的欧盟金融服务市场"目标的体系,将国家级监管机构连接纳入到强大的欧盟网络之中。

financial services, linking national supervisors within a strong Union network.

(9) The ESFS should be an integrated network of national and Union supervisory authorities, leaving day-to-day supervision to the national level. Greater harmonisation and the coherent application of rules for financial institutions and markets across the Union should also be achieved. In addition to the European Supervisory Authority (European Banking Authority) (hereinafter 'the Authority'), a European Supervisory Authority (European Insurance and Occupational Pensions Authority) and a European Supervisory Authority (European Securities and Markets Authority) as well as a Joint Committee of the European Supervisory Authorities (hereinafter 'the Joint Committee') should be established. A European Systemic Risk Board (hereinafter 'the ESRB') should form part of the ESFS for the purposes of the tasks as specified in this Regulation and in Regulation (EU) No 1092/2010 of the European Parliament and of the Council [1].

(10) The European Supervisory Authorities (hereinafter collectively referred to as the 'ESAs') should replace the Committee of European Banking Supervisors established by Commission Decision 2009/78/EC [2], the Committee of European Insurance and Occupational Pensions Supervisors established by Commission Decision 2009/79/EC [3] and the Committee of European Securities Regulators established by Commission Decision 2009/77/EC [4], and should assume all of the tasks and competences of those committees including the continuation of ongoing work and projects, where appropriate. The scope of each European Supervisory Authority's action should be clearly defined. The ESAs should be accountable to the European Parliament and the Council. When that accountability relates to cross-sectoral issues that have been coordinated through the Joint Committee, the ESAs should be accountable, through the Joint Committee, for such coordination.

(11) The Authority should act with a view to improving the functioning of the internal market, in particular by ensuring a high, effective and consistent level of regulation and supervision taking account of the varying interests of all Member States and the different nature of financial institutions. The Authority should protect public values such as the stability of the financial system, the transparency of markets and financial products, and the protection of depositors and investors. The Authority should also prevent regulatory arbitrage and guarantee a level playing field, and strengthen international supervisory coordination, for the benefit of the economy at large, including financial institutions and other stakeholders, consumers and employees. Its tasks should also include promoting supervisory convergence and providing advice to the Union

1 See page 1 of this Official Journal.

2 OJ L 25, 29. 1. 2009, p. 23.

3 OJ L 25, 29. 1. 2009, p. 28.

4 OJ L 25, 29. 1. 2009, p. 18.

(9)欧洲金融监管机构体系应该是一个整合国家层级和欧盟层级监管机构的一体化网络,日常的监管工作仍留待国家层级处理。同时,还应实现金融机构和市场规则在欧盟范围内更高程度的协调和适用的一致性。除了欧洲监管机构(欧洲银行业管理局)(以下简称欧洲银行业管理局)之外,还应设立欧洲监管机构(欧洲保险与职业养老金管理局)、欧洲监管机构(欧洲证券与市场管理局)以及上述三个欧洲监管机构的联合委员会(以下简称联合委员会)。欧洲系统性风险委员会(英文简称ESRB)也应成为欧洲金融监管体系的一部分,以完成本条例以及欧洲议会与欧盟理事会第1092/2010号(欧盟)条例[1]规定的工作。

(10)各欧洲监管机构(英文统称ESA)应取代依据欧盟委员会第2009/78/EC号决定[2]设立的欧洲银行业监管机构委员会、依据欧盟委员会第2009/79/EC号决定[3]设立的欧洲保险与职业养老金监管机构委员会以及依据欧盟委员会第2009/77/EC号决定[4]设立的欧洲证券监管机构委员会,并承担各自的所有职责和职权,包括在适当时继续完成任何正在进行中的职责和项目。对各欧洲监管机构的行动范围应有明确的界定。各欧洲监管机构应对欧洲议会和欧盟理事会负责。如其所承担的责任牵涉到曾经通过联合委员会协调的跨部门问题,则各欧洲监管机构应通过联合委员会对上述协作负责。

(11)欧洲银行业管理局应致力于改善内部市场的运行,尤其是在考虑所有成员国的不同利益以及金融机构的不同性质的基础上,确保高水平、有效和一致的规制和监管。欧洲银行业管理局应保护公共价值观,如金融系统的稳定、市场和金融产品的透明以及对存款人和投资者的保护。欧洲银行业管理局还应为了整体经济利益(包括金融机构以及其他利益相关者、消费者和雇员的利益)而防范监管套利,保证公平的竞争环境,并加强国际监管的相互协调。其职责还应包括推动监管趋同以及就银行业、支付、电子货币规制和监管领域以及相关的公司治理、审计和财务报告事宜向欧盟机构提供建议。欧盟还应委托欧洲银行业管理局对现有和未来的新金融活动承担某些责任。

---

1 请见本《欧盟公报》,第1页。

2 2009年1月29日《欧盟公报》L 25,第23页。

3 2009年1月29日《欧盟公报》L 25,第28页。

4 2009年1月29日《欧盟公报》L 25,第18页。

institutions in the areas of banking, payments, e-money regulation and supervision, and related corporate governance, auditing and financial reporting issues. The Authority should also be entrusted with certain responsibilities for existing and new financial activities.

(12) The Authority should also be able to temporarily prohibit or restrict certain financial activities that threaten the orderly functioning and integrity of financial markets or the stability of the whole or part of the financial system in the Union in the cases specified and under the conditions laid down in the legislative acts referred to in this Regulation. If required to make such temporary prohibition in the case of an emergency situation, the Authority should do so in accordance with and under the conditions laid down in this Regulation. In cases where a temporary prohibition or restriction of certain financial activities has a cross sectoral impact, sectoral legislation should provide that the Authority should consult and coordinate its action with, where relevant, the European Supervisory Authority (European Insurance and Occupational Pensions Authority) and with the European Supervisory Authority (European Securities and Markets Authority), through the Joint Committee.

(13) The Authority should take due account of the impact of its activities on competition and innovation within the internal market, on the Union's global competitiveness, on financial inclusion, and on the Union's new strategy for jobs and growth.

(14) In order to fulfil its objectives, the Authority should have legal personality as well as administrative and financial autonomy.

(15) Based on the work of international bodies, systemic risk should be defined as a risk of disruption in the financial system with the potential to have serious negative consequences for the internal market and the real economy. All types of financial intermediaries, markets and infrastructures may be potentially systemically important to some degree.

(16) Cross-border risk includes all risks caused by economic imbalances or financial failures in all or parts of the Union that have the potential to have significant negative consequences for the transactions between economic operators of two or more Member States, for the functioning of the internal market or for the public finances of the Union or any of its Member States.

(17) The Court of Justice of the European Union in its judgment of 2 May 2006 in Case C-217/04 (United Kingdom of Great Britain and Northern Ireland v. European Parliament and Council of the European Union) held that 'nothing in the wording of Article 95 EC [now Article 114 of the Treaty on the Functioning of the European Union (TFEU)] implies that the addressees of the measures adopted by the Community legislature on the basis of that provision can only be the individual Member States. The

（12）在本条例所述框架立法规定的特定情形下且在满足其所列条件之时，如有金融活动威胁到欧盟金融市场有序运行和诚信度或整体或部分金融系统的稳定，欧洲银行业管理局应能临时禁止或者限制此等金融活动。如在紧急情况下需要实施上述临时禁令，则欧洲银行业管理局应依据本条例所规定的条件实施。临时禁止或者限制某些金融活动会造成跨行业冲击的，行业性立法应规定欧洲银行业管理局在适当时通过联合委员会与两个欧洲监管机构（欧洲保险与职业养老金管理局和欧洲证券与市场管理局）磋商并协调其行动。

（13）欧洲银行业管理局应适当考虑其活动对欧盟内部市场的竞争和创新、欧盟的全球竞争力、金融融入以及欧盟就业和发展新战略所产生的冲击。

（14）为实现其目标，欧洲银行业管理局应有法人身份以及行政管理和财务自主权。

（15）基于国际机构的研究成果，系统性风险应被定义为金融系统发生扰乱并有可能对内部市场和实体经济造成严重消极后果的风险。所有类型的金融中介机构、市场以及基础设施在某种程度上均可能有潜在的系统重要性。

（16）跨境风险包括由欧盟地区的整体或部分经济失衡或金融失败造成的，且可能对2个或以上成员国的经济运营主体之间的交易、欧盟内部市场的运行或欧盟或其任何成员国的公共财政带来严重消极后果的所有风险。

（17）欧盟法院在其2006年5月2日对第C-217/04号案件（大不列颠及北爱尔兰联合王国诉欧洲议会及欧盟理事会）的判决中表明："《欧洲共同体条约》第95条［现《欧洲联盟运行条约》（TFEU）第114条］的措辞并未暗示欧共体立法机构基于该条款所通过的措施只能适用于具体成员国。为促进基于《欧洲共同体条约》第95条的立法能得到统一实施和适用，应制定无法律约束力的辅助性和框架性措施时，立法机构可以认为有必要颁布设立该等欧共体机构的规定，由该机构负责推动协调程序的

legislature may deem it necessary to provide for the establishment of a Community body responsible for contributing to the implementation of a process of harmonisation in situations where, in order to facilitate the uniform implementation and application of acts based on that provision, the adoption of non-binding supporting and framework measures seems appropriate' [1]. The purpose and tasks of the Authority–assisting competent national supervisory authorities in the consistent interpretation and application of Union rules and contributing to financial stability necessary for financial integration – are closely linked to the objectives of the Union acquis concerning the internal market for financial services. The Authority should therefore be established on the basis of Article 114 TFEU.

(18) The following legislative acts lay down the tasks for the competent authorities of Member States, including cooperating with each other and with the Commission: Directive 2006/48/EC of the European Parliament and of the Council of 14 June 2006 relating to the taking up and pursuit of the business of credit institutions [2], Directive 2006/49/EC of the European Parliament and of the Council of 14 June 2006 on the capital adequacy of investment firms and credit institutions [3] and Directive 94/19/EC of the European Parliament and of the Council of 30 May 1994 on deposit–guarantee schemes [4].

(19) Existing Union legislation regulating the field covered by this Regulation also includes Directive 2002/87/EC of the European Parliament and of the Council of 16 December 2002 on the supplementary supervision of credit institutions, insurance undertakings and investment firms in a financial conglomerate [5], Directive 98/78/EC of the European Parliament and of the Council of 27 October 1998 on the supplementary supervision of insurance undertakings in an insurance group [6], Regulation (EC) No 1781/2006 of the European Parliament and of the Council of 15 November 2006 on information on the payer accompanying transfers of funds [7], Directive 2009/110/EC of the European Parliament and of the Council of 16 September 2009 on the taking up, pursuit and prudential supervision of the business of electronic money institutions [8], and the relevant parts of Directive 2005/60/EC of the European Parliament and of the Council of 26 October 2005 on the prevention of the use of the financial system for the purpose of money laundering and terrorist financing [9], of Directive 2002/65/EC of the European

1 European Court Reports 2006 Page I–03771, para. 44.
2 OJ L 177, 30. 6. 2006, p. 1.
3 OJ L 177, 30. 6. 2006, p. 201.
4 OJ L 135, 31. 5. 1994, p. 5.
5 OJ L 35, 11. 2. 2003, p. 1.
6 OJ L 330, 5. 12. 1998, p. 1.
7 OJ L 345, 8. 12. 2006, p. 1.
8 OJ L 267, 10. 10. 2009, p. 7.
9 OJ L 309, 25. 11. 2005, p. 15.

落实”[1]。欧洲银行业管理局的目标和职责在于协助国家级主管部门一致地解释和适用欧盟规则，致力于实现金融一体化所必不可少的金融稳定。该等职责与欧盟金融服务内部市场方面既定之法律所追求的目标紧密关联。因此，欧洲银行业管理局应建立在《欧洲联盟运行条约》第114条的基础上。

（18）下列框架立法规定了成员国主管部门的职责，其中包括相互合作以及与欧盟委员会合作:《欧洲议会与欧盟理事会关于开办和经营信贷机构业务的第2006/48/EC号指令》[2]（2006年6月14日）、《欧洲议会与欧盟理事会关于投资公司和信贷机构资本充足性的第2006/49/EC号指令》[3]（2006年6月14日）以及《欧洲议会与欧盟理事会关于存款担保计划的第94/19/EC号指令》[4]（1994年5月30日）。

（19）对本条例所覆盖的领域进行监管的欧盟现行立法还包括《欧洲议会与欧盟理事会关于对金融集团下属信贷机构、保险公司以及投资公司实施补充监管的第2002/87/EC号指令》[5]（2002年12月16日）、《欧洲议会与欧盟理事会关于对保险集团下属保险公司实施补充监管的第98/78/EC号指令》[6]（1998年10月27日）、《欧洲议会与欧盟理事会关于汇款随附之付款人信息的第1781/2006号（欧共体）条例》[7]（2006年11月15日）、《欧洲议会与欧盟理事会关于开办、经营和审慎监管电子货币机构业务的第2009/110/EC号指令》[8]（2009年9月16日）以及《欧洲议会与欧盟理事会关于防范利用金融系统从事洗钱和恐怖分子融资的第2005/60/EC号指令》[9]（2005年10月26日）、《欧洲

1 《2006年欧洲法院报告》第44段，第I–03771页。
2 2006年6月30日《欧盟公报》L 177，第1页。
3 2006年6月30日《欧盟公报》L 177，第201页。
4 1994年5月31日《欧盟公报》L 135，第5页。
5 2003年2月11日《欧盟公报》L 35，第1页。
6 1998年12月5日《欧盟公报》L 330，第1页。
7 2006年12月8日《欧盟公报》L 345，第1页。
8 2009年10月10日《欧盟公报》L 267，第7页。
9 2005年11月25日《欧盟公报》L 309，第15页。

Parliament and of the Council of 23 September 2002 concerning the distance marketing of consumer financial services [1] and of Directive 2007/64/EC of the European Parliament and of the Council of 13 November 2007 on payment services in the internal market [2].

(20) It is desirable that the Authority promote a consistent approach in the area of deposit guarantees to ensure a level playing field and the equitable treatment of depositors across the Union. As deposit guarantee schemes are subject to oversight in their Member States rather than regulatory supervision, the Authority should be able to exercise its powers under this Regulation in relation to the deposit guarantee scheme itself and its operator.

(21) In accordance with the Declaration (No 39) on Article 290 of the Treaty on the Functioning of the European Union (TFEU), annexed to the Final Act of the Intergovernmental Conference which adopted the Treaty of Lisbon, the elaboration of regulatory technical standards requires assistance of technical expertise in a form which is specific to the financial services area. It is necessary to allow the Authority to provide such expertise also on standards or parts of standards that are not based on a draft technical standard that it has elaborated.

(22) There is a need to introduce an effective instrument to establish harmonised regulatory technical standards in financial services to ensure, also through a single rulebook, a level playing field and adequate protection of depositors, investors and consumers across the Union. As a body with highly specialised expertise, it is efficient and appropriate to entrust the Authority, in areas defined by Union law, with the elaboration of draft regulatory technical standards, which do not involve policy choices.

(23) The Commission should endorse those draft regulatory technical standards by means of delegated acts pursuant to Article 290 TFEU in order to give them binding legal effect. They should be subject to amendment only in very restricted and extraordinary circumstances, since the Authority is the actor in close contact with and knowing best the daily functioning of financial markets. Draft regulatory technical standards would be subject to amendment if they were incompatible with Union law, did not respect the principle of proportionality or ran counter to the fundamental principles of the internal market for financial services as reflected in the *acquis* of Union financial services legislation. The Commission should not change the content of the draft regulatory technical standards prepared by the Authority without prior coordination with the Authority. To ensure a smooth and expeditious adoption process for those standards, the Commission's decision to endorse draft regulatory technical standards should be subject

1 OJ L 271, 9. 10. 2002, p. 16.

2 OJ L 319, 5. 12. 2007, p. 1.

议会与欧盟理事会关于远程营销消费者金融服务的第2002/65/EC号指令》[1](2002年9月23日)以及《欧洲议会与欧盟理事会关于内部市场支付服务的第2007/64/EC号指令》[2](2007年11月13日)的相关部分。

(20)在存款担保领域,欧洲银行业管理局宜推广一套一致的模式,以确保公平的竞争环境,令欧盟各地存款人能享受平等的待遇。由于存款担保计划在各个成员国虽受监控,但不受规制性质的监管,欧洲银行业管理局应能行使其在本条例中规定的与存款担保计划以及存款担保计划运营者相关的权力。

(21)根据通过《里斯本条约》的政府间会议《最后决议》附录中的《关于〈欧洲联盟运行条约〉(TFEU)第290条的声明(第39号)》,对于监管性技术标准的制定,需要金融服务领域专门的技术专长协助。对于那些并非基于欧洲银行业管理局自身制定的技术标准草案之标准或者部分标准,有必要允许欧洲银行业管理局提供上述技术专长。

(22)有必要采取有效的手段,为金融服务制定协调一致的监管性技术标准,同时结合单一规则手册来确保公平的竞争环境以及对欧盟各地存款人、投资者和消费者的充分保护。欧洲银行业管理局作为一个拥有高度专门知识的机构,委托其在欧盟法律界定的领域中制定不涉及政策性选择的监管性技术标准草案是既高效,且适宜的。

(23)欧盟委员会应按照《欧洲联盟运行条约》第290条以授权立法的形式同意和支持该等监管性技术标准草案,以赋予其法律约束力。鉴于欧洲银行业管理局是与金融市场有密切联系并且最了解金融市场日常运行的主体,因此仅能在十分有限和特殊的情况下才能对该等监管性技术标准草案进行修正。监管性技术标准草案与欧盟法律不相容、不符合比例原则,或者违背了欧盟既定的金融服务立法所体现的金融服务内部市场基本原则的,应对其进行修正。未经与欧洲银行业管理局事先协调,欧盟委员会不得变更欧洲银行业管理局起草的监管性技术标准草案内容。为确保顺利、快速地通过该等标准,欧盟委员会应在一定时限内作出同意和支持监管性技术标准草案的决定。

1 2002年10月9日《欧盟公报》L 271,第16页。

2 2007年12月5日《欧盟公报》L 319,第1页。

to a time limit.

(24) Given the technical expertise of the Authority in the areas where regulatory technical standards should be developed, note should be taken of the Commission's stated intention to rely, as a rule, on the draft regulatory technical standards submitted to it by the Authority in view of the adoption of the corresponding delegated acts. However, in cases where the Authority fails to submit a draft regulatory technical standard within the time limits set out by the relevant legislative act, it should be ensured that the result of the exercise of delegated power is actually achieved, and the efficiency of the decision-making process be maintained. In those cases, the Commission should therefore be empowered to adopt regulatory technical standards in the absence of a draft by the Authority.

(25) The Commission should also be empowered to adopt implementing technical standards by means of implementing acts pursuant to Article 291 TFEU.

(26) In areas not covered by regulatory or implementing technical standards, the Authority should have the power to issue guidelines and recommendations on the application of Union law. In order to ensure transparency and to strengthen compliance by national supervisory authorities with those guidelines and recommendations, it should be possible for the Authority to publish the reasons for supervisory authorities' non-compliance with those guidelines and recommendations.

(27) Ensuring the correct and full application of Union law is a core prerequisite for the integrity, transparency, efficiency and orderly functioning of financial markets, the stability of the financial system, and for neutral conditions of competition for financial institutions in the Union. A mechanism should therefore be established whereby the Authority addresses instances of non-application or incorrect application of Union law amounting to a breach thereof. That mechanism should apply in areas where Union law defines clear and unconditional obligations.

(28) To allow for a proportionate response to instances of incorrect or insufficient application of Union law, a three-step mechanism should apply. First, the Authority should be empowered to investigate alleged incorrect or insufficient application of Union law obligations by national authorities in their supervisory practice, concluded by a recommendation. Second, where the competent national authority does not follow the recommendation, the Commission should be empowered to issue a formal opinion taking into account the Authority's recommendation, requiring the competent authority to take the actions necessary to ensure compliance with Union law.

(29) Third, to overcome exceptional situations of persistent inaction by the competent authority concerned, the Authority should be empowered, as a last resort, to adopt decisions addressed to individual financial institutions. That power should be

(24)鉴于欧洲银行业管理局在应制定监管性技术标准之领域拥有技术专长,我们应注意到欧盟委员会声明的如下意向,即其在通过相应的授权立法时一般依赖欧洲银行业管理局向其呈报的监管性技术标准草案。然而,欧洲银行业管理局未在相关框架立法规定的时限内呈报该等草案的,仍应当保证授权之行使获得成效并维持决策程序效率。在该等情形下,欧盟委员会应有权在欧洲银行业管理局未呈报草案的情况下通过监管性技术标准。

(25)欧盟委员会应也有权按《欧洲联盟运行条约》第291条以实施性立法的形式通过实施性技术标准。

(26)在监管性或实施性技术标准未覆盖的领域,欧洲银行业管理局应有权就欧盟法律的适用提出指引和建议。为确保透明度及促进国家级监管机构遵循该等指引和建议,欧洲银行业管理局有可能公布监管机构不遵循该等指引和建议的理由。

(27)确保欧盟法律的正确和全面适用是欧盟金融市场诚信度、透明、有效、有序运行、金融系统稳定以及金融机构竞争中立性的核心前提。因此,应建立一项机制,使欧洲银行业管理局得以处理不适用或不正确适用欧盟法律从而导致违反欧盟法律的情形。该机制应适用于欧盟法律界定了明确、无条件的义务的领域。

(28)为对不正确或不充分适用欧盟法律作出成比例的回应,应采用“三步走”的机制。第一步,欧洲银行业管理局有权对国家级监管机构涉嫌在其监管实践中不正确或不充分履行欧盟法律义务的情况进行调查,而该等调查结论系以一份建议的形式作出;第二步,国家级主管部门没有遵循该建议的,欧盟委员会应有权发出一份反映欧洲银行业管理局建议的正式意见,要求该主管部门采取必要的行动以确保欧盟法律得到遵守。

(29)第三步,为了克服所涉主管部门持续不作为的特殊状况,作为最后手段,欧洲银行业管理局应有权针对具体金融机构作出决定。但是,仅在主管部门不遵循针对其发出的正式意见,且欧盟法律根据现有或未来的欧盟条例可直接适用于金融机构

limited to exceptional circumstances in which a competent authority does not comply with the formal opinion addressed to it and in which Union law is directly applicable to financial institutions by virtue of existing or future Union regulations.

(30) Serious threats to the orderly functioning and integrity of financial markets or the stability of the financial system in the Union require a swift and concerted response at Union level. The Authority should therefore be able to require national supervisory authorities to take specific actions to remedy an emergency situation. The power to determine the existence of an emergency situation should be conferred on the Council, following a request by any of the ESAs, the Commission or the ESRB.

(31) The Authority should be able to require national supervisory authorities to take specific action to remedy an emergency situation. The action undertaken by the Authority in this respect should be without prejudice to the Commission's powers pursuant to Article 258 TFEU to initiate infringement proceedings against the Member State of that supervisory authority for its failure to take such action, and without prejudice to the Commission's right in such circumstances to seek interim measures in accordance with the rules of procedure of the Court of Justice of the European Union. Furthermore, it should be without prejudice to any liability that that Member State might incur in accordance with the case law of the Court of Justice of the European Union if its supervisory authorities fail to take the action required by the Authority.

(32) In order to ensure efficient and effective supervision and a balanced consideration of the positions of the competent authorities in different Member States, the Authority should be able to settle disagreements in cross-border situations between those competent authorities with binding effect, including within colleges of supervisors. A conciliation phase should be provided for during which the competent authorities may reach an agreement. The Authority's competence should cover disagreements on the procedure or content of an action or inaction by a competent authority of a Member State in cases specified in the legally binding Union acts referred to in this Regulation. In such a situation, one of the supervisors involved should be entitled to refer the issue to the Authority, which should act in accordance with this Regulation. The Authority should be empowered to require the competent authorities concerned to take specific action or to refrain from action in order to settle the matter in order to ensure compliance with Union law, with binding effects for the competent authorities concerned. If a competent authority does not comply with the settlement decision addressed to it, the Authority should be empowered to adopt decisions directly addressed to financial institutions in areas of Union law directly applicable to them. The power to adopt such decisions should apply only as a last resort and then only to ensure the correct and consistent application of Union law. In cases where the relevant Union legislation confers discretion on Member States'

的特殊情况下，方可行使上述权力。

（30）欧盟金融市场的有序运行和诚信度或欧盟金融系统稳定面临严重威胁的时候，应在欧盟层面上作出迅速而一致的反应。因此，欧洲银行业管理局应能要求各国家级监管机构采取特定行动对紧急情况进行补救。经任何欧洲监管机构、欧盟委员会或欧洲系统性风险委员会请求，欧盟理事会有权判定是否存在紧急情况。

（31）欧洲银行业管理局应能要求国家级监管机构采取特定行动以对紧急情况作出补救。欧洲银行业管理局就此采取的行动不应影响欧盟委员会因成员国监管机构未采取上述行动而根据《欧洲联盟运行条约》第258条对该成员国启动违法违规诉讼程序的权力，也不应影响欧盟委员会在该等情况下依照欧盟法院程序规则寻求临时措施的权利。此外，成员国由于其监管机构未采取欧洲银行业管理局要求的行动而在欧盟法院判例法下所应承担的任何法律责任，不因欧洲银行业管理局的行动而受影响。

（32）为确保监管兼具效率和成效并平衡考虑各成员国主管部门的立场，欧洲银行业管理局应能以具有约束力的方式解决不同主管部门之间在跨境情形下的分歧，包括监管团内部的分歧。应规定一个调解期，主管部门可在此时间段内达成一致意见。在本条例所述具有法律约束力的欧盟法律文件所指定的情形里，对某成员国主管部门所采取的行动或不采取行动所依据的程序或相关内容出现了分歧的，欧洲银行业管理局应对该等分歧有管辖权。在该状况下，所涉监管机构之一有权将该事宜移交欧洲银行业管理局，由欧洲银行业管理局依照本条例处理。欧洲银行业管理局有权通过要求所涉主管部门采取特定行动或不采取行动的方式来解决有关事宜并确保欧盟法律得到遵守，此等要求应对所涉主管部门具有约束力。如主管部门不遵循对其作出的解决分歧的决定，欧洲银行业管理局有权在欧盟法律直接适用于金融机构的领域，直接对金融机构作出决定。作出上述决定的权力仅能作为最后手段且仅为确保欧盟法律的正确和一致适用而使用。相关欧盟立法授予了成员国主管部门自由裁量权的，欧洲银行业管理局所作出的决定不能替代主管部门依照欧盟法律行使该自由裁量权。

competent authorities, decisions taken by the Authority cannot replace the exercise in compliance with Union law of that discretion.

(33) The crisis has proven that the current system of cooperation between national authorities whose powers are limited to individual Member States is insufficient as regards financial institutions that operate across borders.

(34) Expert Groups set up by Member States to examine the causes of the crisis and make suggestions to improve the regulation and supervision of the financial sector have confirmed that the current arrangements are not a sound basis for the future regulation and supervision of cross-border financial institutions across the Union.

(35) As the de Larosière Report indicates, '[i]n essence, we have two alternatives: the first "chacun pour soi" beggar-thy-neighbour solutions; or the second-enhanced, pragmatic, sensible European cooperation for the benefit of all to preserve an open world economy. This will bring undoubted economic gains'.

(36) Colleges of supervisors play an important role in the efficient, effective and consistent supervision of financial institutions operating across borders. The Authority should contribute to promoting and monitoring the efficient, effective and consistent functioning of the colleges of supervisors and, in that respect, have a leading role in ensuring the consistent and coherent functioning of colleges of supervisors for cross-border financial institutions across the Union. The Authority should therefore have full participation rights in colleges of supervisors with a view to streamlining the functioning of and the information exchange process in the colleges of supervisors and to foster convergence and consistency across colleges in the application of Union law. As the de Larosière Report states, 'competition distortions and regulatory arbitrage stemming from different supervisory practices must be avoided, because they have the potential of undermining financial stability-inter alia by encouraging a shift of financial activity to countries with lax supervision. The supervisory system has to be perceived as fair and balanced'.

(37) Convergence in the fields of crisis prevention, management and resolution, including funding mechanisms, is necessary in order to ensure the internalisation of costs by the financial system and the ability of public authorities to resolve failing financial institutions whilst minimising the impact of failures on the financial system, reliance on taxpayer funds to bail out banks and the use of public sector resources, limiting damage to the economy, and coordinating the application of national resolution measures. In this regard it is imperative to develop a common set of rules on a complete set of tools for the prevention and resolution of failing banks, to deal in particular with the crisis of large, cross-border or interconnected institutions, and the need to confer additional relevant powers to the Authority should be assessed as well as how banks and savings institutions

(33)危机证明,由于国家级监管机构的权力范围局限于其各自所属成员国,目前各国家级监管机构之间的合作制度对于跨境运营的金融机构而言是不充分的。

(34)为检讨危机发生的原因、提出相关建议以改善对金融行业的规制和监管,各成员国设立了专家小组。该专家小组确认了现有安排不足以为欧盟内部跨境金融机构的规制和监管奠定坚实的基础。

(35)正如《德·拉罗西埃报告》所指:“实质上我们有两套方案可供选择:第一个是‘人人为自己’、以邻为壑的解决方案;第二个是在欧洲范围内强化、务实、明智的合作,为各方的利益而维持一个开放的世界经济。这无疑会带来诸多经济成果”。

(36)在对跨境运营的金融机构进行一致的且兼具效率和成效的监管中,各监管团起到重要作用。欧洲银行业管理局应致力于推进和监控各监管团一致的且兼具效率和成效的运作,并在这方面发挥其领导作用,确保监管团对欧盟内跨境金融机构起到相互连贯和一致的作用。因此,欧洲银行业管理局在监管团中应有充分的参与权,以提高监管团运作和信息交流程序的效率,推动在各监管团中能一致趋同地适用欧盟法律。正如《德·拉罗西埃报告》所表明的:“必须避免监管实践的差异造成竞争扭曲和监管套利,因为它们可能会对金融稳定造成损害(如此种差异造成变相鼓励将金融活动转移到监管不严的国家)。欧盟的监管制度必须塑造公平、平衡的公信力。”

(37)在危机防范、管理和清盘的领域,包括经费筹措机制方面,趋同是必要的,以确保有关成本在金融系统内部消化,确保公共机构有能力对濒临倒闭的金融机构进行清盘,最大限度地降低金融机构经营失败对系统的冲击,尽量避免依靠纳税人资金来为银行买单,避免利用公共部门的资源,从而将对经济造成的损害控制在一定限度并协调对国家级清盘措施的适用。为此,有必要针对濒临倒闭银行的预防和清盘所使用的一套完整工具制定一套通用规则,以着重处理大型、跨境或相互关联的机构的危机;同时,对于是否需要授予欧洲银行业管理局额外相关的权力、银行和储蓄机构如何才能优先保护储蓄者,应进行评估。

could prioritise the protection of savers.

(38) In the current review of Directive 94/19/EC and Directive 97/9/EC of the European Parliament and of the Council of 3 March 1997 on investor-compensation schemes [1], the Commission's intention to pay special attention to the need to ensure further harmonisation throughout the Union is noted. In the insurance sector, the Commission's intention to examine the possibility of introducing Union rules protecting insurance policy holders in case of a failing insurance company is also noted. The ESAs should play an important role in those areas and appropriate powers concerning the European guarantee scheme systems should be conferred upon them.

(39) The delegation of tasks and responsibilities can be a useful instrument in the functioning of the network of supervisors in order to reduce the duplication of supervisory tasks, to foster cooperation and thereby streamline the supervisory process, as well as to reduce the burden imposed on financial institutions. This Regulation should therefore provide a clear legal basis for such delegation. Whilst respecting the general rule that delegation should be allowed, Member States should be able to introduce specific conditions for the delegation of responsibilities, for example, regarding information about, and the notification of, delegation arrangements. Delegation of tasks means that tasks are carried out by the Authority or by a national supervisory authority other than the responsible authority, while the responsibility for supervisory decisions remains with the delegating authority. By the delegation of responsibilities, the Authority or a national supervisory authority (the delegate) should be able to decide upon a certain supervisory matter in its own name in lieu of the delegating authority. Delegations should be governed by the principle of allocating supervisory competence to a supervisor which is best placed to take action in the subject matter. A reallocation of responsibilities would be appropriate, for example, for reasons of economies of scale or scope, of coherence in group supervision, and of optimal use of technical expertise among national supervisory authorities. Decisions by the delegate should be recognised by the delegating authority and by other competent authorities as determinative if those decisions are within the scope of the delegation. Relevant Union legislation could further specify the principles for the reallocation of responsibilities upon agreement. The Authority should facilitate and monitor delegation agreements between national supervisory authorities by all appropriate means.

It should be informed in advance of intended delegation agreements, in order to be able to express an opinion where appropriate. It should centralise the publication of such agreements to ensure timely, transparent and easily accessible information about agreements

1 OJ L 84, 26. 3. 1997, p. 22.

(38)在目前对第94/19/EC号指令以及《欧洲议会与欧盟理事会关于投资者补偿计划的第97/9/EC号指令》[1](1997年3月3日)的审评中,欧盟委员会对于确保整个欧盟进一步协调的必要性给予高度重视。在保险业中,欧盟委员会也显然有意审查是否可能在保险公司濒临倒闭时对保户实施欧盟的保护规则。各欧洲监管机构应在该等领域发挥重要作用,并被授予与欧洲担保计划体制相关的适当权力。

(39)在监管机构网络的运行中,职责和责任的委托可减少监管职责的重复并促进合作,从而提高监管程序的效率,同时能减轻金融机构的负担。为此,本条例应为上述委托提供明确的法律依据。在遵守该等委托的一般规则的同时,成员国也应有权为责任委托施加特定的条件,如关于委托安排的信息和通知方面的条件。职责委托的含义是,由欧洲银行业管理局或某个国家级监管机构而非原负责部门来履行职责,但委托部门仍对监管决定负责。通过责任委托,欧洲银行业管理局或国家级监管机构(受托部门)应能以自己名义代表委托部门就某项监管事宜作出决定。委托的原则是将监管职权委托给就相关事项最适宜采取行动的监管机构。出于规模或范围效益、集团监管的相互一致性以及对不同国家级监管机构各自技术专长的优化使用等各种原因的考虑,可对责任进行再分配。受托部门在委托范围内所作决定,应被委托部门和其他主管部门视为有效决定。相关的欧盟立法可进一步阐述经各方一致同意对责任进行再分配的原则。欧洲银行业管理局应通过一切适当的方式协助和监控各国家级监管机构之间达成委托协议。

在委托协议签署之前应通知欧洲银行业管理局,使其能在适当时表达意见。欧洲银行业管理局应统一公布上述协议,以确保所涉各方均能及时、透明和方便地查阅与协议相关的信息。欧洲银行业管理局应确定并传播有关委托活动和委托协议的最佳

1 1997年3月26日《欧盟公报》L 84,第22页。

for all parties concerned. It should identify and disseminate best practices regarding delegation and delegation agreements.

(40) The Authority should actively foster supervisory convergence across the Union with the aim of establishing a common supervisory culture.

(41) Peer reviews are an efficient and effective tool for fostering consistency within the network of financial supervisors. The Authority should therefore develop the methodological framework for such reviews and conduct them on a regular basis. Reviews should focus not only on the convergence of supervisory practices, but also on the capacity of supervisors to achieve high-quality supervisory outcomes, as well as on the independence of those competent authorities. The outcome of peer reviews should be made public with the agreement of the competent authority subject to the review. Best practices should also be identified and made public.

(42) The Authority should actively promote a coordinated Union supervisory response, in particular to ensure the orderly functioning and integrity of financial markets and the stability of the financial system in the Union. In addition to its powers for action in emergency situations, the Authority should therefore be entrusted with a general coordination function within the ESFS. The smooth flow of all relevant information between competent authorities should be a particular focus of the Authority's actions.

(43) In order to safeguard financial stability it is necessary to identify, at an early stage, trends, potential risks and vulnerabilities stemming from the micro-prudential level, across borders and across sectors. The Authority should monitor and assess such developments in the area of its competence and, where necessary, inform the European Parliament, the Council, the Commission, the other European Supervisory Authorities and the ESRB on a regular and, as necessary, on an ad hoc basis. The Authority should also, in cooperation with the ESRB, initiate and coordinate Union-wide stress tests to assess the resilience of financial institutions to adverse market developments, and it should ensure that an as consistent as possible methodology is applied at the national level to such tests. In order to perform its functions properly, the Authority should conduct economic analyses of the markets and the impact of potential market developments.

(44) Given the globalisation of financial services and the increased importance of international standards, the Authority should foster dialogue and cooperation with supervisors outside the Union. It should be empowered to develop contacts and enter into administrative arrangements with the supervisory authorities and administrations of third countries and with international organisations, while fully respecting the existing roles and respective competences of the Member States and the Union institutions. Participation in the work of the Authority should be open to countries which have concluded agreements with the Union whereby they have adopted and are applying Union law, and the Authority

实践。

(40)欧洲银行业管理局应积极促进欧盟范围内的监管趋同,以建立共同的监管文化。

(41)同行审评是促进金融监管机构网络内部一致性的兼具效率和成效的工具。因此,欧洲银行业管理局应为上述审评制定方法论框架,并定期进行审评。审评的焦点不应仅停留在监管实践的趋同,还应着重于监管机构取得高质量监管结果的能力以及该等主管部门的独立性。接受审评的主管部门同意后,同行审评的结果应予公布。欧洲银行业管理局还应确定和公布最佳实践。

(42)欧洲银行业管理局应积极推动欧盟作出协调一致的监管回应,尤其要确保欧盟金融市场的有序运行和诚信度以及金融系统的稳定。因此,除在紧急情况下采取行动的权力之外,欧洲银行业管理局还应被赋予在欧洲金融监管机构体系内的总体协调职能。欧洲银行业管理局的行动应特别注重主管部门之间所有相关信息的顺利交流。

(43)为保护金融稳定,有必要在早期识别来自微观审慎层面的以及跨境和跨行业的趋势、潜在风险以及薄弱环节。欧洲银行业管理局应在其职权管辖范围内监控和评估上述变化,并且在必要的情况下将变化定期通知欧洲议会、欧盟理事会、欧盟委员会、其他欧洲监管机构以及欧洲系统性风险委员会,必要时也可发出临时通知。同时,欧洲银行业管理局应与欧洲系统性风险委员会合作,启动并协调全欧盟的压力测试,以评估金融机构面临不利市场变化时的抗冲击能力,并应确保各成员国实施该等测试的方法尽可能相互一致。为恰当地履行其职能,欧洲银行业管理局应对市场以及潜在市场变化的冲击进行经济分析。

(44)考虑到金融服务的全球化以及国际标准重要性的日益增长,欧洲银行业管理局应推动与非欧盟国家监管机构的对话与合作。欧洲银行业管理局在完全尊重成员国以及欧盟机构现有作用和各自职权范围的同时,应有权与第三国监管机构和行政管理部门以及国际组织建立联系并达成行政安排。与欧盟达成了协议,并在协议中已经采纳或正在适用欧盟法律的国家应能参与欧洲银行业管理局的工作,欧洲银行业管理局也应能和其适用立法与欧盟立法等效的第三国合作。

should be able to cooperate with third countries which apply legislation that has been recognised as equivalent to that of the Union.

(45) The Authority should serve as an independent advisory body to the European Parliament, the Council, and the Commission in the area of its competence. Without prejudice to the competencies of the competent authorities concerned, the Authority should be able to provide its opinion on the prudential assessment of mergers and acquisitions under Directive 2006/48/EC, as amended by Directive 2007/44/EC [1] in those cases in which that Directive requires consultation between competent authorities from two or more Member States.

(46) In order to carry out its duties effectively, the Authority should have the right to request all necessary information. To avoid the duplication of reporting obligations for financial institutions, that information should normally be provided by the national supervisory authorities which are closest to the financial markets and institutions and should take into account already existing statistics. However, as a last resort, the Authority should be able to address a duly justified and reasoned request for information directly to a financial institution where a national competent authority does not or cannot provide such information in a timely fashion. Member States' authorities should be obliged to assist the Authority in enforcing such direct requests. In that context, the work on common reporting formats is essential. The measures for the collection of information should be without prejudice to the legal framework of the European Statistical System and the European System of Central Banks in the field of statistics. This Regulation should therefore be without prejudice both to Regulation (EC) No 223/2009 of the European Parliament and of the Council of 11 March 2009 on European statistics [2] and to Council Regulation (EC) No 2533/98 of 23 November 1998 concerning the collection of statistical information by the European Central Bank [3].

(47) Close cooperation between the Authority and the ESRB is essential to give full effectiveness to the functioning of the ESRB and the follow-up to its warnings and recommendations. The Authority and the ESRB should share any relevant information with each other. Data related to individual undertakings should be provided only upon reasoned request. Upon receipt of warnings or recommendations addressed by the ESRB to the Authority or a national supervisory authority, the Authority should ensure follow-up as

1 Directive 2007/44/EC of the European Parliament and of the Council of 5 September 2007 amending Council Directive 92/49/EEC and Directives 2002/83/EC, 2004/39/EC, 2005/68/EC and 2006/48/EC as regards procedural rules and evaluation criteria for the prudential assessment of acquisitions and increase of holdings in the financial sector (OJ L 247, 21. 9. 2007, p. 1).

2 OJ L 87, 31. 3. 2009, p. 164.

3 OJ L 318, 27. 11. 1998, p. 8.

（45）欧洲银行业管理局应在其职权管辖范围内充当欧洲议会、欧盟理事会以及欧盟委员会的独立咨询机构。在不影响所涉主管部门职权的情况下，第2006/48/EC号指令（经第2007/44/EC号指令修正）[1]要求2个或以上成员国主管部门之间进行磋商的，欧洲银行业管理局应能对该指令项下并购所作的审慎评估提出意见。

（46）为有效履行其职责，欧洲银行业管理局应有权请求获得所有必要信息。为避免金融机构报告责任的重复，该等信息一般应由与金融市场和金融机构联系最紧密的国家级监管机构提供，并应考虑已有的统计数据。然而，国家级主管部门怠于或不能及时提供上述信息的，作为最后手段，欧洲银行业管理局应能直接向金融机构提出有正当理由和经论证的信息请求。各成员国主管部门有义务协助欧洲银行业管理局执行上述直接请求。在该等情况下，与报告通用格式相关的工作至关重要。收集信息的措施不得违背欧洲统计系统和欧洲中央银行体系在统计领域的法律框架。因此，本条例不得违背《欧洲议会与欧盟理事会关于欧洲统计的第223/2009号（欧共体）条例》[2]（2009年3月11日）以及《欧盟理事会关于欧洲中央银行统计信息收集工作的第2533/98号（欧共体）条例》[3]（1998年11月23日）。

（47）欧洲银行业管理局和欧洲系统性风险委员会之间的紧密合作对于欧洲系统性风险委员会的全面有效运行以及对其预警和建议的跟进至关重要。欧洲银行业管理局和欧洲系统性风险委员会彼此应共享任何相关信息。唯有经合理请求，方能提供与具体企业有关的数据。在欧洲银行业管理局或国家级监管机构收到欧洲系统性风险委员会向其发出的预警或建议之后，欧洲银行业管理局应确保予以适当跟进。

1 欧洲议会和欧盟理事会第2007/44/EC号指令（2007年9月5日），在审慎评估收购以及增持金融行业股份的程序规则和估值标准方面修正欧盟理事会第92/49/EEC号指令和第2002/83/EC号指令、第2004/39/EC号指令、第2005/68/EC号指令以及第2006/48/EC号指令（2007年9月21日《欧盟公报》L 247，第1页）。

2 2009年3月31日《欧盟公报》L 87，第164页。

3 1998年11月27日《欧盟公报》L 318，第8页。

appropriate.

(48) The Authority should consult interested parties on regulatory or implementing technical standards, guidelines and recommendations and provide them with a reasonable opportunity to comment on proposed measures. Before adopting draft regulatory or implementing technical standards, guidelines and recommendations, the Authority should carry out an impact study. For reasons of efficiency, a Banking Stakeholder Group should be used for that purpose, and should represent, in balanced proportions, Union credit and investment institutions, representing the diverse models and sizes of financial institutions and businesses, including, as appropriate, institutional investors and other financial institutions which themselves use financial services; small and medium-sized enterprises (SMEs); trade unions; academics; consumers; and other retail users of banking services. The Banking Stakeholder Group should work as an interface with other user groups in the financial services area established by the Commission or by Union legislation.

(49) Members of the Banking Stakeholder Group representing non-profit organisations or academics should receive adequate compensation in order to allow persons that are neither well-funded nor industry representatives to take part fully in the debate on financial regulation.

(50) Member States have a core responsibility for ensuring coordinated crisis management and preserving financial stability in crisis situations, in particular with regard to stabilising and resolving individual failing financial institutions. Decisions by the Authority in emergency or settlement situations affecting the stability of a financial institution should not impinge on the fiscal responsibilities of Member States. A mechanism should be established whereby Member States may invoke this safeguard and ultimately bring the matter before the Council for a decision. However, that safeguard mechanism should not be abused, in particular in relation to a decision taken by the Authority which does not have a significant or material fiscal impact, such as a reduction of income linked to the temporary prohibition of specific activities or products for consumer protection purposes. When taking decisions under the safeguard mechanism, the Council should vote in accordance with the principle where each member has one vote. It is appropriate to confer on the Council a role in this matter given the particular responsibilities of the Member States in this respect. Given the sensitivity of the issue, strict confidentiality arrangements should be ensured.

(51) In its decision-making procedures, the Authority should be bound by Union rules and general principles on due process and transparency. The right of the addressees of the Authority's decisions to be heard should be fully respected. The Authority's acts should form an integral part of Union law.

(52) A Board of Supervisors composed of the heads of the relevant competent

（48）欧洲银行业管理局应就监管性或实施性技术标准、指引和建议向利益相关方征求意见，并给其合理的机会对拟议的措施发表意见。在通过监管性或实施性技术标准草案、指引和建议之前，欧洲银行业管理局应对其影响开展研究。为确保效率，可为此引入银行业利益相关者小组。银行业利益相关者小组应以平衡的比例代表欧盟信贷和投资机构，包括各种模式和规模的金融机构和企业[包括自身使用金融服务的机构投资者以及其他金融机构（如适当）]、中小企业（SME）、工会、学术机构、消费者以及银行业服务的其他零售用户。银行业利益相关者小组应充当与欧洲银行业管理局与欧盟委员会或欧盟立法在金融服务领域建立的其他用户小组对接的部门。

（49）代表非营利组织或学术机构的银行业利益相关者小组成员应获得充足的报酬，让既非资金充裕亦非行业代表的人士能充分参与有关金融监管的讨论。

（50）各成员国负有核心责任，应确保危机管理的协调性并在危机状况下维持金融稳定，特别是在稳定濒临倒闭的具体金融机构的形势并对其进行清盘的时候。在影响金融机构稳定性的紧急情况或争议解决情况下，欧洲银行业管理局所作决定不应影响成员国的财政责任。应建立一项机制，让成员国能借其寻求保障并最终将有关事宜提交欧盟理事会决定。但该项保障机制不得被滥用，特别是当欧洲银行业管理局所作决定对财政收入并未造成突出或重大影响（如为保护消费者利益采取的禁止特定活动或产品的临时措施造成纳税人所得下降的情形）时，不得使用该项机制。欧盟理事会根据保障机制作决定时，应按一人一票的原则投票表决。考虑到成员国在这方面承担的特殊责任，在此问题上应让欧盟理事会发挥一定的作用。鉴于问题的高度敏感性，应确保作出严格的保密安排。

（51）欧洲银行业管理局在进行决策程序时，应受欧盟规则以及关于正当程序和透明度的一般性原则约束。欧洲银行业管理局的决定所涉对象的发言权应得到充分的尊重。欧洲银行业管理局的法律文件应构成欧盟法律不可分割的一部分。

（52）由每一成员国相关主管部门的负责人组成，并由欧洲银行业管理局主席担

authorities in each Member State, and chaired by the Chairperson of the Authority, should be the principal decision-making organ of the Authority. Representatives of the Commission, the ESRB, the European Central Bank, the European Supervisory Authority (European Insurance and Occupational Pensions Authority) and the European Supervisory Authority (European Securities and Markets Authority) should participate as observers. Members of the Board of Supervisors should act independently and only in the Union's interest.

(53) As a general rule, the Board of Supervisors should take its decisions by simple majority in accordance with the principle where each member has one vote. However, for acts of a general nature, including those relating to regulatory and implementing technical standards, guidelines and recommendations, for budgetary matters as well as in respect of requests by a Member State to reconsider a decision by the Authority to temporarily prohibit or restrict cer tain financial activities, it is appropriate to apply the rules of qualified majority voting as laid down in Article 16(4) of the Treaty on European Union and in the Protocol (No 36) on transitional provisions annexed to the Treaty on European Union and to the Treaty on the Functioning of the European Union. Cases concerning the settlement of disagreements between national supervisory authorities should be examined by a restricted, objective panel, composed of members who neither are representatives of the competent authorities which are party to the disagreement nor have any interest in the conflict or direct links to the competent authorities concerned. The composition of the panel should be appropriately balanced. The decision taken by the panel should be approved by the Board of Supervisors by simple majority in accordance with the principle where each member has one vote. However, with regard to decisions taken by the consolidating supervisor, the decision proposed by the panel could be rejected by members representing a blocking minority of the votes as defined in Article 16(4) of the Treaty on European Union and in Article 3 of the Protocol (No 36) on transitional provisions.

(54) A Management Board, composed of the Chairperson of the Authority, of representatives of national supervisory authorities and of the Commission, should ensure that the Authority carries out its mission and performs the tasks assigned to it. The Management Board should be entrusted with the necessary powers, inter alia, to propose the annual and multi-annual work programme, to exercise certain budgetary powers, to adopt the Authority's staff policy plan, to adopt special provisions on the right to access to documents and to propose the annual report.

(55) The Authority should be represented by a full-time Chairperson, appointed by the Board of Supervisors, on the basis of merit, skills, knowledge of financial institutions and markets, and of experience relevant to financial supervision and regulation, following

任主席的监管机构理事会应当是欧洲银行业管理局的主要决策机构。来自欧盟委员会、欧洲系统性风险委员会、欧洲中央银行的代表，以及来自两个欧洲监管机构（欧洲保险与职业养老金管理局以及欧洲证券与市场管理局）的代表，应作为观察员参与。监管机构理事会的理事应独立地且仅为欧盟利益行事。

（53）作为一般规则，监管机构理事会应按一人一票的原则以简单多数通过其决定。然而，对于具有普遍性质的法律文件（包括与监管性和实施性技术标准、指引以及建议有关的法律文件）、预算事项以及成员国向欧洲银行业管理局提出的重新考虑临时禁止或限制某些特定金融活动的请求，应适用《欧洲联盟条约》第16条第4款以及《欧洲联盟条约》和《欧洲联盟运行条约》附录关于过渡规定的《议定书》（第36号）中所规定的特定多数原则。解决各国家级监管机构之间分歧的案件，应由符合下列标准的人员组成的严格客观的专家小组进行审查：并非作为分歧一方的主管部门的代表，并且在所涉主管部门之冲突中无利害关系、与所涉主管部门亦无直接关联的人员。该专家小组的构成应适当平衡。专家小组的决定应由监管机构理事会按一人一票的原则以简单多数通过。然而，关于并表监管机构作出的决定，代表有否决权的少数票的理事有权否决专家小组拟议的决定[有否决权的少数票定义见《欧洲联盟条约》第16条第4款以及关于过渡规定的《议定书（第36号）》第3条]。

（54）由欧洲银行业管理局主席、国家级监管机构代表以及欧盟委员会组成的管理委员会应确保欧洲银行业管理局完成其使命并履行其被赋予的职责。管理委员会应被委以必要的权力，包括但不限于提出年度和跨年度工作计划、行使特定的预算权、通过欧洲银行业管理局的员工政策计划、通过有关文件查阅权的特殊规定以及提出年度报告。

（55）欧洲银行业管理局应由一名全职主席作为代表，该主席人选根据候选人的成就、技能、对金融机构和市场的认识、与金融监管和规制相关的经验等，由监管机构理事会在欧盟委员会的协助下组织和执行公开遴选程序来确定。在指定首任欧洲银

an open selection procedure organised and managed by the Board of Supervisors assisted by the Commission. For the designation of the first Chairperson of the Authority, the Commission should, inter alia, draw up a shortlist of candidates on the basis of merit, skills, knowledge of financial institutions and markets, and experience relevant to financial supervision and regulation. For the subsequent designations, the opportunity of having a shortlist drawn up by the Commission should be reviewed in a report to be established pursuant to this Regulation. Before the selected person takes up his duties, and up to 1 month after his selection by the Board of Supervisors, the European Parliament should be entitled, after having heard the person selected, to object to his designation.

(56) The management of the Authority should be entrusted to an Executive Director, who should have the right to participate in meetings of the Board of Supervisors and the Management Board without the right to vote.

(57) In order to ensure cross-sectoral consistency in the activities of the ESAs, they should coordinate closely through a Joint Committee and reach common positions where appropriate. The Joint Committee should coordinate the functions of the ESAs in relation to financial conglomerates and other cross-sectoral matters. Where relevant, acts also falling within the area of competence of the European Supervisory Authority (European Insurance and Occupational Pensions Authority) or the European Supervisory Authority (European Securities and Markets Authority) should be adopted in parallel by the European Supervisory Authorities concerned. The Joint Committee should be chaired for a 12-month term on a rotating basis by the Chairpersons of the ESAs. The Chairperson of the Joint Committee should be a Vice-Chair of the ESRB. The Joint Committee should have dedicated staff provided by the ESAs to allow for informal information sharing and the development of a common supervisory culture approach across the ESAs.

(58) It is necessary to ensure that the parties affected by decisions adopted by the Authority may have recourse to the necessary remedies. To protect effectively the rights of parties, and for reasons of procedural economy, where the Authority has decision-making powers, parties should be granted a right of appeal to a Board of Appeal. For reasons of efficiency and consistency, the Board of Appeal should be a joint body of the ESAs, independent from their administrative and regulatory structures. The decisions of the Board of Appeal should be subject to appeal before the Court of Justice of the European Union.

(59) In order to guarantee its full autonomy and independence, the Authority should be granted an autonomous budget with revenues mainly from obligatory contributions from national supervisory authorities and from the General Budget of the European Union.

行业管理局主席时，欧盟委员会应基于候选人的成就、技能、对金融机构和市场的认识、与金融监管和规制相关的经验拟定一份候选人名单。对于后续任期，应在根据本条例准备的报告中对是否要求欧盟委员会拟定候选人名单之事进行审议。从获选者到任前，直至其被监管机构理事会选出满1个月期间内，欧洲议会都有权在听取获选者意见后对其任命提出异议。

（56）欧洲银行业管理局的管理应委任给一名执行主任，执行主任有权参与监管机构理事会和管理委员会的会议，但无表决权。

（57）为确保彼此活动的跨行业一致性，各欧洲监管机构应通过联合委员会紧密协调，并在适当时达成共同的立场。联合委员会应协调各欧洲监管机构在金融集团以及其他跨行业事宜方面的职能。在适当时，同时属于欧洲监管机构（欧洲保险与职业养老金管理局或欧洲证券与市场管理局）职权管辖范围的法律文件，应由所涉的各个欧洲监管机构分别通过。联合委员会的主席应由各欧洲监管机构的主席轮流担任，每次任期12个月。联合委员会的主席应为欧洲系统性风险委员会的副主席。各欧洲监管机构应向联合委员会提供专门的员工负责非正式信息共享工作和建设欧洲监管机构共同的监管文化。

（58）有必要确保受欧洲银行业管理局决定影响的当事方可寻求必要的救济。为有效保护各方权利以及出于程序经济的考虑，对于欧洲银行业管理局有决策权的事项，各方应有向行政复议委员会提出行政复议申请的权利。出于效率和一致性原因，行政复议委员会应为各欧洲监管机构之间的联合机构，独立于各自所属的行政和监管结构。针对行政复议委员会的决定，相关方可向欧盟法院提起行政诉讼。

（59）为保证其充分的自主权和独立性，欧洲银行业管理局应有自主的预算，其收入主要来自各国家级监管机构义务缴纳的款项以及欧盟总预算的一部分。欧盟应依据预算部门按照《欧洲议会、欧盟理事会和欧盟委员会关于预算纪律和健全的财务管

Union financing of the Authority is subject to an agreement by the budgetary authority in accordance with Point 47 of the Interinstitutional Agreement between the European Parliament, the Council and the Commission of 17 May 2006 on budgetary discipline and sound financial management [1]. The Union budgetary procedure should be applicable. The auditing of accounts should be undertaken by the Court of Auditors. The overall budget is subject to the discharge procedure.

(60) Regulation (EC) No 1073/1999 of the European Parliament and of the Council of 25 May 1999 concerning investigations conducted by the European Anti-Fraud Office (OLAF) [2] should apply to the Authority. The Authority should also accede to the Interinstitutional Agreement of 25 May 1999 between the European Parliament, the Council of the European Union and the Commission of the European Communities concerning internal investigations by the European Anti-Fraud Office (OLAF). [3]

(61) In order to ensure open and transparent employment conditions and equal treatment of staff, the Staff Regulations of Officials and the Conditions of Employment of Other Servants of the European Communities [4] should apply to the staff of the Authority.

(62) It is essential that business secrets and other confidential information be protected. The confidentiality of information made available to the Authority and exchanged in the network should be subject to stringent and effective confidentiality rules.

(63) Directive 95/46/EC of the European Parliament and of the Council of 24 October 1995 on the protection of individuals with regard to the processing of personal data and on the free movement of such data [5] and Regulation (EC) No 45/2001 of the European Parliament and of the Council of 18 December 2000 on the protection of individuals with regard to the processing of personal data by the Community institutions and bodies and on the free movement of such data [6] are fully applicable to the processing of personal data for the purposes of this Regulation.

(64) In order to ensure the transparent operation of the Authority, Regulation (EC) No 1049/2001 of the European Parliament and of the Council of 30 May 2001 regarding public access to European Parliament, Council and Commission documents [7] should apply to the Authority.

1 OJ C 139, 14. 6. 2006, p. 1.
2 OJ L 136, 31. 5. 1999, p. 1.
3 OJ L 136, 31. 5. 1999, p. 15.
4 OJ L 56, 4. 3. 1968, p. 1.
5 OJ L 281, 23. 11. 1995, p. 31.
6 OJ L 8, 12. 1. 2001, p. 1.
7 OJ L 145, 31. 5. 2001, p. 43

理的机构间协议》[1](2006年5月17日)第47目签署的协议向欧洲银行业管理局提供经费。给其提供的经费应适用欧盟预算程序。其账目应由欧盟审计院进行审计,总体预算则受预算审批程序约束。

(60)《欧洲议会与欧盟理事会关于欧洲反欺诈办公室(OLAF)所开展的调查的第1073/1999号(欧共体)条例》[2](1999年5月25日)应适用于欧洲银行业管理局。同时,欧洲银行业管理局应遵从欧洲议会、欧盟理事会以及欧盟委员会于1999年5月25日签订的《关于欧洲反欺诈办公室(OLAF)内部调查的机构间协议》[3]。

(61)为确保公开透明的聘用条件以及员工的平等待遇,《欧洲共同体官员的人事条例》和《欧洲共同体其他人员的聘用条件》[4]应适用于欧洲银行业管理局工作人员。

(62)保护商业秘密和其他保密信息至关重要。向欧洲银行业管理局提供的以及在监管网络中交换的保密信息均应受严格有效的保密规定约束。

(63)《欧洲议会与欧盟理事会关于处理个人资料时对个人的保护以及该等资料自由流动的第95/46/EC号指令》[5](1995年10月24日)以及《欧洲议会与欧盟理事会关于欧共体机构和单位处理个人资料时对个人的保护以及该等资料自由流动的第45/2001号(欧共体)条例》[6](2000年12月18日)完全适用于根据本条例对个人资料的处理。

(64)为确保欧洲银行业管理局的透明运作,《欧洲议会与欧盟理事会关于公众查阅欧洲议会、欧盟理事会和欧盟委员会文件的第1049/2001号(欧共体)条例》[7](2001年5月30日)应适用于欧洲银行业管理局。

1 2006年6月14日《欧盟公报》C 139,第1页。
2 1999年5月31日《欧盟公报》L 136,第1页。
3 1999年5月31日《欧盟公报》L 136,第15页。
4 1968年3月4日《欧盟公报》L 56,第1页。
5 1995年11月23日《欧盟公报》L 281,第31页。
6 2001年1月12日《欧盟公报》L 8,第1页。
7 2001年5月31日《欧盟公报》L 145,第43页。

(65) Third countries should be allowed to participate in the work of the Authority in accordance with appropriate agreements to be concluded by the Union.

(66) Since the objectives of this Regulation, namely improving the functioning of the internal market by means of ensuring a high, effective and consistent level of prudential regulation and supervision, protecting depositors and investors, protecting the integrity, efficiency and orderly functioning of financial markets, maintaining the stability of the financial system, and strengthening international supervisory coordination, cannot be sufficiently achieved by the Member States and can, therefore, by reason of the scale of the action, be better achieved at Union level, the Union may adopt measures, in accordance with the principle of subsidiarity as set out in Article 5 of the Treaty on European Union. In accordance with the principle of proportionality, as set out in that Article, this Regulation does not go beyond what is necessary in order to achieve those objectives.

(67) The Authority should assume all current tasks and powers of the Committee of European Banking Supervisors. Commission Decision 2009/78/EC should therefore be repealed on the date of the establishment of the Authority and Decision No 716/2009/EC of the European Parliament and of the Council of 16 September 2009 establishing a Community programme to support specific activities in the field of financial services, financial reporting and auditing [1] should be amended accordingly. Given the existing structures and operations of the Committee of European Banking Supervisors, it is important to ensure very close cooperation between the Committee of European Banking Supervisors and the Commission when establishing appropriate transitional arrangements, to ensure that the period during which the Commission is responsible for the administrative establishment and initial administrative operation of the Authority be as limited as possible.

(68) It is appropriate to set a time limit for the application of this Regulation in order to ensure that the Authority is adequately prepared to begin operations and a smooth transition from the Committee of European Banking Supervisors. The Authority should be appropriately financed. At least initially, it should be financed 40% from Union funds and 60% through contributions from Member States, made in accordance with the weighting of votes set out in Article 3(3) of the Protocol (No 36) on transitional provisions.

(69) In order to enable the Authority to be established on 1 January 2011, this Regulation should enter into force on the day following its publication in the Official Journal of the European Union,

1 OJ L 253, 25. 9. 2009, p. 8.

（65）第三国应被允许依照其与欧盟今后缔结的相关协议参与欧洲银行业管理局的工作。

（66）鉴于本条例的目标在于确保高水平、有效和一致的审慎规制和监管以改善欧盟内部市场的运行，保护存款人和投资者，保护金融市场的诚信度、高效和有序运行，维持金融系统的稳定以及加强国际监管协调；上述目的单靠成员国自身无法完全实现，但基于此等目的触及的范围，能在欧盟层面上得到更好的实现，因此，欧盟可根据《欧洲联盟条约》第5条规定的辅助性原则制定相关细则。根据《欧洲联盟条约》第5条规定的比例原则，本条例仅作出实现上述目标的必要规定。

（67）欧洲银行业管理局应承担欧洲银行业监管机构委员会所有的现有职责和权力。因此，欧盟委员会第2009/78/EC号决定应于欧洲银行业管理局成立之日废止，对《欧洲议会与欧盟理事会设立一项支持金融服务领域特定活动、财务报告和审计的欧共体计划的第716/2009/EC号决定》[1]（2009年9月16日）也应作相应修正。考虑到欧洲银行业监管机构委员会的现有结构和运作状况，在作出适当的过渡安排时，确保欧洲银行业监管机构委员会和欧盟委员会之间十分紧密的合作相当重要，以尽量缩短欧盟委员会负担欧洲银行业管理局机构设立和初始行政运作的时间。

（68）应为本条例的适用设定时限，以确保欧洲银行业管理局做好充分的准备启动其运作，并确保欧洲银行业监管机构委员会向欧洲银行业管理局顺利过渡。欧洲银行业管理局应有适当的财政支持，至少在初始阶段，应从欧盟获得40%的经费，另外60%来源于成员国根据关于过渡条款的《议定书》（第36号）第3条第3款规定的加权票数比例缴纳的款项。

（69）为使欧洲银行业管理局于2011年1月1日成立，本条例应于《欧盟公报》公布，公布的次日生效。

1 2009年9月25日《欧盟公报》L 253，第8页。

HAVE ADOPTED THIS REGULATION:

CHAPTER I ESTABLISHMENT AND LEGAL STATUS

Article 1 Establishment and scope of action

1. This Regulation establishes a European Supervisory Authority (European Banking Authority) (hereinafter 'the Authority').

2. The Authority shall act within the powers conferred by this Regulation and within the scope of Directive 2006/48/EC, Directive 2006/49/EC, Directive 2002/87/EC, Regulation (EC) No 1781/2006, Directive 94/19/EC and, to the extent that those acts apply to credit and financial institutions and the competent authorities that supervise them, within the relevant parts of Directive 2005/60/EC, Directive 2002/65/EC, Directive 2007/64/EC and Directive 2009/110/EC, including all directives, regulations, and decisions based on those acts, and of any further legally binding Union act which confers tasks on the Authority.

3. The Authority shall also act in the field of activities of credit institutions, financial conglomerates, investment firms, payment institutions and e-money institutions in relation to issues not directly covered in the acts referred to in paragraph 2, including matters of corporate governance, auditing and financial reporting, provided that such actions by the Authority are necessary to ensure the effective and consistent application of those acts.

4. The provisions of this Regulation are without prejudice to the powers of the Commission, in particular pursuant to Article 258 TFEU, to ensure compliance with Union law.

5. The objective of the Authority shall be to protect the public interest by contributing to the short, medium and long-term stability and effectiveness of the financial system, for the Union economy, its citizens and businesses. The Authority shall contribute to:

(a) improving the functioning of the internal market, including, in particular, a sound, effective and consistent level of regulation and supervision;

(b) ensuring the integrity, transparency, efficiency and orderly functioning of financial markets;

(c) strengthening international supervisory coordination;

(d) preventing regulatory arbitrage and promoting equal conditions of competition;

(e) ensuring the taking of credit and other risks are appropriately regulated and

兹通过本指令如下：

第一章　设立和法律地位

第1条　设立和行动范围

1.本条例设立欧洲监管机构(欧洲银行业管理局)(以下简称欧洲银行业管理局)。

2.欧洲银行业管理局应按本条例授予的权力在第2006/48/EC号指令、第2006/49/EC号指令、第2002/87/EC号指令、第1781/2006号(欧共体)条例、第94/19/EC号指令以及第2005/60/EC号指令、第2002/65/EC号指令、第2007/64/EC号指令和第2009/110/EC号指令适用于信贷和金融机构及其监管主管部门的有关部分(包括所有基于上述法律文件的指令、条例及决定)范围内,以及在将来颁布的赋予欧洲银行业管理局职责的具有法律约束力的任何其他欧盟法律文件范围内行事。

3.欧洲银行业管理局还应在信贷机构、金融集团、投资公司、付款机构和电子货币机构与不直接涵盖在第2款所述法律文件范围内的事项有关的活动领域行事,包括公司治理、审计以及财务报告事宜,前提是欧洲银行业管理局采取的上述行动对于确保该等法律文件的有效、一致适用是必不可少的。

4.本条例的规定不得影响欧盟委员会确保欧盟法律得到遵守的权力,尤其是《欧洲联盟运行条约》第258条中的权力。

5.欧洲银行业管理局的目标是通过为欧盟经济及其公民和企业促进金融系统的短期、中期和长期稳定和有效性以保护公众利益。欧洲银行业管理局应致力于:

(a)改善欧盟内部市场的运行,尤其包括健全、有效、一致的规制和监管;

(b)确保金融市场的诚信度、透明、高效和有序运行;

(c)加强国际监管协调;
(d)防范监管套利并促进竞争的平等条件;
(e)确保对信贷风险及其他风险的涉险行为进行适当的规制和监管;及

supervised; and

(f) enhancing customer protection.

For those purposes, the Authority shall contribute to ensuring the consistent, efficient and effective application of the acts referred to in paragraph 2, foster supervisory convergence, provide opinions to the European Parliament, the Council, and the Commission and undertake economic analyses of the markets to promote the achievement of the Authority's objective.

In the exercise of the tasks conferred upon it by this Regulation, the Authority shall pay particular attention to any systemic risk posed by financial institutions, the failure of which may impair the operation of the financial system or the real economy.

When carrying out its tasks, the Authority shall act independently and objectively and in the interest of the Union alone.

Article 2 European System of Financial Supervision

1. The Authority shall form part of a European System of Financial Supervision (ESFS). The main objective of the ESFS shall be to ensure that the rules applicable to the financial sector are adequately implemented to preserve financial stability and to ensure confidence in the financial system as a whole and sufficient protection for the customers of financial services.

2. The ESFS shall comprise the following:

(a) the European Systemic Risk Board (ESRB), for the purposes of the tasks as specified in Regulation (EU) No 1092/2010 and this Regulation;

(b) the Authority;

(c) the European Supervisory Authority (European Insurance and Occupational Pensions Authority) established by Regulation (EU) No 1094/2010 of the European Parliament and of the Council [1];

(d) the European Supervisory Authority (European Securities and Markets Authority) established by Regulation (EU) No 1095/2010 of the European Parliament and of the Council [2];

(e) the Joint Committee of the European Supervisory Authorities (Joint Committee) for the purposes of carrying out the tasks as specified in Articles 54 to 57 of this Regulation, of Regulation (EU) No 1094/2010 and of Regulation (EU) No 1095/2010;

(f) the competent or supervisory authorities in the Member States as specified in the Union acts referred to in Article 1(2) of this Regulation, of Regulation (EU) No 1094/2010 and of Regulation (EU) No 1095/2010.

---

1 See page 48 of this Official Journal.

2 See page 84 of this Official Journal.

(f)加强对客户的保护。

为此,欧洲银行业管理局应致力于确保第2款所述法律文件得到一致且兼具效率和成效的适用,促进监管趋同,向欧洲议会、欧盟理事会以及欧盟委员会提出意见并对市场进行经济分析,以实现欧洲银行业管理局的目标。

履行本条例所赋予的职责时,欧洲银行业管理局应特别注意金融机构所引起的任何系统性风险,因为金融机构的倒闭可能会对金融系统的运行造成影响或损害实体经济。

欧洲银行业管理局在履行其职责时应仅为欧盟的利益独立客观地行事。

第2条 欧洲金融监管体系

1.欧洲银行业管理局应构成欧洲金融监管体系(ESFS)的一部分。欧洲金融监管体系的主要目标在于确保适用于金融行业的规则得到充分的实施以维护金融稳定,确保公众对金融系统整体的信心,充分保护金融服务的消费者。

2.欧洲金融监管体系应由下列机构组成:

(a)欧洲系统性风险委员会(ESRB),履行第1092/2010号(欧盟)条例以及本条例所规定的职责;

(b)欧洲银行业管理局;

(c)依据《欧洲议会与欧盟理事会第1094/2010号(欧盟)条例》[1]设立的欧洲监管机构(欧洲保险与职业养老金管理局);

(d)依据《欧洲议会与欧盟理事会第1095/2010号(欧盟)条例》[2]设立的欧洲监管机构(欧洲证券与市场管理局);

(e)欧洲监管机构联合委员会(以下简称联合委员会),履行本条例、第1094/2010号(欧盟)条例以及第1095/2010号(欧盟)条例第54条至第57条所规定的职责;

(f)本条例、第1094/2010号(欧盟)条例以及第1095/2010号(欧盟)条例第1条第2款所述欧盟法律文件中规定的成员国主管部门或监管机构。

1 请见本《欧盟公报》,第48页。

2 请见本《欧盟公报》,第84页。

3. The Authority shall cooperate regularly and closely with the ESRB as well as with the European Supervisory Authority (European Insurance and Occupational Pensions Authority) and the European Supervisory Authority (European Securities and Markets Authority) through the Joint Committee, ensuring cross-sectoral consistency of work and reaching joint positions in the area of supervision of financial conglomerates and on other cross-sectoral issues.

4. In accordance with the principle of sincere cooperation pursuant to Article 4(3) of the Treaty on European Union, the parties to the ESFS shall cooperate with trust and full mutual respect, in particular in ensuring the flow of appropriate and reliable information between them.

5. Those supervisory authorities that are party to the ESFS shall be obliged to supervise financial institutions operating in the Union in accordance with the acts referred to in Article 1(2).

Article 3 Accountability of the Authorities

The Authorities referred to in Article 2(2)(a) to (d) shall be accountable to the European Parliament and the Council.

Article 4 Definitions

For the purposes of this Regulation the following definitions apply:

(1) 'financial institutions' means 'credit institutions' as defined in Article 4(1) of Directive 2006/48/EC, 'investment firms' as defined in Article 3(1)(b) of Directive 2006/49/EC, and 'financial conglomerates' as defined in Article 2(14) of Directive 2002/87/EC, save that, with regard to Directive 2005/60/EC, 'financial institutions' means credit institutions and financial institutions as defined in Article 3(1) and (2) of that Directive;

(2) 'competent authorities' means:

(i) competent authorities as defined in Directives 2006/48/EC, 2006/49/EC and 2007/64/EC and as referred to in Directive 2009/110/EC;

(ii) with regard to Directives 2002/65/EC and 2005/60/EC, the authorities competent for ensuring compliance with the requirements of those Directives by credit and financial institutions; and

(iii) with regard to deposit guarantee schemes, bodies which administer deposit-guarantee schemes pursuant to Directive 94/19/EC, or, where the operation of the deposit-guarantee scheme is administered by a private company, the public authority supervising those schemes pursuant to that Directive.

Article 5 Legal status

1. The Authority shall be a Union body with legal personality.

2. In each Member State, the Authority shall enjoy the most extensive legal capacity

3.欧洲银行业管理局应定期与欧洲系统性风险委员会以及通过联合委员会与欧洲保险与两个欧洲监管机构（职业养老金管理局和欧洲证券与市场管理局）紧密合作，确保跨行业工作的一致性，并在金融集团监管领域和其他跨行业问题上取得共同立场。

4.根据《欧洲联盟条约》第4条第3款所指的精诚合作原则，欧洲金融监管体系各方应在合作过程中互相信任和充分尊重，以特别确保各方能够彼此交流适当和可靠的信息。

5.属于欧洲金融监管体系一部分的监管机构有义务依照第1条第2款所述法律文件对在欧盟运营的金融机构进行监管。

第3条　部门问责制

第2条第2款第a项至第d项所述的部门应对欧洲议会和欧盟理事会负责。

第4条　定义

在本条例中适用下列定义：

（1）“金融机构”一词，系指如第2006/48/EC号指令第4条第1款所定义的“信贷机构”、如第2006/49/EC号指令第3条第1款第b项所定义的“投资公司”以及如第2002/87/EC号指令第2条第14款所定义的“金融集团”，但就第2005/60/EC号指令而言，“金融机构”一词，系指如该指令第3条第1款和第2款所定义的信贷机构和金融机构；

（2）“主管部门”一词，系指：

（i）第2006/48/EC号指令、第2006/49/EC号指令以及第2007/64/EC号指令所定义的主管部门以及第2009/110/EC号指令所述的主管部门；

（ii）就第2002/65/EC号指令和第2005/60/EC号指令而言，负责确保信贷机构和金融机构遵循该等指令要求的部门；

（iii）对于存款担保计划而言，按照第94/19/EC号指令负责管理存款担保计划的机构，或（对于由私人公司负责管理的存款担保计划而言）按照该指令监管该等计划的公共机构。

第5条　法律地位

1.欧洲银行业管理局系具有法人身份的欧盟机构。

2.在各成员国内，欧洲银行业管理局享有按该成员国法律授予法人的最广泛的民

accorded to legal persons under national law. It may, in particular, acquire or dispose of movable and immovable property and be a party to legal proceedings.

3. The Authority shall be represented by its Chairperson.

Article 6 Composition

The Authority shall comprise:

(1) a Board of Supervisors, which shall exercise the tasks set out in Article 43;

(2) a Management Board, which shall exercise the tasks set out in Article 47;

(3) a Chairperson, who shall exercise the tasks set out in Article 48;

(4) an Executive Director, who shall exercise the tasks set out in Article 53;

(5) a Board of Appeal, which shall exercise the tasks set out in Article 60.

Article 7 Seat

The Authority shall have its seat in London.

CHAPTER Ⅱ TASKS AND POWERS OF THE AUTHORITY

Article 8 Tasks and powers of the Authority

1. The Authority shall have the following tasks:

(a) to contribute to the establishment of high-quality common regulatory and supervisory standards and practices, in particular by providing opinions to the Union institutions and by developing guidelines, recommendations, and draft regulatory and implementing technical standards which shall be based on the legislative acts referred to in Article 1(2);

(b) to contribute to the consistent application of legally binding Union acts, in particular by contributing to a common supervisory culture, ensuring consistent, efficient and effective application of the acts referred to in Article 1(2), preventing regulatory arbitrage, mediating and settling disagreements between competent authorities, ensuring effective and consistent supervision of financial institutions, ensuring a coherent functioning of colleges of supervisors and taking actions, inter alia, in emergency situations;

(c) to stimulate and facilitate the delegation of tasks and responsibilities among competent authorities;

(d) to cooperate closely with the ESRB, in particular by providing the ESRB with the necessary information for the achievement of its tasks and by ensuring a proper follow up to the warnings and recommendations of the ESRB;

事能力。特别是,欧洲银行业管理局可以获得或处置动产和不动产,并可作为法律程序的当事人。

3.欧洲银行业管理局应由其主席代表。

第6条　构成

欧洲银行业管理局由下列机构和人员组成:

(1)履行第43条所列职责的监管机构理事会;

(2)履行第47条所列职责的管理委员会;

(3)履行第48条所列职责的主席;

(4)履行第53条所列职责的执行主任;

(5)履行第60条所列职责的行政复议委员会。

第7条　总部所在地

欧洲银行业管理局总部位于伦敦。

第二章　欧洲银行业管理局的职责和权力

第8条　欧洲银行业管理局的职责和权力

1.欧洲银行业管理局负有下列职责:

(a)促进制定高水平的通用的规制与监管方面的标准和实践,特别是通过向欧盟机构提供意见以及通过制定指引、建议以及起草以第1条第2款中的框架立法为基础的监管性和实施性技术标准草案;

(b)促进具有法律约束力的欧盟立法的一致适用,特别是通过促成共同的监管文化、确保第1条第2款所述法律文件一致的且兼具效率和成效的适用,防范监管套利,调解和解决主管部门之间的分歧、确保对金融机构的有效和一致监管,确保监管团相互连贯的运行并根据情况(尤其是紧急情况下)采取行动;

(c)促进和推动主管部门之间的职责和责任委托;

(d)与欧洲系统性风险委员会紧密合作,特别是向欧洲系统性风险委员会提供履行其职责所必要的信息以及确保对欧洲系统性风险委员会发布的预警和建议的适当跟进;

(e) to organise and conduct peer review analyses of competent authorities, including issuing guidelines and recommendations and identifying best practices, in order to strengthen consistency in supervisory outcomes;

(f) to monitor and assess market developments in the area of its competence, including where appropriate trends in credit, in particular, to households and SMEs;

(g) to undertake economic analyses of markets to inform the discharge of the Authority's functions;

(h) to foster depositor and investor protection;

(i) to contribute to the consistent and coherent functioning of colleges of supervisors, the monitoring, assessment and measurement of systemic risk, the development and coordination of recovery and resolution plans, providing a high level of protection to depositors and investors throughout the Union and developing methods for the resolution of failing financial institutions and an assessment of the need for appropriate financing instruments, in accordance with Articles 21 to 26;

(j) to fulfil any other specific tasks set out in this Regulation or in other legislative acts;

(k) to publish on its website, and to update regularly, information relating to its field of activities, in particular, within the area of its competence, on registered financial institutions, in order to ensure information is easily accessible by the public;

(l) to take over, as appropriate, all existing and ongoing tasks from the Committee of European Banking Supervisors (CEBS).

2. To achieve the tasks set out in paragraph 1, the Authority shall have the powers set out in this Regulation, in particular to:

(a) develop draft regulatory technical standards in the specific cases referred to in Article 10;

(b) develop draft implementing technical standards in the specific cases referred to in Article 15;

(c) issue guidelines and recommendations, as laid down in Article 16;

(d) issue recommendations in specific cases, as referred to in Article 17(3);

(e) take individual decisions addressed to competent authorities in the specific cases referred to in Articles 18(3) and 19(3);

(f) in cases concerning directly applicable Union law, take individual decisions addressed to financial institutions, in the specific cases referred to in Article 17(6), 18(4) and 19(4);

(g) issue opinions to the European Parliament, the Council, or the Commission as provided for in Article 34;

(h) collect the necessary information concerning financial institutions as provided for

(e)组织和开展主管部门的同行审评分析，包括发布指引和建议以及识别最佳实践，以加强监管结果的一致性；

(f)对其职权管辖范围内的市场变化进行监控和评估，包括在适当时对信贷趋势，特别是向家庭和中小企业发放贷款的趋势进行监控和评估；

(g)进行市场经济分析，为欧洲银行业管理局职能的履行提供信息；

(h)促进对存款人和投资者的保护；

(i)根据第21条至第26条，促进监管团能一致并相互连贯地行使职能，监控、评估和计量系统性风险，制定和协调恢复和清盘计划，向欧盟内的存款人和投资者提供高水平的保护，以及为濒临倒闭的金融机构制定清盘方法并制定评估对适当融资工具之需求的方法；

(j)履行本条例以及其他框架立法中规定的任何其他特定职责；

(k)在其网站上公布有关针对注册金融机构所开展的活动(尤其是在其职权管辖范围内)的相关信息并定期更新，以确保公众能方便地查阅信息；

(l)在适当情况下接手欧洲银行业监管机构委员会(CEBS)所有现有的及持续的职责。

2.为完成第1款所列的职责，欧洲银行业管理局应有本条例规定的权力，特别是：

(a)在第10条所述的特定情形下起草监管性技术标准草案；

(b)在第15条所述的特定情形下起草实施性技术标准草案；

(c)发布第16条规定的指引和建议；

(d)在第17条第3款所述的特定情形下提出建议；

(e)在第18条第3款和第19条第3款所述的特定情形下针对主管部门作出个别决定；

(f)在涉及可直接适用的欧盟法律的案件中，在第17条第6款、第18条第4款和第19条第4款所述的特定情形下，针对金融机构作出个别决定；

(g)按第34条规定向欧洲议会、欧盟理事会或欧盟委员会发布意见；

(h)按第35条规定收集与金融机构有关的必要信息；

in Article 35;

(i) develop common methodologies for assessing the effect of product characteristics and distribution processes on the financial position of institutions and on consumer protection;

(j) provide a centrally accessible database of registered financial institutions in the area of its competence where specified in the acts referred to in Article 1(2).

Article 9 Tasks related to consumer protection and financial activities

1. The Authority shall take a leading role in promoting transparency, simplicity and fair ness in the market for consumer financial products or services across the internal market, including by:

(a) collecting, analysing and reporting on consumer trends;

(b) reviewing and coordinating financial literacy and education initiatives by the competent authorities;

(c) developing training standards for the industry; and

(d) contributing to the development of common disclosure rules.

2. The Authority shall monitor new and existing financial activities and may adopt guidelines and recommendations with a view to promoting the safety and soundness of markets and convergence of regulatory practice.

3. The Authority may also issue warnings in the event that a financial activity poses a serious threat to the objectives laid down in Article 1(5).

4. The Authority shall establish, as an integral part of the Authority, a Committee on financial innovation, which brings together all relevant competent national supervisory authorities with a view to achieving a coordinated approach to the regulatory and supervisory treatment of new or innovative financial activities and providing advice for the Authority to present to the European Parliament, the Council and the Commission.

5. The Authority may temporarily prohibit or restrict certain financial activities that threaten the orderly functioning and integrity of financial markets or the stability of the whole or part of the financial system in the Union in the cases specified and under the conditions laid down in the legislative acts referred to in Article 1(2) or, if so required, in the case of an emergency situation in accordance with and under the conditions laid down in Article 18.

The Authority shall review the decision referred to in the first subparagraph at appropriate intervals and at least every 3 months. If the decision is not renewed after a 3–month period, it shall automatically expire.

A Member State may request the Authority to reconsider its decision. In that case, the Authority shall decide, in accordance with the procedure set out in the second subparagraph of Article 44(1), whether it maintains its decision.

(i)为评估产品特征和分销程序对金融机构的财务状况和消费者保护所产生的影响制定通用的方法论;及

(j)在第1条第2款所述法律文件所规定的职权管辖范围内提供一个可集中查阅数据的注册金融机构数据库。

第9条 与消费者保护和金融活动有关的职责

1.欧洲银行业管理局应通过下列手段在为欧盟内部市场的消费金融产品或服务提升市场透明度、简易性和公平中发挥领导作用:

(a)收集、分析并报告关于消费趋势的信息;

(b)审评并协调主管部门的金融普及和教育新方案;

(c)制定行业培训标准;及

(d)致力于通用披露规则的制定。

2.欧洲银行业管理局应对既有的和新型的金融活动进行监控,并可通过指引和建议以促进市场的安全和稳健以及监管实践的趋同。

3.金融活动对第1条第5款所规定的目标造成严重威胁的,欧洲银行业管理局也可发出预警。

4.欧洲银行业管理局应在金融创新方面设立一个委员会,作为欧洲银行业管理局的组成部分。该委员会集合所有相关国家级主管部门,以便在对新型或创新金融活动作出规制和监管处理时能相互协调,并向欧洲银行业管理局提供呈报给欧洲议会、欧盟理事会和欧盟委员会的建议。

5.欧洲银行业管理局可在第1条第2款所述框架立法规定的情形和条件下,或者在出现第18条所述紧急情况且依据第18条设定的条件有此必要的情形下,决定采取临时措施,禁止或限制威胁到欧盟金融市场有序运行和诚信度以及整个或部分金融系统稳定的某些金融活动。

欧洲银行业管理局应以适当的频率至少每3个月1次对本款第1项所述的决定作审评。决定在3个月期限过后未展延的,应自动失效。

成员国可请求欧洲银行业管理局重新审议其决定。在此情况下,欧洲银行业管理局应依照第44条第1款第2项所列程序决定是否维持其决定。

The Authority may also assess the need to prohibit or restrict certain types of financial activity and, where there is such a need, inform the Commission in order to facilitate the adoption of any such prohibition or restriction.

Article 10 Regulatory technical standards

1. Where the European Parliament and the Council delegate power to the Commission to adopt regulatory technical standards by means of delegated acts pursuant to Article 290 TFEU in order to ensure consistent harmonisation in the areas specifically set out in the legislative acts referred to in Article 1(2), the Authority may develop draft regulatory technical standards. The Authority shall submit its draft standards to the Commission for endorsement.

Regulatory technical standards shall be technical, shall not imply strategic decisions or policy choices and their content shall be delimited by the legislative acts on which they are based.

Before submitting them to the Commission, the Authority shall conduct open public consultations on draft regulatory technical standards and analyse the potential related costs and benefits, unless such consultations and analyses are disproportionate in relation to the scope and impact of the draft regulatory technical standards concerned or in relation to the particular urgency of the matter. The Authority shall also request the opinion of the Banking Stakeholder Group referred to in Article 37.

Where the Authority submits a draft regulatory technical standard, the Commission shall immediately forward it to the European Parliament and the Council.

Within 3 months of receipt of a draft regulatory technical standard, the Commission shall decide whether to endorse it. The Commission may endorse the draft regulatory technical standards in part only, or with amendments, where the Union's interests so require.

Where the Commission intends not to endorse a draft regulatory technical standard or to endorse it in part or with amendments, it shall send the draft regulatory technical standard back to the Authority, explaining why it does not endorse it, or, as the case may be, explaining the reasons for its amendments. Within a period of 6 weeks, the Authority may amend the draft regulatory technical standard on the basis of the Commission's proposed amendments and resubmit it in the form of a formal opinion to the Commission. The Authority shall send a copy of its formal opinion to the European Parliament and to the Council.

If, on the expiry of that six-week period, the Authority has not submitted an amended draft regulatory technical standard, or has submitted a draft regulatory technical standard that is not amended in a way consistent with the Commission's proposed amendments, the Commission may adopt the regulatory technical standard with the

欧洲银行业管理局也可对是否需要禁止或限制特定类型金融活动进行评估，如确实有此需要，则应通知欧盟委员会以促成通过任何上述禁令或限制令。

第10条　监管性技术标准

1.欧洲议会和欧盟理事会按照《欧洲联盟运行条约》第290条授权欧盟委员会以授权立法形式通过监管性技术标准（以确保第1条第2款所述框架立法具体规定之各个领域里的一致协调）时，欧洲银行业管理局可起草监管性技术标准草案。欧洲银行业管理局应将其标准草案呈报欧盟委员会，以获得其同意和支持。

监管性技术标准应是技术性标准，不得含有任何战略决定或政策性选择，并且其内容应限于其所依据的框架立法的范围。

欧洲银行业管理局向欧盟委员会呈报监管性技术标准草案之前，应先公开征求公众意见并分析潜在的相关成本和收益，但是，上述意见征询和分析就所涉监管性技术标准草案的范围和影响而言，或就其特殊紧急性而言不成比例的除外。欧洲银行业管理局还应征求第37条所述的银行业利益相关者小组的意见。

欧洲银行业管理局呈报监管性技术标准草案后，欧盟委员会应立即将其转发给欧洲议会和欧盟理事会。

欧盟委员会收到监管性技术标准草案后3个月内，应决定是否同意和支持该草案。按照对欧盟有利的原则，欧盟委员会可仅同意和支持部分草案，或要求作出修改才同意和支持草案。

欧盟委员会有意否决监管性技术标准草案或仅同意和支持其中的一部分或要求作出修改才同意和支持该草案的，应将草案发回欧洲银行业管理局，并视具体情况对其否决该草案或者就草案需要修改的原因作出解释。欧洲银行业管理局可在6周内根据欧盟委员会的修改建议对监管性技术标准草案进行修改，并以正式意见的形式重新向欧盟委员会呈报。欧洲银行业管理局应将其正式意见的复本发送给欧洲议会和欧盟理事会。

6周期限届满，欧洲银行业管理局仍未呈报监管性技术标准草案修正稿，或呈报的修正稿不符合欧盟委员会的修改建议的，欧盟委员会可在作出其认为适当的修改后通过监管性技术标准草案或否决该草案。

amendments it considers relevant, or reject it.

The Commission may not change the content of a draft regulatory technical standard prepared by the Authority without prior coordination with the Authority, as set out in this Article.

2. Where the Authority has not submitted a draft regulatory technical standard within the time limit set out in the legislative acts referred to in Article 1(2), the Commission may request such a draft within a new time limit.

3. Only where the Authority does not submit a draft regulatory technical standard to the Commission within the time limits in accordance with paragraph 2, may the Commission adopt a regulatory technical standard by means of a delegated act without a draft from the Authority.

The Commission shall conduct open public consultations on draft regulatory technical standards and analyse the potential related costs and benefits, unless such consultations and analyses are disproportionate in relation to the scope and impact of the draft regulatory technical standards concerned or in relation to the particular urgency of the matter. The Commis sion shall also request the opinion or advice of the Banking Stakeholder Group referred to in Article 37.

The Commission shall immediately forward the draft regulatory technical standard to the European Parliament and the Council.

The Commission shall send its draft regulatory technical standard to the Authority. Within a period of 6 weeks, the Authority may amend the draft regulatory technical standard and submit it in the form of a formal opinion to the Commission. The Authority shall send a copy of its formal opinion to the European Parliament and to the Council.

If on the expiry of the six-week period referred to in the fourth subparagraph, the Authority has not submitted an amended draft regulatory technical standard, the Commission may adopt the regulatory technical standard.

If the Authority has submitted an amended draft regulatory technical standard within the six-week period, the Commission may amend the draft regulatory technical standard on the basis of the Authority's proposed amendments or adopt the regulatory technical standard with the amendments it considers relevant. The Commission shall not change the content of the draft regulatory technical standard prepared by the Authority without prior coordination with the Authority, as set out in this Article.

4. The regulatory technical standards shall be adopted by means of regulations or decisions. They shall be published in the Official Journal of the European Union and shall enter into force on the date stated therein.

Article 11 Exercise of the delegation

1. The power to adopt regulatory technical standards referred to in Article 10 shall

依本条规定，未事先与欧洲银行业管理局协调，欧盟委员会不得擅自更改由欧洲银行业管理局起草的监管性技术标准草案的内容。

2.欧洲银行业管理局未在第1条第2款所述框架立法规定的期限内呈报监管性技术标准草案的，欧盟委员会可重新设定期限，要求其提供监管性技术标准草案。

3.唯有当欧洲银行业管理局未在第2款规定的期限内向欧盟委员会呈报监管性技术标准草案时，欧盟委员会方可在无欧洲银行业管理局草案的情况下以授权立法的形式通过监管性技术标准。

欧盟委员会应就监管性技术标准草案公开征求公众意见并分析潜在的相关成本和收益，但是，上述意见征询和分析就所涉监管性技术标准草案的范围和影响而言，或就其特殊紧急性而言不成比例的除外。欧盟委员会也应征求第37条所述的银行业利益相关者小组的意见或建议。

欧盟委员会应立即将其起草的监管性技术标准草案转发给欧洲议会和欧盟理事会。

欧盟委员会应将其监管性技术标准草案发送给欧洲银行业管理局。欧洲银行业管理局可在6周内对监管性技术标准进行修改，并以正式意见的形式呈报欧盟委员会。欧洲银行业管理局应将其正式意见的复本分别发送给欧洲议会和欧盟理事会。

第4项规定的6周期限届满，欧洲银行业管理局仍未呈报监管性技术标准草案修改稿的，欧盟委员会可按原文通过该标准。

欧洲银行业管理局在6周期限内呈报了监管性技术标准草案修改稿的，欧盟委员会可基于欧洲银行业管理局的修改建议对监管性技术标准草案进行修改，或完成其自身认为适当的修改后通过监管性技术标准。依本条规定，未事先与欧洲银行业管理局协调，欧盟委员会不得擅自更改由欧洲银行业管理局起草的监管性技术标准草案的内容。

4.监管性技术标准应以条例或决定的形式通过，在《欧盟公报》公布并自其所示之日起生效。

第11条　委托授权的行使

1.自2010年12月16日起，兹授予欧盟委员会第10条所述通过监管性技术标准的权

be conferred on the Commission for a period of 4 years from 16 December 2010. The Commission shall draw up a report in respect of the delegated power not later than 6 months before the end of the 4-year period. The delegation of power shall be automatically extended for pe riods of an identical duration, unless the European Parliament or the Council revokes it in accordance with Article 14.

2. As soon as it adopts a regulatory technical standard, the Commission shall notify it simultaneously to the European Parliament and to the Council.

3. The power to adopt regulatory technical standards is conferred on the Commission subject to the conditions laid down in Articles 12 to 14.

Article 12 Revocation of the delegation

1. The delegation of power referred to in Article 10 may be revoked at any time by the European Parliament or by the Council.

2. The institution which has commenced an internal procedure for deciding whether to revoke a delegation of power shall endeavour to inform the other institution and the Commission within a reasonable time before the final decision is taken, indicating the delegated power which could be subject to revocation.

3. The decision of revocation shall put an end to the delegation of the power specified in that decision. It shall take effect immediately or at a later date specified therein. It shall not affect the validity of the regulatory technical standards already in force. It shall be published in the Official Journal of the European Union.

Article 13 Objections to regulatory technical standards

1. The European Parliament or the Council may object to a regulatory technical standard within a period of 3 months from the date of notification of the regulatory technical standard adopted by the Commission. At the initiative of the European Parliament or the Council that period shall be extended by 3 months.

Where the Commission adopts a regulatory technical standard which is the same as the draft regulatory technical standard submitted by the Authority, the period during which the European Parliament and the Council may object shall be 1 month from the date of notification. At the initiative of the European Parliament or the Council that period shall be extended by 1 month.

2. If, on the expiry of the period referred to in paragraph 1, neither the European Parliament nor the Council has objected to the regulatory technical standard, it shall be published in the Official Journal of the European Union and shall enter into force on the date stated therein.

The regulatory technical standard may be published in the Official Journal of the European Union and enter into force before the expiry of that period if the European Parliament and the Council have both informed the Commission of their intention not to

力,权力有效期为4年。欧盟委员会应在该4年期限届满的6个月前就被委托的权力起草一份报告。除非欧洲议会或欧盟理事会依照第14条撤销委托授权,否则委托授权期限届满后应自动展延,每次展延的期限与原期限相同。

2.欧盟委员会应在通过监管性技术标准后立即同时通知欧洲议会和欧盟理事会。

3.授予欧盟委员会的通过监管性技术标准的权力受制于第12条至第14条规定的条件。

第12条　委托授权的撤销

1.欧洲议会或欧盟理事会可以随时撤销第10条所述的委托授权。

2.欧洲议会或欧盟理事会已经启动决定是否撤销某项委托授权的内部程序的,应当尽力在作出最终决定前的合理时间内通知彼此以及欧盟委员会,指明可能被撤销的委托授权。

3.撤销决定将使其列明的委托授权效力终止。撤销决定应立即生效,或在决定中规定的较晚日期生效。撤销决定不影响已生效的监管性技术标准的效力。撤销决定应在《欧盟公报》公布。

第13条　对监管性技术标准的异议

1.欧洲议会或欧盟理事会可在欧盟委员会通过的监管性技术标准的通知日起3个月期限内对该等标准提出异议。经欧洲议会或欧盟理事会主动要求,该期限可延长3个月。

欧盟委员会依照欧洲银行业管理局呈报的监管性技术标准草案原文通过了该标准,欧洲议会和欧盟理事会提出异议的期限为通知日起的1个月。经欧洲议会或欧盟理事会主动要求,该期限可延长1个月。

2.第1款所述期限届满时,欧洲议会和欧盟理事会均未对监管性技术标准提出异议的,该监管性技术标准应在《欧盟公报》公布,并自其规定的生效日期起生效。

在第1款所述期限届满前,欧洲议会和欧盟理事会均已通知欧盟委员会其无意提出异议的,监管性技术标准可提前在《欧盟公报》公布并生效。

raise objections.

3. If either the European Parliament or the Council objects to a regulatory technical standard within the period referred to in paragraph 1, it shall not enter into force. In accordance with Article 296 TFEU, the institution which objects shall state the reasons for objecting to the regulatory technical standard.

Article 14 Non-endorsement or amendment of draft regulatory technical standards

1. In the event that the Commission does not endorse a draft regulatory technical standard or amends it as provided for in Article 10, the Commission shall inform the Authority, the European Parliament and the Council, stating its reasons.

2. Where appropriate, the European Parliament or the Council may invite the responsible Commissioner, together with the Chairperson of the Authority, within 1 month of the notice referred to in paragraph 1, for an ad hoc meeting of the competent committee of the European Parliament or the Council to present and explain their differences.

Article 15 Implementing technical standards

1. The Authority may develop implementing technical standards, by means of implementing acts pursuant to Article 291 TFEU, in the areas specifically set out in the legislative acts referred to in Article 1(2). Implementing technical standards shall be technical, shall not imply strategic decisions or policy choices and their content shall be to determine the conditions of application of those acts. The Authority shall submit its draft implementing technical standards to the Commission for endorsement.

Before submitting draft implementing technical standards to the Commission, the Authority shall conduct open public consultations and shall analyse the potential related costs and benefits, unless such consultations and analyses are disproportionate in relation to the scope and impact of the draft implementing technical standards concerned or in relation to the particular urgency of the matter. The Authority shall also request the opinion of the Banking Stakeholder Group referred to in Article 37.

Where the Authority submits a draft implementing technical standard, the Commission shall immediately forward it to the European Parliament and the Council.

Within 3 months of receipt of a draft implementing technical standard, the Commission shall decide whether to endorse it. The Commission may extend that period by 1 month. The Commission may endorse the draft implementing technical standard in part only, or with amendments, where the Union's interests so require.

Where the Commission intends not to endorse a draft implementing technical standard or intends to endorse it in part or with amendments, it shall send it back to the Authority explaining why it does not intend to endorse it, or, as the case may be, explaining the reasons for its amendments. Within a period of 6 weeks, the Authority may

3.欧洲议会或欧盟理事会在第1款所述期限内对监管性技术标准提出异议的，该标准不得生效。根据《欧洲联盟运行条约》第296条的规定，对监管性技术标准提出异议的机构应说明异议理由。

第14条　不同意或修改监管性技术标准草案

1.欧盟委员会按第10条规定不同意和支持监管性技术标准草案或对其作出修改的，欧盟委员会应通知欧洲银行业管理局、欧洲议会和欧盟理事会并陈述理由。

2.在适当时，欧洲议会或欧盟理事会可邀请负责的委员与欧洲银行业管理局的主席一同在第1款所指通知发出后1个月内参加欧洲议会或欧盟理事会有关委员会的临时会议，陈述其分歧并对之作出解释。

第15条　实施性技术标准

1.欧洲银行业管理局可在第1条第2款所述框架立法具体规定的领域按照《欧洲联盟运行条约》第291条以实施性立法的形式制定实施性技术标准。实施性技术标准应是技术性标准，不应涉及任何战略决定或政策选择；其内容应是确定上述框架立法的适用条件。欧洲银行业管理局应将实施性技术标准草案呈报欧盟委员会，以获得其同意和支持。

欧洲银行业管理局向欧盟委员会呈报实施性技术标准草案之前，应先公开征求公众意见并分析潜在的相关成本和收益，但是，上述意见征询和分析就所涉实施性技术标准草案的范围和影响而言，或就其特殊紧急性而言不成比例的除外。欧洲银行业管理局还应征求第37条所述的银行业利益相关者小组的意见。

欧洲银行业管理局呈报实施性技术标准草案后，欧盟委员会应立即将其转发给欧洲议会和欧盟理事会。

欧盟委员会收到实施性技术标准草案后3个月内，应决定是否同意和支持该草案。欧盟委员会可将该期限延长1个月。按照对欧盟有利的原则，欧盟委员会可仅同意和支持部分草案，或要求作出修改才同意和支持草案。

欧盟委员会有意否决实施性技术标准草案或仅同意和支持其中的一部分或要求作出修改才同意和支持该草案的，应将草案发回欧洲银行业管理局，并视具体情况对其否决该草案或者就草案需要修改的原因作出解释。欧洲银行业管理局可在6周内根据欧盟委员会的修改建议对实施性技术标准草案进行修改，并以正式意见的形式重

amend the draft implementing technical standard on the basis of the Commission's proposed amendments and resubmit it in the form of a formal opinion to the Commission. The Authority shall send a copy of its formal opinion to the European Parliament and to the Council.

If, on the expiry of the six-week period referred to in the fifth subparagraph, the Authority has not submitted an amended draft implementing technical standard, or has submitted a draft implementing technical standard that is not amended in a way consistent with the Commission's proposed amendments, the Commission may adopt the implementing technical standard with the amendments it considers relevant or reject it.

The Commission shall not change the content of a draft implementing technical standard prepared by the Authority without prior coordination with the Authority, as set out in this Article.

2. In cases where the Authority has not submitted a draft implementing technical standard within the time limit set out in the legislative acts referred to in Article 1(2), the Commission may request such a draft within a new time limit.

3. Only where the Authority does not submit a draft implementing technical standard to the Commission within the time limits in accordance with paragraph 2, may the Commission adopt an implementing technical standard by means of an implementing act without a draft from the Authority.

The Commission shall conduct open public consultations on draft implementing technical standards and analyse the potential related costs and benefits, unless such consultations and analyses are disproportionate in relation to the scope and impact of the draft implementing technical standards concerned or in relation to the particular urgency of the matter. The Commission shall also request the opinion or advice of the Banking Stakeholder Group referred to in Article 37.

The Commission shall immediately forward the draft implementing technical standard to the European Parliament and the Council.

The Commission shall send the draft implementing technical standard to the Authority. Within a period of 6 weeks, the Authority may amend the draft implementing technical standard and submit it in the form of a formal opinion to the Commission. The Authority shall send a copy of its formal opinion to the European Parliament and to the Council.

If, on the expiry of the six-week period referred to in the fourth subparagraph, the Authority has not submitted an amended draft implementing technical standard, the Commission may adopt the implementing technical standard.

If the Authority has submitted an amended draft implementing technical standard within that six-week period, the Commission may amend the draft implementing technical

新向欧盟委员会呈报。欧洲银行业管理局应将其正式意见的复本发送给欧洲议会和欧盟理事会。

第5项所述的6周期限届满，欧洲银行业管理局仍未呈报实施性技术标准草案修改稿，或呈报的修改稿不符合欧盟委员会的修改建议的，欧盟委员会可在作出其认为适当的修改后通过实施性技术标准草案或否决该草案。

依本条规定，未事先与欧洲银行业管理局协调，欧盟委员会不得擅自更改由欧洲银行业管理局起草的实施性技术标准草案的内容。

2.欧洲银行业管理局未在第1条第2款所述框架立法规定的期限内呈报实施性技术标准草案的，欧盟委员会可重新设定期限，要求其提供实施性技术标准草案。

3.唯有当欧洲银行业管理局未在第2款规定的期限内向欧盟委员会呈报实施性技术标准草案时，欧盟委员会方可在无欧洲银行业管理局草案的情况下以实施性立法的形式通过实施性技术标准。

欧盟委员会应就实施性技术标准草案公开征求公众意见，并分析潜在的相关成本和收益，但是，上述意见征询和分析就所涉实施性技术标准草案的范围和影响而言，或就其特殊紧急性而言不成比例的除外。欧盟委员会也应征求第37条所述的银行业利益相关者小组的意见或建议。

欧盟委员会应立即将实施性技术标准草案转发给欧洲议会和欧盟理事会。

欧盟委员会应将实施性技术标准草案发送给欧洲银行业管理局。欧洲银行业管理局可在6周内对实施性技术标准进行修改，并以正式意见的形式呈报欧盟委员会。欧洲银行业管理局应将其正式意见的复本分别发给欧洲议会和欧盟理事会。

第4项所述的6周期限届满，欧洲银行业管理局仍未呈报实施性技术标准草案修改稿的，欧盟委员会可按原文通过该标准。

欧洲银行业管理局在6周期限内呈报了实施性技术标准草案修改稿的，欧盟委员会可基于欧洲银行业管理局的修改建议对实施性技术标准草案进行修改，或完成其

standard on the basis of the Authority's proposed amendments or adopt the implementing technical standard with the amendments it considers relevant.

The Commission shall not change the content of the draft implementing technical standards prepared by the Authority without prior coordination with the Authority, as set out in this Article.

4. The implementing technical standards shall be adopted by means of regulations or decisions. They shall be published in the Official Journal of the European Union and shall enter into force on the date stated therein.

Article 16 Guidelines and recommendations

1. The Authority shall, with a view to establishing consistent, efficient and effective supervisory practices within the ESFS, and to ensuring the common, uniform and consistent application of Union law, issue guidelines and recommendations addressed to competent authorities or financial institutions.

2. The Authority shall, where appropriate, conduct open public consultations regarding the guidelines and recommendations and analyse the related potential costs and benefits. Such consultations and analyses shall be proportionate in relation to the scope, nature and impact of the guidelines or recommendations. The Authority shall, where appropriate, also request opinions or advice from the Banking Stakeholder Group referred to in Article 37.

3. The competent authorities and financial institutions shall make every effort to comply with those guidelines and recommendations.

Within 2 months of the issuance of a guideline or recommendation, each competent authority shall confirm whether it complies or intends to comply with that guideline or recommendation. In the event that a competent authority does not comply or does not intend to comply, it shall inform the Authority, stating its reasons.

The Authority shall publish the fact that a competent authority does not comply or does not intend to comply with that guideline or recommendation. The Authority may also decide, on a case-by-case basis, to publish the reasons provided by the competent authority for not complying with that guideline or recommendation. The competent authority shall receive advanced notice of such publication.

If required by that guideline or recommendation, financial institutions shall report, in a clear and detailed way, whether they comply with that guideline or recommendation.

4. In the report referred to in Article 43(5) the Authority shall inform the European Parliament, the Council and the Commission of the guidelines and recommendations that have been issued, stating which competent authority has not complied with them, and outlining how the Authority intends to ensure that the competent authority concerned follow its recommendations and guidelines in the future.

自身认为适当的修改后通过实施性技术标准。

依本条规定，未事先与欧洲银行业管理局协调，欧盟委员会不得擅自更改由欧洲银行业管理局起草的实施性技术标准草案的内容。

4.实施性技术标准应以条例或决定的形式通过，在《欧盟公报》公布并自其所示之日起生效。

第16条　指引和建议

1.为在欧洲金融监管体系内建立一致的且兼具效率和成效的监管实践，确保欧盟法律的共同、统一和一致的适用，欧洲银行业管理局应针对主管部门或金融机构提出指引和建议。

2.在适当时，欧洲银行业管理局应就指引和建议公开征求公众意见并分析潜在的相关成本和收益。上述意见征询和分析应与指引或建议的范围、性质和影响成比例。在适当时，欧洲银行业管理局还应征求第37条所述银行业利益相关者小组的意见或建议。

3.主管部门和金融机构应尽其所能遵循该等指引和建议。

指引或建议发布后2个月内，各主管部门应确认其是否遵循或有意遵循该指引或建议。主管部门不遵循或不愿遵循的，应通知欧洲银行业管理局并陈述理由。

欧洲银行业管理局应公布主管部门不遵循或不愿遵循该指引或建议的事实。欧洲银行业管理局还可根据具体情况决定公布主管部门所提出的不遵循该指引或建议的理由。公布上述事实或理由应提前通知主管部门。

如指引或建议要求以清楚详尽的方式报告其是否遵循该指引或建议，金融机构应遵守该等要求。

4.在第43条第5款所述的报告中，欧洲银行业管理局应将其已发布的指引或建议通知欧洲议会、欧盟理事会和欧盟委员会，列明未遵循上述指引和建议的主管部门，并简要说明欧洲银行业管理局计划如何确保所涉主管部门未来切实遵循其建议和指引。

Article 17 Breach of Union law

1. Where a competent authority has not applied the acts referred to in Article 1(2), or has applied them in a way which appears to be a breach of Union law, including the regulatory technical standards and implementing technical standards established in accordance with Articles 10 to 15, in particular by failing to ensure that a financial institution satisfies the requirements laid down in those acts, the Authority shall act in accordance with the powers set out in paragraphs 2, 3 and 6 of this Article.

2. Upon a request from one or more competent authorities, the European Parliament, the Council, the Commission or the Banking Stakeholder Group, or on its own initiative, and after having informed the competent authority concerned, the Authority may investigate the alleged breach or non-application of Union law.

Without prejudice to the powers laid down in Article 35, the competent authority shall, without delay, provide the Authority with all information which the Authority considers necessary for its investigation.

3. The Authority may, not later than 2 months from initiating its investigation, address a recommendation to the competent authority concerned setting out the action necessary to comply with Union law.

The competent authority shall, within 10 working days of receipt of the recommendation, inform the Authority of the steps it has taken or intends to take to ensure compliance with Union law.

4. Where the competent authority has not complied with Union law within 1 month from receipt of the Authority's recommendation, the Commission may, after having been informed by the Authority, or on its own initiative, issue a formal opinion requiring the competent authority to take the action necessary to comply with Union law. The Commission's formal opinion shall take into account the Authority's recommendation.

The Commission shall issue such a formal opinion no later than 3 months after the adoption of the recommendation. The Commission may extend this period by 1 month.

The Authority and the competent authorities shall provide the Commission with all necessary information.

5. The competent authority shall, within 10 working days of receipt of the formal opinion referred to in paragraph 4, inform the Commission and the Authority of the steps it has taken or intends to take to comply with that formal opinion.

6. Without prejudice to the powers of the Commission pursuant to Article 258 TFEU, where a competent authority does not comply with the formal opinion referred to in paragraph 4 within the period of time specified therein, and where it is necessary to remedy in a timely manner such non-compliance in order to maintain or restore neutral conditions of competition in the market or ensure the orderly functioning and integrity of

第17条　违反欧盟法律

1.对于第1条第2款所述法律文件，包括依照第10条至第15条的规定制定的监管性技术标准和实施性技术标准，某主管部门未予适用，或者似以违反欧盟法律的方式适用，尤其是未能确保金融机构满足该等法律文件所列要求的，欧洲银行业管理局应依照本条第2款、第3款和第6款授予的权力行事。

2.欧洲银行业管理局可经一个或多个主管部门、欧洲议会、欧盟理事会、欧盟委员会或银行业利益相关者小组请求对涉嫌违反或不适用欧盟法律的情况进行调查，亦可主动进行调查，但调查应提前通知所涉主管部门。

在不影响第35条所规定的权力的情况下，主管部门应按照欧洲银行业管理局的要求立即向其提供调查所必要的一切信息。

3.欧洲银行业管理局可在启动调查后2个月内向所涉主管部门提出建议，提出为遵循欧盟法律所需采取的行动。

主管部门应在收到建议后10个工作日内通知欧洲银行业管理局其为遵循欧盟法律而已采取或有意采取的措施。

4.主管部门在收到欧洲银行业管理局建议1个月内仍未遵守欧盟法律的，欧盟委员会可在接到欧洲银行业管理局通知后发布正式意见，亦可主动发布正式意见，要求主管部门采取必要的行动以遵守欧盟法律。欧盟委员会的正式意见应考虑欧洲银行业管理局的建议。

欧盟委员会应最迟于建议通过后3个月(含)内发布上述正式意见。欧盟委员会可将此期限延长1个月。

欧洲银行业管理局和主管部门应向欧盟委员会提供所有必要信息。

5.主管部门应在收到第4款所述正式意见后10个工作日内通知欧盟委员会和欧洲银行业管理局其为遵循该正式意见而已采取或有意采取的措施。

6.在不影响欧盟委员会在《欧洲联盟运行条约》第258条中的权力的情况下，某主管部门未在第4款所述正式意见确定的期限内遵循该正式意见，且有必要及时对上述不遵循进行补救以维持或恢复市场的竞争中立性或确保金融系统的有序运行和诚信度的，欧洲银行业管理局可在第1条第2款所述法律文件的相关要求可直接适用于金融机构的情况下，针对金融机构作出个别决定，要求其采取必要的行动以履行其在欧

the financial system, the Authority may, where the relevant requirements of the acts referred to in Article 1(2) are directly applicable to financial institutions, adopt an individual decision addressed to a financial institution requiring the necessary action to comply with its obligations under Union law including the cessation of any practice.

The decision of the Authority shall be in conformity with the formal opinion issued by the Commission pursuant to paragraph 4.

7. Decisions adopted under paragraph 6 shall prevail over any previous decision adopted by the competent authorities on the same matter.

When taking action in relation to issues which are subject to a formal opinion pursuant to paragraph 4 or a decision pursuant to paragraph 6, competent authorities shall comply with the formal opinion or the decision, as the case may be.

8. In the report referred to in Article 43(5), the Authority shall set out which competent authorities and financial institutions have not complied with the formal opinions or decisions referred to in paragraphs 4 and 6 of this Article.

Article 18 Action in emergency situations

1. In the case of adverse developments which may seriously jeopardise the orderly functioning and integrity of financial markets or the stability of the whole or part of the financial system in the Union, the Authority shall actively facilitate and, where deemed necessary, coordinate any actions undertaken by the relevant national competent supervisory authorities.

In order to be able to perform that facilitating and coordinating role, the Authority shall be fully informed of any relevant developments, and shall be invited to participate as an observer in any relevant gathering by the relevant national competent supervisory authorities.

2. The Council, in consultation with the Commission and the ESRB and, where appropriate, the ESAs, may adopt a decision addressed to the Authority, determining the existence of an emergency situation for the purposes of this Regulation, following a request by the Authority, the Commission or the ESRB. The Council shall review that decision at appropriate intervals and at least once a month. If the decision is not renewed at the end of a 1-month period, it shall automatically expire. The Council may declare the discontinuation of the emergency situation at any time.

Where the ESRB or the Authority considers that an emergency situation may arise, it shall issue a confidential recommendation addressed to the Council and provide it with an assessment of the situation. The Council shall then assess the need for a meeting. In that process, due care of confidentiality shall be guaranteed.

If the Council determines the existence of an emergency situation, it shall duly inform the European Parliament and the Commission without delay.

盟法律中的义务，包括停办任何业务。

欧洲银行业管理局的决定应与欧盟委员会根据第4款所发布的正式意见一致。

7.根据第6款所作出的决定应优先适用于主管部门之前就相同事宜所作出的决定。

针对第4款下的正式意见或第6款下的决定涉及的问题采取行动时，主管部门应严格遵循相关的正式意见或决定（视具体情况而定）。

8.在第43条第5款所述的报告中，欧洲银行业管理局应列出未遵循本条第4款所述的正式意见或第6款所述的决定的主管部门和金融机构。

第18条　紧急情况下的行动

1.如果发生可能严重危害欧盟金融市场有序运行和诚信度或整个或部分欧盟金融系统稳定的不利变化状况，则欧洲银行业管理局应积极促进并在其认为必要时协调相关的国家级监管主管部门采取的任何行动。

为了能够起到促进和协调的作用，欧洲银行业管理局应充分知悉任何相关的变化情况，并获邀作为观察员参加相关的国家级监管主管部门的任何相关集会。

2.经欧洲银行业管理局、欧盟委员会或欧洲系统性风险委员会请求，欧盟理事会可在与欧盟委员会和欧洲系统性风险委员会磋商以及在适当时与各欧洲监管机构磋商后，向欧洲银行业管理局发出决定，以确定是否存在本条例所指的紧急情况。欧盟理事会应以适当的频率并至少每月1次对该项决定进行审评。如1个月期限届满时决定未展延，则应自动失效。欧盟理事会可随时宣布紧急情况终止。

如欧洲系统性风险委员会或欧洲银行业管理局认为可能会出现紧急情况，应向欧盟理事会发出保密建议，并附对紧急情况的评估。欧盟理事会随后应判断是否有必要召开会议。在该过程中保密的注意义务应得到遵守。

欧盟理事会判定存在紧急情况的，应立即向欧洲议会和欧盟委员会发出通知。

3. Where the Council has adopted a decision pursuant to paragraph 2, and in exceptional circumstances where coordinated action by national authorities is necessary to respond to adverse developments which may seriously jeopardise the orderly functioning and integrity of financial markets or the stability of the whole or part of the financial system in the Union, the Authority may adopt individual decisions requiring competent authorities to take the necessary action in accordance with the legislation referred to in Article 1(2) to address any such developments by ensuring that financial institutions and competent authorities satisfy the requirements laid down in that legislation.

4. Without prejudice to the powers of the Commission pursuant to Article 258 TFEU, where a competent authority does not comply with the decision of the Authority referred to in paragraph 3 within the period laid down in that decision, the Authority may, where the relevant requirements laid down in the legislative acts referred to in Article 1(2) including in regulatory technical standards and implementing technical standards adopted in accordance with those acts are directly applicable to financial institutions, adopt an individual decision addressed to a financial institution requiring the necessary action to comply with its obligations under that legislation, including the cessation of any practice. This shall apply only in situations in which a competent authority does not apply the legislative acts referred to in Article 1(2), including regulatory technical standards and implementing technical standards adopted in accordance with those acts, or applies them in a way which appears to be a manifest breach of those acts, and where urgent remedying is necessary to restore the orderly functioning and integrity of financial markets or the stability of the whole or part of the financial system in the Union.

5. Decisions adopted under paragraph 4 shall prevail over any previous decision adopted by the competent authorities on the same matter.

Any action by the competent authorities in relation to issues which are subject to a decision pursuant to paragraph 3 or 4 shall be compatible with those decisions.

Article 19 Settlement of disagreements between competent authorities in cross-border situations

1. Without prejudice to the powers laid down in Article 17, where a competent authority disagrees about the procedure or content of an action or inaction of a competent authority of another Member State in cases specified in the acts referred to in Article 1(2), the Authority, at the request of one or more of the competent authorities concerned, may assist the authorities in reaching an agreement in accordance with the procedure set out in paragraphs 2 to 4 of this Article.

In cases specified in the legislation referred to in Article 1(2), and where on the basis of objective criteria, disagreement between competent authorities from different Member States can be determined, the Authority may, on its own initiative, assist the

3.欧盟理事会已经作出第2款中的决定，并且为应对可严重危害欧盟金融市场有序运行和诚信度或整个或部分金融系统稳定的不利变化而有必要协调国家级监管机构的行动的，欧洲银行业管理局可作出个别决定，要求主管部门按照第1条第2款所述立法采取必要的行动，以确保金融机构和主管部门符合该等立法的要求，以应对上述不利变化。

4.在不影响欧盟委员会在《欧洲联盟运行条约》第258条中的权力的情况下，第3款所述的欧洲银行业管理局的决定未在该决定规定的时限内为某主管部门所遵守的，欧洲银行业管理局可对金融机构作出个别决定，要求其采取必要的行动（包括停办任何业务），以遵循其在该立法中的义务，前提是第1条第2款所述法律的相关要求以及据其通过的相关监管性技术标准和实施性技术标准所规定的相关要求能够直接适用于金融机构。上述规定仅适用于下列情况：对于第1条第2款所述框架立法，包括根据该等框架立法通过的相关监管性技术标准和实施性技术标准，某主管部门未予适用，或者似以明显违反欧盟法律的方式适用，并且有必要作出紧急补救以恢复欧盟金融市场的有序运行和诚信度或整个或部分欧盟金融系统的稳定。

5.根据第4款作出的决定应优先适用于主管部门之前就相同事宜所作出的任何决定。

主管部门就第3款或第4款中的决定所涉问题采取的任何行动均应符合该等决定。

第19条　跨境情况下主管部门之间分歧的解决

1.在不影响第17条所规定的权力的情况下，某主管部门对另一成员国主管部门在第1条第2款所述法律文件规定的情况下采取的行动或不采取行动所依据的程序或相关内容有异议的，经一个或多个所涉主管部门请求，欧洲银行业管理局可协助各部门依照本条第2款至第4款规定的程序达成一致。

在第1条第2款所述立法规定的情况下，不同成员国主管部门之间的分歧可以基于客观的标准予以判定的，欧洲银行业管理局可主动协助各部门依照第2款至第4款规定的程序达成一致。

authorities in reaching an agreement in accordance with the procedure set out in paragraphs 2 to 4.

2. The Authority shall set a time limit for conciliation between the competent authorities taking into account any relevant time periods specified in the acts referred to in Article 1(2) and the complexity and urgency of the matter. At that stage the Authority shall act as a mediator.

3. If the competent authorities concerned fail to reach an agreement within the conciliation phase referred to in paragraph 2, the Authority may, in accordance with the procedure set out in the third and fourth subparagraph of Article 44(1) take a decision requiring them to take specific action or to refrain from action in order to settle the matter, with binding effects for the competent authorities concerned, in order to ensure compliance with Union law.

4. Without prejudice to the powers of the Commission pursuant to Article 258 TFEU, where a competent authority does not comply with the decision of the Authority, and thereby fails to ensure that a financial institution complies with requirements directly applicable to it by virtue of the acts referred to in Article 1(2), the Authority may adopt an individual decision addressed to a financial institution requiring the necessary action to comply with its obligations under Union law, including the cessation of any practice.

5. Decisions adopted under paragraph 4 shall prevail over any previous decision adopted by the competent authorities on the same matter. Any action by the competent authorities in relation to facts which are subject to a decision pursuant to paragraph 3 or 4 shall be compatible with those decisions.

6. In the report referred to in Article 50(2), the Chairperson of the Authority shall set out the nature and type of disagreements between competent authorities, the agreements reached and the decisions taken to settle such disagreements.

Article 20 Settlement of disagreements between competent authorities across sectors

The Joint Committee shall, in accordance with the procedure laid down in Articles 19 and 56, settle cross-sectoral disagreements that may arise between competent authorities as defined in Article 4(2) of this Regulation, of Regulation (EU) 1094/2010 and of Regulation (EU) 1095/2010 respectively.

Article 21 Colleges of supervisors

1. The Authority shall contribute to promoting and monitoring the efficient, effective and consistent functioning of the colleges of supervisors referred to in Directive 2006/48/EC and foster the coherence of the application of Union law among the colleges of supervisors. With the objective of converging supervisory best practices, staff from the Authority shall be able to participate in the activities of the colleges of supervisors,

2.欧洲银行业管理局应在考虑到第1条第2款所述法律文件规定的任何相关期限以及所涉事项的复杂性和紧迫性后，为主管部门之间的调解设定时限。在该阶段欧洲银行业管理局应作为调解者行事。

3.所涉主管部门未在第2款所述的调解期达成一致的，欧洲银行业管理局可依照第44条第1款第3项和第4项规定的程序作出决定，要求所涉主管部门采取特定行动或不采取行动来解决有关问题，以确保其遵守欧盟法律，该决定对所涉主管部门均具有约束效力。

4.在不影响欧盟委员会在《欧洲联盟运行条约》第258条中的权力的情形下，某主管部门不遵循欧洲银行业管理局的决定，因而无法确保金融机构遵守第1条第2款所述法律文件中可直接适用于该金融机构的要求的，欧洲银行业管理局可针对该金融机构作出个别决定，要求其采取必要的行动，包括停办任何业务，以遵守其在欧盟法律中的义务。

5.根据第4款作出的决定应优先适用于主管部门之前就相同事宜所作出的任何决定。主管部门就第3款或第4款中的决定所涉问题采取的任何行动均应符合该等决定。

6.在第50条第2款所述的报告中，欧洲银行业管理局的主席应说明主管部门之间分歧的性质和类型、达成的一致意见以及为解决该等分歧而作出的决定。

第20条　跨行业主管部门分歧的解决

联合委员会应根据第19条和第56条规定的程序解决本条例、第1094/2010号（欧盟）条例以及第1095/2010号（欧盟）条例各自第4条第2款所界定的主管部门之间的跨行业分歧。

第21条　监管团

1.欧洲银行业管理局应致力于推动并监控第2006/48/EC号指令所述监管团一致的且兼具效率和成效的运行，并促使各监管团在适用欧盟法律时保持一致性。为达到最佳监管实践趋同之目的，欧洲银行业管理局的工作人员应能参加监管团的活动，包括由2个或多个主管部门共同进行的现场检查。

including on-site examinations, carried out jointly by two or more competent authorities.

2. The Authority shall lead in ensuring a consistent and coherent functioning of colleges of supervisors for cross-border institutions across the Union, taking account of the systemic risk posed by financial institutions referred to in Article 23.

For the purpose of this paragraph and of paragraph 1 of this Article, the Authority shall be considered a 'competent authority' within the meaning of the relevant legislation.

The Authority may:

(a) collect and share all relevant information in cooperation with the competent authorities in order to facilitate the work of the college and establish and manage a central system to make such information accessible to the competent authorities in the college;

(b) initiate and coordinate Union-wide stress tests in accordance with Article 32 to assess the resilience of financial institutions, in particular the systemic risk posed by financial institutions as referred to in Article 23, to adverse market developments, and evaluate the potential for systemic risk to increase in situations of stress, ensuring that a consistent methodology is applied at the national level to such tests and, where appropriate, address a recommendation to the competent authority to correct issues identified in the stress test;

(c) promote effective and efficient supervisory activities, including evaluating the risks to which financial institutions are or might be exposed as determined under the supervisory review process or in stress situations;

(d) oversee, in accordance with the tasks and powers specified in this Regulation, the tasks carried out by the competent authorities; and

(e) request further deliberations of a college in any cases where it considers that the decision would result in an incorrect application of Union law or would not contribute to the objective of convergence of supervisory practices. It may also require the consolidating supervisor to schedule a meeting of the college or add a point to the agenda of a meeting.

3. The Authority may develop draft regulatory and implementing technical standards to ensure uniform conditions of application with respect to the provisions regarding the operational functioning of colleges of supervisors and issue guidelines and recommendations adopted pursuant to Article 16 to promote convergence in supervisory functioning and best practices adopted by the colleges of supervisors.

4. The Authority shall have a legally binding mediation role to resolve disputes between competent authorities in accordance with the procedure set out in Article 19. The Authority may take supervisory decisions directly applicable to the institution concerned in accordance with Article 19.

2.欧洲银行业管理局在考虑到第23条所述金融机构所产生的系统性风险的前提下,应在确保监管团对欧盟各跨境机构的监管发挥相互一致的功能中起到领导作用。

就本款以及本条第1款而言,欧洲银行业管理局应被视为相关立法所定义的“主管部门”。

欧洲银行业管理局可:

(a)与主管部门合作收集并共享所有相关信息,以推进监管团的工作,以及建立和管理一个中央信息系统,使监管团中的各主管部门能够查阅上述信息;

(b)根据第32条启动并协调欧盟范围内的压力测试,以评估金融机构在不利市场变化下的抗冲击能力,特别是评估第23条所述金融机构产生的系统性风险;评估在压力状况下系统性风险增加的可能性,确保各成员国实施该等测试的方法具有一致性,以及在适当时向主管部门提出更正压力测试中发现的问题的建议;

(c)推广高效率和高成效的监管活动,包括评估在监管审查过程中确定的、金融机构正在或可能面临的风险或金融机构在压力状况下正在或可能面临的风险;

(d)根据本条例所规定的职责和权力,对主管部门履行职责的情况进行监控;及

(e)在其认为某监管团的决定会导致欧盟法律的不正确适用或不利于监管实践趋同目的的任何情况下,要求该监管团进一步审议该决定。欧洲银行业管理局还可要求并表监管机构为监管团安排会议或增加会议议程。

3.欧洲银行业管理局可起草监管性和实施性技术标准草案以确保有关监管团具体运作的条款具有统一的适用条件,并发布根据第16条所制定的指引和建议,以推动各监管团的监管运作方式以及所采用的最佳实践的趋同。

4.欧洲银行业管理局应在依照第19条规定的程序解决主管部门之间的争议中发挥具有法律约束力的调解作用。根据第19条,欧洲银行业管理局可作出直接适用于所涉机构的监管决定。

Article 22 General provisions

1. The Authority shall duly consider systemic risk as defined by Regulation (EU) No 1092/2010. It shall address any risk of disruption in financial services that:

(a) is caused by an impairment of all or parts of the financial system; and

(b) has the potential to have serious negative consequences for internal market and the real economy.

The Authority shall consider, where appropriate, the monitoring and assessment of systemic risk as developed by the ESRB and the Authority and respond to warnings and recommendations by the ESRB in accordance with Article 17 of Regulation (EU) No 1092/2010.

2. The Authority shall, in collaboration with the ESRB, develop a common set of quantitative and qualitative indicators (risk dashboard) to identify and measure systemic risk.

The Authority shall also develop an adequate stress-testing regime to help identifying those institutions that may pose systemic risk. These institutions shall be subject to strengthened supervision, and where necessary, to the recovery and resolution procedures referred to in Article 25.

3. Without prejudice to the acts referred to in Article 1(2), the Authority shall draw up, as necessary, additional guidelines and recommendations for financial institutions, to take account of the systemic risk posed by them.

The Authority shall ensure that the systemic risk posed by financial institutions is taken into account when developing draft regulatory and implementing technical standards in the areas laid down in the legislative acts referred to in Article 1(2).

4. Upon a request from one or more competent authorities, the European Parliament, the Council or the Commission, or on its own initiative, the Authority may conduct an inquiry into a particular type of financial institution or type of product or type of conduct in order to assess potential threats to the stability of the financial system and make appropriate recommendations for action to the competent authorities concerned.

For those purposes, the Authority may use the powers conferred on it under this Regulation, including Article 35.

5. The Joint Committee shall ensure overall and cross-sectoral coordination of the activities carried out in accordance with this Article.

Article 23 Identification and measurement of systemic risk

1. The Authority shall, in consultation with the ESRB, develop criteria for the identification and measurement of systemic risk and an adequate stress-testing regime which includes an evaluation of the potential for systemic risk posed by financial institutions to increase in situations of stress. The financial institutions that may pose a systemic risk shall be subject to strengthened supervision, and where necessary, the

第22条　一般条款

1.欧洲银行业管理局应充分考虑第1092/2010号(欧盟)条例所界定的系统性风险。欧洲银行业管理局应处理符合下列条件的任何金融系统发生扰乱的风险:

(a)由整个或部分金融系统的损害所造成的;并且

(b)可能会对欧盟内部市场和实体经济造成严重负面后果的。

欧洲银行业管理局应适时考虑由欧洲系统性风险委员会和欧洲银行业管理局所进行的系统性风险监控和评估,并按照第1092/2010号(欧盟)条例第17条对欧洲系统性风险委员会所提出的预警和建议作出回应。

2.欧洲银行业管理局应与欧洲系统性风险委员会合作,制定用以识别和计量系统性风险的一组通用的定量和定性指标(风险监控表)。

欧洲银行业管理局还应建立适当的压力测试机制来帮助识别可能带来系统性风险的机构。应加强对此等机构的监管,并在必要时对其适用第25条所述的恢复和清盘程序。

3.在不影响第1条第2款所述法律文件的情况下,在必要时,欧洲银行业管理局应考虑金融机构所带来的系统性风险,就其起草额外的指引和建议。

在第1条第2款所述框架立法所规定的领域起草监管性和实施性技术标准草案时,欧洲银行业管理局应确保已考虑了金融机构所带来的系统性风险。

4.欧洲银行业管理局可经一个或多个主管部门、欧洲议会、欧盟理事会或欧盟委员会请求对某一特定类型的金融机构或产品或行为进行调查,亦可主动进行调查,以评估其对金融系统稳定的潜在威胁,并对所涉主管部门提出适当的行动建议。

欧洲银行业管理局可为该等目的行使本条例(包括第35条)授予的权力。

5.联合委员会应确保根据本条所开展的活动的全面和跨行业协调。

第23条　识别和计量系统性风险

1.欧洲银行业管理局应与欧洲系统性风险委员会磋商,制定识别和计量系统性风险的标准,并建立完善的压力测试机制,该机制应包含对于压力状况下金融机构系统性风险增加的可能性的评估。应加强对可能带来系统性风险的金融机构的监管,并在必要时对其适用第25条所述的恢复和清盘程序。

recovery and resolution procedures referred to in Article 25.

2. The Authority shall take fully into account the relevant international approaches when developing the criteria for the identification and measurement of systemic risk posed by financial institutions, including those established by the Financial Stability Board, the International Monetary Fund and the Bank for International Settlements.

Article 24 Permanent capacity to respond to systemic risks

1. The Authority shall ensure it has specialised and ongoing capacity to respond effectively to the materialisation of systemic risks as referred to in Articles 22 and 23, in particular, with respect to institutions that pose a systemic risk.

2. The Authority shall fulfil the tasks conferred upon it in this Regulation and in the legislation referred to in Article 1(2), and shall contribute to ensuring a coherent and coordinated crisis management and resolution regime in the Union.

Article 25 Recovery and resolution procedures

1. The Authority shall contribute to and participate actively in the development and coordination of effective and consistent recovery and resolution plans, procedures in emergency situations and preventive measures to minimise the systemic impact of any failure.

2. The Authority may identify best practices aimed at facilitating the resolution of failing institutions and, in particular, cross-border groups, in ways which avoid contagion, ensuring that appropriate tools, including sufficient resources, are available and allow the institution or the group to be resolved in an orderly, cost-efficient and timely manner.

3. The Authority may develop regulatory and implementing technical standards as specified in the legislative acts referred to in Article 1(2) in accordance with the procedure laid down in Articles 10 to 15.

Article 26 European system of deposit guarantee schemes

1. The Authority shall contribute to strengthening the European system of national deposit guarantee schemes by acting under the powers conferred to it in this Regulation to ensure the correct application of Directive 94/19/EC with the aim of ensuring that national deposit guarantee schemes are adequately funded by contributions from financial institutions including from those financial institutions established and taking deposits within the Union but headquartered outside the Union as provided for in Directive 94/19/EC and provide a high level of protection to all depositors in a harmonised framework throughout the Union, which leaves the stabilising safeguard role of mutual guarantee schemes intact, provided they comply with Union legislation.

2. Article 16 concerning the Authority's powers to adopt guidelines and recommendations shall apply to deposit guarantee schemes.

3. The Authority may develop regulatory and implementing technical standards as

2.在制定识别和计量金融机构的系统性风险标准时，欧洲银行业管理局应充分考虑相关国际处理方法，包括金融稳定委员会、国际货币基金组织以及国际清算银行所制定的方法。

第24条　持续应对系统性风险的能力

1.欧洲银行业管理局应确保有专门和持续的能力对第22条和第23条所述系统性风险的具体结果特别是对产生系统性风险的机构作出有效回应。

2.欧洲银行业管理局应履行本条例以及第1条第2款所述立法赋予的职责，并应致力于确保欧盟具备相互一致和协调的危机管理和清盘机制。

第25条　恢复和清盘程序

1.欧洲银行业管理局应促进并积极参与下列各项的制定和协调工作：紧急情况下有效、一致的恢复和清盘计划和程序，以及将任何金融机构倒闭的系统性影响降到最低的预防性措施。

2.欧洲银行业管理局可识别旨在以避免风险传播的方式促进濒临倒闭机构（尤其是跨境集团）清盘的最佳实践，以确保有适当的工具（包括充分资源）可供使用，保障能以有序且有成本效益的方式及时对机构或者集团进行清盘。

3.欧洲银行业管理局可依照第10条至第15条规定的程序，制定第1条第2款所述框架立法指明的监管性和实施性技术标准。

第26条　欧洲存款担保计划体系

1.欧洲银行业管理局应通过运用其在本条例下的权力，致力于强化欧洲国家级存款担保计划体系，保障第94/19/EC号指令正确适用，以确保国家级存款担保计划从金融机构（包括第94/19/EC号指令所规定的那些在欧盟内设立并接受存款但总部位于欧盟之外的金融机构）处收到充足的缴款以获得充足的经费，并确保在全欧盟协调一致的框架中给予所有存款人高水平的保护。因此，在符合欧盟立法的前提下，互助担保计划维持稳定的保障性角色将不改变。

2.第16条关于欧洲银行业管理局制定指引和建议的权力的规定应适用于存款担保计划。

3.欧洲银行业管理局可依照第10条至第15条规定的程序起草第1条第2款所述框

specified in the legislative acts referred to in Article 1(2) in accordance with the procedure laid down in Articles 10 to 15.

4. The review of this Regulation provided for in Article 81 shall, in particular, examine the convergence of the European system of national deposit guarantee schemes.

Article 27 European system of bank resolution and funding arrangements

1. The Authority shall contribute to developing methods for the resolution of failing financial institutions, in particular those that may pose a systemic risk, in ways which avoid contagion and allow them to be wound down in an orderly and timely manner, including, where applicable, coherent and robust funding mechanisms as appropriate.

2. The Authority shall contribute to the assessment of the need for a system of coherent, robust and credible funding mechanisms, with appropriate financing instruments linked to a set of coordinated national crisis management arrangements.

The Authority shall contribute to the work on the level playing field issues and cumulative impacts of any systems of levies and contributions on financial institutions that may be introduced to ensure fair burden sharing and incentives to contain systemic risk as a part of a coherent and credible resolution framework.

The review of this Regulation provided for in Article 81 shall, in particular, examine the possible enhancement of the role of the Authority in a framework of crisis prevention, management and resolution, and, if necessary, the creation of a European resolution fund.

Article 28 Delegation of tasks and responsibilities

1. Competent authorities may, with the consent of the delegate, delegate tasks and responsibilities to the Authority or other competent authorities subject to the conditions set out in this Article. Member States may set out specific arrangements regarding the delegation of responsibilities that have to be complied with before their competent authorities enter into such delegation agreements, and may limit the scope of delegation to what is necessary for the effective supervision of cross-border financial institutions or groups.

2. The Authority shall stimulate and facilitate the delegation of tasks and responsibilities between competent authorities by identifying those tasks and responsibilities that can be delegated or jointly exercised and by promoting best practices.

3. The delegation of responsibilities shall result in the reallocation of competences laid down in the acts referred to in Article 1(2). The law of the delegate authority shall govern the procedure, enforcement and administrative and judicial review relating to the delegated responsibilities.

4. The competent authorities shall inform the Authority of delegation agreements into which they intend to enter. They shall put the agreements into effect at the earliest 1 month after informing the Authority.

架立法指明的监管性和实施性技术标准。

4.本条例第81条规定的对本条例的审评应特别就欧洲国家级存款担保计划体系的趋同进行审查。

第27条　欧洲银行清盘系统和资金安排

1.欧洲银行业管理局应致力于制定濒临倒闭的金融机构,特别是那些可能产生系统性风险的金融机构的相关清盘方法。此等清盘方法应避免风险的传播,允许金融机构能有序、及时地停业清理,包括建立相互一致且完善的适当经费筹措机制(如适用)。

2.欧洲银行业管理局应致力于评估符合下列条件的经费筹措机制的必要性:相互一致、强大和可信,并且具有适当的融资工具,与一系列相互协调的国家级危机管理安排相配套。

欧洲银行业管理局应致力于下列两方面的工作:公平竞争问题;以及对金融机构实行各种计征费和缴款制度对金融机构产生的累积效应,该等制度可能会作为一个相互一致且可信的清盘框架的一部分,以确保公平的成本分担,并由此为金融机构创造足够的动力去遏制系统性风险。

根据本条例第81条规定对本条例进行审评时,应特别考察欧洲银行业管理局在危机预防、管理和清盘框架中以及(必要时)在设立欧洲清盘基金中发挥的作用能否有所加强。

第28条　职责和责任的委托

1.经受托人同意,主管部门可按本条所列条件将职责和责任委托给欧洲银行业管理局或其他主管部门。成员国可规定在其主管部门达成上述委托协议前所应遵循的责任委托的特殊安排,并可将委托范围限定在对跨境金融机构或集团进行有效监管必要的范围内。

2.欧洲银行业管理局应通过识别可以委托或可以共同履行的职责和责任以及推广最佳实践的方式,来促进和推动主管部门之间的职责和责任委托。

3.责任委托会产生第1条第2款所述法律文件所规定的职权的再分配。受托部门的法律应对与被委托的责任有关的程序、执法以及行政和司法审查进行规制。

4.主管部门应将其拟缔结的委托协议通知欧洲银行业管理局。该等协议最早应在通知欧洲银行业管理局1个月后生效。

The Authority may give an opinion on the intended agreement within 1 month of being informed.

The Authority shall publish, by appropriate means, any delegation agreement as concluded by the competent authorities, in order to ensure that all parties concerned are informed appropriately.

Article 29 Common supervisory culture

1. The Authority shall play an active role in building a common Union supervisory culture and consistent supervisory practices, as well as in ensuring uniform procedures and consistent approaches throughout the Union. The Authority shall carry out, at a minimum, the following activities:

(a) providing opinions to competent authorities;

(b) promoting an effective bilateral and multilateral exchange of information between competent authorities, with full respect for the applicable confidentiality and data protection provisions provided for in the relevant Union legislation;

(c) contributing to developing high-quality and uniform supervisory standards, including reporting standards, and international accounting standards in accordance with Article 1(3);

(d) reviewing the application of the relevant regulatory and implementing technical standards adopted by the Commission, and of the guidelines and recommendations issued by the Authority and proposing amendments where appropriate; and

(e) establishing sectoral and cross-sectoral training programmes, facilitating personnel exchanges and encouraging competent authorities to intensify the use of secondment schemes and other tools.

2. The Authority may, as appropriate, develop new practical instruments and convergence tools to promote common supervisory approaches and practices.

Article 30 Peer reviews of competent authorities

1. The Authority shall periodically organise and conduct peer reviews of some or all of the activities of competent authorities, to further strengthen consistency in supervisory out comes. To that end, the Authority shall develop methods to allow for objective assessment and comparison between the authorities reviewed. When conducting peer reviews, existing information and evaluations already made with regard to the competent authority concerned shall be taken into account.

2. The peer review shall include an assessment of, but shall not be limited to:

(a) the adequacy of resources and governance arrangements of the competent authority, with particular regard to the effective application of the regulatory technical standards and implementing technical standards referred to in Articles 10 to 15 and of the acts referred to in Article 1(2) and the capacity to respond to market developments;

欧洲银行业管理局可在收到上述拟缔结的协议通知后的1个月内发表意见。

欧洲银行业管理局应以适当的方式公布主管部门所缔结的任何委托协议，以确保所涉各方均得到适当的通知。

第29条　共同的监管文化

1.欧洲银行业管理局应在建立共同的欧盟监管文化和一致的监管实践以及确保欧盟有统一的程序和一致的方法中发挥积极的作用。欧洲银行业管理局至少应开展下列活动：

(a)向主管部门提供意见；

(b)推进主管部门在充分遵守相关欧盟立法适用的保密和数据保护规定的前提下进行有效的双边或多边信息交流；

(c)根据第1条第3款的规定致力于制定高质量和统一的监管标准，包括报告标准，以及国际会计标准；

(d)审评欧盟委员会所通过的相关监管性和实施性技术标准以及欧洲银行业管理局所发布的指引和建议的适用，并在适当时提出修改建议；及

(e)制订行业或跨行业培训计划，促进人员交流并鼓励主管部门更多地使用人员借调计划以及其他工具。

2.欧洲银行业管理局可根据情况开发新的实用工具和趋同手段来推广共同的监管方法和实践。

第30条　主管部门的同行审评

1.欧洲银行业管理局应针对主管部门的部分或全部活动定期组织和开展同行审评，以进一步加强监管结果的一致性。为此，欧洲银行业管理局应制定相关方法，以实现被审评部门之间的客观评价和比较。开展同行审评时，应考虑到与所涉主管部门有关的现有信息以及过去已作过的评价结果。

2.同行审评应包括但不限于下列方面的评价：

(a)主管部门资源和治理安排的充分性，特别是对于第10条至第15条的规定所述监管性技术标准和实施性技术标准以及第1条第2款所述法律文件的有效适用而言是否充分，以及应对市场变化的能力；

(b) the degree of convergence reached in the application of Union law and in supervisory practice, including regulatory technical standards and implementing technical standards, guidelines and recommendations adopted pursuant to Articles 10 to 16, and the extent to which the supervisory practice achieves the objectives set out in Union law;

(c) best practices developed by some competent authorities which might be of benefit for other competent authorities to adopt;

(d) the effectiveness and the degree of convergence reached with regard to the enforcement of the provisions adopted in the implementation of Union law, including the administrative measures and sanctions imposed against persons responsible where those provisions have not been complied with.

3. On the basis of a peer review, the Authority may issue guidelines and recommendations pursuant to Article 16. In accordance with Article 16 (3), the competent authorities shall endeavour to follow those guidelines and recommendations. The Authority shall take into account the outcome of the peer review when developing draft regulatory technical or implementing technical standards in accordance with Articles 10 to 15.

4. The Authority shall make the best practices that can be identified from those peer reviews publicly available. In addition, all other results of peer reviews may be disclosed publicly, subject to the agreement of the competent authority that is the subject of the peer review.

Article 31 Coordination function

The Authority shall fulfil a general coordination role between competent authorities, in particular in situations where adverse developments could potentially jeopardise the orderly functioning and integrity of financial markets or the stability of the financial system in the Union.

The Authority shall promote a coordinated Union response, inter alia, by:

(a) facilitating the exchange of information between the competent authorities;

(b) determining the scope and, where possible and appropriate, verifying the reliability of information that should be made available to all the competent authorities concerned;

(c) without prejudice to Article 19, carrying out non-binding mediation upon a request from the competent authorities or on its own initiative;

(d) notifying the ESRB of any potential emergency situations without delay;

(e) taking all appropriate measures in case of developments which may jeopardise the functioning of the financial markets with a view to facilitating the coordination of actions undertaken by relevant competent authorities;

(f) centralising information received from competent authorities in accordance with

(b)欧盟法律的适用以及监管实践(包括根据第10条至第16条制定的监管性技术标准和实施性技术标准、指引和建议)所达到的趋同程度,以及监管实践在多大程度上实现了欧盟法律设定的目标;

(c)某些主管部门制定的可能值得其他主管部门采用的最佳实践;

(d)欧盟法律实施当中制定的规定,在执行时所达到的有效程度和趋同程度,包括发生违反该等规定的行为时对相关负责人施加的行政措施和处罚。

3.欧洲银行业管理局可在同行审评的基础上依据第16条发布指引和建议。根据第16条第3款,主管部门应尽力遵循该等指引和建议。欧洲银行业管理局在根据第10条至第15条的规定起草监管性和实施性技术标准草案时,应考虑同行审评的结果。

4.对于从该等同行审评中识别出的最佳实践,欧洲银行业管理局应予公布。此外,在作为同行审评对象的主管部门同意披露的前提下,同行审评的所有其他结果也可向公众披露。

第31条　协调职能

欧洲银行业管理局尤应在发生可能对欧盟金融市场有序运行和诚信度或金融系统稳定造成危害的不利变化时在主管部门之间发挥总协调作用。

欧洲银行业管理局应通过相关措施促进欧盟内部相互协调的回应,包括但不限于:

(a)促进主管部门之间的信息交流;

(b)确定应向所有所涉主管部门提供的信息范围,在可能和适当时对其可靠性予以核实;

(c)在不影响第19条的情况下,经主管部门请求开展无约束力的调解,亦可主动开展调解;

(d)立即通知欧洲系统性风险委员会任何可能发生的紧急情况;

(e)在发生可能危害金融市场运行的变化时,采取所有适当的措施以为相关主管部门行动间的协调工作提供方便;

(f)根据第21条和第35条汇总从主管部门接收到的信息,此等信息为主管部门就

Articles 21 and 35 as the result of the regulatory reporting obligations for institutions active in more than one Member State. The Authority shall share that information with the other competent authorities concerned.

Article 32 Assessment of market developments

1. The Authority shall monitor and assess market developments in the area of its competence and, where necessary, inform the European Supervisory Authority (European Insurance and Occupational Pensions Authority) and the European Supervisory Authority (European Securities and Markets Authority), the ESRB and the European Parliament, the Council and the Commission about the relevant micro-prudential trends, potential risks and vulnerabilities. The Authority shall include in its assessments an economic analysis of the markets in which financial institutions operate and an assessment of the impact of potential market developments on such institutions.

2. The Authority shall, in cooperation with the ESRB, initiate and coordinate Union-wide assessments of the resilience of financial institutions to adverse market developments. To that end, it shall develop the following, for application by the competent authorities:

(a) common methodologies for assessing the effect of economic scenarios on an institution's financial position;

(b) common approaches to communication on the outcomes of these assessments of the resilience of financial institutions;

(c) common methodologies for assessing the effect of particular products or distribution processes on an institution's financial position and on depositors, investors and customer information.

3. Without prejudice to the tasks of the ESRB set out in Regulation (EU) No 1092/2010, the Authority shall, at least once a year, and more frequently as necessary, provide assessments to the European Parliament, the Council, the Commission and the ESRB of trends, potential risks and vulnerabilities in its area of competence.

The Authority shall include a classification of the main risks and vulnerabilities in these assessments and, where necessary, recommend preventative or remedial actions.

4. The Authority shall ensure an adequate coverage of cross-sectoral developments, risks and vulnerabilities by closely cooperating with the European Supervisory Authority (European Insurance and Occupational Pensions Authority) and the European Supervisory Authority (European Securities and Markets Authority) through the Joint Committee.

Article 33 International relations

1. Without prejudice to the respective competences of the Member States and the Union institutions, the Authority may develop contacts and enter into administrative

在多个成员国境内开展业务的金融机构履行监管报告义务所形成的。欧洲银行业管理局应与其他所涉主管部门共享该等信息。

第32条　对市场变化的评估

1.欧洲银行业管理局应对其职权管辖范围内的市场变化进行监控和评估,并在必要时将相关的微观审慎趋势、潜在风险及薄弱环节通知两个欧洲监管机构(欧洲保险与职业养老金管理局和欧洲证券与市场管理局)、欧洲系统性风险委员会以及欧洲议会、欧盟理事会和欧盟委员会。欧洲银行业管理局的评估还应包括对金融机构所在市场的经济分析以及对该等机构受潜在市场变化影响的评估。

2.欧洲银行业管理局应与欧洲系统性风险委员会合作,在欧盟范围内启动和协调对金融机构面临不利市场变化时的抗冲击能力的评估。为此,欧洲银行业管理局应制定下列方式和方法供主管部门使用:

(a)评估不同的经济场景对金融机构财务状况影响的通用方法;

(b)对金融机构的抗冲击能力评估结果进行交流所采用的通用方法;

(c)评估特殊产品或销售方法对金融机构的财务状况以及存款人、投资者和客户信息影响的通用方法。

3.在不影响欧洲系统性风险委员会在第1092/2010号(欧盟)条例中的职责的情况下,欧洲银行业管理局应至少每年1次并在必要时更频繁地为欧洲议会、欧盟理事会、欧盟委员会和欧洲系统性风险委员会提供其职权管辖范围内对趋势、潜在风险和薄弱环节的评估结果。

欧洲银行业管理局应在此等评估中对主要风险和薄弱环节进行分类,并在必要时提出预防或补救行动的建议。

4.欧洲银行业管理局应通过联合委员会与两个欧洲监管机构(欧洲保险与职业养老金管理局和欧洲证券与市场管理局)紧密合作,确保其监管工作充分覆盖跨行业变化、风险和薄弱环节。

第33条　国际关系

1.在不影响成员国和欧盟机构各自职权的情况下,欧洲银行业管理局可与监管机构、国际组织以及第三国的行政管理部门建立联系并达成行政安排。该等安排既不得

arrangements with supervisory authorities, international organisations and the administrations of third countries. Those arrangements shall not create legal obligations in respect of the Union and its Member States nor shall they prevent Member States and their competent authorities from concluding bilateral or multilateral arrangements with those third countries.

2. The Authority shall assist in preparing equivalence decisions pertaining to supervisory regimes in third countries in accordance with the acts referred to in Article 1 (2).

3. In the report referred to in Article 43(5), the Authority shall set out the administrative arrangements agreed upon with international organisations or administrations in third countries and the assistance provided in preparing equivalence decisions.

Article 34 Other tasks

1. The Authority may, upon a request from the European Parliament, the Council or the Commission, or on its own initiative, provide opinions to the European Parliament, the Council and the Commission on all issues related to its area of competence.

2. With regard to prudential assessments of mergers and acquisitions falling within the scope of Directive 2006/48/EC, as amended by Directive 2007/44/EC, and which according to that Directive require consultation between competent authorities from two or more Member States, the Authority may, on application of one of the competent authorities concerned, issue and publish an opinion on a prudential assessment, except in relation to the criteria in Article 19a(1)(e) of Directive 2006/48/EC. The opinion shall be issued promptly and in any event before the end of the assessment period in accordance with Directive 2006/48/EC, as amended by Directive 2007/44/EC. Article 35 shall apply to the areas in respect of which the Authority may issue an opinion.

Article 35 Collection of information

1. At the request of the Authority, the competent authorities of the Member States shall provide the Authority with all the necessary information to carry out the duties assigned to it by this Regulation, provided that they have legal access to the relevant information and that the request for information is necessary in relation to the nature of the duty in question.

2. The Authority may also request information to be provided at recurring intervals and in specified formats. Such requests shall, where possible, be made using common reporting formats.

3. Upon a duly justified request from a competent authority of a Member State, the Authority may provide any information that is necessary to enable the competent authority to carry out its duties, in accordance with the professional secrecy obligations laid down in sectoral legislation and in Article 70.

为欧盟及其成员国设定法律义务，也不得妨碍成员国及其主管部门与该等第三国缔结双边或多边安排。

2.根据第1条第2款所述法律文件，欧洲银行业管理局应协助完成关于第三国监管体制的等效性决定。

3.在第43条第5款所述的报告中，欧洲银行业管理局应列出与国际组织或第三国行政管理部门所缔结的行政安排以及在作出等效性决定中所提供的协助。

第34条　其他职责

1.经欧洲议会、欧盟理事会或欧盟委员会请求，欧洲银行业管理局可就与其职权管辖范围内的一切有关的问题向欧洲议会、欧盟理事会和欧盟委员会提供意见，亦可自行提供该等意见。

2.对于在第2006/48/EC号指令（经第2007/44/EC号指令修正）范围内且根据该指令需要2个或多个成员国主管部门进行磋商的并购，经其中一个所涉主管部门申请，欧洲银行业管理局可发布并公开关于此类并购审慎评估的意见，但是，涉及第2006/48/EC号指令第19a条第1款第e项中的评估标准的情况除外。该等意见应迅速发布，并且任何情况下均应于第2006/48/EC号指令（经第2007/44/EC号指令修正）规定的评估期限结束前发布。第35条适用于欧洲银行业管理局可发布意见的领域。

第35条　信息的收集

1.经欧洲银行业管理局请求，在该等成员国主管部门自身能合法获得相关信息并且该信息就所涉职责性质而言确属必要的前提下，各成员国主管部门应向欧洲银行业管理局提供履行其在本条例中的职责所必要的一切信息。

2.欧洲银行业管理局还可请求主管部门定期以指定的格式提供信息。如果可能，上述请求应使用通用的报告格式。

3.收到某成员国主管部门有正当理由的请求后，欧洲银行业管理局可提供该主管部门履行职责所必要的任何信息，但须遵守行业立法以及第70条所规定的职业保密义务。

4. Before requesting information in accordance with this Article and in order to avoid the duplication of reporting obligations, the Authority shall take account of any relevant existing statistics produced and disseminated by the European Statistical System and the European System of Central Banks.

5. Where information is not available or is not made available by the competent authorities in a timely fashion, the Authority may address a duly justified and reasoned request to other supervisory authorities, to the ministry responsible for finance where it has at its disposal prudential information, to the national central bank or to the statistical office of the Member State concerned.

6. Where information is not available or is not made available under paragraph 1 or 5 in a timely fashion, the Authority may address a duly justified and reasoned request directly to the relevant financial institutions. The reasoned request shall explain why the information concerning the respective individual financial institutions is necessary.

The Authority shall inform the relevant competent authorities of requests in accordance with this paragraph and with paragraph 5.

At the request of the Authority, the competent authorities shall assist the Authority in collecting the information.

7. The Authority may use confidential information received pursuant to this Article only for the purposes of carrying out the duties assigned to it by this Regulation.

Article 36 Relationship with the ESRB

1. The Authority shall cooperate closely and on a regular basis with the ESRB.

2. The Authority shall provide the ESRB with regular and timely information necessary for the achievement of its tasks. Any data necessary for the achievement of its tasks that are not in summary or aggregate form shall be provided, without delay, to the ESRB upon a reasoned request, as specified in Article 15 of Regulation (EU) No 1092/2010. The Authority, in cooperation with the ESRB, shall have in place adequate internal procedures for the trans mission of confidential information, in particular information regarding individual financial institutions.

3. The Authority shall, in accordance with paragraphs 4 and 5, ensure a proper follow-up to ESRB warnings and recommendations referred to in Article 16 of Regulation (EU) No 1092/2010.

4. On receipt of a warning or recommendation from the ESRB addressed to the Authority, the Authority shall convene a meeting of the Board of Supervisors without delay and assess the implications of such a warning or recommendation for the fulfilment of its tasks.

It shall decide, by the relevant decision-making procedure, on any actions to be

4.为了避免报告义务的重复，在根据本条规定提出信息请求前，欧洲银行业管理局应参考由欧洲统计系统和欧洲中央银行体系提供和发布的任何现有的相关统计数据。

5.主管部门无法或未及时提供信息的，欧洲银行业管理局可向所涉成员国的其他监管机构、财政部（如其掌握了审慎信息）、成员国中央银行或统计局提出有正当理由和经论证的信息请求。

6.未能获得信息或未能根据第1款或第5款及时获得信息的，欧洲银行业管理局可直接向相关的金融机构提出有正当理由和经论证的信息请求。该等信息请求应说明需要各个相关金融机构提供信息的原因。

欧洲银行业管理局应通知相关主管部门按照本款和第5款提出的请求。

经欧洲银行业管理局请求，主管部门应协助欧洲银行业管理局收集信息。

7.欧洲银行业管理局仅可以出于履行本条例赋予的职责的目的使用根据本条接收到的保密信息。

第36条　与欧洲系统性风险委员会的关系

1.欧洲银行业管理局应紧密并定期地与欧洲系统性风险委员会开展合作。

2.欧洲银行业管理局应定期并及时地向欧洲系统性风险委员会提供完成其职责所必要的信息。按第1092/2010号（欧盟）条例第15条的规定，经欧洲系统性风险委员会合理请求，任何为完成其职责所必要的且非摘要或汇总格式的数据均应立即提供给欧洲系统性风险委员会。欧洲银行业管理局应与欧洲系统性风险委员会合作，为保密信息特别是与具体金融机构有关的信息的发送设置充分的内部程序。

3.欧洲银行业管理局应依照第4款和第5款确保对第1092/2010号（欧盟）条例第16条所述欧洲系统性风险委员会预警和建议进行恰当的跟进。

4.收到欧洲系统性风险委员会向欧洲银行业管理局提出的预警或建议后，欧洲银行业管理局应立即召开监管机构理事会会议，并对该预警或建议对于其履行职责的影响进行评估。

欧洲银行业管理局依据本条例所授予的权力对预警和建议提出的问题采取任何

taken in accordance with the powers conferred upon it by this Regulation for addressing the issues identified in the warnings and recommendations.

If the Authority does not act on a recommendation, it shall explain to the ESRB and the Council its reasons for not doing so.

5. On receipt of a warning or recommendation from the ESRB addressed to a competent national supervisory authority, the Authority shall, where relevant, use the powers conferred upon it by this Regulation to ensure a timely follow-up.

Where the addressee intends not to follow the recommendation of the ESRB, it shall inform and discuss with the Board of Supervisors its reasons for not acting.

The competent authority shall take due account of the views of the Board of Supervisors when informing the Council and the ESRB in accordance with Article 17 of Regulation (EU) No 1092/2010.

6. In discharging the tasks set out in this Regulation, the Authority shall take the utmost account of the warnings and recommendations of the ESRB.

Article 37 Banking Stakeholder Group

1. To help facilitate consultation with stakeholders in areas relevant to the tasks of the Authority, a Banking Stakeholder Group shall be established. The Banking Stakeholder Group shall be consulted on actions taken in accordance with Articles 10 to 15 concerning regulatory technical standards and implementing technical standards and, to the extent that these do not concern individual financial institutions, Article 16 concerning guidelines and recommendations. If actions must be taken urgently and consultation becomes impossible, the Banking Stakeholder Group shall be informed as soon as possible.

The Banking Stakeholder Group shall meet at least four times a year.

2. The Banking Stakeholder Group shall be composed of 30 members, representing in balanced proportions credit and investment institutions operating in the Union, their employees' representatives as well as consumers, users of banking services and representatives of SMEs. At least five of its members shall be independent top-ranking academics. Ten of its members shall represent financial institutions, three of whom shall represent cooperative and savings banks.

3. The members of the Banking Stakeholder Group shall be appointed by the Board of Supervisors, following proposals from the relevant stakeholders. In making its decision, the Board of Supervisors shall, to the extent possible, ensure an appropriate geographical and gender balance and representation of stakeholders across the Union.

4. The Authority shall provide all necessary information subject to professional secrecy as set out in Article 70 and ensure adequate secretarial support for the Banking Stakeholder Group. Adequate compensation shall be provided to members of the Banking

行动的，应通过相关的决策程序作出决定。

欧洲银行业管理局不针对建议采取任何行动的，应向欧洲系统性风险委员会和欧盟理事会说明理由。

5.收到欧洲系统性风险委员会向国家级主管部门发出的预警或建议后，欧洲银行业管理局应在适当时运用本条例所授予的权力确保及时采取跟进行动。

被建议方无意遵循欧洲系统性风险委员会的建议的，应通知监管机构理事会并与其讨论其不采取行动的理由。

主管部门应在根据第1092/2010号（欧盟）条例第17条通知欧盟理事会和欧洲系统性风险委员会时，充分考虑监管机构理事会的意见。

6.欧洲银行业管理局在履行本条例所规定的职责时，应充分考虑欧洲系统性风险委员会的预警和建议。

第37条　银行业利益相关者小组

1.为了便于就欧洲银行业管理局职责相关领域征求利益相关者的意见，应设立一个银行业利益相关者小组。根据第10条至第15条的规定所采取的与监管性技术标准和实施性技术标准有关的行动，以及在不涉及具体金融机构的范围内根据第16条的规定所采取的与指引和建议有关的行动，均应征求银行业利益相关者小组的意见。在必须采取紧急行动而不可能提前征求其意见的情况下，应尽早通知银行业利益相关者小组。

银行业利益相关者小组每年至少应召开4次会议。

2.银行业利益相关者小组应由30名成员组成，以平衡的比例代表在欧盟运营的信贷和投资机构、其员工代表以及消费者、银行业服务用户以及中小企业代表。其中至少应有5名成员是独立的一流学者；应有10名成员代表金融机构，其中3名代表合作银行和储蓄银行。

3.银行业利益相关者小组成员的人选应由监管机构理事会根据相关的利益相关者的提议任命。作出决定时，监管机构理事会应尽可能确保该利益相关者小组成员在欧盟范围内适当的地理分布平衡和性别平衡。

4.欧洲银行业管理局应在遵循第70条规定的职业保密义务前提下为银行业利益相关者小组提供一切必要信息，并确保为其提供适当的秘书支持。对银行业利益相关者小组中代表非营利机构的成员（行业代表除外）提供充足的报酬。银行业利益相关

Stakeholder Group representing non-profit organisations, excluding industry representatives. The Banking Stakeholder Group may establish working groups on technical issues. Members of the Banking Stakeholder Group shall serve for a period of 21/2 years, following which a new selection procedure shall take place.

The members of the Banking Stakeholder Group may serve two successive terms.

5. The Banking Stakeholder Group may submit opinions and advice to the Authority on any issue related to the tasks of the Authority with particular focus on the tasks set out in Articles 10 to 16 and Articles 29, 30 and 32.

6. The Banking Stakeholder Group shall adopt its rules of procedure by a majority of two-thirds of its members.

7. The Authority shall make public the opinions and advice of the Banking Stakeholder Group and the results of its consultations.

Article 38 Safeguards

1. The Authority shall ensure that no decision adopted pursuant to Article 18 or 19 impinges in any way on the fiscal responsibilities of Member States.

2. Where a Member State considers that a decision taken pursuant to Article 19(3) impinges on its fiscal responsibilities, it may notify the Authority and the Commission within 2 weeks after notification of the Authority's decision to the competent authority that the decision will not be implemented by the competent authority.

In its notification, the Member State shall clearly and specifically explain why and how the decision impinges on its fiscal responsibilities.

In the case of such notification, the decision of the Authority shall be suspended.

Within a period of 1 month from the notification by the Member State, the Authority shall inform the Member State as to whether it maintains its decision or whether it amends or revokes it. If the decision is maintained or amended, the Authority shall state that fiscal responsibilities are not affected.

Where the Authority maintains its decision, the Council shall take a decision, by a majority of the votes cast, at one of its meetings not later than 2 months after the Authority has informed the Member State as set out in the fourth subparagraph, as to whether the Authority's decision is maintained.

Where the Council, after having considered the matter, does not take a decision to maintain the Authority's decision in accordance with the fifth subparagraph, the Authority's decision shall be terminated.

3. Where a Member State considers that a decision taken pursuant to Article 18(3) impinges on its fiscal responsibilities, it may notify the Authority, the Commission and the Council within 3 working days after notification of the Authority's decision to the competent authority that the decision will not be implemented by the competent authority.

者小组可就技术性问题设立工作组。银行业利益相关者小组成员的任期为两年半，任期结束后进行新一轮的遴选。

银行业利益相关者小组的成员可连任2期。

5.银行业利益相关者小组可针对与欧洲银行业管理局职责（特别是第10条至第16条以及第29条、第30条和第32条所列职责）有关的任何问题向欧洲银行业管理局呈报意见和建议。

6.银行业利益相关者小组通过其程序规则时，应经2/3成员的同意。

7.欧洲银行业管理局应公布银行业利益相关者小组的意见和建议及其磋商结果。

第38条　保障措施

1.欧洲银行业管理局应确保根据第18条或第19条作出的任何决定不会以任何方式对成员国的财政责任造成影响。

2.如有成员国认为根据第19条第3款作出的决定影响了其财政责任，则在欧洲银行业管理局通知主管部门其决定后的2周内，该成员国可通知欧洲银行业管理局和欧盟委员会该成员国将不实施该项决定。

成员国应在其通知中清楚具体地说明该项决定为何以及如何会影响其财政责任。

在成员国作出上述通知的情况下，欧洲银行业管理局的决定应暂停执行。

欧洲银行业管理局应在成员国发出通知后1个月内通知成员国是否维持决定还是修改或撤销决定。在维持或修改其决定的情形下，欧洲银行业管理局应声明成员国的财政责任未受影响。

欧洲银行业管理局维持其决定的，欧盟理事会应在欧洲银行业管理局按第4项通知成员国之后2个月内召开的任何欧盟理事会会议中，通过多数票投票决定是否维持欧洲银行业管理局的决定。

欧盟理事会经审议后未根据第5项决定维持欧洲银行业管理局的决定的，应终止欧洲银行业管理局的决定。

3.如有成员国认为欧洲银行业管理局根据第18条第3款作出的决定影响了其财政责任，则在欧洲银行业管理局通知主管部门其决定后的3个工作日内，该成员国可通知欧洲银行业管理局、欧盟委员会和欧盟理事会该成员国将不实施该项决定。

In its notification, the Member State shall clearly and specifically explain why and how the decision impinges on its fiscal responsibilities.

In the case of such notification, the decision of the Authority shall be suspended.

The Council shall, within 10 working days, convene a meeting and take a decision, by a simple majority of its members, as to whether the Authority's decision is revoked.

Where the Council, after having considered the matter, does not take a decision to revoke the Authority's decision in accordance with the fourth subparagraph, the suspension of the Authority's decision shall be terminated.

4. Where the Council has taken a decision in accordance with paragraph 3 not to revoke a decision of the Authority relating to Article 18(3), and the Member State concerned still considers that the decision of the Authority impinges upon its fiscal responsibilities, that Member State may notify the Commission and the Authority and request the Council to re-examine the matter. The Member State concerned shall clearly set out the reasons for its disagreement with the decision of the Council.

Within a period of 4 weeks after the notification referred to in the first subparagraph, the Council shall confirm its original decision or take a new decision in accordance with paragraph 3.

The period of 4 weeks may be extended by four additional weeks by the Council, if the particular circumstances of the case so require.

5. Any abuse of this Article, in particular in relation to a decision by the Authority which does not have a significant or material fiscal impact, shall be prohibited as incompatible with the internal market.

Article 39 Decision-making procedures

1. Before taking the decisions provided for in this Regulation, the Authority shall inform any named addressee of its intention to adopt the decision, setting a time limit within which the addressee may express its views on the matter, taking full account of the urgency, complexity and potential consequences of the matter. This applies mutatis mutandis to recommendations as referred to in Article 17(3).

2. The decisions of the Authority shall state the reasons on which they are based.

3. The addressees of decisions of the Authority shall be informed of the legal remedies available under this Regulation.

4. Where the Authority has taken a decision pursuant to Article 18(3) or (4), it shall review that decision at appropriate intervals.

5. The decisions which the Authority takes pursuant to Articles 17, 18 or 19 shall be made public and shall state the identity of the competent authority or financial institution concerned and the main content of the decision, unless such publication is in conflict with the legitimate interests of financial institutions in the protection of their business secrets

成员国应在其通知中清楚具体地说明该项决定为何以及如何影响其财政责任。

在成员国作出上述通知的情况下，欧洲银行业管理局的决定应暂停执行。

欧盟理事会应在10个工作日内召开会议，理事以简单多数票决定是否撤销欧洲银行业管理局的决定。

欧盟理事会经审议后并未根据第4项决定撤销欧洲银行业管理局的决定的，应终止欧洲银行业管理局决定的暂停执行。

4.欧盟理事会根据第3款决定不撤销欧洲银行业管理局与第18条第3款有关的决定，而所涉成员国仍认为欧洲银行业管理局的决定影响了其财政责任的，该成员国可通知欧盟委员会和欧洲银行业管理局并要求欧盟理事会重新审查该事宜。所涉成员国应清楚说明其对欧盟理事会决定持异议的理由。

第1项所述的通知发出后4周内，欧盟理事会可重申其原决定或根据第3款作出新的决定。

案件有特殊情况的，欧盟理事会可将上述4周期限再延长4周。

5.任何滥用本条款的行为，特别是在欧洲银行业管理局的决定并不对成员国的财政责任造成任何重大或实质性影响的情况下滥用本条款，均应被视为与欧盟内部市场不相容而被禁止。

第39条　决策程序

1.在作出本条例所规定的决定前，欧洲银行业管理局应通知该等决定所针对的任何具名对象其有意作出该决定，并在充分考虑事宜的紧迫性、复杂性和潜在后果的情况下设定时限，允许决定所针对的对象就该事宜表达观点。第17条第3款所述的建议比照上述规定处理。

2.欧洲银行业管理局发布的决定应阐明决定所基于的理由。

3.应通知欧洲银行业管理局决定所针对的对象其可根据本条例获得的法律救济。

4.欧洲银行业管理局根据第18条第3款或第4款作出决定后，应以适当的频率审评该项决定。

5.欧洲银行业管理局应公布其根据第17条、第18条或第19条作出的决定并说明所涉主管部门或金融机构的身份以及决定的主要内容，除非公布上述内容与金融机构保护其商业秘密的合法权益有冲突，或可能严重危害欧盟金融市场有序运行和诚信度或整个或部分金融系统的稳定。

or could seriously jeopardise the orderly functioning and integrity of financial markets or the stability of the whole or part of the financial system of the Union.

CHAPTER Ⅲ ORGANISATION

SECTION 1 Board of Supervisors

Article 40 Composition

1. The Board of Supervisors shall be composed of:

(a) the Chairperson, who shall be non-voting;

(b) the head of the national public authority competent for the supervision of credit institutions in each Member State, who shall meet in person at least twice a year;

(c) one representative of the Commission, who shall be non-voting;

(d) one representative of the European Central Bank, who shall be non-voting;

(e) one representative of the ESRB, who shall be non-voting;

(f) one representative of each of the other two European Supervisory Authorities, who shall be non-voting.

2. The Board of Supervisors shall convene meetings with the Banking Stakeholder Group regularly, at least twice a year.

3. Each competent authority shall be responsible for nominating a high-level alternate from its authority, who may replace the member of the Board of Supervisors referred to in paragraph 1(b), where that person is prevented from attending.

4. Where the authority referred to in paragraph 1(b) is not a central bank, the member of the Board of Supervisors referred to in that point may decide to bring a representative from the Member State's central bank, who shall be non-voting.

5. In Member States where more than one authority is responsible for the supervision according to this Regulation, those authorities shall agree on a common representative. Nevertheless, when an item to be discussed by the Board of Supervisors does not fall within the competence of the national authority being represented by the member referred to in paragraph 1(b), that member may bring a representative from the relevant national authority, who shall be non-voting.

6. For the purpose of acting within the scope of Directive 94/19/EC, the member of the Board of Supervisors referred to in paragraph 1(b) may, where appropriate, be accompanied by a representative from the relevant bodies which administer deposit-guarantee schemes in each Member State, who shall be non-voting.

第三章 组织结构

第1节 监管机构理事会

第40条 构成

1.监管机构理事会组成如下：

（a）主席，无表决权；

（b）每个成员国内主管信贷机构监管的国家级公共机构的负责人，该等负责人每年应至少亲自出席2次会议；

（c）欧盟委员会1名代表，无表决权；

（d）欧洲中央银行1名代表，无表决权；

（e）欧洲系统性风险委员会1名代表，无表决权；

（f）另外2个欧洲监管机构各自1名代表，无表决权。

2.监管机构理事会应定期召开与银行业利益相关者小组的会议，每年至少2次。

3.各主管部门应负责从其部门中指定1名高级别的替补人员，以在第1款第b项所述的监管机构理事会理事不能参加会议时代替其出席。

4.第1款第b项所述的部门并非中央银行的，该项中的监管机构理事会的理事可决定携1名成员国中央银行的代表与会，该代表无投票权。

5.某成员国如有多个部门负责本条例下的监管工作，则该等部门应指定1名共同的代表。然而，监管机构理事会讨论的事项不属于第1款第b项中的理事所代表的国家级监管机构的职权范围的，该成员可携1名来自相关国家级监管机构的代表与会，该代表无投票权。

6.为在第94/19/EC号指令的范围内行事，第1款第b项所述监管机构理事会的理事可在适当时由其所属成员国负责管理存款担保计划的相关机构代表陪同，该代表无表决权。

7. The Board of Supervisors may decide to admit observers.

The Executive Director may participate in meetings of the Board of Supervisors, without the right to vote.

Article 41 Internal committees and panels

1. The Board of Supervisors may establish internal committees or panels for specific tasks attributed to the Board of Supervisors, and may provide for the delegation of certain clearly defined tasks and decisions to internal committees or panels, to the Management Board or to the Chairperson.

2. For the purposes of Article 19, the Board of Supervisors shall convoke an independent panel to facilitate an impartial settlement of the disagreement, consisting of the Chairperson and two of its members, who are not representatives of the competent authorities which are party to the disagreement and who have neither any interest in the conflict nor direct links to the competent authorities concerned.

3. Subject to Article 19(2), the panel shall propose a decision for final adoption by the Board of Supervisors, in accordance with the procedure set out in the third subparagraph of Article 44(1).

4. The Board of Supervisors shall adopt rules of procedure for the panel referred to in paragraph 2.

Article 42 Independence

When carrying out the tasks conferred upon it by this Regulation, the Chairperson and the voting members of the Board of Supervisors shall act independently and objectively in the sole interest of the Union as a whole and shall neither seek nor take instructions from Union institutions or bodies, from any government of a Member State or from any other public or private body.

Neither Member States, the Union institutions or bodies, nor any other public or private body shall seek to influence the members of the Board of Supervisors in the performance of their tasks.

Article 43 Tasks

1. The Board of Supervisors shall give guidance to the work of the Authority and shall be in charge of taking the decisions referred to in Chapter Ⅱ.

2. The Board of Supervisors shall adopt the opinions, recommendations, and decisions, and issue the advice referred to in Chapter Ⅱ.

3. The Board of Supervisors shall appoint the Chairperson.

4. The Board of Supervisors shall adopt, before 30 September of each year, on the basis of a proposal by the Management Board, the work programme of the Authority for the coming year, and shall transmit it for information to the European Parliament, the Council and the Commission.

7.监管机构理事会可决定设立观察员。

执行主任可参与监管机构理事会的会议,但无表决权。

第41条　内部委员会和专家小组

1.监管机构理事会可为其承担的特别职责设立内部委员会或专家小组,并可允许将某些清楚界定的职责和决定委托给内部委员会或专家小组、管理委员会或主席。

2.出于第19条之目的,监管机构理事会应召集独立的专家小组,促进分歧的公正解决,该专家小组由监管机构理事会主席和2名成员组成,他们应为非分歧一方主管部门的代表,在所涉主管部门的冲突中无利害关系,与所涉主管部门亦无直接关联。

3.在遵守第19条第2款的前提下,专家小组应向监管机构理事会提出决定建议,以供后者依照第44条第1款第3项规定的程序最终通过。

4.监管机构理事会应通过第2款所述专家小组的程序规则。

第42条　独立性

监管机构理事会主席以及有表决权的成员履行本条例所赋予的职责时,应仅代表欧盟整体利益独立客观地行事,不得寻求或听从欧盟机构或单位、任何成员国政府或任何其他公共或私人机构的指示。

各成员国、欧盟机构或单位以及任何其他公共或私人机构均不得试图影响监管机构理事会理事履行其职责。

第43条　职责

1.监管机构理事会应为欧洲银行业管理局的工作提供指导并负责作出第二章所述的决定。

2.监管机构理事会应制定第二章所述的意见、建议和决定,并发布第二章所述的建议。

3.监管机构理事会应任命1名主席。

4.监管机构理事会应于每年9月30日前根据管理委员会的提议通过欧洲银行业管理局下一年度的工作计划,并将其发送给欧洲议会、欧盟理事会和欧盟委员会供其参考。

The work programme shall be adopted without prejudice to the annual budgetary procedure and shall be made public.

5. The Board of Supervisors shall, on the basis of a proposal by the Management Board, adopt the annual report on the activities of the Authority, including on the performance of the Chairperson's duties, on the basis of the draft report referred to in Article 53(7) and shall transmit that report to the European Parliament, the Council, the Commission, the Court of Auditors and the European Economic and Social Committee by 15 June each year. The report shall be made public.

6. The Board of Supervisors shall adopt the multi-annual work programme of the Authority, and shall transmit it for information to the European Parliament, the Council and the Commission.

The multi-annual work programme shall be adopted without prejudice to the annual budgetary procedure and shall be made public.

7. The Board of Supervisors shall adopt the budget in accordance with Article 63.

8. The Board of Supervisors shall exercise disciplinary authority over the Chairperson and the Executive Director and may remove them from office in accordance with Article 48(5) or 51(5) respectively.

Article 44 Decision-making

1. Decisions of the Board of Supervisors shall be taken by a simple majority of its members. Each member shall have one vote.

With regard to the acts specified in Articles 10 to 16 and measures and decisions adopted under the third subparagraph of Article 9(5) and Chapter Ⅵ and by way of derogation from the first subparagraph of this paragraph, the Board of Supervisors shall take decisions on the basis of a qualified majority of its members, as defined in Article 16 (4) of the Treaty on European Union and in Article 3 of the Protocol (No 36) on transitional provisions.

With regard to decisions in accordance with Article 19(3), for decisions taken by the consolidating supervisor, the decision proposed by the panel shall be considered as adopted, if approved by a simple majority, unless it is rejected by members representing a blocking minority of the votes as defined in Article 16(4) of the Treaty on European Union and in Article 3 of the Protocol (No 36) on transitional provisions.

For all other decisions in accordance with Article 19(3), the decision proposed by the panel shall be adopted by a simple majority of the members of the Board of Supervisors. Each member shall have one vote.

2. Meetings of the Board of Supervisors shall be convened by the Chairperson at his own initiative or at the request of one third of its members, and shall be chaired by the Chairperson.

工作计划的通过不得影响年度预算程序，并应予公布。

5.监管机构理事会应根据管理委员会的提议在第53条第7款所述的报告草案基础上通过关于欧洲银行业管理局活动，包括主席职责履行情况的年度报告，并于每年6月15日前将该报告发送给欧洲议会、欧盟理事会、欧盟委员会、欧盟审计院以及欧洲经济与社会委员会。该报告应予公布。

6.监管机构理事会应通过欧洲银行业管理局的跨年度工作计划，并将其发送给欧洲议会、欧盟理事会和欧盟委员会供其参考。

跨年度工作计划的通过不得影响年度预算程序并应予公布。

7.监管机构理事会按照第63条的规定通过预算。

8.监管机构理事会对主席和执行主任行使纪律处分权，并可根据第48条第5款或第51条第5款免除其职务。

第44条　决策

1.监管机构理事会应以简单多数票通过决定。每名理事均有一票表决权。

作为本款第1项的例外，对于第10条至第16条所指明的法律文件以及依据第9条第5款第3项和第六章所采取的措施和作出的决定，监管机构理事会应以特定多数票通过决定，该特定多数票的定义见《欧洲联盟条约》第16条第4款以及关于过渡条款的《议定书（第36号）》第3条。

就第19条第3款下的决定而言，对于由并表监管机构作出的决定，专家小组提议的决定经简单多数票同意应视为通过，但是，被起否决作用的少数票的成员否决的情况除外，起否决作用的少数票的定义见《欧洲联盟条约》第16条第4款以及关于过渡规定的《议定书（第36号）》第3条。

对于所有其他根据第19条第3款所作的决定，由专家小组提议的决定应由监管机构理事会按简单多数票通过，每名理事均有一票表决权。

2.监管机构理事会会议应由主席主动召集或经1/3理事请求召集，由主席主持。

3. The Board of Supervisors shall adopt and make public its rules of procedure.

4. The rules of procedure shall set out in detail the arrangements governing voting, including, where appropriate, the rules governing quorums. The non-voting members and the observers, with the exception of the Chairperson and the Executive Director, shall not attend any discussions within the Board of Supervisors relating to individual financial institutions, unless otherwise provided for in Article 75(3) or in the acts referred to in Article 1(2).

SECTION 2 Management Board

Article 45 Composition

1. The Management Board shall be composed of the Chairperson and six other members of the Board of Supervisors, elected by and from the voting members of the Board of Supervisors.

Other than the Chairperson, each member of the Management Board shall have an alternate, who may replace him if he is prevented from attending.

The term of office of the members elected by the Board of Supervisors shall be 2 1/2 years. That term may be extended once. The composition of the Management Board shall be balanced and proportionate and shall reflect the Union as a whole. Mandates shall be overlapping and an appropriate rotating arrangement shall apply.

2. Decisions by the Management Board shall be adopted on the basis of a majority of the members present. Each member shall have one vote.

The Executive Director and a representative of the Commission shall participate in meetings of the Management Board without the right to vote.

The representative of the Commission shall have the right to vote on matters referred to in Article 63.

The Management Board shall adopt and make public its rules of procedure.

3. Meetings of the Management Board shall be convened by the Chairperson at his own initiative or at the request of at least a third of its members, and shall be chaired by the Chairperson.

The Management Board shall meet prior to every meeting of the Board of Supervisors and as often as the Management Board deems necessary. It shall meet at least five times a year.

4. The members of the Management Board may, subject to the rules of procedure, be assisted by advisers or experts. The non-voting members, with the exception of the Executive Director, shall not attend any discussions within the Management Board relating to individual financial institutions.

Article 46 Independence

The members of the Management Board shall act independently and objectively in

3.监管机构理事会应通过并公布其程序规则。

4.程序规则应详细规定表决安排,在适当时应包括关于法定人数的规则。除主席和执行主任外,无表决权的成员和观察员不得参加监管机构理事会关于具体金融机构的任何讨论,但是第75条第3款或者第1条第2款所述法律文件另有规定的情况除外。

第2节 管理委员会

第45条 构成

1.管理委员会应由监管机构理事会主席和其他6名委员组成,该6名委员从监管机构理事会有表决权的理事中选出。

除主席之外,管理委员会的每名委员均应有1名替补人员,在其无法出席会议时代替其出席。

监管机构理事会所选出的管理委员会委员任期为两年半。该任期可延长1次。管理委员会的构成应是平衡并且成比例的,并应反映欧盟整体情况。不同管理委员会委员的任期应当有所重叠,并应实行适当的轮换安排。

2.管理委员会的决定应由出席会议的委员多数同意后通过。每名委员均有一票表决权。

执行主任和欧盟委员会的1名代表应出席管理委员会的会议,但无表决权。

欧盟委员会的代表应有权就第63条所述事项进行表决。

管理委员会应通过并公布其程序规则。

3.管理委员会的会议应由主席主动召集或经至少1/3成员请求召集,由主席主持。

管理委员会应在每次监管机构理事会会议前及其认为必要的其他时间召开会议,每年至少应召开5次会议。

4.管理委员会的委员可按程序规则获得顾问或专家的协助。除执行主任之外,无表决权的委员不得参与管理委员会内部关于具体金融机构的讨论。

第46条 独立性

管理委员会委员应仅代表欧盟整体利益独立客观地行事,不得寻求或听从欧盟

the sole interest of the Union as a whole and shall neither seek nor take instructions from the Union institutions or bodies, from any government of a Member State or from any other public or private body.

Neither Member States, the Union institutions or bodies, nor any other public or private body shall seek to influence the members of the Management Board in the performance of their tasks.

Article 47 Tasks

1. The Management Board shall ensure that the Authority carries out its mission and performs the tasks assigned to it in accordance with this Regulation.

2. The Management Board shall propose, for adoption by the Board of Supervisors, an annual and multi-annual work programme.

3. The Management Board shall exercise its budgetary powers in accordance with Articles 63 and 64.

4. The Management Board shall adopt the Authority's staff policy plan and, pursuant to Article 68(2), the necessary implementing measures of the Staff Regulations of Officials of the European Communities (hereinafter 'the Staff Regulations').

5. The Management Board shall adopt the special provisions on right of access to the documents of the Authority, in accordance with Article 72.

6. The Management Board shall propose an annual report on the activities of the Authority, including on the Chairperson's duties, on the basis of the draft report referred to in Article 53(7) to the Board of Supervisors for approval.

7. The Management Board shall adopt and make public its rules of procedure.

8. The Management Board shall appoint and remove the members of the Board of Appeal in accordance with Article 58(3) and (5).

SECTION 3 Chairperson

Article 48 Appointment and tasks

1. The Authority shall be represented by a Chairperson, who shall be a full-time independent professional.

The Chairperson shall be responsible for preparing the work of the Board of Supervisors and shall chair the meetings of the Board of Supervisors and the Management Board.

2. The Chairperson shall be appointed by the Board of Supervisors on the basis of merit, skills, knowledge of financial institutions and markets, and of experience relevant to financial supervision and regulation, following an open selection procedure.

Before taking up his duties, and up to 1 month after the selection by the Board of Supervisors, the European Parliament may, after having heard the candidate selected by

机构或单位、任何成员国政府或任何其他公共或私人机构的指示。

各成员国、欧盟机构或单位以及任何其他公共或私人机构均不得试图影响管理委员会委员履行其职责。

第47条　职责

1.管理委员会应确保欧洲银行业管理局完成本条例所赋予的使命和职责。

2.管理委员会应提出年度和跨年度工作计划，交由监管机构理事会通过。

3.管理委员会应根据第63条和第64条行使预算权。

4.管理委员会应通过欧洲银行业管理局的人事政策计划，并根据第68条第2款制定实施《欧洲共同体官员的人事条例》（以下简称《人事条例》）的必要措施。

5.根据第72条规定，管理委员会应通过关于欧洲银行业管理局文件查阅权的特殊规定。

6.在第53条第7款所述报告草案的基础上，管理委员会应将关于欧洲银行业管理局活动（包括主席职责）的年度报告呈报监管机构理事会审批。

7.管理委员会应通过并公布其程序规则。

8.管理委员会应根据第58条第3款和第5款任免行政复议委员会的委员。

第3节　主　　席

第48条　任命和职责

1.欧洲银行业管理局由主席代表。主席应为全职、独立的专业人士。

主席负责筹备监管机构理事会的工作，并主持监管机构理事会以及管理委员会的会议。

2.主席由监管机构理事会根据其成就、技能、对金融机构和市场的认识、与金融监管和规制相关的经验，经过公开遴选程序任命。

在获选者到任前，直至其被监管机构理事会选出满1个月期间内，欧洲议会都有权在听取获选者意见后对其任命提出异议。

the Board of Supervisors, object to the designation of the selected person.

The Board of Supervisors shall also elect, from among its members, an alternate who shall carry out the functions of the Chairperson in his absence. That alternate shall not be elected from among the members of the Management Board.

3. The Chairperson's term of office shall be 5 years and may be extended once.

4. In the course of the 9 months preceding the end of the 5 year term of office of the Chairperson, the Board of Supervisors shall evaluate:

(a) the results achieved in the first term of office and the way they were achieved;

(b) the Authority's duties and requirements in the coming years.

The Board of Supervisors, taking into account the evaluation, may extend the term of office of the Chairperson once subject to confirmation by the European Parliament.

5. The Chairperson may be removed from office only by the European Parliament following a decision of the Board of Supervisors.

The Chairperson shall not prevent the Board of Supervisors from discussing matters relating to the Chairperson, in particular the need for his removal, and shall not be involved in deliberations concerning such a matter.

Article 49 Independence

Without prejudice to the role of the Board of Supervisors in relation to the tasks of the Chairperson, the Chairperson shall neither seek nor take instructions from the Union institutions or bodies, from any government of a Member State or from any other public or private body.

Neither Member States, the Union institutions or bodies, nor any other public or private body shall seek to influence the Chairperson in the performance of his tasks.

In accordance with the Staff Regulations referred to in Article 68, the Chairperson shall, after leaving service, continue to be bound by the duty to behave with integrity and discretion as regards the acceptance of certain appointments or benefits.

Article 50 Report

1. The European Parliament and the Council may invite the Chairperson or his alternate to make a statement, while fully respecting his independence. The Chairperson shall make a statement before the European Parliament and answer any questions put by its members, whenever so requested.

2. The Chairperson shall report in writing on the main activities of the Authority to the European Parliament when requested and at least 15 days before making the statement referred to in paragraph 1.

3. In addition to the information referred to in Articles 11 to 18 and Articles 20 and 33, the report shall also include any relevant information requested by the European Parliament on an ad-hoc basis.

监管机构理事会还应从其理事中选出1名替补人员，在主席缺席的情况下代为行使其职能。该替补人员不得为管理委员会的委员。

3.主席的任期为5年，可延长1次。

4.在主席5年任期结束前的9个月期间内，监管机构理事会可对下列方面作出评价：

(a)主席在首期任期内取得的工作成果以及取得该成果的方式；

(b)未来几年欧洲银行业管理局的职责和要求。

在上述评价的基础上，监管机构理事会可经欧洲议会确认后将主席任期延长1次。

5.只有在监管机构理事会作出罢免决定后，欧洲议会方能免除主席职务。

主席不得妨碍监管机构理事会讨论与主席有关的事宜，特别是围绕罢免其职务所进行的必要讨论，并且不得参与涉及上述事宜的审议。

第49条　独立性

不影响监管机构理事会就主席的职责发挥作用的情况下，主席不得寻求或听从欧盟机构或单位、任何成员国政府或任何其他公共或私人机构的指示。

各成员国、欧盟机构或单位或任何其他公共或私人机构均不得试图影响主席履行其职责。

根据第68条所述的《人事条例》，主席离职后在接受某些任命或利益方面仍应受诚信和谨慎义务约束。

第50条　报告

1.欧洲议会和欧盟理事会可在充分尊重主席独立性的前提下要求主席或其替补人员作出陈述。任何时候经欧洲议会要求，主席均应向后者作出陈述并回答其议员所提出的任何问题。

2.经欧洲议会要求并至少在进行第1款提及的陈述的15日前，主席应就欧洲银行业管理局的主要活动向欧洲议会提交书面报告。

3.除了第11条至第18条以及第20条和第33条所述的信息外，报告还应包括欧洲议会专门要求提供的任何相关信息。

SECTION 4 Executive Director

Article 51 Appointment

1. The Authority shall be managed by an Executive Director, who shall be a full-time independent professional.

2. The Executive Director shall be appointed by the Board of Supervisors, after confirmation by the European Parliament, on the basis of merit, skills, knowledge of financial institutions and markets, and experience relevant to financial supervision and regulation and managerial experience, following an open selection procedure.

3. The Executive Director's term of office shall be 5 years and may be extended once.

4. In the course of the 9 months preceding the end of the Executive Director's term of office, the Board of Supervisors shall evaluate in particular:

(a) the results achieved in the first term of office and the way they were achieved;

(b) the Authority's duties and requirements in the coming years.

The Board of Supervisors, taking into account the evaluation referred to in the first subparagraph, may extend the term of office of the Executive Director once.

5. The Executive Director may be removed from office only upon a decision of the Board of Supervisors.

Article 52 Independence

Without prejudice to the respective roles of the Management Board and the Board of Supervisors in relation to the tasks of the Executive Director, the Executive Director shall neither seek nor take instructions from the Union institutions or bodies, from any government of a Member State or from any other public or private body.

Neither Member States, the Union institutions or bodies, nor any other public or private body shall seek to influence the Executive Director in the performance of his tasks.

In accordance with the Staff Regulations referred to in Article 68, the Executive Director shall, after leaving service, continue to be bound by the duty to behave with integrity and discretion as regards the acceptance of certain appointments or benefits.

Article 53 Tasks

1. The Executive Director shall be in charge of the management of the Authority and shall prepare the work of the Management Board.

2. The Executive Director shall be responsible for implementing the annual work programme of the Authority under the guidance of the Board of Supervisors and under the control of the Management Board.

3. The Executive Director shall take the necessary measures, notably the adoption of

第4节 执行主任

第51条 任命

1.欧洲银行业管理局应由1名执行主任负责管理,执行主任应为全职、独立的专业人士。

2.执行主任应由监管机构理事会根据其成就、技能、对金融机构和市场的认识、与金融监管和规制相关的经验以及管理经验,经过公开遴选程序并经欧洲议会确认后任命。

3.执行主任的任期为5年,可延长1次。

4.执行主任任期结束前的9个月期间内,监管机构理事会尤其可对下列方面进行评价:

(a)执行主任在首期任期内取得的工作成果以及取得该成果的方式;

(b)未来几年欧洲银行业管理局的职责和要求。

在第1项所述评价的基础上,监管机构理事会可将执行主任的任期延长1次。

5.经监管机构理事会作出决定后方能免除执行主任职务。

第52条 独立性

不影响管理委员会和监管机构理事会就执行主任的职责发挥各自作用的情况下,执行主任不得寻求或听从欧盟机构或单位、任何成员国政府或任何其他公共或私人机构的指示。

各成员国、欧盟机构或单位以及任何其他公共或私人机构均不得试图影响执行主任履行其职责。

根据第68条所述的《人事条例》,执行主任离职后在接受某些任命或利益方面仍应受诚信和谨慎义务约束。

第53条 职责

1.执行主任应负责管理欧洲银行业管理局并布置管理委员会的工作。

2.执行主任应在监管机构理事会的指导以及管理委员会的管理下,负责实施欧洲银行业管理局的年度工作计划。

3.根据本条例,执行主任应采取必要的措施,特别是应通过内部行政指示和通知

internal administrative instructions and the publication of notices, to ensure the functioning of the Authority, in accordance with this Regulation.

4. The Executive Director shall prepare a multi-annual work programme, as referred to in Article 47(2).

5. Each year, by 30 June, the Executive Director shall prepare a work programme for the following year, as referred to in Article 47(2).

6. The Executive Director shall draw up a preliminary draft budget of the Authority pursuant to Article 63 and shall implement the budget of the Authority pursuant to Article 64.

7. Each year the Executive Director shall prepare a draft report with a section on the regulatory and supervisory activities of the Authority and a section on financial and administrative matters.

8. The Executive Director shall exercise in respect to the Authority's staff the powers laid down in Article 68 and manage staff matters.

CHAPTER Ⅳ JOINT BODIES OF THE EUROPEAN SUPERVISORY AUTHORITIES

SECTION 1 Joint Committee of European Supervisory Authorities

Article 54 Establishment

1. The Joint Committee of the European Supervisory Authorities is hereby established.

2. The Joint Committee shall serve as a forum in which the Authority shall cooperate regularly and closely and ensure cross-sectoral consistency with the European Supervisory Authority (European Insurance and Occupational Pensions Authority) and the European Supervisory Authority (European Securities and Markets Authority), in particular regarding:

— financial conglomerates,

— accounting and auditing,

— micro-prudential analyses of cross-sectoral developments, risks and vulnerabilities for financial stability,

— retail investment products,

— measures combating money laundering, and

来确保欧洲银行业管理局的有效运行。

4.执行主任应制订第47条第2款所述的跨年度工作计划。

5.每年6月30日前,执行主任应为下一年度制订第47条第2款所述的工作计划。

6. 执行主任应根据第63条起草欧洲银行业管理局初步预算草案并根据第64条实施欧洲银行业管理局的预算。

7.执行主任每年均应起草一份报告草案,其中一节关于欧洲银行业管理局的规制和监管活动,另一节关于财务和行政管理事宜。

8.执行主任应对欧洲银行业管理局的工作人员行使第68条规定的权力,并负责管理人事。

第四章　欧洲监管机构的联合机构

第1节　欧洲监管机构联合委员会

第54条　设立

1.特此设立欧洲监管机构联合委员会。

2.联合委员会应充当欧洲银行业管理局与两个欧洲监管机构(欧洲保险与职业养老金管理局和欧洲证券与市场管理局)之间的平台,该等机构通过此一平台得以开展定期紧密合作并保持跨行业监管一致性,尤其是在下列几个方面:

——金融集团,
——会计和审计,
——对金融稳定的跨行业变化、风险和薄弱环节的微观审慎分析,

——零售投资产品,
——打击洗钱活动的措施,和

— information exchange with the ESRB and developing the relationship between the ESRB and the ESAs.

3. The Joint Committee shall have a dedicated staff provided by the ESAs that shall act as a secretariat. The Authority shall contribute adequate resources to administrative, infrastructure and operational expenses.

4. In the event that a financial institution reaches across different sectors, the Joint Committee shall resolve disagreements in accordance with Article 56.

Article 55 Composition

1. The Joint Committee shall be composed of the Chairpersons of the ESAs, and, where applicable, the Chairperson of any Sub-Committee established pursuant to Article 57.

2. The Executive Director, a representative of the Commission and the ESRB shall be invited to the meetings of the Joint Committee, as well as of any Sub-Committees referred to in Article 57, as observers.

3. The Chairperson of the Joint Committee shall be appointed on an annual rotational basis from among the Chairpersons of the ESAs. The Chairperson of the Joint Committee shall be a Vice-Chair of the ESRB.

4. The Joint Committee shall adopt and publish its own rules of procedure. The rules may specify further participants in the meetings of the Joint Committee.

The Joint Committee shall meet at least once every 2 months.

Article 56 Joint positions and common acts

Within the scope of its tasks in Chapter Ⅱ, and in particular with respect to the implementation of Directive 2002/87/EC, where relevant, the Authority shall reach joint positions with the European Supervisory Authority (European Insurance and Occupational Pensions Authority) and with the European Supervisory Authority (European Securities and Markets Authority), as appropriate.

Acts pursuant to Articles 10 to 15, 17, 18 or 19 of this Regulation in relation to the application of Directive 2002/87/EC and of any other Union acts referred to in Article 1 (2) that also fall within the area of competence of the European Supervisory Authority (European Insurance and Occupational Pensions Authority) or the European Supervisory Authority (European Securities and Markets Authority) shall be adopted, in parallel, by the Authority, the European Supervisory Authority (European Insurance and Occupational Pensions Authority), and the European Supervisory Authority (European Securities and Markets Authority), as appropriate.

Article 57 Sub-Committees

1. For the purposes of Article 56, a Sub-Committee on Financial Conglomerates to the Joint Committee shall be established.

——与欧洲系统性风险委员会的信息交流以及欧洲系统性风险委员会和各欧洲监管机构之间关系的建立。

3.各欧洲监管机构应为联合委员会提供1名专职工作人员作为秘书。欧洲银行业管理局应为行政、基础设施和运营开支提供充足的资源。

4.对于涉足多个行业的金融机构,联合委员会应依照第56条的规定解决分歧。

第55条　构成

1.联合委员会应由各欧洲监管机构的主席以及依据第57条设立的任何分委员会的主席(如有)组成。

2.执行主任以及欧盟委员会和欧洲系统性风险委员会应各有1名代表被邀请作为观察员参加联合委员会以及第57条所述的任何分委员会的会议。

3.联合委员会的主席应每年由各欧洲监管机构的主席轮流担任。联合委员会的主席应兼任欧洲系统性风险委员会的副主席。

4.联合委员会应通过并公布其程序规则。除上述参会人员外,规则可具体规定其他可参加联合委员会会议的人选。

联合委员会应至少每2个月召开1次会议。

第56条　共同立场和通用法律文件

在第二章所述的欧洲银行业管理局职责范围内,特别是与实施第2002/87/EC号指令有关的职责(如适用)范围内,欧洲银行业管理局应与欧洲监管机构(欧洲保险与职业养老金管理局或欧洲证券与市场管理局)(视具体情况而定)达成共同立场。

本条例第10条至第15条、第17条、第18条或第19条中与第2002/87/EC指令以及第1条第2款所述欧盟立法的适用有关的,并且同时也属于欧洲监管机构(欧洲保险与职业养老金管理局或欧洲证券与市场管理局)职权管辖范围的立法,应同时由欧洲银行业管理局与欧洲监管机构(欧洲保险与职业养老金管理局或欧洲证券与市场管理局)(视具体情况而定)共同通过。

第57条　分委员会

1.为了第56条之目的,应在联合委员会下设立一个金融集团分委员会。

2. The Sub-Committee shall be composed of the individuals referred to in Article 55 (1), and one high-level representative from the current staff of the relevant competent authority from each Member State.

3. The Sub-Committee shall elect a Chairperson from among its members, who shall also be a member of the Joint Committee.

4. The Joint Committee may establish further Sub-Committees.

SECTION 2 Board of Appeal

Article 58 Composition and operation

1. The Board of Appeal shall be a joint body of the ESAs.

2. The Board of Appeal shall be composed of six members and six alternates, who shall be individuals of a high repute with a proven record of relevant knowledge and professional experience, including supervisory experience, to a sufficiently high level in the fields of banking, insurance, occupational pensions, securities markets or other financial services, excluding current staff of the competent authorities or other national or Union institutions involved in the activities of the Authority. The Board of Appeal shall have sufficient legal expertise to provide expert legal advice on the legality of the Authority's exercise of its powers.

The Board of Appeal shall designate its President.

3. Two members of the Board of Appeal and two alternates shall be appointed by the Management Board of the Authority from a short-list proposed by the Commission, following a public call for expressions of interest published in the Official Journal of the European Union, and after consultation of the Board of Supervisors.

The other members shall be appointed in accordance with Regulation (EU) No 1094/2010 and Regulation (EU) No 1095/2010.

4. The term of office of the members of the Board of Appeal shall be 5 years. That term may be extended once.

5. A member of the Board of Appeal appointed by the Management Board of the Authority shall not be removed during his term of office, unless he has been found guilty of serious misconduct and the Management Board takes a decision to that effect after consulting the Board of Supervisors.

6. The decisions of the Board of Appeal shall be adopted on the basis of a majority of at least four of its six members. Where the appealed decision falls within the scope of this Regulation, the deciding majority shall include at least one of the two members of the Board of Appeal appointed by the Authority.

7. The Board of Appeal shall be convened by its President when necessary.

8. The ESAs shall ensure adequate operational and secretarial support for the Board

2.分委员会应由第55条第1款所述的个人以及各成员国相关主管部门现任工作人员中选派的高级别代表组成。

3.分委员会应从其委员中选出1名主席，该主席应同时为联合委员会的委员。

4.联合委员会还可进一步设立其他分委员会。

第2节 行政复议委员会

第58条 构成和运作

1.行政复议委员会应为各个欧洲监管机构之间的一个联合机构。

2.行政复议委员会应由6名委员和6名替补委员组成，其应具有良好声誉，并且能证明其在银行业、保险、职业养老金、证券市场或其他金融服务领域有足够的相关知识和专业经验（包括监管经验），但其中不得有参与欧洲银行业管理局活动的主管部门或其他国家级或欧盟机构的现任工作人员。行政复议委员会应具备足够的法律专业知识就欧洲银行业管理局权力行使的合法性提供专业的法律意见。

行政复议委员会应指定1名主席。

3.在《欧盟公报》上发布征寻公告并咨询监管机构理事会的意见后，由欧洲银行业管理局的管理委员会从欧盟委员会提议的一份候选人短名单中任命行政复议委员会的2名委员以及2名替补委员。

其他委员应根据第1094/2010号（欧盟）条例以及第1095/2010号（欧盟）条例任命。

4.行政复议委员会委员的任期为5年。任期可延长1次。

5.由欧洲银行业管理局管理委员会任命的行政复议委员会委员不得在其任期内被免职，但是，被发现有严重不当行为并且管理委员会在咨询监管机构理事会的意见后决定免除其职务的除外。

6.行政复议委员会的决定应由其6名委员中的至少4名同意后方能通过。行政复议所涉欧洲银行业管理局决定属于本条例管辖范围的，同意行政复议决定的委员中应至少包括由欧洲银行业管理局任命的2名行政复议委员会委员的其中1名。

7.行政复议委员会应在必要时由其主席召集。

8.各欧洲监管机构应确保通过联合委员会对行政复议委员会提供充分的运作和

of Appeal through the Joint Committee.

Article 59 Independence and impartiality

1. The members of the Board of Appeal shall be independent in making their decisions. They shall not be bound by any instructions. They shall not perform any other duties in relation to the Authority, its Management Board or its Board of Supervisors.

2. Members of the Board of Appeal shall not take part in any appeal proceedings in which they have any personal interest, if they have previously been involved as representatives of one of the parties to the proceedings, or if they have participated in the decision under appeal.

3. If, for one of the reasons referred to in paragraphs 1 and 2 or for any other reason, a member of a Board of Appeal considers that another member should not take part in any appeal proceedings, he shall inform the Board of Appeal accordingly.

4. Any party to the appeal proceedings may object to the participation of a member of the Board of Appeal on any of the grounds referred to in paragraphs 1 and 2, or if suspected of bias.

No objection may be based on the nationality of members nor shall it be admissible if, while being aware of a reason for objecting, the party to the appeal proceedings has nonetheless taken a procedural step other than objecting to the composition of the Board of Appeal.

5. The Board of Appeal shall decide on the action to be taken in the cases specified in paragraphs 1 and 2 without the participation of the member concerned.

For the purpose of taking that decision, the member concerned shall be replaced on the Board of Appeal by his alternate. Where the alternate is in a similar situation, the Chairperson shall designate a replacement from among the available alternates.

6. The members of the Board of Appeal shall undertake to act independently and in the public interest.

For that purpose, they shall make a declaration of commitments and a declaration of interests indicating either the absence of any interest which may be considered prejudicial to their independence or any direct or indirect interest which might be considered prejudicial to their independence.

Those declarations shall be made public, annually and in writing.

秘书支持。

第59条　独立性与公正性

1.行政复议委员会的委员应独立作出决定。他们不受任何指示的约束，不得履行与欧洲银行业管理局、其管理委员会或其监管机构理事会有关的任何其他职责。

2.如果行政复议程序涉及行政复议委员会某委员的个人利益，或其之前曾作为行政复议程序一方当事人的代表涉案或曾经参与作出被复议的欧洲银行业管理局决定，则其不得参与行政复议程序。

3.出于第1款和第2款所述的理由之一或任何其他理由，有行政复议委员会委员认为其他委员不应参与任何行政复议程序的，应将该情况通知行政复议委员会。

4.基于第1款和第2款所述的任何理由或在涉嫌有失公允的情况下，行政复议程序的任何一方均可申请行政复议委员会委员回避。

不能以委员的国籍为由申请回避；当行政复议程序的一方当事人明知有理由申请回避而不提出申请且继续行政复议程序的，之后不得再提出回避申请。

5.行政复议委员会应就第1款和第2款所指情况下所需采取的行动作出决定，作上述决定时所涉委员不得参与。

为作出该决定，所涉委员应由其替补委员代替其出席行政复议委员会。该名替补人员处于类似状况的，主席应从其他可供选择的替补人员当中指定1名出席。

6.行政复议委员会的委员应承诺独立地出于公众利益行事。

为此，行政复议委员会的委员应作出承诺声明和利害关系声明，说明其本人不存在可被视为对其独立性产生影响的任何利害关系或任何直接或间接利益。

该等声明应每年以书面形式公布。

CHAPTER V REMEDIES

Article 60 Appeals

1. Any natural or legal person, including competent authorities, may appeal against a decision of the Authority referred to in Articles 17, 18 and 19 and any other decision taken by the Authority in accordance with the Union acts referred to in Article 1(2) which is addressed to that person, or against a decision which, although in the form of a decision addressed to another person, is of direct and individual concern to that person.

2. The appeal, together with a statement of grounds, shall be filed in writing at the Authority within 2 months of the date of notification of the decision to the person concerned, or, in the absence of a notification, of the day on which the Authority published its decision.

The Board of Appeal shall decide upon the appeal within 2 months after the appeal has been lodged.

3. An appeal lodged pursuant to paragraph 1 shall not have suspensive effect.

However, the Board of Appeal may, if it considers that circumstances so require, suspend the application of the contested decision.

4. If the appeal is admissible, the Board of Appeal shall examine whether it is well-founded. It shall invite the parties to the appeal proceedings to file observations on its own notifications or on communications from the other parties to the appeal proceedings, within specified time limits. Parties to the appeal proceedings shall be entitled to make oral representations.

5. The Board of Appeal may confirm the decision taken by the competent body of the Authority, or remit the case to the competent body of the Authority. That body shall be bound by the decision of the Board of Appeal and that body shall adopt an amended decision regarding the case concerned.

6. The Board of Appeal shall adopt and make public its rules of procedure.

7. The decisions taken by the Board of Appeal shall be reasoned and shall be made public by the Authority.

Article 61 Actions before the Court of Justice of the European Union

1. Proceedings may be brought before the Court of Justice of the European Union, in accordance with Article 263 TFEU, contesting a decision taken by the Board of Appeal or, in cases where there is no right of appeal before the Board of Appeal, by the Authority.

第五章 救 济

第60条 行政复议

1.任何自然人或法人,包括主管部门,均可针对欧洲银行业管理局的下列决定提出行政复议申请:第17条、第18条以及第19条所述的决定;根据第1条第2款所述欧盟立法作出的针对上述主体的任何其他决定;对于尽管表面看来是针对其他人作出的,但实际上与上述主体本人有直接和个人关系的决定,也可提出行政复议申请。

2.所涉主体可在欧洲银行业管理局向其发出决定通知的2个月内,或者未作通知的,在其决定公布之日起的2个月内,以书面形式向欧洲银行业管理局提出行政复议申请并附上一份行政复议申请理由说明。

行政复议委员会应在行政复议申请提交后2个月内作出行政复议决定。

3.根据第1款提交的行政复议申请对所涉决定无暂停效力。

然而,行政复议委员会可在其认为必要的情况下,暂停实施受到质疑的决定。

4.对于可受理的行政复议申请,行政复议委员会应审查是否有充足的理由。行政复议委员会应要求行政复议程序的各当事人在规定的时限内提交其对行政复议委员会所发通知的意见或者对从行政复议程序其他当事人收到的信函的意见。行政复议程序的各当事人均有权作口头陈述。

5.行政复议委员会可确认欧洲银行业管理局的主管机构的决定,或将案件退回欧洲银行业管理局的主管机构。该机构应受行政复议委员会的决定约束,并应就所涉案件修改其决定。

6.行政复议委员会应通过并公布其程序规则。

7.行政复议委员会的决定应有合理依据并应由欧洲银行业管理局予以公布。

第61条 在欧盟法院的行政诉讼

1.根据《欧洲联盟运行条约》第263条,如行政复议委员会的决定受到质疑,或者在相关方无权向行政复议委员会提出行政复议申请的情况下,欧洲银行业管理局可向欧盟法院提起行政诉讼。

2. Member States and the Union institutions, as well as any natural or legal person, may institute proceedings before the Court of Justice of the European Union against decisions of the Authority, in accordance with Article 263 TFEU.

3. In the event that the Authority has an obligation to act and fails to take a decision, proceedings for failure to act may be brought before the Court of Justice of the European Union in accordance with Article 265 TFEU.

4. The Authority shall be required to take the necessary measures to comply with the judgment of the Court of Justice of the European Union.

CHAPTER VI FINANCIAL PROVISIONS

Article 62 Budget of the Authority

1. The revenues of the Authority, a European body in accordance with Article 185 of Council Regulation (EC Euratom) No 1605/2002 of 25 June 2002 on the Financial Regulation applicable to the general budget of the European Communities [1] (hereinafter the 'Financial Regulation'), shall consist, in particular, of any combination of the following:

(a) obligatory contributions from the national public authorities competent for the supervision of financial institutions, which shall be made in accordance with a formula based on the weighting of votes set out in Article 3(3) of Protocol (No 36) on transitional provisions. For the purposes of this Article, Article 3(3) of Protocol (No 36) on transitional provisions shall continue to apply beyond the deadline of 31 October 2014 therein established;

(b) a subsidy from the Union, entered in the General Budget of the European Union (Commission Section);

(c) any fees paid to the Authority in the cases specified in the relevant instruments of Union law.

2. The expenditure of the Authority shall include, at least, staff, remuneration, administrative, infrastructure, professional training and operational expenses.

3. Revenue and expenditure shall be in balance.

4. Estimates of all Authority revenue and expenditure shall be prepared for each financial year, corresponding to the calendar year, and shall be presented in the budget of the Authority.

---

1 OJ L 248, 16. 9. 2002, p. 1.

2.各成员国和欧盟机构，以及任何自然人或法人，均可根据《欧洲联盟运行条约》第263条就欧洲银行业管理局的决定向欧盟法院提起行政诉讼。

3.欧洲银行业管理局有义务采取行动但未作决定的，相关方可根据《欧洲联盟运行条约》第265条就其不采取行动向欧盟法院提起行政诉讼。

4.欧洲银行业管理局应采取必要措施以执行欧盟法院的判决。

第六章 财务规定

第62条 欧洲银行业管理局的预算

1.根据《欧盟理事会关于适用于欧洲共同体总预算的财务条例的第1605/2002号(欧共体和欧洲原子能共同体)条例》[1](2002年6月25日)(以下简称《财务条例》)的第185条，欧洲机构欧洲银行业管理局的收入应主要包括下列各项的任意组合：

(a)来自主管金融机构监管的国家级公共机构的义务缴款，该等缴款的计算公式应以关于过渡条款的《议定书(第36号)》第3条第3款所规定的加权票数为基础。为本条之目的，关于过渡条款的《议定书(第36号)》第3条第3款应在其设定的到期日2014年10月31日之后继续适用；

(b)在欧盟《总预算》(欧盟委员会部分)中列支的欧盟补助；

(c)欧洲银行业管理局在欧盟法律相关法律文件所具体规定的情况下收取的任何费用。

2.欧洲银行业管理局的开支至少应包括人员、薪酬、行政管理、基础设施、专业培训和运营费用。

3.欧洲银行业管理局应保持收支平衡。

4.欧洲银行业管理局预算中应包含欧洲银行业管理局每个会计年度(与日历年度一致)所有收支的估算。

1 2002年9月16日《欧盟公报》L 248，第1页。

Article 63 Establishment of the budget

1. By 15 February each year, the Executive Director shall draw up a draft statement of estimates of revenue and expenditure for the following financial year, and shall forward it to the Management Board and the Board of Supervisors, together with the establishment plan. Each year, the Board of Supervisors shall, on the basis of the draft statement drawn up by the Executive Director and approved by the Management Board, produce a statement of estimates of revenue and expenditure of the Authority for the following financial year. That statement of estimates, including a draft establishment plan, shall be transmitted by the Board of Supervisors to the Commission by 31 March. Prior to adoption of the statement of estimates, the draft prepared by the Executive Director shall be approved by the Management Board.

2. The statement of estimates shall be transmitted by the Commission to the European Parliament and to the Council (hereinafter referred to together as the 'budgetary authority'), together with the draft budget of the European Union.

3. On the basis of the statement of estimates, the Commission shall enter in the draft budget of the European Union the estimates it deems necessary in respect of the establishment plan and the amount of the subsidy to be charged to the General Budget of the European Union in accordance with Articles 313 and 314 TFEU.

4. The budgetary authority shall adopt the establishment plan for the Authority. The budgetary authority shall authorise the appropriations for the subsidy to the Authority.

5. The budget of the Authority shall be adopted by the Board of Supervisors. It shall become final after the final adoption of the General Budget of the European Union. Where necessary, it shall be adjusted accordingly.

6. The Management Board shall, without delay, notify the budgetary authority of its intention to implement any project which may have significant financial implications for the funding of its budget, in particular any project relating to property, such as the rental or purchase of buildings. It shall inform the Commission thereof. If either branch of the budgetary authority intends to issue an opinion, it shall, within 2 weeks of receipt of the information on the project, notify the Authority of its intention to issue such an opinion. In the absence of a reply, the Authority may proceed with the planned operation.

7. For the first year of operation of the Authority, ending on 31 December 2011, the financing of the Authority by the Union is subject to an agreement by the budgetary authority as provided for in Point 47 of the Interinstitutional Agreement on budgetary discipline and sound financial management.

Article 64 Implementation and control of the budget

1. The Executive Director shall act as authorising officer and shall implement the Authority's budget.

第63条　预算制订

1.每年2月15日前，执行主任应起草下个会计年度收支的估算报表草案，并和预算制订计划一起转发给管理委员会和监管机构理事会。监管机构理事会每年均应在执行主任起草并经管理委员会批准的报表草案的基础上，制定关于欧洲银行业管理局下个会计年度收支的估算报表。监管机构理事会应将该估算报表连同一份预算制订计划草案于3月31日前发送给欧盟委员会。在通过估算报表前，执行委员会制定的草案应先获得管理委员会批准。

2.欧盟委员会应将估算报表连同欧盟的预算草案一起发送给欧洲议会和欧盟理事会（以下统称预算部门）。

3.根据《欧洲联盟运行条约》第313条和第314条，欧盟委员会应在估算报表的基础上将其认为对预算制订计划属于必要的估算金额以及应在欧盟总预算中列支的补助额纳入欧盟的预算草案。

4.预算部门应通过欧洲银行业管理局的预算制订计划。预算部门应核准将补助划拨给欧洲银行业管理局。

5.欧洲银行业管理局的预算应由监管机构理事会通过。在欧盟总预算最终通过后，欧洲银行业管理局的预算也随之通过，必要时应根据欧盟总预算对其作相应调整。

6.管理委员会如有意实施任何可能会对其预算经费产生重大财务影响的项目，特别是与物业（如租用或购买建筑物）有关的任何项目，应立即通知预算部门。管理委员会应将上述意向如实通知欧盟委员会。任一预算部门有意就上述项目提出意见的，应在收到项目信息后2周内将该意向通知欧洲银行业管理局。如预算部门未针对管理委员会通知作出答复，则欧洲银行业管理局可按计划开展项目。

7.根据《关于预算纪律和健全的财务管理的机构间协议》的第47目，在欧洲银行业管理局运作的首年（即于2011年12月31日结束的年度），在向欧洲银行业管理局提供经费前，欧盟应先获得预算部门的同意。

第64条　预算的实施和控制

1.执行主任应作为欧洲银行业管理局的预算核准官员，并应负责实施欧洲银行业管理局的预算。

2. By 1 March following the completion of each financial year, the Authority's accounting officer shall forward to the Commission's accounting officer and to the Court of Auditors the provisional accounts, accompanied by the report on budgetary and financial management during the financial year. The Authority's accounting officer shall also send the report on budgetary and financial management to the members of the Board of Supervisors, the European Parliament and the Council by 31 March of the following year.

The Commission's accounting officer shall then consolidate the provisional accounts of the institutions and decentralised bodies in accordance with Article 128 of the Financial Regulation.

3. After receiving the observations of the Court of Auditors on the provisional accounts of the Authority in accordance with Article 129 of the Financial Regulation, the Executive Director, acting on his own responsibility, shall draw up the final accounts of the Authority and transmit them, for opinion, to the Management Board.

4. The Management Board shall deliver an opinion on the final accounts of the Authority.

5. The Executive Director shall transmit those final accounts, accompanied by the opinion of the Management Board, by 1 July following the completion of the financial year, to the Members of the Board of Supervisors, the European Parliament, the Council, the Commission and the Court of Auditors.

6. The final accounts shall be published.

7. The Executive Director shall send the Court of Auditors a reply to the latter's observations by 30 September. He shall also send a copy of that reply to the Management Board and the Commission.

8. The Executive Director shall submit to the European Parliament, at the latter's request and as provided for in Article 146(3) of the Financial Regulation, any information necessary for the smooth application of the discharge procedure for the financial year in question.

9. The European Parliament, following a recommendation from the Council acting by qualified majority, shall, before 15 May of the year N+2, grant a discharge to the Authority for the implementation of the budget comprising revenue from the General Budget of the European Union and competent authorities for the financial year N.

Article 65 Financial rules

The financial rules applicable to the Authority shall be adopted by the Management Board after consulting the Commission. Those rules may not depart from Commission Regulation (EC, Euratom) No 2343/2002 of 19 November 2002 on the framework Financial

2.在每个会计年度结束后至下一年度的3月1日前，欧洲银行业管理局的会计官员应将该会计年度的临时财务报表连同关于该会计年度预算和财务管理的报告转发给欧盟委员会的会计官员以及欧盟审计院。欧洲银行业管理局的会计官员还应在次年3月31日前将预算和财务管理报告发送给监管机构理事会的理事、欧洲议会和欧盟理事会。

根据《财务条例》第128条，欧盟委员会的会计官员应对其所收到的各机构和派出单位的临时财务报表进行合并工作。

3.收到欧盟审计院根据《财务条例》第129条对欧洲银行业管理局临时财务报表作出的评述后，执行主任应自行负责起草欧洲银行业管理局的最终报表并将其发送给管理委员会以征求其意见。

4.管理委员会应提交关于欧洲银行业管理局最终报表的意见。

5.执行主任应在会计年度结束之后下一年度的7月1日前将该等最终报表连同管理委员会的意见发送给监管机构理事会理事、欧洲议会、欧盟理事会、欧盟委员会以及欧盟审计院。

6.最终报表应予公布。

7.执行主任应在9月30日前就欧盟审计院的评述向其作出答复。执行主任还应将一份该答复发送给管理委员会和欧盟委员会。

8.经欧洲议会要求，以及根据《财务条例》第146条第3款，执行主任应向其递交所涉会计年度的预算审批程序顺利实施所必要的任何信息。

9.欧洲议会应在第N+2年的5月15日前依照欧盟理事会经特定多数通过的建议，批准欧洲银行业管理局对第N个会计年度包括来自欧盟总预算和主管部门的收入的预算的实施结果。

第65条　财务规则

欧洲银行业管理局所适用的财务规则应由管理委员会在咨询欧盟委员会意见后通过。该等规则不得偏离《欧盟委员会关于〈欧盟理事会关于适用于欧洲共同体总预算的财务条例的第1605/2002号（欧共体和欧洲原子能共同体）条例〉第185条所指机构

Regulation for the bodies referred to in Article 185 of Council Regulation (EC, Euratom) No 1605/2002 on the Financial Regulation applicable to the general budget of the European Communities [1] unless the specific operational needs for the functioning of the Authority so require and only with the prior agreement of the Commission.

Article 66 Anti-fraud measures

1. For the purposes of combating fraud, corruption and any other illegal activity, Regulation (EC) No 1073/1999 shall apply to the Authority without any restriction.

2. The Authority shall accede to the Interinstitutional Agreement concerning internal investigations by OLAF and shall immediately adopt appropriate provisions for all staff of the Authority.

3. The funding decisions and the agreements and the implementing instruments resulting from them shall explicitly stipulate that the Court of Auditors and OLAF may, if need be, carry out on-the-spot checks on the beneficiaries of monies disbursed by the Authority as well as on the staff responsible for allocating these monies.

CHAPTER VII GENERAL PROVISIONS

Article 67 Privileges and immunities

The Protocol (No 7) on the privileges and immunities of the European Union annexed to the Treaty on European Union and to the TFEU shall apply to the Authority and its staff.

Article 68 Staff

1. The Staff Regulations, the Conditions of Employment of Other Servants and the rules adopted jointly by the Union institutions for the purpose of applying them shall apply to the staff of the Authority, including its Executive Director and its Chairperson.

2. The Management Board, in agreement with the Commission, shall adopt the necessary implementing measures, in accordance with the arrangements provided for in Article 110 of the Staff Regulations.

3. In respect of its staff, the Authority shall exercise the powers conferred on the appointing authority by the Staff Regulations and on the authority entitled to conclude contracts by the Conditions of Employment of Other Servants.

4. The Management Board shall adopt provisions to allow national experts from Member States to be seconded to the Authority.

---

1 OJ L 357, 31. 12. 2002, p. 72.

的框架性〈财务条例〉的第2343/2002号(欧共体和欧洲原子能共同体)条例》[1](2002年11月19日),但是,出于欧洲银行业管理局运行的特殊运营需要并且仅在经欧盟委员会事先同意的情况下除外。

第66条　反欺诈措施

1.为反欺诈、腐败以及其他非法活动之目的,第1073/1999号(欧共体)条例应不受限制地适用于欧洲银行业管理局。

2.欧洲银行业管理局应加入《关于欧洲反欺诈办公室内部调查的机构间协议》,并应立即通过针对欧洲银行业管理局所有工作人员的适当规定。

3.经费筹措决定以及由此产生的协议和实施性法律文件应明确规定欧盟审计院和欧洲反欺诈办公室可在必要时对欧洲银行业管理局支出款项的受益人以及负责分配该等款项的工作人员进行现场调查。

第七章　一般条款

第67条　特殊权利和豁免

《欧洲联盟条约》和《欧洲联盟运行条约》附录关于欧盟的特殊权利和豁免的《议定书(第7号)》应适用于欧洲银行业管理局及其工作人员。

第68条　工作人员

1.《人事条例》、《其他人员的聘用条件》以及欧盟机构为上述文件的适用联合通过的规则应适用于欧洲银行业管理局的工作人员,包括其执行主任和主席。

2.根据《人事条例》第110条所规定的安排,管理委员会与欧盟委员会达成一致后应制定必要的实施细则。

3.欧洲银行业管理局应对其工作人员行使《人事条例》授予的任命权以及《其他人员的聘用条件》授予的签订聘用合同的权力。

4.管理委员会应通过相关规定以允许从各成员国借调国内的专家到欧洲银行业管理局。

1　2002年12月31日《欧盟公报》L 357,第72页。

Article 69 Liability of the Authority

1. In the case of non-contractual liability, the Authority shall, in accordance with the general principles common to the laws of the Member States, make good any damage caused by it or by its staff in the performance of their duties. The Court of Justice of the European Union shall have jurisdiction in any dispute over the remedying of such damage.

2. The personal financial liability and disciplinary liability of Authority staff towards the Authority shall be governed by the relevant provisions applying to the staff of the Authority.

Article 70 Obligation of professional secrecy

1. Members of the Board of Supervisors and the Management Board, the Executive Director, and members of the staff of the Authority including officials seconded by Member States on a temporary basis and all other persons carrying out tasks for the Authority on a contractual basis shall be subject to the requirements of professional secrecy pursuant to Article 339 TFEU and the relevant provisions in Union legislation, even after their duties have ceased.

Article 16 of the Staff Regulations shall apply to them.

In accordance with the Staff Regulations, the staff shall, after leaving service, continue to be bound by the duty to behave with integrity and discretion as regards the acceptance of certain appointments or benefits.

Neither Member States, the Union institutions or bodies, nor any other public or private body shall seek to influence staff members of the Authority in the performance of their tasks.

2. Without prejudice to cases covered by criminal law, any confidential information received by persons referred to in paragraph 1 whilst performing their duties may not be divulged to any person or authority whatsoever, except in summary or aggregate form, such that individual financial institutions cannot be identified.

Moreover, the obligation under paragraph 1 and the first subparagraph of this paragraph shall not prevent the Authority and the national supervisory authorities from using the information for the enforcement of the acts referred to in Article 1(2), and in particular for legal procedures for the adoption of decisions.

3. Paragraphs 1 and 2 shall not prevent the Authority from exchanging information with national supervisory authorities in accordance with this Regulation and other Union legislation applicable to financial institutions.

That information shall be subject to the conditions of professional secrecy referred to in paragraphs 1 and 2. The Authority shall lay down in its internal rules of procedure the practical arrangements for implementing the confidentiality rules referred to in paragraphs 1 and 2.

第69条　欧洲银行业管理局的责任

1.对于欧洲银行业管理局或其工作人员在履行职责时造成的不属于合同责任的任何损害，欧洲银行业管理局应根据各成员国国内法律通用的一般原则进行赔偿。欧盟法院应对上述损害赔偿引发的任何争议有司法管辖权。

2.欧洲银行业管理局工作人员对欧洲银行业管理局承担的个人财务责任和违纪责任应受适用于欧洲银行业管理局工作人员的相关规定管辖。

第70条　职业保密义务

1.监管机构理事会的理事和管理委员会的委员、执行主任、欧洲银行业管理局工作人员（包括成员国暂时借调的官员）以及所有其他按合同为欧洲银行业管理局履行职责的人员在欧洲银行业管理局任职期间以及任职结束后均应遵守《欧洲联盟运行条约》第339条以及欧盟立法相关条款规定的职业保密要求。

《人事条例》第16条应适用于上述人员。

根据《人事条例》，工作人员离职后在接受特定任命和利益时应继续受诚信和谨慎义务约束。

各成员国、欧盟机构或单位或任何公共或私人机构均不得试图影响欧洲银行业管理局工作人员履行其职责。

2.第1款所指人员在履行职责时收到的任何保密信息均不得泄露给任何个人或部门，但是，以无法识别具体金融机构的摘要或汇总形式披露的除外。上述规定不影响相关情形下刑法的适用。

另外，第1款以及本款第1项中的义务应不妨碍欧洲银行业管理局和各国家级监管机构将信息用于执行第1条第2款所述立法，特别是用于通过决定的法律程序。

3.第1款和第2款应不妨碍欧洲银行业管理局根据本条例以及其他适用于金融机构的欧盟立法与各国家级监管机构交换信息。

该等信息受第1款和第2款所述职业保密条件的约束。欧洲银行业管理局应在其内部程序规则中规定实施第1款和第2款所述保密规则的具体安排。

4. The Authority shall apply Commission Decision 2001/844/EC/ECSC, Euratom of 29 November 2001 amending its internal Rules of Procedure [1].

Article 71 Data protection

This Regulation shall be without prejudice to the obligations of Member States relating to their processing of personal data under Directive 95/46/EC or the obligations of the Authority relating to its processing of personal data under Regulation (EC) No 45/2001 when fulfilling its responsibilities.

Article 72 Access to documents

1. Regulation (EC) No 1049/2001 shall apply to documents held by the Authority.

2. The Management Board shall, by 31 May 2011, adopt practical measures for applying Regulation (EC) No 1049/2001.

3. Decisions taken by the Authority pursuant to Article 8 of Regulation (EC) No 1049/2001 may be the subject of a complaint to the Ombudsman or of proceedings before the Court of Justice of the European Union, following an appeal to the Board of Appeal, as appropriate, in accordance with the conditions laid down in Articles 228 and 263 TFEU respectively.

Article 73 Language arrangements

1. Council Regulation No 1 determining the languages to be used by the European Economic Community [2] shall apply to the Authority.

2. The Management Board shall decide on the internal language arrangements for the Authority.

3. The translation services required for the functioning of the Authority shall be provided by the Translation Centre for the Bodies of the European Union.

Article 74 Headquarters Agreement

The necessary arrangements concerning the accommodation to be provided for the Authority in the Member State where its seat is located and the facilities to be made available by that Member State, as well as the specific rules applicable in that Member State to the Executive Director, the members of the Management Board, the staff of the Authority and members of their families shall be laid down in a Headquarters Agreement between the Authority and that Member State concluded after obtaining the approval of the Management Board.

That Member State shall provide the best possible conditions to ensure the proper functioning of the Authority, including multi-lingual, European-oriented schooling and appropriate transport connections.

---

1 OJ L 317, 3. 12. 2001, p. 1.

2 OJ 17, 6. 10. 1958, p. 385.

4.欧洲银行业管理局应适用修改其内部程序规则的欧盟委员会第2001/844/EC/ECSC号(欧洲原子能共同体)决定[1](2001年11月29日)。

第71条 数据保护

本条例不影响成员国在第95/46/EC号指令下与个人数据处理有关的义务或欧洲银行业管理局在履行职责过程中应遵循的第45/2001号(欧共体)条例下与个人数据处理有关的义务。

第72条 文件查阅权

1.第1049/2001号(欧共体)条例应适用于欧洲银行业管理局所持有的文件。

2.管理委员会应在2011年5月31日前制定适用第1049/2001号(欧共体)条例的具体措施。

3.针对欧洲银行业管理局根据第1049/2001号(欧共体)条例第8条作出的决定,在适当情况下所涉人员可首先向行政复议委员会提出行政复议申请,若对行政复议结果不服,可再分别依照《欧洲联盟运行条约》第228条和第263条所列条件向申诉官申诉或向欧盟法院提起行政诉讼。

第73条 语言安排

1.确定欧洲经济共同体所用语言的欧盟理事会第1号条例[2]应适用于欧洲银行业管理局。

2.管理委员会应就欧洲银行业管理局的内部语言安排作出决定。

3.欧洲银行业管理局运行所需的翻译服务应由欧盟翻译中心提供。

第74条 《总部协议》

获得管理委员会批准之后,欧洲银行业管理局与其总部所在的成员国之间应缔结一份《总部协议》,规定该成员国应向欧洲银行业管理局提供的住宿条件和供其使用的设施相关的必要安排,以及该成员国适用于执行主任、管理委员会委员、欧洲银行业管理局工作人员及其家属的具体规则。

该成员国应尽可能提供最好的条件以确保欧洲银行业管理局的稳健运行,包括多语的欧洲模式教育以及适当的交通便利。

1 2001年12月3日《欧盟公报》L 317,第1页。

2 1958年10月6日《欧盟公报》17,第385页。

Article 75 Participation of third countries

1. Participation in the work of the Authority shall be open to third countries which have concluded agreements with the Union whereby they have adopted and are applying Union law in the areas of competence of the Authority as referred to in Article 1(2).

2. The Authority may cooperate with the countries referred to in paragraph 1, applying legislation which has been recognised as equivalent in the areas of competence of the Authority referred to in Article 1(2), as provided for in international agreements concluded by the Union in accordance with Article 216 TFEU.

3. Under the relevant provisions of the agreements referred to in paragraphs 1 and 2, arrangements shall be made specifying, in particular, the nature, scope and procedural aspects of the involvement of the countries referred to in paragraph 1 in the work of the Authority, including provisions relating to financial contributions and to staff. They may provide for representation, as an observer, on the Board of Supervisors, but shall ensure that those countries do not attend any discussions relating to individual financial institutions, except where there is a direct interest.

CHAPTER Ⅷ TRANSITIONAL AND FINAL PROVISIONS

Article 76 Preparatory actions

1. Following the entry into force of this Regulation, and before the establishment of the Authority, CEBS shall act in close cooperation with the Commission to prepare for the replacement of CEBS by the Authority.

2. Once the Authority has been established, the Commission shall be responsible for the administrative establishment and initial administrative operation of the Authority until the Authority has appointed an Executive Director.

For that purpose, until such time as the Executive Director takes up his duties following his appointment by the Board of Supervisors in accordance with Article 51, the Commission may assign one official on an interim basis in order to fulfil the functions of the Executive Director. That period shall be limited to the time necessary for the appointment of an Executive Director of the Authority.

The interim Executive Director may authorise all payments covered by credits provided in the budget of the Authority, once approved by the Management Board and may conclude contracts, including staff contracts following the adoption of the Authority's establishment plan.

第75条　第三国的参与

1.第三国与欧盟缔结了相关协议,因此已经采纳并正在适用第1条第2款所述欧洲银行业管理局职权管辖范围内的欧盟法律的,应能参与欧洲银行业管理局的工作。

2.根据欧盟依照《欧洲联盟运行条约》第216条缔结的国际协议,欧洲银行业管理局可与第1款所述的国家合作适用已被认定在欧洲银行业管理局第1条第2款所述职权管辖范围内与欧盟立法等效的立法。

3.根据第1款和第2款所述协议的相关规定,应作出相应安排,以特别指明第1款所述国家涉入欧洲银行业管理局工作的性质、范围和程序,包括与费用分摊和工作人员有关的规定。根据该等安排,第三国可作为监管机构理事会的观察员,但应确保该等国家不参与任何与具体金融机构有关的讨论,存在直接利害关系的除外。

第八章　过渡规定和最终条款

第76条　筹备活动

1.本条例生效后至欧洲银行业管理局成立前的期间内,欧洲银行业监管机构委员会应与欧盟委员会紧密合作,为欧洲银行业管理局取代欧洲银行业监管机构委员会做好筹备工作。

2.欧洲银行业管理局成立后,在欧洲银行业管理局任命执行主任之前,应由欧盟委员会负责欧洲银行业管理局的行政设立和初始行政运作。

为此,在监管机构理事会根据第51条任命执行主任之后,直至执行主任到任之前,欧盟委员会可临时委派一名官员履行执行主任的职能。该段时间应限于欧洲银行业管理局任命执行主任所必要的时期。

临时执行主任经管理委员会批准,可核准欧洲银行业管理局预算贷方项目所涵盖的所有支出,并可签订合同,包括在通过欧洲银行业管理局预算制订计划后签订的劳动合同。

3. Paragraphs 1 and 2 are without prejudice to the powers of the Board of Supervisors and the Management Board.

4. The Authority shall be considered the legal successor of CEBS. By the date of establishment of the Authority, all assets and liabilities and all pending operations of CEBS shall be automatically transferred to the Authority. CEBS shall establish a statement showing its closing asset and liability situation as of the date of that transfer. That statement shall be audited and approved by CEBS and by the Commission.

Article 77 Transitional staff provisions

1. By way of derogation from Article 68, all employment contracts and secondment agreements concluded by CEBS or its Secretariat and in force on 1 January 2011 shall be honoured until their expiry date. They may not be extended.

2. All members of staff under contracts referred to in paragraph 1 shall be offered the possibility of concluding temporary agent contracts pursuant to Article 2(a) of the Conditions of Employment of Other Servants at the various grades as set out in the Authority's establishment plan.

An internal selection limited to staff who have contracts with CEBS or its Secretariat shall be carried out after the entry into force of this Regulation by the authority authorised to conclude contracts in order to check the ability, efficiency and integrity of those to be engaged. The internal selection procedure shall take full account of the skills and experience demonstrated by the individuals' performance prior to the engagement.

3. Depending on the type and level of functions to be performed, successful applicants shall be offered temporary agents' contracts of a duration corresponding at least to the time remaining under the prior contract.

4. The relevant national law relating to labour contracts and other relevant instruments shall continue to apply to staff members with prior contracts who choose not to apply for temporary agent's contracts or who are not offered temporary agents contracts in accordance with paragraph 2.

Article 78 National provisions

The Member States shall make such provision as is appropriate to ensure the effective application of this Regulation.

Article 79 Amendments

Decision No 716/2009/EC is hereby amended in so far as CEBS is removed from the list of beneficiaries set out in Section B of the Annex to that Decision.

Article 80 Repeal

Commission Decision 2009/78/EC, establishing CEBS, is hereby repealed with effect from 1 January 2011.

3.第1款和第2款不影响监管机构理事会和管理委员会的权力。

4.欧洲银行业管理局应被视为欧洲银行业监管机构委员会的合法继任机构。在欧洲银行业管理局成立之日,欧洲银行业监管机构委员会的所有资产和债务以及所有待执行的运营事务将自动转移给欧洲银行业管理局。欧洲银行业监管机构委员会应制定一份报表表明其截至转移当日期末资产和债务的情况。该报表应由欧洲银行业监管机构委员会和欧盟委员会审计和批准。

第77条 过渡期人事规定

1.作为第68条的例外,欧洲银行业监管机构委员会或其秘书处签订的并于2011年1月1日有效的所有劳动合同和借调协议,均应履行至到期日,不得延期。

2.第1款所述合同下的所有工作人员均应有机会按照欧洲银行业管理局的预算制订计划所列各种级别签订符合《其他人员的聘用条件》第2条第a款的临时劳动合同。

本条例生效后,获得授权签订合同的部门应开展内部遴选,遴选对象仅限于与欧洲银行业监管机构委员会或其秘书处有合同关系的工作人员,以对拟聘用人员的能力、效率和诚信进行审查。内部遴选程序应充分考虑候选人被聘用前在工作中所展现出的个人技能和经验。

3.根据待履行职能的类型和级别,被录用的申请人应获得临时劳动合同,该等合同的期限应至少相当于先前合同未履行的时间。

4.与劳动合同有关的国内法律以及其他相关法律文件应继续适用于之前签订过合同,但选择不申请临时劳动合同或未根据第2款获得临时劳动合同的工作人员。

第78条 成员国的规定

各成员国应制定适当的规定以确保本条例的有效适用。

第79条 修正

应对第716/2009/EC号决定作出修正,从附录第B节所列的受益者名单中删除欧洲银行业监管机构委员会。

第80条 废止

设立欧洲银行业监管机构委员会的欧盟委员会第2009/78/EC号决定特此于2011年1月1日废止。

Article 81 Review

1. By 2 January 2014, and every 3 years thereafter, the Commission shall publish a general report on the experience acquired as a result of the operation of the Authority and the procedures laid down in this Regulation. That report shall evaluate, inter alia:

(a) the convergence in supervisory practices reached by competent authorities:

(i) the convergence in functional independence of the competent authorities and in standards equivalent to corporate governance;

(ii) the impartiality, objectivity and autonomy of the Authority;

(b) the functioning of the colleges of supervisors;

(c) the progress achieved towards convergence in the fields of crisis prevention, management and resolution, including Union funding mechanisms;

(d) the role of the Authority as regards systemic risk;

(e) the application of the safeguard clause established in Article 38;

(f) the application of the binding mediation role established in Article 19.

2. The report referred to in paragraph 1 shall also examine whether:

(a) it is appropriate to continue separate supervision of banking, insurance, occupational pensions, securities and financial markets;

(b) it is appropriate to undertake prudential supervision and supervise the conduct of business separately or by the same supervisor;

(c) it is appropriate to simplify and reinforce the architecture of the ESFS in order to increase the coherence between the macro and the micro levels and between the ESAs;

(d) the evolution of the ESFS is consistent with that of the global evolution;

(e) there is sufficient diversity and excellence within the ESFS;

(f) accountability and transparency in relation to publication requirements are adequate;

(g) the resources of the Authority are adequate to carry out its responsibilities;

(h) it is appropriate for the seat of the Authority to be maintained or to move the ESAs to a single seat to enhance better coordination between them.

3. Concerning the issue of direct supervision of institutions or infrastructures of pan-European reach and taking account of market developments, the Commission shall draw up an annual report on the appropriateness of entrusting the Authority with further supervisory responsibilities in this area.

4. The report and any accompanying proposals, as appropriate, shall be forwarded to the European Parliament and to the Council.

Article 82 Entry into force

This Regulation shall enter into force on the day following its publication in the Official Journal of the European Union.

第81条 审评

1.2014年1月2日前，欧盟委员会应发布一份综合报告，说明其在欧洲银行业管理局运营和本条例所列程序方面取得的经验，并于此后每3年发布一份该等综合报告。该报告应评价的问题包括但不限于：

(a)各主管部门所达到的监管实践的趋同：

(i)各主管部门职能上的独立性趋同以及与公司治理等效之标准的趋同；

(ii)欧洲银行业管理局的公正性、客观性和自主性；

(b)监管团的运作；

(c)在危机预防、管理和清盘领域(包括欧盟经费筹措机制)取得的趋同程度；

(d)欧洲银行业管理局在系统性风险方面所起的作用；

(e)第38条所确立的保障条款的适用；

(f)第19条所设定的有约束力的调解角色的应用。

2.第1款所述的报告还应对下列事项进行审查：

(a)是否宜继续对银行业、保险、职业养老金、证券以及金融市场进行分业监管；

(b)是否宜分别开展审慎监管和业务活动监管或由一个监管机构同时进行上述两项监管；

(c)是否宜简化和加强欧洲金融监管机构体系的结构，以加强宏观和微观层面以及各欧洲监管机构之间的相互一致性；

(d)欧洲金融监管机构体系的发展是否与全球发展一致；

(e)欧洲金融监管机构体系内是否具有足够的多样性和卓越性；

(f)在公开相关要求方面是否有充分的问责制和透明度；

(g)欧洲银行业管理局的资源是否能保证其充分履行责任；

(h)欧洲银行业管理局的地点是否宜保持不变，还是应将各欧洲监管机构迁至同一地点以加强相互之间的协调。

3.对于泛欧范围内的机构或基础设施的直接监管问题，考虑到市场的发展，欧盟委员会应起草一份关于是否应在此领域赋予欧洲银行业管理局更多监管责任的年度报告。

4.报告及随附的任何提议(如有)均应转发给欧洲议会和欧盟理事会。

第82条 生效

本条例应于《欧盟公报》公布，公布的次日生效。

It shall apply from 1 January 2011, with the exception of Article 76 and Article 77 (1) and (2), which shall apply as from the date of its entry into force.

The Authority shall be established on 1 January 2011.

This Regulation shall be binding in its entirety and directly applicable in all Member States.

Done at Strasbourg, 24 November 2010.

For the European Parliament
The President
J. BUZEK

For the Council
The President
O. CHASTEL

本条例应于2011年1月1日起适用，但第76条以及第77条第1款和第2款应从本条例生效之日起适用。

欧洲银行业管理局应于2011年1月1日成立。

本条例所有内容对各成员国均具有约束力,并可直接适用于所有成员国。

2010年11月24日于斯特拉斯堡通过。

欧洲议会议长 欧盟理事会主席

J.布泽克 O.查斯特尔

REGULATION (EU) NO 1094/2010 OF THE EUROPEAN PARLIAMENT AND OF THE COUNCIL

欧洲议会与欧盟理事会第1094/2010号(欧盟)条例

REGULATION (EU) No 1094/2010 OF THE EUROPEAN PARLIAMENT AND OF THE COUNCIL

of 24 November 2010 establishing a European Supervisory Authority (European Insurance and Occupational Pensions Authority), amending Decision No 716/2009/EC and repealing Commission Decision 2009/79/EC

THE EUROPEAN PARLIAMENT AND THE COUNCIL OF THE EUROPEANU - NION,

Having regard to the Treaty on the Functioning of the European Union, and in particular Article 114 thereof,

Having regard to the proposal from the European Commission,

Having regard to the opinion of the European Central Bank [1],

Having regard to the opinion of the European Economic and Social Committee [2],

Acting in accordance with the ordinary legislative procedure [3],

Whereas:

(1) The financial crisis in 2007 and 2008 exposed important shortcomings in financial supervision, both in particular cases and in relation to the financial system as a whole. Nationally based supervisory models have lagged behind financial globalisation and the integrated and interconnected reality of European financial markets, in which many financial institutions operate across borders. The crisis exposed shortcomings in the areas of cooperation, coordination, consistent application of Union law and trust between national supervisors.

(2) Before and during the financial crisis, the European Parliament has called for a

1 OJ C 13, 20.1.2010, p. 1.

2 Opinion of 22 January 2010 (not yet published in the Official Journal).

3 Position of the European Parliament of 22 September 2010 (not yet published in the Official Journal) and decision of the Council of17 November 2010.

欧洲议会与欧盟理事会
第 1094/2010 号(欧盟)条例

(本条例于 2010 年 11 月 24 日通过,设立欧洲监管机构欧洲保险与职业养老金管理局并修正第 716/2009/EC 号决定和废止欧盟委员会第 2009/79/EC 号决定)

欧洲议会和欧盟理事会,

根据《欧洲联盟运行条约》,特别是其中的第114条,

根据欧盟委员会的提议,
根据欧洲中央银行的意见[1],
根据欧洲经济与社会委员会的意见[2],
依照正常的立法程序[3],
鉴于下列情形,通过本条例:

(1)2007年和2008年的金融危机暴露出金融监管的重要缺陷,不论就特殊事例而言抑或就金融系统整体而言。局限于国家这一层级的监管模式已落后于金融全球化的步伐,亦无法适应众多金融机构已实现跨境运营的欧洲金融市场在一体化和相互关联方面的现实态势。危机暴露出的问题体现在国家级监管机构之间的合作与协调不够、欧盟法律适用一致性的缺乏及相互信任的不足这几个方面。

(2)欧洲议会在其于金融危机发生前及其持续期间,呼吁进一步整合欧洲的金融

1 2010 年 1 月 20 日《欧盟公报》C 13,第 1 页。
2 2010 年 1 月 22 日的意见(尚未在《欧盟公报》公布)。
3 2010 年 9 月 22 日欧洲议会立场(尚未在《欧盟公报》公布)以及 2010 年 11 月 17 日欧盟理事会决定。

move towards more integrated European supervision in order to ensure a true level playing field for all actors at the level of the Union and to reflect the increasing integration of financial markets in the Union (in its resolutions of 13 April 2000 on the Commission communication on implementing the framework for financial markets: Action Plan [1], of 21 November 2002 on prudential supervision rules in the European Union [2], of 11 July 2007 on financial services policy (2005 to 2010) White Paper [3], of 23 September 2008 with recommendations to the Commission on hedge funds and private equity [4] and of 9 October 2008 with recommendations to the Commission on Lamfalussy follow-up: future structure of supervision [5], and in its positions of 22 April 2009 on the amended proposal for a directive of the European Parliament and of the Council on the taking-up and pursuit of the business of Insurance and Reinsurance (Solvency Ⅱ) [6] and of 23 April 2009 on the proposal for a regulation of the European Parliament and of the Council on Credit Rating Agencies [7].

(3) In November 2008, the Commission mandated a High-Level Group chaired by Jacques de Larosière to make recommendations on how to strengthen European supervisory arrangements with a view to better protecting the citizen and rebuilding trust in the financial system. In its final report presented on 25 February 2009 (the 'de Larosière Report'), the High-Level Group recommended that the supervisory framework be strengthened to reduce the risk and severity of future financial crises. It recommended reforms to the structure of supervision of the financial sector in the Union. The group also concluded that a European System of Financial Supervisors should be created, comprising three European Supervisory Authorities, one for the banking sector, one for the securities sector and one for the insurance and occupational pensions sector, and recommended the creation of a European Systemic Risk Council. The report represented the reforms the experts considered were needed and on which work had to begin immediately.

(4) In its Communication of 4 March 2009 entitled 'Driving European Recovery', the Commission proposed to put forward draft legislation creating a European system of financial supervision and a European systemic risk board. In its Communication of 27 May 2009 entitled 'European Financial Supervision', it provided more detail about the possible architecture of such a new supervisory framework reflecting the main thrust of the de Larosière Report.

1 OJ C 40, 7.2.2001, p. 453.
2 OJ C 25 E, 29.1.2004, p. 394.
3 OJ C 175 E, 10.7.2008, p. 392.
4 OJ C 8 E, 14.1.2010, p. 26.
5 OJ C 9 E, 15.1.2010, p. 48.
6 OJ C 184 E, 8.7.2010, p. 214.
7 OJ C 184 E, 8.7.2010, p. 292.

监管,以便确保能在欧盟这一层级为所有市场主体提供真正公平的竞争环境,并反映欧盟金融市场不断一体化的现实[请参见:欧洲议会2000年4月13日关于欧盟委员会通报《落实金融市场框架:行动计划》的决议[1]、2002年11月21日关于欧盟审慎监管规则的决议[2]、2007年7月11日关于《2005年至2010年金融服务政策白皮书》的决议[3]、2008年9月23日关于对冲基金和私募股权的决议(含向欧盟委员会提出的建议)[4]、2008年10月9日关于《莱姆法路西的后续行动:未来监管结构》的决议(含向欧盟委员会提出的建议)[5]、2009年4月22日对《欧洲议会与欧盟理事会关于开办和经营保险与再保险业务的指令》(保险偿付能力标准Ⅱ)的修正稿提案所持立场[6]以及2009年4月23日对《欧洲议会与欧盟理事会关于信用评级机构的条例》的提案所持立场[7]。]

(3)2008年11月,欧盟委员会委托一个高级工作组在雅克·德·拉罗西埃的领导下,就如何加强欧洲监管安排以更好地保护公众利益并重建公众对金融系统的信任提出建议。在其于2009年2月25日提交的最终报告(《德·拉罗西埃报告》)中,高级工作组建议强化监管框架以降低未来出现金融危机的风险及其严重程度,并建议对欧盟金融行业的监管结构进行改革,该小组还得出了应成立欧洲金融监管机构体系的结论,欧洲金融监管机构体系应由银行、证券以及保险与职业养老金三大金融行业的欧洲监管机构(ESA)组成,并建议创设一个欧洲系统性风险理事会。此份报告阐述了专家们认为需要进行的改革以及必须立刻开展的工作。

(4)在2009年3月4日名为《推动欧洲复苏》的通报中,欧盟委员会提议起草相关立法草案以创建欧洲金融监管体系和欧洲系统性风险委员会,并在其2009年5月27日名为《欧洲金融监管》的通报中提供了该新监管框架可能之架构的更多细节,体现了《德·拉罗西埃报告》的要旨。

---

1 2001年2月7日《欧盟公报》C 40,第453页。
2 2004年1月29日《欧盟公报》C 25 E,第394页。
3 2008年7月10日《欧盟公报》C 175 E,第392页。
4 2010年1月14日《欧盟公报》C 8 E,第26页。
5 2010年1月15日《欧盟公报》C 9 E,第48页。
6 2010年7月8日《欧盟公报》C 184 E,第214页。
7 2010年7月8日《欧盟公报》C 184 E,第292页。

(5) The European Council, in its conclusions of 19 June 2009, confirmed that a European System of Financial Supervisors, comprising three new European Supervisory Authorities, should be established. The system should be aimed at upgrading the quality and consistency of national supervision, strengthening oversight of cross-border groups and establishing a European single rulebook applicable to all financial institutions in the internal market. It emphasised that the European Supervisory Authorities should also have supervisory powers in relation to credit rating agencies and invited the Commission to prepare concrete proposals on how the European System of Financial Supervisors could play a strong role in crisis situations, while stressing that decisions taken by the European Supervisory Authorities should not impinge on the fiscal responsibilities of Member States.

(6) The financial and economic crisis has created real and serious risks to the stability of the financial system and the functioning of the internal market. Restoring and maintaining a stable and reliable financial system is an absolute prerequisite to preserving trust and coherence in the internal market, and thereby to preserve and improve the conditions for the establishment of a fully integrated and functioning internal market in the field of financial services. Moreover, deeper and more integrated financial markets offer better opportunities for financing and risk diversification, and thus help to improve the capacity of the economies to absorb shocks.

(7) The Union has reached the limits of what can be done with the present status of the Committees of European Supervisors. The Union cannot remain in a situation where there is no mechanism to ensure that national supervisors arrive at the best possible supervisory decisions for cross-border financial institutions; where there is insufficient cooperation and information exchange between national supervisors; where joint action by national authorities requires complicated arrangements to take account of the patchwork of regulatory and supervisory requirements; where national solutions are most often the only feasible option in responding to problems at the level of the Union; and where different interpretations of the same legal text exist. The European System of Financial Supervision (hereinafter the ESFS') should be designed to overcome those deficiencies and provide a system that is in line with the objective of a stable and single Union financial market for financial services, linking national supervisors within a strong Union network.

(8) ESFS should be an integrated network of national and Union supervisory authorities, leaving day-to-day supervision to the national level. Greater harmonisation and the coherent application of rules for financial institutions and markets across the Union should also be achieved. In addition to the European Supervisory Authority (European Insurance and Occupational Pensions Authority) (hereinafter the Authority'), a European Supervisory Authority (European Banking Authority) and a European Supervisory Authority (European Securities and Markets Authority) as well as a Joint Committee of the

(5)欧洲理事会在其2009年6月19日的结论中确认,应当建立一个由3个新的欧洲监管机构组成的欧洲金融监管机构体系。该体系应旨在改善国家级监管工作的质量和一致性、加强对跨境集团的监控、建立适用于欧盟内部市场所有金融机构的欧洲单一规则手册。欧洲理事会还强调了欧洲监管机构对信用评级机构的监管权,并要求欧盟委员会针对欧洲金融监管机构体系在危机情况下如何发挥强有力作用制定具体的提案,但同时也强调欧洲监管机构作出的决策不应影响成员国的财政责任。

(6)金融与经济危机对金融系统稳定以及内部市场运行带来了真实而严重的风险。恢复与维持一个稳定可靠的金融系统,无疑是维持公众对内部市场的信任和内部市场自身凝聚力的先决条件,建立一个彻底一体化和全面运行的金融服务内部市场所需条件也因而能得到维持和改善。此外,更为深化和一体化的金融市场为融资和风险分散提供了更好的机会,从而有助于提高各经济体化解冲击的能力。

(7)以欧洲监管机构委员会现有的身份和状态,欧盟已穷尽各种可能。欧盟不能面对下列困境坐视不管:欧盟缺乏一套能确保国家级监管机构对跨境金融机构作出尽可能最佳的监管决定的机制;国家级监管机构之间缺乏足够的合作和信息交流;鉴于各国规制和监管要求的差异,国家级监管机构需要复杂的安排才能作出共同行动;目前为止,应对欧盟层级问题最常见且唯一可行的解决方案往往只是国家层级的解决方案;不同成员国对同一法律文本存在各种不同的解释。欧洲金融监管体系(英文简称ESFS)应旨在克服该等不足,并建立符合"稳定和单一的欧盟金融服务市场"目标的体系,将国家级监管机构连接纳入到强大的欧盟网络之中。

(8)欧洲金融监管机构体系应该是一个整合国家层级和欧盟层级监管机构的一体化网络,日常的监管工作仍留待国家层级处理。同时,还应实现金融机构和市场规则在欧盟范围内更高程度的协调和适用的一致性。除了欧洲监管机构(欧洲保险与职业养老金管理局)(以下简称欧洲保险与职业养老金管理局)之外,还应设立欧洲监管机构(欧洲银行业管理局)、欧洲监管机构(欧洲证券与市场管理局)以及上述三个欧洲监管机构的联合委员会(以下简称联合委员会)。欧洲系统性风险委员会(英文简称ESRB)也应成为欧洲金融监管体系的一部分,以完成本条例以及欧洲议会与欧盟理事

European Supervisory Authorities (hereinafter the Joint Committee') should be established. A European Systemic Risk Board (hereinafter the ESRB') should form part of the ESFS for the purposes of the tasks as specified in this Regulation and in Regulation (EU) No 1092/2010 of the European Parliament and of the Council [1].

(9) The European Supervisory Authorities (hereinafter collectively referred to as the 'ESAs') should replace the Committee of European Banking Supervisors established by Commission Decision 2009/78/EC [2], the Committee of European Insurance and Occupational Pensions Supervisors established by Commission Decision 2009/79/EC [3] and the Committee of European Securities Regulators established by Commission Decision 2009/77/EC [4], and should assume all of the tasks and competences of those committees including the continuation of ongoing work and projects, where appropriate. The scope of each European Supervisory Authority's action should be clearly defined. The ESAs should be accountable to the European Parliament and the Council. When that accountability relates to cross-sectoral issues that have been coordinated through the Joint Committee, the ESAs should be accountable, through the Joint Committee, for such coordination.

(10) The Authority should act with a view to improving the functioning of the internal market, in particular by ensuring a high, effective and consistent level of regulation and supervision taking account of the varying interests of all Member States and the different nature of financial institutions. The Authority should protect public values such as the stability of the financial system, the transparency of markets and financial products, and the protection of policyholders, pension scheme members and beneficiaries. The Authority should also prevent regulatory arbitrage, guarantee a level playing field, and strengthen international supervisory coordination, for the benefit of the economy at large, including financial institutions and other stakeholders, consumers and employees. Its tasks should also include promoting supervisory convergence and providing advice to the Union institutions in the area of insurance, reinsurance and occupational retirement provision regulation and supervision, and related corporate governance, auditing and financial reporting issues. The Authority should also be entrusted with certain responsibilities for existing and new financial activities.

(11) The Authority should also be able to temporarily prohibit or restrict certain financial activities that threaten the orderly functioning and integrity of financial markets or the stability of the whole or part of the financial system in the Union in the cases

1 See page 1 of this Official Journal.

2 OJ L 25, 29.1.2009, p. 23.

3 OJ L 25, 29.1.2009, p. 28.

4 OJ L 25, 29.1.2009, p. 18.

会第1092/2010号(欧盟)条例[1]规定的工作。

(9)各欧洲监管机构(英文统称ESA)应取代依据欧盟委员会第2009/78/EC号决定[2]设立的欧洲银行业监管机构委员会、依据欧盟委员会第2009/79/EC号决定[3]设立的欧洲保险与职业养老金监管机构委员会以及依据欧盟委员会第2009/77/EC号决定[4]设立的欧洲证券监管机构委员会,并承担各自的所有职责和职权,包括在适当时继续完成任何正在进行中的职责和项目。对各欧洲监管机构的行动范围应有明确的界定。各欧洲监管机构应对欧洲议会和欧盟理事会负责。如其所承担的责任牵涉到曾经通过联合委员会协调的跨行业问题,则各欧洲监管机构应通过联合委员会对上述协作负责。

(10)欧洲保险与职业养老金管理局应致力于改善内部市场的运行,尤其是在考虑所有成员国的不同利益以及金融机构的不同性质的基础上,确保高水平、有效和一致的规制和监管。欧洲保险与养老金管理局应保护公共价值观,如金融系统的稳定、市场和金融产品的透明以及对保单持有人、养老金计划成员以及其他受益人的保护。欧洲保险与养老金管理局还应为了整体经济利益(包括金融机构以及其他利益相关者、消费者和雇员的利益)而防范监管套利并保证公平的竞争环境,并加强国际监管的相互协调。其职责还应包括推动监管趋同以及就保险、再保险和职业退休金规制和监管领域以及相关的公司治理、审计和财务报告事宜向欧盟机构提供建议。欧盟还应委托欧洲保险与职业养老金管理局对现有和未来的新金融活动承担某些责任。

(11)在本条例所述框架立法规定的特定情形下且在满足其所列条件之时,如有金融活动威胁到欧盟金融市场有序运行和诚信度或整体或部分金融系统的稳定,欧洲保险与职业养老金管理局应能临时禁止或者限制此等金融活动。如在紧急情况下

1 请见本《欧盟公报》,第1页。
2 2009年1月29日《欧盟公报》L 25,第23页。
3 2009年1月29日《欧盟公报》L 25,第28页。
4 2009年1月29日《欧盟公报》L 25,第18页。

specified and under the conditions laid down in the legislative acts referred to in this Regulation. If required to make such temporary prohibition in the case of an emergency situation, the Authority should do so in accordance with and under the conditions laid down in this Regulation. In cases where a temporary prohibition or restriction of certain financial activities has a cross-sectoral impact, sectoral legislation should provide that the Authority consult and coordinate its action with, where relevant, the European Supervisory Authority (European Banking Authority) and the European Supervisory Authority (European Securities and Markets Authority), through the Joint Committee.

(12) The Authority should take due account of the impact of its activities on competition and innovation within the internal market, on the Union's global competitiveness, on financial inclusion, and on the Union's new strategy for jobs and growth.

(13) In order to fulfil its objectives, the Authority should have legal personality as well as administrative and financial autonomy.

(14) Based on the work of international bodies, systemic risk should be defined as a risk of disruption in the financial system with the potential to have serious negative consequences for the internal market and the real economy. All types of financial intermediaries, markets and infrastructures may be potentially systemically important to some degree.

(15) Cross-border risk includes all risks caused by economic imbalances or financial failures in all or parts of the Union that have the potential to have significant negative consequences for the transactions between economic operators of two or more Member States, for the functioning of the internal market or for the public finances of the Union or any of its Member States.

(16) The Court of Justice of the European Union in its judgment of 2 May 2006 in Case C-217/04 (United Kingdom of Great Britain and Northern Ireland v. European Parliament and Council of the European Union) held that 'nothing in the wording of Article 95 EC [now Article 114 of the Treaty on the Functioning of the European Union (TFEU)] implies that the addressees of the measures adopted by the Community legislature on the basis of that provision can only be the individual Member States. The legislature may deem it necessary to provide for the establishment of a Community body responsible for contributing to the implementation of a process of harmonisation in situations where, in order to facilitate the uniform implementation and application of acts based on that provision, the adoption of non-binding supporting and framework measures seems appropriate'[1]. The purpose and tasks of the Authority-assisting competent national

1 OJ L 339, 27.12.1984, p. 21.

需要实施上述临时禁令，则欧洲保险与职业养老金管理局应依据本条例所规定的条件实施。临时禁止或者限制某些金融活动会造成跨行业冲击的，行业性立法应规定欧洲保险与职业养老金管理局在适当时通过联合委员会与两个欧洲监管机构（欧洲银行业管理局和欧洲证券与市场管理局）磋商并协调其行动。

（12）欧洲保险与职业养老金管理局应适当考虑其活动对欧盟内部市场的竞争和创新、欧盟全球竞争力、金融融入以及欧盟就业和发展新战略所产生的冲击。

（13）为实现其目标，欧洲保险与职业养老金管理局应有法人身份以及行政管理和财务自主权。

（14）基于国际机构的研究成果，系统性风险应被定义为金融系统发生扰乱并有可能对内部市场和实体经济造成严重消极后果的风险。所有类型的金融中介机构、市场以及基础设施在某种程度上均可能有潜在的系统重要性。

（15）跨境风险包括由欧盟地区的整体或部分经济不平衡或金融失败造成的，且可能对2个或以上成员国的经济运营主体之间的交易、欧盟内部市场的运行或欧盟或其任何成员国的公共财政带来严重消极后果的所有风险。

（16）欧盟法院在其2006年5月2日对第C-217/04号案件（大不列颠及北爱尔兰联合王国诉欧洲议会及欧盟理事会）的判决中表明："《欧洲共同体条约》第95条［现《欧洲联盟运行条约》（TFEU）第114条］的措辞并未暗示欧共体立法机构基于该条款所通过的措施只能适用于具体成员国。为促进基于《欧洲共同体条约》第95条的立法能得到统一实施和适用，应制定无法律约束力的辅助性和框架性措施时，立法机构可以认为有必要颁布设立该等欧共体机构的规定，由该机构负责推动协调程序的落实"[1]。欧洲保险与职业养老金管理局的目标和职责在于协助国家级主管部门一致地解释和适用欧盟规则，致力于实现金融一体化所必不可少的金融稳定。该等职责与欧盟金融服务内部市场方面既定之法律所追求的目标紧密关联。因此，欧洲保险与职业养老金管理局应建立在《欧洲联盟运行条约》第114条的基础上。

1 1984年12月27日《欧盟公报》L 39，第21页。

supervisory authorities in the consistent interpretation and application of Union rules and contributing to financial stability necessary for financial integration–are closely linked to the objectives of the Union *acquis* concerning the internal market for financial services. The Authority should therefore be established on the basis of Article 114 TFEU.

(17) The following legislative acts lay down the tasks for the competent authorities of Member States, including cooperating with each other and with the Commission: Directive 2009/138/EC of the European Parliament and of the Council of 25 November 2009 on the taking-up and pursuit of the business of Insurance and Reinsurance (Solvency II) [1], with the exception of Title IV thereof, Directive 2002/92/EC of the European Parliament and of the Council of 9 December 2002 on insurance mediation [2], Directive 2003/41/EC of the European Parliament and of the Council of 3 June 2003 on the activities and supervision of institutions for occupational retirement provision [3], Directive 2002/87/EC of the European Parliament and of the Council of 16 December 2002 on the supplementary supervision of credit institutions, insurance undertakings and investment firms in a financial conglomerate [4], Council Directive 64/225/EEC of 25 February 1964 on the abolition of restrictions on freedom of establishment and freedom to provide services in respect of reinsurance and retrocession [5], Council Directive 73/239/EEC of 24 July 1973 on the coordination of laws, regulations and administrative provisions relating to the taking up and pursuit of the business of direct insurance other than life assurance [6], Council Directive 73/240/EEC of 24 July 1973 abolishing restrictions on freedom of establishment in the business of direct insurance other than life assurance [7], Council Directive 76/580/EEC of 29 June 1976 amending Directive 73/239/EEC on the coordination of laws, regulations and administrative provisions relating to the taking up and pursuit of the business of direct insurance other than life assurance [8], Council Directive 78/473/EEC of 30 May 1978 on the coordination of laws, regulations and administrative provisions relating to Community co-insurance [9], Council Directive 84/641/EEC of 10 December 1984 amending, particularly as regards tourist assistance, the First Council Directive 73/239/EEC on the coordination of laws, regulations and administrative provisions relating to the taking-up and pursuit of the business of direct insurance other

1 OJ L 335, 17.12.2009, p. 1.
2 OJ L 9, 15.1.2003, p. 3.
3 OJ L 235, 23.9.2003, p. 10.
4 OJ L 35, 11.2.2003, p. 1.
5 OJ 56, 4.4.1964, p. 878.
6 OJ L 228, 16.8.1973, p. 3.
7 OJ L 228, 16.8.1973, p. 20.
8 OJ L 189, 13.7.1976, p. 13.
9 OJ L 151, 7.6.1978, p. 25.

（17）下列框架立法规定了成员国主管部门的职责，其中包括相互合作以及与欧盟委员会合作：《欧洲议会与欧盟理事会关于开办和经营保险与再保险业务的第2009/138/EC号指令》（保险偿付能力标准Ⅱ）[1]（2009年11月25日通过，不包括其中的第四章）、《欧洲议会与欧盟理事会关于保险调解的第2002/92/EC号指令》[2]（2002年12月9日）、《欧洲议会与欧盟理事会关于职业退休金管理机构的活动和监管的第2003/41/EC号指令》[3]（2003年6月3日）、《欧洲议会与欧盟理事会对金融集团下属信贷机构、保险公司以及投资公司实施补充监管的第2002/87/EC号指令》[4]（2002年12月16日）、《欧洲经济共同体理事会关于废止新设业务限制及提供再保险和转分保限制的第64/225/EEC号指令》[5]（1964年2月25日）、《欧洲经济共同体理事会协调关于开办和经营直接保险（寿险除外）业务的法律、法规和规章的第73/239/EEC号指令》[6]（1973年7月24日）、《欧洲经济共同体理事会关于废止新设直接保险（寿险除外）业务限制的第73/240/EEC号指令》[7]（1973年7月24日）、《欧洲经济共同体理事会修正〈协调关于开办和经营直接保险（寿险除外）业务的法律、法规和规章的第73/239/EEC号指令〉的第76/580/EEC号指令》[8]（1976年6月29日）、《欧洲经济共同体理事会协调关于欧共体共同保险的法律、法规和规章的第78/473/EEC号指令》[9]（1978年5月30日）、《欧洲经济共同体理事会特别针对旅游协助修正〈欧洲经济共同体理事会协调关于开办和经营直接保险（寿险除外）业务的法律、法规和规章的73/239/EEC第一号指令〉的第84/641/EEC

1 2009年12月17日《欧盟公报》L 335，第1页。
2 2003年1月15日《欧盟公报》L 9，第3页。
3 2003年9月23日《欧盟公报》L 235，第10页。
4 2003年2月11日《欧盟公报》L 35，第1页。
5 1964年4月4日《欧盟公报》56，第878页。
6 1973年8月16日《欧盟公报》L 228，第3页。
7 1973年8月16日《欧盟公报》L 228，第20页。
8 1976年7月13日《欧盟公报》L 189，第13页。
9 1978年6月7日《欧盟公报》L 151，第25页。

than life assurance [1], Council Directive 87/344/EEC of 22 June 1987 on the coordination of laws, regulations and administrative provisions relating to legal expenses insurance [2], Council Directive 88/357/EEC of 22 June 1988 on the coordination of laws, regulations and administrative provisions relating to direct insurance other than life assurance and laying down provisions to facilitate the effective exercise of freedom to provide services [3], Council Directive 92/49/EEC of 18 June 1992 on the coordination of laws, regulations and administrative provisions relating to direct insurance other than life assurance (third non-life insurance Directive) [4], Directive 98/78/EC of the European Parliament and of the Council of 27 October 1998 on the supplementary supervision of insurance undertakings in an insurance group [5], Directive 2001/17/EC of the European Parliament and of the Council of 19 March 2001 on the reorganisation and winding -up of insurance undertakings [6], Directive 2002/83/EC of the European Parliament and of the Council of 5 November 2002 concerning life assurance [7] and Directive 2005/68/EC of the European Parliament and of the Council of 16 November 2005 on reinsurance [8]. However, with regard to institutions for occupational retirement provision, the Authority's actions should be without prejudice to national social and labour law.

(18) Existing Union legislation regulating the field covered by this Regulation also includes the relevant parts of Directive 2005/60/EC of the European Parliament and of the Council of 26 October 2005 on the prevention of the use of the financial system for the purpose of money laundering and terrorist financing [9], and of Directive 2002/65/EC of the European Parliament and of the Council of 23 September 2002 concerning the distance marketing of consumer financial services [10]

(19) It is desirable that the Authority contribute to the assessment of the need for a European network of national insurance guarantee schemes which is adequately funded and sufficiently harmonised.

(20) In accordance with the Declaration (No 39) on Article 290 of the Treaty on the Functioning of the European Union (TFEU), annexed to the Final Act of the

1 OJ L 339, 27.12.1984, p. 21.
2 OJ L 185, 4.7.1987, p. 77.
3 OJ L 172, 4.7.1988, p. 1.
4 OJ L 228, 11.8.1992, p. 1.
5 OJ L 330, 5.12.1998, p. 1.
6 OJ L 110, 20.4.2001, p. 28.
7 OJ L 345, 19.12.2002, p. 1.
8 OJ L 323, 9.12.2005, p. 1.
9 OJ L 309, 25.11.2005, p. 15.
10 OJ L 271, 9.10.2002, p. 16.

号指令》[1]（1984年12月10日）、《欧洲经济共同体理事会协调关于诉讼费用保险的法律、法规和规章的第87/344/EEC号指令》[2]（1987年6月22日）、《欧洲经济共同体理事会协调关于直接保险（寿险除外）的法律、法规和规章以及制定相关条款以便有效行使提供服务自由权的第88/357/EEC号指令》[3]（1988年6月22日）、《欧洲经济共同体理事会协调关于直接保险（寿险除外）的法律、法规和规章的第92/49/EEC号指令》[4]（第三非寿险指令，1992年6月18日通过）、《欧洲议会与欧盟理事会关于对保险集团下属保险公司实施补充监管的第98/78/EC号指令》[5]（1998年10月27日）、《欧洲议会与欧盟理事会关于保险公司的重组和停业清理的第2001/17/EC号指令》[6]（2001年3月19日）、《欧洲议会与欧盟理事会关于寿险的第2002/83/EC号指令》[7]（2002年11月5日）以及《欧洲议会与欧盟理事会关于再保险的第2005/68/EC号指令》[8]（2005年11月16日）。然而，欧洲保险与职业养老金管理局就职业退休金管理机构所采取的行动不应影响成员国国内的社会保障和劳动法。

（18）对本条例所覆盖的领域进行监管的欧盟现行立法还包括《欧洲议会与欧盟理事会关于防范利用金融系统从事洗钱和恐怖分子融资的第2005/60/EC号指令》[9]（2005年10月26日）和《欧洲议会与欧盟理事会关于远程营销消费者金融服务的第2002/65/EC号指令》[10]（2002年9月23日）中的相关部分。

（19）欧洲保险与职业养老金管理局宜致力于评估建立资金充足并充分协调一致的欧洲国家级保险担保计划体系的必要性。

（20）根据通过《里斯本条约》的政府间会议《最后决议》附录中的《关于〈欧洲联盟运行条约〉（TFEU）第290条的声明（第39号）》，对于监管性技术标准的制定，需要金融

1 1984年12月27日《欧盟公报》L 339，第21页。
2 1987年7月4日《欧盟公报》L 185，第77页。
3 1988年7月4日《欧盟公报》L 172，第1页。
4 1992年8月11日《欧盟公报》L 228，第1页。
5 1998年12月5日《欧盟公报》L 330，第1页。
6 2001年4月20日《欧盟公报》L 110，第28页。
7 2002年12月19日《欧盟公报》L 345，第1页。
8 2005年12月9日《欧盟公报》L 323，第1页。
9 2005年11月25日《欧盟公报》L 309，第15页。
10 2002年10月9日《欧盟公报》L 271，第16页。

Intergovernmental Conference which adopted the Treaty of Lisbon, the elaboration of regulatory technical standards requires assistance of technical expertise in a form which is specific to the financial services area. It is necessary to allow the Authority to provide such expertise also on standards or parts of standards that are not based on a draft technical standard that it has elaborated.

(21) There is a need to introduce an effective instrument to establish harmonised regulatory technical standards in financial services to ensure, also through a single rulebook, a level playing field and adequate protection of policyholders, pension scheme members and other beneficiaries across the Union. As a body with highly specialised expertise, it is efficient and appropriate to entrust the Authority, in areas defined by Union law, with the elaboration of draft regulatory technical standards, which do not involve policy choices.

(22) The Commission should endorse those draft regulatory technical standards by means of delegated acts under Article 290 TFEU in order to give them binding legal effect. They should be subject to amendment only in very restricted and extraordinary circumstances, since the Authority is the actor in close contact with and knowing best the daily functioning of financial markets. Draft regulatory technical standards would be subject to amendment if they were incompatible with Union law, did not respect the principle of proportionality or ran counter to the fundamental principles of the internal market for financial services as reflected in the *acquis* of Union financial services legislation. The Commission should not change the content of the draft regulatory technical standards prepared by the Authority without prior coordination with the Authority. To ensure a smooth and expeditious adoption process for those standards, the Commission's decision to endorse draft regulatory technical standards should be subject to a time limit.

(23) Given the technical expertise of the Authority in the areas where regulatory technical standards should be developed, note should be taken of the Commission's stated intention to rely, as a rule, on the draft regulatory technical standards submitted to it by the Authority in view of the adoption of the corresponding delegated acts. However, in cases where the Authority fails to submit a draft regulatory technical standard within the time limits set out by the relevant legislative act, it should be ensured that the result of the exercise of delegated power is actually achieved, and the efficiency of the decision-making process be maintained. In those cases, the Commission should therefore be empowered to adopt regulatory technical standards in the absence of a draft by the Authority.

(24) The Commission should also be empowered to adopt implementing technical standards by means of implementing acts under Article 291 TFEU.

服务领域专门的技术专长协助。对于那些并非基于欧洲保险与职业养老金管理局自身制定的技术标准草案之标准或者部分标准,也有必要允许欧洲保险与职业养老金管理局提供上述技术专长。

(21)有必要采取有效的手段,为金融服务制定协调一致的监管性技术标准,同时结合单一规则手册来确保公平的竞争环境以及对欧盟各地保单持有人、养老金计划成员以及其他受益人的充分保护。欧洲保险与职业养老金管理局作为一个拥有高度专门知识的机构,委托其在欧盟法律界定的领域中制定不涉及政策性选择的监管性技术标准草案是既高效,且适宜的。

(22)欧盟委员会应按照《欧洲联盟运行条约》第290条以授权立法的形式同意和支持该等监管性技术标准草案,以赋予其法律约束力。鉴于欧洲保险与职业养老金管理局是与金融市场有密切联系并且最了解金融市场日常运行的主体,因此仅能在十分有限和特殊的情况下才能对该等监管性技术标准草案进行修正。监管性技术标准草案与欧盟法律不相容、不符合比例原则,或者违背了欧盟既定的金融服务立法所体现的金融服务内部市场基本原则的,应对其进行修正。未经与欧洲保险与职业养老金管理局事先协调,欧盟委员会不得变更欧洲保险与职业养老金管理局起草的监管性技术标准草案内容。为确保顺利、快速地通过该等标准,欧盟委员会应在一定的时限内作出同意和支持监管性技术标准草案的决定。

(23)鉴于欧洲保险与职业养老金管理局在应制定监管性技术标准之领域拥有技术专长,应注意到欧盟委员会声明的如下意向,即其在通过相应的授权立法时一般依赖欧洲保险与职业养老金管理局向其呈报的监管性技术标准草案。然而,欧洲保险与职业养老金管理局未在相关框架立法规定的时限内呈报该等草案的,仍应当保证授权之行使获得成效并维持决策程序效率。在该等情形下,欧盟委员会应有权在欧洲保险与职业养老金管理局未呈报草案的情况下通过监管性技术标准。

(24)欧盟委员会应也有权按《欧洲联盟运行条约》第291条以实施性立法的形式通过实施性技术标准。

(25) In areas not covered by regulatory or implementing technical standards, the Authority should have the power to issue guidelines and recommendations on the application of Union law. In order to ensure transparency and to strengthen compliance by national supervisory authorities with those guidelines and recommendations, it should be possible for the Authority to publish the reasons for supervisory authorities' non-compliance with those guidelines and recommendations.

(26) Ensuring the correct and full application of Union law is a core prerequisite for the integrity, transparency, efficiency and orderly functioning of financial markets, the stability of the financial system, and for neutral conditions of competition for financial institutions in the Union. A mechanism should therefore be established whereby the Authority addresses instances of non-application or incorrect application of Union law amounting to a breach thereof. That mechanism should apply in areas where Union law defines clear and unconditional obligations.

(27) To allow for a proportionate response to instances of incorrect or insufficient application of Union law, a three-step mechanism should apply. First, the Authority should be empowered to investigate alleged incorrect or insufficient application of Union law obligations by national authorities in their supervisory practice, concluded by a recommendation. Second, where the competent national authority does not follow the recommendation, the Commission should be empowered to issue a formal opinion taking into account the Authority's recommendation, requiring the competent authority to take the actions necessary to ensure compliance with Union law.

(28) Third, to overcome exceptional situations of persistent inaction by the competent authority concerned, the Authority should be empowered, as a last resort, to adopt decisions addressed to individual financial institutions. That power should be limited to exceptional circumstances in which a competent authority does not comply with the formal opinion addressed to it and in which Union law is directly applicable to financial institutions by virtue of existing or future Union regulations.

(29) Serious threats to the orderly functioning and integrity of financial markets or the stability of the financial system in the Union require a swift and concerted response at Union level. The Authority should therefore be able to require national supervisory authorities to take specific actions to remedy an emergency situation. The power to determine the existence of an emergency situation should be conferred on the Council, following a request by any of the ESAs, the Commission or the ESRB.

(30) The Authority should be able to require national supervisory authorities to take specific action to remedy an emergency situation. The action undertaken by the Authority in this respect should be without prejudice to the Commission's powers under Article 258 TFEU to initiate infringement proceedings against the Member State of that supervisory

（25）在监管性或实施性技术标准未覆盖的领域，欧洲保险与职业养老金管理局应有权就欧盟法律的适用提出指引和建议。为确保透明度及促进国家级监管机构遵循该等指引和建议，欧洲保险与职业养老金管理局有可能公布监管机构不遵循该等指引和建议的理由。

（26）确保欧盟法律的正确和全面适用是欧盟金融市场诚信度、透明、有效、有序运行、金融系统稳定以及金融机构竞争中立性的核心前提。因此，应建立一项机制，使欧洲保险与职业养老金管理局得以处理不适用或不正确适用欧盟法律从而导致违反欧盟法律的情形。该机制应适用于欧盟法律界定了明确、无条件的义务的领域。

（27）为对不正确或不充分适用欧盟法律作出成比例的回应，应采用“三步走”的机制。第一步，欧洲保险与职业养老金管理局有权对国家级监管机构涉嫌在其监管实践中不正确或不充分履行欧盟法律义务的情况进行调查，而该等调查结论系以一份建议的形式作出；第二步，国家级主管部门没有遵循该建议的，欧盟委员会应有权发出一份反映欧洲保险与职业养老金管理局建议的正式意见，要求该主管部门采取必要的行动以确保欧盟法律得到遵守。

（28）第三步，为了克服所涉主管部门持续不作为的特殊状况，作为最后手段，欧洲保险与职业养老金管理局应有权针对具体金融机构作出决定，但是，仅在主管部门不遵循针对其发出的正式意见，且欧盟法律根据现有或未来的欧盟条例可直接适用于金融机构的特殊情况下，方可行使上述权力。

（29）欧盟金融市场的有序运行和诚信度或欧盟金融系统稳定面临严重威胁的时候，应在欧盟层面上作出迅速而一致的反应。因此，欧洲保险与职业养老金管理局应能要求各国家级监管机构采取特定行动对紧急情况进行补救。经任何欧洲监管机构、欧盟委员会或欧洲系统性风险委员会请求，欧盟理事会有权判定是否存在紧急情况。

（30）欧洲保险与职业养老金管理局应能要求国家级监管机构采取特定行动以对紧急情况作出补救。欧洲保险与职业养老金管理局就此采取的行动不应影响欧盟委员会因成员国监管机构未采取上述行动而根据《欧洲联盟运行条约》第258条对该成员国启动违法违规诉讼程序的权力，也不应影响欧盟委员会在该等情况下依照欧盟

authority for its failure to take such action, and without prejudice to the Commission's right in such circumstances to seek interim measures in accordance with the rules of procedure of the Court of Justice of the European Union. Furthermore, it should be without prejudice to any liability that Member State might incur in accordance with the case law of the Court of Justice of the European Union if its supervisory authorities fail to take the action required by the Authority.

(31) In order to ensure efficient and effective supervision and a balanced consideration of the positions of the competent authorities in different Member States, the Authority should be able to settle disagreements in cross-border situations between those competent authorities with binding effect, including within colleges of supervisors. A conciliation phase should be provided for during which the competent authorities may reach an agreement. The Authority's competence should cover disagreements on the procedure or content of an action or inaction by a competent authority of aMember State in cases specified in the legally binding Union acts referred to in this Regulation. In such a situation, one of the supervisors involved should be entitled to refer the issue to the Authority, which should act in accordance with this Regulation. The Authority should be empowered to require the competent authorities concerned to take specific action or to refrain from action in order to settle the matter in order to ensure compliance with Union law, with binding effects for the competent authorities concerned. If a competent authority does not comply with the settlement decision addressed to it, the Authority should be empowered to adopt decisions directly addressed to financial institutions in areas of Union law directly applicable to them. The power to adopt such decisions should apply only as a last resort and then only to ensure the correct and consistent application of Union law. In cases where the relevant Union legislation confers discretion on Member States' competent authorities, decisions taken by the Authority cannot replace the exercise in compliance with Union law of that discretion.

(32) The crisis has proven that the current system of cooperation between national authorities whose powers are limited to individual Member States is insufficient as regards financial institutions that operate across borders.

(33) Expert Groups set up by Member States to examine the causes of the crisis and make suggestions to improve the regulation and supervision of the financial sector have confirmed that the current arrangements are not a sound basis for the future regulation and supervision of cross-border financial institutions across the Union.

(34) As the de Larosière Report indicates, '[i]n essence, we have two alternatives: the first "chacun pour soi" beggar-thy-neighbour solutions; or the second-enhanced, pragmatic, sensible European cooperation for the benefit of all to preserve an open world economy. This will bring undoubted economic gains'.

法院程序规则寻求临时措施的权利。此外,成员国由于其监管机构未采取欧洲保险与职业养老金管理局要求的行动而在欧盟法院判例法下所应承担的任何法律责任,不因欧洲保险与职业养老金管理局的行动而受影响。

(31)为确保监管兼具效率和成效并平衡考虑各成员国主管部门的立场,欧洲保险与职业养老金管理局应能以具有约束力的方式解决不同主管部门之间在跨境情形下的分歧,包括监管团内部的分歧。应规定一个调解期,主管部门可在此时间段内达成一致意见。在本条例所述具有法律约束力的欧盟法律文件所指定的情形里,对某成员国主管部门所采取的行动或不采取行动所依据的程序或相关内容出现了分歧的,欧洲保险与职业养老金管理局应对该等分歧有管辖权。在该状况下,所涉监管机构之一有权将该事宜移交欧洲保险与职业养老金管理局,由欧洲保险与职业养老金管理局依照本条例处理。欧洲保险与职业养老金管理局有权通过要求所涉主管部门采取特定行动或不采取行动的方式来解决有关事宜并确保欧盟法律得到遵守,此等要求应对所涉主管部门具有约束力。如主管部门不遵循对其作出解决分歧的决定,欧洲保险与职业养老金管理局有权在欧盟法律直接适用于金融机构的领域,直接对金融机构作出决定。作出上述决定的权力仅能作为最后手段且仅为确保欧盟法律的正确和一致适用而使用。相关欧盟立法授予了成员国主管部门自由裁量权的,欧洲保险与职业养老金管理局所作出的决定不能替代主管部门依照欧盟法律行使该自由裁量权。

(32)危机证明,由于国家级监管机构的权力范围局限于其各自所属成员国,目前各国家级监管机构之间的合作制度对于跨境运营的金融机构而言是不充分的。

(33)为检讨危机发生的原因、提出相关建议以改善对金融行业的规制和监管,各成员国设立了专家小组。该专家小组确认了现有安排不足以为欧盟内部跨境金融机构的规制和监管奠定坚实的基础。

(34)正如《德·拉罗西埃报告》所指:“实质上我们有两套方案可供选择:一个是‘人人为自己’、以邻为壑的解决方案;第二个是在欧洲范围内强化、务实、明智的合作,为各方的利益而维持一个开放的世界经济。这无疑会带来诸多经济成果。”

(35) Colleges of supervisors play an important role in the efficient, effective and consistent supervision of financial institutions operating across borders. The Authority should contribute to promoting and monitoring the efficient, effective and consistent functioning of the colleges of supervisors and, in that respect, have a leading role in ensuring the consistent and coherent functioning of colleges of supervisors for cross-border financial institutions across the Union. The Authority should therefore have full participation rights in colleges of supervisors with a view to streamlining the functioning of and the information exchange process in the colleges of supervisors and to foster convergence and consistency across colleges in the application of Union law. As the de Larosière Report states, 'competition distortions and regulatory arbitrage stemming from different supervisory practices must be avoided, because they have the potential of undermining financial stability–inter alia by encouraging a shift of financial activity to countries with lax supervision. The supervisory system has to be perceived as fair and balanced'.

(36) Convergence in the fields of crisis prevention, management and resolution, including funding mechanisms, is necessary in order to ensure that public authorities are able to resolve failing financial institutions whilst minimising the impact of failures on the financial system, reliance on taxpayer funds to bail out insurance or reinsurance undertakings and the use of public sector resources, limiting damage to the economy, and coordinating the application of national resolution measures. In this regard, the Commission should be able to request the Authority to contribute to the assessment referred to in Article 242 of Directive 2009/138/EC, in particular as regards the cooperation of supervisory authorities within, and functionality of, the colleges of supervisors; the supervisory practices concerning setting the capital add-ons; the assessment of the benefit of enhancing group supervision and capital management within a group of insurance or reinsurance undertakings, including possible measures to enhance the sound cross-border management of insurance groups, notably in respect of risks and assets; and reporting on any new developments and progress concerning a set of coordinated national crisis management arrangements, including the necessity or otherwise of a system of coherent and credible funding mechanisms, with appropriate financing instruments.

(37) In the current review of Directive 94/19/EC of the European Parliament and the Council of 30 May 1994 on deposit-guarantee schemes [1] and Directive 97/9/EC of the European Parliament and of the Council of 3 March 1997 on investor-compensation schemes [2], the Commission's intention to pay special attention to the need to ensure

---

1 OJ L 135, 31.5.1994, p. 5.

2 OJ L 84, 26.3.1997, p. 22.

(35)在对跨境运营的金融机构进行一致的且兼具效率和成效的监管中,各监管团起到重要作用。欧洲保险与职业养老金管理局应致力于推进和监控各监管团一致的且兼具效率和成效的运作,并在这方面发挥其领导作用,确保监管团对欧盟内跨境金融机构起到相互连贯和一致的作用。因此,欧洲保险与职业养老金管理局在监管团中应有充分的参与权,以提高监管团运作和信息交流程序的效率,推动在各监管团中能一致趋同地适用欧盟法律。正如《德·拉罗西埃报告》所表明的:"必须避免监管实践的差异造成竞争扭曲和监管套利,因为它们可能会对金融稳定造成损害(如此种差异造成变相鼓励将金融活动转移到监管不严的国家)。欧盟的监管制度必须塑造公平、平衡的公信力。"

(36)在危机防范、管理和清盘的领域,包括经费筹措机制方面,趋同是必要的,以确保公共机构有能力对濒临倒闭的金融机构进行清盘,最大限度地降低金融机构经营失败对系统的冲击,尽量避免依靠纳税人资金来为保险或再保险公司买单,避免利用公共部门的资源,从而将对经济造成的损害控制在一定限度并协调对国家级清盘措施的适用。为此,欧盟委员会应能要求欧洲保险与职业养老金管理局致力于第2009/138/EC号指令第242条所述的评估,尤其是对监管团内监管机构的合作以及监管团作用的评估;致力于与要求进行资本追加有关的监管实践;致力于评估加强保险或再保险公司集团内的集团监管和资本管理的益处,包括加强对保险集团的良好跨境管理特别是风险和资产管理的可能措施;致力于报告与成员国在危机管理方面作出的各种协调的国家级安排有关的任何新发展和进展,包括建立具有适当融资工具的相互连贯并可信的经费筹措机制的必要性。

(37)在目前对《欧洲议会与欧盟理事会关于存款担保计划的第94/19/EC号指令》[1](1994年5月30日)以及《欧洲议会与欧盟理事会关于投资者补偿计划的第97/9/EC号指令》[2](1997年3月3日)的审评中,欧盟委员会对于确保整个欧盟进一步协调的必要性给予高度重视。在保险业中,欧盟委员会也显然有意审查是否可能在保险公司濒临倒闭

1 1994年5月31日《欧盟公报》L 135,第5页。
2 1997年3月26日《欧盟公报》L 84,第22页。

further harmonisation throughout the Union is noted. In the insurance sector, the Commission's intention to examine the possibility of introducing Union rules protecting insurance policy holders in case of a failing insurance company is also noted. The ESAs should play an important role in those areas and appropriate powers concerning the European network of national insurance guarantee schemes should be conferred upon them.

(38) The delegation of tasks and responsibilities can be a useful instrument in the functioning of the network of supervisors in order to reduce the duplication of supervisory tasks, to foster cooperation and thereby streamline the supervisory process, as well as to reduce the burden imposed on financial institutions. This Regulation should therefore provide a clear legal basis for such delegation. Whilst respecting the general rule that delegation should be allowed, Member States should be able to introduce specific conditions for the delegation of responsibilities, for example, regarding information about, and the notification of, delegation arrangements. Delegation of tasks means that tasks are carried out by the Authority or by a national supervisory authority other than the responsible authority, while the responsibility for supervisory decisions remains with the delegating authority. By the delegation of responsibilities, the Authority or a national supervisory authority (the delegate) should be able to decide upon a certain supervisory matter in its own name in lieu of the delegating authority. Delegations should be governed by the principle of allocating supervisory competence to a supervisor which is best placed to take action in the subject matter. A reallocation of responsibilities would be appropriate, for example, for reasons of economies of scale or scope, of coherence in group supervision, and of optimal use of technical expertise among national supervisory authorities. Decisions by the delegate should be recognised by the delegating authority and by other competent authorities as determinative if those decisions are within the scope of the delegation. Relevant Union legislation could further specify the principles for the reallocation of responsibilities upon agreement.

The Authority should facilitate and monitor delegation agreements between national supervisory authorities by all appropriate means. It should be informed in advance of intended delegation agreements, in order to be able to express an opinion where appropriate. It should centralise the publication of such agreements to ensure timely, transparent and easily accessible information about agreements for all parties concerned. It should identify and disseminate best practices regarding delegation and delegation agreements.

(39) The Authority should actively foster supervisory convergence across the Union with the aim of establishing a common supervisory culture.

(40) Peer reviews are an efficient and effective tool for fostering consistency within

时对保单持有人实施欧盟的保护规则。各欧洲监管机构应在该等领域发挥重要作用，并被授予与欧洲国家级保险担保计划体系相关的适当权力。

(38)在监管机构网络的运行中，职责和责任的委托可减少监管职责的重复并促进合作，从而提高监管程序的效率，同时能减轻金融机构的负担。为此，本条例应为上述委托提供明确的法律依据。在遵守该等委托的一般规则的同时，成员国也应有权为责任委托施加特定的条件，如关于委托安排的信息和通知方面的条件。职责委托的含义是，由欧洲保险与职业养老金管理局或某个国家级监管机构而非原负责部门来履行职责，但委托部门仍对监管决定负责。通过责任委托，欧洲保险与职业养老金管理局或国家级监管机构(受托部门)应能以自己名义代表委托部门就某项监管事宜作出决定。委托的原则是将监管职权委托给就相关事项最适宜采取行动的监管机构。出于规模或范围效益、集团监管的相互一致性以及对不同国家级监管机构各自技术专长的优化使用等各种原因的考虑，可对责任进行再分配。受托部门在委托范围内所作决定，应被委托部门和其他主管部门视为有效决定。相关的欧盟立法可进一步阐述经各方一致同意对责任进行再分配的原则。

欧洲保险与职业养老金管理局应通过一切适当的方式协助和监控各国家级监管机构之间的委托协议。在委托协议签署之前应通知欧洲保险与职业养老金管理局，使其能在适当时表达意见。欧洲保险与职业养老金管理局应统一公布上述协议，以确保所涉各方均能及时、透明和方便地查阅有关协议的信息。欧洲保险与职业养老金管理局应确定并传播有关委托活动和委托协议的最佳实践。

(39)欧洲保险与职业养老金管理局应积极促进欧盟范围内的监管趋同，以建立共同的监管文化。

(40)同行审评是促进金融监管机构网络内部一致性的兼具效率和成效的工具。

the network of financial supervisors. The Authority should therefore develop the methodological framework for such reviews and conduct them on a regular basis. Reviews should focus not only on the convergence of supervisory practices, but also on the capacity of supervisors to achieve high-quality supervisory outcomes, as well as on the independence of those competent authorities. The outcome of peer reviews should be made public with the agreement of the competent authority subject to the review. Best practices should also be identified and made public.

(41) The Authority should actively promote a coordinated Union supervisory response, in particular to ensure the orderly functioning and integrity of financial markets and the stability of the financial system in the Union. In addition to its powers for action in emergency situations, the Authority should therefore be entrusted with a general coordination function within the ESFS. The smooth flow of all relevant information between competent authorities should be a particular focus of the Authority's actions.

(42) In order to safeguard financial stability it is necessary to identify, at an early stage, trends, potential risks and vulnerabilities stemming from the micro-prudential level, across borders and across sectors. The Authority should monitor and assess such developments in the area of its competence and, where necessary, inform the European Parliament, the Council, the Commission, the other European Supervisory Authorities and the ESRB on a regular and, as necessary, on an ad hoc basis. The Authority should also, in cooperation with the ESRB, initiate and coordinate Union-wide stress tests to assess the resilience of financial institutions to adverse market developments, and it should ensure that an as consistent as possible methodology is applied at the national level to such tests. In order to perform its functions properly, the Authority should conduct economic analyses of the markets and the impact of potential market developments.

(43) Given the globalisation of financial services and the increased importance of international standards, the Authority should foster dialogue and cooperation with supervisors outside the Union. It should be empowered to develop contacts and enter into administrative arrangements with the supervisory authorities and administrations of third countries and with international organisations, while fully respecting the existing roles and respective competences of the Member States and the Union institutions. Participation in the work of the Authority should be open to countries which have concluded agreements with the Union whereby they have adopted and are applying Union law, and the Authority should be able to cooperate with third countries which apply legislation that has been recognised as equivalent to that of the Union.

(44) The Authority should serve as an independent advisory body to the European Parliament, the Council, and the Commission in the area of its competence. Without prejudice to the competencies of the competent authorities concerned, the Authority

因此，欧洲保险与职业养老金管理局应为上述审评制定方法论框架，并定期进行审评。审评的焦点不应仅停留在监管实践的趋同，还应着重于监管机构取得高质量监管结果的能力以及该等主管部门的独立性。接受审评的主管部门同意后，同行审评的结果应予公布。欧洲保险与职业养老金管理局还应确定和公布最佳实践。

(41)欧洲保险与职业养老金管理局应积极推动欧盟作出协调一致的监管回应，尤其要确保欧盟金融市场的有序运行和诚信度以及金融系统的稳定。因此，除在紧急情况下采取行动的权力之外，欧洲保险与职业养老金管理局还应被赋予在欧洲金融监管机构体系内的总体协调职能。欧洲保险与职业养老金管理局的行动应特别注重主管部门之间所有相关信息的顺利交流。

(42)为保护金融稳定，有必要在早期识别来自微观审慎层面的以及跨境和跨行业的趋势、潜在风险以及薄弱环节。欧洲保险与职业养老金管理局应在其职权管辖范围内监控和评估上述变化，并且在必要的情况下将变化定期通知欧洲议会、欧盟理事会、欧盟委员会、其他欧洲监管机构以及欧洲系统性风险委员会，必要时也可发出临时通知。同时，欧洲保险与职业养老金管理局应与欧洲系统性风险委员会合作，启动并协调全欧盟的压力测试，以评估金融机构面临不利市场变化时的抗冲击能力，并应确保各成员国实施该等测试方的方法尽可能相互一致。为恰当地履行其职能，欧洲保险与职业养老金管理局应对市场以及潜在市场变化的冲击进行经济分析。

(43)考虑到金融服务的全球化以及国际标准重要性的日益增长，欧洲保险与职业养老金管理局应推动与非欧盟国家监管机构的对话与合作。欧洲保险与职业养老金管理局在完全尊重成员国以及欧盟机构现有作用和各自职权范围的同时，应有权与第三国监管机构和行政管理部门以及国际组织建立联系并达成行政安排。与欧盟达成了协议，并在协议中已经采纳或正在适用欧盟法律的国家应能参与欧洲保险与职业养老金管理局的工作，欧洲保险与职业养老金管理局也应能和其适用立法与欧盟立法等效的第三国合作。

(44)欧洲保险与职业养老金管理局应在其职权管辖范围内充当欧洲议会、欧盟理事会以及欧盟委员会的独立咨询机构。在不影响所涉主管部门职权的情况下，第92/49/EEC号指令、第2002/83/EC号指令和第2005/68/EC号指令（经第2007/44/EC号指

should be able to provide its opinion on the prudential assessment of mergers and acquisitions under Directive 92/49/EEC and Directives 2002/83/EC and 2005/68/EC, as amended by Directive 2007/44/EC [1] in those cases in which that Directive requires consultation between competent authorities from two or more Member States.

(45) In order to carry out its duties effectively, the Authority should have the right to request all necessary information. To avoid the duplication of reporting obligations for financial institutions, that information should normally be provided by the national supervisory authorities which are closest to the financial markets and institutions and should take into account already existing statistics. However, as a last resort, the Authority should be able to address a duly justified and reasoned request for information directly to a financial institution where a national competent authority does not or cannot provide such information in a timely fashion. Member States' authorities should be obliged to assist the Authority in enforcing such direct requests. In that context, the work on common reporting formats is essential. The measures for the collection of information should be without prejudice to the legal framework of the European Statistical System and the European System of Central Banks in the field of statistics. This Regulation should therefore be without prejudice both to Regulation (EC) No 223/2009 of the European Parliament and of the Council of 11 March 2009 on European statistics [2] and to Council Regulation (EC) No 2533/98 of 23 November 1998 concerning the collection of statistical information by the European Central Bank [3].

(46) Close cooperation between the Authority and the ESRB is essential to give full effectiveness to the functioning of the ESRB and the follow-up to its warnings and recommendations. The Authority and the ESRB should share any relevant information with each other. Data related to individual undertakings should be provided only upon reasoned request. Upon receipt of warnings or recommendations addressed by the ESRB to the Authority or a national supervisory authority, the Authority should ensure follow-up as appropriate.

(47) The Authority should consult interested parties on regulatory or implementing technical standards, guidelines and recommendations and provide them with a reasonable opportunity to comment on proposed measures. Before adopting draft regulatory or

1 Directive 2007/44/EC of the European Parliament and of the Council of 5 September 2007 amending Council Directive 92/49/EEC and Directives 2002/83/EC, 2004/39/EC, 2005/68/EC and 2006/48/EC as regards procedural rules and evaluation criteria for the prudential assessment of acquisitions and increase of holdings in the financial sector (OJ L 247, 21.9.2007, p. 1).

2 OJ L 87, 31.3.2009, p. 164.

3 OJ L 318, 27.11.1998, p. 8.

令修正)[1]要求2个或以上成员国主管部门之间进行磋商的,欧洲保险与职业养老金管理局应能对上述指令项下并购所作的审慎评估提出意见。

(45)为有效履行其职责,欧洲保险与职业养老金管理局应有权请求获得所有必要信息。为避免金融机构报告责任的重复,该等信息一般应由与金融市场和金融机构联系最紧密的国家级监管机构提供,并应考虑已有的统计数据。然而,国家级主管部门怠于或不能及时提供上述信息的,作为最后手段,欧洲保险与职业养老金管理局应能直接向金融机构提出有正当理由和经论证的信息请求。各成员国主管部门有义务协助欧洲保险与职业养老金管理局执行上述直接请求。在该等情况下,与报告通用格式相关的工作至关重要。收集信息的措施不得违背欧洲统计系统和欧洲中央银行体系在统计领域的法律框架。因此,本条例不得违背《欧洲议会与欧盟理事会关于欧洲统计的第223/2009号(欧共体)条例》[2](2009年3月11日)以及《欧盟理事会关于欧洲中央银行统计信息收集工作的第2533/98号(欧共体)条例》[3](1998年11月23日)。

(46)欧洲保险与职业养老金管理局和欧洲系统性风险委员会之间的紧密合作对于欧洲系统性风险委员会的全面有效运行以及对其预警和建议的跟进至关重要。欧洲保险与职业养老金管理局和欧洲系统性风险委员会彼此应共享任何相关信息。唯有经合理请求,方能提供与具体企业有关的数据。在欧洲保险与职业养老金管理局或国家级监管机构收到欧洲系统性风险委员会向其发出的预警或建议之后,欧洲保险与职业养老金管理局应确保予以适当跟进。

(47)欧洲保险与职业养老金管理局应就监管性或实施性技术标准、指引和建议向利益相关方征求意见,并给其合理的机会对拟议的措施发表意见。在通过监管性或实施性技术标准草案、指引和建议之前,欧洲保险与职业养老金管理局应对其影响开

---

1 欧洲议会和欧盟理事会第 2007/44/EC 号指令(2007 年 9 月 5 日),在审慎评估收购以及增持金融行业股份的程序规则和估值标准方面修正欧盟理事会第 92/49/EEC 号指令和第 2002/83/EC 号指令、第 2004/39/EC 号指令、第 2005/68/EC 号指令以及第 2006/48/EC 号指令(2007 年 9 月 21 日《欧盟公报》L 247,第 1 页)。

2 2009 年 3 月 31 日《欧盟公报》L 87,第 164 页。

3 1998 年 11 月 27 日《欧盟公报》L 318,第 8 页。

implementing technical standards, guidelines and recommendations, the Authority should carry out an impact study. For reasons of efficiency, an Insurance and Reinsurance Stakeholder Group and an Occupational Pensions Stakeholder Group should be used for that purpose and should represent, in balanced proportions and respectively, the relevant financial institutions operating in the Union, representing the diverse business models and sizes of financial institutions and businesses; small and medium-sized enterprises (SMEs); trade unions; academics; consumers; other retail users of those financial institutions; and representatives of relevant professional associations. Those stakeholder groups should work as an interface with other user groups in the financial services area established by the Commission or by Union legislation.

(48) Members of the stakeholder groups representing non-profit organisations or academics should receive adequate compensation in order to allow persons that are neither well-funded nor industry representatives to take part fully in the debate on financial regulation.

(49) The stakeholder groups should be consulted by the Authority and should be able to submit opinions and advice to the Authority on issues related to the optional application to institutions covered by Directive 2002/83/EC or Directive 2003/41/EC.

(50) Member States have a core responsibility for ensuring coordinated crisis management and preserving financial stability in crisis situations, in particular with regard to stabilising and resolving individual failing financial institutions. Decisions by the Authority in emergency or settlement situations affecting the stability of a financial institution should not impinge on the fiscal responsibilities of Member States. A mechanism should be established whereby Member States may invoke this safeguard and ultimately bring the matter before the Council for a decision. However, that safeguard mechanism should not be abused, in particular in relation to a decision taken by the Authority which does not have a significant or material fiscal impact, such as a reduction of income linked to the temporary prohibition of specific activities or products for consumer protection purposes. When taking decisions under the safeguard mechanism, the Council should vote in accordance with the principle where each member has one vote. It is appropriate to confer on the Council a role in this matter given the particular responsibilities of the Member States in this respect. Given the sensitivity of the issue, strict confidentiality arrangements should be ensured.

(51) In its decision-making procedures, the Authority should be bound by Union rules and general principles on due process and transparency. The right of the addressees of the Authority's decisions to be heard should be fully respected. The Authority's acts

展研究。为确保效率,可为此引入保险和再保险利益相关者小组以及职业养老金利益相关者小组。该等利益相关者小组应以平衡的比例代表在欧盟运营的相关金融机构,包括各种模式和规模的金融机构和企业、中小企业(SMEs)、工会、学术机构、消费者、该等金融机构的其他零售用户以及相关专业协会的代表。保险和再保险利益相关者小组以及职业养老金利益相关者小组应充当与欧洲保险与职业养老金管理局与欧盟委员会或欧盟立法在金融服务领域建立的其他用户小组对接的部门。

(48)代表非营利组织或学术机构的利益相关者小组成员应获得充足的报酬,让既非资金充裕亦非行业代表的人士能充分参与有关金融监管的讨论。

(49)欧洲保险与职业养老金管理局应征求利益相关者小组的意见,而利益相关者小组也应能就第2002/83/EC号指令或第2003/41/EC号指令所覆盖的由各机构自行选择是否适用的事宜向欧洲保险与职业养老金管理局呈报意见和建议。

(50)各成员国负有核心责任,应确保危机管理的协调性并在危机状况下维持金融稳定,特别是在稳定濒临倒闭的具体金融机构的形势并对其进行清盘的时候。在影响金融机构稳定性的紧急情况或争议解决情况下,欧洲保险与职业养老金管理局所作决定不应影响成员国的财政责任。应建立一项机制,让成员国能借其寻求该等保障并最终将有关事宜提交欧盟理事会决定。但该项保障机制不得被滥用,特别是当欧洲保险与职业养老金管理局所作决定对财政收入并未造成突出或重大影响(如为保护消费者利益采取的禁止特定活动或产品的临时措施造成纳税人所得下降的情形)时,不得使用该项机制。欧盟理事会根据保障机制作决定时,应按一人一票的原则投票表决。考虑到成员国在这方面承担的特殊责任,在此问题上应让欧盟理事会发挥一定的作用。鉴于问题的高度敏感性,应确保作出严格的保密安排。

(51)欧洲保险与职业养老金管理局在进行决策程序时,应受欧盟规则以及关于正当程序和透明度的一般性原则约束。欧洲保险与职业养老金管理局的决定所涉对象的发言权应得到充分的尊重。欧洲保险与职业养老金管理局的法律文件应构成欧

should form an integral part of Union law.

(52) A Board of Supervisors composed of the heads of the relevant competent authorities in each Member State, and chaired by the Chairperson of the Authority, should be the principal decision-making organ of the Authority. Representatives of the Commission, the ESRB, the European Supervisory Authority (European Banking Authority) and the European Supervisory Authority (European Securities and Markets Authority) should participate as observers. Members of the Board of Supervisors should act independently and only in the Union's interest.

(53) As a general rule, the Board of Supervisors should take its decisions by simple majority in accordance with the principle where each member has one vote. However, for acts of a general nature, including those relating to regulatory and implementing technical standards, guidelines and recommendations, for budgetary matters as well as in respect of requests by a Member State to reconsider a decision by the Authority to temporarily prohibit or restrict certain financial activities, it is appropriate to apply the rules of qualified majority voting as laid down in Article 16(4) of the Treaty on European Union and in the Protocol (No 36) on transitional provisions annexed to the Treaty on European Union and to the Treaty on the Functioning of the European Union. Cases concerning the settlement of disagreements between national supervisory authorities should be examined by a restricted, objective panel, composed of members who neither are representatives of the competent authorities which are party to the disagreement nor have any interest in the conflict or direct links to the competent authorities concerned. The composition of the panel should be appropriately balanced. The decision taken by the panel should be approved by the Board of Supervisors by simple majority in accordance with the principle where each member has one vote. However, with regard to decisions taken by the consolidating supervisor, the decision proposed by the panel could be rejected by members representing a blocking minority of the votes as defined in Article 16(4) of the Treaty on European Union and in Article 3 of the Protocol (No 36) on transitional provisions.

(54) A Management Board, composed of the Chairperson of the Authority, of representatives of national supervisory authorities and of the Commission, should ensure that the Authority carries out its mission and performs the tasks assigned to it. The Management Board should be entrusted with the necessary powers, inter alia, to propose the annual and multi-annual work programme, to exercise certain budgetary powers, to adopt the Authority's staff policy plan, to adopt special provisions on the right to access to documents and to propose the annual report.

(55) The Authority should be represented by a full-time Chairperson, appointed by the Board of Supervisors, on the basis of merit, skills, knowledge of financial institutions

盟法律不可分割的一部分。

(52)由每一成员国相关主管部门的负责人组成,并由欧洲保险与职业养老金管理局主席担任主席的监管机构理事会应当是欧洲保险与职业养老金管理局的主要决策机构。来自欧盟委员会、欧洲系统性风险委员会,以及来自两个欧洲监管机构(欧洲银行业管理局和欧洲证券与市场管理局)的代表,应作为观察员参与监管机构理事会。监管机构理事会的理事应独立地且仅为欧盟利益行事。

(53)作为一般规则,监管机构理事会应按一人一票的原则以简单多数通过其决定。然而,对于具有普遍性质的法律文件(包括与监管性和实施性技术标准、指引以及建议有关的法律文件)、预算事项以及成员国向欧洲保险与职业养老金管理局提出的重新考虑临时禁止或限制某些特定金融活动的请求,应适用《欧洲联盟条约》第16条第4款以及《欧洲联盟条约》和《欧洲联盟运行条约》附录关于过渡规定的《议定书(第36号)》中所规定的特定多数原则。解决各国家级监管机构之间分歧的案件,应由符合下列标准的人员组成的严格客观的专家小组进行审查:并非作为分歧一方的主管部门的代表,并且在所涉主管部门之冲突中无利害关系、与所涉主管部门亦无直接关联的人员。该专家小组的构成应适当平衡。专家小组的决定应由监管机构理事会按一人一票的原则以简单多数通过。然而,关于并表监管机构作出的决定,代表有否决权的少数票的理事有权否决专家小组拟议的决定[有否决权的少数票定义见《欧洲联盟条约》第16条第4款以及关于过渡规定的《议定书(第36号)》第3条]。

(54)由欧洲保险与职业养老金管理局主席、国家级监管机构代表以及欧盟委员会组成的管理委员会应确保欧洲保险与职业养老金管理局完成其使命并履行其被赋予的职责。管理委员会应被委以必要的权力,包括但不限于提出年度和跨年度工作计划、行使特定的预算权、通过欧洲保险与职业养老金管理局的员工政策计划、通过有关文件查阅权的特殊规定以及提出年度报告。

(55)欧洲保险与职业养老金管理局应由一名全职主席作为代表,该主席人选根据候选人的成就、技能、对金融机构和市场的认识、与金融监管和规制相关的经验等,

and markets, and of experience relevant to financial supervision and regulation, following an open selection procedure organised and managed by the Board of Supervisors assisted by the Commission. For the designation of the first Chairperson of the Authority, the Commission should, inter alia, draw up a shortlist of candidates on the basis of merit, skills, knowledge of financial institutions and markets, and experience relevant to financial supervision and regulation. For the subsequent designations, the opportunity of having a shortlist drawn up by the Commission should be reviewed in a report to be established pursuant to this Regulation. Before the selected person takes up his duties, and up to 1 month after his selection by the Board of Supervisors, the European Parliament should be entitled, after having heard the person selected, to object to his designation.

(56) The management of the Authority should be entrusted to an Executive Director, who should have the right to participate in meetings of the Board of Supervisors and the Management Board without the right to vote.

(57) In order to ensure cross-sectoral consistency in the activities of the ESAs, they should coordinate closely through a Joint Committee and reach common positions where appropriate. The Joint Committee should coordinate the functions of the ESAs in relation to financial conglomerates and other cross-sectoral matters. Where relevant, acts also falling within the area of competence of the European Supervisory Authority (European Banking Authority) or the European Supervisory Authority (European Securities and Markets Authority) should be adopted in parallel by the European Supervisory Authorities concerned. The Joint Committee should be chaired for a 12-month term on a rotating basis by the Chairpersons of the ESAs. The Chairperson of the Joint Committee should be a Vice-Chair of the ESRB. The Joint Committee should have dedicated staff provided by the ESAs to allow for informal information sharing and the development of a common supervisory culture approach across the ESAs.

(58) It is necessary to ensure that the parties affected by decisions adopted by the Authority may have recourse to the necessary remedies. To protect effectively the rights of parties, and for reasons of procedural economy, where the Authority has decision-making powers, parties should be granted a right of appeal to a Board of Appeal. For reasons of efficiency and consistency, the Board of Appeal should be a joint body of the ESAs, independent from their administrative and regulatory structures. The decisions of the Board of Appeal should be subject to appeal before the Court of Justice of the European Union.

(59) In order to guarantee its full autonomy and independence, the Authority should be granted an autonomous budget with revenues mainly from obligatory contributions from national supervisory authorities and from the General Budget of the European Union.

由监管机构理事会在欧盟委员会的协助下组织和执行公开遴选程序来确定。在指定首任欧洲保险与职业养老金管理局主席时,欧盟委员会应基于候选人的成就、技能、对金融机构和市场的认识、与金融监管和规制相关的经验拟定一份候选人名单。对于后续任期,应在根据本条例准备的报告中对是否要求欧盟委员会拟定候选人名单之事进行审议。在获选者到任前,直至其被监管机构理事会选出满1个月期间内,欧洲议会都有权在听取获选者意见后对其任命提出异议。

(56)欧洲保险与职业养老金管理局的管理应委任给1名执行主任,执行主任有权参与监管机构理事会和管理委员会的会议,但无表决权。

(57)为确保彼此活动的跨行业一致性,各欧洲监管机构应通过联合委员会紧密协调,并在适当时达成共同的立场。联合委员会应协调各欧洲监管机构在金融集团以及其他跨行业事宜方面的职能。在适当时,同时属于欧洲监管机构(欧洲银行业管理局或欧洲证券与市场管理局)职权的管辖范围的法律文件,应由所涉的各个欧洲监管机构分别通过。联合委员会的主席应由各欧洲监管机构的主席轮流担任,每次任期12个月。联合委员会的主席应为欧洲系统性风险委员会的副主席。各欧洲监管机构应向联合委员会提供专门的员工负责非正式信息共享工作和建设欧洲监管机构共同的监管文化。

(58)有必要确保受欧洲保险与职业养老金管理局决定影响的当事方可寻求必要的救济。为有效保护各方权利以及出于程序经济的考虑,对于欧洲保险与职业养老金管理局有决策权的事项,各方应有向行政复议委员会提出行政复议申请的权利。出于效率和一致性原因,行政复议委员会应为各欧洲监管机构之间的联合机构,独立于各自所属的行政和监管结构。针对行政复议委员会的决定,相关方可向欧盟法院提起行政诉讼。

(59)为保证其充分的自主权和独立性,欧洲保险与职业养老金管理局应有自主的预算,其收入主要来自各国家级监管机构义务缴纳的款项以及欧盟总预算的一部分。欧盟应依据预算部门按照《欧洲议会、欧盟理事会和欧盟委员会关于预算纪律和

Union financing of the Authority is subject to an agreement by the budgetary authority in accordance with Point 47 of the Interinstitutional Agreement between the European Parliament, the Council and the Commission of 17 May 2006 on budgetary discipline and sound financial management [1]. The Union budgetary procedure should be applicable. The auditing of accounts should be undertaken by the Court of Auditors. The overall budget is subject to the discharge procedure.

(60) Regulation (EC) No 1073/1999 of the European Parliament and of the Council of 25 May 1999 concerning investigations conducted by the European Anti-Fraud Office (OLAF) [2] should apply to the Authority. The Authority should also accede to the Interinstitutional Agreement of 25 May 1999 between the European Parliament, the Council of the European Union and the Commission of the European Communities concerning internal investigations by the European Anti-Fraud Office (OLAF) [3].

(61) In order to ensure open and transparent employment conditions and equal treatment of staff, the Staff Regulations of Officials and the Conditions of Employment of Other Servants of the European Communities [4] should apply to the staff of the Authority.

(62) It is essential that business secrets and other confidential information be protected. The confidentiality of information made available to the Authority and exchanged in the network should be subject to stringent and effective confidentiality rules.

(63) Directive 95/46/EC of the European Parliament and of the Council of 24 October 1995 on the protection of individuals with regard to the processing of personal data and on the free movement of such data [5] and Regulation (EC) No 45/2001 of the European Parliament and of the Council of 18 December 2000 on the protection of individuals with regard to the processing of personal data by the Community institutions and bodies and on the free movement of such data [6] are fully applicable to the processing of personal data for the purposes of this Regulation.

(64) In order to ensure the transparent operation of the Authority, Regulation (EC) No 1049/2001 of the European Parliament and of the Council of 30 May 2001 regarding public access to European Parliament, Council and Commission documents [7] should apply to the Authority.

(65) Third countries should be allowed to participate in the work of the Authority in

1 OJ C 139, 14.6.2006, p. 1.
2 OJ L 136, 31.5.1999, p. 1.
3 OJ L 136, 31.5.1999, p. 15.
4 OJ L 56, 4.3.1968, p. 1.
5 OJ L 281, 23.11.1995, p. 31.
6 OJ L 8, 12.1.2001, p. 1.
7 OJ L 145, 31.5.2001, p. 43.

健全的财务管理的机构间协议》[1](2006年5月17日)第47目签署的协议向欧洲保险与职业养老金管理局提供经费。给其提供的经费应适用欧盟预算程序。其账目应由欧盟审计院进行审计,总体预算则受预算审批程序约束。

(60)《欧洲议会与欧盟理事会关于欧洲反欺诈办公室(OLAF)所开展的调查的第1073/1999号(欧共体)条例》[2](1999年5月25日)应适用于欧洲保险与职业养老金管理局。同时,欧洲保险与职业养老金管理局应遵从欧洲议会、欧盟理事会以及欧盟委员会1999年5月25日签订的《关于欧洲反欺诈办公室(OLAF)内部调查的机构间协议》[3]。

(61)为确保公开透明的聘用条件以及员工的平等待遇,《欧洲共同体官员的人事条例》和《欧洲共同体其他人员的聘用条件》[4]应适用于欧洲保险与职业养老金管理局工作人员。

(62)保护商业秘密和其他保密信息至关重要。向欧洲保险与职业养老金管理局提供的以及在监管网络中交换的保密信息均应受严格有效的保密规定约束。

(63)《欧洲议会与欧盟理事会关于处理个人资料时对个人的保护以及该等资料自由流动的第95/46/EC号指令》[5](1995年10月24日)以及《欧洲议会与欧盟理事会关于欧共体机构和单位处理个人资料时对个人的保护以及该等资料自由流动的第45/2001号(欧共体)条例》[6](2000年12月18日)完全适用于根据本条例对个人资料的处理。

(64)为确保欧洲保险与职业养老金管理局的透明运作,《欧洲议会与欧盟理事会关于公众查阅欧洲议会、欧盟理事会和欧盟委员会文件的第1049/2001号(欧共体)条例》[7](2001年5月30日)应适用于欧洲保险与职业养老金管理局。

(65)第三国应被允许依照其与欧盟今后缔结的相关协议参与欧洲保险与职业养

1 2006年6月14日《欧盟公报》C 139,第1页。
2 1999年5月31日《欧盟公报》L 136,第1页。
3 1999年5月31日《欧盟公报》L 136,第15页。
4 1968年3月4日《欧盟公报》L 56,第1页。
5 1995年11月23日《欧盟公报》L 281,第31页。
6 2001年1月12日《欧盟公报》L 8,第1页。
7 2001年5月31日《欧盟公报》L 145,第43页。

accordance with appropriate agreements to be concluded by the Union.

(66) Since the objectives of this Regulation, namely improving the functioning of the internal market by means of ensuring a high, effective and consistent level of prudential regulation and supervision, protecting policyholders, pension scheme members and other beneficiaries, protecting the integrity, efficiency and orderly functioning of financial markets, maintaining the stability of the financial system, and strengthening international supervisory coordination, cannot be sufficiently achieved by the Member States and can, therefore, by reason of the scale of the action, be better achieved at Union level, the Union may adopt measures, in accordance with the principle of subsidiarity as set out in Article 5 of the Treaty on European Union. In accordance with the principle of proportionality, as set out in that Article, this Regulation does not go beyond what is necessary in order to achieve those objectives.

(67) The Authority should assume all current tasks and powers of the Committee of European Insurance and Occupational Pensions Supervisors. Commission Decision 2009/79/EC should therefore be repealed on the date of the establishment of the Authority, and Decision No 716/2009/EC of the European Parliament and of the Council of 16 September 2009 establishing a Community programme to support specific activities in the field of financial services, financial reporting and auditing [1] should be amended accordingly. Given the existing structures and operations of the Committee of European Insurance and Occupational Pensions Supervisors, it is important to ensure very close cooperation between the Committee of European Insurance and Occupational Pensions Supervisors and the Commission when establishing appropriate transitional arrangements, to ensure that the period during which the Commission is responsible for the administrative establishment and initial administrative operation of the Authority be as limited as possible.

(68) It is appropriate to set a time limit for the application of this Regulation in order to ensure that the Authority is adequately prepared to begin operations and a smooth transition from the Committee of European Insurance and Occupational Pensions Supervisors. The Authority should be appropriately financed. At least initially, it should be financed 40 % from Union funds and 60 % through contributions from Member States, made in accordance with the weighting of votes set out in Article 3(3) of the Protocol (No 36) on transitional provisions.

(69) In order to enable the Authority to be established on 1 January 2011, this Regulation should enter into force on the day following its publication in the Official Journal of the European Union.

---

1 OJ L 253, 25.9.2009, p. 8.

老金管理局的工作。

（66）鉴于本条例的目标在于确保高水平、有效和一致的审慎规制和监管以改善欧盟内部市场的运行，保护保单持有人、养老金计划成员以及其他受益人，保护金融市场的诚信度、高效和有序运行，维持金融系统的稳定以及加强国际监管协调；上述目的单靠成员国自身无法完全实现，但基于此等目的触及的范围，能在欧盟层面上得到更好的实现，因此，欧盟可根据《欧洲联盟条约》第5条规定的辅助性原则制定相关细则。根据《欧洲联盟条约》第5条规定的比例原则，本条例仅作出实现上述目标的必要规定。

（67）欧洲保险与职业养老金管理局应承担欧洲保险与职业养老金监管机构委员会所有的现有职责和权力。因此，欧盟委员会第2009/79/EC号决定应于欧洲保险与职业养老金管理局成立之日废止，对《欧洲议会与欧盟理事会设立一项支持金融服务领域特定活动、财务报告和审计的欧共体计划的第716/2009/EC号决定》[1]（2009年9月16日）也应作相应修正。考虑到欧洲保险与职业养老金监管机构委员会的现有结构和运作状况，在作出适当的过渡安排时，确保欧洲保险与职业养老金监管机构委员会和欧盟委员会之间十分紧密的合作相当重要，以尽量缩短欧盟委员会负担欧洲保险与职业养老金管理局机构设立和初始行政运作的时间。

（68）应为本条例的适用设定时限，以确保欧洲保险与职业养老金管理局做好充分的准备启动其运作，并确保从欧洲保险与职业养老金监管机构委员会向欧洲保险与职业养老金管理局顺利过渡。欧洲保险与职业养老金管理局应有适当的财政支持，至少在初始阶段，应从欧盟获得40%的经费，另外60%来源于成员国根据关于过渡条款的《议定书（第36号）》第3条第3款规定的加权票数比例缴纳的款项。

（69）为使欧洲保险与职业养老金管理局于2011年1月1日成立，本条例应于《欧盟公报》公布，公布的次日生效。

1 2009年9月25日《欧盟公报》L 253，第8页。

HAVE ADOPTED THIS REGULATION:

CHAPTER I ESTABLISHMENT AND LEGAL STATUS

Article 1 Establishment and scope of action

1. This Regulation establishes a European Supervisory Authority (European Insurance and Occupational Pensions Authority) (hereinafter the 'Authority').

2. The Authority shall act within the powers conferred by this Regulation and within the scope of Directive 2009/138/EC with the exception of Title Ⅳ thereof, of Directives 2002/92/EC, 2003/41/EC, 2002/87/EC, 64/225/EEC, 73/239/EEC, 73/240/EEC, 76/580/EEC, 78/473/EEC, 84/641/EEC, 87/344/EEC, 88/357/EEC, 92/49/EEC, 98/78/EC, 2001/17/EC, 2002/83/EC, 2005/68/EC and, to the extent that those acts apply to insurance undertakings, reinsurance undertakings, institutions for occupational retirement provision and insurance intermediaries, within the relevant parts of Directives 2005/60/EC and 2002/65/EC, including all directives, regulations, and decisions based on those acts, and of any further legally binding Union act which confers tasks on the Authority.

3. The Authority shall also act in the field of activities of insurance undertakings, reinsurance undertakings, financial conglomerates, institutions for occupational retirement provision and insurance intermediaries, in relation to issues not directly covered in the acts referred to in paragraph 2, including matters of corporate governance, auditing and financial reporting, provided that such actions by the Authority are necessary to ensure the effective and consistent application of those acts.

4. With regard to institutions for occupational retirement provision, the Authority shall act without prejudice to national social and labour law.

5. The provisions of this Regulation are without prejudice to the powers of the Commission, in particular under Article 258 TFEU, to ensure compliance with Union law.

6. The objective of the Authority shall be to protect the public interest by contributing to the short, medium and long-term stability and effectiveness of the financial system, for the Union economy, its citizens and businesses. The Authority shall contribute to:

(a) improving the functioning of the internal market, including in particular a sound, effective and consistent level of regulation and supervision,

(b) ensuring the integrity, transparency, efficiency and orderly functioning of financial markets,

兹通过本指令如下：

第一章　设立和法律地位

第1条　设立和行动范围

1.本条例设立欧洲监管机构(欧洲保险与职业养老金管理局)(以下简称欧洲保险与职业养老金管理局)。

2.欧洲保险与职业养老金管理局应按本条例授予的权力在第2009/138/EC号指令(不包括第四章)、第2002/92/EC号指令、第2003/41/EC号指令、第2002/87/EC号指令、第64/225/EEC号指令、第73/239/EEC号指令、第73/240/EEC号指令、第76/580/EEC号指令、第78/473/EEC号指令、第84/641/EEC号指令、第87/344/EEC号指令、第88/357/EEC号指令、第92/49/EEC号指令、第98/78/EC号指令、第2001/17/EC号指令、第2002/83/EC号指令、第2005/68/EC号指令以及第2005/60/EC号指令和第2002/65/EC号指令适用于保险公司、再保险公司、职业退休金管理机构和保险中介机构的有关部分(包括所有基于上述法律文件的指令、条例及决定)范围内,以及在将来颁布的赋予欧洲保险与职业养老金管理局职责的具有法律约束力的任何其他欧盟法律文件范围内行事。

3.欧洲保险与职业养老金管理局还应在保险公司、再保险公司、金融集团、职业退休金管理机构和保险中介机构与不直接涵盖在第2款所述法律文件范围内的事项有关的活动领域行事,包括公司治理、审计以及财务报告事宜,前提是欧洲保险与职业养老金管理局采取的上述行动对于确保该等法律文件的有效、一致适用是必不可少的。

4.欧洲保险与职业养老金管理局就职业退休金管理机构所采取的行动不应违背成员国国内的社会保障和劳动法。

5.本条例的规定不得影响欧盟委员会确保欧盟法律得到遵守的权力,尤其是《欧洲联盟运行条约》第258条中的权力。

6.欧洲保险与职业养老金管理局的目标是通过为欧盟经济及其公民和企业促进金融系统的短期、中期和长期稳定和有效性以保护公众利益。欧洲保险与职业养老金管理局应致力于：

(a)改善欧盟内部市场的运行,尤其包括健全、有效、一致的规制和监管;

(b)确保金融市场的诚信度、透明、高效和有序运行;

(c) strengthening international supervisory coordination,

(d) preventing regulatory arbitrage and promoting equal conditions of competition,

(e) ensuring the taking of risks related to insurance, reinsurance and occupational pensions activities is appropriately regulated and supervised, and

(f) enhancing customer protection.

For those purposes, the Authority shall contribute to ensuring the consistent, efficient and effective application of the acts referred to in paragraph 2, foster supervisory convergence, provide opinions to the European Parliament, the Council, and the Commission and undertake economic analyses of the markets to promote the achievement of the Authority's objective.

In the exercise of the tasks conferred upon it by this Regulation, the Authority shall pay particular attention to any potential systemic risk posed by financial institutions, the failure of which may impair the operation of the financial system or the real economy.

When carrying out its tasks, the Authority shall act independently and objectively and in the interest of the Union alone.

Article 2 European System of Financial Supervision

1. The Authority shall form part of a European System of Financial Supervision (ESFS). The main objective of the ESFS shall be to ensure that the rules applicable to the financial sector are adequately implemented to preserve financial stability and to ensure confidence in the financial system as a whole and sufficient protection for the customers of financial services.

2. The ESFS shall comprise the following:

(a) the European Systemic Risk Board (ESRB), for the purposes of the tasks as specified in Regulation (EU) No 1092/2010 and this Regulation;

(b) the Authority;

(c) the European Supervisory Authority (European Banking Authority) established by Regulation (EU) No 1093/2010 of the European Parliament and of the Council [1];

(d) the European Supervisory Authority (European Securities and Markets Authority) established by Regulation (EU) No 1095/2010 of the European Parliament and of the Council [2];

(e) the Joint Committee of the European Supervisory Authorities (Joint Committee) for the purposes of carrying out the tasks as specified in Articles 54 to 57 of this Regulation, of Regulation (EU) No 1093/2010 and of Regulation (EU) No 1095/2010;

(f) the competent or supervisory authorities in the Member States as specified in the

1 See page 12 of this Official Journal.

2 See page 84 of this Official Journal.

(c)加强国际监管协调;

(d)防范监管套利并促进竞争的平等条件;

(e)确保对信贷风险及其他风险的涉险行为进行适当的规制和监管;及

(f)加强对客户的保护。

为此,欧洲保险与职业养老金管理局应致力于确保第2款所述法律文件得到一致且兼具效率和成效的适用,促进监管趋同,向欧洲议会、欧盟理事会以及欧盟委员会提出意见并对市场进行经济分析,以实现欧洲保险与职业养老金管理局的目标。

履行本条例所赋予的职责时,欧洲保险与职业养老金管理局应特别注意金融机构可能引起的任何系统性风险,因为金融机构的倒闭可能会对金融系统的运行造成影响或损害实体经济。

欧洲保险与职业养老金管理局在履行其职责时应仅为欧盟的利益独立客观地行事。

第2条　欧洲金融监管体系

1.欧洲保险与职业养老金管理局应构成欧洲金融监管体系(ESFS)的一部分。欧洲金融监管体系的主要目标在于确保适用于金融行业的规则得到充分的实施以维护金融稳定,确保公众对金融系统整体的信心,充分保护金融服务的客户。

2.欧洲金融监管体系应由下列机构组成:

(a)欧洲系统性风险委员会(ESRB),履行第1092/2010号(欧盟)条例以及本条例所规定的职责;

(b)欧洲保险与职业养老金管理局;

(c)依据欧洲议会与欧盟理事会第1093/2010号(欧盟)条例[1]设立的欧洲监管机构(欧洲银行业管理局);

(d)依据欧洲议会与欧盟理事会第1095/2010号(欧盟)条例[2]设立的欧洲监管机构(欧洲证券与市场管理局);

(e)欧洲监管机构联合委员会(以下简称联合委员会),履行本条例、第1093/2010号(欧盟)条例以及第1095/2010号(欧盟)条例第54条至第57条所规定的职责;

(f)本条例、第1093/2010号(欧盟)条例以及第1095/2010号(欧盟)条例第1条第2款

1　请见本《欧盟公报》,第12页。

2　请见本《欧盟公报》,第84页。

Union acts referred to in Article 1(2) of this Regulation, of Regulation (EU) No 1093/2010 and of Regulation (EU) No 1095/2010;

3. The Authority shall cooperate regularly and closely with the ESRB as well as with the European Supervisory Authority (European Banking Authority) and the European Supervisory Authority (European Securities and Markets Authority) through the Joint Committee, ensuring cross-sectoral consistency of work and reaching joint positions in the area of supervision of financial conglomerates and on other cross-sectoral issues.

4. In accordance with the principle of sincere cooperation under Article 4(3) of the Treaty on European Union, the parties to the ESFS shall cooperate with trust and full mutual respect, in particular in ensuring the flow of appropriate and reliable information between them.

5. Those supervisory authorities that are party to the ESFS shall be obliged to supervise financial institutions operating in the Union in accordance with the acts referred to in Article 1(2).

Article 3 Accountability of the Authorities

The Authorities referred to in Article 2(2)(a) to (d) shall be accountable to the European Parliament and the Council.

Article 4 Definitions

For the purposes of this Regulation the following definitions apply:

(1) 'financial institutions' means undertakings, entities and natural and legal persons subject to any of the legislative acts referred to in Article 1(2). With regard to Directive 2005/60/EC, 'financial institutions' means only insurance undertakings and insurance intermediaries as defined in that Directive;

(2) 'competent authorities' means:

(i) supervisory authorities as defined in Directive 2009/138/EC, and competent authorities as defined in Directive 2003/41/EC and 2002/92/EC;

(ii) with regard to Directives 2002/65/EC and 2005/60/EC, the authorities competent for ensuring compliance with the requirements of those Directives by financial institutions as defined in point (1).

Article 5 Legal status

1. The Authority shall be a Union body with legal personality.

2. In each Member State, the Authority shall enjoy the most extensive legal capacity accorded to legal persons under national law. It may, in particular, acquire or dispose of movable and immovable property and be a party to legal proceedings.

3. The Authority shall be represented by its Chairperson.

Article 6 Composition

The Authority shall comprise:

所述欧盟法律文件中规定的成员国主管部门或监管机构。

3.欧洲保险与职业养老金管理局应定期与欧洲系统性风险委员会以及通过联合委员会与两个欧洲监管机构(欧洲银行业管理局和欧洲证券与市场管理局)紧密合作,确保跨行业工作的一致性,并在金融集团监管领域和其他跨行业问题上取得共同立场。

4.根据《欧洲联盟条约》第4条第3款所指的精诚合作原则,欧洲金融监管体系各方应在合作过程中互相信任和充分尊重,以特别确保各方能够彼此交流适当和可靠的信息。

5.属于欧洲金融监管体系一部分的监管机构有义务依照第1条第2款所述法律文件对在欧盟运营的金融机构进行监管。

第3条　部门问责制

第2条第2款第a项至第d项所述的部门应对欧洲议会和欧盟理事会负责。

第4条　定义

在本条例中适用下列定义:

(1)"金融机构"一词,系指第1条第2款所述任何框架立法规定的公司、实体以及自然人和法人。但就第2005/60/EC号指令而言,"金融机构"一词,仅指如该指令所定义的保险公司和保险中介机构;

(2)"主管部门"一词,系指:

(i)如第2009/138/EC号指令所定义的监管机构以及如第2003/41/EC号指令和第2002/92/EC号指令所定义的主管部门;

(ii)就第2002/65/EC号指令和第2005/60/EC号指令而言,负责确保第1目所定义的金融机构遵循该等指令要求的部门。

第5条　法律地位

1.欧洲保险与职业养老金管理局系具有法人身份的欧盟机构。

2.在各成员国内,欧洲保险与职业养老金管理局享有按该成员国国内法律授予法人的最广泛的民事能力。特别是,欧洲保险与职业养老金管理局可以获得或处置动产和不动产,并可作为法律程序的当事人。

3.欧洲保险与职业养老金管理局应由其主席代表。

第6条　构成

欧洲保险与职业养老金管理局由下列机构和人员组成:

(1) a Board of Supervisors, which shall exercise the tasks set out in Article 43;

(2) a Management Board, which shall exercise the tasks set out in Article 47;

(3) a Chairperson, who shall exercise the tasks set out in Article 48;

(4) an Executive Director, who shall exercise the tasks set out in Article 53;

(5) a Board of Appeal, which shall exercise the tasks set out in Article 60.

Article 7 Seat

The Authority shall have its seat in Frankfurt am Main.

CHAPTER Ⅱ TASKS AND POWERS OF THE AUTHORITY

Article 8 Tasks and powers of the Authority

1. The Authority shall have the following tasks:

(a) to contribute to the establishment of high-quality common regulatory and supervisory standards and practices, in particular by providing opinions to the Union institutions and by developing guidelines, recommendations, and draft regulatory and implementing technical standards which shall be based on the legislative acts referred to in Article 1(2);

(b) to contribute to the consistent application of legally binding Union acts, in particular by contributing to a common supervisory culture, ensuring consistent, efficient and effective application of the acts referred to in Article 1(2), preventing regulatory arbitrage, mediating and settling disagreements between competent authorities, ensuring effective and consistent supervision of financial institutions, ensuring a coherent functioning of colleges of supervisors and taking actions, inter alia, in emergency situations;

(c) to stimulate and facilitate the delegation of tasks and responsibilities among competent authorities;

(d) to cooperate closely with the ESRB, in particular by providing the ESRB with the necessary information for the achievement of its tasks and by ensuring a proper follow up to the warnings and recommendations of the ESRB;

(e) to organise and conduct peer review analyses of competent authorities, including issuing guidelines and recommendations and identifying best practices, in order to strengthen consistency in supervisory outcomes;

(f) to monitor and assess market developments in the area of its competences;

(g) to undertake economic analyses of markets to inform the discharge of the

(1)履行第43条所列职责的监管机构理事会;
(2)履行第47条所列职责的管理委员会;
(3)履行第48条所列职责的主席;
(4)履行第53条所列职责的执行主任;
(5)履行第60条所列职责的行政复议委员会。

第7条　总部所在地

欧洲保险与职业养老金管理局总部位于美因河畔的法兰克福。

第二章　欧洲保险与职业养老金管理局的职责和权力

第8条　欧洲保险与职业养老金管理局的职责和权力

1.欧洲保险与职业养老金管理局负有下列职责:

(a)促进制定高水平的通用的规制与监管方面的标准和实践,特别是通过向欧盟机构提供意见以及通过制定指引、建议以及起草以第1条第2款中的框架立法为基础的监管性和实施性技术标准草案;

(b)促进具有法律约束力的欧盟立法的一致适用,特别是通过促成共同的监管文化、确保第1条第2款所述法律文件一致的且兼具效率和成效的适用,防范监管套利,调解和解决主管部门之间的分歧,确保对金融机构的有效和一致监管,确保监管团相互连贯的运行并根据情况(尤其是紧急情况下)采取行动;

(c)促进和推动主管部门之间的职责和责任委托;

(d)与欧洲系统性风险委员会紧密合作,特别是向欧洲系统性风险委员会提供履行其职责所必要的信息以及确保对欧洲系统性风险委员会发布的预警和建议的适当跟进;

(e)组织和开展主管部门的同行审评分析,包括发布指引和建议以及识别最佳实践,以加强监管结果的一致性;

(f)对其职权管辖范围内的市场变化进行监控和评估;
(g)进行市场经济分析,为欧洲保险与职业养老金管理局职能的履行提供信息;

Authority's functions;

(h) to foster the protection of policyholders, pension scheme members and beneficiaries;

(i) to contribute to the consistent and coherent functioning of colleges of supervisors, the monitoring, assessment and measurement of systemic risk, the development and coordination of recovery and resolution plans, providing a high level of protection to policy holders, to beneficiaries and throughout the Union, in accordance with Articles 21 to 26;

(j) to fulfil any other specific tasks set out in this Regulation or in other legislative acts;

(k) to publish on its website, and to update regularly, information relating to its field of activities, in particular, within the area of its competence, on registered financial institutions, in order to ensure information is easily accessible by the public;

(l) to take over, as appropriate, all existing and ongoing tasks from the Committee of European Insurance and Occupational Pensions Supervisors (CEIOPS);

2. To achieve the tasks set out in paragraph 1, the Authority shall have the powers set out in this Regulation, in particular to:

(a) develop draft regulatory technical standards in the specific cases referred to in Article 10;

(b) develop draft implementing technical standards in the specific cases referred to in Article 15;

(c) issue guidelines and recommendations, as laid down in Article 16;

(d) issue recommendations in specific cases, as referred to in Article 17(3);

(e) take individual decisions addressed to competent authorities in the specific cases referred to in Articles 18(3) and 19(3);

(f) in cases concerning directly applicable Union law, take individual decisions addressed to financial institutions, in the specific cases referred to in Article 17(6), in Article 18(4) and in Article 19(4);

(g) issue opinions to the European Parliament, the Council, or the Commission as provided for in Article 34;

(h) collect the necessary information concerning financial institutions as provided for in Article 35;

(i) develop common methodologies for assessing the effect of product characteristics and distribution processes on the financial position of institutions and on consumer protection;

(j) provide a centrally accessible database of registered financial institutions in the area of its competence where specified in the acts referred to in Article 1(2).

(h)促进对保单持有人、养老金计划成员以及受益人的保护;

(i)根据第21条至第26条,促进监管团能一致并相互连贯地行使职能,监控、评估和计量系统性风险,制定和协调恢复和清盘计划,向欧盟内的保单持有人和受益人养老金计划成员[1]提供高度的保护;

(j)履行本条例以及其他框架立法中规定的任何其他特定职责;

(k)在其网站上公布有关针对注册金融机构所开展的活动(尤其是在其职权管辖范围内)的相关信息并定期更新,以确保公众能方便地查阅信息;

(l)在适当情况下接手欧洲保险与职业养老金监管机构委员会(CEIOPS)所有现有的及持续的职责。

2.为完成第1款所列的职责,欧洲保险与职业养老金管理局应有本条例规定的权力,特别是:

(a)在第10条所述的特定情形下起草监管性技术标准草案;

(b)在第15条所述的特定情形下起草实施性技术标准草案;

(c)发布第16条规定的指引和建议;

(d)在第17条第3款所述的特定情形下提出建议;

(e)在第18条第3款和第19条第3款所述的特定情形下针对主管部门作出个别决定;

(f)在涉及可直接适用的欧盟法律的案件中,在第17条第6款、第18条第4款和第19条第4款所述的特定情形下,针对金融机构作出个别决定;

(g)按第34条规定向欧洲议会、欧盟理事会或欧盟委员会发布意见;

(h)按第35条规定收集与金融机构有关的必要信息;

(i)为评估产品特征和分销程序对机构的财务状况和消费者保护所产生的影响制定通用的方法论;及

(j)在第1条第2款所述法律文件所规定的职权管辖范围内提供一个可集中查阅数据的注册金融机构数据库。

1 英文原文似有错漏,似应增加"养老金计划成员"一项,已在译文中添加。——译者注

Article 9 Tasks related to consumer protection and financial activities

1. The Authority shall take a leading role in promoting transparency, simplicity and fairness in the market for consumer financial products or services across the internal market, including by:

(a) collecting, analysing and reporting on consumer trends;

(b) reviewing and coordinating financial literacy and education initiatives by the competent authorities;

(c) developing training standards for the industry; and

(d) contributing to the development of common disclosure rules.

2. The Authority shall monitor new and existing financial activities and may adopt guidelines and recommendations with a view to promoting the safety and soundness of markets and convergence of regulatory practice.

3. The Authority may also issue warnings in the event that a financial activity poses a serious threat to the objectives laid down in Article 1(6).

4. The Authority shall establish, as an integral part of the Authority, a Committee on financial innovation, which brings together all relevant competent national supervisory authorities with a view to achieving a coordinated approach to the regulatory and supervisory treatment of new or innovative financial activities and providing advice for the Authority to present to the European Parliament, the Council and the Commission.

5. The Authority may temporarily prohibit or restrict certain financial activities that threaten the orderly functioning and integrity of financial markets or the stability of the whole or part of the financial system in the Union in the cases specified and under the conditions laid down in the legislative acts referred to in Article 1(2) or, if so required, in the case of an emergency situation in accordance with and under the conditions laid down in Article 18.

The Authority shall review the decision referred to in the first subparagraph at appropriate intervals and at least every 3 months. If the decision is not renewed after a three-month period, it shall automatically expire.

A Member State may request the Authority to reconsider its decision. In that case, the Authority shall decide in accordance with the procedure set out in the second subparagraph of Article 44(1), whether it maintains its decision.

The Authority may also assess the need to prohibit or restrict certain types of financial activity and, where there is such a need, inform the Commission in order to facilitate the adoption of any such prohibition or restriction.

Article 10 Regulatory technical standards

1. Where the European Parliament and the Council delegate power to the Commission to adopt regulatory technical standards by means of delegated acts under

第9条　与消费者保护和金融活动有关的职责

1.欧洲保险与职业养老金管理局应至少通过下列手段在为欧盟内部市场的消费金融产品或服务提升市场透明度、简易性和公平中发挥领导作用：

(a)收集、分析并报告关于消费趋势的信息；

(b)审评并协调主管部门的金融普及和教育新方案；

(c)制定行业培训标准；及

(d)致力于通用披露规则的制定。

2.欧洲保险与职业养老金管理局应对既有的和新型的金融活动进行监控，并可通过指引和建议以促进市场的安全和稳健以及监管实践的趋同。

3.金融活动对第1条第6款所规定的目标造成严重威胁，欧洲保险与职业养老金管理局也可发出预警。

4.欧洲保险与职业养老金管理局应在金融创新方面设立一个委员会，作为欧洲保险与职业养老金管理局的组成部分。该委员会集合所有相关国家级主管部门，以便在对新型或创新金融活动作出规制和监管处理时能相互协调，并向欧洲保险与职业养老金管理局提供呈报给欧洲议会、欧盟理事会和欧盟委员会的建议。

5.欧洲保险与职业养老金管理局可在第1条第2款所述框架立法规定的情形和条件下，或者在出现第18条所述紧急情况且依据第18条设定的条件有此必要的情形下，决定采取临时措施，禁止或限制威胁到欧盟金融市场有序运行和诚信度以及整个或部分金融系统稳定的某些金融活动。

欧洲保险与职业养老金管理局应以适当的频率至少每3个月1次对本款第1项所述的决定作审评。决定在3个月期限过后未展延的，应自动失效。

成员国可请求欧洲保险与职业养老金管理局重新审议其决定。在此情况下，欧洲保险与职业养老金管理局应依照第44条第1款第2项所列程序决定是否维持其决定。

欧洲保险与职业养老金管理局也可对是否需要禁止或限制特定类型金融活动进行评估，如确实有此需要，则应通知欧盟委员会以促成通过任何上述禁令或限制令。

第10条　监管性技术标准

1.欧洲议会和欧盟理事会按照《欧洲联盟运行条约》第290条授权欧盟委员会以授权立法形式通过监管性技术标准（以确保第1条第2款所述框架立法具体规定之各个

Article 290 TFEU in order to ensure consistent harmonisation in the areas specifically set out in the legislative acts referred to in Article 1(2), the Authority may develop draft regulatory technical standards. The Authority shall submit its draft standards to the Commission for endorsement.

Regulatory technical standards shall be technical, shall not imply strategic decisions or policy choices and their content shall be delimited by the legislative acts on which they are based.

Before submitting them to the Commission, the Authority shall conduct open public consultations on draft regulatory technical standards and analyse the potential related costs and benefits, unless such consultations and analyses are disproportionate in relation to the scope and impact of the draft regulatory technical standards concerned or in relation to the particular urgency of the matter. The Authority shall also request the opinion of the relevant stakeholder group referred to in Article 37.

Where the Authority submits a draft regulatory technical standard, the Commission shall immediately forward it to the European Parliament and the Council.

Within 3 months of receipt of a draft regulatory technical standard, the Commission shall decide whether to endorse it. The Commission may endorse the draft regulatory technical standards in part only, or with amendments, where theUnion's interests so require.

Where the Commission intends not to endorse a draft regulatory technical standard, or to endorse it in part or with amendments, it shall send the draft regulatory technical standard back to the Authority, explaining why it does not endorse it, or, as the case may be, explaining the reasons for its amendments. Within a period of 6 weeks, the Authority may amend the draft regulatory technical standard on the basis of the Commission's proposed amendments and resubmit it in the form of a formal opinion to the Commission. The Authority shall send a copy of its formal opinion to the European Parliament and to the Council.

If, on the expiry of that six-week period, the Authority has not submitted an amended draft regulatory technical standard, or has submitted a draft regulatory technical standard that is not amended in a way consistent with the Commission's proposed amendments, the Commission may adopt the regulatory technical standard with the amendments it considers relevant or reject it.

The Commission may not change the content of a draft regulatory technical standard prepared by the Authority without prior coordination with the Authority, as set out in this Article.

2. Where the Authority has not submitted a draft regulatory technical standard within the time limit set out in the legislative acts referred to in Article 1(2), the Commission may request such a draft within a new time limit.

领域里的一致协调)时,欧洲保险与职业养老金管理局可起草监管性技术标准草案。欧洲保险与职业养老金管理局应将其标准草案呈报欧盟委员会,以获得其同意和支持。

监管性技术标准应是技术性标准,不得含有任何战略决定或政策性选择,并且其内容应限于其所依据的框架立法的范围。

欧洲保险与职业养老金管理局向欧盟委员会呈报监管性技术标准草案之前,应先公开征求公众意见并分析潜在的相关成本和收益,但是,上述意见征询和分析就所涉监管性技术标准草案的范围和影响而言,或就其特殊紧急性而言不成比例的除外。欧洲保险与职业养老金管理局还应征求第37条所述的相关利益相关者小组的意见。

欧洲保险与职业养老金管理局呈报监管性技术标准草案后,欧盟委员会应立即将其转发给欧洲议会和欧盟理事会。

欧盟委员会收到监管性技术标准草案后3个月内,应决定是否同意和支持该草案。按照对欧盟有利的原则,欧盟委员会可仅同意和支持部分草案,或要求作出修改后才同意和支持草案。

欧盟委员会有意否决监管性技术标准草案或仅同意和支持其中的一部分或要求作出修改才同意和支持该草案的,应将草案发回欧洲保险与职业养老金管理局,并视具体情况对其否决该草案或者就草案需要修改的原因作出解释。欧洲保险与职业养老金管理局可在6周内根据欧盟委员会的修改建议对监管性技术标准草案进行修改,并以正式意见的形式重新向欧盟委员会呈报。欧洲保险与职业养老金管理局应将其正式意见的复本发送给欧洲议会和欧盟理事会。

6周期限届满,欧洲保险与职业养老金管理局仍未呈报监管性技术标准草案修正稿,或呈报的修正稿不符合欧盟委员会的修改建议的,欧盟委员会可在作出其认为适当的修改后通过监管性技术标准草案或否决该草案。

依本条规定,未事先与欧洲保险与职业养老金管理局协调,欧盟委员会不得擅自更改由欧洲保险与职业养老金管理局起草的监管性技术标准草案的内容。

2.欧洲保险与职业养老金管理局未在第1条第2款所述框架立法规定的期限内呈报监管性技术标准草案的,欧盟委员会可重新设定期限,要求其提供监管性技术标准草案。

3. Only where the Authority does not submit a draft regulatory technical standard to the Commission within the time limits in accordance with paragraph 2, may the Commission adopt a regulatory technical standard by means of a delegated act without a draft from the Authority.

The Commission shall conduct open public consultations on draft regulatory technical standards and analyse the potential related costs and benefits, unless such consultations and analyses are disproportionate in relation to the scope and impact of the draft regulatory technical standards concerned or in relation to the particular urgency of the matter. The Commission shall also request the opinion or advice of the relevant stakeholder group referred to in Article 37.

The Commission shall immediately forward the draft regulatory technical standard to the European Parliament and the Council.

The Commission shall send its draft regulatory technical standard to the Authority. Within a period of 6 weeks, the Authority may amend the draft regulatory technical standard and submit it in the form of a formal opinion to the Commission. The Authority shall send a copy of its formal opinion to the European Parliament and to the Council.

If, on the expiry of the six-week period referred to in the fourth subparagraph, the Authority has not submitted an amended draft regulatory technical standard, the Commission may adopt the regulatory technical standard.

If the Authority has submitted an amended draft regulatory technical standard within the six-week period, the Commission may amend the draft regulatory technical standard on the basis of the Authority's proposed amendments or adopt the regulatory technical standard with the amendments it considers relevant. The Commission shall not change the content of the draft regulatory technical standard prepared by the Authority without prior coordination with the Authority, as set out in this Article.

4. The regulatory technical standards shall be adopted by means of regulations or decisions. They shall be published in the Official Journal of the European Union and shall enter into force on the date stated therein.

Article 11 Exercise of the delegation

1. The power to adopt regulatory technical standards referred to in Article 10 shall be conferred on the Commission for a period of four years from 16 December 2010. The Commission shall draw up a report in respect of the delegated power not later than 6 months before the end of the four-year period. The delegation of power shall be automatically extended for periods of an identical duration, unless the European Parliament or the Council revokes it in accordance with Article 14.

2. As soon as it adopts a regulatory technical standard, the Commission shall notify it simultaneously to the European Parliament and to the Council.

3.唯有当欧洲保险与职业养老金管理局未在第2款规定的期限内向欧盟委员会呈报监管性技术标准草案时,欧盟委员会方可在无欧洲保险与职业养老金管理局草案的情况下以授权立法的形式通过监管性技术标准。

欧盟委员会应就监管性技术标准草案公开征求公众意见并分析潜在的相关成本和收益,但是,上述意见征询和分析就所涉监管性技术标准草案的范围和影响而言,或就其特殊紧急性而言不成比例的除外。欧盟委员会也应征求第37条所述及的相关利益相关者小组的意见或建议。

欧盟委员会应立即将其起草的监管性技术标准草案转发给欧洲议会和欧盟理事会。

欧盟委员会应将其监管性技术标准草案发送给欧洲保险与职业养老金管理局。欧洲保险与职业养老金管理局可在6周内对监管性技术标准进行修改,并以正式意见的形式呈报欧盟委员会。欧洲保险与职业养老金管理局应将其正式意见的复本分别发送给欧洲议会和欧盟理事会。

第4项规定的6周期限届满,欧洲保险与职业养老金管理局仍未呈报监管性技术标准草案修改稿的,欧盟委员会可按原文通过该标准。

欧洲保险与职业养老金管理局在6周期限内呈报了监管性技术标准草案修改稿的,欧盟委员会可基于欧洲保险与职业养老金管理局的修改建议对监管性技术标准草案进行修改,或完成其自身认为适当的修改后通过监管性技术标准。依本条规定,未事先与欧洲保险与职业养老金管理局协调,欧盟委员会不得擅自更改由欧洲保险与职业养老金管理局起草的监管性技术标准草案的内容。

4.监管性技术标准应以条例或决定的形式通过,在《欧盟公报》公布并自其所示之日起生效。

第11条　委托授权的行使

1.自2010年12月16日起,兹授予欧盟委员会第10条所述通过监管性技术标准的权力,权力有效期为4年。欧盟委员会应在该4年期限届满的6个月前就被委托的权力起草一份报告。除非欧洲议会或欧盟理事会依照第14条撤销委托授权,否则委托授权期限届满后应自动展延,每次展延的期限与原期限相同。

2.欧盟委员会应在通过监管性技术标准后立即同时通知欧洲议会和欧盟理事会。

3. The power to adopt regulatory technical standards is conferred on the Commission subject to the conditions laid down in Articles 12 to 14.

Article 12 Revocation of the delegation

1. The delegation of power referred to in Article 10 may be revoked at any time by the European Parliament or by the Council.

2. The institution which has commenced an internal procedure for deciding whether to revoke a delegation of power shall endeavour to inform the other institution and the Commission within a reasonable time before the final decision is taken, indicating the delegated power which could be subject to revocation.

3. The decision of revocation shall put an end to the delegation of the power specified in that decision. It shall take effect immediately or at a later date specified therein. It shall not affect the validity of the regulatory technical standards already in force. It shall be published in the Official Journal of the European Union.

Article 13 Objections to regulatory technical standards

1. The European Parliament or the Council may object to a regulatory technical standard within a period of 3 months from the date of notification of the regulatory technical standard adopted by the Commission. At the initiative of the European Parliament or the Council that period shall be extended by 3 months.

Where the Commission adopts a regulatory technical standard which is the same as the draft regulatory technical standard submitted by the Authority, the period during which the European Parliament and the Council may object shall be 1 month from the date of notification. At the initiative of the European Parliament or the Council that period shall be extended by 1 month.

2. If, on the expiry of the period referred to in paragraph 1, neither the European Parliament nor the Council has objected to the regulatory technical standard, it shall be published in the Official Journal of the European Union and shall enter into force on the date stated therein. The regulatory technical standard may be published in the Official Journal of the European Union and enter into force before the expiry of that period if the European Parliament and the Council have both informed the Commission of their intention not to raise objections.

3. If either the European Parliament or the Council objects to a regulatory technical standard within the period referred to in paragraph 1, it shall not enter into force. In accordance with Article 296 TFEU, the institution which objects shall state the reasons for objecting to the regulatory technical standard.

Article 14 Non-endorsement or amendment of draft regulatory technical standards

1. In the event that the Commission does not endorse a draft regulatory technical

3.授予欧盟委员会的通过监管性技术标准的权力受制于第12条至第14条规定的条件。

第12条 委托授权的撤销

1.欧洲议会或欧盟理事会可以随时撤销第10条所述的委托授权。

2.欧洲议会或欧盟理事会已经启动决定是否撤销某项委托授权的内部程序的,应当尽力在作出最终决定前的合理时间内通知彼此以及欧盟委员会,指明可能被撤销的委托授权。

3.撤销决定将使其列明的委托授权效力终止。撤销决定应立即生效,或在决定中规定的较晚日期生效。撤销决定不影响已生效的监管性技术标准的效力。撤销决定应在《欧盟公报》公布。

第13条 对监管性技术标准的异议

1.欧洲议会或欧盟理事会可在欧盟委员会通过的监管性技术标准的通知日起3个月期限内对该等标准提出异议。经欧洲议会或欧盟理事会主动要求,该期限可延长3个月。

欧盟委员会依照欧洲保险与职业养老金管理局呈报的监管性技术标准草案原文通过了该标准,欧洲议会和欧盟理事会提出异议的期限为通知日起的1个月。经欧洲议会或欧盟理事会主动要求,该期限可延长1个月。

2.第1款所述期限届满时,欧洲议会和欧盟理事会均未对监管性技术标准提出异议的,监管性技术标准应在《欧盟公报》公布,并自其规定的生效日期起生效。在第1款所述期限届满前,欧洲议会和欧盟理事会均已通知欧盟委员会其无意提出异议的,该监管性技术标准可提前在《欧盟公报》公布并生效。

3.欧洲议会或欧盟理事会在第1款所述期限内对监管性技术标准提出异议的,该标准不得生效。根据《欧洲联盟运行条约》第296条的规定,对监管性技术标准提出异议的机构应说明异议理由。

第14条 不同意或修改监管性技术标准草案

1.欧盟委员会按第10条规定不同意和支持监管性技术标准草案或对其作出修改

standard or amends it as provided for in Article 10, the Commission shall inform the Authority, the European Parliament and the Council, stating its reasons.

2. Where appropriate, the European Parliament or the Council may invite the responsible Commissioner, together with the Chairperson of the Authority, within 1 month of the notice referred to in paragraph 1, for an ad hoc meeting of the competent committee of the European Parliament or the Council to present and explain their differences.

Article 15 Implementing technical standards

1. The Authority may develop implementing technical standards, by means of implementing acts under Article 291 TFEU, in the areas specifically set out in the legislative acts referred to in Article 1(2). Implementing technical standards shall be technical, shall not imply strategic decisions or policy choices and their content shall be to determine the conditions of application of those acts. The Authority shall submit its draft implementing technical standards to the Commission for endorsement.

Before submitting draft implementing technical standards to the Commission, the Authority shall conduct open public consultations and shall analyse the potential related costs and benefits, unless such consultations and analyses are disproportionate in relation to the scope and impact of the draft implementing technical standards concerned or in relation to the particular urgency of the matter. The Authority shall also request the opinion of the relevant stakeholder group referred to in Article 37.

Where the Authority submits a draft implementing technical standard, the Commission shall immediately forward it to the European Parliament and the Council.

Within 3 months of receipt of a draft implementing technical standard, the Commission shall decide whether to endorse it. The Commission may extend that period by 1 month. The Commission may endorse the draft implementing technical standard in part only, or with amendments, where theUnion's interests so require.

Where the Commission intends not to endorse a draft implementing technical standard or intends to endorse it in part or with amendments, it shall send it back to the Authority explaining why it does not intend to endorse it, or, as the case may be, explaining the reasons for its amendments. Within a period of 6 weeks, the Authority may amend the draft implementing technical standard on the basis of the Commission's proposed amendments and resubmit it in the form of a formal opinion to the Commission. The Authority shall send a copy of its formal opinion to the European Parliament and to the Council.

If, on the expiry of the six-week period referred to in the fifth subparagraph, the Authority has not submitted an amended draft implementing technical standard, or has submitted a draft implementing technical standard that is not amended in a way consistent

的,欧盟委员会应通知欧洲保险与职业养老金管理局、欧洲议会和欧盟理事会并陈述理由。

2.在适当时,欧洲议会或欧盟理事会可邀请负责的委员与欧洲保险与职业养老金管理局的主席一同在第1款所指通知发出后1个月内参加欧洲议会或欧盟理事会有关委员会的临时会议,陈述其分歧并对之作出解释。

第15条 实施性技术标准

1.欧洲保险与职业养老金管理局可在第1条第2款所述框架立法具体规定的领域按照《欧洲联盟运行条约》第291条以实施性立法的形式制定实施性技术标准。实施性技术标准应是技术性标准,不应涉及任何战略决定或政策选择;其内容应是确定上述框架立法的适用条件。欧洲保险与职业养老金管理局应将实施性技术标准草案呈报欧盟委员会,以获得其同意和支持。

欧洲保险与职业养老金管理局向欧盟委员会呈报实施性技术标准草案之前,应先公开征求公众意见并分析潜在的相关成本和收益,但是,上述意见征询和分析就所涉实施性技术标准草案的范围和影响而言,或就其特殊紧急性而言不成比例的除外。欧洲保险与职业养老金管理局还应征求第37条所述的相关利益相关者小组的意见。

欧洲保险与职业养老金管理局呈报实施性技术标准草案后,欧盟委员会应立即将其转发给欧洲议会和欧盟理事会。

欧盟委员会收到实施性技术标准草案后3个月内,应决定是否同意和支持该草案。欧盟委员会可将该期限延长1个月。按照对欧盟有利的原则,欧盟委员会可仅同意和支持部分草案,或要求作出修改才同意和支持草案。

欧盟委员会有意否决实施性技术标准草案或仅同意和支持其中的一部分或要求作出修改才同意和支持该草案的,应将草案发回欧洲保险与职业养老金管理局,并视具体情况对其否决该草案或者就草案需要修改的原因作出解释。欧洲保险与职业养老金管理局可在6周内根据欧盟委员会的修改建议对实施性技术标准草案进行修改,并以正式意见的形式重新向欧盟委员会呈报。欧洲保险与职业养老金管理局应将其正式意见的复本发送给欧洲议会和欧盟理事会。

第5项所述的6周期限届满,欧洲保险与职业养老金管理局仍未呈报实施性技术标准草案修改稿,或呈报的修改稿不符合欧盟委员会的修改建议的,欧盟委员会可在作出其认为适当的修改后通过实施性技术标准草案或否决该草案。

with the Commission's proposed amendments, the Commission may adopt the implementing technical standard with the amendments it considers relevant or reject it.

The Commission shall not change the content of a draft implementing technical standard prepared by the Authority without prior coordination with the Authority, as set out in this Article.

2. In cases where the Authority has not submitted a draft implementing technical standard within the time limit set out in the legislative acts referred to in Article 1(2), the Commission may request such a draft within a new time limit.

3. Only where the Authority does not submit a draft implementing technical standard to the Commission within the time limits in accordance with paragraph 2, may the Commission adopt an implementing technical standard by means of an implementing act without a draft from the Authority.

The Commission shall conduct open public consultations on draft implementing technical standards and analyse the potential related costs and benefits, unless such consultations and analyses are disproportionate in relation to the scope and impact of the draft implementing technical standards concerned or in relation to the particular urgency of the matter. The Commission shall also request the opinion or advice of the relevant stakeholder group referred to in Article 37.

The Commission shall immediately forward the draft implementing technical standard to the European Parliament and the Council.

The Commission shall send the draft implementing technical standard to the Authority. Within a period of 6 weeks, the Authority may amend the draft implementing technical standard and submit it in the form of a formal opinion to the Commission. The Authority shall send a copy of its formal opinion to the European Parliament and to the Council.

If, on the expiry of the six-week period referred to in the fourth subparagraph, the Authority has not submitted an amended draft implementing technical standard, the Commission may adopt the implementing technical standard.

If the Authority has submitted an amended draft implementing technical standard within that six-week period, the Commission may amend the draft implementing technical standard on the basis of the Authority's proposed amendments or adopt the implementing technical standard with the amendments it considers relevant.

The Commission shall not change the content of the draft implementing technical standards prepared by the Authority without prior coordination with the Authority, as set out in this Article.

4. The implementing technical standards shall be adopted by means of regulations or decisions. They shall be published in the Official Journal of the European Union and shall

依本条规定，未事先与欧洲保险与职业养老金管理局协调，欧盟委员会不得擅自更改由欧洲保险与职业养老金管理局起草的实施性技术标准草案的内容。

2.欧洲保险与职业养老金管理局未在第1条第2款所述框架立法规定的期限内呈报实施性技术标准草案的，欧盟委员会可重新设定期限，要求其提供实施性技术标准草案。

3.唯有当欧洲保险与职业养老金管理局未在第2款规定的期限内向欧盟委员会呈报实施性技术标准草案时，欧盟委员会方可在无欧洲保险与职业养老金管理局草案的情况下以实施性立法的形式通过实施性技术标准。

欧盟委员会应就实施性技术标准草案公开征求公众意见，并分析潜在的相关成本和收益，但是，上述意见征询和分析就所涉实施性技术标准草案的范围和影响而言，或就其特殊紧急性而言不成比例的除外。欧盟委员会也应征求第37条所述的相关利益相关者小组的意见或建议。

欧盟委员会应立即将实施性技术标准草案转发给欧洲议会和欧盟理事会。

欧盟委员会应将实施性技术标准草案发送给欧洲保险与职业养老金管理局。欧洲保险与职业养老金管理局可在6周内对实施性技术标准进行修改，并以正式意见的形式呈报欧盟委员会。欧洲保险与职业养老金管理局应将其正式意见的复本分别发给欧洲议会和欧盟理事会。

第4项所述的6周期限届满，欧洲保险与职业养老金管理局仍未呈报实施性技术标准草案修改稿的，欧盟委员会可按原文通过该标准。

欧洲保险与职业养老金管理局在6周期限内呈报了实施性技术标准草案修改稿的，欧盟委员会可基于欧洲保险与职业养老金管理局的修改建议对实施性技术标准草案进行修改，或完成其自身认为适当的修改后通过实施性技术标准。

依本条规定，未事先与欧洲保险与职业养老金管理局协调，欧盟委员会不得擅自更改由欧洲保险与职业养老金管理局起草的实施性技术标准草案的内容。

4.实施性技术标准应以条例或决定的形式通过，在《欧盟公报》公布并自其所示之日起生效。

enter into force on the date stated therein.

Article 16 Guidelines and recommendations

1. The Authority shall, with a view to establishing consistent, efficient and effective supervisory practices within the ESFS, and to ensuring the common, uniform and consistent application of Union law, issue guidelines and recommendations addressed to competent authorities or financial institutions.

2. The Authority shall, where appropriate, conduct open public consultations regarding the guidelines and recommendations and analyse the related potential costs and benefits. Such consultations and analyses shall be proportionate in relation to the scope, nature and impact of the guidelines or recommendations. The Authority shall, where appropriate, also request opinions or advice from the relevant stakeholder group referred to in Article 37.

3. The competent authorities and financial institutions shall make every effort to comply with those guidelines and recommendations.

Within 2 months of the issuance of a guideline or recommendation, each competent authority shall confirm whether it complies or intends to comply with that guideline or recommendation. In the event that a competent authority does not comply or does not intend to comply, it shall inform the Authority, stating its reasons.

The Authority shall publish the fact that a competent authority does not comply or does not intend to comply with that guideline or recommendation. The Authority may also decide, on a case-by-case basis, to publish the reasons provided by the competent authority for not complying with that guideline or recommendation. The competent authority shall receive advanced notice of such publication.

If required by that guideline or recommendation, financial institutions shall report, in a clear and detailed way, whether they comply with that guideline or recommendation.

4. In the report referred to in Article 43(5) the Authority shall inform the European Parliament, the Council and the Commission of the guidelines and recommendations that have been issued, stating which competent authority has not complied with them, and outlining how the Authority intends to ensure that the competent authority concerned follow its recommendations and guidelines in the future.

Article 17 Breach of Union law

1. Where a competent authority has not applied the acts referred to in Article 1(2) or has applied them in a way which appears to be a breach of Union law, including the regulatory technical standards and implementing technical standards established in accordance with Articles 10 to 15, in particular by failing to ensure that a financial institution satisfies the requirements laid down in those acts, the Authority shall act in accordance with the powers set out in paragraphs 2, 3 and 6 of this Article.

第16条　指引和建议

1.为在欧洲金融监管体系内建立一致的且兼具效率和成效的监管实践,确保欧盟法律的共同、统一和一致的适用,欧洲保险与职业养老金管理局应针对主管部门或金融机构提出指引和建议。

2.在适当时,欧洲保险与职业养老金管理局应就指引和建议公开征求公众意见并分析潜在的相关成本和收益。上述意见征询和分析应与指引或建议的范围、性质和影响成比例。在适当时,欧洲保险与职业养老金管理局还应征求第37条所述相关利益相关者小组的意见或建议。

3.主管部门和金融机构应尽其所能遵循该等指引和建议。

指引或建议发布后2个月内,各主管部门应确认其是否遵循或有意遵循该指引或建议。主管部门不遵循或不愿遵循的,应通知欧洲保险与职业养老金管理局并陈述理由。

欧洲保险与职业养老金管理局应公布主管部门不遵循或不愿遵循该指引或建议的事实。欧洲保险与职业养老金管理局还可根据具体情况决定公布主管部门所提出的不遵循该指引或建议的理由。公布上述事实或理由应提前通知主管部门。

如指引或建议要求以清楚详尽的方式报告其是否遵循该指引或建议,金融机构应遵守该等要求。

4.在第43条第5款所述的报告中,欧洲保险与职业养老金管理局应将其已发布的指引或建议通知欧洲议会、欧盟理事会和欧盟委员会,列明未遵循上述指引和建议的主管部门,并简要说明欧洲保险与职业养老金管理局计划如何确保所涉主管部门未来切实遵循其建议和指引。

第17条　违反欧盟法律

1.对于第1条第2款所述法律文件,包括依照第10条至第15条的规定制定的监管性技术标准和实施性技术标准,某主管部门未予适用,或者似以违反欧盟法律的方式适用,尤其是未能确保金融机构满足该等法律文件所列要求的,欧洲保险与职业养老金管理局应依照本条第2款、第3款和第6款授予的权力行事。

2. Upon a request from one or more competent authorities, the European Parliament, the Council, the Commission or the relevant stakeholder group, or on its own initiative and after having informed the competent authority concerned, the Authority may investigate the alleged breach or non-application of Union law.

Without prejudice to the powers laid down in Article 35, the competent authority shall, without delay, provide the Authority with all information which the Authority considers necessary for its investigation.

3. The Authority may, not later than 2 months from initiating its investigation, address a recommendation to the competent authority concerned setting out the action necessary to comply with Union law.

The competent authority shall, within ten working days of receipt of the recommendation, inform the Authority of the steps it has taken or intends to take to ensure compliance with Union law.

4. Where the competent authority has not complied with Union law within 1 month from receipt of the Authority's recommendation, the Commission may, after having been informed by the Authority, or on its own initiative, issue a formal opinion requiring the competent authority to take the action necessary to comply with Union law. The Commission's formal opinion shall take into account the Authority's recommendation.

The Commission shall issue such a formal opinion no later than 3 months after the adoption of the recommendation. The Commission may extend this period by 1 month.

The Authority and the competent authorities shall provide the Commission with all necessary information.

5. The competent authority shall, within ten working days of receipt of the formal opinion referred to in paragraph 4, inform the Commission and the Authority of the steps it has taken or intends to take to comply with that formal opinion.

6. Without prejudice to the powers of the Commission under Article 258 TFEU, where a competent authority does not comply with the formal opinion referred to in paragraph 4 within the period of time specified therein, and where it is necessary to remedy in a timely manner such non-compliance in order to maintain or restore neutral conditions of competition in the market or ensure the orderly functioning and integrity of the financial system, the Authority may, where the relevant requirements of the acts referred to in Article 1(2) are directly applicable to financial institutions, adopt an individual decision addressed to a financial institution requiring the necessary action to comply with its obligations under Union law including the cessation of any practice.

The decision of the Authority shall be in conformity with the formal opinion issued by the Commission pursuant to paragraph 4.

7. Decisions adopted under paragraph 6 shall prevail over any previous decision

2.欧洲保险与职业养老金管理局可经一个或多个主管部门、欧洲议会、欧盟理事会、欧盟委员会或相关利益相关者小组请求对涉嫌违反或不适用欧盟法律的情况进行调查,亦可主动进行调查,但调查应提前通知所涉主管部门。

在不影响第35条所规定的权力的情况下,主管部门应按照欧洲保险与职业养老金管理局的要求立即向其提供调查所必要的一切信息。

3.欧洲保险与职业养老金管理局可在启动调查后2个月内向所涉主管部门提出建议,提出为遵循欧盟法律所需采取的行动。

主管部门应在收到建议后10个工作日内通知欧洲保险与职业养老金管理局其为遵循欧盟法律而已采取或有意采取的措施。

4.主管部门在收到欧洲保险与职业养老金管理局建议1个月内仍未遵守欧盟法律的,欧盟委员会可在接到欧洲保险与职业养老金管理局通知后发布正式意见,亦可主动发布正式意见,要求主管部门采取必要的行动以遵守欧盟法律。欧盟委员会的正式意见应考虑欧洲保险与职业养老金管理局的建议。

欧盟委员会应最迟于建议通过后3个月(含)内发布上述正式意见。欧盟委员会可将此期限延长1个月。

欧洲保险与职业养老金管理局和主管部门应向欧盟委员会提供所有必要信息。

5.主管部门应在收到第4款所述正式意见后10个工作日内通知欧盟委员会和欧洲保险与职业养老金管理局其为遵循该正式意见而已采取或有意采取的措施。

6.在不影响欧盟委员会在《欧洲联盟运行条约》第258条中的权力的情况下,某主管部门未在第4款所述正式意见确定的期限内遵循该正式意见,且有必要及时对上述不遵循进行补救以维持或恢复市场的竞争中立性或确保金融系统的有序运行和诚信度的,欧洲保险与职业养老金管理局可在第1条第2款所述法律文件的相关要求可直接适用于金融机构的情况下,针对金融机构作出个别决定,要求其采取必要的行动以履行其在欧盟法律中的义务,包括停办任何业务。

欧洲保险与职业养老金管理局的决定应与欧盟委员会根据第4款所发布的正式意见一致。

7.根据第6款所作出的决定应优先适用于主管部门之前就相同事宜所作出的

adopted by the competent authorities on the same matter.

When taking action in relation to issues which are subject to a formal opinion pursuant to paragraph 4 or a decision pursuant to paragraph 6, competent authorities shall comply with the formal opinion or the decision, as the case may be.

8. In the report referred to in Article 43(5), the Authority shall set out which competent authorities and financial institutions have not complied with the formal opinions or decisions referred to in paragraphs 4 and 6 of this Article.

Article 18 Action in emergency situations

1. In the case of adverse developments which may seriously jeopardise the orderly functioning and integrity of financial markets or the stability of the whole or part of the financial system in the Union, the Authority shall actively facilitate and, where deemed necessary, coordinate any actions undertaken by the relevant national competent supervisory authorities.

In order to be able to perform that facilitating and coordinating role, the Authority shall be fully informed of any relevant developments, and shall be invited to participate as an observer in any relevant gathering by the relevant national competent supervisory authorities.

2. The Council, in consultation with the Commission and the ESRB and, where appropriate, the ESAs, may adopt a decision addressed to the Authority, determining the existence of an emergency situation for the purposes of this Regulation, following a request by the Authority, the Commission or the ESRB. The Council shall review that decision at appropriate intervals and at least once a month. If the decision is not renewed at the end of a one-month period, it shall automatically expire. The Council may declare the discontinuation of the emergency situation at any time.

Where the ESRB or the Authority considers that an emergency situation may arise, it shall issue a confidential recommendation addressed to the Council and provide it with an assessment of the situation. The Council shall then assess the need for a meeting. In that process, due care of confidentiality shall be guaranteed.

If the Council determines the existence of an emergency situation, it shall duly inform the European Parliament and the Commission without delay.

3. Where the Council has adopted a decision pursuant to paragraph 2, and in exceptional circumstances where coordinated action by national authorities is necessary to respond to adverse developments which may seriously jeopardise the orderly functioning and integrity of financial markets or the stability of the whole or part of the financial system in the Union, the Authority may adopt individual decisions requiring competent authorities to take the necessary action in accordance with the legislation referred to in Article 1(2) to address any such developments by ensuring that financial institutions and

决定。

针对第4款下的正式意见或第6款下的决定涉及的问题采取行动时，主管部门应严格遵循相关的正式意见或决定（视具体情况而定）。

8.在第43条第5款所述的报告中，欧洲保险与职业养老金管理局应列出未遵循本条第4款所述的正式意见或第6款所述的决定的主管部门和金融机构。

第18条　紧急情况下的行动

1.如果发生可能严重危害欧盟金融市场有序运行和诚信度或整个或部分欧盟金融系统稳定的不利变化状况，则欧洲保险与职业养老金管理局应积极促进并在其认为必要时协调相关的国家级监管主管部门采取的任何行动。

为了能够起到促进和协调的作用，欧洲保险与职业养老金管理局应充分知悉任何相关的变化情况，并获邀作为观察员参加相关的国家级监管主管部门的任何相关集会。

2.经欧洲保险与职业养老金管理局、欧盟委员会或欧洲系统性风险委员会请求，欧盟理事会可在与欧盟委员会和欧洲系统性风险委员会磋商以及在适当时与各欧洲监管机构磋商后，向欧洲保险与职业养老金管理局发出决定，以确定是否存在本条例所指的紧急情况。欧盟理事会应以适当的频率并至少每月1次对该项决定进行审评。如1个月期限届满时决定未展延，则应自动失效。欧盟理事会可随时宣布紧急情况终止。

如欧洲系统性风险委员会或欧洲保险与职业养老金管理局认为可能会出现紧急情况，应向欧盟理事会发出保密建议，并附对紧急情况的评估。欧盟理事会随后应判断是否有必要召开会议。在该过程中保密的注意义务应得到遵守。

欧盟理事会判定存在紧急情况的，应立即向欧洲议会和欧盟委员会发出通知。

3.欧盟理事会已经作出第2款中的决定，并且为应对可严重危害欧盟金融市场有序运行和诚信度或整个或部分金融系统稳定的不利变化而有必要协调国家级监管机构的行动的，欧洲保险与职业养老金管理局可作出个别决定，要求主管部门按照第1条第2款所述立法采取必要的行动，以确保金融机构和主管部门符合该等立法的要求，以应对上述不利变化。

competent authorities satisfy the requirements laid down in that legislation.

4. Without prejudice to the powers of the Commission under Article 258 TFEU, where a competent authority does not comply with the decision of the Authority referred to in paragraph 3 within the period laid down in that decision, the Authority may, where the relevant requirements laid down in the legislative acts referred to in Article 1 (2) including in regulatory technical standards and implementing technical standards adopted in accordance with those acts are directly applicable to financial institutions, adopt an individual decision addressed to a financial institution requiring the necessary action to comply with its obligations under that legislation, including the cessation of any practice. This shall apply only in situations in which a competent authority does not apply the legislative acts referred to in Article 1(2), including regulatory technical standards and implementing technical standards adopted in accordance with those acts, or applies them in a way which appears to be a manifest breach of those acts, and where urgent remedying is necessary to restore the orderly functioning and integrity of financial markets or the stability of the whole or part of the financial system in the Union.

5. Decisions adopted under paragraph 4 shall prevail over any previous decision adopted by the competent authorities on the same matter.

Any action by the competent authorities in relation to issues which are subject to a decision pursuant to paragraph 3 or 4 shall be compatible with those decisions.

Article 19 Settlement of disagreements between competent authorities in cross-border situations

1. Without prejudice to the powers laid down in Article 17, where a competent authority disagrees about the procedure or content of an action or inaction of a competent authority of another Member State in cases specified in the acts referred to in Article 1 (2), the Authority, at the request of one or more of the competent authorities concerned, may assist the authorities in reaching an agreement in accordance with the procedure set out in paragraphs 2 to 4 of this Article.

In cases specified in the legislation referred to in Article 1(2), and where on the basis of objective criteria, disagreement between competent authorities from different Member States can be determined, the Authority may, on its own initiative, assist the authorities in reaching an agreement in accordance with the procedure set out in paragraphs 2 to 4.

2. The Authority shall set a time limit for conciliation between the competent authorities taking into account any relevant time periods specified in the acts referred to in Article 1(2) and the complexity and urgency of the matter. At that stage the Authority shall act as a mediator.

3. If the competent authorities concerned fail to reach an agreement within the

4.在不影响欧盟委员会在《欧洲联盟运行条约》第258条中的权力的情况下，第3款所述的欧洲保险与职业养老金管理局的决定未在该决定规定的时限内为某主管部门所遵守的，欧洲保险与职业养老金管理局可对金融机构作出个别决定，要求其采取必要的行动（包括停办任何业务），以遵循其在该立法中的义务，前提是第1条第2款所述法律的相关要求以及据其通过的相关监管性技术标准和实施性技术标准所规定的相关要求能够直接适用于金融机构。上述规定仅适用于下列情况：对于第1条第2款所述框架立法，包括根据该等框架立法通过的相关监管性技术标准和实施性技术标准，某主管部门未予适用，或者似以明显违反欧盟法律的方式适用，并且有必要作出紧急补救以恢复欧盟金融市场的有序运行和诚信度或整个或部分欧盟金融系统的稳定。

5.根据第4款作出的决定应优先适用于主管部门之前就相同事宜所作出的任何决定。

主管部门就第3款或第4款中的决定所涉问题采取的任何行动均应符合该等决定。

第19条　跨境情况下主管部门之间分歧的解决

1.在不影响第17条所规定的权力的情况下，某主管部门对另一成员国主管部门在第1条第2款所述法律文件规定的情况下采取的行动或不采取行动所依据的程序或相关内容有异议的，经一个或多个所涉主管部门请求，欧洲保险与职业养老金管理局可协助各部门依照本条第2款至第4款规定的程序达成一致。

在第1条第2款所述立法规定的情况下，不同成员国主管部门之间的分歧可以基于客观的标准予以判定的，欧洲保险与职业养老金管理局可主动协助各部门依照第2款至第4款规定的程序达成一致。

2.欧洲保险与职业养老金管理局应在考虑到第1条第2款所述法律文件规定的任何相关期限以及所涉事项的复杂性和紧迫性后，为主管部门之间的调解设定时限。在该阶段欧洲保险与职业养老金管理局应作为调解者行事。

3.所涉主管部门未在第2款所述的调解期达成一致的，欧洲保险与职业养老金管

conciliation phase referred to in paragraph 2, the Authority may, in accordance with the procedure set out in the third and fourth subparagraph of Article 44(1) take a decision requiring them to take specific action or to refrain from action in order to settle the matter, with binding effects for the competent authorities concerned, in order to ensure compliance with Union law.

4. Without prejudice to the powers of the Commission under Article 258 TFEU, where a competent authority does not comply with the decision of the Authority, and thereby fails to ensure that a financial institution complies with requirements directly applicable to it by virtue of the acts referred to in Article 1(2), the Authority may adopt an individual decision addressed to a financial institution requiring the necessary action to comply with its obligations under Union law, including the cessation of any practice.

5. Decisions adopted under paragraph 4 shall prevail over any previous decision adopted by the competent authorities on the same matter. Any action by the competent authorities in relation to facts which are subject to a decision pursuant to paragraph 3 or 4 shall be compatible with those decisions.

6. In the report referred to in Article 50(2), the Chairperson of the Authority shall set out the nature and type of disagreements between competent authorities, the agreements reached and the decisions taken to settle such disagreements.

Article 20 Settlement of disagreements between competent authorities across sectors

The Joint Committee shall, in accordance with the procedure laid down in Article 19 and Article 56, settle cross-sectoral disagreements that may arise between competent authorities as defined in Article 4(2) of this Regulation, of Regulation (EU) No 1093/2010 and of Regulation (EU) No 1095/2010 respectively.

Article 21 Colleges of supervisors

1. The Authority shall contribute to promoting and monitoring the efficient, effective and consistent functioning of the colleges of supervisors referred to in Directive 2009/138/EC and foster the coherence of the application of Union law among the colleges of supervisors. With the objective of converging supervisory best practices, staff from the Authority shall be able to participate in the activities of the colleges of supervisors, including on-site examinations, carried out jointly by two or more competent authorities.

2. The Authority shall lead in ensuring a consistent and coherent functioning of colleges of supervisors for cross-border institutions across the Union, taking account of the systemic risk posed by financial institutions referred to in Article 23.

For the purpose of this paragraph and of paragraph 1 of this Article, the Authority shall be considered a 'competent authority' within the meaning of the relevant legislation.

The Authority may:

理局可依照第44条第1款第3项和第4项规定的程序作出决定，要求所涉主管部门采取特定行动或不采取行动来解决有关问题，以确保其遵守欧盟法律，该决定对所涉主管部门均具有约束效力。

4.在不影响欧盟委员会在《欧洲联盟运行条约》第258条中的权力的情形下，如果某主管部门不遵循欧洲保险与职业养老金管理局的决定，因而无法确保金融机构遵守第1条第2款所述法律文件中可直接适用于该金融机构的要求，则欧洲保险与职业养老金管理局可针对该金融机构作出个别决定，要求其采取必要的行动，包括停办任何业务，以遵守其在欧盟法律中的义务。

5.根据第4款作出的决定应优先适用于主管部门之前就相同事宜所作出的任何决定。主管部门就第3款或第4款中的决定所涉问题采取的任何行动均应符合该等决定。

6.在第50条第2款所述的报告中，欧洲保险与职业养老金管理局的主席应说明主管部门之间分歧的性质和类型、达成的一致意见以及为解决该等分歧而作出的决定。

第20条　跨行业主管部门分歧的解决

联合委员会应根据第19条和第56条规定的程序解决本条例、第1093/2010号(欧盟)条例以及第1095/2010号(欧盟)条例各自第4条第2款所界定的主管部门之间的跨行业分歧。

第21条　监管团

1.欧洲保险与职业养老金管理局应致力于推动并监控第2009/138/EC号指令所述监管团一致的且兼具效率和成效的运行，并促使各监管团在适用欧盟法律时保持一致性。为达到最佳监管实践趋同之目的，欧洲保险与职业养老金管理局的工作人员应能参加监管团的活动，包括由2个或多个主管部门共同进行的现场检查。

2.欧洲保险与职业养老金管理局在考虑到第23条所述金融机构所产生的系统性风险的前提下，应在确保监管团对欧盟各跨境机构的监管发挥相互一致的功能中起到领导作用。

就本款以及本条第1款而言，欧洲保险与职业养老金管理局应被视为相关立法所定义的“主管部门”。

欧洲保险与职业养老金管理局可：

(a) collect and share all relevant information in cooperation with the competent authorities in order to facilitate the work of the college and establish and manage a central system to make such information accessible to the competent authorities in the college;

(b) initiate and coordinate Union-wide stress tests in accordance with Article 32 to assess the resilience of financial institutions, in particular the systemic risk posed by financial institutions as referred to in Article 23, to adverse market developments, and evaluate the potential for systemic risk to increase in situations of stress, ensuring that a consistent methodology is applied at the national level to such tests and, where appropriate, address a recommendation to the competent authority to correct issues identified in the stress test;

(c) promote effective and efficient supervisory activities, including evaluating the risks to which financial institutions are or might be exposed as determined under the supervisory review process or in stress situations;

(d) oversee, in accordance with the tasks and powers specified in this Regulation, the tasks carried out by the competent authorities; and

(e) request further deliberations of a college in any cases where it considers that the decision would result in an incorrect application of Union law or would not contribute to the objective of convergence of supervisory practices. It may also require the group supervisor to schedule a meeting of the college or add a point to the agenda of a meeting.

3. The Authority may develop draft regulatory and implementing technical standards to ensure uniform conditions of application with respect to the provisions regarding the operational functioning of colleges of supervisors and issue guidelines and recommendations adopted under Article 16 to promote convergence in supervisory functioning and best practices adopted by the colleges of supervisors.

4. The Authority shall have a legally binding mediation role to resolve disputes between competent authorities in accordance with the procedure set out in Article 19. The Authority may take supervisory decisions directly applicable to the institution concerned in accordance with Article 19.

Article 22 General provisions

1. The Authority shall duly consider systemic risk as defined by Regulation (EU) No 1092/2010. It shall address any risk of disruption in financial services that:

(a) is caused by an impairment of all or parts of the financial system; and

(b) has the potential to have serious negative consequences for internal market and the real economy.

The Authority shall consider, where appropriate, the monitoring and assessment of systemic risk as developed by the ESRB and the Authority and respond to warnings and

（a）与主管部门合作收集并共享所有相关信息，以推进监管团的工作，以及建立和管理一个中央信息系统，使监管团中的各主管部门能够查阅上述信息；

（b）根据第32条启动并协调欧盟范围内的压力测试，以评估金融机构在不利市场变化下的抗冲击能力，特别是评估第23条所述金融机构产生的系统性风险；评估在压力状况下系统性风险增加的可能性，确保各成员国实施该等测试的方法相互一致，以及在适当时向主管部门提出更正压力测试中发现的问题的建议；

（c）推广高效率和高成效的监管活动，包括评估在监管审查过程中确定的、金融机构正在或可能面临的风险或金融机构在压力状况下正在或可能面临的风险；

（d）根据本条例所规定的职责和权力，对主管部门履行职责的情况进行监控；及

（e）在其认为某监管团的决定会导致欧盟法律的不正确适用或不利于监管实践趋同目的的任何情况下，要求该监管团进一步审议该决定。欧洲保险与职业养老金管理局还可要求集团监管机构为监管团安排会议或增加会议议程。

3.欧洲保险与职业养老金管理局可起草监管性和实施性技术标准草案以确保有关监管团具体运作的条款具有统一的适用条件，并发布根据第16条所制定的指引和建议，以推动各监管团的监管运作方式以及所采用的最佳实践的趋同。

4.欧洲保险与职业养老金管理局应在依照第19条规定的程序解决主管部门之间的争议中发挥具有法律约束力的调解作用。根据第19条，欧洲保险与职业养老金管理局可作出直接适用于所涉机构的监管决定。

第22条　一般条款

1.欧洲保险与职业养老金管理局应充分考虑第1092/2010号（欧盟）条例所界定的系统性风险。欧洲保险与职业养老金管理局应处理符合下列条件的任何金融系统发生扰乱的风险：

（a）由整个或部分金融系统的损害所造成的；并且

（b）可能会对欧盟内部市场和实体经济造成严重负面后果的。

欧洲保险与职业养老金管理局应适时考虑由欧洲系统性风险委员会和欧洲保险与职业养老金管理局所进行的系统性风险监控和评估，并按照第1092/2010号（欧盟）

recommendations by the ESRB in accordance with Article 17 of Regulation (EU) No 1092/2010.

2. The Authority shall, in collaboration with the ESRB, and in accordance with Article 23(1), develop a common approach to the identification and measurement of systemic importance, including quantitative and qualitative indicators as appropriate.

These indicators shall be a critical element in the determination of appropriate supervisory actions. The Authority shall monitor the degree of convergence in the determinations made, with a view to promoting a common approach.

3. Without prejudice to the acts referred to in Article 1(2), the Authority shall draw up, as necessary, additional guidelines and recommendations for financial institutions, to take account of the systemic risk posed by them.

The Authority shall ensure that the systemic risk posed by financial institutions is taken into account when developing draft regulatory and implementing technical standards in the areas laid down in the legislative acts referred to in Article 1(2).

4. Upon a request from one or more competent authorities, the European Parliament, the Council or the Commission, or on its own initiative, the Authority may conduct an inquiry into a particular type of financial institution or type of product or type of conduct in order to assess potential threats to the stability of the financial system and make appropriate recommendations for action to the competent authorities concerned.

For those purposes, the Authority may use the powers conferred on it under this Regulation, including Article 35.

5. The Joint Committee shall ensure overall and cross-sectoral coordination of the activities carried out in accordance with this Article.

Article 23 Identification and measurement of systemic risk

1. The Authority shall, in consultation with the ESRB, develop criteria for the identification and measurement of systemic risk and an adequate stress testing regime which includes an evaluation of the potential for systemic risk that may be posed by financial institutions to increase in situations of stress.

The Authority shall develop an adequate stress testing regime to help identify those financial institutions that may pose a systemic risk. These institutions shall be subject to strengthened supervision, and where necessary, to the recovery and resolution procedures referred to in Article 25.

2. The Authority shall take fully into account the relevant international approaches when developing the criteria for the identification and measurement of systemic risk that may be posed by insurance, re-insurance and occupational pensions institutions, including those established by the Financial Stability Board, the International Monetary Fund, the International Association of Insurance Supervisors and the Bank for International

条例第17条对欧洲系统性风险委员会所提出的预警和建议作出回应。

2.根据第23条第1款,欧洲保险与职业养老金管理局应与欧洲系统性风险委员会合作,制定用以识别和计量系统重要性的通用方法,包括制定适当的定量和定性指标。

该等指标应为决定监管行动是否适当的关键要素。欧洲保险与职业养老金管理局应出于推广通用方法之目的监控所作决定的趋同程度。

3.在不影响第1条第2款所述法律文件的情况下,在必要时,欧洲保险与职业养老金管理局应考虑金融机构所带来的系统性风险,就其起草额外的指引和建议。

在第1条第2款所述框架立法所规定的领域起草监管性和实施性技术标准草案时,欧洲保险与职业养老金管理局应确保已考虑了金融机构所带来的系统性风险。

4.欧洲保险与职业养老金管理局可经一个或多个主管部门、欧洲议会、欧盟理事会或欧盟委员会请求对某一特定类型的金融机构或产品或行为进行调查,亦可主动进行调查,以评估对金融系统稳定的潜在威胁,并对所涉主管部门提出适当的行动建议。

欧洲保险与职业养老金管理局可为该等目的行使本条例(包括第35条)授予的权力。

5.联合委员会应确保根据本条所开展的活动的全面和跨行业协调。

第23条　识别和计量系统性风险

1.欧洲保险与职业养老金管理局应与欧洲系统性风险委员会磋商,制定识别和计量系统性风险的标准,并建立完善的压力测试机制,该机制应包含对于压力状况下金融机构系统性风险增加的可能性的评估。

欧洲保险与职业养老金管理局应建立完善的压力测试机制,以便识别可能带来系统性风险的金融机构。应加强对此等机构的监管,并在必要时对其适用第25条所述的恢复和清盘程序。

2.在制定识别和计量保险、再保险和职业养老金管理机构系统性风险的标准时,欧洲保险与职业养老金管理局应充分考虑相关国际处理方法,包括金融稳定委员会、国际货币基金组织、国际保险监管机构协会以及国际清算银行所制定的方法。

Settlements.

Article 24 Permanent capacity to respond to systemic risks

1. The Authority shall ensure it has specialised and ongoing capacity to respond effectively to the materialisation of systemic risks as referred to in Articles 22 and 23, in particular with respect to institutions that pose a systemic risk.

2. The Authority shall fulfil the tasks conferred upon it in this Regulation and in the legislation referred to in Article 1(2), and shall contribute to ensuring a coherent and coordinated crisis management and resolution regime in the Union.

Article 25 Recovery and resolution procedures

1. The Authority shall contribute to and participate actively in the development and coordination of effective and consistent recovery and resolution plans, procedures in emergency situations and preventive measures to minimise the systemic impact of any failure.

2. The Authority may identify best practices aimed at facilitating the resolution of failing institutions and, in particular, cross-border groups, in ways which avoid contagion, ensuring that appropriate tools, including sufficient resources, are available and allow the institution or the group to be resolved in an orderly, cost-efficient and timely manner.

3. The Authority may develop regulatory and implementing technical standards as specified in the legislative acts referred to in Article 1(2) in accordance with the procedure laid down in Articles 10 to 15.

Article 26 Development of a European network of national insurance guarantee schemes

The Authority may contribute to the assessment of the need for a European network of national insurance guarantee schemes which is adequately funded and sufficiently harmonised.

Article 27 Crisis prevention, management and resolution

The Authority may be requested by the Commission to contribute to the assessment referred to in Article 242 of Directive 2009/138/EC, in particular as regards the cooperation of supervisory authorities within, and functionality of, colleges of supervisors; the supervisory practices concerning setting the capital add-ons; the assessment of the benefit of enhancing group supervision and capital management within a group of insurance or reinsurance undertakings, including possible measures to enhance a sound cross-border management of insurance groups, in particular in respect of risks and asset management; and may report on any new developments and progress concerning:

(a) a harmonised framework for early intervention;

(b) practices in centralised group risk management and functioning of group internal models including stress testing;

第24条　持续应对系统性风险的能力

1.欧洲保险与职业养老金管理局应确保有专门和持续的能力对第22条和第23条所述系统性风险的具体结果特别是对产生系统性风险的机构作出有效回应。

2.欧洲保险与职业养老金管理局应履行本条例以及第1条第2款所述立法赋予的职责,并应致力于确保欧盟具备相互一致和协调的危机管理和清盘机制。

第25条　恢复和清盘程序

1.欧洲保险与职业养老金管理局应促进并积极参与下列各项的制定和协调工作:紧急情况下有效、一致的恢复和清盘计划和程序,以及将任何金融机构倒闭的系统性影响降到最低的预防性措施。

2.欧洲保险与职业养老金管理局可识别旨在以避免风险传播的方式促进濒临倒闭机构(尤其是跨境集团)清盘的最佳实践,以确保有适当的工具(包括充分资源)可供使用,保障能以有序且有成本效益的方式及时对机构或者集团进行清盘。

3.欧洲保险与职业养老金管理局可依照第10条至第15条规定的程序,制定第1条第2款所述框架立法指明的监管性和实施性技术标准。

第26条　建立欧洲国家级保险担保计划体系

欧洲保险与职业养老金管理局可致力于评估建立资金充裕和充分协调一致的欧洲国家级保险担保计划体系的必要。

第27条　危机预防、管理和清盘

欧盟委员会可要求欧洲保险与职业养老金管理局致力于第2009/138/EC号指令第242条所述的评估,特别是与监管团内监管机构的合作以及监管团的功能有关的评估;致力于与要求资本追加有关的监管实践;致力于评估加强保险或再保险公司集团内的集团监管和资本管理的益处,包括加强对保险集团的良好跨境管理特别是风险和资产管理的可能的措施;并可对下列事项的任何新发展和进展作出报告:

(a)早期干预框架的协调一致;

(b)统一的集团风险管理实践以及集团内部模型(包括压力测试)的运作;

(c) intra-group transactions and risk concentrations;

(d) the behaviour of diversification and concentration effects over time;

(e) a harmonised framework for asset transferability, insolvency and winding-up procedures which eliminates the relevant national company or corporate law barriers to asset transferability;

(f) an equivalent level of protection of policy holders and beneficiaries of the undertakings of the same group, particularly in crisis situations;

(g) a harmonised and adequately funded Union-wide solution for insurance guarantee schemes.

Having regard to point (f), the Authority may also report on any new developments and progress concerning a set of coordinated national crisis management arrangements and including the necessity or otherwise of a system of coherent and credible funding mechanisms, with appropriate financing instruments.

The review of this Regulation provided for in Article 81 shall, in particular, examine the possible enhancement of the role of the Authority in a framework of crisis prevention, management and resolution.

Article 28 Delegation of tasks and responsibilities

1. Competent authorities may, with the consent of the delegate, delegate tasks and responsibilities to the Authority or other competent authorities subject to the conditions set out in this Article. Member States may set out specific arrangements regarding the delegation of responsibilities that have to be complied with before their competent authorities enter into such delegation agreements, and may limit the scope of delegation to what is necessary for the effective supervision of cross-border financial institutions or groups.

2. The Authority shall stimulate and facilitate the delegation of tasks and responsibilities between competent authorities by identifying those tasks and responsibilities that can be delegated or jointly exercised and by promoting best practices.

3. The delegation of responsibilities shall result in the reallocation of competences laid down in the acts referred to in Article 1(2). The law of the delegate authority shall govern the procedure, enforcement and administrative and judicial review relating to the delegated responsibilities.

4. The competent authorities shall inform the Authority of delegation agreements into which they intend to enter. They shall put the agreements into effect at the earliest 1 month after informing the Authority.

The Authority may give an opinion on the intended agreement within 1 month of being informed.

The Authority shall publish, by appropriate means, any delegation agreement as

(c)集团内部交易和风险集中；
(d)分散和集中行为随时间推移产生的影响；
(e)有关资产可转让性、资不抵债和停业清理程序方面协调一致的框架，该框架消除了相关成员国公司法对资产可转让性所构成的障碍；

(f)尤其在出现危机时，对同一集团下属各公司保户和受益人的同等水平的保护；

(g)欧盟范围内协调一致且资金充足的保险担保计划解决方案。

根据第f目，欧洲保险与职业养老金管理局还可报告与成员国在危机管理方面作出的各种协调的国家级安排有关的任何新发展和进展，包括建立具有适当融资工具的相互连贯并可信的经费筹措机制的必要性。

根据第81条规定对本条例进行审评时，应特别审查欧洲保险与职业养老金管理局在危机预防、管理和清盘框架中发挥的作用能否有所加强。

第28条　职责和责任的委托

1.经受托人同意，主管部门可按本条所列条件将职责和责任委托给欧洲保险与职业养老金管理局或其他主管部门。成员国可规定在其主管部门达成上述委托协议前所应遵循的责任委托的特殊安排，并可将委托范围限定在对跨境金融机构或集团进行有效监管必要的范围内。

2.欧洲保险与职业养老金管理局应通过识别可以委托或可以共同履行的职责和责任以及推广最佳实践的方式，来促进和推动主管部门之间的职责和责任委托。

3.责任委托会产生第1条第2款所述法律文件所规定的职权的再分配。受托部门的法律应对与被委托的责任有关的程序、执法以及行政和司法审查进行规制。

4.主管部门应将其拟缔结的委托协议通知欧洲保险与职业养老金管理局。该等协议最早应在通知欧洲保险与职业养老金管理局1个月后生效。

欧洲保险与职业养老金管理局可在收到上述拟缔结的协议通知后的1个月内发表意见。

欧洲保险与职业养老金管理局应以适当的方式公布主管部门所缔结的任何委托

concluded by the competent authorities, in order to ensure that all parties concerned are informed appropriately.

Article 29 Common supervisory culture

1. The Authority shall play an active role in building a common Union supervisory culture and consistent supervisory practices, as well as in ensuring uniform procedures and consistent approaches throughout the Union. The Authority shall carry out, at a minimum, the following activities:

(a) providing opinions to competent authorities;

(b) promoting an effective bilateral and multilateral exchange of information between competent authorities, with full respect for the applicable confidentiality and data protection provisions provided for in the relevant Union legislation;

(c) contributing to developing high quality and uniform supervisory standards, including reporting standards, and international accounting standards in accordance with Article 1(3);

(d) reviewing the application of the relevant regulatory and implementing technical standards adopted by the Commission, and of the guidelines and recommendations issued by the Authority and proposing amendments where appropriate; and

(e) establishing sectoral and cross-sectoral training programmes, facilitating personnel exchanges and encouraging competent authorities to intensify the use of secondment schemes and other tools.

2. The Authority may, as appropriate, develop new practical instruments and convergence tools to promote common supervisory approaches and practices.

Article 30 Peer reviews of competent authorities

1. The Authority shall periodically organise and conduct peer reviews of some or all of the activities of competent authorities, to further strengthen consistency in supervisory outcomes. To that end, the Authority shall develop methods to allow for objective assessment and comparison between the authorities reviewed. When conducting peer reviews, existing information and evaluations already made with regard to the competent authority concerned shall be taken into account.

2. The peer review shall include an assessment of, but shall not be limited to:

(a) the adequacy of resources and governance arrangements of the competent authority, with particular regard to the effective application of the regulatory technical standards and implementing technical standards referred to in Articles 10 to 15 and of the acts referred to in Article 1(2) and the capacity to respond to market developments;

(b) the degree of convergence reached in the application of Union law and in supervisory practice, including regulatory technical standards and implementing technical standards, guidelines and recommendations adopted under Articles 10 to 16, and the

协议，以确保所涉各方均得到适当的通知。

第29条　共同的监管文化

1.欧洲保险与职业养老金管理局应在建立共同的欧盟监管文化和一致的监管实践以及确保欧盟有统一的程序和一致的方法中发挥积极的作用。欧洲保险与职业养老金管理局至少应开展下列活动：

(a)向主管部门提供意见；

(b)推进主管部门在充分遵守相关欧盟立法适用的保密和数据保护规定的前提下进行有效的双边或多边信息交流；

(c)根据第1条第3款的规定致力于制定高质量和统一的监管标准，包括报告标准，以及国际会计标准；

(d)审评欧盟委员会所通过的相关监管性和实施性技术标准以及欧洲保险与职业养老金管理局所发布的指引和建议的适用，并在适当时提出修改建议；及

(e)制定行业或跨行业培训计划，促进人员交流并鼓励主管部门更多地使用人员借调计划以及其他工具。

2.在适当情况下，欧洲保险与职业养老金管理局可开发新的实用工具和趋同手段来推广共同的监管方法和实践。

第30条　主管部门的同行审评

1.欧洲保险与职业养老金管理局应针对主管部门的部分或全部活动定期组织和开展同行审评，以进一步加强监管结果的一致性。为此，欧洲保险与职业养老金管理局应制定相关方法，以实现被审查部门之间的客观评价和比较。开展同行审评时，应考虑到与所涉主管部门有关的现有信息以及过去已作过的评价结果。

2.同行审评应包括但不限于下列方面的评价：

(a)主管部门资源和治理安排的充分性，特别是对于第10条至第15条所述监管性技术标准和实施性技术标准以及第1条第2款所述法律文件的有效适用而言是否充分，以及应对市场变化的能力；

(b)欧盟法律的适用以及监管实践(包括根据第10条至第16条制定的监管性技术标准和实施性技术标准、指引和建议)所达到的趋同程度，以及监管实践在多大程度上实现了欧盟法律设定的目标；

extent to which the supervisory practice achieves the objectives set out in Union law;

(c) best practices developed by some competent authorities which might be of benefit for other competent authorities to adopt;

(d) the effectiveness and the degree of convergence reached with regard to the enforcement of the provisions adopted in the implementation of Union law, including the administrative measures and sanctions imposed against persons responsible where those provisions have not been complied with.

3. On the basis of a peer review, the Authority may issue guidelines and recommendations pursuant to Article 16. In accordance with Article 16(3), the competent authorities shall endeavour to follow those guidelines and recommendations. The Authority shall take into account the outcome of the peer review when developing draft regulatory technical or implementing technical standards in accordance with Articles 10 to 15.

4. The Authority shall make the best practices that can be identified from those peer reviews publicly available. In addition, all other results of peer reviews may be disclosed publicly, subject to the agreement of the competent authority that is the subject of the peer review.

Article 31 Coordination function

The Authority shall fulfil a general coordination role between competent authorities, in particular in situations where adverse developments could potentially jeopardise the orderly functioning and integrity of financial markets or the stability of the financial system in the Union.

The Authority shall promote a coordinated Union response, inter alia, by:

(a) facilitating the exchange of information between the competent authorities;

(b) determining the scope and, where possible and appropriate, verifying the reliability of information that should be made available to all the competent authorities concerned;

(c) without prejudice to Article 19, carrying out non-binding mediation upon a request from the competent authorities or on its own initiative;

(d) notifying the ESRB of any potential emergency situations without delay;

(e) taking all appropriate measures in case of developments which may jeopardise the functioning of the financial markets with a view to facilitating the coordination of actions undertaken by relevant competent authorities;

(f) centralising information received from competent authorities in accordance with Articles 21 and 35 as the result of the regulatory reporting obligations for institutions active in more than oneMember State. The Authority shall share that information with the other competent authorities concerned.

(c)某些主管部门制定的可能值得其他主管部门采用的最佳实践；

(d)欧盟法律实施当中制定的规定，在执行时所达到的有效程度和趋同程度，包括发生违反该等规定的行为时对相关负责人施加的行政措施和处罚。

3.欧洲保险与职业养老金管理局可在同行审评的基础上依据第16条发布指引和建议。根据第16条第3款，主管部门应尽力遵循该等指引和建议。欧洲保险与职业养老金管理局在根据第10条至第15条的规定起草监管性和实施性技术标准草案时，应考虑同行审评的结果。

4.对于从该等同行审评中识别出的最佳实践，欧洲保险与职业养老金管理局应予公布。此外，在作为同行审评对象的主管部门同意披露的前提下，同行审评的所有其他结果也可向公众披露。

第31条　协调职能

欧洲保险与职业养老金管理局尤应在发生可能对欧盟金融市场有序运行和诚信度或金融系统稳定造成危害的不利变化时在主管部门之间发挥总协调作用。

欧洲保险与职业养老金管理局应通过相关措施促进欧盟内部相互协调的回应，包括但不限于：

(a)促进主管部门之间的信息交流；

(b)确定应向所有所涉主管部门提供的信息范围，在可能和适当时对其可靠性予以核实；

(c)在不影响第19条的情况下，经主管部门请求开展无约束力的调解，亦可主动开展调解；

(d)立即通知欧洲系统性风险委员会任何可能发生的紧急情况；

(e)在发生可能危害金融市场运行的变化时，采取所有适当的措施以为相关主管部门行动间的协调工作提供方便；

(f)根据第21条和第35条汇总从主管部门接收到的信息，此等信息为主管部门就在多个成员国境内开展业务的金融机构履行监管报告义务所形成的。欧洲保险与职业养老金管理局应与其他所涉主管部门共享该等信息。

Article 32 Assessment of market developments

1. The Authority shall monitor and assess market developments in the area of its competence and, where necessary, inform the European Supervisory Authority (European Banking Authority) and the European Supervisory Authority (European Securities and Markets Authority), the ESRB and the European Parliament, the Council and the Commission about the relevant micro-prudential trends, potential risks and vulnerabilities. The Authority shall include in its assessments an economic analysis of the markets in which financial institutions operate and an assessment of the impact of potential market developments on such institutions.

2. The Authority shall, in cooperation with the ESRB, initiate and coordinate Union-wide assessments of the resilience of financial institutions to adverse market developments. To that end, it shall develop the following, for application by the competent authorities:

(a) common methodologies for assessing the effect of economic scenarios on an institution's financial position;

(b) common approaches to communication on the outcomes of these assessments of the resilience of financial institutions;

(c) common methodologies for assessing the effect of particular products or distribution processes on an institution's financial position and on policyholders, pension scheme members, beneficiaries and customer information.

3. Without prejudice to the tasks of the ESRB set out in Regulation (EU) No 1092/2010, the Authority shall, at least once a year, and more frequently as necessary, provide assessments to the European Parliament, the Council, the Commission and the ESRB of trends, potential risks and vulnerabilities in its area of competence.

The Authority shall include a classification of the main risks and vulnerabilities in these assessments and, where necessary, recommend preventative or remedial actions.

4. The Authority shall ensure an adequate coverage of cross-sectoral developments, risks and vulnerabilities by closely cooperating with the European Supervisory Authority (European Banking Authority) and the European Supervisory Authority (European Securities and Markets Authority) through the Joint Committee.

Article 33 International relations

1. Without prejudice to the respective competences of the Member States and the Union institutions, the Authority may develop contacts and enter into administrative arrangements with supervisory authorities, international organisations and the administrations of third countries. Those arrangements shall not create legal obligations in respect of the Union and its Member States nor shall they prevent Member States and their competent authorities from concluding bilateral or multilateral arrangements with

第32条 对市场变化的评估

1.欧洲保险与职业养老金管理局应对其职权管辖范围内的市场变化进行监控和评估,并在必要时将相关的微观审慎趋势、潜在风险及薄弱环节通知两个欧洲监管机构(欧洲银行业管理局和欧洲证券与市场管理局)、欧洲系统性风险委员会以及欧洲议会、欧盟理事会和欧盟委员会。欧洲保险与职业养老金管理局的评估还应包括对金融机构所在市场的经济分析以及对该等机构受潜在市场变化影响的评估。

2.欧洲保险与职业养老金管理局应与欧洲系统性风险委员会合作,在欧盟范围内启动和协调对金融机构面临不利市场变化时的抗冲击能力的评估。为此,欧洲保险与职业养老金管理局应制定下列方式和方法供主管部门使用:

(a)评估不同的经济场景对金融机构财务状况影响的通用方法;

(b)对金融机构抗冲击能力评估结果进行交流所采用的通用方法;

(c)评估特殊产品或销售方法对金融机构的财务状况以及保单持有人、养老金计划成员、受益人和客户信息影响的通用方法。

3.在不影响欧洲系统性风险委员会在第1092/2010号(欧盟)条例中的职责的情况下,欧洲保险与职业养老金管理局应至少每年1次并在必要时更频繁地为欧洲议会、欧盟理事会、欧盟委员会和欧洲系统性风险委员会提供其职权管辖范围内对趋势、潜在风险和薄弱环节的评估结果。

欧洲保险与职业养老金管理局应在此等评估中对主要风险和薄弱环节进行分类,并在必要时提出预防或补救行动的建议。

4.欧洲保险与职业养老金管理局应通过联合委员会与两个欧洲监管机构(欧洲银行业管理局和欧洲证券与市场管理局)紧密合作,确保其监管工作充分覆盖跨行业变化、风险和薄弱环节。

第33条 国际关系

1.在不影响成员国和欧盟机构各自职权的情况下,欧洲保险与职业养老金管理局可与监管机构、国际组织以及第三国的行政管理部门建立联系并达成行政安排。该等安排既不得为欧盟及其成员国设定法律义务,也不得妨碍成员国及其主管部门与该等第三国缔结双边或多边安排。

those third countries.

2. The Authority shall assist in preparing equivalence decisions pertaining to supervisory regimes in third countries in accordance with the acts referred to in Article 1 (2).

3. In the report referred to in Article 43(5), the Authority shall set out the administrative arrangements agreed upon with international organisations or administrations in third countries and the assistance provided in preparing equivalence decisions.

Article 34 Other tasks

1. The Authority may, upon a request from the European Parliament, the Council or the Commission, or on its own initiative, provide opinions to the European Parliament, the Council and the Commission on all issues related to its area of competence.

2. With regard to prudential assessments of mergers and acquisitions falling within the scope of Directive 92/49/EEC and Directives 2002/83/EC and 2005/68/EC, as amended by Directive 2007/44/EC, and which, according to those Directives, require consultation between competent authorities from two or more Member States, the Authority may, on application of one of the competent authorities concerned, issue and publish an opinion on a prudential assessment, except in relation to the criteria in Article 15b(1)(e) of Directive 92/49/EEC, Article 15b(1)(e) of Directive 2002/83/EC and Article 19a (1)(e) of Directive 2005/68/EC. The opinion shall be issued promptly and in any event before the end of the assessment period in accordance with Directive 92/49/EEC and Directives 2002/83/EC and 2005/68/EC, as amended by Directive 2007/44/EC. Article 35 shall apply to the areas in respect of which the Authority may issue an opinion.

Article 35 Collection of information

1. At the request of the Authority, the competent authorities of the Member States shall provide the Authority with all the necessary information to carry out the duties assigned to it by this Regulation, provided that they have legal access to the relevant information and that the request for information is necessary in relation to the nature of the duty in question.

2. The Authority may also request information to be provided at recurring intervals and in specified formats. Such requests shall, where possible, be made using common reporting formats.

3. Upon a duly justified request from a competent authority of a Member State, the Authority may provide any information that is necessary to enable the competent authority to carry out its duties, in accordance with the professional secrecy obligations laid down in sectoral legislation and in Article 70.

4. Before requesting information in accordance with this Article and in order to avoid

2.根据第1条第2款所述法律文件,欧洲保险与职业养老金管理局应协助完成关于第三国监管体制的等效性决定。

3.在第43条第5款所述的报告中,欧洲保险与职业养老金管理局应列出与国际组织或第三国行政管理部门所缔结的行政安排以及在作出等效性决定中所提供的协助。

第34条　其他职责

1.经欧洲议会、欧盟理事会或欧盟委员会请求,欧洲保险与职业养老金管理局可就与其职权管辖范围内的一切有关的问题向欧洲议会、欧盟理事会和欧盟委员会提供意见,亦可自行提供该等意见。

2.对于在第92/49/EEC号指令和第2002/83/EC号指令与第2005/68/EC号指令(经第2007/44/EC号指令修正)范围内且根据该等指令需要两个或多个成员国主管部门进行磋商的并购,经其中一个所涉主管部门申请,欧洲保险与职业养老金管理局可发布并公开关于此类并购的审慎评估的意见,但是,涉及第92/49/EEC号指令第15b条第1款第e项、第2002/83/EC号指令第15b条第1款第e项以及第2005/68/EC号指令第19a条第1款第e项中的评估标准的情况除外。该等意见应迅速发布,并且任何情况下均应于第92/49/EEC号指令以及第2002/83/EC号指令与第2005/68/EC号指令(经第2007/44/EC号指令修正)规定的评估期限结束前发布。第35条适用于欧洲保险与职业养老金管理局可发布意见的领域。

第35条　信息的收集

1.经欧洲保险与职业养老金管理局请求,各成员国主管部门应向欧洲保险与职业养老金管理局提供履行其在本条例中的职责所必要的一切信息,前提是该等成员国主管部门能够合法查阅相关的信息,并且就所涉职责的性质而言信息请求是必要的。

2.欧洲保险与职业养老金管理局还可请求主管部门定期以指定的格式提供信息。如果可能,上述请求应使用通用的报告格式。

3.收到某成员国主管部门有正当理由的请求后,欧洲保险与职业养老金管理局可提供该主管部门履行职责所必要的任何信息,但须遵守行业立法以及第70条所规定的职业保密义务。

4.为了避免报告义务的重复,在根据本条规定提出信息请求前,欧洲保险与职业

the duplication of reporting obligations, the Authority shall take account of any relevant existing statistics produced and disseminated by the European Statistical System and the European System of Central Banks.

5. Where information is not available or is not made available by the competent authorities in a timely fashion, the Authority may address a duly justified and reasoned request to other supervisory authorities, to the ministry responsible for finance where it has at its disposal prudential information, to the national central bank or to the statistical office of the Member State concerned.

6. Where information is not available or is not made available under paragraph 1 or 5 in a timely fashion, the Authority may address a duly justified and reasoned request directly to the relevant financial institutions. The reasoned request shall explain why the information concerning the respective individual financial institutions is necessary.

The Authority shall inform the relevant competent authorities of requests in accordance with this paragraph and with paragraph 5.

At the request of the Authority, the competent authorities shall assist the Authority in collecting the information.

7. The Authority may use confidential information received under this Article only for the purposes of carrying out the duties assigned to it by this Regulation.

Article 36 Relationship with the ESRB

1. The Authority shall cooperate closely and on a regular basis with the ESRB.

2. The Authority shall provide the ESRB with regular and timely information necessary for the achievement of its tasks. Any data necessary for the achievement of its tasks that are not in summary or aggregate form shall be provided, without delay, to the ESRB upon a reasoned request, as specified in Article 15 of Regulation (EU) No 1092/2010. The Authority, in cooperation with the ESRB, shall have in place adequate internal procedures for the transmission of confidential information, in particular information regarding individual financial institutions.

3. The Authority shall, in accordance with paragraphs 4 and 5, ensure a proper follow-up to ESRB warnings and recommendations referred to in Article 16 of Regulation (EU) No 1092/2010.

4. On receipt of a warning or recommendation from the ESRB addressed to the Authority, the Authority shall convene a meeting of the Board of Supervisors without delay and assess the implications of such a warning or recommendation for the fulfilment of its tasks.

It shall decide, by the relevant decision-making procedure, on any actions to be taken in accordance with the powers conferred upon it by this Regulation for addressing

养老金管理局应参考由欧洲统计系统和欧洲中央银行体系提供和发布的任何现有的相关统计数据。

5.主管部门无法或未及时提供信息的,欧洲保险与职业养老金管理局可向所涉成员国的其他监管机构、财政部(如其掌握了审慎信息)、成员国中央银行或统计局提出有正当理由和经论证的信息请求。

6.未能获得信息或未能根据第1款或第5款及时获得信息的,欧洲保险与职业养老金管理局可直接向相关的金融机构提出有正当理由和经论证的信息请求。该等信息请求应说明需要各个相关金融机构提供信息的原因。

欧洲保险与职业养老金管理局应通知相关主管部门按照本款和第5款提出的请求。

经欧洲保险与职业养老金管理局请求,主管部门应协助欧洲保险与职业养老金管理局收集信息。

7.欧洲保险与职业养老金管理局仅可以出于履行本条例赋予其职责的目的使用根据本条接收到的保密信息。

第36条　与欧洲系统性风险委员会的关系

1.欧洲保险与职业养老金管理局应紧密并定期地与欧洲系统性风险委员会开展合作。

2.欧洲保险与职业养老金管理局应定期并及时地向欧洲系统性风险委员会提供完成其职责所必要的信息。按第1092/2010号(欧盟)条例第15条的规定,经欧洲系统性风险委员会合理请求,任何为完成其职责所必要的且非摘要或汇总格式的数据均应立即提供给欧洲系统性风险委员会。欧洲保险与职业养老金管理局应与欧洲系统性风险委员会合作,为保密信息特别是与具体金融机构有关的信息的发送设置充分的内部程序。

3.欧洲保险与职业养老金管理局应依照第4款和第5款确保对第1092/2010号(欧盟)条例第16条所述欧洲系统性风险委员会预警和建议进行恰当的跟进。

4.收到欧洲系统性风险委员会向欧洲保险与职业养老金管理局提出的预警或建议后,欧洲保险与职业养老金管理局应立即召开监管机构理事会会议,并对该预警或建议对于其履行职责的意义进行评估。

欧洲保险与职业养老金管理局依据本条例所授予的权力对预警和建议提出的问题采取任何行动的,应通过相关的决策程序作出决定。

the issues identified in the warnings and recommendations.

If the Authority does not act on a recommendation, it shall explain to the ESRB and the Council its reasons for not doing so.

5. On receipt of a warning or recommendation from the ESRB addressed to a competent national supervisory authority, the Authority shall, where relevant, use the powers conferred upon it by this Regulation to ensure a timely follow-up.

Where the addressee intends not to follow the recommendation of the ESRB, it shall inform and discuss with the Board of Supervisors its reasons for not acting.

The competent authority shall take due account of the views of the Board of Supervisors when informing the Council and the ESRB in accordance with Article 17 of Regulation (EU) No 1092/2010.

6. In discharging the tasks set out in this Regulation, the Authority shall take the utmost account of the warnings and recommendations of the ESRB.

Article 37 Insurance and Reinsurance Stakeholder Group and Occupational Pensions Stakeholder Group

1. To help facilitate consultation with stakeholders in areas relevant to the tasks of the Authority, an Insurance and Reinsurance Stakeholder Group and an Occupational Pensions Stakeholder Group shall be established (hereinafter collectively referred to as the 'Stakeholder Groups'). The Stakeholder Groups shall be consulted on actions taken in accordance with Articles 10 to 15 concerning regulatory technical standards and implementing technical standards, and, to the extent that these do not concern individual financial institutions, Article 16 concerning guidelines and recommendations. If actions must be taken urgently and consultation becomes impossible, the Stakeholder Groups shall be informed as soon as possible.

The Stakeholder Groups shall meet at least four times a year. They may, together, discuss areas of mutual interest and shall inform each other of the other issues being discussed.

Members of one stakeholder group may be also members of the other stakeholder group.

2. The Insurance and Reinsurance Stakeholder Group shall be composed of 30 members, representing in balanced proportions insurance and reinsurance undertakings and insurance intermediaries operating in the Union, and their employees' representatives, as well as consumers, users of insurance and reinsurance services, representatives of SMEs and representatives of relevant professional associations. At least five of its members shall be independent top-ranking academics. Ten of its members shall represent insurance undertakings, reinsurance undertakings or insurance intermediaries, three of whom shall represent cooperative and mutual insurers or reinsurers.

欧洲保险与职业养老金管理局不针对建议采取任何行动的，应向欧洲系统性风险委员会和欧盟理事会说明理由。

5.收到欧洲系统性风险委员会向国家级监管机构发出的预警或建议后，欧洲保险与职业养老金管理局应在适当时运用本条例所授予的权力确保及时采取跟进行动。

被建议方无意遵循欧洲系统性风险委员会的建议的，应通知监管机构理事会并与其讨论其不采取行动的理由。

主管部门应在根据第1092/2010号（欧盟）条例第17条通知欧盟理事会和欧洲系统性风险委员会时，充分考虑监管机构理事会的意见。

6.欧洲保险与职业养老金管理局在履行本条例所规定的职责时，应充分考虑欧洲系统性风险委员会的预警和建议。

第37条　保险和再保险利益相关者小组以及职业养老金利益相关者小组

1.为了便于就欧洲保险与职业养老金管理局职责相关领域征求利益相关者的意见，应设立一个保险和再保险利益相关者小组以及一个职业养老金利益相关者小组（以下统称利益相关者小组）。根据第10条至第15条的规定所采取的与监管性技术标准和实施性技术标准有关的行动，以及在不涉及具体金融机构的范围内根据第16条的规定所采取的与指引和建议有关的行动，均应征求利益相关者小组的意见。在必须采取紧急行动而不可能提前征求其意见的情况下，应尽早通知利益相关者小组。

利益相关者小组每年至少应召开4次会议，可以一起对存在共同利益的领域进行讨论，并应互相通知各自正在讨论的其他事宜。

其中一个利益相关者小组的成员可同时担任其他利益相关者小组的成员。

2.保险和再保险利益相关者小组应由30名成员组成，以平衡的比例代表在欧盟运营的保险和再保险公司以及保险中介机构、其员工代表以及消费者、保险和再保险服务用户、中小企业代表以及相关专业协会的代表。其中至少应有5名成员是独立的一流学者；应有10名成员代表保险公司、再保险公司或保险中介机构，其中3名代表合作和互助保险公司或再保险公司。

3. The Occupational Pensions Stakeholder Group shall be composed of 30 members, representing in balanced proportions institutions for occupational retirement provision operating in the Union, representatives of employees, representatives of beneficiaries, representatives of SMEs and representatives of relevant professional associations. At least five of its members shall be independent top-ranking academics. Ten of its members shall represent institutions for occupational retirement provision.

4. The members of the Stakeholder Groups shall be appointed by the Board of Supervisors, following proposals from the relevant stakeholders. In making its decision, the Board of Supervisors shall, to the extent possible, ensure an appropriate geographical and gender balance and representation of stakeholders across the Union.

5. The Authority shall provide all necessary information subject to professional secrecy as set out in Article 70 and ensure adequate secretarial support for the Stakeholder Groups. Adequate compensation shall be provided to members of the Stakeholder Groups representing non-profit organisations, excluding industry representatives. The Stakeholder Groups may establish working groups on technical issues. Members of the Stakeholder Groups shall serve for a period of two-and-a-half years, following which a new selection procedure shall take place.

The members of the Stakeholder Groups may serve two successive terms.

6. The Stakeholder Groups may submit opinions and advice to the Authority on any issue related to the tasks of the Authority with particular focus on the tasks set out in Articles 10 to 16, and Articles 29, 30 and 32.

7. The Stakeholder Groups shall adopt their rules of procedure on the basis of the agreement of a two-thirds majority of their respective members.

8. The Authority shall make public the opinions and advice of the Stakeholder Groups and the results of their consultations.

Article 38 Safeguards

1. The Authority shall ensure that no decision adopted under Articles 18 or 19 impinges in any way on the fiscal responsibilities of Member States.

2. Where a Member State considers that a decision taken under Article 19 (3) impinges on its fiscal responsibilities, it may notify the Authority and the Commission within 2 weeks after notification of the Authority's decision to the competent authority that the decision will not be implemented by the competent authority.

In its notification, the Member State shall clearly and specifically explain why and how the decision impinges on its fiscal responsibilities.

In the case of such notification, the decision of the Authority shall be suspended.

Within a period of 1 month from the notification by the Member State, the Authority

3.职业养老金利益相关者小组应由30名成员组成,以平衡的比例代表在欧盟运营的职业退休金管理机构、员工代表、受益人代表、中小企业代表以及相关专业协会的代表。其中至少应有5名成员是独立的一流学者;应有10名成员代表职业退休金管理机构。

4.利益相关者小组成员的人选应由监管机构理事会根据相关的利益相关者的提议任命。作出决定时,监管机构理事会应尽可能确保该利益相关者小组成员在欧盟范围内适当的地理分布平衡和性别平衡。

5.欧洲保险与职业养老金管理局应在遵循第70条规定的职业保密义务前提下为利益相关者小组提供一切必要信息,并确保为其提供充分的秘书支持。对利益相关者小组中代表非营利机构的成员(行业代表除外)提供充足的报酬。利益相关者小组可就技术性问题设立工作组。利益相关者小组成员的任期为两年半,任期结束后进行新一轮的遴选。

利益相关者小组的成员可连任2期。

6.利益相关者小组可针对与欧洲保险与职业养老金管理局职责(特别是第10条至第16条以及第29条、第30条和第32条所列职责)有关的任何问题向欧洲保险与职业养老金管理局呈报意见和建议。

7.利益相关者小组通过其程序规则时,应经2/3成员的同意。

8.欧洲保险与职业养老金管理局应公布利益相关者小组的意见和建议及其磋商结果。

第38条　保障措施

1.欧洲保险与职业养老金管理局应确保根据第18条或第19条作出的任何决定不会以任何方式对成员国的财政责任造成影响。

2.如有成员国认为根据第19条第3款作出的决定影响了其财政责任,则在欧洲保险与职业养老金管理局通知主管部门其决定后的2周内,该成员国可通知欧洲保险与职业养老金管理局和欧盟委员会该成员国将不实施该项决定。

成员国应在其通知中清楚具体地说明该项决定为何以及如何会影响其财政责任。

在成员国作出上述通知的情况下,欧洲保险与职业养老金管理局的决定应暂停执行。

欧洲保险与职业养老金管理局应在成员国发出通知后1个月内通知成员国是否

shall inform the Member State as to whether it maintains its decision or whether it amends or revokes it. If the decision is maintained or amended, the Authority shall state that fiscal responsibilities are not affected.

Where the Authority maintains its decision, the Council shall take a decision, by a majority of the votes cast, at one of its meetings not later than 2 months after the Authority has informed the Member State as set out in the fourth subparagraph, as to whether the Authority's decision is maintained.

Where the Council, after having considered the matter, does not take a decision to maintain the Authority's decision in accordance with the fifth subparagraph, the Authority's decision shall be terminated.

3. Where a Member State considers that a decision taken under Article 18 (3) impinges on its fiscal responsibilities, it may notify the Authority, the Commission and the Council, within three working days after notification of the Authority's decision to the competent authority, that the decision will not be implemented by the competent authority.

In its notification, the Member State shall clearly and specifically explain why and how the decision impinges on its fiscal responsibilities.

In the case of such notification, the decision of the Authority shall be suspended.

The Council shall, within ten working days, convene a meeting and take a decision, by a simple majority of its members, as to whether the Authority's decision is revoked.

Where the Council, after having considered the matter, does not take a decision to revoke the Authority's decision in accordance with the fourth subparagraph, the suspension of the Authority's decision shall be terminated.

4. Where the Council has taken a decision in accordance with paragraph 3 not to revoke a decision of the Authority relating to Article 18(3), and the Member State concerned still considers that the decision of the Authority impinges upon its fiscal responsibilities, that Member State may notify the Commission and the Authority and request the Council to re-examine the matter. The Member State concerned shall clearly set out the reasons for its disagreement with the decision of the Council.

Within a period of 4 weeks after the notification referred to in the first subparagraph, the Council shall confirm its original decision or take a new decision in accordance with paragraph 3.

The period of 4 weeks may be extended by four additional weeks by the Council, if the particular circumstances of the case so require.

5. Any abuse of this Article, in particular in relation to a decision by the Authority which does not have a significant or material fiscal impact, shall be prohibited as incompatible with the internal market.

维持决定还是修改或撤销决定。在维持或修改其决定的情形下，欧洲保险与职业养老金管理局应声明成员国的财政责任未受影响。

欧洲保险与职业养老金管理局维持其决定的，欧盟理事会应在欧洲保险与职业养老金管理局按第4项通知成员国之后2个月内召开的任何欧盟理事会会议中，通过多数票投票决定是否维持欧洲保险与职业养老金管理局的决定。

欧盟理事会经审议后未根据第5项决定维持欧洲保险与职业养老金管理局的决定的，应终止欧洲保险与职业养老金管理局的决定。

3.如有成员国认为欧洲保险与职业养老金管理局根据第18条第3款作出的决定影响了其财政责任，则在欧洲保险与职业养老金管理局通知主管部门其决定后的3个工作日内，该成员国可通知欧洲保险与职业养老金管理局、欧盟委员会和欧盟理事会该成员国将不实施该项决定。

成员国应在其通知中清楚具体地说明该项决定为何以及如何影响其财政责任。

在成员国作出上述通知的情况下，欧洲保险与职业养老金管理局的决定应暂停执行。

欧盟理事会应在10个工作日内召开会议，理事以简单多数票决定是否撤销欧洲保险与职业养老金管理局的决定。

欧盟理事会经审议后并未根据第4项决定撤销欧洲保险与职业养老金管理局的决定的，应终止欧洲保险与职业养老金管理局决定的暂停执行。

4.欧盟理事会根据第3款决定不撤销欧洲保险与职业养老金管理局与第18条第3款有关的决定，而所涉成员国仍认为欧洲保险与职业养老金管理局的决定影响了其财政责任的，该成员国可通知欧盟委员会和欧洲保险与职业养老金管理局并要求欧盟理事会重新审查该事宜。所涉成员国应清楚说明其对欧盟理事会决定持异议的理由。

第1项所述通知发出后4周内，欧盟理事会可重申其原决定或根据第3款作出新的决定。

案件有特殊情况的，欧盟理事会可将上述4周期限再延长4周。

5.任何滥用本条款的行为，特别是在欧洲保险与职业养老金管理局的决定并不对成员国的财政责任造成任何重大或实质性影响的情况下滥用本条款，均应被视为与欧盟内部市场不相容而被禁止。

Article 39 Decision-making procedures

1. Before taking the decisions provided for in this Regulation, the Authority shall inform any named addressee of its intention to adopt the decision, setting a time limit within which the addressee may express its views on the matter, taking full account of the urgency, complexity and potential consequences of the matter. This applies mutatis mutandis to recommendations as referred to in Article 17(3).

2. The decisions of the Authority shall state the reasons on which they are based.

3. The addressees of decisions of the Authority shall be informed of the legal remedies available under this Regulation.

4. Where the Authority has taken a decision pursuant to Article 18(3) or (4), it shall review that decision at appropriate intervals.

5. The decisions which the Authority takes pursuant to Articles 17, 18 or 19 shall be made public and shall state the identity of the competent authority or financial institution concerned and the main content of the decision, unless such publication is in conflict with the legitimate interests of financial institutions in the protection of their business secrets or could seriously jeopardise the orderly functioning and integrity of financial markets or the stability of the whole or part of the financial system of the Union.

CHAPTER Ⅲ ORGANISATION

SECTION 1 Board of Supervisors

Article 40 Composition

1. The Board of Supervisors shall be composed of:

(a) the Chairperson, who shall be non-voting;

(b) the head of the national public authority competent for the supervision of financial institutions in each Member State, who shall meet in person at least twice a year;

(c) one representative of the Commission, who shall be non-voting;

(d) one representative of the ESRB, who shall be non-voting;

(e) one representative of each of the other two European Supervisory Authorities, who shall be non-voting;

2. The Board of Supervisors shall convene meetings with the Stakeholder Groups regularly, at least twice a year.

3. Each competent authority shall be responsible for nominating a High-Level alternate from its authority, who may replace the member of the Board of Supervisors referred to in

第39条 决策程序

1.在作出本条例所规定的决定前,欧洲保险与职业养老金管理局应通知该等决定所针对的任何具名对象其有意作出该决定,并在充分考虑事宜的紧迫性、复杂性和潜在后果的情况下设定时限,允许决定所针对的对象就该事宜表达观点。第17条第3款所述的建议比照上述规定处理。

2.欧洲保险与职业养老金管理局发布的决定应阐明决定所基于的理由。

3.应通知欧洲保险与职业养老金管理局决定所针对的对象其可根据本条例获得的法律救济。

4.欧洲保险与职业养老金管理局根据第18条第3款或第4款作出决定后,应以适当的频率审评该项决定。

5.欧洲保险与职业养老金管理局应公布其根据第17条、第18条或第19条作出的决定并说明所涉主管部门或金融机构的身份以及决定的主要内容,除非公布上述内容与金融机构保护其商业秘密的合法权益有冲突,或可能严重危害欧盟金融市场有序运行和诚信度或整个或部分金融系统的稳定。

第三章 组 织 结 构

第1节 监管机构理事会

第40条 构成

1.监管机构理事会组成如下:

(a)主席,无表决权;

(b)每个成员国内主管金融机构监管的国家级公共机构的负责人,该等负责人每年应至少亲自出席2次会议;

(c)欧盟委员会1名代表,无表决权;

(d)欧洲系统性风险委员会1名代表,无表决权;

(e)另外两个欧洲监管机构各自1名代表,无表决权。

2.监管机构理事会应定期召开与利益相关者小组的会议,每年至少2次。

3.各主管部门应负责从其部门中指定1名高级别的替补人员,以在第1款第b项所述的监管机构理事会理事不能参加会议时代替其出席。

paragraph 1(b), where that person is prevented from attending.

4. In Member States where more than one authority is responsible for the supervision according to this Regulation, those authorities shall agree on a common representative. Nevertheless, when an item to be discussed by the Board of Supervisors does not fall within the competence of the national authority being represented by the member referred to in paragraph 1(b), that member may bring a representative from the relevant national authority, who shall be non-voting.

5. The Board of Supervisors may decide to admit observers.

The Executive Director may participate in meetings of the Board of Supervisors, without the right to vote.

Article 41 Internal committees and panels

1. The Board of Supervisors may establish internal committees or panels for specific tasks attributed to the Board of Supervisors, and may provide for the delegation of certain clearly defined tasks and decisions to internal committees or panels, to the Management Board or to the Chairperson.

2. For the purposes of Article 19, the Board of Supervisors shall convoke an independent panel to facilitate an impartial settlement of the disagreement, consisting of the Chairperson and two of its members, who are not representatives of the competent authorities which are party to the disagreement and who have neither any interest in the conflict nor direct links to the competent authorities concerned.

3. Subject to Article 19(2), the panel shall propose a decision for final adoption by the Board of Supervisors, in accordance with the procedure set out in the third subparagraph of Article 44(1).

4. The Board of Supervisors shall adopt rules of procedure for the panel referred to in paragraph 2.

Article 42 Independence

When carrying out the tasks conferred upon it by this Regulation, the Chairperson and the voting members of the Board of Supervisors shall act independently and objectively in the sole interest of the Union as a whole and shall neither seek nor take instructions from Union institutions or bodies, from any government of a Member State or from any other public or private body.

Neither Member States, the Union institutions or bodies, nor any other public or private body shall seek to influence the members of the Board of Supervisors in the performance of their tasks.

Article 43 Tasks

1. The Board of Supervisors shall give guidance to the work of the Authority and shall be in charge of taking the decisions referred to in Chapter II.

4.某成员国如有多个部门负责本条例下的监管工作，则该等部门应指定1名共同的代表。然而，监管机构理事会讨论的事项不属于第1款第b项中的理事所代表的国家级监管机构的职权范围的，该成员可携1名来自相关国家级监管机构的代表与会，该代表无投票权。

5.监管机构理事会可决定设立观察员。

执行主任可参与监管机构理事会的会议，但无表决权。

第41条　内部委员会和专家小组

1.监管机构理事会可为其承担的特别职责设立内部委员会或专家小组，并可允许将某些清楚界定的职责和决定委托给内部委员会或专家小组、管理委员会或主席。

2.出于第19条之目的，监管机构理事会应召集独立的专家小组，促进分歧的公正解决，该专家小组由监管机构理事会主席和2名成员组成，他们应为非分歧一方主管部门代表，在所涉主管部门的冲突中无利害关系，与所涉主管部门亦无直接关联。

3.在遵守第19条第2款的前提下，专家小组应向监管机构理事会提出决定建议，以供后者依照第44条第1款第3项规定的程序最终通过。

4.监管机构理事会应通过第2款所述专家小组的程序规则。

第42条　独立性

监管机构理事会主席以及有表决权的成员履行本条例所赋予的职责时，应仅代表欧盟整体利益独立客观地行事，不得寻求或听从欧盟机构或单位、任何成员国政府或任何其他公共或私人机构的指示。

各成员国、欧盟机构或单位以及任何其他公共或私人机构均不得试图影响监管机构理事会理事履行其职责。

第43条　职责

1.监管机构理事会应为欧洲保险与职业养老金管理局的工作提供指导并负责作出第二章所述的决定。

2. The Board of Supervisors shall adopt the opinions, recommendations, and decisions, and issue the advice referred to in Chapter Ⅱ.

3. The Board of Supervisors shall appoint the Chairperson.

4. The Board of Supervisors shall adopt, before 30 September of each year, on the basis of a proposal by the Management Board, the work programme of the Authority for the coming year, and shall transmit it for information to the European Parliament, the Council and the Commission.

The work programme shall be adopted without prejudice to the annual budgetary procedure and shall be made public.

5. The Board of Supervisors shall, on the basis of a proposal by the Management Board, adopt the annual report on the activities of the Authority, including on the performance of the Chairperson's duties, on the basis of the draft report referred to in Article 53(7) and shall transmit that report to the European Parliament, the Council, the Commission, the Court of Auditors and the European Economic and Social Committee by 15 June each year. The report shall be made public.

6. The Board of Supervisors shall adopt the multi-annual work programme of the Authority, and shall transmit it for information to the European Parliament, the Council and the Commission.

The multi-annual work programme shall be adopted without prejudice to the annual budgetary procedure and shall be made public.

7. The Board of Supervisors shall adopt the budget in accordance with Article 63.

8. The Board of Supervisors shall exercise disciplinary authority over the Chairperson and the Executive Director and may remove them from office in accordance with Article 48(5) or Article 51(5) respectively.

Article 44 Decision making

1. Decisions of the Board of Supervisors shall be taken by a simple majority of its members. Each member shall have one vote.

With regard to the acts specified in Articles 10 to 16 and measures and decisions adopted under the third subparagraph of Article 9(5) and Chapter VI and by way of derogation from the first subparagraph of this paragraph, the Board of Supervisors shall take decisions on the basis of a qualified majority of its members, as defined in Article 16(4) of the Treaty on European Union and in Article 3 of the Protocol (No 36) on transitional provisions.

With regard to decisions in accordance with Article 19(3), for decisions taken by the group supervisor, the decision proposed by the panel shall be considered as adopted, if approved by a simple majority, unless it is rejected by members representing a blocking minority of the votes as defined in Article 16(4) of the Treaty on European Union and in

2.监管机构理事会应制定第二章所述的意见、建议和决定，并发布第二章所述的建议。

3.监管机构理事会应任命一名主席。

4.监管机构理事会应于每年9月30日前根据管理委员会的提议通过欧洲保险与职业养老金管理局下一年度的工作计划，并将其发送给欧洲议会、欧盟理事会和欧盟委员会供其参考。

工作计划的通过不得影响年度预算程序，并应予公布。

5.监管机构理事会应根据管理委员会的提议在第53条第7款所述的报告草案基础上通过关于欧洲保险与职业养老金管理局活动，包括主席职责履行情况的年度报告，并于每年6月15日前将该报告发送给欧洲议会、欧盟理事会、欧盟委员会、欧盟审计院以及欧洲经济与社会委员会。该报告应予公布。

6.监管机构理事会应通过欧洲保险与职业养老金管理局的跨年度工作计划，并将其发送给欧洲议会、欧盟理事会和欧盟委员会供其参考。

跨年度工作计划的通过不得影响年度预算程序并应予公布。

7.监管机构理事会按照第63条的规定通过预算。

8.监管机构理事会对主席和执行主任行使纪律处分权，并可根据第48条第5款或第51条第5款免除其职务。

第44条　决策

1.监管机构理事会应以简单多数票通过决定。每名理事均有一票表决权。

作为本款第1项的例外，对于第10条至第16条所指明的法律文件以及依据第9条第5款第3项和第六章所采取的措施和作出的决定，监管机构理事会应以特定多数票通过决定，该特定多数票的定义见《欧洲联盟条约》第16条第4款以及关于过渡条款的《议定书（第36号）》第3条。

就第19条第3款下的决定而言，对于由集团监管机构作出的决定，专家小组提议的决定经简单多数票同意应视为通过，但是，被起否决作用的少数票的成员否决的除外，起否决作用的少数票的定义见《欧洲联盟条约》第16条第4款以及关于过渡规定的《议定书（第36号）》第3条。

Article 3 of the Protocol (No 36) on transitional provisions.

For all other decisions in accordance with Article 19(3), the decision proposed by the panel shall be adopted by a simple majority of the members of the Board of Supervisors. Each member shall have one vote.

2. Meetings of the Board of Supervisors shall be convened by the Chairperson at his own initiative or at the request of one third of its members, and shall be chaired by the Chairperson.

3. The Board of Supervisors shall adopt and make public its rules of procedure.

4. The rules of procedure shall set out in detail the arrangements governing voting, including, where appropriate, the rules governing quorums. The non-voting members and the observers, with the exception of the Chairperson and the Executive Director, shall not attend any discussions within the Board of Supervisors relating to individual financial institutions, unless otherwise provided for in Article 75(3) or in the acts referred to in Article 1(2).

SECTION 2 Management Board

Article 45 Composition

1. The Management Board shall be composed of the Chairperson and six other members of the Board of Supervisors, elected by and from the voting members of the Board of Supervisors.

Other than the Chairperson, each member of the Management Board shall have an alternate, who may replace him if he is prevented from attending.

The term of office of the members elected by the Board of Supervisors shall be two-and-a-half years. That term may be extended once. The composition of the Management Board shall be balanced and proportionate and shall reflect the Union as a whole. Mandates shall be overlapping and an appropriate rotating arrangement shall apply.

2. Decisions by the Management Board shall be adopted on the basis of a majority of the members present. Each member shall have one vote.

The Executive Director and a representative of the Commission shall participate in meetings of the Management Board without the right to vote.

The representative of the Commission shall have the right to vote on matters referred to in Article 63.

The Management Board shall adopt and make public its rules of procedure.

3. Meetings of the Management Board shall be convened by the Chairperson at his own initiative or at the request of at least a third of its members, and shall be chaired by the Chairperson.

The Management Board shall meet prior to every meeting of the Board of Supervisors

对于所有其他根据第19条第3款所作的决定，由专家小组提议的决定应由监管机构理事会按简单多数票通过，每名理事均有一票表决权。

2.监管机构理事会会议应由主席主动召集或经1/3理事请求召集，由主席主持。

3.监管机构理事会应通过并公布其程序规则。

4.程序规则应详细规定表决安排，在适当时应包括关于法定人数的规则。除主席和执行主任外，无表决权的成员和观察员不得参加监管机构理事会关于具体金融机构的任何讨论，但是第75条第3款或者第1条第2款所述法律文件另有规定的除外。

第2节 管理委员会

第45条 构成

1.管理委员会应由监管机构理事会主席和其他6名委员组成，该6名委员从监管机构理事会有表决权的理事中选出。

除主席之外，管理委员会的每名委员均应有1名替补人员，在其无法出席会议时代替其出席。

监管机构理事会所选出的管理委员会委员任期为两年半。该任期可延长1次。管理委员会的构成应是平衡并且成比例的，并应反映欧盟整体情况。不同管理委员会委员的任期应当有所重叠，并应实行适当的轮换安排。

2.管理委员会的决定应由出席会议的委员多数同意后通过。每名委员均有一票表决权。

执行主任和欧盟委员会的1名代表应出席管理委员会的会议，但无表决权。

欧盟委员会的代表应有权就第63条所述事项进行表决。

管理委员会应通过并公布其程序规则。

3.管理委员会的会议应由主席主动召集或经至少1/3成员请求召集，由主席主持。

管理委员会应在每次监管机构理事会会议前及其认为必要的其他时间召开会

and as often as the Management Board deems necessary. It shall meet at least five times a year.

4. The members of the Management Board may, subject to the rules of procedure, be assisted by advisers or experts. The non-voting members, with the exception of the Executive Director, shall not attend any discussions within the Management Board relating to individual financial institutions.

Article 46 Independence

The members of the Management Board shall act independently and objectively in the sole interest of the Union as a whole and shall neither seek nor take instructions from the Union institutions or bodies, from any government of a Member State or from any other public or private body.

Neither Member States, the Union institutions or bodies, nor any other public or private body shall seek to influence the members of the Management Board in the performance of their tasks.

Article 47 Tasks

1. The Management Board shall ensure that the Authority carries out its mission and performs the tasks assigned to it in accordance with this Regulation.

2. The Management Board shall propose, for adoption by the Board of Supervisors, an annual and multi-annual work programme.

3. The Management Board shall exercise its budgetary powers in accordance with Articles 63 and 64.

4. The Management Board shall adopt the Authority's staff policy plan and, pursuant to Article 68(2), the necessary implementing measures of the Staff Regulations of Officials of the European Communities (hereinafter the 'Staff Regulations').

5. The Management Board shall adopt the special provisions on right of access to the documents of the Authority, in accordance with Article 72.

6. The Management Board shall propose an annual report on the activities of the Authority, including on the Chairperson's duties, on the basis of the draft report referred to in Article 53(7) to the Board of Supervisors for approval.

7. The Management Board shall adopt and make public its rules of procedure.

8. The Management Board shall appoint and remove the members of the Board of Appeal in accordance with Article 58(3) and (5).

SECTION 3 Chairperson

Article 48 Appointment and tasks

1. The Authority shall be represented by a Chairperson, who shall be a full-time independent professional.

议,每年至少应召开5次会议。

4.管理委员会的委员可按程序规则获得顾问或专家的协助。除执行主任之外,无表决权的委员不得参与管理委员会内部关于具体金融机构的讨论。

第46条　独立性

管理委员会委员应仅代表欧盟整体利益独立客观地行事,不得寻求或听从欧盟机构或单位、任何成员国政府或任何其他公共或私人机构的指示。

各成员国、欧盟机构或单位以及任何其他公共或私人机构均不得试图影响管理委员会委员履行其职责。

第47条　职责

1.管理委员会应确保欧洲保险与职业养老金管理局完成本条例所赋予的使命和职责。

2.管理委员会应提出年度和跨年度工作计划,交由监管机构理事会通过。

3.管理委员会应根据第63条和第64条行使预算权。

4.管理委员会应通过欧洲保险与职业养老金管理局的人事政策计划,并根据第68条第2款制定实施《欧洲共同体官员的人事条例》(以下简称《人事条例》)的必要措施。

5.根据第72条的规定,管理委员会应通过关于欧洲保险与职业养老金管理局文件查阅权的特殊规定。

6.在第53条第7款所述报告草案的基础上,管理委员会应将关于欧洲保险与职业养老金管理局活动(包括主席职责)的年度报告呈报监管机构理事会审批。

7.管理委员会应通过并公布其程序规则。

8.管理委员会应根据第58条第3款和第5款任免行政复议委员会的委员。

第3节　主　　席

第48条　任命和职责

1.欧洲保险与职业养老金管理局由主席代表。主席应为全职、独立的专业人士。

The Chairperson shall be responsible for preparing the work of the Board of Supervisors and shall chair the meetings of the Board of Supervisors and the Management Board.

2. The Chairperson shall be appointed by the Board of Supervisors on the basis of merit, skills, knowledge of financial institutions and markets, and of experience relevant to financial supervision and regulation, following an open selection procedure.

Before taking up his duties, and up to 1 month after the selection by the Board of Supervisors, the European Parliament may, after having heard the candidate selected by the Board of Supervisors, object to the designation of the selected person.

The Board of Supervisors shall also elect, from among its members, an alternate who shall carry out the functions of the Chairperson in his absence. That alternate shall not be elected from among the members of the Management Board.

3. The Chairperson's term of office shall be 5 years and may be extended once.

4. In the course of the 9 months preceding the end of the five-year term of office of the Chairperson, the Board of Supervisors shall evaluate:

(a) the results achieved in the first term of office and the way they were achieved;

(b) the Authority's duties and requirements in the coming years.

The Board of Supervisors, taking into account the evaluation, may extend the term of office of the Chairperson once subject to confirmation by the European Parliament.

5. The Chairperson may be removed from office only by the European Parliament following a decision of the Board of Supervisors.

The Chairperson shall not prevent the Board of Supervisors from discussing matters relating to the Chairperson, in particular the need for his removal, and shall not be involved in deliberations concerning such a matter.

Article 49 Independence

Without prejudice to the role of the Board of Supervisors in relation to the tasks of the Chairperson, the Chairperson shall neither seek nor take instructions from the Union institutions or bodies, from any government of a Member State or from any other public or private body.

Neither Member States, the Union institutions or bodies nor any other public or private body shall seek to influence the Chairperson in the performance of his tasks.

In accordance with the Staff Regulations referred to in Article 68, the Chairperson shall, after leaving service, continue to be bound by the duty to behave with integrity and discretion as regards the acceptance of certain appointments or benefits.

Article 50 Report

1. The European Parliament and the Council may invite the Chairperson or his alternate to make a statement, while fully respecting his independence. The Chairperson

主席负责筹备监管机构理事会的工作，并主持监管机构理事会以及管理委员会的会议。

2.主席由监管机构理事会根据其成就、技能、对金融机构和市场的认识、与金融监管和规制相关的经验，经过公开遴选程序任命。

在获选者到任前，直至其被监管机构理事会选出满1个月期间内，欧洲议会都有权在听取获选者意见后对其任命提出异议。

监管机构理事会还应从其理事中选出1名替补人员，在主席缺席的情况下代为行使其职能。该替补人员不得为管理委员会的委员。

3.主席的任期为5年，可延长1次。

4.在主席5年任期结束前的9个月期间内，监管机构理事会可对下列方面作出评价：

(a)主席在首期任期内取得的工作成果以及取得该成果的方式；

(b)未来几年欧洲保险与职业养老金管理局的职责和要求。

在上述评价的基础上，监管机构理事会可经欧洲议会确认后将主席任期延长1次。

5.只有在监管机构理事会作出罢免决定后，欧洲议会方能免除主席职务。

主席不得妨碍监管机构理事会讨论与主席有关的事宜，特别是围绕罢免其职务所进行的必要讨论，并且不得参与涉及上述事宜的审议。

第49条　独立性

不影响监管机构理事会就主席的职责发挥作用的情况下，主席不得寻求或听从欧盟机构或单位、任何成员国政府或任何其他公共或私人机构的指示。

各成员国、欧盟机构或单位或任何其他公共或私人机构均不得试图影响主席履行其职责。

根据第68条所述的《人事条例》，主席离职后在接受某些任命或利益方面仍应受诚信和谨慎义务约束。

第50条　报告

1.欧洲议会和欧盟理事会可在充分尊重主席独立性的前提下要求主席或其替补人员作出陈述。任何时候经欧洲议会要求，主席均应向后者作出陈述并回答其议员所

shall make a statement before the European Parliament and answer any questions put by its members whenever so requested.

2. The Chairperson shall report in writing on the main activities of the Authority to the European Parliament when requested and at least 15 days before making the statement referred to in paragraph 1.

3. In addition to the information referred to in Articles 11 to 18 and Articles 20 and 33, the report shall also include any relevant information requested by the European Parliament on an ad-hoc basis.

SECTION 4 Executive Director

Article 51 Appointment

1. The Authority shall be managed by an Executive Director, who shall be a full-time independent professional.

2. The Executive Director shall be appointed by the Board of Supervisors, after confirmation by the European Parliament, on the basis of merit, skills, knowledge of financial institutions and markets, and experience relevant to financial supervision and regulation and managerial experience, following an open selection procedure.

3. The Executive Director's term of office shall be 5 years and may be extended once.

4. In the course of the 9 months preceding the end of the Executive Director's term of office, the Board of Supervisors shall evaluate in particular:

(a) the results achieved in the first term of office and the way they were achieved;

(b) the Authority's duties and requirements in the coming years.

The Board of Supervisors, taking into account the evaluation referred to in the first subparagraph, may extend the term of office of the Executive Director once.

5. The Executive Director may be removed from office only upon a decision of the Board of Supervisors.

Article 52 Independence

Without prejudice to the respective roles of the Management Board and the Board of Supervisors in relation to the tasks of the Executive Director, the Executive Director shall neither seek nor take instructions from the Union institutions or bodies, from any government of a Member State, or from any other public or private body.

Neither Member States, the Union institutions or bodies, nor any other public or private body shall seek to influence the Executive Director in the performance of his tasks.

In accordance with the Staff Regulations referred to in Article 68, the Executive Director shall, after leaving service, continue to be bound by the duty to behave with

提出的任何问题。

2.经欧洲议会要求并至少在进行第1款提及的陈述的15日前，主席应就欧洲保险与职业养老金管理局的主要活动向欧洲议会提交书面报告。

3.除了第11条至第18条以及第20条和第33条所述的信息外，报告还应包括欧洲议会专门要求提供的任何相关信息。

第4节 执行主任

第51条 任命

1.欧洲保险与职业养老金管理局应由一名执行主任负责管理，执行主任应为全职、独立的专业人士。

2.执行主任应由监管机构理事会根据其成就、技能、对金融机构和市场的认识、与金融监管和规制相关的经验以及管理经验，经过公开遴选程序并经欧洲议会确认后任命。

3.执行主任的任期为5年，可延长1次。

4.执行主任任期结束前的9个月期间内，监管机构理事会尤其可对下列方面进行评价：

(a)执行主任在首期任期内取得的工作成果以及取得该成果的方式；

(b)未来几年欧洲保险与职业养老金管理局的职责和要求。

在第1项所述评价的基础上，监管机构理事会可将执行主任的任期延长1次。

5.经监管机构理事会作出决定后方能免除执行主任职务。

第52条 独立性

不影响管理委员会和监管机构理事会就执行主任的职责发挥各自作用的情况下，执行主任不得寻求或听从欧盟机构或单位、任何成员国政府或任何其他公共或私人机构的指示。

各成员国、欧盟机构或单位以及任何其他公共或私人机构均不得试图影响执行主任履行其职责。

根据第68条所述的《人事条例》，执行主任离职后在接受某些任命或利益方面仍应受诚信和谨慎义务约束。

integrity and discretion as regards the acceptance of certain appointments or benefits.

Article 53 Tasks

1. The Executive Director shall be in charge of the management of the Authority and shall prepare the work of the Management Board.

2. The Executive Director shall be responsible for implementing the annual work programme of the Authority under the guidance of the Board of Supervisors and under the control of the Management Board.

3. The Executive Director shall take the necessary measures, notably the adoption of internal administrative instructions and the publication of notices, to ensure the functioning of the Authority, in accordance with this Regulation.

4. The Executive Director shall prepare a multi-annual work programme, as referred to in Article 47(2).

5. Each year, by 30 June, the Executive Director shall prepare a work programme for the following year, as referred to in Article 47(2).

6. The Executive Director shall draw up a preliminary draft budget of the Authority pursuant to Article 63 and shall implement the budget of the Authority pursuant to Article 64.

7. Each year the Executive Director shall prepare a draft report with a section on the regulatory and supervisory activities of the Authority and a section on financial and administrative matters.

8. The Executive Director shall exercise in respect to the Authority's staff the powers laid down in Article 68 and manage staff matters.

CHAPTER Ⅳ JOINT BODIES OF THE EUROPEAN SUPERVISORY AUTHORITIES

SECTION 1 Joint Committee of European Supervisory Authorities

Article 54 Establishment

1. The Joint Committee of the European Supervisory Authorities is hereby established.

2. The Joint Committee shall serve as a forum in which the Authority shall cooperate regularly and closely and ensure cross-sectoral consistency with the European Supervisory Authority (European Banking Authority) and the European Supervisory Authority (European

第53条　职责

1.执行主任应负责管理欧洲保险与职业养老金管理局并布置管理委员会的工作。

2.执行主任应在监管机构理事会的指导以及管理委员会的管理下,负责实施欧洲保险与职业养老金管理局的年度工作计划。

3.根据本条例,执行主任应采取必要的措施,特别是应通过内部行政指示和通知来确保欧洲保险与职业养老金管理局的有效运行。

4.执行主任应制定第47条第2款所述的跨年度工作计划。

5.每年6月30日前,执行主任应为下一年度制定第47条第2款所述的工作计划。

6.执行主任应根据第63条起草欧洲保险与职业养老金管理局初步预算草案并根据第64条实施欧洲保险与职业养老金管理局的预算。

7.执行主任每年均应起草一份报告草案,其中一节关于欧洲保险与职业养老金管理局的规制和监管活动,另一节关于财务和行政管理事宜。

8.执行主任应对欧洲保险与职业养老金管理局的工作人员行使第68条规定的权力,并负责管理人事。

第四章　欧洲监管机构的联合机构

第1节　欧洲监管机构联合委员会

第54条　设立

1.特此设立欧洲监管机构联合委员会。

2.联合委员会应充当欧洲保险与职业养老金管理局与两个欧洲监管机构(欧洲银行业管理局和欧洲证券与市场管理局)之间的平台,该等机构通过此一平台得以开展定期紧密合作并保持跨行业监管一致性,尤其是在下列几个方面:

Securities and Markets Authority), in particular regarding:

— financial conglomerates,

— accounting and auditing,

— micro-prudential analyses of cross-sectoral developments, risks and vulnerabilities for financial stability,

— retail investment products,

— measures combating money laundering; and,

— information exchange with the ESRB and developing the relationship between the ESRB and the ESAs,

3. The Joint Committee shall have a dedicated staff provided by the ESAs that shall act as a secretariat. The Authority shall contribute adequate resources to administrative, infrastructure and operational expenses.

4. In the event that a financial institution reaches across different sectors, the Joint Committee shall resolve disagreements in accordance with Article 56.

Article 55 Composition

1. The Joint Committee shall be composed of the Chairpersons of the ESAs, and, where applicable, the Chairperson of any Sub-Committee established under Article 57.

2. The Executive Director, a representative of the Commission and the ESRB shall be invited to the meetings of the Joint Committee, as well as of any Sub-Committees referred to in Article 57, as observers.

3. The Chairperson of the Joint Committee shall be appointed on an annual rotational basis from among the Chairpersons of the ESAs. The Chairperson of the Joint Committee shall be a Vice-Chair of the ESRB.

4. The Joint Committee shall adopt and publish its own rules of procedure. The rules may specify further participants in the meetings of the Joint Committee.

The Joint Committee shall meet at least once every 2 months.

Article 56 Joint positions and common acts

Within the scope of its tasks in Chapter II, and in particular with respect to the implementation of Directive 2002/87/EC, where relevant, the Authority shall reach joint positions with the European Supervisory Authority (European Banking Authority) and with the European Supervisory Authority (European Securities and Markets Authority), as appropriate.

Acts under Articles 10 to 15, 17, 18 or 19 of this Regulation in relation to the application of Directive 2002/87/EC and of any other Union acts referred to in Article 1 (2) that also fall within the area of competence of the European Supervisory Authority (European Banking Authority) or the European Supervisory Authority (European Securities and Markets Authority) shall be adopted, in parallel, by the Authority, the European

——金融集团，
——会计和审计，
——对金融稳定的跨行业变化、风险和薄弱环节的微观审慎分析，

——零售投资产品，
——打击洗钱活动的措施，及
——与欧洲系统性风险委员会的信息交流以及欧洲系统性风险委员会和各欧洲监管机构之间关系的建立。

3.各欧洲监管机构应为联合委员会提供一名专职的工作人员作为秘书。欧洲保险与职业养老金管理局应为行政、基础设施和运营开支提供充足的资源。

4.对于涉足多个行业的金融机构，联合委员会应依照第56条的规定解决分歧。

第55条　构成

1.联合委员会应由各欧洲监管机构的主席以及依据第57条设立的任何分委员会的主席（如有）组成。

2.执行主任以及欧盟委员会和欧洲系统性风险委员会应各有一名代表被邀请作为观察员参加联合委员会以及第57条所述的任何分委员会的会议。

3.联合委员会的主席应每年由各欧洲监管机构的主席轮流担任。联合委员会的主席应兼任欧洲系统性风险委员会的副主席。

4.联合委员会应通过并公布其程序规则。除上述参会人员外，规则可具体规定其他可参加联合委员会会议的人选。

联合委员会应至少每2个月召开1次会议。

第56条　共同立场和通用法律文件

在第二章所述的欧洲保险与职业养老金管理局职责范围内，特别是与实施第2002/87/EC号指令有关的职责（如适用）范围内，欧洲保险与职业养老金管理局应与欧洲监管机构（欧洲银行业管理局或欧洲证券与市场管理局）（视具体情况而定）达成共同立场。

本条例第10条至第15条、第17条、第18条或第19条中与第2002/87/EC指令以及第1条第2款所述欧盟立法的适用有关的，并且同时也属于欧洲监管机构（欧洲银行业管理局或欧洲证券与市场管理局）职权管辖范围的立法，应同时由欧洲保险与职业养老金管理局与欧洲监管机构（欧洲银行业管理局或欧洲证券与市场管理局）（视具体情况而定）共同通过。

Supervisory Authority (European Banking Authority), and the European Supervisory Authority (European Securities and Market Authority), as appropriate.

Article 57 Sub-Committees

1. For the purposes of Article 56, a Sub-Committee on Financial Conglomerates to the Joint Committee shall be established.

2. The Sub-Committee shall be composed of the individuals referred to in Article 55 (1), and one High-Level representative from the current staff of the relevant competent authority from each Member State.

3. The Sub-Committee shall elect a Chairperson from among its members, who shall also be a member of the Joint Committee.

4. The Joint Committee may establish further Sub-Committees.

SECTION 2 Board of Appeal

Article 58 Composition and operation

1. The Board of Appeal shall be a joint body of the ESAs.

2. The Board of Appeal shall be composed of six members and six alternates, who shall be individuals of a high repute with a proven record of relevant knowledge and professional experience, including supervisory experience, to a sufficiently high level in the fields of banking, insurance, occupational pensions, securities markets or other financial services, excluding current staff of the competent authorities or other national or Union institutions involved in the activities of the Authority. The Board of Appeal shall have sufficient legal expertise to provide expert legal advice on the legality of the Authority's exercise of its powers.

The Board of Appeal shall designate its President.

3. Two members of the Board of Appeal and two alternates shall be appointed by the Management Board of the Authority from a short-list proposed by the Commission, following a public call for expressions of interest published in the Official Journal of the European Union, and after consultation of the Board of Supervisors.

The other members shall be appointed in accordance with Regulation (EU) No 1093/2010 and Regulation (EU) No 1095/2010.

4. The term of office of the members of the Board of Appeal shall be 5 years. That term may be extended once.

5. A member of the Board of Appeal appointed by the Management Board of the Authority shall not be removed during his term of office unless he has been found guilty of serious misconduct and the Management Board takes a decision to that effect after consulting the Board of Supervisors.

6. The decisions of the Board of Appeal shall be adopted on the basis of a majority

第57条 分委员会

1.为了第56条之目的,应在联合委员会下设立一个金融集团分委员会。

2.分委员会应由第55条第1款所述的个人以及各成员国相关主管部门现任工作人员中选派的高级别代表组成。

3.分委员会应从其委员中选出一名主席,该主席应同时为联合委员会的委员。

4.联合委员会还可进一步设立其他分委员会。

第2节 行政复议委员会

第58条 构成和运作

1.行政复议委员会应为各个欧洲监管机构之间的一个联合机构。

2.行政复议委员会应由6名委员和6名替补委员组成,其应具有良好声誉,并且能证明其在银行业、保险、职业养老金、证券市场或其他金融服务领域有足够的相关知识和专业经验(包括监管经验),但其中不得有参与欧洲保险与职业养老金管理局活动的主管部门或其他国家级或欧盟机构的现任工作人员。行政复议委员会应具备足够的法律专业知识就欧洲保险与职业养老金管理局权力行使的合法性提供专业的法律意见。

行政复议委员会应指定一名主席。

3.在《欧盟公报》上发布征寻公告并咨询监管机构理事会的意见后,由欧洲保险与职业养老金管理局的管理委员会从欧盟委员会提议的一份候选人短名单中任命行政复议委员会的2名委员以及2名替补委员。

其他委员应根据第1093/2010号(欧盟)条例以及第1095/2010号(欧盟)条例任命。

4.行政复议委员会委员的任期为5年。任期可延长1次。

5.由欧洲保险与职业养老金管理局管理委员会任命的行政复议委员会委员不得在其任期内被免职,但是,被发现有严重不当行为并且管理委员会在咨询监管机构理事会的意见后决定免除其职务的除外。

6.行政复议委员会的决定应由其6名委员中的至少4名同意后方能通过。行政复议

of at least four of its six members. Where the appealed decision falls within the scope of this Regulation, the deciding majority shall include at least one of the two members of the Board of Appeal appointed by the Authority.

7. The Board of Appeal shall be convened by its President when necessary.

8. The ESAs shall ensure adequate operational and secretarial support for the Board of Appeal through the Joint Committee.

Article 59 Independence and impartiality

1. The members of the Board of Appeal shall be independent in making their decisions. They shall not be bound by any instructions. They shall not perform any other duties in relation to the Authority, its Management Board or its Board of Supervisors.

2. Members of the Board of Appeal shall not take part in any appeal proceedings in which they have any personal interest if they have previously been involved as representatives of one of the parties to the proceedings, or if they have participated in the decision under appeal.

3. If, for one of the reasons referred to in paragraphs 1 and 2 or for any other reason, a member of a Board of Appeal considers that another member should not take part in any appeal proceedings, he shall inform the Board of Appeal accordingly.

4. Any party to the appeal proceedings may object to the participation of a member of the Board of Appeal on any of the grounds referred to in paragraphs 1 and 2, or if suspected of bias.

No objection may be based on the nationality of members nor shall it be admissible if, while being aware of a reason for objecting, the party to the appeal proceedings has nonetheless taken a procedural step other than objecting to the composition of the Board of Appeal.

5. The Board of Appeal shall decide on the action to be taken in the cases specified in paragraphs 1 and 2 without the participation of the member concerned.

For the purpose of taking that decision, the member concerned shall be replaced on the Board of Appeal by his alternate. Where the alternate is in a similar situation, the Chairperson shall designate a replacement from among the available alternates.

6. The members of the Board of Appeal shall undertake to act independently and in the public interest.

For that purpose, they shall make a declaration of commitments and a declaration of interests indicating either the absence of any interest which may be considered prejudicial to their independence or any direct or indirect interest which might be considered prejudicial to their independence.

Those declarations shall be made public, annually and in writing.

所涉欧洲保险与职业养老金管理局决定属于本条例管辖范围的，同意行政复议决定的委员中应至少包括由欧洲保险与职业养老金管理局任命的2名行政复议委员会委员其中的1名。

7.行政复议委员会应在必要时由其主席召集。

8.各欧洲监管机构应确保通过联合委员会对行政复议委员会提供充分的运作和秘书支持。

第59条　独立性与公正性

1.行政复议委员会的委员应独立作出决定。他们不受任何指示的约束，不得履行与欧洲保险与职业养老金管理局、其管理委员会或其监管机构理事会有关的任何其他职责。

2.如果行政复议程序涉及行政复议委员会某委员的个人利益，或其之前曾作为行政复议程序一方当事人的代表涉案或曾经参与作出被复议的欧洲保险与职业养老金管理局决定，则其不得参与行政复议程序。

3.出于第1款和第2款所述的理由之一或任何其他理由，有行政复议委员会委员认为其他委员不应参与任何行政复议程序的，应将该情况通知行政复议委员会。

4.基于第1款和第2款所述的任何理由或在涉嫌有失公允的情况下，行政复议程序的任何一方均可申请行政复议委员会委员回避。

不能以委员的国籍为由申请回避；当行政复议程序的一方当事人明知有理由申请回避而不提出申请且继续行政复议程序的，之后不得再提出回避申请。

5.行政复议委员会应就第1款和第2款所指情况下所需采取的行动作出决定，作上述决定时所涉委员不得参与。

为作出该决定，所涉委员应由其替补委员代替其出席行政复议委员会。该名替补人员处于类似状况的，主席应从其他可供选择的替补人员当中指定1名出席。

6.行政复议委员会的委员应承诺独立地出于公众利益行事。

为此，行政复议委员会的委员应作出承诺声明和利害关系声明，说明其本人不存在可被视为对其独立性产生影响的任何利害关系或任何直接或间接利益。

该等声明应每年以书面形式公布。

CHAPTER V REMEDIES

Article 60 Appeals

1. Any natural or legal person, including competent authorities, may appeal against a decision of the Authority referred to in Articles 17, 18 and 19 and any other decision taken by the Authority in accordance with the Union acts referred to in Article 1 (2) which is addressed to that person, or against a decision which, although in the form of a decision addressed to another person, is of direct and individual concern to that person.

2. The appeal, together with a statement of grounds, shall be filed in writing at the Authority within 2 months of the date of notification of the decision to the person concerned, or, in the absence of a notification, of the day on which the Authority published its decision.

The Board of Appeal shall decide upon the appeal within 2 months after the appeal has been lodged.

3. An appeal lodged pursuant to paragraph 1 shall not have suspensive effect.

However, the Board of Appeal may, if it considers that circumstances so require, suspend the application of the contested decision.

4. If the appeal is admissible, the Board of Appeal shall examine whether it is well-founded. It shall invite the parties to the appeal proceedings to file observations on its own notifications or on communications from the other parties to the appeal proceedings, within specified time limits. Parties to the appeal proceedings shall be entitled to make oral representations.

5. The Board of Appeal may confirm the decision taken by the competent body of the Authority, or remit the case to the competent body of the Authority. That body shall be bound by the decision of the Board of Appeal and that body shall adopt an amended decision regarding the case concerned.

6. The Board of Appeal shall adopt and make public its rules of procedure.

7. The decisions taken by the Board of Appeal shall be reasoned and shall be made public by the Authority.

Article 61 Actions before the Court of Justice of the European Union

1. Proceedings may be brought before the Court of Justice of the European Union, in accordance with Article 263 TFEU, contesting a decision taken by the Board of Appeal or, in cases where there is no right of appeal before the Board of Appeal, by the Authority.

第五章 救 济

第60条 行政复议

1.任何自然人或法人,包括主管部门,均可针对欧洲保险与职业养老金管理局的下列决定提出行政复议申请:第17条、第18条以及第19条所述的决定;根据第1条第2款所述欧盟立法作出的针对上述主体的任何其他决定;对于尽管表面看来是针对其他人作出的,但实际上与上述主体本人有直接和个人关系的决定,也可提出行政复议申请。

2.所涉主体可在欧洲保险与职业养老金管理局向其发出决定通知的2个月内,或者未作通知的,在其决定公布之日起的2个月内,以书面形式向欧洲保险与职业养老金管理局提出行政复议申请并附上一份行政复议申请理由说明。

行政复议委员会应在行政复议申请提交后2个月内作出行政复议决定。

3.根据第1款提交的行政复议申请对所涉决定无暂停效力。

然而,行政复议委员会可在其认为必要的情况下,暂停实施受到质疑的决定。

4.对于可受理的行政复议申请,行政复议委员会应审查是否有充足的理由。行政复议委员会应要求行政复议程序的各当事人在规定的时限内提交其对行政复议委员会所发通知的意见或者对从行政复议程序其他当事人收到的信函的意见。行政复议程序的各当事人均有权作口头陈述。

5.行政复议委员会可确认欧洲保险与职业养老金管理局的主管机构的决定,或将案件退回欧洲保险与职业养老金管理局的主管机构。该机构应受行政复议委员会的决定约束,并应就所涉案件修改其决定。

6.行政复议委员会应通过并公布其程序规则。

7.行政复议委员会的决定应有合理依据并应由欧洲保险与职业养老金管理局予以公布。

第61条 在欧盟法院的行政诉讼

1.根据《欧洲联盟运行条约》第263条,如行政复议委员会的决定受到质疑,或者在相关方无权向行政复议委员会提出行政复议申请的情况下,欧洲保险与职业养老金管理局可向欧盟法院提起行政诉讼。

2. Member States and the Union institutions, as well as any natural or legal person, may institute proceedings before the Court of Justice of the European Union against decisions of the Authority, in accordance with Article 263 TFEU.

3. In the event that the Authority has an obligation to act and fails to take a decision, proceedings for failure to act may be brought before the Court of Justice of the European Union in accordance with Article 265 TFEU.

4. The Authority shall be required to take the necessary measures to comply with the judgment of the Court of Justice of the European Union.

CHAPTER Ⅵ FINANCIAL PROVISIONS

Article 62 Budget of the Authority

1. The revenues of the Authority, a European body in accordance with Article 185 of Council Regulation (EC, Euratom) No 1605/2002 of 25 June 2002 on the Financial Regulation applicable to the general budget of the European Communities [1] (hereinafter the 'Financial Regulation'), shall consist, in particular, of any combination of the following:

(a) obligatory contributions from the national public authorities competent for the supervision of financial institutions, which shall be made in accordance with a formula based on the weighting of votes set out in Article 3(3) of Protocol (No 36) on transitional provisions. For the purposes of this Article, Article 3(3) of Protocol (No 36) on transitional provisions shall continue to apply beyond the deadline of 31 October 2014 therein established;

(b) a subsidy from theUnion, entered in the General Budget of the European Union (Commission Section);

(c) any fees paid to the Authority in the cases specified in the relevant instruments of Union law.

2. The expenditure of the Authority shall include, at least, staff, remuneration, administrative, infrastructure, professional training and operational expenses.

3. Revenue and expenditure shall be in balance.

4. Estimates of all Authority revenue and expenditure shall be prepared for each financial year, corresponding to the calendar year, and shall be presented in the budget of the Authority.

1 OJ L 248, 16.9.2002, p. 1.

2.各成员国和欧盟机构，以及任何自然人或法人，均可根据《欧洲联盟运行条约》第263条就欧洲保险与职业养老金管理局的决定向欧盟法院提起行政诉讼。

3.欧洲保险与职业养老金管理局有义务采取行动但未作决定的，相关方可根据《欧洲联盟运行条约》第265条就其不采取行动向欧盟法院提起行政诉讼。

4.欧洲保险与职业养老金管理局应采取必要措施以执行欧盟法院的判决。

第六章 财务规定

第62条 欧洲保险与职业养老金管理局的预算

1.根据《欧盟理事会关于适用于欧洲共同体总预算的财务条例的第1605/2002号（欧共体和欧洲原子能共同体）条例》[1]（2002年6月25日）（以下简称《财务条例》）的第185条，欧洲机构欧洲保险与职业养老金管理局的收入应主要包括下列各项的任意组合：

（a）来自主管金融机构监管的国家级公共机构的义务缴款，该等缴款的计算公式应以关于过渡条款的《议定书（第36号）》第3条第3款所规定的加权票数为基础。为本条之目的，关于过渡条款的《议定书（第36号）》第3条第3款应在其设定的到期日2014年10月31日之后继续适用；

（b）在欧盟总预算（欧盟委员会部分）中列支的欧盟补助；

（c）欧洲保险与职业养老金管理局在欧盟法律相关法律文件所具体规定的情况下收取的任何费用。

2.欧洲保险与职业养老金管理局的开支至少应包括人员、薪酬、行政管理、基础设施、专业培训和运营费用。

3.欧洲保险与职业养老金管理局应保持收支平衡。

4.欧洲保险与职业养老金管理局预算中应包含欧洲保险与职业养老金管理局每个会计年度（与日历年度一致）所有收支的估算。

1 2002年9月16日《欧盟公报》L 248，第1页。

Article 63 Establishment of the budget

1. By 15 February each year, the Executive Director shall draw up a draft statement of estimates of revenue and expenditure for the following financial year, and shall forward it to the Management Board and the Board of Supervisors, together with the establishment plan. Each year, the Board of Supervisors shall, on the basis of the draft statement drawn up by the Executive Director and approved by the Management Board, produce a statement of estimates of revenue and expenditure of the Authority for the following financial year. That statement of estimates, including a draft establishment plan, shall be transmitted by the Board of Supervisors to the Commission by 31 March. Prior to adoption of the statement of estimates, the draft prepared by the Executive Director shall be approved by the Management Board.

2. The statement of estimates shall be transmitted by the Commission to the European Parliament and to the Council (hereinafter referred to together as the 'budgetary authority'), together with the draft budget of the European Union.

3. On the basis of the statement of estimates, the Commission shall enter in the draft budget of the European Union the estimates it deems necessary in respect of the establishment plan and the amount of the subsidy to be charged to the General Budget of the European Union in accordance with Articles 313 and 314 TFEU.

4. The budgetary authority shall adopt the establishment plan for the Authority. The budgetary authority shall authorise the appropriations for the subsidy to the Authority.

5. The budget of the Authority shall be adopted by the Board of Supervisors. It shall become final after the final adoption of the General Budget of the European Union. Where necessary, it shall be adjusted accordingly.

6. The Management Board shall, without delay, notify the budgetary authority of its intention to implement any project which may have significant financial implications for the funding of its budget, in particular any project relating to property, such as the rental or purchase of buildings. It shall inform the Commission thereof. If either branch of the budgetary authority intends to issue an opinion, it shall, within 2 weeks of receipt of the information on the project, notify the Authority of its intention to issue such an opinion. In the absence of a reply, the Authority may proceed with the planned operation.

7. For the first year of operation of the Authority, ending on 31 December 2011, the financing of the Authority by the Union is subject to an agreement by the budgetary authority as provided for in Point 47 of the Interinstitutional Agreement on budgetary discipline and sound financial management.

Article 64 Implementation and control of the budget

1. The Executive Director shall act as authorising officer and shall implement the Authority's budget.

第63条 预算制定

1.每年2月15日前,执行主任应起草下个会计年度收支的估算报表草案,并和预算制定计划一起转发给管理委员会和监管机构理事会。监管机构理事会每年均应在执行主任起草并经管理委员会批准的报表草案的基础上,制定关于欧洲保险与职业养老金管理局下个会计年度收支的估算报表。监管机构理事会应将该估算报表连同一份预算制定计划草案于3月31日前发送给欧盟委员会。在通过估算报表前,执行委员会制定的草案应先获得管理委员会批准。

2.欧盟委员会应将估算报表连同欧盟的预算草案一起发送给欧洲议会和欧盟理事会(以下统称预算部门)。

3.根据《欧洲联盟运行条约》第313条和第314条,欧盟委员会应在估算报表的基础上将其认为对预算制定计划属于必要的估算金额以及应在欧盟总预算中列支的补助额纳入欧盟的预算草案。

4.预算部门应通过欧洲保险与职业养老金管理局的预算制定计划。预算部门应核准将补助划拨给欧洲保险与职业养老金管理局。

5.欧洲保险与职业养老金管理局的预算应由监管机构理事会通过。在欧盟总预算最终通过后,欧洲保险与职业养老金管理局的预算也随之通过,必要时应根据欧盟总预算对其作相应调整。

6.管理委员会有意实施任何可能会对其预算经费产生重大财务影响的项目,特别是与物业(例如租用或购买建筑物)有关的任何项目,应立即通知预算部门。管理委员会应将上述意向如实通知欧盟委员会。任一预算部门有意就上述项目提出意见的,应在收到项目信息后两周内将该意向通知欧洲保险与职业养老金管理局。如预算部门未针对管理委员会通知作出答复,则欧洲保险与职业养老金管理局可按计划开展项目。

7.根据《关于预算纪律和健全的财务管理的机构间协议》的第47目,在欧洲保险与职业养老金管理局运作的首年(即于2011年12月31日结束的年度),在向欧洲保险与职业养老金管理局提供经费前欧盟应先获得预算部门的同意。

第64条 预算的实施和控制

1.执行主任应作为欧洲保险与职业养老金管理局的预算核准官员,并应负责实施欧洲保险与职业养老金管理局的预算。

2. By 1 March following the completion of each financial year, the Authority's accounting officer shall forward to the Commission's accounting officer and to the Court of Auditors the provisional accounts, accompanied by the report on budgetary and financial management during the financial year. The Authority's accounting officer shall also send the report on budgetary and financial management to the members of the Board of Supervisors, the European Parliament and the Council by 31 March of the following year.

The Commission's accounting officer shall then consolidate the provisional accounts of the institutions and decentralised bodies in accordance with Article 128 of the Financial Regulation.

3. After receiving the observations of the Court of Auditors on the provisional accounts of the Authority in accordance with Article 129 of the Financial Regulation, the Executive Director, acting on his own responsibility, shall draw up the final accounts of the Authority and transmit them, for opinion, to the Management Board.

4. The Management Board shall deliver an opinion on the final accounts of the Authority.

5. The Executive Director shall transmit those final accounts, accompanied by the opinion of the Management Board, by 1 July following the completion of the financial year, to the Members of the Board of Supervisors, the European Parliament, the Council, the Commission and the Court of Auditors.

6. The final accounts shall be published.

7. The Executive Director shall send the Court of Auditors a reply to the latter's observations by 30 September. He shall also send a copy of that reply to the Management Board and the Commission.

8. The Executive Director shall submit to the European Parliament, at the latter's request and as provided for in Article 146(3) of the Financial Regulation, any information necessary for the smooth application of the discharge procedure for the financial year in question.

9. The European Parliament, following a recommendation from the Council acting by qualified majority, shall, before 15 May of the year N+2, grant a discharge to the Authority for the implementation of the budget comprising revenue from the General Budget of the European Union and competent authorities for the financial year N.

Article 65 Financial rules

The financial rules applicable to the Authority shall be adopted by the Management Board after consulting the Commission. Those rules may not depart from Commission Regulation (EC, Euratom) No 2343/2002 of 19 November 2002 on the framework Financial Regulation for the bodies referred to in Article 185 of Council Regulation (EC,

2.在每个会计年度结束后至下一年度的3月1日前，欧洲保险与职业养老金管理局的会计官员应将该会计年度的临时财务报表连同关于该会计年度预算和财务管理的报告转发给欧盟委员会的会计官员以及欧盟审计院。欧洲保险与职业养老金管理局的会计官员还应在次年3月31日前将预算和财务管理报告发送给监管机构理事会的理事、欧洲议会和欧盟理事会。

根据《财务条例》第128条，欧盟委员会的会计官员应对其所收到的各机构和派出单位的临时财务报表进行合并工作。

3.收到欧盟审计院根据《财务条例》第129条对欧洲保险与职业养老金管理局临时财务报表作出的评述后，执行主任应自行负责起草欧洲保险与职业养老金管理局的最终报表并将其发送给管理委员会以征求其意见。

4.管理委员会应提交关于欧洲保险与职业养老金管理局最终报表的意见。

5.执行主任应在会计年度结束之后下一年度的7月1日前将该等最终报表连同管理委员会的意见发送给监管机构理事会理事、欧洲议会、欧盟理事会、欧盟委员会以及欧盟审计院。

6.最终报表应予公布。

7.执行主任应在9月30日前就欧盟审计院的评述向其作出答复。执行主任还应将一份该答复发送给管理委员会和欧盟委员会。

8.经欧洲议会要求，以及根据《财务条例》第146条第3款，执行主任应向其递交所涉会计年度的预算审批程序顺利实施所必要的任何信息。

9.欧洲议会应在第N+2年的5月15日前依照欧盟理事会经特定多数通过的建议，批准欧洲保险与职业养老金管理局对第N个会计年度包括来自欧盟总预算和主管部门的收入的预算的实施。

第65条　财务规则

欧洲保险与职业养老金管理局所适用的财务规则应由管理委员会在咨询欧盟委员会意见后通过。该等规则不得偏离《欧盟委员会关于〈欧盟理事会关于适用于欧洲共同体总预算的财务条例的第1605/2002号（欧共体和欧洲原子能共同体）条例〉第185条所指机构的框架性〈财务条例〉的第2343/2002号（欧共体和欧洲原子能共同体）条

Euratom) No 1605/2002 on the Financial Regulation applicable to the general budget of the European Communities [1] unless the specific operational needs for the functioning of the Authority so require and only with the prior agreement of the Commission.

Article 66 Anti-fraud measures

1. For the purposes of combating fraud, corruption and any other illegal activity, Regulation (EC) No 1073/1999 shall apply to the Authority without any restriction.

2. The Authority shall accede to the Interinstitutional Agreement concerning internal investigations by OLAF and shall immediately adopt appropriate provisions for all staff of the Authority.

3. The funding decisions and the agreements and the implementing instruments resulting from them shall explicitly stipulate that the Court of Auditors and OLAF may, if need be, carry out on-the-spot checks on the beneficiaries of monies disbursed by the Authority as well as on the staff responsible for allocating these monies.

CHAPTER Ⅶ GENERAL PROVISIONS

Article 67 Privileges and immunities

The Protocol (No 7) on the privileges and immunities of the European Union annexed to the Treaty on European Union and to the TFEU shall apply to the Authority and its staff.

Article 68 Staff

1. The Staff Regulations, the Conditions of Employment of Other Servants and the rules adopted jointly by the Union institutions for the purpose of applying them shall apply to the staff of the Authority, including its Executive Director and its Chairperson.

2. The Management Board, in agreement with the Commission, shall adopt the necessary implementing measures, in accordance with the arrangements provided for in Article 110 of the Staff Regulations.

3. In respect of its staff, the Authority shall exercise the powers conferred on the appointing authority by the Staff Regulations and on the authority entitled to conclude contracts by the Conditions of Employment of Other Servants.

4. The Management Board shall adopt provisions to allow national experts from Member States to be seconded to the Authority.

1 OJ L 357, 31.12.2002, p. 72.

例》[1]（2002年11月19日），但是，出于欧洲保险与职业养老金管理局运行的特殊运营需要并且仅在经欧盟委员会事先同意的情况下除外。

第66条　反欺诈措施

1.为反欺诈、腐败以及其他非法活动之目的，第1073/1999号（欧共体）条例应不受限制地适用于欧洲保险与职业养老金管理局。

2.欧洲保险与职业养老金管理局应加入《关于欧洲反欺诈办公室内部调查的机构间协议》，并应立即通过针对欧洲保险与职业养老金管理局所有工作人员的适当规定。

3.经费筹措决定以及由此产生的协议和实施性法律文件应明确规定欧盟审计院和欧洲反欺诈办公室可在必要时对欧洲保险与职业养老金管理局支出款项的受益人以及负责分配该等款项的工作人员进行现场调查。

第七章　一般条款

第67条　特殊权利和豁免

《欧洲联盟条约》和《欧洲联盟运行条约》附录关于欧盟的特殊权利和豁免的《议定书（第7号）》应适用于欧洲保险与职业养老金管理局及其工作人员。

第68条　工作人员

1.《人事条例》、《其他人员的聘用条件》以及欧盟机构为上述文件的适用联合通过的规则应适用于欧洲保险与职业养老金管理局的工作人员，包括其执行主任和主席。

2.根据《人事条例》第110条所规定的安排，管理委员会与欧盟委员会达成一致后应制定必要的实施细则。

3.欧洲保险与职业养老金管理局应对其工作人员行使《人事条例》授予的任命权以及《其他人员的聘用条件》授予的签订聘用合同的权力。

4.管理委员会应通过相关规定以允许从各成员国借调国内的专家到欧洲保险与职业养老金管理局。

1　2002年12月31日《欧盟公报》L 357，第72页。

Article 69 Liability of the Authority

1. In the case of non-contractual liability, the Authority shall, in accordance with the general principles common to the laws of the Member States, make good any damage caused by it or by its staff in the performance of their duties. The Court of Justice of the European Union shall have jurisdiction in any dispute over the remedying of such damage.

2. The personal financial liability and disciplinary liability of Authority staff towards the Authority shall be governed by the relevant provisions applying to the staff of the Authority.

Article 70 Obligation of professional secrecy

1. Members of the Board of Supervisors and the Management Board, the Executive Director, and members of the staff of the Authority including officials seconded by Member States on a temporary basis and all other persons carrying out tasks for the Authority on a contractual basis shall be subject to the requirements of professional secrecy pursuant to Article 339 TFEU and the relevant provisions in Union legislation, even after their duties have ceased.

Article 16 of the Staff Regulations shall apply to them.

In accordance with the Staff Regulations, the staff shall, after leaving service, continue to be bound by the duty to behave with integrity and discretion as regards the acceptance of certain appointments or benefits.

Neither Member States, the Union institutions or bodies, nor any other public or private body shall seek to influence staff members of the Authority in the performance of their tasks.

2. Without prejudice to cases covered by criminal law, any confidential information received by persons referred to in paragraph 1 whilst performing their duties may not be divulged to any person or authority whatsoever, except in summary or aggregate form, such that individual financial institutions cannot be identified.

Moreover, the obligation under paragraph 1 and the first subparagraph of this paragraph shall not prevent the Authority and the national supervisory authorities from using the information for the enforcement of the acts referred to in Article 1(2), and in particular for legal procedures for the adoption of decisions.

3. Paragraphs 1 and 2 shall not prevent the Authority from exchanging information with national supervisory authorities in accordance with this Regulation and other Union legislation applicable to financial institutions.

That information shall be subject to the conditions of professional secrecy referred to in paragraphs 1 and 2. The Authority shall lay down in its internal rules of procedure the practical arrangements for implementing the confidentiality rules referred to in paragraphs 1 and 2.

第69条 欧洲保险与职业养老金管理局的责任

1.对于欧洲保险与职业养老金管理局或其工作人员在履行职责时造成的不属于合同责任的任何损害，欧洲保险与职业养老金管理局应根据各成员国国内法律通用的一般原则进行赔偿。欧盟法院应对上述损害赔偿引发的任何争议有司法管辖权。

2.欧洲保险与职业养老金管理局工作人员对欧洲保险与职业养老金管理局承担的个人财务责任和违纪责任应受适用于欧洲保险与职业养老金管理局工作人员的相关规定管辖。

第70条 职业保密义务

1.监管机构理事会的理事和管理委员会的委员、执行主任、欧洲保险与职业养老金管理局工作人员（包括成员国暂时借调的官员）以及所有其他按合同为欧洲保险与职业养老金管理局履行职责的人员在欧洲保险与职业养老金管理局任职期间以及任职结束后均应遵守《欧洲联盟运行条约》第339条以及欧盟立法相关条款规定的职业保密要求。

《人事条例》第16条应适用于上述人员。

根据《人事条例》，工作人员离职后在接受特定任命和利益时应继续受诚信和谨慎义务约束。

各成员国、欧盟机构或单位或任何公共或私人机构均不得试图影响欧洲保险与职业养老金管理局工作人员履行其职责。

2.第1款所指人员在履行职责时收到的任何保密信息均不得泄露给任何个人或部门，但是，以无法识别具体金融机构的摘要或汇总形式披露的除外。上述规定不影响相关情形下刑法的适用。

另外，第1款以及本款第1项中的义务应不妨碍欧洲保险与职业养老金管理局和各国家级监管机构将信息用于执行第1条第2款所述立法，特别是用于通过决定的法律程序。

3.第1款和第2款应不妨碍欧洲保险与职业养老金管理局根据本条例以及其他适用于金融机构的欧盟立法与各国家级监管机构交换信息。

该等信息受第1款和第2款所述职业保密条件的约束。欧洲保险与职业养老金管理局应在其内部程序规则中规定实施第1款和第2款所述保密规则的具体安排。

4. The Authority shall apply Commission Decision 2001/844/EC, ECSC, Euratom of 29 November 2001 amending its internal Rules of Procedure [1].

Article 71 Data protection

This Regulation shall be without prejudice to the obligations of Member States relating to their processing of personal data under Directive 95/46/EC or the obligations of the Authority relating to its processing of personal data under Regulation (EC) No 45/2001 when fulfilling its responsibilities.

Article 72 Access to documents

1. Regulation (EC) No 1049/2001 shall apply to documents held by the Authority.

2. The Management Board shall, by 31 May 2011, adopt practical measures for applying Regulation (EC) No 1049/2001.

3. Decisions taken by the Authority pursuant to Article 8 of Regulation (EC) No 1049/2001 may be the subject of a complaint to the Ombudsman or of proceedings before the Court of Justice of the European Union, following an appeal to the Board of Appeal, as appropriate, in accordance with the conditions laid down in Articles 228 and 263 TFEU respectively.

Article 73 Language arrangements

1. Council Regulation No 1 determining the languages to be used by the European Economic Community [2] shall apply to the Authority.

2. The Management Board shall decide on the internal language arrangements for the Authority.

3. The translation services required for the functioning of the Authority shall be provided by the Translation Centre for the Bodies of the European Union.

Article 74 Headquarters Agreement

The necessary arrangements concerning the accommodation to be provided for the Authority in the Member State where its seat is located and the facilities to be made available by that Member State, as well as the specific rules applicable in that Member State to the Executive Director, the members of the Management Board, the staff of the Authority and members of their families shall be laid down in a Headquarters Agreement between the Authority and that Member State concluded after obtaining the approval of the Management Board.

That Member State shall provide the best possible conditions to ensure the proper functioning of the Authority, including multilingual, European-oriented schooling and

1 OJ L 317, 3.12.2001, p. 1

2 OJ 17, 6.10.1958, p. 385.

4.欧洲保险与职业养老金管理局应适用修改其内部程序规则的欧盟委员会2001/844/EC/ECSC号(欧洲原子能共同体)决定[1](2001年11月29日)。

第71条　数据保护

本条例不影响成员国在第95/46/EC号指令下与个人数据处理有关的义务或欧洲保险与职业养老金管理局在履行职责过程中应遵循的第45/2001号(欧共体)条例下与个人数据处理有关的义务。

第72条　文件查阅权

1.第1049/2001号(欧共体)条例应适用于欧洲保险与职业养老金管理局所持有的文件。

2.管理委员会应在2011年5月31日前制定适用第1049/2001号(欧共体)条例的具体措施。

3.针对欧洲保险与职业养老金管理局根据第1049/2001号(欧共体)条例第8条作出的决定,在适当情况下所涉人员可首先向行政复议委员会提出行政复议申请,若对行政复议结果不服,可再分别依照《欧洲联盟运行条约》第228条和第263条所列条件向申诉官申诉或向欧盟法院提起行政诉讼。

第73条　语言安排

1.确定欧洲经济共同体所用语言的欧盟理事会第1号条例[2]应适用于欧洲保险与职业养老金管理局。

2.管理委员会应就欧洲保险与职业养老金管理局的内部语言安排作出决定。

3.欧洲保险与职业养老金管理局运行所需的翻译服务应由欧盟翻译中心提供。

第74条　《总部协议》

获得管理委员会批准之后,欧洲保险与职业养老金管理局与其总部所在的成员国之间应缔结一份《总部协议》,规定该成员国应向欧洲保险与职业养老金管理局提供的住宿条件和供其使用的设施相关的必要安排,以及该成员国适用于执行主任、管理委员会委员、欧洲保险与职业养老金管理局工作人员及其家属的具体规则。

该成员国应尽可能提供最好的条件以确保欧洲保险与职业养老金管理局的稳健运行,包括多语的欧洲模式教育以及适当的交通便利。

1　2001年12月3日《欧盟公报》L 317,第1页。

2　1958年10月6日《欧盟公报》17,第385页。

appropriate transport connections.

Article 75 Participation of third countries

1. Participation in the work of the Authority shall be open to third countries which have concluded agreements with the Union whereby they have adopted and are applying Union law in the areas of competence of the Authority as referred to in Article 1(2).

2. The Authority may cooperate with the countries referred to in paragraph 1 applying legislation which has been recognised as equivalent in the areas of competence of the Authority referred to in Article 1(2), as provided for in international agreements concluded by the Union in accordance with Article 216 TFEU.

3. Under the relevant provisions of the agreements referred to in paragraphs 1 and 2, arrangements shall be made specifying, in particular, the nature, scope and procedural aspects of the involvement of the countries referred to in paragraph 1 in the work of the Authority, including provisions relating to financial contributions and to staff. They may provide for representation, as an observer, on the Board of Supervisors, but shall ensure that those countries do not attend any discussions relating to individual financial institutions, except where there is a direct interest.

CHAPTER Ⅷ TRANSITIONAL AND FINAL PROVISIONS

Article 76 Preparatory actions

1. Following the entry into force of this Regulation, and before the establishment of the Authority, CEIOPS shall act in close cooperation with the Commission to prepare for the replacement of CEIOPS by the Authority.

2. Once the Authority has been established, the Commission shall be responsible for the administrative establishment and initial administrative operation of the Authority until the Authority has appointed an Executive Director.

For that purpose, until such time as the Executive Director takes up his duties following his appointment by the Board of Supervisors in accordance with Article 51, the Commission may assign one official on an interim basis in order to fulfil the functions of the Executive Director. That period shall be limited to the time necessary for the appointment of an Executive Director of the Authority.

The interim Executive Director may authorise all payments covered by credits provided in the budget of the Authority, once approved by the Management Board and

第75条　第三国的参与

1.第三国与欧盟缔结了相关协议，因此已经采纳并正在适用第1条第2款所述欧洲保险与职业养老金管理局职权管辖范围内的欧盟法律的，应能参与欧洲保险与职业养老金管理局的工作。

2.根据欧盟依照《欧洲联盟运行条约》第216条缔结的国际协议，欧洲保险与职业养老金管理局可与第1款所述的国家合作适用已被认定在欧洲保险与职业养老金管理局第1条第2款所述职权管辖范围内与欧盟立法等效的立法。

3.根据第1款和第2款所述协议的相关规定，应作出相应安排，以特别指明第1款所述国家涉入欧洲保险与职业养老金管理局工作的性质、范围和程序，包括与费用分摊和工作人员有关的规定。根据该等安排，第三国可作为监管机构理事会的观察员，但应确保该等国家不参与任何与具体金融机构有关的讨论，存在直接利害关系的除外。

第八章　过渡规定和最终条款

第76条　筹备活动

1.本条例生效后至欧洲保险与职业养老金管理局成立前的期间内，欧洲保险与职业养老金监管机构委员会应与欧盟委员会紧密合作，为欧洲保险与职业养老金管理局取代欧洲保险与职业养老金监管机构委员会做好筹备工作。

2.欧洲保险与职业养老金管理局成立后，在欧洲保险与职业养老金管理局任命执行主任之前，应由欧盟委员会负责欧洲保险与职业养老金管理局的行政设立和初始行政运作。

为此，在监管机构理事会根据第51条任命执行主任之后，直至执行主任到任之前，欧盟委员会可临时委派一名官员履行执行主任的职能。该段时间应限于欧洲保险与职业养老金管理局任命执行主任所必要的时期。

临时执行主任经管理委员会批准，可核准欧洲保险与职业养老金管理局预算贷方项目所涵盖的所有支出，并可签订合同，包括在通过欧洲保险与职业养老金管理局

may conclude contracts, including staff contracts following the adoption of the Authority's establishment plan.

3. Paragraphs 1 and 2 are without prejudice to the powers of the Board of Supervisors and the Management Board.

4. The Authority shall be considered the legal successor of CEIOPS. By the date of establishment of the Authority, all assets and liabilities and all pending operations of CEIOPS shall be automatically transferred to the Authority. CEIOPS shall establish a statement showing its closing asset and liability situation as of the date of that transfer. That statement shall be audited and approved by CEIOPS and by the Commission.

Article 77 Transitional staff provisions

1. By way of derogation from Article 68, all employment contracts and secondment agreements concluded by CEIOPS or its Secretariat and in force on 1 January 2011 shall be honoured until their expiry date. They may not be extended.

2. All members of staff under contracts referred to in paragraph 1 shall be offered the possibility of concluding temporary agent contracts under Article 2(a) of the Conditions of Employment of Other Servants at the various grades as set out in the Authority's establishment plan.

An internal selection limited to staff who have contracts with CEIOPS or its Secretariat shall be carried out after the entry into force of this Regulation by the authority authorised to conclude contracts in order to check the ability, efficiency and integrity of those to be engaged. The internal selection procedure shall take full account of the skills and experience demonstrated by the individuals' performance prior to the engagement.

3. Depending on the type and level of functions to be performed, successful applicants shall be offered temporary agent's contracts of a duration corresponding at least to the time remaining under the prior contract.

4. The relevant national law relating to labour contracts and other relevant instruments shall continue to apply to staff members with prior contracts who choose not to apply for temporary agent's contracts or who are not offered temporary agents contracts in accordance with paragraph 2.

Article 78 National provisions

The Member States shall make such provision as is appropriate to ensure the effective application of this Regulation.

Article 79 Amendments

Decision No 716/2009/EC is hereby amended in so far as CEIOPS is removed from the list of beneficiaries set out in Section B of the Annex to that Decision.

预算制定计划后签订的劳动合同。

3.第1款和第2款不影响监管机构理事会和管理委员会的权力。

4.欧洲保险与职业养老金管理局应被视为欧洲保险与职业养老金监管机构委员会的合法继任机构。在欧洲保险与职业养老金管理局成立之日,欧洲保险与职业养老金监管机构委员会的所有资产和债务以及所有待执行的运营事务将自动转移给欧洲保险与职业养老金管理局。欧洲保险与职业养老金管理局监管机构委员会应制定一份报表表明其截至转移当日期末资产和债务的情况。该报表应由欧洲保险与职业养老金监管机构委员会和欧盟委员会审计和批准。

第77条　过渡期人事规定

1.作为第68条的例外,欧洲保险与职业养老金监管机构委员会或其秘书处签订的,并于2011年1月1日有效的所有劳动合同和借调协议,均应履行至到期日,不得延期。

2.第1款所述合同下的所有工作人员均应有机会按照欧洲保险与职业养老金管理局的预算制定计划所列各种级别签订符合《其他人员的聘用条件》第2条第a款的临时劳动合同。

本条例生效后,获得授权签订合同的部门应开展内部遴选,遴选对象仅限于与欧洲保险与职业养老金监管机构委员会或其秘书处有合同关系的工作人员,以对拟聘用人员的能力、效率和诚信进行审查。内部遴选程序应充分考虑候选人聘用前在工作中所展现出的个人技能和经验。

3.根据待履行职能的类型和级别,被录用的申请人应获得临时劳动合同,该等合同的期限应至少相当于先前合同未履行的时间。

4.与劳动合同有关的国内法律以及其他相关法律文件应继续适用于之前签订过合同,但选择不申请临时劳动合同或未根据第2款获得临时劳动合同的工作人员。

第78条　成员国的规定

各成员国应制定适当的规定以确保本条例的有效适用。

第79条　修正

应对第716/2009/EC号决定作出修正,从附录第B节所列的受益者名单中删除欧洲保险与职业养老金监管机构委员会。

Article 80 Repeal

Commission Decision 2009/79/EC, establishing CEIOPS, is hereby repealed with effect from 1 January 2011.

Article 81 Review

1. By 2 January 2014, and every 3 years thereafter, the Commission shall publish a general report on the experience acquired as a result of the operation of the Authority and the procedures laid down in this Regulation. That report shall evaluate, inter alia:

(a) the convergence in supervisory practices reached by competent authorities,

(i) the convergence in functional independence of the competent authorities and in standards equivalent to corporate governance;

(ii) the impartiality, objectivity and autonomy of the Authority;

(b) the functioning of the colleges of supervisors;

(c) the progress achieved towards convergence in the fields of crisis prevention, management and resolution, includingUnion funding mechanisms;

(d) the role of the Authority as regards systemic risk;

(e) the application of the safeguard clause established in Article 38;

(f) the application of the binding mediation role established in Article 19.

2. The report referred to in paragraph 1 shall also examine whether:

(a) it is appropriate to continue separate supervision of banking, insurance, occupational pensions, securities and financial markets;

(b) it is appropriate to undertake prudential supervision and supervise the conduct of business separately or by the same supervisor;

(c) it is appropriate to simplify and reinforce the architecture of the ESFS in order to increase the coherence between the macro and the micro levels and between the ESAs;

(d) the evolution of the ESFS is consistent with that of the global evolution;

(e) there is sufficient diversity and excellence within the ESFS;

(f) accountability and transparency in relation to publication requirements are adequate;

(g) the resources of the Authority are adequate to carry out its responsibilities;

(h) it is appropriate for the seat of the Authority to be maintained or to move the ESAs to a single seat to enhance better coordination between them.

3. Concerning the issue of direct supervision of institutions or infrastructures of pan-European reach and taking account of market developments, the Commission shall draw up an annual report on the appropriateness of entrusting the Authority with further supervisory responsibilities in this area.

4. The report and any accompanying proposals, as appropriate, shall be forwarded to the European Parliament and to the Council.

第80条　废止

设立欧洲保险与职业养老金监管机构委员会的欧盟委员会第2009/79/EC号决定特此于2011年1月1日废止。

第81条　审评

1.2014年1月2日前，欧盟委员会应发布一份综合报告，说明其在欧洲保险与职业养老金管理局运营和本条例所列程序方面取得的经验，并于此后每3年发布一份该等综合报告。该报告应评价的问题包括但不限于：

(a)各主管部门所达到的监管实践的趋同：

(i)各主管部门职能上的独立性趋同以及与公司治理等效之标准的趋同；

(ii)欧洲保险与职业养老金管理局的公正性、客观性和自主性；

(b)监管团的运作；

(c)在危机预防、管理和清盘领域(包括欧盟经费筹措机制)取得的趋同程度；

(d)欧洲保险与职业养老金管理局在系统性风险方面所起的作用；

(e)第38条所确立的保障条款的适用；

(f)第19条所设定的有约束力的调解角色的应用。

2.第1款所述的报告还应对下列事项进行审查：

(a)是否宜继续对银行业、保险、职业养老金、证券以及金融市场进行分业监管；

(b)是否宜分别开展审慎监管和业务活动监管或由一个监管机构同时进行上述两项监管；

(c)是否宜简化和加强欧洲金融监管机构体系的结构，以加强宏观和微观层级以及各欧洲监管机构之间的相互一致性；

(d)欧洲金融监管机构体系的发展是否与全球发展一致；

(e)欧洲金融监管机构体系内是否有足够的多样性和卓越性；

(f)在公开相关要求方面是否有充分的问责制和透明度；

(g)欧洲保险与职业养老金管理局的资源是否能保证其充分履行责任；

(h)欧洲保险与职业养老金管理局的地点是否宜保持不变，还是应将各欧洲监管机构迁至同一地点以加强相互之间的协调。

3.对于泛欧范围内的机构或基础设施的直接监管问题，考虑到市场的发展，欧盟委员会应起草一份关于是否应在此领域赋予欧洲保险与职业养老金管理局更多监管责任的年度报告。

4.报告及随附的任何提议(如有)均应转发给欧洲议会和欧盟理事会。

Article 82 Entry into force

This Regulation shall enter into force on the day following its publication in the Official Journal of the European Union.

It shall apply from 1 January 2011, with the exception of Article 76 and Article 77 (1) and (2), which shall apply as from the date of its entry into force.

The Authority shall be established on 1 January 2011.

This Regulation shall be binding in its entirety and directly applicable in all Member States.

Done atStrasbourg, 24 November 2010.

For the Council
The President
J. BUZEK

For the European Parliament
The President
O. CHASTEL

第82条　生效

本条例应于《欧盟公报》公布,公布的次日生效。

本条例应于2011年1月1日起适用，但第76条以及第77条第1款和第2款应从本条例生效之日起适用。

欧洲保险与职业养老金管理局应于2011年1月1日成立。

本条例所有内容对各成员国均具有约束力,并可直接适用于所有成员国。

2010年11月24日于斯特拉斯堡通过。

欧洲议会议长[1]　　　　欧盟理事会主席[2]

J.布泽克　　　　O.查斯特尔

1　英文为欧盟理事会主席,疑为欧洲议会议长,在译文中相应修改。——译者注

2　英文为欧洲议会议长,疑为欧盟理事会主席,已在译文中相应修改。——译者注

REGULATION (EU) NO 1095/2010 OF THE EUROPEAN PARLIAMENT AND OF THE COUNCIL

欧洲议会与欧盟理事会第 1095/2010 号(欧盟)条例

REGULATION (EU) NO 1095/2010 OF THE EUROPEAN PARLIAMENT AND OF THE COUNCIL

of 24 November 2010 establishing a European Supervisory Authority (European Securities and Markets Authority), amending Decision No 716/2009/EC and repealing Commission Decision 2009/77/EC

THE EUROPEAN PARLIAMENT AND THE COUNCIL OF THE EUROPEAN UNION,

Having regard to the Treaty on the Functioning of the European Union, and in particular Article 114 thereof,

Having regard to the proposal from the European Commission,

Having regard to the opinion of the European Central Bank [1],

Having regard to the opinion of the European Economic and Social Committee [2],

Acting in accordance with the ordinary legislative procedure [3],

Whereas:

(1) The financial crisis in 2007 and 2008 exposed important shortcomings in financial supervision, both in particular cases and in relation to the financial system as a whole. Nationally based supervisory models have lagged behind financial globalisation and the integrated and interconnected reality of European financial markets, in which many financial institutions operate across borders. The crisis exposed shortcomings in the areas of cooperation, coordination, consistent application of Union law and trust between national supervisors.

(2) Before and during the financial crisis, the European Parliament has called for a

1 OJ C 13, 20.1.2010, p. 1.

2 Opinion of 22 January 2010 (not yet published in the Official Jour-nal).

3 Position of the European Parliament of 22 September 2010 (not yet published in the Official Journal) and decision of the Council of 17 November 2010.

欧洲议会与欧盟理事会
第1095/2010号(欧盟)条例

(本条例于2010年11月24日通过,设立欧洲监管机构欧洲证券与市场管理局并修正第716/2009/EC号决定和废止欧盟委员会第2009/77/EC号决定)

欧洲议会和欧盟理事会,

根据《欧洲联盟运行条约》,特别是其中的第114条,

根据欧盟委员会的提议,

根据欧洲中央银行的意见[1],

根据欧洲经济与社会委员会的意见[2],

依照正常的立法程序[3],

鉴于下列情形,通过本条例:

(1)2007年和2008年的金融危机暴露出金融监管的重要缺陷,不论就特殊事例而言抑或就金融系统整体而言。局限于国家这一层级的监管模式已落后于金融全球化的步伐,亦无法适应众多金融机构已实现跨境运营的欧洲金融市场在一体化和相互关联方面的现实态势。危机暴露出的问题体现在国家级监管机构之间的合作与协调不够、欧盟法律适用一致性的缺乏及相互信任的不足这几个方面。

(2)欧洲议会在其于金融危机发生前及其持续期间,呼吁进一步整合欧洲的金融

1 2010年1月20日《欧盟公报》C 13,第1页。

2 2010年1月22日的意见(尚未在《欧盟公报》公布)。

3 2010年9月22日欧洲议会立场(尚未在《欧盟公报》公布)以及2010年11月17日欧盟理事会决定。

move towards more integrated European supervision in order to ensure a true level playing field for all actors at the level of the Union and to reflect the increasing integration of financial markets in the Union (in its resolutions of 13 April 2000 on the Commission communication on implementing the framework for financial markets: Action Plan [1], of 21 November 2002 on prudential supervision rules in the European Union [2] of 11 July 2007 on financial services policy (2005 to 2010) White Paper [3], of 23 September 2008 with recommendations to the Commission on hedge funds and private equity [4] and of 9 October 2008 with recommendations to the Commission on Lamfalussy follow-up: future structure of supervision [5], and in its positions of 22 April 2009 on the amended proposal for a directive of the European Parliament and of the Council on the taking-up and pursuit of the business of Insurance and Reinsurance (Solvency II) [6] and of 23 April 2009 on the proposal for a regulation of the European Parliament and of the Council on Credit Rating Agencies [7]).

(3) In November 2008, the Commission mandated a High-Level Group chaired by Jacques de Larosière to make recommendations on how to strengthen European supervisory arrangements with a view to better protecting the citizen and rebuilding trust in the financial system. In its final report presented on 25 February 2009 (the 'de Larosière Report'), the High-Level Group recommended that the supervisory framework be strengthened to reduce the risk and severity of future financial crises. It recommended reforms to the structure of supervision of the financial sector in the Union. The group also concluded that a European System of Financial Supervisors should be created, comprising three European Supervisory Authorities, one for the banking sector, one for the securities sector and one for the insurance and occupational pensions sector and recommended the creation of a European Systemic Risk Council. The report represented the reforms the experts considered were needed and on which work had to begin immediately.

(4) In its Communication of 4 March 2009 entitled 'Driving European Recovery', the Commission proposed to put forward draft legislation creating a European system of financial supervision and a European systemic risk board. In its Communication of 27 May 2009 entitled 'European Financial Supervision', it provided more detail about the possible architecture of such a new supervisory framework reflecting the main thrust of the de Larosière Report.

1 OJ C 40, 7.2.2001, p. 453.
2 OJ C 25 E, 29.1.2004, p. 394.
3 OJ C 175 E, 10.7.2008, p. 392.
4 OJ C 8 E, 14.1.2010, p. 26.
5 OJ C 9 E, 15.1.2010, p. 48.
6 OJ C 184 E, 8.7.2010, p. 214.
7 OJ C 184 E, 8.7.2010, p. 292.

监管，以便确保能在欧盟这一层级为所有市场主体提供真正公平的竞争环境，并反映欧盟金融市场不断一体化的现实［请参见：欧洲议会2000年4月13日关于欧盟委员会通报《落实金融市场框架：行动计划》的决议[1]、2002年11月21日关于欧盟审慎监管规则的决议[2]、2007年7月11日关于《2005年至2010年金融服务政策白皮书》的决议[3]、2008年9月23日关于对冲基金和私募股权的决议（含向欧盟委员会提出的建议）[4]、2008年10月9日关于《莱姆法路西的后续行动：未来监管结构》的决议（含向欧盟委员会提出的建议）[5]、2009年4月22日对《欧洲议会与欧盟理事会关于开办和经营保险与再保险业务的指令》（保险偿付能力标准Ⅱ）的修正稿提案所持立场[6]以及2009年4月23日对《欧洲议会与欧盟理事会关于信用评级机构的条例》的提案所持立场[7]］。

（3）2008年11月，欧盟委员会委托一个高级工作组在雅克·德·拉罗西埃的领导下，就如何加强欧洲监管安排以更好保护公众利益并重建公众对金融系统的信任提出建议。在其于2009年2月25日提交的最终报告（《德·拉罗西埃报告》）中，高级工作组建议强化监管框架以降低未来出现金融危机的风险及其严重程度，并建议对欧盟金融行业的监管结构进行改革，该小组还得出了应成立欧洲金融监管机构体系的结论，欧洲金融监管机构体系应由银行、证券以及保险与职业养老金三大金融行业的欧洲监管机构组成，并建议创设一个欧洲系统性风险理事会。此份报告阐述了专家们认为需要进行的改革以及必须立刻开展的工作。

（4）在2009年3月4日名为《推动欧洲复苏》的通报中，欧盟委员会提议起草相关立法草案以创建欧洲金融监管体系和欧洲系统性风险委员会，并在其2009年5月27日名为《欧洲金融监管》的通报中提供了该新监管框架可能之架构的更多细节，体现了《德·拉罗西埃报告》的要旨。

---

1 2001年2月7日《欧盟公报》C 40，第453页。
2 2004年1月29日《欧盟公报》C 25 E，第394页。
3 2008年7月10日《欧盟公报》C 175 E，第392页。
4 2010年1月14日《欧盟公报》C 8 E，第26页。
5 2010年1月15日《欧盟公报》C 9 E，第48页。
6 2010年7月8日《欧盟公报》C 184 E，第214页。
7 2010年7月8日《欧盟公报》C 184 E，第292页。

(5) The European Council, in its conclusions of 19 June 2009, confirmed that a European System of Financial Supervisors, comprising three new European Supervisory Authorities, should be established. The system should be aimed at upgrading the quality and consistency of national supervision, strengthening oversight of cross-border groups and establishing a European single rulebook applicable to all financial market participants in the internal market. It emphasised that the European Supervisory Authorities should also have supervisory powers in relation to credit rating agencies and invited the Commission to prepare concrete proposals on how the European System of Financial Supervisors could play a strong role in crisis situations, while stressing that decisions taken by the European Supervisory Authorities should not impinge on the fiscal responsibilities of Member States. The Commission has presented a Proposal for a Regulation amending Regulation (EC) No 1060/2009 of the European Parliament and of the Council of 16 September 2009 on credit rating agencies [1]. The European Parliament and the Council should consider that proposal in order to ensure that European Supervisory Authority (European Securities and Markets Authority) (hereinafter the Authority') will have adequate supervisory powers over credit rating agencies, bearing in mind that the Authority should execute exclusive supervisory powers over Credit Rating Agencies entrusted to it in Regulation (EC) No 1060/2009. For that purpose, the Authority should have appropriate powers of investigation and enforcement as specified in the relevant legislation, as well as the possibility of charging fees.

(6) On 17 June 2010, the European Council agreed that 'Member States should introduce systems of levies and taxes on financial institutions to ensure fair burden-sharing and to set incentives to contain systemic risk. Such levies or taxes should be part of a credible resolution framework. Further work is urgently required on their main features and issues of level playing field and cumulative impacts of various regulatory measures should be carefully assessed'.

(7) The financial and economic crisis has created real and serious risks to the stability of the financial system and the functioning of the internal market. Restoring and maintaining a stable and reliable financial system is an absolute prerequisite to preserving trust and coherence in the internal market, and thereby to preserve and improve the conditions for the establishment of a fully integrated and functioning internal market in the field of financial services. Moreover, deeper and more integrated financial markets offer better opportunities for financing and risk diversification, and thus help to improve the capacity of the economies to absorb shocks.

(8) The Union has reached the limits of what can be done with the present status of

1 OJ L 302, 17.11.2009, p. 1.

(5)欧洲理事会在其2009年6月19日的结论中确认,应当建立一个由三个新的欧洲监管机构组成的欧洲金融监管机构体系。该体系应旨在改善国家级监管工作的质量和一致性、加强对跨境集团的监控、建立适用于欧盟内部市场所有金融市场参与者的欧洲单一规则手册。欧洲理事会还强调了欧洲监管机构对信用评级机构的监管权,并要求欧盟委员会针对欧洲金融监管机构体系在危机情况下如何发挥强有力作用制定具体的提案,但同时也强调欧洲监管机构作出的决策不应影响成员国的财税责任。欧盟委员会呈报了一份关于修正《欧洲议会与欧盟理事会关于信用评级机构的第1060/2009号(欧共体)条例》[1](2009年9月16日)的条例提案。欧洲议会和欧盟理事会应对该提案予以考虑,以在坚持第1060/2009(欧共体)号条例授予欧洲监管机构欧洲证券与市场管理局(以下简称欧洲证券与市场管理局)对信用评级机构的专有监管权的原则下,确保欧洲证券与市场管理局对信用评级机构有充分的监管权力。为此,欧洲证券与市场管理局应有相关立法所规定的适当的调查权和执法权,并有可能收取相关费用。

(6)2010年6月17日,欧洲理事会同意:"成员国应实行对金融机构的计征费和税费制度,以确保公平的责任分担、激励金融机构遏制系统性风险,该等计征费或税费应作为一个可信的清盘框架的一部分。欧盟迫切需要就上述制度的主要特征开展进一步工作,同时应对公平竞争问题和各种监管措施累加造成的影响作审慎评估。"

(7)金融与经济危机对金融系统稳定以及内部市场运行带来了真实而严重的风险。恢复与维持一个稳定可靠的金融系统,无疑是维持公众对内部市场的信任和内部市场自身凝聚力的先决条件,建立一个彻底一体化和全面运行的金融服务内部市场所需条件也因而能得到维持和改善。此外,更为深化和一体化的金融市场为融资和风险分散提供了更好的机会,从而有助于提高各经济体化解冲击的能力。

(8)以欧洲监管机构委员会现有的身份和状态,欧盟已穷尽各种可能。欧盟不能

1 2009年11月17日《欧盟公报》L 302,第1页。

the Committees of European Supervisors. The Union cannot remain in a situation where there is no mechanism to ensure that national supervisors arrive at the best possible supervisory decisions for cross-border financial market participants; where there is insufficient cooperation and information exchange between national supervisors; where joint action by national authorities requires complicated arrangements to take account of the patchwork of regulatory and supervisory requirements; where national solutions are most often the only feasible option in responding to problems at the level of the Union; and where different interpretations of the same legal text exist. The European System of Financial Supervision (hereinafter 'the ESFS') should be designed to overcome those deficiencies and provide a system that is in line with the objective of a stable and single Union financial market for financial services, linking national supervisors within a strong Union network.

(9) The ESFS should be an integrated network of national and Union supervisory authorities, leaving day-to-day supervision to the national level. Greater harmonisation and the coherent application of rules for financial market participants across the Union should also be achieved. In addition to the Authority, a European Supervisory Authority (European Banking Authority) and a European Supervisory Authority (European Insurance and Occupational Pensions Authority) as well as a Joint Committee of the European Supervisory Authorities (hereinafter the Joint Committee') should be established. A European Systemic Risk Board (hereinafter 'the ESRB') should form part of the ESFS for the purposes of the tasks as specified in this Regulation and in Regulation (EU) No 1092/2010 of the European Parliament and of the Council [1].

(10) The European Supervisory Authorities (hereinafter collectively referred to as the 'ESAs') should replace the Committee of European Banking Supervisors established by Commission Decision 2009/78/EC [2], the Committee of European Insurance and Occupational Pensions Supervisors established by Commission Decision 2009/79/EC [3] and the Committee of European Securities Regulators established by Commission Decision 2009/77/EC [4], and should assume all of the tasks and competences of those committees including the continuation of ongoing work and projects, where appropriate. The scope of each European Supervisory Authority's action should be clearly defined. The ESAs should be accountable to the European Parliament and the Council. When that accountability relates to cross-sectoral issues that have been coordinated through the Joint Committee,

1 See page 1 of this Official Journal.
2 OJ L 25, 29.1.2009, p. 23.
3 OJ L 25, 29.1.2009, p. 28.
4 OJ L 25, 29.1.2009, p. 18.

面对下列困境坐视不管：欧盟缺乏一套能确保国家级监管机构对跨境金融市场参与者作出尽可能最佳的监管决定的机制；国家级监管机构之间缺乏足够的合作和信息交流；鉴于各国规制和监管要求的差异，国家级监管机构需要复杂的安排才能作出共同行动；目前为止，应对欧盟层级问题最常见且唯一可行的解决方案往往只是国家层级的解决方案；不同成员国对同一法律文本存在各种不同的解释。欧洲金融监管体系（英文简称ESFS）应旨在克服该等不足，并建立符合"稳定和单一的欧盟金融服务市场"目标的体系，将国家级监管机构连接纳入强大的欧盟网络之中。

（9）欧洲金融监管机构体系应该是一个整合国家层级和欧盟层级监管机构的一体化网络，日常的监管工作仍留待国家层级处理。同时，还应实现金融市场参与者规则在欧盟范围内更高程度的协调和适用的一致性。除了欧洲监管机构（欧洲证券与市场管理局）之外，还应设立欧洲监管机构（欧洲银行业管理局）、欧洲监管机构（欧洲保险与职业养老金管理局）以及上述三个欧洲监管机构的联合委员会（以下简称联合委员会）。欧洲系统性风险委员会（英文简称ESRB）也应成为欧洲金融监管体系的一部分，以完成本条例以及欧洲议会与欧盟理事会第1092/2010号（欧盟）条例[1]规定的工作。

（10）各欧洲监管机构（英文统称ESA）应取代依据欧盟委员会第2009/78/EC号决定[2]设立的欧洲银行业监管机构委员会、依据欧盟委员会第2009/79/EC号决定[3]设立的欧洲保险与职业养老金监管机构委员会以及依据欧盟委员会第2009/77/EC号决定[4]设立的欧洲证券监管机构委员会，并承担各自的所有职责和职权，包括在适当时继续完成任何正在进行中的职责和项目。对各欧洲监管机构的行动范围应有明确的界定。各欧洲监管机构应对欧洲议会和欧盟理事会负责。如其所承担的责任牵涉到曾经通过联合委员会协调的跨行业问题，则各欧洲监管机构应通过联合委员会对上述协作负责。

1 请见本《欧盟公报》，第1页。
2 2009年1月29日《欧盟公报》L 25，第23页。
3 2009年1月29日《欧盟公报》L 25，第28页。
4 2009年1月29日《欧盟公报》L 25，第18页。

the ESAs should be accountable, through the Joint Committee, for such coordination.

(11) The Authority should act with a view to improving the functioning of the internal market, in particular by ensuring a high, effective and consistent level of regulation and supervision taking account of the varying interests of all Member States and the different nature of financial market participants. The Authority should protect public values such as the integrity and stability of the financial system, the transparency of markets and financial products and the protection of investors. The Authority should also prevent regulatory arbitrage and guarantee a level playing field, and strengthen international supervisory coordination, for the benefit of the economy at large, including financial institutions and other stakeholders, consumers and employees. Its tasks should also include promoting supervisory convergence and providing advice to the Union institutions in the areas of its responsibility. The Authority should also be entrusted with certain responsibilities for existing and new financial activities.

(12) The Authority should also be able to temporarily prohibit or restrict certain financial activities that threaten the orderly functioning and integrity of financial markets or the stability of the whole or part of the financial system in the Union in the cases specified and under the conditions laid down in the legislative acts referred to in this Regulation. If required to make such temporary prohibition in the case of an emergency situation, the Authority should do so in accordance with and under the conditions laid down in this Regulation. In cases where a temporary prohibition or restriction of certain financial activities has a cross-sectoral impact, sectoral legislation should provide that the Authority should consult and coordinate its action with, where relevant, the European Supervisory Authority (European Banking Authority) and the European Supervisory Authority (European Insurance and Occupational Pensions Authority), through the Joint Committee.

(13) The Authority should take due account of the impact of its activities on competition and innovation within the internal market, on the Union's global competitiveness, on financial inclusion, and on the Union's new strategy for jobs and growth.

(14) In order to fulfil its objectives, the Authority should have legal personality as well as administrative and financial autonomy.

(15) Based on the work of international bodies, systemic risk should be defined as a risk of disruption in the financial system with the potential to have serious negative consequences for the internal market and the real economy. All types of financial intermediaries, markets and infrastructures may be potentially systemically important to some degree.

(16) Cross-border risk includes all risks caused by economic imbalances or financial

（11）欧洲证券与市场管理局应致力于改善内部市场的运行，尤其是在考虑所有成员国的不同利益以及金融市场参与者的不同性质的基础上，确保高水平、有效和一致的规制和监管。欧洲证券与市场管理局应保护公共价值观，如金融系统的诚信度和稳定、市场和金融产品的透明以及对投资者的保护。欧洲证券与市场管理局还应为了整体经济利益（包括金融机构以及其他利益相关者、消费者和雇员的利益）而防范监管套利，保证公平的竞争环境，并加强国际监管的相互协调。其职责还应包括推动监管趋同以及向其责任范围内的欧盟机构提供建议。欧盟还应委托欧洲证券与市场管理局对现有和未来的新金融活动承担某些责任。

（12）在本条例所述框架立法规定的特定情形下且在满足其所列条件之时，如有金融活动威胁到欧盟金融市场有序运行和诚信度或整体或部分金融系统的稳定，欧洲证券与市场管理局应能临时禁止或者限制此等金融活动。如在紧急情况下需要实施上述临时禁令，则欧洲证券与市场管理局应依据本条例所规定的条件实施。临时禁止或者限制某些金融活动会造成跨行业冲击的，行业性立法应规定欧洲证券与市场管理局在适当时通过联合委员会与两个欧洲监管机构（欧洲银行业管理局和欧洲保险与职业养老金管理局）磋商并协调其行动。

（13）欧洲证券与市场管理局应适当考虑其活动对欧盟内部市场的竞争和创新、欧盟的全球竞争力、金融融入以及欧盟就业和发展新战略所产生的冲击。

（14）为实现其目标，欧洲证券与市场管理局应有法人身份以及行政管理和财务自主权。

（15）基于国际机构的研究成果，系统性风险应被定义为金融系统发生扰乱并有可能对内部市场和实体经济造成严重消极后果的风险。所有类型的金融中介机构、市场以及基础设施在某种程度上均可能有潜在的系统重要性。

（16）跨境风险包括由欧盟地区的整体或部分经济不平衡或金融失败造成的，且

failures in all or parts of the Union that have the potential to have significant negative consequences for the transactions between economic operators of two or more Member States, for the functioning of the internal market or for the public finances of the Union or any of its Member States.

(17) The Court of Justice of the European Union in its judgment of 2 May 2006 in Case C–217/04 (United Kingdom of Great Britain and Northern Ireland v. European Parliament and Council of the European Union) held that: 'nothing in the wording of Article 95 EC [now Article 114 of the Treaty on the Functioning of the European Union (TFEU)] implies that the addressees of the measures adopted by the Community legislature on the basis of that provision can only be the individual Member States. The legislature may deem it necessary to provide for the establishment of a Community body responsible for contributing to the implementation of a process of harmonisation in situations where, in order to facilitate the uniform implementation and application of acts based on that provision, the adoption of non–binding supporting and framework measures seems appropriate' [1]. The purpose and tasks of the Authority–assisting competent national supervisory authorities in the consistent interpretation and application of Union rules and contributing to financial stability necessary for financial integration – are closely linked to the objectives of the Union *acquis* concerning the internal market for financial services. The Authority should therefore be established on the basis of Article 114 TFEU.

(18) The following legislative acts lay down the tasks for competent authorities of Member States, including cooperating with each other and with the Commission: Directive 97/9/EC of the European Parliament and of the Council of 3 March 1997 on investor–compensation schemes [2], Directive 98/26/EC of the European Parliament and of the Council of 19 May 1998 on settlement finality in payment and securities settlement systems [3], Directive 2001/34/EC of the European Parliament and of the Council of 28 May 2001 on the admission of securities to official stock exchange listing and on information to be published on those securities [4], Directive 2002/47/EC of the European Parliament and of the Council of 6 June 2002 on financial collateral arrangements [5], Directive 2003/6/EC of the European Parliament and of the Council of 28 January 2003 on insider dealing and market manipulation (market abuse) [6], Directive 2003/71/EC of the European Parliament and of the Council of 4 November 2003 on the prospectus to be published when securities

1 European Court Reports 2006 Page I–03771, para 44.
2 OJ L 84, 26.3.1997, p. 22.
3 OJ L 166, 11.6.1998, p. 45.
4 OJ L 184, 6.7.2001, p. 1.
5 OJ L 168, 27.6.2002, p. 43.
6 OJ L 96, 12.4.2003, p. 16.

可能对2个或以上成员国的经济运营主体之间的交易、欧盟内部市场的运行或欧盟或其任何成员国的公共财政带来严重消极后果的所有风险。

（17）欧盟法院在其2006年5月2日对第C-217/04号案件（大不列颠及北爱尔兰联合王国诉欧洲议会及欧盟理事会）的判决中表明："《欧洲共同体条约》第95条［现《欧洲联盟运行条约》（TFEU）第114条］的措辞并未暗示欧共体立法机构基于该条款所通过的措施只能适用于具体成员国。为促进基于《欧洲共同体条约》第95条的立法能得到统一实施和适用，应制定无法律约束力的辅助性和框架性措施时，立法机构可以认为有必要颁布设立该等欧共体机构的规定，由该机构负责推动协调程序的落实"[1]。欧洲证券与市场管理局的目标和职责在于协助国家级主管部门一致地解释和适用欧盟规则，致力于实现金融一体化所必不可少的金融稳定。该等职责与欧盟金融服务内部市场方面既定之法律所追求的目标紧密关联。因此，欧洲证券与市场管理局应建立在《欧洲联盟运行条约》第114条的基础上。

（18）下列框架立法规定了成员国主管部门的职责，其中包括相互合作以及与欧盟委员会合作：《欧洲议会与欧盟理事会关于投资者补偿计划的第97/9/EC号指令》[2]（1997年3月3日）、《欧洲议会与欧盟理事会关于支付系统和证券结算系统中的结算终结性的第98/26/EC号指令》[3]（1998年5月19日）、《欧洲议会与欧盟理事会关于证券获准在证券交易所正式上市以及应公布的与该等证券有关的信息的第2001/34/EC号指令》[4]（2001年5月28日）、《欧洲议会与欧盟理事会关于金融抵押品安排的第2002/47/EC号指令》[5]（2002年6月6日）、《欧洲议会与欧盟理事会关于内幕交易和市场操纵（市场滥用）的第2003/6/EC号指令》[6]（2003年1月28日）、《欧洲议会与欧盟理事会关于向公众发行证券或证券获准交易时所应公布的招募说明书的第2003/71/EC号指令（修正

1 《2006年欧洲法院报告》第44段，第I-03771页。
2 1997年3月26日《欧盟公报》L 84，第22页。
3 1998年6月11日《欧盟公报》L 166，第45页。
4 2001年7月6日《欧盟公报》L 184，第1页。
5 2002年6月27日《欧盟公报》L 168，第43页。
6 2003年4月12日《欧盟公报》L 96，第16页。

are offered to the public or admitted to trading and amending Directive 2001/34/EC [1], Directive 2004/39/EC of the European Parliament and of the Council of 21 April 2004 on markets in financial instruments [2], Directive 2004/109/EC of the European Parliament and of the Council of 15 December 2004 on the harmonisation of transparency requirements in relation to information about issuers whose securities are admitted to trading on a regulated market [3], Directive 2006/49/EC of the European Parliament and the Council of 14 June 2006 on the capital adequacy of investment firms and credit institutions [4], without prejudice to the competence of the European Supervisory Authority (European Banking Authority), as far as prudential supervision is concerned, Directive 2009/65/EC of the European Parliament and of the Council of 13 July 2009 on the coordination of laws, regulations and administrative provisions relating to undertakings for collective investment in transferable securities (UCITS) [5], any future legislation in the area of Alternative Investment Fund Managers (AIFM) and Regulation (EC) No 1060/2009.

(19) Existing Union legislation regulating the field covered by this Regulation also includes Directive 2002/87/EC of the European Parliament and of the Council of 16 December 2002 on the supplementary supervision of credit institutions, insurance undertakings and investment firms in a financial conglomerate [6], Directive 98/78/EC of the European Parliament and of the Council of 27 October 1998 on the supplementary supervision of insurance undertakings in an insurance group [7], Regulation (EC) No 1781/2006 of the European Parliament and of the Council of 15 November 2006 on information on the payer accompanying transfers of funds [8], and the relevant parts of Directive 2005/60/EC of the European Parliament and of the Council of 26 October 2005 on the prevention of the use of the financial system for the purpose of money laundering and terrorist financing [9] and of Directive 2002/65/EC of the European Parliament and of the Council of 23 September 2002 concerning the distance marketing of consumer financial services [10].

(20) It is desirable that the Authority promote a consistent approach in the area of

1 OJ L 345, 31.12.2003, p. 64.
2 OJ L 145, 30.4.2004, p. 1.
3 OJ L 390, 31.12.2004, p. 38.
4 OJ L 177, 30.6.2006, p. 201.
5 OJ L 302, 17.11.2009, p. 32.
6 OJ L 35, 11.2.2003, p. 1.
7 OJ L 330, 5.12.1998, p. 1.
8 OJ L 345, 8.12.2006, p. 1.
9 OJ L 309, 25.11.2005, p. 15.
10 OJ L 271, 9.10.2002, p. 16.

〈第2001/34/EC号指令〉)》[1]（2003年11月4日）、《欧洲议会与欧盟理事会关于金融工具市场的第2004/39/EC号指令》[2]（2004年4月21日）、《欧洲议会与欧盟理事会关于协调证券获准在受监管市场交易的发行人的信息透明度要求的第2004/109/EC号指令》[3]（2004年12月15日）、《欧洲议会与欧盟理事会关于投资公司和信贷机构资本充足性的第2006/49/EC号指令》[4]（2006年6月14日），以及《欧洲议会与欧盟理事会协调关于可转让证券集合投资计划（UCITS）的法律、法规和规章的第2009/65/EC号指令》[5]（2009年7月13日）、将来颁布的关于另类投资基金管理人（AIFM）的其他立法以及第1060/2009号（欧共体）条例在不影响欧洲监管机构（欧洲银行业管理局）职权的情况下涉及审慎监管的部分。

（19）对本条例所覆盖的领域进行监管的欧盟现行立法还包括《欧洲议会与欧盟理事会关于对金融集团下属信贷机构、保险公司以及投资公司实施补充监管的第2002/87/EC号指令》[6]（2002年12月16日）、《欧洲议会与欧盟理事会关于对保险集团下属保险公司实施补充监管的第98/78/EC号指令》[7]（1998年10月27日）、《欧洲议会与欧盟理事会关于汇款随附之付款人信息的第1781/2006号（欧共体）条例》[8]（2006年11月15日）、《欧洲议会与欧盟理事会关于防范利用金融系统从事洗钱和恐怖分子融资的第2005/60/EC号指令》[9]（2005年10月26日）以及《欧洲议会与欧盟理事会关于远程营销消费者金融服务的第2002/65/EC号指令》[10]（2002年9月23日）的相关部分。

（20）在投资者补偿计划领域，欧洲证券与市场管理局宜推广一套一致的模式，以

1 2003年12月31日《欧盟公报》L 345，第64页。
2 2004年4月30日《欧盟公报》L 145，第1页。
3 2004年12月31日《欧盟公报》L 390，第38页。
4 2006年6月30日《欧盟公报》L 177，第201页。
5 2009年11月17日《欧盟公报》L 302，第32页。
6 2003年2月11日《欧盟公报》L 35，第1页。
7 1998年12月5日《欧盟公报》L 330，第1页。
8 2006年12月8日《欧盟公报》L 345，第1页。
9 2005年11月25日《欧盟公报》L 309，第15页。
10 2002年10月9日《欧盟公报》L 271，第16页。

investor compensation schemes to ensure a level playing field and the equitable treatment of investors across the Union. As investor compensation schemes are subject to oversight in their Member States rather than regulatory supervision, the Authority should be able to exercise its powers under this Regulation in relation to the investor compensation scheme itself and its operator.

(21) In accordance with the Declaration (No 39) on Article 290 of the Treaty on the Functioning of the European Union (TFEU), annexed to the Final Act of the Intergovernmental Conference which adopted the Treaty of Lisbon, the elaboration of regulatory technical standards requires assistance of technical expertise in a form which is specific to the financial services area. It is necessary to allow the Authority to provide such expertise also on standards or parts of standards that are not based on a draft technical standard that it has elaborated.

(22) There is a need to introduce an effective instrument to establish harmonised regulatory technical standards in financial services to ensure, also through a single rulebook, a level playing field and adequate protection of investors and consumers across the Union. As a body with highly specialised expertise, it is efficient and appropriate to entrust the Authority, in areas defined by Union law, with the elaboration of draft regulatory technical standards, which do not involve policy choices.

(23) The Commission should endorse those draft regulatory technical standards by means of delegated acts under Article 290 TFEU in order to give them binding legal effect. They should be subject to amendment only in very restricted and extraordinary circumstances, since the Authority is the actor in close contact with and knowing best the daily functioning of financial markets. Draft regulatory technical standards would be subject to amendment if they were incompatible with Union law, did not respect the principle of proportionality or ran counter to the fundamental principles of the internal market for financial services as reflected in the *acquis* of Union financial services legislation. The Commission should not change the content of the draft regulatory technical standards prepared by the Authority without prior coordination with the Authority. To ensure a smooth and expeditious adoption process for those standards, the Commission's decision to endorse draft regulatory technical standards should be subject to a time limit.

(24) Given the technical expertise of the Authority in the areas where regulatory technical standards should be developed, note should be taken of the Commission's stated intention to rely, as a rule, on the draft regulatory technical standards submitted to it by the Authority in view of the adoption of the corresponding delegated acts. However, in cases where the Authority fails to submit a draft regulatory technical standard within the time limits set out by the relevant legislative act, it should be ensured that the result of

确保公平的竞争环境,令欧盟各地投资者能享受平等的待遇。由于投资者补偿计划在各个成员国虽受监控,但不受规制性质的监管,欧洲证券与市场管理局应能行使其在本条例下关于投资者补偿计划以及投资者补偿计划运营者的权力。

(21)根据通过《里斯本条约》的政府间会议《最后决议》附录中的《关于〈欧洲联盟运行条约〉(TFEU)第290条的声明(第39号)》,对于监管性技术标准的制定,需要金融服务领域专门的技术专长协助。对于那些并非基于欧洲证券与市场管理局自身制定的技术标准草案之标准或者部分标准,也有必要允许欧洲证券与市场管理局提供上述技术专长。

(22)有必要采取有效的手段,为金融服务制定协调一致的监管性技术标准,同时结合单一规则手册来确保公平的竞争环境以及对欧盟各地投资者和消费者的充分保护。欧洲证券与市场管理局作为一个拥有高度专门知识的机构,委托其在欧盟法律界定的领域中制定不涉及政策性选择的监管性技术标准草案是高效且适宜的。

(23)欧盟委员会应按照《欧洲联盟运行条约》第290条以授权立法的形式同意和支持该等监管性技术标准草案,以赋予其法律约束力。鉴于欧洲证券与市场管理局是与金融市场有密切联系并且最了解金融市场日常运行的主体,因此仅能在十分有限和特殊的情况下才能对该等监管性技术标准草案进行修正。如果监管性技术标准草案与欧盟法律不相容、不符合比例原则,或者违背了欧盟既定的金融服务立法所体现的金融服务内部市场基本原则,则应对其进行修正。未经与欧洲证券与市场管理局事先协调,欧盟委员会不得变更欧洲证券与市场管理局起草的监管性技术标准草案内容。为确保顺利、快速地通过该等标准,欧盟委员会应在一定的时限内作出同意和支持监管性技术标准草案的决定。

(24)鉴于欧洲证券与市场管理局在应制定监管性技术标准之领域拥有技术专长,我们应注意到欧盟委员会声明的如下意向,即其在通过相应的授权立法时一般依赖欧洲证券与市场管理局向其呈报的监管性技术标准草案。然而,欧洲证券与市场管理局未在相关框架立法规定的时限内呈报该等草案的,仍应当保证委托授权之行使获得成效并维持决策程序效率。在该等情形下,欧盟委员会应有权在欧洲证券与市场管理局未呈报草案的情况下通过监管性技术标准。

the exercise of delegated power is actually achieved, and the efficiency of the decision-making process be maintained. In those cases, the Commission should therefore be empowered to adopt regulatory technical standards in the absence of a draft by the Authority.

(25) The Commission should also be empowered to adopt implementing technical standards by means of implementing acts under Article 291 TFEU.

(26) In areas not covered by regulatory or implementing technical standards, the Authority should have the power to issue guidelines and recommendations on the application of Union law. In order to ensure transparency and to strengthen compliance by national supervisory authorities with those guidelines and recommendations, it should be possible for the Authority to publish the reasons for supervisory authorities' non-compliance with those guidelines and recommendations.

(27) Ensuring the correct and full application of Union law is a core prerequisite for the integrity, transparency, efficiency and orderly functioning of financial markets, the stability of the financial system, and for neutral conditions of competition for financial market participants in the Union. A mechanism should therefore be established whereby the Authority addresses instances of non-application or incorrect application of Union law amounting to a breach thereof. That mechanism should apply in areas where Union law defines clear and unconditional obligations.

(28) To allow for a proportionate response to instances of incorrect or insufficient application of Union law, a three-step mechanism should apply. First, the Authority should be empowered to investigate alleged incorrect or insufficient application of Union law obligations by national authorities in their supervisory practice, concluded by a recommendation. Second, where the competent national authority does not follow the recommendation, the Commission should be empowered to issue a formal opinion taking into account the Authority's recommendation, requiring the competent authority to take the actions necessary to ensure compliance with Union law.

(29) Third, to overcome exceptional situations of persistent inaction by the competent authority concerned, the Authority should be empowered, as a last resort, to adopt decisions addressed to individual financial market participants. That power should be limited to exceptional circumstances in which a competent authority does not comply with the formal opinion addressed to it and in which Union law is directly applicable to financial market participants by virtue of existing or future Union regulations.

(30) Serious threats to the orderly functioning and integrity of financial markets or the stability of the financial system in the Union require a swift and concerted response at Union level. The Authority should therefore be able to require national supervisory authorities to take specific actions to remedy an emergency situation.

(25)欧盟委员会应也有权按《欧洲联盟运行条约》第291条以实施性立法的形式通过实施性技术标准。

(26)在监管性或实施性技术标准未覆盖的领域,欧洲证券与市场管理局应有权就欧盟法律的适用提出指引和建议。为确保透明度及促进国家级监管机构遵循该等指引和建议,欧洲证券与市场管理局有可能公布监管机构不遵循该等指引和建议的理由。

(27)确保欧盟法律的正确和全面适用是欧盟金融市场诚信度、透明、有效、有序运行、金融系统稳定以及金融市场参与者竞争中立性的核心前提。因此,应建立一项机制,使欧洲证券与市场管理局得以处理不适用或不正确适用欧盟法律从而导致违反欧盟法律的情形。该机制应适用于欧盟法律界定了明确、无条件的义务的领域。

(28)为对不正确或不充分适用欧盟法律作出成比例的回应,应采用“三步走”的机制。第一步,欧洲证券与市场管理局有权对国家级监管机构涉嫌在其监管实践中不正确或不充分履行欧盟法律义务的情况进行调查,而该等调查结论系以一份建议的形式作出;第二步,国家级主管部门没有遵循该建议的,欧盟委员会应有权发出一份反映欧洲证券与市场管理局建议的正式意见,要求该主管部门采取必要的行动以确保欧盟法律得到遵守。

(29)第三步,为了克服所涉主管部门持续不作为的特殊状况,作为最后手段,欧洲证券与市场管理局有权针对具体金融市场参与者作出决定,但是,仅在主管部门不遵循针对其发出的正式意见,且欧盟法律根据现有或未来的欧盟条例可直接适用于金融市场参与者的特殊情况下,方可行使上述权力。

(30)欧盟金融市场的有序运行和诚信度或欧盟金融系统稳定面临严重威胁的时候,应在欧盟层面作出迅速而一致的反应。因此,欧洲证券与市场管理局应能要求各国家级监管机构采取特定行动对紧急情况进行补救。经任何欧洲监管机构、欧盟委员会或欧洲系统性风险委员会请求,欧盟理事会有权判定是否存在紧急情况。

The power to determine the existence of an emergency situation should be conferred on the Council, following a request by any of the ESAs, the Commission or the ESRB.

(31) The Authority should be able to require national supervisory authorities to take specific action to remedy an emergency situation. The action undertaken by the Authority in this respect should be without prejudice to the Commission's powers under Article 258 TFEU to initiate infringement proceedings against the Member State of that supervisory authority for its failure to take such action, and without prejudice to the Commission's right in such circumstances to seek interim measures in accordance with the rules of procedure of the Court of Justice of the European Union. Furthermore, it should be without prejudice to any liability that that Member State might incur in accordance with the case law of the Court of Justice of the European Union if its supervisory authorities fail to take the action required by the Authority.

(32) In order to ensure efficient and effective supervision and a balanced consideration of the positions of the competent authorities in different Member States, the Authority should be able to settle disagreements in cross-border situations between those competent authorities with binding effect, including within colleges of supervisors. A conciliation phase should be provided for during which the competent authorities may reach an agreement. The Authority's competence should cover disagreements on the procedure or content of an action or inaction by a competent authority of a Member State in cases specified in the legally binding Union acts referred to in this Regulation. In such a situation, one of the supervisors involved should be entitled to refer the issue to the Authority, which should act in accordance with this Regulation. The Authority should be empowered to require the competent authorities concerned to take specific action or to refrain from action in order to settle the matter in order to ensure compliance with Union law, with binding effects for the competent authorities concerned. If a competent authority does not comply with the settlement decision addressed to it, the Authority should be empowered to adopt decisions directly addressed to financial market participants in areas of Union law directly applicable to them. The power to adopt such decisions should apply only as a last resort and then only to ensure the correct and consistent application of Union law. In cases where the relevant Union legislation confers discretion on Member States' competent authorities, decisions taken by the Authority cannot replace the exercise in compliance with Union law of that discretion.

(33) The crisis has proven that the current system of cooperation between national authorities whose powers are limited to individual Member States is insufficient as regards financial institutions that operate across borders.

(31)欧洲证券与市场管理局应能要求国家级监管机构采取特定行动以对紧急情况作出补救。欧洲证券与市场管理局就此采取的行动不应影响欧盟委员会因成员国监管机构未采取上述行动而根据《欧洲联盟运行条约》第258条对该成员国启动违法违规诉讼程序的权力,也不应影响欧盟委员会在该等情况下依照欧盟法院程序规则寻求临时措施的权利。此外,成员国由于其监管机构未采取欧洲证券与市场管理局要求的行动而在欧盟法院判例法下所应承担的任何法律责任,不因欧洲证券与市场管理局的行动而受影响。

(32)为确保监管兼具效率和成效并平衡考虑各成员国主管部门的立场,欧洲证券与市场管理局应能以具有约束力的方式解决不同主管部门之间在跨境情形下的分歧,包括监管团内部的分歧。应规定一个调解期,主管部门可在此时间段内达成一致意见。在本条例所述具有法律约束力的欧盟法律文件所指定的情形里,对某成员国主管部门所采取的行动或不采取行动所依据的程序或相关内容出现了分歧的,欧洲证券与市场管理局应对该等分歧有管辖权。在该状况下,所涉监管机构之一有权将该事宜移交欧洲证券与市场管理局,由欧洲证券与市场管理局依照本条例处理。欧洲证券与市场管理局有权通过要求所涉主管部门采取特定行动或不采取行动的方式来解决有关事宜并确保欧盟法律得到遵守,此等要求应对所涉主管部门具有约束力。如主管部门不遵循对其作出的解决分歧的决定,欧洲证券与市场管理局有权在欧盟法律直接适用于金融市场参与者的领域,直接对金融市场参与者作出决定。作出上述决定的权力仅能作为最后手段且仅为确保欧盟法律的正确和一致适用而使用。相关欧盟立法授予了成员国主管部门自由裁量权的,欧洲证券与市场管理局所作出的决定不能替代主管部门依照欧盟法律行使该自由裁量权。

(33)危机证明,由于国家级监管机构的权力范围局限于其各自所属成员国,目前各国家级监管机构之间的合作制度对于跨境运营的金融机构而言是不充分的。

(34) Expert Groups set up by Member States to examine the causes of the crisis and make suggestions to improve the regulation and supervision of the financial sector have confirmed that the current arrangements are not a sound basis for the future regulation and supervision of cross-border financial institutions across the Union.

(35) As the de Larosière Report indicates, '[i]n essence, we have two alternatives: the first "chacun pour soi" beggar-thy-neighbour solutions; or the second-enhanced, pragmatic, sensible European cooperation for the benefit of all to preserve an open world economy. This will bring undoubted economic gains'.

(36) Colleges of supervisors play an important role in the efficient, effective and consistent supervision of financial market participants operating across borders. The Authority should contribute to promoting and monitoring the efficient, effective and consistent functioning of the colleges of supervisors and, in that respect, have a leading role in ensuring the consistent and coherent functioning of colleges of supervisors for cross-border financial institutions across the Union. The Authority should therefore have full participation rights in colleges of supervisors with a view to streamlining the functioning of and the information exchange process in the colleges of supervisors and to foster convergence and consistency across colleges in the application of Union law. As the de Larosière Report states,'competition distortions and regulatory arbitrage stemming from different supervisory practices must be avoided, because they have the potential of undermining financial stability-inter alia by encouraging a shift of financial activity to countries with lax supervision. The supervisory system has to be perceived as fair and balanced'.

(37) In the areas of its competence, the Authority should contribute to, and participate actively in the development and coordination of effective and consistent recovery and resolution plans, procedures in emergency situations and preventive measures to ensure the internalisation of costs by the financial system, in order to minimise the systemic impact of any failure and the reliance on taxpayer funds to bail out financial market participants. It should contribute to developing methods for the resolution of failing key financial market participants in ways which avoid contagion, which allow them to be wound down in an orderly and timely manner, and which, where applicable, include coherent and credible funding mechanisms as appropriate.

(38) In the current review of Directive 94/19/EC of the European Parliament and of the Council of 30 May 1994 on deposit-guarantee schemes [1] and Directive 97/9/EC, the Commission's intention to pay special attention to the need to ensure further

1 OJ L 135, 31.5.1994, p. 5.

(34)为检讨危机发生的原因、提出相关建议以改善对金融行业的规制和监管,各成员国设立了专家小组。该专家小组确认了现有安排不足以为欧盟内部跨境金融机构的规制和监管奠定坚实的基础。

(35)正如《德·拉罗西埃报告》所指:"实质上我们有两套方案可供选择:一个是'人人为自己'、以邻为壑的解决方案;第二个是在欧洲范围内强化、务实、明智的合作,为各方的利益而维持一个开放的世界经济。这无疑会带来诸多经济成果。"

(36)在对跨境运营的金融市场参与者进行一致的且兼具效率和成效的监管中,各监管团起到重要作用。欧洲证券与市场管理局应致力于推进和监控各监管团一致的且兼具效率和成效的运作,并在这方面发挥其领导作用,确保监管团对欧盟内跨境金融机构起到相互连贯和一致的作用。因此,欧洲证券与市场管理局在监管团中应有充分的参与权,以提高监管团运作和信息交流程序的效率,推动在各监管团中能一致趋同地适用欧盟法律。正如《德·拉罗西埃报告》所表明的:"必须避免监管实践的差异造成竞争扭曲和监管套利,因为它们可能会对金融稳定造成损害(如此种差异造成变相鼓励将金融活动转移到监管不严的国家)。欧盟的监管制度必须塑造公平、平衡的公信力"。

(37)欧洲证券与市场管理局应在其职权管辖范围内致力于并积极参与制定和协调紧急情况下有效、一致的恢复和清盘计划、程序以及预防不利情况的措施,以确保有关成本在金融系统内部消化,同时最大程度地降低金融机构经营失败对系统的冲击,尽量避免依靠纳税人资金来为金融市场参与者买单。欧洲证券与市场管理局应致力于制定针对濒临倒闭的关键金融市场参与者的清盘方法,此等清盘方法应避免风险的传播,使濒临倒闭的关键金融市场参与者能有序、及时地停业清理,包括一套相互一致且强大的适当经费筹措机制。

(38)在目前对《欧洲议会与欧盟理事会关于存款担保计划的第94/19/EC号指令》[1](1994年5月30日)以及第97/9/EC号指令的审评中,欧盟委员会对于确保整个欧盟进一步协调的必要性给予高度重视。在保险业中,欧盟委员会也显然有意审查是否可能在

1 1994年5月31日《欧盟公报》L 135,第5页。

harmonisation throughout the Union is noted. In the insurance sector, the Commission's intention to examine the possibility of introducing Union rules protecting insurance policy holders in case of a failing insurance company is also noted. The ESAs should play an important role in those areas and appropriate powers concerning the European guarantee scheme systems should be conferred upon them.

(39) The delegation of tasks and responsibilities can be a useful instrument in the functioning of the network of supervisors in order to reduce the duplication of supervisory tasks, to foster cooperation and thereby streamline the supervisory process, as well as to reduce the burden imposed on financial market participants. This Regulation should therefore provide a clear legal basis for such delegation. Whilst respecting the general rule that delegation should be allowed, Member States should be able to introduce specific conditions for the delegation of responsibilities, for example regarding information about, and the notification of, delegation arrangements. Delegation of tasks means that tasks are carried out by the Authority or by a national supervisory authority other than the responsible authority, while the responsibility for supervisory decisions remains with the delegating authority. By the delegation of responsibilities, the Authority or a national supervisory authority (the delegate) should be able to decide upon a certain supervisory matter in its own name in lieu of the delegating authority. Delegations should be governed by the principle of allocating supervisory competence to a supervisor which is best placed to take action in the subject matter. A reallocation of responsibilities would be appropriate, for example, for reasons of economies of scale or scope, of coherence in group supervision, and of optimal use of technical expertise among national supervisory authorities. Decisions by the delegate should be recognised by the delegating authority and by other competent authorities as determinative if those decisions are within the scope of the delegation. Relevant Union legislation could further specify the principles for the reallocation of responsibilities upon agreement. The Authority should facilitate and monitor delegation agreements between national supervisory authorities by all appropriate means.

It should be informed in advance of intended delegation agreements, in order to be able to express an opinion where appropriate. It should centralise the publication of such agreements to ensure timely, transparent and easily accessible information about agreements for all parties concerned. It should identify and disseminate best practices regarding delegation and delegation agreements.

(40) The Authority should actively foster supervisory convergence across the Union with the aim of establishing a common supervisory culture.

(41) Peer reviews are an efficient and effective tool for fostering consistency within the network of financial supervisors. The Authority should therefore develop the

保险公司濒临倒闭时对保户实施欧盟的保护规则。各欧洲监管机构应在该等领域发挥重要作用,并被授予与欧洲担保计划体制相关的适当权力。

(39)在监管机构网络的运行中,职责和责任的委托可减少监管职责的重复并促进合作,从而提高监管程序的效率,同时能减轻金融市场参与者的负担。为此,本条例应为上述委托提供明确的法律依据。在遵守该等委托的一般规则的同时,成员国也应有权为责任委托施加特定的条件,如关于委托安排的信息和通知方面的条件。职责委托的含义是,由欧洲证券与市场管理局或某个国家级监管机构而非原负责部门来履行职责,但委托部门仍对监管决定负责。通过责任委托,欧洲证券与市场管理局或国家级监管机构(受托部门)应能以自己名义代表委托部门就某项监管事宜作出决定。委托的原则是将监管职权委托给就相关事项最适宜采取行动的监管机构。出于规模或范围效益、集团监管的相互一致性以及对不同国家级监管机构各自技术专长的优化使用等各种原因的考虑,可对责任进行再分配。受托部门在委托范围内所作决定,应被委托部门和其他主管部门视为有效决定。相关的欧盟立法可进一步阐述经各方一致同意对责任进行再分配的原则。欧洲证券与市场管理局应通过一切适当的方式协助和监控各国家级监管机构之间达成委托协议。

在委托协议签署之前应通知欧洲证券与市场管理局,使其能在适当时表达意见。欧洲证券与市场管理局应统一公布上述协议,以确保所涉各方均能及时、透明和方便地查阅有关协议的信息。欧洲证券与市场管理局应确定并传播有关委托活动和委托协议的最佳实践。

(40)欧洲证券与市场管理局应积极促进欧盟范围内的监管趋同,以建立共同的监管文化。

(41)同行审评是促进金融监管机构网络内部一致性的兼具效率和成效的工具。因此,欧洲证券与市场管理局应为上述审评制定方法论框架,并定期进行审评。审评

methodological framework for such reviews and conduct them on a regular basis. Reviews should focus not only on the convergence of supervisory practices but also on the capacity of supervisors to achieve high quality supervisory outcomes as well as on the independence of those competent authorities. The outcome of peer reviews should be made public with the agreement of the competent authority subject to the review. Best practices should also be identified and made public.

(42) The Authority should actively promote a coordinated Union supervisory response, in particular to ensure the orderly functioning and integrity of financial markets and the stability of the financial system in the Union. In addition to its powers for action in emergency situations, the Authority should therefore be entrusted with a general coordination function within the ESFS. The smooth flow of all relevant information between competent authorities should be a particular focus of the Authority's actions.

(43) In order to safeguard financial stability it is necessary to identify, at an early stage, trends, potential risks and vulnerabilities stemming from the micro-prudential level, across borders and across sectors. The Authority should monitor and assess such developments in the area of its competence and, where necessary, inform the European Parliament, the Council, the Commission, the other European Supervisory Authorities and the ESRB on a regular and, as necessary, on an ad hoc basis. The Authority should also, in cooperation with the ESRB, initiate and coordinate Union-wide stress tests to assess the resilience of financial market participants to adverse market developments, and it should ensure that an as consistent as possible methodology is applied at the national level to such tests. In order to perform its functions properly, the Authority should conduct economic analyses of the markets and the impact of potential market developments.

(44) Given the globalisation of financial services and the increased importance of international standards, the Authority should foster dialogue and cooperation with supervisors outside the Union. It should be empowered to develop contacts and enter into administrative arrangements with the supervisory authorities and administrations of third countries and with international organisations, while fully respecting the existing roles and respective competences of the Member States and the Union institutions. Participation in the work of the Authority should be open to countries which have concluded agreements with the Union whereby they have adopted and are applying Union law, and the Authority should be able to cooperate with third countries which apply legislation that has been recognised as equivalent to that of the Union.

(45) The Authority should serve as an independent advisory body to the European Parliament, the Council, and the Commission in the area of its competence. Without

的焦点不应仅停留在监管实践的趋同，还应着重于监管机构取得高质量监管结果的能力以及该等主管部门的独立性。接受审评的主管部门同意后，同行审评的结果应予公布。欧洲证券与市场管理局还应确定和公布最佳实践。

(42)欧洲证券与市场管理局应积极推动欧盟作出协调一致的监管回应，尤其要确保欧盟金融市场的有序运行和诚信度以及金融系统的稳定。因此，除在紧急情况下采取行动的权力之外，欧洲证券与市场管理局还应被赋予在欧洲金融监管机构体系内的总体协调职能。欧洲证券与市场管理局的行动应特别注重主管部门之间所有相关信息的顺利交流。

(43)为保护金融稳定，有必要在早期识别来自微观审慎层面的以及跨境和跨行业的趋势、潜在风险以及薄弱环节。欧洲证券与市场管理局应在其职权管辖范围内监控和评估上述变化，并且在必要的情况下将变化定期通知欧洲议会、欧盟理事会、欧盟委员会、其他欧洲监管机构以及欧洲系统性风险委员会，必要时也可发出临时通知。同时，欧洲证券与市场管理局应与欧洲系统性风险委员会合作，启动并协调全欧盟的压力测试，以评估金融市场参与者面临不利市场变化时的抗冲击能力，并应确保各成员国实施该等测试方的方法尽可能相互一致。为恰当地履行其职能，欧洲证券与市场管理局应对市场以及潜在市场变化的冲击进行经济分析。

(44)考虑到金融服务的全球化以及国际标准重要性的日益增长，欧洲证券与市场管理局应推动与非欧盟国家监管机构的对话与合作。欧洲证券与市场管理局在完全尊重成员国以及欧盟机构现有作用和各自职权范围的同时，应有权与第三国监管机构和行政管理部门以及国际组织建立联系并达成行政安排。与欧盟达成了协议，并在协议中已经采纳或正在适用欧盟法律的国家应能参与欧洲证券与市场管理局的工作，欧洲证券与市场管理局也应能和其适用立法与欧盟立法等效的第三国合作。

(45)欧洲证券与市场管理局应在其职权管辖范围内充当欧洲议会、欧盟理事会以及欧盟委员会的独立咨询机构。在不影响所涉主管部门职权的情况下，《欧洲议会

prejudice to the competencies of the competent authorities concerned, the Authority should be able to provide its opinion on the prudential assessment of mergers and acquisitions under Directive 2004/39/EC of the European Parliament and of the Council of 21 April 2004 on markets in financial instruments [1], as amended by Directive 2007/44/EC [2] in those cases in which that Directive requires consultation between competent authorities from two or more Member States.

(46) In order to carry out its duties effectively, the Authority should have the right to request all necessary information. To avoid the duplication of reporting obligations for financial market participants, that information should normally be provided by the national supervisory authorities which are closest to the financial markets and financial market participants and should take into account already existing statistics. However, as a last resort, the Authority should be able to address a duly justified and reasoned request for information directly to a financial market participant where a national competent authority does not or cannot provide such information in a timely fashion. Member States' authorities should be obliged to assist the Authority in enforcing such direct requests. In that context, the work on common reporting formats is essential. The measures for the collection of information should be without prejudice to the legal framework of the European Statistical System and the European System of Central Banks in the field of statistics. This Regulation should therefore be without prejudice both to Regulation (EC) No 223/2009 of the European Parliament and of the Council of 11 March 2009 on European statistics [3] and to Council Regulation (EC) No 2533/98 of 23 November 1998 concerning the collection of statistical information by the European Central Bank [4].

(47) Close cooperation between the Authority and the ESRB is essential to give full effectiveness to the functioning of the ESRB and the follow-up to its warnings and recommendations. The Authority and the ESRB should share any relevant information with each other. Data related to individual undertakings should be provided only upon reasoned request. Upon receipt of warnings or recommendations addressed by the ESRB to the Authority or a national supervisory authority, the Authority should ensure follow-up as appropriate.

(48) The Authority should consult interested parties on regulatory or implementing

---

1 OJ L 145, 30.4.2004, p. 1.

2 Directive 2007/44/EC of the European Parliament and of the Council of 5 September 2007 amending Council Directive 92/49/EEC and Directives 2002/83/EC, 2004/39/EC, 2005/68/EC and 2006/48/EC as regards procedural rules and evaluation criteria for the prudential assessment of acquisitions and increase of holdings in the financial sector (OJ L 247, 21.9.2007, p. 1).

3 OJ L 87, 31.3.2009, p. 164.

4 OJ L 318, 27.11.1998, p. 8.

与欧盟理事会关于金融工具市场的第2004/39/EC号指令》[1]（2004年4月21日通过，经第2007/44/EC号指令[2]修正）要求2个或以上成员国主管部门之间进行磋商的，欧洲证券与市场管理局应能对该指令项下并购所作的审慎评估提出意见。

（46）为有效履行其职责，欧洲证券与市场管理局应有权请求获得所有必要信息。为避免金融市场参与者报告责任的重复，该等信息一般应由与金融市场和金融市场参与者联系最紧密的国家级监管机构提供，并应考虑已有的统计数据。然而，国家级主管部门怠于或不能及时提供上述信息的，作为最后手段，欧洲证券与市场管理局应能直接向金融市场参与者提出有正当理由和经论证的信息请求。各成员国主管部门有义务协助欧洲证券与市场管理局执行上述直接请求。在该等情况下，与报告通用格式相关的工作至关重要。收集信息的措施不得违背欧洲统计系统和欧洲中央银行体系在统计领域的法律框架。因此，本条例不得违背《欧洲议会与欧盟理事会关于欧洲统计的第223/2009号（欧共体）条例》[3]（2009年3月11日）以及《欧盟理事会关于欧洲中央银行统计信息收集工作的第2533/98号（欧共体）条例》[4]（1998年11月23日）。

（47）欧洲证券与市场管理局和欧洲系统性风险委员会之间的紧密合作对于欧洲系统性风险委员会的全面有效运行以及对其预警和建议的跟进至关重要。欧洲证券与市场管理局和欧洲系统性风险委员会彼此应共享任何相关信息。唯有经合理请求，方能提供与具体企业有关的数据。在欧洲证券与市场管理局或国家级监管机构收到欧洲系统性风险委员会向其发出的预警或建议之后，欧洲证券与市场管理局应确保予以适当跟进。

（48）欧洲证券与市场管理局应就监管性或实施性技术标准、指引和建议向利益

1 2004年4月30日《欧盟公报》L 145，第1页。

2 欧洲议会和欧盟理事会第2007/44/EC号指令（2007年9月5日），在审慎评估收购以及增持金融行业股份的程序规则和评估标准方面修正欧盟理事会第92/49/EEC号指令和第2002/83/EC号指令、第2004/39/EC号指令、第2005/68/EC号指令以及第2006/48/EC号指令（2007年9月21日《欧盟公报》L 247，第1页）。

3 2009年3月31日《欧盟公报》L 87，第164页。

4 1998年11月27日《欧盟公报》L 318，第8页。

technical standards, guidelines and recommendations and provide them with a reasonable opportunity to comment on proposed measures. Before adopting draft regulatory or implementing technical standards, guidelines and recommendations, the Authority should carry out an impact study. For reasons of efficiency, a Securities and Markets Stakeholder Group should be used for that purpose, and should represent, in balanced proportions, financial market participants, small and medium-sized enterprises (SMEs), academics and consumers and other retail users of financial services. The Securities and Markets Stakeholder Group should work as an interface with other user groups in the financial services area established by the Commission or by Union legislation.

(49) Members of the Securities and Markets Stakeholder Group representing non-profit organisations or academics should receive adequate compensation in order to allow persons that are neither well-funded nor industry representatives to take part fully in the debate on financial regulation.

(50) Member States have a core responsibility for ensuring coordinated crisis management and preserving financial stability in crisis situations, in particular with regard to stabilising and resolving individual failing financial market participants. Decisions by the Authority in emergency or settlement situations affecting the stability of a financial market participant should not impinge on the fiscal responsibilities of Member States. A mechanism should be established whereby Member States may invoke this safeguard and ultimately bring the matter before the Council for a decision. However, that safeguard mechanism should not be abused, in particular in relation to a decision taken by the Authority which does not have a significant or material fiscal impact, such as a reduction of income linked to the temporary prohibition of specific activities or products for consumer protection purposes. When taking decisions under the safeguard mechanism, the Council should vote, in accordance with the principle where each member has one vote. It is appropriate to confer on the Council a role in this matter given the particular responsibilities of the Member States in this respect. Given the sensitivity of the issue, strict confidentiality arrangements should be ensured.

(51) In its decision-making procedures, the Authority should be bound by Union rules and general principles on due process and transparency. The right of the addressees of the Authority's decisions to be heard should be fully respected. The Authority's acts should form an integral part of Union law.

(52) A Board of Supervisors composed of the heads of the relevant competent authorities in each Member State, and chaired by the Chairperson of the Authority, should be the principal decision-making organ of the Authority. Representatives of the Commission, the ESRB, the European Supervisory Authority (European Insurance and Occupational Pensions Authority) and the European Supervisory Authority (European Banking Authority)

相关方征求意见,并给其合理的机会对拟议的措施发表意见。在通过监管性或实施性技术标准草案、指引和建议之前,欧洲证券与市场管理局应对其影响开展研究。为确保效率,可为此引入证券与市场利益相关者小组。证券与市场利益相关者小组应以平衡的比例代表代表金融市场参与者、中小企业(SME)、学术机构和消费者以及金融服务的其他零售用户。证券与市场利益相关者小组应充当与欧洲证券与市场管理局与欧盟委员会或欧盟立法在金融服务领域建立的其他用户小组对接的部门。

(49)代表非营利组织或学术机构的证券与市场利益相关者小组成员应获得充足的报酬,让既非资金充裕亦非行业代表的人士能充分参与有关金融监管的讨论。

(50)各成员国负有核心责任,应确保危机管理的协调性并在危机状况下维持金融稳定,特别是在稳定濒临倒闭的具体金融市场参与者的形势并对其进行清盘的时候。在影响金融市场参与者稳定性的紧急情况或争议解决情况下,欧洲证券与市场管理局所作决定不应影响成员国的财政责任。应建立一项机制,让成员国能借其寻求该等保障并最终将有关事宜提交欧盟理事会决定。但该项保障机制不得被滥用,特别是当欧洲证券与市场管理局所作决定对财政收入并未造成突出或重大影响(如为保护消费者利益采取的禁止特定活动或产品的临时措施造成纳税人所得下降的情形)时,不得使用该项机制。欧盟理事会根据保障机制作决定时,应按一人一票原则投票表决。考虑到成员国在这方面承担的特殊责任,在此问题上应让欧盟理事会发挥一定的作用。鉴于问题的高度敏感性,应确保作出严格的保密安排。

(51)欧洲证券与市场管理局在进行决策程序时,应受欧盟规则以及关于正当程序和透明度的一般性原则约束。欧洲证券与市场管理局的决定所涉对象的发言权应得到充分的尊重。欧洲证券与市场管理局的法律文件应构成欧盟法律不可分割的一部分。

(52)由每一成员国相关主管部门的负责人组成,并由欧洲证券与市场管理局主席担任主席的监管机构理事会应当是欧洲证券与市场管理局的主要决策机构。来自欧盟委员会和欧洲系统性风险委员会的代表,以及来自两个欧洲监管机构(欧洲保险与职业养老金管理局以及欧洲银行业管理局)的代表,应作为观察员参与。监管机构理事会的理事应独立地且仅为欧盟利益行事。

should participate as observers. Members of the Board of Supervisors should act independently and only in the Union's interest.

(53) As a general rule, the Board of Supervisors should take its decisions by simple majority in accordance with the principle where each member has one vote. However, for acts of a general nature, including those relating to regulatory and implementing technical standards, guidelines and recommendations, for budgetary matters as well as in respect of requests by a Member State to reconsider a decision by the Authority to temporarily prohibit or restrict certain financial activities, it is appropriate to apply the rules of qualified majority voting as laid down in Article 16(4) of the Treaty on European Union and in the Protocol (No 36) on transitional provisions annexed to the Treaty on European Union and to the Treaty on the Functioning of the European Union. Cases concerning the settlement of disagreements between national supervisory authorities should be examined by a restricted, objective panel, composed of members who neither are representatives of the competent authorities which are party to the disagreement nor have any interest in the conflict or direct links to the competent authorities concerned. The composition of the panel should be appropriately balanced. The decision taken by the panel should be approved by the Board of Supervisors by simple majority in accordance with the principle where each member has one vote. However, with regard to decisions taken by the consolidating supervisor, the decision proposed by the panel could be rejected by members representing a blocking minority of the votes as defined in Article 16(4) of the Treaty on European Union and in Article 3 of the Protocol (No 36) on transitional provisions.

(54) A Management Board, composed of the Chairperson of the Authority, of representatives of national supervisory authorities and of the Commission, should ensure that the Authority carries out its mission and performs the tasks assigned to it. The Management Board should be entrusted with the necessary powers, inter alia, to propose the annual and multi-annual work programme, to exercise certain budgetary powers, to adopt the Authority's staff policy plan, to adopt special provisions on the right to access to documents and to propose the annual report.

(55) The Authority should be represented by a full time Chairperson, appointed by the Board of Supervisors on the basis of merit, skills, knowledge of financial institutions and markets, and of experience relevant to financial supervision and regulation, following an open selection procedure organised and managed by the Board of Supervisors assisted by the Commission. For the designation of the first Chairperson of the Authority, the Commission should, inter alia, draw up a shortlist of candidates on the basis of merit, skills, knowledge of financial institutions and markets, and experience relevant to financial supervision and regulation. For the subsequent designations, the opportunity of

(53)作为一般规则,监管机构理事会应按一人一票原则以简单多数通过其决定。然而,对于具有普遍性质的法律文件(包括与监管性和实施性技术标准、指引以及建议有关的法律文件)、预算事项以及成员国向欧洲证券与市场管理局提出的重新考虑临时禁止或限制某些特定金融活动的请求,应适用《欧洲联盟条约》第16条第4款以及《欧洲联盟条约》和《欧洲联盟运行条约》附录关于过渡规定的《议定书(第36号)》中所规定的特定多数原则。解决各国家级监管机构之间分歧的案件,应由符合下列标准的人员组成的严格客观的专家小组进行审查:并非作为分歧一方的主管部门的代表,并且在所涉主管部门之冲突中无利害关系、与所涉主管部门亦无直接关联的人员。该专家小组的构成应适当平衡。专家小组的决定应由监管机构理事会按一人一票原则以简单多数通过。然而,关于并表监管机构作出的决定,代表有否决权的少数票的理事有权否决专家小组拟议的决定[有否决权的少数票定义见《欧洲联盟条约》第16条第4款以及关于过渡规定的《议定书(第36号)》第3条]。

(54)由欧洲证券与市场管理局主席、国家级监管机构代表以及欧盟委员会组成的管理委员会应确保欧洲证券与市场管理局完成其使命并履行其被赋予的职责。管理委员会应被委以必要的权力,包括但不限于提出年度和跨年度工作计划、行使特定的预算权、通过欧洲证券与市场管理局的员工政策计划、通过有关文件查阅权的特殊规定以及提出年度报告。

(55)欧洲证券与市场管理局应由1名全职主席作为代表,该主席人选根据候选人的成就、技能、对金融机构和市场的认识、与金融监管和规制相关的经验等,由监管机构理事会在欧盟委员会的协助下组织和执行公开遴选程序来确定。在指定首任欧洲证券与市场管理局主席时,欧盟委员会应基于候选人的成就、技能、对金融机构和市场的认识、与金融监管和规制相关的经验拟定一份候选人名单。对于后续任期,应在根据本条例准备的报告中对是否要求欧盟委员会拟定候选人名单之事进行审议。在获选者到任前,直至其被监管机构理事会选出满1个月期间内,欧洲议会都有权在听取获选者意见后对其任命提出异议。

having a shortlist drawn up by the Commission should be reviewed in a report to be established pursuant to this Regulation. Before the selected person takes up his duties, and up to 1 month after his selection by the Board of Supervisors, the European Parliament should be entitled, after having heard the person selected, to object to his designation.

(56) The management of the Authority should be entrusted to an Executive Director, who should have the right to participate in meetings of the Board of Supervisors and the Management Board without the right to vote.

(57) In order to ensure cross-sectoral consistency in the activities of the ESAs, they should coordinate closely through a Joint Committee and reach common positions where appropriate. The Joint Committee should coordinate the functions of the ESAs in relation to financial conglomerates and other cross sectoral matters. Where relevant, acts also falling within the area of competence of the European Supervisory Authority (European Insurance and Occupational Pensions Authority) or the European Supervisory Authority (European Banking Authority) should be adopted in parallel by the European Supervisory Authorities concerned. The Joint Committee should be chaired for a 12-month term on a rotating basis by the Chairpersons of the ESAs. The Chairperson of the Joint Committee should be a Vice-Chair of the ESRB. The Joint Committee should have dedicated staff provided by the ESAs to allow for informal information sharing and the development of a common supervisory culture approach across the ESAs.

(58) It is necessary to ensure that the parties affected by decisions adopted by the Authority may have recourse to the necessary remedies. To protect effectively the rights of parties, and for reasons of procedural economy, where the Authority has decision-making powers, parties should be granted a right of appeal to a Board of Appeal. For reasons of efficiency and consistency, the Board of Appeal should be a joint body of the ESAs, independent from their administrative and regulatory structures. The decisions of the Board of Appeal should be subject to appeal before the Court of Justice of the European Union.

(59) In order to guarantee its full autonomy and independence, the Authority should be granted an autonomous budget with revenues mainly from obligatory contributions from national supervisory authorities and from the General Budget of the European Union. Union financing of the Authority is subject to an agreement by the budgetary authority in accordance with Point 47 of the Interinstitutional Agreement between the European Parliament, the Council and the Commission of 17 May 2006 on budgetary discipline and sound financial management [1]. The Union budgetary procedure should be applicable. The

1 OJ C 139, 14.6.2006, p. 1.

(56)欧洲证券与市场管理局的管理应委任给1名执行主任，执行主任有权参与监管机构理事会和管理委员会的会议，但无表决权。

(57)为确保彼此活动的跨行业一致性，各欧洲监管机构应通过联合委员会紧密协调，并在适当时达成共同的立场。联合委员会应协调各欧洲监管机构在金融集团以及其他跨行业事宜方面的职能。在适当时，同时属于欧洲监管机构(欧洲保险与职业养老金管理局或欧洲银行业管理局)职权的管辖范围的法律文件，应由所涉的各个欧洲监管机构分别通过。联合委员会的主席应由各欧洲监管机构的主席轮流担任，每次任期12个月。联合委员会的主席应为欧洲系统性风险委员会的副主席。各欧洲监管机构应向联合委员会提供专门的员工负责非正式信息共享工作和建设欧洲监管机构共同的监管文化。

(58)有必要确保受欧洲证券与市场管理局决定影响的当事方可寻求必要的救济。为有效保护各方权利以及出于程序经济的考虑，对于欧洲证券与市场管理局有决策权的事项，各方应有向行政复议委员会提出行政复议申请的权利。出于效率和一致性原因，行政复议委员会应为各欧洲监管机构之间的联合机构，独立于各自所属的行政和监管结构。针对行政复议委员会的决定，相关方可向欧盟法院提起行政诉讼。

(59)为保证其充分的自主权和独立性，欧洲证券与市场管理局应有自主的预算，其收入主要来自各国家级监管机构义务缴纳的款项以及欧盟总预算的一部分。欧盟应依据预算部门按照《欧洲议会、欧盟理事会和欧盟委员会关于预算纪律和健全的财务管理的机构间协议》[1](2006年5月17日)第47目签署的协议向欧洲证券与市场管理局提供经费。给其提供的经费应适用欧盟预算程序。其账目应由欧盟审计院进行审计，总体预算则受预算审批程序约束。

1 2006年6月14日《欧盟公报》C 139，第1页。

auditing of accounts should be undertaken by the Court of Auditors. The overall budget is subject to the discharge procedure.

(60) Regulation (EC) No 1073/1999 of the European Parliament and of the Council of 25 May 1999 concerning investigations conducted by the European Anti-Fraud Office (OLAF) [1] should apply to the Authority. The Authority should also accede to the Interinstitutional Agreement of 25 May 1999 between the European Parliament, the Council of the European Union and the Commission of the European Communities concerning internal investigations by the European Anti-Fraud Office (OLAF). [2]

(61) In order to ensure open and transparent employment conditions and equal treatment of staff, Staff Regulations of Officials and the Conditions of Employment of Other Servants of the European Communities [3] should apply to the staff of the Authority.

(62) It is essential that business secrets and other confidential information be protected. The confidentiality of information made available to the Authority and exchanged in the network should be subject to stringent and effective confidentiality rules.

(63) Directive 95/46/EC of the European Parliament and of the Council of 24 October 1995 on the protection of individuals with regard to the processing of personal data and on the free movement of such data [4] and Regulation (EC) No 45/2001 of the European Parliament and of the Council of 18 December 2000 on the protection of individuals with regard to the processing of personal data by the Community institutions and bodies and on the free movement of such data [5] are fully applicable to the processing of personal data for the purposes of this Regulation.

(64) In order to ensure the transparent operation of the Authority, Regulation (EC) No 1049/2001 of the European Parliament and of the Council of 30 May 2001 regarding public access to European Parliament, Council and Commission documents [6] should apply to the Authority.

(65) Third countries should be allowed to participate in the work of the Authority in accordance with appropriate agreements to be concluded by the Union.

(66) Since the objectives of this Regulation, namely improving the functioning of the internal market by means of ensuring a high, effective and consistent level of prudential regulation and supervision, protecting investors, protecting the integrity, efficiency and orderly functioning of financial markets, maintaining the stability of the financial system,

---

1 OJ L 136, 31.5.1999, p. 1.
2 OJ L 136, 31.5.1999, p. 15.
3 OJ L 56, 4.3.1968, p. 1.
4 OJ L 281, 23.11.1995, p. 31.
5 OJ L 8, 12.1.2001, p. 1.
6 OJ L 145, 31.5.2001, p. 43.

（60）《欧洲议会与欧盟理事会关于欧洲反欺诈办公室（OLAF）所开展的调查的第1073/1999号（欧共体）条例》[1]（1999年5月25日）应适用于欧洲证券与市场管理局。同时，欧洲证券与市场管理局应遵从欧洲议会、欧盟理事会以及欧盟委员会于1999年5月25日签订的《关于欧洲反欺诈办公室（OLAF）内部调查的机构间协议》[2]。

（61）为确保公开透明的聘用条件以及员工的平等待遇，《欧洲共同体官员的人事条例》和《欧洲共同体其他人员的聘用条件》[3]应适用于欧洲证券与市场管理局工作人员。

（62）保护商业秘密和其他保密信息至关重要。向欧洲证券与市场管理局提供的以及在监管网络中交换的保密信息均应受严格有效的保密规定约束。

（63）《欧洲议会与欧盟理事会关于处理个人资料时对个人的保护以及该等资料自由流动的第95/46/EC号指令》[4]（1995年10月24日）以及《欧洲议会与欧盟理事会关于欧共体机构和单位处理个人资料时对个人的保护以及该等资料自由流动的第45/2001号（欧共体）条例》[5]（2000年12月18日）完全适用于根据本条例对个人资料的处理。

（64）为确保欧洲证券与市场管理局的透明运作，《欧洲议会与欧盟理事会关于公众查阅欧洲议会、欧盟理事会和欧盟委员会文件的第1049/2001号（欧共体）条例》[6]（2001年5月30日）应适用于欧洲证券与市场管理局。

（65）第三国应被允许依照其与欧盟今后缔结的相关协议参与欧洲证券与市场管理局的工作。

（66）鉴于本条例的目标在于确保高水平、有效和一致的审慎规制和监管以改善欧盟内部市场的运行，保护投资者，保护金融市场的诚信度、高效和有序运行，维持金融系统的稳定以及加强国际监管协调；上述目的单靠成员国自身无法完全实现，但基于此等目的触及的范围，能在欧盟层面上得到更好的实现，因此，欧盟可根据《欧洲联

1 1999年5月31日《欧盟公报》L 136，第1页。
2 1999年5月31日《欧盟公报》L 136，第15页。
3 1968年3月4日《欧盟公报》L 56，第1页。
4 1995年11月23日《欧盟公报》L 281，第31页。
5 2001年1月12日《欧盟公报》L 8，第1页。
6 2001年5月31日《欧盟公报》L 145，第43页。

and strengthening international supervisory coordination, cannot be sufficiently achieved by the Member States and can, therefore, by reason of the scale of the action, be better achieved at Union level, the Union may adopt measures, in accordance with the principle of subsidiarity as set out in Article 5 of the Treaty on European Union. In accordance with the principle of proportionality, as set out in that Article, this Regulation does not go beyond what is necessary in order to achieve those objectives.

(67) The Authority should assume all current tasks and powers of the Committee of European Securities Regulators. Commission Decision 2009/77/EC should therefore be repealed on the date of the establishment of the Authority and Decision No 716/2009/EC of the European Parliament and of the Council of 16 September 2009 establishing a Community programme to support specific activities in the field of financial services, financial reporting and auditing [1], should be amended accordingly. Given the existing structures and operations of the Committee of European Securities Regulators, it is important to ensure very close cooperation between the Committee of European Securities Regulators and the Commission when establishing appropriate transitional arrangements, to ensure that the period during which the Commission is responsible for the administrative establishment and initial administrative operation of the Authority be as limited as possible.

(68) It is appropriate to set a time limit for the application of this Regulation in order to ensure that the Authority is adequately prepared to begin operations and a smooth transition from the Committee of European Securities Regulators. The Authority should be appropriately financed. At least initially, it should be financed 40% from Union funds and 60% through contributions from Member States, made in accordance with the weighting of votes set out in Article 3(3) of the Protocol (No 36) on transitional provisions.

(69) In order to enable the Authority to be established on 1 January 2011, this Regulation should enter into force on the day following its publication in the Official Journal of the European Union,

HAVE ADOPTED THIS REGULATION:

1 OJ L 253, 25.9.2009, p. 8.

盟条约》第5条规定的辅助性原则制定相关细则。根据《欧洲联盟条约》第5条规定的比例原则，本条例仅作出实现上述目标的必要规定。

(67)欧洲证券与市场管理局应承担欧洲证券监管机构委员会所有的现有职责和权力。因此，欧盟委员会第2009/77/EC号决定应于欧洲证券与市场管理局成立之日废止，对《欧洲议会与欧盟理事会设立一项支持金融服务领域特定活动、财务报告和审计的欧共体计划的第716/2009/EC号决定》[1](2009年9月16日)也应作相应修正。考虑到欧洲证券监管机构委员会的现有结构和运作状况，在作出适当的过渡安排时，确保欧洲证券监管机构委员会和欧盟委员会之间十分紧密的合作相当重要，以尽量缩短欧盟委员会负担欧洲证券与市场管理局机构设立和初始行政运作的时间。

(68)应为本条例的适用设定时限，以确保欧洲证券与市场管理局做好充分的准备启动其运作，并确保欧洲证券监管机构委员会向欧洲证券与市场管理局顺利过渡。欧洲证券与市场管理局应有适当的财政支持，至少在初始阶段，应从欧盟获得40%的经费，另外60%来源于成员国根据关于过渡条款的《议定书(第36号)》第3条第3款规定的加权票数比例缴纳的款项。

(69)为使欧洲证券与市场管理局于2011年1月1日成立，本条例应于《欧盟公报》公布，公布的次日生效。

兹通过本指令如下：

1 2009年9月25日《欧盟公报》L 253，第8页。

CHAPTER I ESTABLISHMENT AND LEGAL STATUS

Article 1 Establishment and scope of action

1. This Regulation establishes a European Supervisory Authority (European Securities and Markets Authority) (hereinafter the Authority').

2. The Authority shall act within the powers conferred by this Regulation and within the scope of Directive 97/9/EC, Directive 98/26/EC, Directive 2001/34/EC, Directive 2002/47/EC, Directive 2003/6/EC, Directive 2003/71/EC, Directive 2004/39/EC, Directive 2004/109/EC, Directive 2009/65/EC and to Directive 2006/49/EC, without prejudice to the competence of the European Supervisory Authority (European Banking Authority) in terms of prudential supervision, any future legislation in the area of Alternative Investment Fund Managers (AIFM), and Regulation (EC) No 1060/2009, and, to the extent that these acts apply to firms providing investment services or to collective investment undertakings marketing their units or shares and the competent authorities that supervise them, within the relevant parts of, Directive 2002/87/EC, Directive 2005/60/EC, Directive 2002/65/EC, including all directives, regulations, and decisions based on those acts, and of any further legally binding Union act which confers tasks on the Authority.

3. The Authority shall also act in the field of activities of market participants in relation to issues not directly covered in the acts referred to in paragraph 2, including matters of corporate governance, auditing and financial reporting, provided that such actions by the Authority are necessary to ensure the effective and consistent application of those acts. The Authority shall also take appropriate action in the context of take-over bids, clearing and settlement and derivative issues.

4. The provisions of this Regulation are without prejudice to the powers of the Commission, in particular under Article 258 TFEU, to ensure compliance with Union law.

5. The objective of the Authority shall be to protect the public interest by contributing to the short, medium and long-term stability and effectiveness of the financial system, for the Union economy, its citizens and businesses. The Authority shall contribute to:

(a) improving the functioning of the internal market, including in particular a sound, effective and consistent level of regulation and supervision,

(b) ensuring the integrity, transparency, efficiency and orderly functioning of financial markets,

第一章 设立和法律地位

第1条 设立和行动范围

1.本条例设立欧洲监管机构(欧洲证券与市场管理局)(以下简称欧洲证券与市场管理局)。

2.欧洲证券与市场管理局应按本条例授予的权力,在不影响欧洲监管机构(欧洲银行业管理局)的审慎监管职权的情况下,在第97/9/EC号指令、第98/26/EC号指令、第2001/34/EC号指令、第2002/47/EC号指令、第2003/6/EC号指令、第2003/71/EC号指令、第2004/39/EC号指令、第2004/109/EC号指令、第2009/65/EC号指令及第2006/49/EC号指令范围内,以及在未来颁布的另类投资基金管理人(AIFM)领域的立法以及第1060/2009号(欧共体)条例范围内,在第2002/87/EC号指令、第2005/60/EC号指令、第2002/65/EC号指令适用于提供投资服务的公司或营销其投资单位或份额的集合投资计划及其监管主管部门的有关部分(包括所有基于上述法律文件的指令、条例及决定)范围内,以及在将来颁布的赋予欧洲证券与市场管理局职责的具有法律约束力的任何其他欧盟法律文件范围内行事。

3.欧洲证券与市场管理局还应在市场参与者与不直接涵盖在第2款所述法律文件范围内的事项有关的领域行事,包括公司治理、审计以及财务报告事宜,前提是欧洲证券与市场管理局采取的上述行动对于确保该等法律文件的有效、一致适用是必不可少的。欧洲证券与市场管理局还应就收购竞标、清算和结算以及衍生品事宜采取适当的行动。

4.本条例的规定不得影响欧盟委员会确保欧盟法律得到遵守的权力,尤其是《欧洲联盟运行条约》第258条中的权力。

5.欧洲证券与市场管理局的目标是通过为欧盟经济及其公民和企业促进金融系统的短期、中期和长期稳定和有效性以保护公众利益。欧洲证券与市场管理局应致力于:

(a)改善欧盟内部市场的运行,尤其包括健全、有效、一致的规制和监管;

(b)确保金融市场的诚信度、透明、高效和有序运行;

(c) strengthening international supervisory coordination,

(d) preventing regulatory arbitrage and promoting equal conditions of competition,

(e) ensuring the taking of investment and other risks are appropriately regulated and supervised, and

(f) enhancing customer protection.

For those purposes, the Authority shall contribute to ensuring the consistent, efficient and effective application of the acts referred to in paragraph 2, foster supervisory convergence, provide opinions to the European Parliament, the Council, and the Commission and undertake economic analyses of the markets to promote the achievement of the Authority's objective.

In the exercise of the tasks conferred upon it by this Regulation, the Authority shall pay particular attention to any systemic risk posed by financial market participants, the failure of which may impair the operation of the financial system or the real economy.

When carrying out its tasks, the Authority shall act independently and objectively and in the interest of theUnion alone.

Article 2 European System of Financial Supervision

1. The Authority shall form part of a European System of Financial Supervision (ESFS). The main objective of the ESFS shall be to ensure that the rules applicable to the financial sector are adequately implemented to preserve financial stability and to ensure confidence in the financial system as a whole and sufficient protection for the customers of financial services.

2. The ESFS shall comprise the following:

(a) the European Systemic Risk Board (ESRB), for the purposes of the tasks as specified in Regulation (EU) No 1092/2010 [1] and this Regulation;

(b) the Authority;

(c) the European Supervisory Authority (European Banking Authority) established by Regulation (EU) No 1093/2010 of the European Parliament and of the Council [2];

(d) the European Supervisory Authority (European Insurance and Occupational Pensions Authority) established by Regulation (EU) No 1094/2010 of the European Parliament and of the Council [3];

(e) the Joint Committee of the European Supervisory Authorities ('Joint Committee') for the purposes of carrying out the tasks as specified in Articles 54 to 57 of this Regulation, of Regulation (EU) No 1093/2010 and of Regulation (EU) No 1094/2010;

---

1 See page 1 of this Official Journal.

2 See page 12 of this Official Journal.

3 See page 48 of this Official Journal.

(c)加强国际监管协调；

(d)防范监管套利并促进竞争的平等条件；

(e)确保对投资风险及其他风险的涉险行为进行适当的规制和监管；及

(f)加强对客户的保护。

为此，欧洲证券与市场管理局应致力于确保第2款所述法律文件得到一致且兼具效率和成效的适用，促进监管趋同，向欧洲议会、欧盟理事会以及欧盟委员会提出意见并对市场进行经济分析，以实现欧洲证券与市场管理局的目标。

履行本条例所赋予的职责时，欧洲证券与市场管理局应特别注意金融市场参与者所引起的任何系统性风险，因为金融市场参与者的倒闭可能会对金融系统的运行造成影响或损害实体经济。

欧洲证券与市场管理局在履行其职责时应仅为欧盟的利益独立客观地行事。

第2条　欧洲金融监管体系

1.欧洲证券与市场管理局应构成欧洲金融监管体系(ESFS)的一部分。欧洲金融监管体系的主要目标在于确保适用于金融行业的规则得到充分的实施以维护金融稳定，确保公众对金融系统整体的信心，充分保护金融服务的客户。

2.欧洲金融监管体系应由下列机构组成：

(a)欧洲系统性风险委员会(ESRB)，履行第1092/2010号(欧盟)条例[1]以及本条例所规定的职责；

(b)欧洲证券与市场管理局；

(c)依据欧洲议会与欧盟理事会第1093/2010号(欧盟)条例[2]设立的欧洲监管机构(欧洲银行业管理局)；

(d)依据欧洲议会与欧盟理事会第1094/2010号(欧盟)条例[3]设立的欧洲监管机构(欧洲保险与职业养老金管理局)；

(e)欧洲监管机构联合委员会(以下简称联合委员会)，履行本条例、第1093/2010号(欧盟)条例以及第1094/2010号(欧盟)条例第54条至第57条所规定的职责；

---

1 请见本《欧盟公报》，第1页。

2 请见本《欧盟公报》，第12页。

3 请见本《欧盟公报》，第48页。

(f) the competent or supervisory authorities in the Member States as specified in the Union acts referred to in Article 1(2) of this Regulation, of Regulation (EU) No 1093/2010 and of Regulation (EU) No 1094/2010.

3. The Authority shall cooperate regularly and closely with the ESRB as well as with the European Supervisory Authority (European Banking Authority) and the European Supervisory Authority (European Insurance and Occupational Pensions Authority) through the Joint Committee, ensuring cross-sectoral consistency of work and reaching joint positions in the area of supervision of financial conglomerates and on other cross-sectoral issues.

4. In accordance with the principle of sincere cooperation under Article 4(3) of the Treaty on European Union, the parties to the ESFS shall cooperate with trust and full mutual respect, in particular in ensuring the flow of appropriate and reliable information between them.

5. Those supervisory authorities that are party to the ESFS shall be obliged to supervise financial market participants operating in the Union in accordance with the acts referred to in Article 1(2).

Article 3 Accountability of the Authorities

The Authorities referred to in Article 2(2)(a) to (d) shall be accountable to the European Parliament and the Council.

Article 4 Definitions

For the purposes of this Regulation the following definitions apply:

(1) 'financial market participant' means any person in relation to whom a requirement in the legislation referred to in Article 1(2) or a national law implementing such legislation applies;

(2) 'key financial market participant' means a financial market participant whose regular activity or financial viability has or is likely to have a significant effect on the stability, integrity or efficiency of the financial markets in theUnion;

(3) 'competent authorities' means:

(i) competent authorities and/or supervisory authorities as defined in the legislation referred to in Article 1(2);

(ii) with regard to Directives 2002/65/EC and 2005/60/EC, the authorities competent for ensuring compliance with the requirements of those Directives by firms providing investment services and by collective investment undertakings marketing their units or shares;

(iii) with regard to investor compensation schemes, bodies which administer national compensation schemes pursuant to Directive 97/9/EC, or in the case where the operation of the investor compensation scheme is administered by a private company, the public

(f)本条例、第1093/2010号(欧盟)条例以及第1094/2010号(欧盟)条例第1条第2款所述欧盟法律文件中规定的成员国主管部门或监管机构。

3.欧洲证券与市场管理局应定期与欧洲系统性风险委员会以及通过联合委员会与两个欧洲监管机构(欧洲银行业管理局和欧洲保险与职业养老金管理局)紧密合作,确保跨行业工作的一致性,并在金融集团监管领域和其他跨行业问题上取得共同立场。

4.根据《欧洲联盟条约》第4条第3款所指的精诚合作原则,欧洲金融监管体系各方应在合作过程中互相信任和充分尊重,以特别确保各方能够彼此交流适当和可靠的信息。

5.属于欧洲金融监管体系一部分的监管机构有义务依照第1条第2款所述法律文件对在欧盟运营的金融市场参与者进行监管。

第3条　部门问责制

第2条第2款第a项至第d项所述的部门应对欧洲议会和欧盟理事会负责。

第4条　定义

在本条例中适用下列定义:

(1)"金融市场参与者"一词,系指适用第1条第2款所述立法规定的条件的任何人,或适用实施该项立法的成员国国内法律的任何人;

(2)"关键金融市场参与者"一词,系指其日常活动或财务生存能力实际上或很可能会对欧盟金融市场的稳定、诚信度或效率造成重大影响的金融市场参与者;

(3)"主管部门"一词,系指:

(i)如第1条第2款所述立法定义的主管部门和/或监管机构;

(ii)就第2002/65/EC号指令和第2005/60/EC号指令而言,负责确保提供投资服务的公司和营销其投资单位或份额的集合投资计划遵循该等指令要求的部门;

(iii)对于投资者补偿计划而言,按照第97/9/EC号指令负责管理国家级补偿计划的机构,或(对于由私人公司负责管理的投资者补偿计划而言)按照该指令监管该等计划的公共机构。

authority supervising those schemes pursuant to that Directive.

Article 5 Legal status

1. The Authority shall be a Union body with legal personality.

2. In each Member State, the Authority shall enjoy the most extensive legal capacity accorded to legal persons under national law. It may, in particular, acquire or dispose of movable and immovable property and be a party to legal proceedings.

3. The Authority shall be represented by its Chairperson.

Article 6 Composition

The Authority shall comprise:

(1) a Board of Supervisors, which shall exercise the tasks set out in Article 43;

(2) a Management Board, which shall exercise the tasks set out in Article 47;

(3) a Chairperson, who shall exercise the tasks set out in Article 48;

(4) an Executive Director, who shall exercise the tasks set out in Article 53;

(5) a Board of Appeal, which shall exercise the tasks set out in Article 60.

Article 7 Seat

The Authority shall have its seat inParis.

CHAPTER Ⅱ TASKS AND POWERS OF THE AUTHORITY

Article 8 Tasks and powers of the Authority

1. The Authority shall have the following tasks:

(a) to contribute to the establishment of high-quality common regulatory and supervisory standards and practices, in particular by providing opinions to the Union institutions and by developing guidelines, recommendations, and draft regulatory and implementing technical standards which shall be based on the legislative acts referred to in Article 1(2);

(b) to contribute to the consistent application of legally binding Union acts, in particular by contributing to a common supervisory culture, ensuring consistent, efficient and effective application of the acts referred to in Article 1(2), preventing regulatory arbitrage, mediating and settling disagreements between competent authorities, ensuring effective and consistent supervision of financial market participants, ensuring a coherent functioning of colleges of supervisors and taking actions, inter alia, in emergency situations;

(c) to stimulate and facilitate the delegation of tasks and responsibilities among

第5条　法律地位

1.欧洲证券与市场管理局系具有法人身份的欧盟机构。

2.在各成员国内,欧洲证券与市场管理局享有按该成员国国内法律授予法人的最广泛的民事能力。特别是欧洲证券与市场管理局可以获得或处置动产和不动产,并可作为法律程序的当事人。

3.欧洲证券与市场管理局应由其主席代表。

第6条　构成

欧洲证券与市场管理局由下列机构和人员组成:

(1)履行第43条所列职责的监管机构理事会;

(2)履行第47条所列职责的管理委员会;

(3)履行第48条所列职责的主席;

(4)履行第53条所列职责的执行主任;

(5)履行第60条所列职责的行政复议委员会。

第7条　总部所在地

欧洲证券与市场管理局总部位于巴黎。

第二章　欧洲证券与市场管理局的职责和权力

第8条　欧洲证券与市场管理局的职责和权力

1.欧洲证券与市场管理局负有下列职责:

(a)促进制定高水平的通用的规制与监管方面的标准和实践,特别是通过向欧盟机构提供意见以及通过制定指引、建议以及起草以第1条第2款中的框架立法为基础的监管性和实施性技术标准草案;

(b)促进具有法律约束力的欧盟立法的一致适用,特别是通过促成共同的监管文化、确保第1条第2款所述法律文件一致的且兼具效率和成效的适用,防范监管套利,调解和解决主管部门之间的分歧、确保对金融市场参与者的有效和一致监管,确保监管团相互连贯的运行并根据情况(尤其是紧急情况下)采取行动;

(c)促进和推动主管部门之间的职责和责任委托;

competent authorities;

(d) to cooperate closely with the ESRB, in particular by providing the ESRB with the necessary information for the achievement of its tasks and by ensuring a proper follow up to the warnings and recommendations of the ESRB;

(e) to organise and conduct peer review analyses of competent authorities, including issuing guidelines and recommendations and identifying best practices, in order to strengthen consistency in supervisory outcomes;

(f) to monitor and assess market developments in the area of its competence;

(g) to undertake economic analyses of markets to inform the discharge of the Authority's functions;

(h) to foster investor protection;

(i) to contribute to the consistent and coherent functioning of colleges of supervisors, the monitoring, assessment and measurement of systemic risk, the development and coordination of recovery and resolution plans, providing a high level of protection to investors throughout the Union and developing methods for the resolution of failing financial market participants and an assessment of the need for appropriate financing instruments, in accordance with Articles 21 to 26;

(j) to fulfil any other specific tasks set out in this Regulation or in other legislative acts;

(k) to publish on its website, and to update regularly, information relating to its field of activities, in particular, within the area of its competence, on registered financial market participants, in order to ensure information is easily accessible by the public;

(l) to take over, as appropriate, all existing and ongoing tasks from the Committee of European Securities Regulators (CESR).

2. To achieve the tasks set out in paragraph 1, the Authority shall have the powers set out in this Regulation, in particular to:

(a) develop draft regulatory technical standards in the specific cases referred to in Article 10;

(b) develop draft implementing technical standards in the specific cases referred to in Article 15;

(c) issue guidelines and recommendations, as laid down in Article 16;

(d) issue recommendations in specific cases, as referred to in Article 17(3);

(e) take individual decisions addressed to competent authorities in the specific cases referred to in Articles 18(3) and 19(3);

(f) in cases concerning directly applicable Union law, take individual decisions addressed to financial market participants, in the specific cases referred to in Article 17(6), in Article 18(4) and in Article 19(4);

(d)与欧洲系统性风险委员会紧密合作，特别是向欧洲系统性风险委员会提供履行其职责所必要的信息以及确保对欧洲系统性风险委员会发布的预警和建议的适当跟进；

(e)组织和开展主管部门的同行审评分析，包括发布指引和建议以及识别最佳实践，以加强监管结果的一致性；

(f)对其职权管辖范围内的市场变化进行监控和评估；

(g)进行市场经济分析，为欧洲证券与市场管理局职能的履行提供信息；

(h)促进对投资者的保护；

(i)根据第21条至第26条，促进监管团能一致并相互连贯地行使职能，监控、评估和计量系统性风险，制定和协调恢复和清盘计划，向欧盟内的投资者提供高水平的保护，以及为濒临倒闭的金融市场参与者制定清盘方法并制定评估对适当融资工具之需求的方法；

(j)履行本条例以及其他框架立法中规定的任何其他特定职责；

(k)在其网站上公布有关针对注册金融市场参与者所开展的活动(尤其是在其职权管辖范围内)的相关信息并定期更新，以确保公众能方便地查阅信息；

(l)在适当情况下接手欧洲证券监管机构委员会(CESR)所有现有的及持续的职责。

2.为完成第1款所列的职责，欧洲证券与市场管理局应有本条例规定的权力，特别是：

(a)在第10条所述的特定情形下起草监管性技术标准草案；

(b)在第15条所述的特定情形下起草实施性技术标准草案；

(c)发布第16条规定的指引和建议；

(d)在第17条第3款所述的特定情形下提出建议；

(e)在第18条第3款和第19条第3款所述的特定情形下针对主管部门作出个别决定；

(f)在涉及可直接适用的欧盟法律的案件中，在第17条第6款、第18条第4款和第19条第4款所述的特定情形下，针对金融市场参与者作出个别决定；

(g) issue opinions to the European Parliament, the Council, or the Commission as provided for in Article 34;

(h) collect the necessary information concerning financial market participants as provided for in Article 35;

(i) develop common methodologies for assessing the effect of product characteristics and distribution processes on the financial position of financial market participants and on consumer protection;

(j) provide a centrally accessible database of registered financial market participants in the area of its competence where specified in the acts referred to in Article 1(2).

Article 9 Tasks related to consumer protection and financial activities

1. The Authority shall take a leading role in promoting transparency, simplicity and fairness in the market for consumer financial products or services across the internal market, including by:

(a) collecting, analysing and reporting on consumer trends;

(b) reviewing and coordinating financial literacy and education initiatives by the competent authorities;

(c) developing training standards for the industry; and

(d) contributing to the development of common disclosure rules.

2. The Authority shall monitor new and existing financial activities and may adopt guidelines and recommendations with a view to promoting the safety and soundness of markets and convergence of regulatory practice.

3. The Authority may also issue warnings in the event that a financial activity poses a serious threat to the objectives laid down in Article 1(5).

4. The Authority shall establish, as an integral part of the Authority, a Committee on financial innovation, which brings together all relevant competent national supervisory authorities with a view to achieving a coordinated approach to the regulatory and supervisory treatment of new or innovative financial activities and providing advice for the Authority to present to the European Parliament, the Council and the Commission.

5. The Authority may temporarily prohibit or restrict certain financial activities that threaten the orderly functioning and integrity of financial markets or the stability of the whole or part of the financial system in the Union in the cases specified and under the conditions laid down in the legislative acts referred to in Article 1(2) or if so required in the case of an emergency situation in accordance with and under the conditions laid down in Article 18.

The Authority shall review the decision referred to in the first subparagraph at appropriate intervals and at least every 3 months. If the decision is not renewed after a three-month period, it shall automatically expire.

(g)按第34条规定向欧洲议会、欧盟理事会或欧盟委员会发布意见;

(h)按第35条规定收集与金融市场参与者有关的必要信息;

(i)为评估产品特征和分销程序对金融市场参与者的财务状况和消费者保护所产生的影响制定通用的方法论;及

(j)在第1条第2款所述法律文件所规定的职权管辖范围内提供一个可集中查阅数据的注册金融市场参与者数据库。

第9条 与消费者保护和金融活动有关的职责

1.欧洲证券与市场管理局应通过下列手段在为欧盟内部市场的消费金融产品或服务提升市场透明度、简易性和公平中发挥领导作用:

(a)收集、分析并报告关于消费趋势的信息;

(b)审评并协调主管部门的金融普及和教育新方案;

(c)制定行业培训标准;及

(d)致力于通用披露规则的制定。

2.欧洲证券与市场管理局应对既有的和新型的金融活动进行监控,并可通过指引和建议以促进市场的安全和稳健以及监管实践的趋同。

3.金融活动对第1条第5款所规定的目标造成严重威胁的,欧洲证券与市场管理局也可发出预警。

4.欧洲证券与市场管理局应在金融创新方面设立一个委员会,作为欧洲证券与市场管理局的组成部分。该委员会集合所有相关国家级主管部门,以便在对新型或创新金融活动作出规制和监管处理时能相互协调,并向欧洲证券与市场管理局提供呈报给欧洲议会、欧盟理事会和欧盟委员会的建议。

5.欧洲证券与市场管理局可在第1条第2款所述框架立法规定的情形和条件下,或者在出现第18条所述紧急情况且依据第18条设定的条件有必要的情形下,决定采取临时措施,禁止或限制威胁到欧盟金融市场有序运行和诚信度以及整个或部分金融系统稳定的某些金融活动。

欧洲证券与市场管理局应以适当的频率至少每3个月1次对本款第1项所述的决定作审评。决定在3个月期限过后未展延的,应自动失效。

A Member State may request the Authority to reconsider its decision. In that case, the Authority shall decide in accordance with the procedure set out in the second subparagraph of Article 44(1), whether it maintains its decision.

The Authority may also assess the need to prohibit or restrict certain types of financial activity and, where there is such a need, inform the Commission in order to facilitate the adoption of any such prohibition or restriction.

Article 10 Regulatory technical standards

1. Where the European Parliament and the Council delegate power to the Commission to adopt regulatory technical standards by means of delegated acts under Article 290 TFEU in order to ensure consistent harmonisation in the areas specifically set out in the legislative acts referred to in Article 1(2), the Authority may develop draft regulatory technical standards. The Authority shall submit its draft standards to the Commission for endorsement.

Regulatory technical standards shall be technical, shall not imply strategic decisions or policy choices and their content shall be delimited by the legislative acts on which they are based.

Before submitting them to the Commission, the Authority shall conduct open public consultations on draft regulatory technical standards and analyse the potential related costs and benefits, unless such consultations and analyses are disproportionate in relation to the scope and impact of the draft regulatory technical standards concerned or in relation to the particular urgency of the matter. The Authority shall also request the opinion of the Securities and Markets Stakeholder Group referred to in Article 37.

Where the Authority submits a draft regulatory technical standard, the Commission shall immediately forward it to the European Parliament and the Council.

Within 3 months of receipt of a draft regulatory technical standard, the Commission shall decide whether to endorse it. The Commission may endorse the draft regulatory technical standards in part only, or with amendments, where theUnion's interests so require.

Where the Commission intends not to endorse a draft regulatory technical standard or to endorse it in part or with amendments, it shall send the draft regulatory technical standard back to the Authority, explaining why it does not endorse it, or, as the case may be, explaining the reasons for its amendments. Within a period of 6 weeks, the Authority may amend the draft regulatory technical standard on the basis of the Commission's proposed amendments and resubmit it in the form of a formal opinion to the Commission. The Authority shall send a copy of its formal opinion to the European Parliament and to the Council.

If, on the expiry of that six-week period, the Authority has not submitted an amended

成员国可请求欧洲证券与市场管理局重新审议其决定。在此情况下,欧洲证券与市场管理局应依照第44条第1款第2项所列程序决定是否维持其决定。

欧洲证券与市场管理局也可对是否需要禁止或限制特定类型金融活动进行评估,如确实有此需要,则应通知欧盟委员会以促成通过任何上述禁令或限制令。

第10条　监管性技术标准

1.欧洲议会和欧盟理事会按照《欧洲联盟运行条约》第290条授权欧盟委员会以授权立法形式通过监管性技术标准(以确保第1条第2款所述框架立法具体规定之各个领域里的一致协调)时,欧洲证券与市场管理局可起草监管性技术标准草案。欧洲证券与市场管理局应将其标准草案呈报欧盟委员会,以获得其同意和支持。

监管性技术标准应是技术性标准,不得含有任何战略决定或政策性选择,并且其内容应限于其所依据的框架立法的范围。

欧洲证券与市场管理局向欧盟委员会呈报监管性技术标准草案之前,应先公开征求公众意见并分析潜在的相关成本和收益,但是,上述意见征询和分析就所涉监管性技术标准草案的范围和影响而言,或就其特殊紧急性而言不成比例的除外。欧洲证券与市场管理局还应征求第37条所述的证券与市场利益相关者小组的意见。

欧洲证券与市场管理局呈报监管性技术标准草案后,欧盟委员会应立即将其转发给欧洲议会和欧盟理事会。

欧盟委员会收到监管性技术标准草案后3个月内,应决定是否同意和支持该草案。按照对欧盟有利的原则,欧盟委员会可仅同意和支持部分草案,或要求作出修改才同意和支持草案。

欧盟委员会有意否决监管性技术标准草案或仅同意和支持其中的一部分或要求作出修改才同意和支持该草案的,应将草案发回欧洲证券与市场管理局,并视具体情况对其否决该草案或者就草案需要修改的原因作出解释。欧洲证券与市场管理局可在6周内根据欧盟委员会的修改建议对监管性技术标准草案进行修改,并以正式意见的形式重新向欧盟委员会呈报。欧洲证券与市场管理局应将其正式意见的复本发送给欧洲议会和欧盟理事会。

6周期限届满,欧洲证券与市场管理局仍未呈报监管性技术标准草案修正稿,或

draft regulatory technical standard, or has submitted a draft regulatory technical standard that is not amended in a way consistent with the Commission's proposed amendments, the Commission may adopt the regulatory technical standard with the amendments it considers relevant, or reject it.

The Commission may not change the content of a draft regulatory technical standard prepared by the Authority without prior coordination with the Authority, as set out in this Article.

2. Where the Authority has not submitted a draft regulatory technical standard within the time limit set out in the legislative acts referred to in Article 1(2), the Commission may request such a draft within a new time limit.

3. Only where the Authority does not submit a draft regulatory technical standard to the Commission within the time limits in accordance with paragraph 2, may the Commission adopt a regulatory technical standard by means of a delegated act without a draft from the Authority.

The Commission shall conduct open public consultations on draft regulatory technical standards and analyse the potential related costs and benefits, unless such consultations and analyses are disproportionate in relation to the scope and impact of the draft regulatory technical standards concerned or in relation to the particular urgency of the matter. The Commission shall also request the opinion or advice of the Securities and Markets Stakeholder Group referred to in Article 37.

The Commission shall immediately forward the draft regulatory technical standard to the European Parliament and the Council.

The Commission shall send its draft regulatory technical standard to the Authority. Within a period of 6 weeks, the Authority may amend the draft regulatory technical standard and submit it in the form of a formal opinion to the Commission. The Authority shall send a copy of its formal opinion to the European Parliament and to the Council.

If, on the expiry of the six-week period referred to in the fourth subparagraph, the Authority has not submitted an amended draft regulatory technical standard, the Commission may adopt the regulatory technical standard.

If the Authority has submitted an amended draft regulatory technical standard within the six-week period, the Commission may amend the draft regulatory technical standard on the basis of the Authority's proposed amendments or adopt the regulatory technical standard with the amendments it considers relevant. The Commission shall not change the content of the draft regulatory technical standard prepared by the Authority without prior coordination with the Authority, as set out in this Article.

4. The regulatory technical standards shall be adopted by means of regulations or decisions. They shall be published in the Official Journal of the European Union and shall

呈报的修正稿不符合欧盟委员会的修改建议的,欧盟委员会可在作出其认为适当的修改后通过监管性技术标准草案或否决该草案。

依本条规定,未事先与欧洲证券与市场管理局协调,欧盟委员会不得擅自更改由欧洲证券与市场管理局起草的监管性技术标准草案的内容。

2.欧洲证券与市场管理局未在第1条第2款所述框架立法规定的期限内呈报监管性技术标准草案的,欧盟委员会可重新设定期限,要求其提供监管性技术标准草案。

3.唯有当欧洲证券与市场管理局未在第2款规定的期限内向欧盟委员会呈报监管性技术标准草案时,欧盟委员会方可在无欧洲证券与市场管理局草案的情况下以授权立法的形式通过监管性技术标准。

欧盟委员会应就监管性技术标准草案公开征求公众意见并分析潜在的相关成本和收益,但是,上述意见征询和分析就所涉监管性技术标准草案的范围和影响而言,或就其特殊紧急性而言不成比例的除外。欧盟委员会也应征求第37条所述的证券与市场利益相关者小组的意见或建议。

欧盟委员会应立即将其起草的监管性技术标准草案转发给欧洲议会和欧盟理事会。

欧盟委员会应将其监管性技术标准草案发送给欧洲证券与市场管理局。欧洲证券与市场管理局可在6周内对监管性技术标准进行修改,并以正式意见的形式呈报欧盟委员会。欧洲证券与市场管理局应将其正式意见的复本分别发送给欧洲议会和欧盟理事会。

第4项规定的6周期限届满,欧洲证券与市场管理局仍未呈报监管性技术标准草案修改稿的,欧盟委员会可按原文通过该标准。

欧洲证券与市场管理局在6周期限内呈报了监管性技术标准草案修改稿的,欧盟委员会可基于欧洲证券与市场管理局的修改建议对监管性技术标准草案进行修改,或完成其自身认为适当的修改后通过监管性技术标准。依本条规定,未事先与欧洲证券与市场管理局协调,欧盟委员会不得擅自更改由欧洲证券与市场管理局起草的监管性技术标准草案的内容。

4.监管性技术标准应以条例或决定的形式通过,在《欧盟公报》公布并自其所示之日起生效。

enter into force on the date stated therein.

Article 11 Exercise of the delegation

1. The power to adopt regulatory technical standards referred to in Article 10 shall be conferred on the Commission for a period of 4 years from 16 December 2010. The Commission shall draw up a report in respect of the delegated power not later than 6 months before the end of the four-year period. The delegation of power shall be automatically extended for periods of an identical duration, unless the European Parliament or the Council revokes it in accordance with Article 14.

2. As soon as it adopts a regulatory technical standard, the Commission shall notify it simultaneously to the European Parliament and to the Council.

3. The power to adopt regulatory technical standards is conferred on the Commission subject to the conditions laid down in Articles 12 to 14.

Article 12 Revocation of the delegation

1. The delegation of power referred to in Article 10 may be revoked at any time by the European Parliament or by the Council.

2. The institution which has commenced an internal procedure for deciding whether to revoke a delegation of power shall endeavour to inform the other institution and the Commission within a reasonable time before the final decision is taken, indicating the delegated power which could be subject to revocation.

3. The decision of revocation shall put an end to the delegation of the power specified in that decision. It shall take effect immediately or at a later date specified therein. It shall not affect the validity of the regulatory technical standards already in force. It shall be published in the Official Journal of the European Union.

Article 13 Objections to regulatory technical standards

1. The European Parliament or the Council may object to a regulatory technical standard within a period of 3 months from the date of notification of the regulatory technical standard adopted by the Commission. At the initiative of the European Parliament or the Council that period shall be extended by 3 months.

Where the Commission adopts a regulatory technical standard which is the same as the draft regulatory technical standard submitted by the Authority, the period during which the European Parliament and the Council may object shall be 1 month from the date of notification. At the initiative of the European Parliament or the Council that period shall be extended by 1 month.

2. If, on the expiry of the period referred to in paragraph 1, neither the European Parliament nor the Council has objected to the regulatory technical standard, it shall be published in the Official Journal of the European Union and shall enter into force on the date stated therein.

第11条　委托授权的行使

1.自2010年12月16日起，兹授予欧盟委员会第10条所述通过监管性技术标准的权力，权力有效期为4年。欧盟委员会应在该4年期限届满的6个月前就被委托的权力起草一份报告。除非欧洲议会或欧盟理事会依照第14条撤销委托授权，否则委托授权期限届满后应自动展延，每次展延的期限与原期限相同。

2.欧盟委员会应在通过监管性技术标准后立即同时通知欧洲议会和欧盟理事会。

3.授予欧盟委员会的通过监管性技术标准的权力受制于第12条至第14条规定的条件。

第12条　委托授权的撤销

1.欧洲议会或欧盟理事会可以随时撤销第10条所述的委托授权。

2.欧洲议会或欧盟理事会已经启动决定是否撤销某项委托授权的内部程序的，应当尽力在作出最终决定前的合理时间通知彼此以及欧盟委员会，指明可能被撤销的委托授权。

3.撤销决定将使其列明的委托授权效力终止。撤销决定应立即生效，或在决定中规定的较晚日期生效。撤销决定不影响已生效的监管性技术标准的效力。撤销决定应在《欧盟公报》公布。

第13条　对监管性技术标准的异议

1.欧洲议会或欧盟理事会可在欧盟委员会通过的监管性技术标准的通知日起3个月期限内对该等标准提出异议。经欧洲议会或欧盟理事会主动要求，该期限可延长3个月。

欧盟委员会依照欧洲证券与市场管理局呈报的监管性技术标准草案原文通过了该标准的，欧洲议会和欧盟理事会提出异议的期限为通知日起的1个月。经欧洲议会或欧盟理事会主动要求，该期限可延长1个月。

2.第1款所述期限届满时，欧洲议会和欧盟理事会均未对监管性技术标准提出异议的，该监管性技术标准应在《欧盟公报》公布，并自其规定的生效日期起生效。

The regulatory technical standard may be published in the Official Journal of the European Union and enter into force before the expiry of that period if the European Parliament and the Council have both informed the Commission of their intention not to raise objections.

3. If either the European Parliament or the Council objects to a regulatory technical standard within the period referred to in paragraph 1, it shall not enter into force. In accordance with Article 296 TFEU, the institution which objects shall state the reasons for objecting to the regulatory technical standard.

Article 14 Non-endorsement or amendment of draft regulatory technical standards

1. In the event that the Commission does not endorse a draft regulatory technical standard or amends it as provided for in Article 10, the Commission shall inform the Authority, the European Parliament and the Council, stating its reasons.

2. Where appropriate, the European Parliament or the Council may invite the responsible Commissioner, together with the Chairperson of the Authority, within 1 month of the notice referred to in paragraph 1, for an ad hoc meeting of the competent committee of the European Parliament or the Council to present and explain their differences.

Article 15 Implementing technical standards

1. The Authority may develop implementing technical standards, by means of implementing acts under Article 291 TFEU, in the areas specifically set out in the legislative acts referred to in Article 1(2). Implementing technical standards shall be technical, shall not imply strategic decisions or policy choices and their content shall be to determine the conditions of application of those acts. The Authority shall submit its draft implementing technical standards to the Commission for endorsement.

Before submitting draft implementing technical standards to the Commission, the Authority shall conduct open public consultations and shall analyse the potential, related costs and benefits, unless such consultations and analyses are disproportionate in relation to the scope and impact of the draft implementing technical standards concerned or in relation to the particular urgency of the matter. The Authority shall also request the opinion of the Securities and Markets Stakeholder Group referred to in Article 37.

Where the Authority submits a draft implementing technical standard, the Commission shall immediately forward it to the European Parliament and the Council.

Within 3 months of receipt of a draft implementing technical standard, the Commission shall decide whether to endorse it. The Commission may extend that period by 1 month. The Commission may endorse the draft implementing technical standard in part only, or with amendments, where theUnion's interests so require.

Where the Commission intends not to endorse a draft implementing technical

在第1款所述期限届满前，欧洲议会和欧盟理事会均已通知欧盟委员会其无意提出异议的，监管性技术标准可提前在《欧盟公报》公布并生效。

3.欧洲议会或欧盟理事会在第1款所述期限内对监管性技术标准提出异议的，该标准不得生效。根据《欧洲联盟运行条约》第296条的规定，对监管性技术标准提出异议的机构应说明异议理由。

第14条　不同意或修改监管性技术标准草案

1.欧盟委员会按第10条规定不同意和支持监管性技术标准草案或对其作出修改的，欧盟委员会应通知欧洲证券与市场管理局、欧洲议会和欧盟理事会并陈述理由。

2.在适当时，欧洲议会或欧盟理事会可邀请负责的委员与欧洲证券与市场管理局的主席一同在第1款所指通知发出后1个月内参加欧洲议会或欧盟理事会有关委员会的临时会议，陈述其分歧并对之作出解释。

第15条　实施性技术标准

1.欧洲证券与市场管理局可在第1条第2款所述框架立法具体规定的领域按照《欧洲联盟运行条约》第291条以实施性立法的形式制定实施性技术标准。实施性技术标准应是技术性标准，不应涉及任何战略决定或政策选择；其内容应是确定上述框架立法的适用条件。欧洲证券与市场管理局应将实施性技术标准草案呈报欧盟委员会，以获得其同意和支持。

欧洲证券与市场管理局向欧盟委员会呈报实施性技术标准草案之前，应先公开征求公众意见并分析潜在的相关成本和收益，但是，上述意见征询和分析就所涉实施性技术标准草案的范围和影响而言，或就其特殊紧急性而言不成比例的除外。欧洲证券与市场管理局还应征求第37条所述的证券与市场利益相关者小组的意见。

欧洲证券与市场管理局呈报实施性技术标准草案后，欧盟委员会应立即将其转发给欧洲议会和欧盟理事会。

欧盟委员会收到实施性技术标准草案后3个月内，应决定是否同意和支持该草案。欧盟委员会可将该期限延长1个月。按照对欧盟有利的原则，欧盟委员会可仅同意和支持部分草案，或要求作出修改后才同意和支持草案。

欧盟委员会有意否决实施性技术标准草案或仅同意和支持其中的一部分或要求

standard or intends to endorse it in part or with amendments, it shall send it back to the Authority explaining why it does not intend to endorse it, or as the case may be, explaining the reasons for its amendments. Within a period of 6 weeks, the Authority may amend the draft implementing technical standard on the basis of the Commission's proposed amendments and resubmit it in the form of a formal opinion to the Commission. The Authority shall send a copy of its formal opinion to the European Parliament and to the Council.

If, on the expiry of the six-week period referred to in the fifth subparagraph, the Authority has not submitted an amended draft implementing technical standard, or has submitted a draft implementing technical standard that is not amended in a way consistent with the Commission's proposed amendments, the Commission may adopt the implementing technical standard with the amendments it considers relevant or reject it.

The Commission shall not change the content of a draft implementing technical standard prepared by the Authority without prior coordination with the Authority, as set out in this Article.

2. In cases where the Authority has not submitted a draft implementing technical standard within the time limit set out in the legislative acts referred to in Article 1(2), the Commission may request such a draft within a new time limit.

3. Only where the Authority does not submit a draft implementing technical standard to the Commission within the time limits in accordance with paragraph 2, may the Commission adopt an implementing technical standard by means of an implementing act without a draft from the Authority.

The Commission shall conduct open public consultations on draft implementing technical standards and analyse the potential related costs and benefits, unless such consultations and analyses are disproportionate in relation to the scope and impact of the draft implementing technical standards concerned or in relation to the particular urgency of the matter. The Commission shall also request the opinion or advice of the Securities and Markets Stakeholder Group referred to in Article 37.

The Commission shall immediately forward the draft implementing technical standard to the European Parliament and the Council.

The Commission shall send the draft implementing technical standard to the Authority. Within a period of 6 weeks, the Authority may amend the draft implementing technical standard and submit it in the form of a formal opinion to the Commission. The Authority shall send a copy of its formal opinion to the European Parliament and to the Council.

If, on the expiry of the six-week period referred to in the fourth subparagraph, the Authority has not submitted an amended draft implementing technical standard, the

作出修改才同意和支持该草案的，应将草案发回欧洲证券与市场管理局，并视具体情况对其否决该草案或者就草案需要修改的原因作出解释。欧洲证券与市场管理局可在6周内根据欧盟委员会的修改建议对实施性技术标准草案进行修改，并以正式意见的形式重新向欧盟委员会呈报。欧洲证券与市场管理局应将其正式意见的复本发送给欧洲议会和欧盟理事会。

第5项所述的6周期限届满，欧洲证券与市场管理局仍未呈报实施性技术标准草案修改稿，或呈报的修改稿不符合欧盟委员会的修改建议的，欧盟委员会可在作出其认为适当的修改后通过实施性技术标准草案或否决该草案。

依本条规定，未事先与欧洲证券与市场管理局协调，欧盟委员会不得擅自更改由欧洲证券与市场管理局起草的实施性技术标准草案的内容。

2.欧洲证券与市场管理局未在第1条第2款所述框架立法规定的期限内呈报实施性技术标准草案的，欧盟委员会可重新设定期限，要求其提供实施性技术标准草案。

3.唯有当欧洲证券与市场管理局未在第2款规定的期限内向欧盟委员会呈报实施性技术标准草案时，欧盟委员会方可在无欧洲证券与市场管理局草案的情况下以实施性立法的形式通过实施性技术标准。

欧盟委员会应就实施性技术标准草案公开征求公众意见，并分析潜在的相关成本和收益，但是，上述意见征询和分析就所涉实施性技术标准草案的范围和影响而言，或就其特殊紧急性而言不成比例的除外。欧盟委员会也应征求第37条所述的证券与市场利益相关者小组的意见或建议。

欧盟委员会应立即将实施性技术标准草案转发给欧洲议会和欧盟理事会。

欧盟委员会应将实施性技术标准草案发送给欧洲证券与市场管理局。欧洲证券与市场管理局可在6周内对实施性技术标准进行修改，并以正式意见的形式呈报欧盟委员会。欧洲证券与市场管理局应将其正式意见的复本分别发给欧洲议会和欧盟理事会。

第4项所述的6周期限届满，欧洲证券与市场管理局仍未呈报实施性技术标准草案修改稿的，欧盟委员会可按原文通过该标准。

Commission may adopt the implementing technical standard.

If the Authority has submitted an amended draft implementing technical standard within that six-week period, the Commission may amend the draft implementing technical standard on the basis of the Authority's proposed amendments or adopt the implementing technical standard with the amendments it considers relevant.

The Commission shall not change the content of the draft implementing technical standards prepared by the Authority without prior coordination with the Authority, as set out in this Article.

4. The implementing technical standards shall be adopted by means of regulations or decisions. They shall be published in the Official Journal of the European Union and shall enter into force on the date stated therein.

Article 16 Guidelines and recommendations

1. The Authority shall, with a view to establishing consistent, efficient and effective supervisory practices within the ESFS, and to ensuring the common, uniform and consistent application of Union law, issue guidelines and recommendations addressed to competent authorities or financial market participants.

2. The Authority shall, where appropriate, conduct open public consultations regarding the guidelines and recommendations and analyse the related potential costs and benefits. Such consultations and analyses shall be proportionate in relation to the scope, nature and impact of the guidelines or recommendations. The Authority shall, where appropriate, also request opinions or advice from the Securities and Markets Stakeholder Group referred to in Article 37.

3. The competent authorities and financial market participants shall make every effort to comply with those guidelines and recommendations.

Within 2 months of the issuance of a guideline or recommendation, each competent authority shall confirm whether it complies or intends to comply with that guideline or recommendation. In the event that a competent authority does not comply or does not intend to comply, it shall inform the Authority, stating its reasons.

The Authority shall publish the fact that a competent authority does not comply or does not intend to comply with that guideline or recommendation. The Authority may also decide, on a case by case basis, to publish the reasons provided by the competent authority for not complying with that guideline or recommendation. The competent authority shall receive advanced notice of such publication.

If required by that guideline or recommendation, financial market participants shall report, in a clear and detailed way, whether they comply with that guideline or recommendation.

4. In the report referred to in Article 43(5) the Authority shall inform the European

欧洲证券与市场管理局在6周期限内呈报了实施性技术标准草案修改稿的，欧盟委员会可基于欧洲证券与市场管理局的修改建议对实施性技术标准草案进行修改，或完成其自身认为适当的修改后通过实施性技术标准。

依本条规定，未事先与欧洲证券与市场管理局协调，欧盟委员会不得擅自更改由欧洲证券与市场管理局起草的实施性技术标准草案的内容。

4.实施性技术标准应以条例或决定的形式通过，在《欧盟公报》公布并自其所示之日起生效。

第16条　指引和建议

1.为在欧洲金融监管体系内建立一致的且兼具效率和成效的监管实践，确保欧盟法律的共同、统一和一致的适用，欧洲证券与市场管理局应针对主管部门或金融市场参与者提出指引和建议。

2.在适当时，欧洲证券与市场管理局应就指引和建议公开征求公众意见并分析潜在的相关成本和收益。上述意见征询和分析应与指引或建议的范围、性质和影响成比例。在适当时，欧洲证券与市场管理局还应征求第37条所述证券与市场利益相关者小组的意见或建议。

3.主管部门和金融市场参与者应尽其所能遵循该等指引和建议。

指引或建议发布后2个月内，各主管部门应确认其是否遵循或有意遵循该指引或建议。主管部门不遵循或不愿遵循的，应通知欧洲证券与市场管理局并陈述理由。

欧洲证券与市场管理局应公布主管部门不遵循或不愿遵循该指引或建议的事实。欧洲证券与市场管理局还可根据具体情况决定公布主管部门所提出的不遵循该指引或建议的理由。公布上述事实或理由应提前通知主管部门。

如指引或建议要求以清楚详尽的方式报告其是否遵循该指引或建议，金融市场参与者应遵守该等要求。

4.在第43条第5款所述的报告中，欧洲证券与市场管理局应将其已发布的指引或

Parliament, the Council and the Commission of the guidelines and recommendations that have been issued, stating which competent authority has not complied with them, and outlining how the Authority intends to ensure that the competent authority concerned follow its recommendations and guidelines in the future.

Article 17 Breach of Union law

1. Where a competent authority has not applied the acts referred to in Article 1(2), or has applied them in a way which appears to be a breach of Union law, including the regulatory technical standards and implementing technical standards established in accordance with Articles 10 to 15, in particular by failing to ensure that a financial market participant satisfies the requirements laid down in those acts, the Authority shall act in accordance with the powers set out in paragraphs 2, 3 and 6 of this Article.

2. Upon a request from one or more competent authorities, the European Parliament, the Council, the Commission or the Securities and Markets Stakeholder Group, or on its own initiative, and after having informed the competent authority concerned, the Authority may investigate the alleged breach or non-application of Union law.

Without prejudice to the powers laid down in Article 35, the competent authority shall, without delay, provide the Authority with all information which the Authority considers necessary for its investigation.

3. The Authority may, not later than 2 months from initiating its investigation, address a recommendation to the competent authority concerned setting out the action necessary to comply with Union law.

The competent authority shall, within ten working days of receipt of the recommendation, inform the Authority of the steps it has taken or intends to take to ensure compliance with Union law.

4. Where the competent authority has not complied with Union law within 1 month from receipt of the Authority's recommendation, the Commission may, after having been informed by the Authority or on its own initiative, issue a formal opinion requiring the competent authority to take the action necessary to comply with Union law. The Commission's formal opinion shall take into account the Authority's recommendation.

The Commission shall issue such a formal opinion no later than 3 months after the adoption of the recommendation. The Commission may extend this period by 1 month.

The Authority and the competent authorities shall provide the Commission with all necessary information.

5. The competent authority shall, within ten working days of receipt of the formal opinion referred to in paragraph 4, inform the Commission and the Authority of the steps it has taken or intends to take to comply with that formal opinion.

6. Without prejudice to the powers of the Commission under Article 258 TFEU,

建议通知欧洲议会、欧盟理事会和欧盟委员会，列明未遵循上述指引和建议的主管部门，并简要说明欧洲证券与市场管理局计划如何确保所涉主管部门未来切实遵循其建议和指引。

第17条　违反欧盟法律

1.对于第1条第2款所述法律文件，包括依照第10条至第15条的规定制定的监管性技术标准和实施性技术标准，某主管部门未予适用，或者似以违反欧盟法律的方式适用，尤其是未能确保金融市场参与者满足该等法律文件所列要求的，欧洲证券与市场管理局应依照本条第2款、第3款和第6款授予的权力行事。

2.欧洲证券与市场管理局可经一个或多个主管部门、欧洲议会、欧盟理事会、欧盟委员会或证券与市场利益相关者小组请求对涉嫌违反或不适用欧盟法律的情况进行调查，亦可主动进行调查，但调查应提前通知所涉主管部门。

在不影响第35条所规定的权力的情况下，主管部门应按照欧洲证券与市场管理局的要求立即向其提供调查所必要的一切信息。

3.欧洲证券与市场管理局可在启动调查后2个月内向所涉主管部门提出建议，提出为遵循欧盟法律所需采取的行动。

主管部门应在收到建议后10个工作日内通知欧洲证券与市场管理局其为遵循欧盟法律而已采取或有意采取的措施。

4.主管部门在收到欧洲证券与市场管理局建议1个月内仍未遵守欧盟法律的，欧盟委员会可在接到欧洲证券与市场管理局通知后发布正式意见，亦可主动发布正式意见，要求主管部门采取必要的行动以遵守欧盟法律。欧盟委员会的正式意见应考虑欧洲证券与市场管理局的建议。

欧盟委员会应最迟于建议通过后3个月（含）内发布上述正式意见。欧盟委员会可将此期限延长1个月。

欧洲证券与市场管理局和主管部门应向欧盟委员会提供所有必要信息。

5.主管部门应在收到第4款所述正式意见后10个工作日内通知欧盟委员会和欧洲证券与市场管理局其为遵循该正式意见而已采取或有意采取的措施。

6.在不影响欧盟委员会在《欧洲联盟运行条约》第258条中的权力的情况下，某主

where a competent authority does not comply with the formal opinion referred to in paragraph 4 within the period of time specified therein, and where it is necessary to remedy in a timely manner such noncompliance in order to maintain or restore neutral conditions of competition in the market or ensure the orderly functioning and integrity of the financial system, the Authority may, where the relevant requirements of the acts referred to in Article 1(2) are directly applicable to financial market participants, adopt an individual decision addressed to a financial market participant requiring the necessary action to comply with its obligations under Union law including the cessation of any practice.

The decision of the Authority shall be in conformity with the formal opinion issued by the Commission pursuant to paragraph 4.

7. Decisions adopted under paragraph 6 shall prevail over any previous decision adopted by the competent authorities on the same matter.

When taking action in relation to issues which are subject to a formal opinion pursuant to paragraph 4 or a decision pursuant to paragraph 6, competent authorities shall comply with the formal opinion or the decision, as the case may be.

8. In the report referred to in Article 43(5), the Authority shall set out which competent authorities and financial market participants have not complied with the formal opinions or decisions referred to in paragraphs 4 and 6 of this Article.

Article 18 Action in emergency situations

1. In the case of adverse developments which may seriously jeopardise the orderly functioning and integrity of financial markets or the stability of the whole or part of the financial system in the Union, the Authority shall actively facilitate and, where deemed necessary, coordinate any actions undertaken by the relevant national competent supervisory authorities.

In order to be able to perform that facilitating and coordinating role, the Authority shall be fully informed of any relevant developments, and shall be invited to participate as an observer in any relevant gathering by the relevant national competent supervisory authorities.

2. The Council, in consultation with the Commission and the ESRB and, where appropriate, the ESAs, may adopt a decision addressed to the Authority, determining the existence of an emergency situation for the purposes of this Regulation, following a request by the Authority, the Commission or the ESRB. The Council shall review that decision at appropriate intervals and at least once a month. If the decision is not renewed at the end of a one-month period, it shall automatically expire. The Council may declare the discontinuation of the emergency situation at any time.

Where the ESRB or the Authority considers that an emergency situation may arise, it

管部门未在第4款所述正式意见确定的期限内遵循该正式意见，且有必要及时对上述不遵循进行补救以维持或恢复市场的竞争中立性或确保金融系统的有序运行和诚信度的，欧洲证券与市场管理局可在第1条第2款所述法律文件的相关要求可直接适用于金融市场参与者的情况下，针对金融市场参与者作出个别决定，要求其采取必要的行动以履行其在欧盟法律中的义务，包括停办任何业务。

欧洲证券与市场管理局的决定应与欧盟委员会根据第4款所发布的正式意见一致。

7.根据第6款所作出的决定应优先适用于主管部门之前就相同事宜所作出的决定。

针对第4款下的正式意见或第6款下的决定涉及的问题采取行动时，主管部门应严格遵循相关的正式意见或决定（视具体情况而定）。

8.在第43条第5款所述的报告中，欧洲证券与市场管理局应列出未遵循本条第4款所述的正式意见或第6款所述的决定的主管部门和金融市场参与者。

第18条　紧急情况下的行动

1.如果发生可能严重危害欧盟金融市场有序运行和诚信度或整个或部分欧盟金融系统稳定的不利变化状况，则欧洲证券与市场管理局应积极促进并在其认为必要时协调相关的国家级监管主管部门采取的任何行动。

为了能够起到促进和协调的作用，欧洲证券与市场管理局应充分知悉任何相关的变化情况，并获邀作为观察员参加相关的国家级监管主管部门的任何相关集会。

2.经欧洲证券与市场管理局、欧盟委员会或欧洲系统性风险委员会请求，欧盟理事会可在与欧盟委员会和欧洲系统性风险委员会磋商以及在适当时与各欧洲监管机构磋商后，向欧洲证券与市场管理局发出决定，以确定是否存在本条例所指的紧急情况。欧盟理事会应以适当的频率并至少每月1次对该项决定进行审评。如1个月期限届满时决定未展延，则应自动失效。欧盟理事会可随时宣布紧急情况终止。

如欧洲系统性风险委员会或欧洲证券与市场管理局认为可能会出现紧急情况，

shall issue a confidential recommendation addressed to the Council and provide it with an assessment of the situation. The Council shall then assess the need for a meeting. In that process, due care of confidentiality shall be guaranteed.

If the Council determines the existence of an emergency situation, it shall duly inform the European Parliament and the Commission without delay.

3. Where the Council has adopted a decision pursuant to paragraph 2, and in exceptional circumstances where coordinated action by national authorities is necessary to respond to adverse developments which may seriously jeopardise the orderly functioning and integrity of financial markets or the stability of the whole or part of the financial system in the Union, the Authority may adopt individual decisions requiring competent authorities to take the necessary action in accordance with the legislation referred to in Article 1(2) to address any such developments by ensuring that financial market participants and competent authorities satisfy the requirements laid down in that legislation.

4. Without prejudice to the powers of the Commission under Article 258 TFEU, where a competent authority does not comply with the decision of the Authority referred to in paragraph 3 within the period laid down in that decision, the Authority may, where the relevant requirements laid down in the legislative acts referred to in Article 1(2) including in regulatory technical standards and implementing technical standards adopted in accordance with those acts are directly applicable to financial market participants, adopt an individual decision addressed to a financial market participant requiring the necessary action to comply with its obligations under that legislation, including the cessation of any practice. This shall apply only in situations in which a competent authority does not apply the legislative acts referred to in Article 1(2), including regulatory technical standards and implementing technical standards adopted in accordance with those acts, or applies them in a way which appears to be a manifest breach of those acts, and where urgent remedying is necessary to restore the orderly functioning and integrity of financial markets or the stability of the whole or part of the financial system in the Union.

5. Decisions adopted under paragraph 4 shall prevail over any previous decision adopted by the competent authorities on the same matter.

Any action by the competent authorities in relation to issues which are subject to a decision pursuant to paragraph 3 or 4 shall be compatible with those decisions.

Article 19 Settlement of disagreements between competent authorities in cross-border situations

1. Without prejudice to the powers laid down in Article 17, where a competent authority disagrees about the procedure or content of an action or inaction of a competent

应向欧盟理事会发出保密建议,并附对紧急情况的评估。欧盟理事会随后应判断是否有必要召开会议。在该过程中保密的注意义务应得到遵守。

欧盟理事会判定存在紧急情况的,应立即向欧洲议会和欧盟委员会发出通知。

3.欧盟理事会已经作出第2款中的决定,并且为应对可严重危害欧盟金融市场有序运行和诚信度或整个或部分金融系统稳定的不利变化而有必要协调国家级监管机构的行动的,欧洲证券与市场管理局可作出个别决定,要求主管部门按照第1条第2款所述立法采取必要的行动,以确保金融市场参与者和主管部门符合该等立法的要求,以应对上述不利变化。

4.在不影响欧盟委员会在《欧洲联盟运行条约》第258条中的权力的情况下,第3款所述的欧洲证券与市场管理局的决定未在该决定规定的时限内为某主管部门所遵守的,欧洲证券与市场管理局可对金融市场参与者作出个别决定,要求其采取必要的行动(包括停办任何业务),以遵循其在该立法中的义务,前提是第1条第2款所述法律的相关要求以及据其通过的相关监管性技术标准和实施性技术标准所规定的相关要求能够直接适用于金融市场参与者。上述规定仅适用于下列情况:对于第1条第2款所述框架立法,包括根据该等框架立法通过的相关监管性技术标准和实施性技术标准,某主管部门未予适用,或者似以明显违反欧盟法律的方式适用,并且有必要作出紧急补救以恢复欧盟金融市场的有序运行和诚信度或整个或部分欧盟金融系统的稳定。

5.根据第4款作出的决定应优先适用于主管部门之前就相同事宜所作出的任何决定。

主管部门就第3款或第4款中的决定所涉问题采取的任何行动均应符合该等决定。

第19条　跨境情况下主管部门之间分歧的解决

1.在不影响第17条所规定的权力的情况下,某主管部门对另一成员国主管部门在第1条第2款所述法律文件规定的情况下采取的行动或不采取行动所依据的程序或相

authority of another Member State in cases specified in the acts referred to in Article 1(2), the Authority, at the request of one or more of the competent authorities concerned may assist the authorities in reaching an agreement in accordance with the procedure set out in paragraphs 2 to 4 of this Article.

In cases specified in the legislation referred to in Article 1(2), and where on the basis of objective criteria, disagreement between competent authorities from different Member States can be determined, the Authority may, on its own initiative, assist the authorities in reaching an agreement in accordance with the procedure set out in paragraphs 2 to 4.

2. The Authority shall set a time limit for conciliation between the competent authorities taking into account any relevant time periods specified in the acts referred to in Article 1(2) and the complexity and urgency of the matter. At that stage the Authority shall act as a mediator.

3. If the competent authorities concerned fail to reach an agreement within the conciliation phase referred to in paragraph 2, the Authority may, in accordance with the procedure set out in the third and fourth subparagraph of Article 44(1) take a decision requiring them to take specific action or to refrain from action in order to settle the matter, with binding effects for the competent authorities concerned, in order to ensure compliance with Union law.

4. Without prejudice to the powers of the Commission under Article 258 TFEU, where a competent authority does not comply with the decision of the Authority, and thereby fails to ensure that a financial market participant complies with requirements directly applicable to it by virtue of the acts referred to in Article 1(2), the Authority may adopt an individual decision addressed to a financial market participant requiring the necessary action to comply with its obligations under Union law, including the cessation of any practice.

5. Decisions adopted under paragraph 4 shall prevail over any previous decision adopted by the competent authorities on the same matter. Any action by the competent authorities in relation to facts which are subject to a decision pursuant to paragraph 3 or 4 shall be compatible with those decisions.

6. In the report referred to in Article 50(2), the Chairperson of the Authority shall set out the nature and type of disagreements between competent authorities, the agreements reached and the decisions taken to settle such disagreements.

Article 20 Settlement of disagreements between competent authorities across sectors

The Joint Committee shall, in accordance with the procedure laid down in Article 19 and Article 56, settle cross-sectoral disagreements that may arise between competent

关内容有异议的，经一个或多个所涉主管部门请求，欧洲证券与市场管理局可协助各部门依照本条第2款至第4款规定的程序达成一致。

在第1条第2款所述立法规定的情况下，不同成员国主管部门之间的分歧可以基于客观的标准予以判定的，欧洲证券与市场管理局可主动协助各部门依照第2款至第4款规定的程序达成一致。

2.欧洲证券与市场管理局应在考虑到第1条第2款所述法律文件规定的任何相关期限以及所涉事项的复杂性和紧迫性后，为主管部门之间的调解设定时限。在该阶段欧洲证券与市场管理局应作为调解者行事。

3.所涉主管部门未在第2款所述的调解期达成一致的，欧洲证券与市场管理局可依照第44条第1款第3项和第4项规定的程序作出决定，要求所涉主管部门采取特定行动或不采取行动来解决有关问题，以确保其遵守欧盟法律，该决定对所涉主管部门均具有约束效力。

4.在不影响欧盟委员会在《欧洲联盟运行条约》第258条中的权力的情形下，如果某主管部门不遵循欧洲证券与市场管理局的决定，因而无法确保金融市场参与者遵守第1条第2款所述法律文件中可直接适用于该金融市场参与者的要求，则欧洲证券与市场管理局可针对金融市场参与者作出个别决定，要求其采取必要的行动，包括停办任何业务，以遵守其在欧盟法律中的义务。

5.根据第4款作出的决定应优先适用于主管部门之前就相同事宜所作出的任何决定。主管部门就第3款或第4款中的决定所涉问题采取的任何行动均应符合该等决定。

6.在第50条第2款所述的报告中，欧洲证券与市场管理局的主席应说明主管部门之间分歧的性质和类型、达成的一致意见以及为解决该等分歧而作出的决定。

第20条　跨行业主管部门分歧的解决

联合委员会应根据第19条和第56条规定的程序解决本条例、第1093/2010号（欧盟）条例以及第1094/2010号（欧盟）条例各自第4条第2款所界定的主管部门之间的跨

authorities as defined in Article 4(2) of this Regulation, of Regulation (EU) No 1093/2010 and of Regulation (EU) No 1094/2010 respectively.

Article 21 Colleges of supervisors

1. The Authority shall contribute to promoting and monitoring the efficient, effective and consistent functioning of the colleges of supervisors established in the legislative acts referred to in Article 1(2) and foster the coherence of the application of Union law among the colleges of supervisors. With the objective of converging supervisory best practices, staff from the Authority shall be able to participate in the activities of the colleges of supervisors, including on-site examinations, carried out jointly by two or more competent authorities.

2. The Authority shall lead in ensuring a consistent and coherent functioning of colleges of supervisors for cross-border institutions across the Union, taking account of the systemic risk posed by financial market participants referred to in Article 23.

For the purpose of this paragraph and of paragraph 1 of this Article, the Authority shall be considered a 'competent authority' within the meaning of the relevant legislation.

The Authority may:

(a) collect and share all relevant information in cooperation with the competent authorities in order to facilitate the work of the college and establish and manage a central system to make such information accessible to the competent authorities in the college;

(b) initiate and coordinate Union-wide stress tests in accordance with Article 32 to assess the resilience of financial market participants, in particular the systemic risk posed by key financial market participants as referred to in Article 23, to adverse market developments, and evaluate the potential for systemic risk posed by key financial market participants to increase in situations of stress, ensuring that a consistent methodology is applied at the national level to such tests and, where appropriate, address a recommendation to the competent authority to correct issues identified in the stress test;

(c) promote effective and efficient supervisory activities, including evaluating the risks to which financial market participants are or might be exposed in stress situations;

(d) oversee, in accordance with the tasks and powers specified in this Regulation, the tasks carried out by the competent authorities, and

(e) request further deliberations of a college in any cases where it considers that the decision would result in an incorrect application of Union law or would not contribute to the objective of convergence of supervisory practices. It may also require to schedule a meeting of the college or add a point to the agenda of a meeting.

3. The Authority may develop draft regulatory and implementing technical standards to ensure uniform conditions of application with respect to the provisions regarding the operational functioning of colleges of supervisors and issue guidelines and recommendations

行业分歧。

第21条　监管团

1.欧洲证券与市场管理局应致力于推动并监控第1条第2款所述框架立法设立的监管团一致的且兼具效率和成效的运行，并促使各监管团在适用欧盟法律时保持一致性。为达到最佳监管实践趋同之目的，欧洲证券与市场管理局的工作人员应能参加监管团的活动，包括由2个或多个主管部门共同进行的现场检查。

2.欧洲证券与市场管理局在考虑到第23条所述金融市场参与者所产生的系统性风险的前提下，应在确保监管团对欧盟各跨境机构的监管发挥相互一致的功能中起到领导作用。

就本款以及本条第1款而言，欧洲证券与市场管理局应被视为相关立法所定义的“主管部门”。

欧洲证券与市场管理局可以：

(a)与主管部门合作收集并共享所有相关信息，以推进监管团的工作，以及建立和管理一个中央信息系统，使监管团中的各主管部门能够查阅上述信息；

(b)根据第32条启动并协调欧盟范围内的压力测试，以评估金融市场参与者在不利市场变化下的抗冲击能力，特别是评估第23条所述金融机构产生的系统性风险；评估在压力情况下关键金融市场参与者所带来的系统性风险增加的可能性，确保各成员国实施该等测试的方法相互一致，以及在适当时向主管部门提出更正压力测试中发现的问题的建议；

(c)推广高效率和高成效的监管活动，包括评估金融市场参与者在压力状况下正在或可能面临的风险；

(d)根据本条例所规定的职责和权力，对主管部门履行职责的情况进行监控；及

(e)在其认为某监管团的决定会导致欧盟法律的不正确适用或不利于监管实践趋同目的的任何情况下，要求该监管团进一步审议该决定。欧洲证券与市场管理局还可要求为监管团安排会议或增加会议议程。

3.欧洲证券与市场管理局可起草监管性和实施性技术标准草案以确保有关监管团具体运作的条款具有统一的适用条件，并发布根据第16条所制定的指引和建议，以推动各监管团的监管运作方式以及所采用的最佳实践的趋同。

adopted under Article 16 to promote convergence in supervisory functioning and best practices adopted by the colleges of supervisors.

4. The Authority shall have a legally binding mediation role to resolve disputes between competent authorities in accordance with the procedure set out in Article 19. The Authority may take supervisory decisions directly applicable to the financial market participant concerned in accordance with Article 19.

Article 22 General provisions

1. The Authority shall duly consider systemic risk as defined by Regulation (EU) No 1092/2010. It shall address any risk of disruption in financial services that:

(a) is caused by an impairment of all or parts of the financial system; and

(b) has the potential to have serious negative consequences for internal market and the real economy.

The Authority shall consider, where appropriate, the monitoring and assessment of systemic risk as developed by the ESRB and the Authority and respond to warnings and recommendations by the ESRB in accordance with Article 17 of Regulation (EU) No 1092/2010.

2. The Authority shall, in collaboration with the ESRB, and in accordance with Article 23 develop a common approach for the identification and measurement of systemic risk posed by key financial market participants, including quantitative and qualitative indicators as appropriate.

Those indicators shall be a critical element in the determination of appropriate supervisory actions. The Authority shall monitor the degree of convergence in the determinations made, with a view to promoting a common approach.

3. Without prejudice to the acts referred to in Article 1(2), the Authority shall draw up, as necessary, additional guidelines and recommendations for key financial market participants, to take account of the systemic risk posed by them.

The Authority shall ensure that the systemic risk posed by key financial market participants is taken into account when developing draft regulatory and implementing technical standards in the areas laid down in the legislative acts referred to in Article 1 (2).

4. Upon a request from one or more competent authorities, the European Parliament, the Council or the Commission, or on its own initiative, the Authority may conduct an inquiry into a particular type of financial activity or type of product or type of conduct in order to assess potential threats to the integrity of financial markets or the stability of the financial system and make appropriate recommendations for action to the competent authorities concerned.

For those purposes, the Authority may use the powers conferred on it under this

4.欧洲证券与市场管理局应在依照第19条规定的程序解决主管部门之间的争议中发挥具有法律约束力的调解作用。根据第19条,欧洲证券与市场管理局可作出直接适用于所涉金融市场参与者的监管决定。

第22条　一般条款

1.欧洲证券与市场管理局应充分考虑第1092/2010号(欧盟)条例所界定的系统性风险。欧洲证券与市场管理局应处理符合下列条件的任何金融系统发生扰乱的风险:

(a)由整个或部分金融系统的损害所造成的;并且

(b)可能会对欧盟内部市场和实体经济造成严重负面后果的。

欧洲证券与市场管理局应适时考虑由欧洲系统性风险委员会和欧洲证券与市场管理局所进行的系统性风险监控和评估,并按照第1092/2010号(欧盟)条例第17条对欧洲系统性风险委员会所提出的预警和建议作出回应。

2.根据第23条,欧洲证券与市场管理局应与欧洲系统风险委员会合作,制定用以识别和计量关键金融市场参与者带来的系统性风险的通用方法,包括制定适当的定量和定性指标。

该等指标应为决定监管行动是否适当的关键要素。欧洲证券与市场管理局应出于推广通用方法之目的监控所作决定的趋同程度。

3.在不影响第1条第2款所述法律文件的情况下,在必要时,欧洲证券与市场管理局应考虑关键金融市场参与者所带来的系统性风险,就其起草额外的指引和建议。

在第1条第2款所述框架立法所规定的领域起草监管性和实施性技术标准草案时,欧洲证券与市场管理局应确保已考虑了关键金融市场参与者所带来的系统性风险。

4.欧洲证券与市场管理局可经一个或多个主管部门、欧洲议会、欧盟理事会或欧盟委员会请求对某一特定类型的金融活动或产品或行为进行调查,亦可主动进行调查,以评估对金融市场的诚信度或金融系统稳定的潜在威胁,并对所涉主管部门提出适当的行动建议。

欧洲证券与市场管理局可为该等目的行使本条例(包括第35条)授予的权力。

Regulation, including Article 35.

5. The Joint Committee shall ensure overall and cross-sectoral coordination of the activities carried out in accordance with this Article.

Article 23 Identification and measurement of systemic risk

1. The Authority shall, in consultation with the ESRB, develop criteria for the identification and measurement of systemic risk and an adequate stress testing regime which includes an evaluation of the potential for systemic risk posed by financial market participants to increase in situations of stress. The financial market participants that may pose a systemic risk shall be subject to strengthened supervision, and where necessary, the recovery and resolution procedures referred to in Article 25.

2. The Authority shall take fully into account the relevant international approaches when developing the criteria for the identification and measurement of systemic risk posed by financial market participants, including those established by the Financial Stability Board, the International Monetary Fund and the Bank for International Settlements.

Article 24 Permanent capacity to respond to systemic risks

1. The Authority shall ensure it has specialised and ongoing capacity to respond effectively to the materialisation of systemic risks as referred to in Articles 22 and 23, in particular with respect to institutions that pose a systemic risk.

2. The Authority shall fulfil the tasks conferred upon it in this Regulation and in the legislation referred to in Article 1(2), and shall contribute to ensuring a coherent and coordinated crisis management and resolution regime in the Union.

Article 25 Recovery and resolution procedures

1. The Authority shall contribute to and participate actively in the development and coordination of effective and consistent recovery and resolution plans, procedures in emergency situations and preventive measures to minimize the systemic impact of any failure.

2. The Authority may develop regulatory and implementing technical standards as specified in the legislative acts referred to in Article 1(2) in accordance with the procedure laid down in Articles 10 to 15.

Article 26 European system of national Investor Compensation Schemes

1. The Authority shall contribute to strengthening the European system of national Investor Compensation Schemes (ICS) by acting under the powers conferred to it in this Regulation to ensure the correct application of Directive 97/9/EC with the aim of ensuring that national Investor Compensation Schemes are adequately funded by contributions from the concerned financial market participants, including where appropriate financial market participants headquartered in third-countries, and provide a high level of protection to all investors in a harmonised framework throughout the Union.

5.联合委员会应确保根据本条所开展的活动的全面和跨行业协调。

第23条　识别和计量系统性风险

1.欧洲证券与市场管理局应与欧洲系统性风险委员会磋商，制定识别和计量系统性风险的标准，并建立完善的压力测试机制，该机制应包含对于压力状况下金融市场参与者系统性风险增加的可能性的评估。应加强对可能带来系统性风险的金融市场参与者的监管，并在必要时对其适用第25条所述的恢复和清盘程序。

2.在制定识别和计量金融市场参与者的系统性风险标准时，欧洲证券与市场管理局应充分考虑相关国际处理方法，包括金融稳定委员会、国际货币基金组织以及国际清算银行所制定的方法。

第24条　持续应对系统性风险的能力

1.欧洲证券与市场管理局应确保有专门和持续的能力对第22条和第23条所述系统性风险的具体结果特别是对产生系统性风险的机构作出有效回应。

2.欧洲证券与市场管理局应履行本条例以及第1条第2款所述立法赋予的职责，并应致力于确保欧盟具备相互一致和协调的危机管理和清盘机制。

第25条　恢复和清盘程序

1.欧洲证券与市场管理局应促进并积极参与下列各项的制定和协调工作：紧急情况下有效、一致的恢复和清盘计划和程序，以及将任何金融机构倒闭的系统性影响降到最低的预防性措施。

2.欧洲证券与市场管理局可依照第10条至第15条规定的程序，制定第1条第2款所述框架立法指明的监管性和实施性技术标准。

第26条　欧洲国家级投资者补偿计划体系

1.欧洲证券与市场管理局应通过运用其本条例下的权力，致力于强化欧洲国家级投资者补偿计划体系（ICS），保障第97/9/EC号指令正确适用，以确保国家级投资者补偿计划从所涉金融市场参与者（适当时包括总部位于第三国的金融市场参与者）处收到充足的缴款以获得充足的经费，并确保在全欧盟协调一致的框架中给予所有投资者高水平的保护。

2. Article 16 concerning the Authority's powers to adopt guidelines and recommendations shall apply to Investor Compensation Schemes.

3. The Authority may develop regulatory and implementing technical standards as specified in the legislative acts referred to in Article 1(2) in accordance with the procedure laid down in Articles 10 to 15.

4. The review of this Regulation provided for in Article 81 shall in particular examine the convergence of the European system of national Investor Compensation Schemes.

Article 27 European system of resolution and funding arrangements

1. In the areas of its competence, the Authority shall contribute to developing methods for the resolution of failing key financial market participants in ways which avoid contagion, allow them to be wound down in an orderly and timely manner, and, where applicable, including coherent and credible funding mechanisms as appropriate.

2. The Authority shall contribute to the work on the level playing field issues and cumulative impacts of any systems of levies and contributions on financial institutions that may be introduced to ensure fair burden sharing and incentives to contain systemic risk as a part of a coherent and credible resolution framework.

The review of this Regulation provided for in Article 81 shall in particular examine the possible enhancement of the role of the Authority in a framework of crisis prevention, management and resolution.

Article 28 Delegation of tasks and responsibilities

1. Competent authorities may, with the consent of the delegate, delegate tasks and responsibilities to the Authority or other competent authorities subject to the conditions set out in this Article. Member States may set out specific arrangements regarding the delegation of responsibilities that have to be complied with before their competent authorities enter into such delegation agreements, and may limit the scope of delegation to what is necessary for the effective supervision of cross-border financial market participants or groups.

2. The Authority shall stimulate and facilitate the delegation of tasks and responsibilities between competent authorities by identifying those tasks and responsibilities that can be delegated or jointly exercised and by promoting best practices.

3. The delegation of responsibilities shall result in the reallocation of competences laid down in the acts referred to in Article 1(2). The law of the delegate authority shall govern the procedure, enforcement and administrative and judicial review relating to the delegated responsibilities.

4. The competent authorities shall inform the Authority of delegation agreements into which they intend to enter. They shall put the agreements into effect at the earliest 1

2.第16条关于欧洲证券与市场管理局制定指引和建议的权力的规定应适用于投资者补偿计划。

3.欧洲证券与市场管理局可依照第10条至第15条规定的程序起草第1条第2款所述框架立法指明的监管性和实施性技术标准。

4.第81条规定的对本条例的审评应特别就欧洲国家级投资者补偿计划体系的趋同进行审查。

第27条　欧洲清盘系统和资金安排

1.在其职权管辖范围内,欧洲证券与市场管理局应致力于制定濒临倒闭的关键金融市场参与者的相关清盘方法。此等清盘方法应避免风险的传播,允许关键金融市场参与者能有序、及时地停业清理,包括在可能的情况下建立相互一致且可信的适当经费筹措机制。

2.欧洲证券与市场管理局应致力于下列两方面的工作:公平竞争问题;及对金融机构实行各种计征费和缴款制度对金融机构产生的累积效应,该等制度可能会作为一个相互一致且可信的清盘框架的一部分,以确保公平的成本分担,并由此为金融机构创造足够的动力去遏制系统性风险。

根据第81条规定对本条例进行审评时,应特别审查欧洲证券与市场管理局在危机预防、管理和清盘框架中发挥的作用能否有所加强。

第28条　职责和责任的委托

1.经受托人同意,主管部门可按本条所列条件将职责和责任委托给欧洲证券与市场管理局或其他主管部门。成员国可规定在其主管部门达成上述委托协议前所应遵循的责任委托的特殊安排,并可将委托范围限定在对跨境金融市场参与者或集团进行有效监管必要的范围内。

2.欧洲证券与市场管理局应通过识别可以委托或可以共同履行的职责和责任以及推广最佳实践的方式,来促进和推动主管部门之间的职责和责任委托。

3.责任委托会产生第1条第2款所述法律文件所规定的职权的再分配。受托部门的法律应对与被委托的责任有关的程序、执法以及行政和司法审查进行规制。

4.主管部门应将其拟缔结的委托协议通知欧洲证券与市场管理局。该等协议最早应在通知欧洲证券与市场管理局1个月后生效。

month after informing the Authority.

The Authority may give an opinion on the intended agreement within 1 month of being informed.

The Authority shall publish, by appropriate means, any delegation agreement as concluded by the competent authorities, in order to ensure that all parties concerned are informed appropriately.

Article 29 Common supervisory culture

1. The Authority shall play an active role in building a common Union supervisory culture and consistent supervisory practices, as well as in ensuring uniform procedures and consistent approaches throughout the Union. The Authority shall carry out, at a minimum, the following activities:

(a) providing opinions to competent authorities;

(b) promoting an effective bilateral and multilateral exchange of information between competent authorities, with full respect for the applicable confidentiality and data protection provisions provided for in the relevant Union legislation;

(c) contributing to developing high-quality and uniform supervisory standards, including reporting standards, and international accounting standards in accordance with Article 1(3);

(d) reviewing the application of the relevant regulatory and implementing technical standards adopted by the Commission, and of the guidelines and recommendations issued by the Authority and proposing amendments where appropriate; and

(e) establishing sectoral and cross-sectoral training programmes, facilitating personnel exchanges and encouraging competent authorities to intensify the use of secondment schemes and other tools.

2. The Authority may, as appropriate, develop new practical instruments and convergence tools to promote common supervisory approaches and practices.

Article 30 Peer reviews of competent authorities

1. The Authority shall periodically organise and conduct peer reviews of some or all of the activities of competent authorities, to further strengthen consistency in supervisory outcomes. To that end, the Authority shall develop methods to allow for objective assessment and comparison between the authorities reviewed. When conducting peer reviews, existing information and evaluations already made with regard to the competent authority concerned shall be taken into account.

2. The peer review shall include an assessment of, but shall not be limited to:

(a) the adequacy of resources and governance arrangements of the competent authority, with particular regard to the effective application of the regulatory technical standards and implementing technical standards referred to in Articles 10 to 15 and of the

欧洲证券与市场管理局可在收到上述拟缔结的协议通知后的1个月内发表意见。

欧洲证券与市场管理局应以适当的方式公布主管部门所缔结的任何委托协议，以确保所涉各方均得到适当的通知。

第29条　共同的监管文化

1.欧洲证券与市场管理局应在建立共同的欧盟监管文化和一致的监管实践以及确保欧盟有统一的程序和一致的方法中发挥积极的作用。欧洲证券与市场管理局至少应开展下列活动：

(a)向主管部门提供意见；

(b)推进主管部门在充分遵守相关欧盟立法适用的保密和数据保护规定的前提下进行有效的双边或多边信息交流；

(c)根据第1条第3款的规定致力于制定高质量和统一的监管标准,包括报告标准，以及国际会计标准；

(d)审评欧盟委员会所通过的相关监管性和实施性技术标准以及欧洲证券与市场管理局所发布的指引和建议的适用,并在适当时提出修改建议;及

(e)制订行业或跨行业培训计划,促进人员交流并鼓励主管部门更多地使用人员借调计划以及其他工具。

2.在适当情况下,欧洲证券与市场管理局可开发新的实用工具和趋同手段来推广共同的监管方法和实践。

第30条　主管部门的同行审评

1.欧洲证券与市场管理局应针对主管部门的部分或全部活动定期组织和开展同行审评,以进一步加强监管结果的一致性。为此,欧洲证券与市场管理局应制定相关方法,以实现被审查部门之间的客观评价和比较。开展同行审评时,应考虑到与所涉主管部门有关的现有信息以及过去已作过的评价结果。

2.同行审评应包括但不限于下列方面的评价：

(a)主管部门资源和治理安排的充分性,特别是对于第10条至第15条所述监管性技术标准和实施性技术标准以及第1条第2款所述法律文件的有效适用而言是否充分,以及应对市场变化的能力；

acts referred to in Article 1(2) and the capacity to respond to market developments;

(b) the degree of convergence reached in the application of Union law and in supervisory practice, including regulatory technical standards and implementing technical standards, guidelines and recommendations adopted under Articles 10 to 16, and the extent to which the supervisory practice achieves the objectives set out in Union law;

(c) best practices developed by some competent authorities which might be of benefit for other competent authorities to adopt;

(d) the effectiveness and the degree of convergence reached with regard to the enforcement of the provisions adopted in the implementation of Union law, including the administrative measures and sanctions imposed against persons responsible where those provisions have not been complied with.

3. On the basis of a peer review, the Authority may issue guidelines and recommendations pursuant to Article 16. In accordance with Article 16(3), the competent authorities shall endeavour to follow those guidelines and recommendations. The Authority shall take into account the outcome of the peer review when developing draft regulatory technical or implementing technical standards in accordance with Articles 10 to 15.

4. The Authority shall make the best practices that can be identified from those peer reviews publicly available. In addition, all other results of peer reviews may be disclosed publicly, subject to the agreement of the competent authority that is the subject of the peer review.

Article 31 Coordination function

The Authority shall fulfil a general coordination role between competent authorities, in particular in situations where adverse developments could potentially jeopardise the orderly functioning and integrity of financial markets or the stability of the financial system in the Union.

The Authority shall promote a coordinated Union response, inter alia, by:

(a) facilitating the exchange of information between the competent authorities;

(b) determining the scope and, where possible and appropriate, verifying the reliability of information that should be made available to all the competent authorities concerned;

(c) without prejudice to Article 19, carrying out non-binding mediation upon a request from the competent authorities or on its own initiative;

(d) notifying the ESRB of any potential emergency situations without delay;

(e) taking all appropriate measures in case of developments which may jeopardise the functioning of the financial markets with a view to facilitating the coordination of actions undertaken by relevant competent authorities;

(b)欧盟法律的适用以及监管实践(包括根据第10条至第16条制定的监管性技术标准和实施性技术标准、指引和建议)所达到的趋同程度,以及监管实践在多大程度上实现了欧盟法律设定的目标;

(c)某些主管部门制定的可能值得其他主管部门采用的最佳实践;

(d)欧盟法律实施当中制定的规定,在执行时所达到的有效程度和趋同程度,包括发生违反该等规定的行为时对相关负责人施加的行政措施和处罚。

3.欧洲证券与市场管理局可在同行审评的基础上依据第16条发布指引和建议。根据第16条第3款,主管部门应尽力遵循该等指引和建议。欧洲证券与市场管理局在根据第10条至第15条的规定起草监管性和实施性技术标准草案时,应考虑同行审评的结果。

4.对于从该等同行审评中识别出的最佳实践,欧洲证券与市场管理局应予公布。此外,在作为同行审评对象的主管部门同意披露的前提下,同行审评的所有其他结果也可向公众披露。

第31条 协调职能

欧洲证券与市场管理局尤应在发生可能对欧盟金融市场有序运行和诚信度或金融系统稳定造成危害的不利变化时在主管部门之间发挥总协调作用。

欧洲证券与市场管理局应通过相关措施促进欧盟内部相互协调的回应,包括但不限于:

(a)促进主管部门之间的信息交流;

(b)确定应向所有所涉主管部门提供的信息范围,在可能和适当时对其可靠性予以核实;

(c)在不影响第19条的情况下,经主管部门请求开展无约束力的调解,亦可主动开展调解;

(d)立即通知欧洲系统性风险委员会任何可能发生的紧急情况;

(e)在发生可能危害金融市场运行的变化时,采取所有适当的措施以为相关主管部门行动间的协调工作提供方便;

(f) centralising information received from competent authorities in accordance with Articles 21 and 35 as the result of the regulatory reporting obligations for financial market participants active in more than one Member State. The Authority shall share that information with the other competent authorities concerned.

Article 32 Assessment of market developments

1. The Authority shall monitor and assess market developments in the area of its competence and, where necessary, inform the European Supervisory Authority (European Banking Authority), and the European Supervisory Authority (European Insurance and Occupational Pensions Authority), the ESRB and the European Parliament, the Council and the Commission about the relevant microprudential trends, potential risks and vulnerabilities. The Authority shall include in its assessments an economic analysis of the markets in which financial market participants operate, and an assessment of the impact of potential market developments on such institutions.

2. The Authority shall, in cooperation with the ESRB, initiate and coordinate Union-wide assessments of the resilience of financial market participants to adverse market developments. To that end, it shall develop the following, for application by the competent authorities:

(a) common methodologies for assessing the effect of economic scenarios on the financial position of a financial market participant;

(b) common approaches to communication on the outcomes of these assessments of the resilience of financial market participants;

(c) common methodologies for assessing the effect of particular products or distribution processes on the financial position of a financial market participant and on investors and customer information.

3. Without prejudice to the tasks of the ESRB set out in Regulation (EU) No 1092/2010, the Authority shall, at least once a year, and more frequently as necessary, provide assessments to the European Parliament, the Council, the Commission and the ESRB of trends, potential risks and vulnerabilities in its area of competence.

The Authority shall include a classification of the main risks and vulnerabilities in these assessments and, where necessary, recommend preventative or remedial actions.

4. The Authority shall ensure an adequate coverage of cross-sectoral developments, risks and vulnerabilities by closely cooperating with the European Supervisory Authority (European Banking Authority) and the European Supervisory Authority (European Insurance and Occupational Pensions Authority) through the Joint Committee.

Article 33 International relations

1. Without prejudice to the respective competences of the Member States and the Union institutions, the Authority may develop contacts and enter into administrative

(f)根据第21条和第35条汇总从主管部门接收到的信息,此等信息为主管部门就在多个成员国境内开展业务的金融市场参与者履行监管报告义务所形成的。欧洲证券与市场管理局应与其他所涉主管部门共享该等信息。

第32条　对市场变化的评估

1.欧洲证券与市场管理局应对其职权管辖范围内的市场变化进行监控和评估,并在必要时将相关的微观审慎趋势、潜在风险及薄弱环节通知两个欧洲监管机构(欧洲银行业管理局和欧洲保险与职业养老金管理局)、欧洲系统性风险委员会以及欧洲议会、欧盟理事会和欧盟委员会。欧洲证券与市场管理局的评估还应包括对金融市场参与者所在市场的经济分析以及对该等金融市场参与者受潜在市场变化影响的评估。

2.欧洲证券与市场管理局应与欧洲系统性风险委员会合作,在欧盟范围内启动和协调对金融市场参与者面临不利市场变化时的抗冲击能力的评估。为此,欧洲证券与市场管理局应制定下列方式和方法供主管部门使用:

(a)评估不同的经济场景对金融市场参与者财务状况影响的通用方法;

(b)对金融市场参与者的抗冲击能力评估结果进行交流所采用的通用方法;

(c)评估特殊产品或销售方法对金融市场参与者的财务状况以及投资者和客户信息影响的通用方法。

3.在不影响欧洲系统性风险委员会在第1092/2010号(欧盟)条例中的职责的情况下,欧洲证券与市场管理局应至少每年1次并在必要时更频繁地为欧洲议会、欧盟理事会、欧盟委员会和欧洲系统性风险委员会提供其职权管辖范围内对趋势、潜在风险和薄弱环节的评估结果。

欧洲证券与市场管理局应在此等评估中对主要风险和薄弱环节进行分类,并在必要时提出预防或补救行动的建议。

4.欧洲证券与市场管理局应通过联合委员会与两个欧洲监管机构(欧洲银行业管理局和欧洲保险与职业养老金管理局)紧密合作,确保其监管工作充分覆盖跨行业变化、风险和薄弱环节。

第33条　国际关系

1.在不影响成员国和欧盟机构各自职权的情况下,欧洲证券与市场管理局可与监管机构、国际组织以及第三国的行政管理部门建立联系并达成行政安排。该等安排既

arrangements with supervisory authorities, international organisations and the administrations of third countries. Those arrangements shall not create legal obligations in respect of the Union and its Member States nor shall they prevent Member States and their competent authorities from concluding bilateral or multilateral arrangements with those third countries.

2. The Authority shall assist in preparing equivalence decisions pertaining to supervisory regimes in third countries in accordance with the acts referred to in Article 1 (2).

3. In the report referred to in Article 43(5), the Authority shall set out the administrative arrangements agreed upon with international organisations or administrations in third countries and the assistance provided in preparing equivalence decisions.

Article 34 Other tasks

1. The Authority may, upon a request from the European Parliament, the Council or the Commission, or on its own initiative, provide opinions to the European Parliament, the Council and the Commission on all issues related to its area of competence.

2. With regard to prudential assessments of mergers and acquisitions falling within the scope of Directive 2004/39/EC, as amended by Directive 2007/44/EC, and which according to that Directive require consultation between competent authorities from two or more Member States, the Authority may, on application of one of the competent authorities concerned, issue and publish an opinion on a prudential assessment, except in relation to the criteria in Article 10b(e) of Directive 2004/39/EC. The opinion shall be issued promptly and in any event before the end of the assessment period in accordance with Directive 2004/39/EC, as amended by Directive 2007/44/EC. Article 35 shall apply to the areas in respect of which the Authority may issue an opinion.

Article 35 Collection of information

1. At the request of the Authority, the competent authorities of the Member States shall provide the Authority with all the necessary information to carry out the duties assigned to it by this Regulation, provided that they have legal access to the relevant information, and that the request for information is necessary in relation to the nature of the duty in question.

2. The Authority may also request information to be provided at recurring intervals and in specified formats. Such requests shall, where possible, be made using common reporting formats.

3. Upon a duly justified request from a competent authority of a Member State, the Authority may provide any information that is necessary to enable the competent authority to carry out its duties, in accordance with the professional secrecy obligations laid down in

不得为欧盟及其成员国设定法律义务，也不得妨碍成员国及其主管部门与该等第三国缔结双边或多边安排。

2.根据第1条第2款所述法律文件，欧洲证券与市场管理局应协助完成关于第三国监管体制的等效性决定。

3.在第43条第5款所述的报告中，欧洲证券与市场管理局应列出与国际组织或第三国行政管理部门所缔结的行政安排以及在作出等效性决定中所提供的协助。

第34条　其他职责

1.经欧洲议会、欧盟理事会或欧盟委员会请求，欧洲证券与市场管理局可就与其职权管辖范围内的一切有关的问题向欧洲议会、欧盟理事会和欧盟委员会提供意见，亦可自行提供该等意见。

2.对于在第2004/39/EC号指令（经第2007/44/EC号指令修正）范围内且根据该指令需要2个或多个成员国主管部门进行磋商的并购，经其中一个所涉主管部门申请，欧洲证券与市场管理局可发布并公开关于此类并购审慎评估的意见，但是，涉及第2004/39/EC号指令第10 b条第e款中的评估标准的情况除外。该等意见应迅速发布，并且任何情况下均应于第2004/39/EC号指令（经第2007/44/EC号指令修正）规定的评估期限结束前发布。第35条适用于欧洲证券与市场管理局可发布意见的领域。

第35条　信息的收集

1.经欧洲证券与市场管理局请求，各成员国主管部门应向欧洲证券与市场管理局提供履行其在本条例中的职责所必要的一切信息，前提是该等成员国主管部门能够合法查阅相关的信息，并且就所涉职责的性质而言信息请求是必要的。

2.欧洲证券与市场管理局还可请求主管部门定期以指定的格式提供信息。如果可能，上述请求应使用通用的报告格式。

3.收到某成员国主管部门有正当理由的请求后，欧洲证券与市场管理局可提供该主管部门履行职责所必要的任何信息，但须遵守行业立法以及第70条所规定的职业保密义务。

sectoral legislation and in Article 70.

4. Before requesting information in accordance with this Article and in order to avoid the duplication of reporting obligations, the Authority shall take account of any relevant existing statistics produced and disseminated by the European Statistical System and the European System of Central Banks.

5. Where information is not available or is not made available by the competent authorities in a timely fashion, the Authority may address a duly justified and reasoned request to other supervisory authorities, to the ministry responsible for finance where it has at its disposal prudential information, to the national central bank or to the statistical office of the Member State concerned.

6. Where information is not available or is not made available under paragraph 1 or 5 in a timely fashion, the Authority may address a duly justified and reasoned request directly to the relevant financial market participants. The reasoned request shall explain why the information concerning the respective individual financial market participants is necessary.

The Authority shall inform the relevant competent authorities of requests in accordance with this paragraph and with paragraph 5.

At the request of the Authority, the competent authorities shall assist the Authority in collecting the information.

7. The Authority may use confidential information received under this Article only for the purposes of carrying out the duties assigned to it by this Regulation.

Article 36 Relationship with the ESRB

1. The Authority shall cooperate closely and on a regular basis with the ESRB.

2. The Authority shall provide the ESRB with regular and timely information necessary for the achievement of its tasks. Any data necessary for the achievement of its tasks that are not in summary or aggregate form shall be provided, without delay, to the ESRB upon a reasoned request, as specified in Article 15 of Regulation (EU) No 1092/2010. The Authority, in cooperation with the ESRB, shall have in place adequate internal procedures for the transmission of confidential information, in particular information regarding individual financial market participants.

3. The Authority shall, in accordance with paragraphs 4 and 5, ensure a proper follow-up to ESRB warnings and recommendations referred to in Article 16 of Regulation (EU) No 1092/2010.

4. On receipt of a warning or recommendation from the ESRB addressed to the Authority, the Authority shall convene a meeting of the Board of Supervisors without delay and assess the implications of such a warning or recommendation for the fulfilment of its tasks.

4.为了避免报告义务的重复,在根据本条规定提出信息请求前,欧洲证券与市场管理局应参考由欧洲统计系统和欧洲中央银行体系提供和发布的任何现有的相关统计数据。

5.主管部门无法或未及时提供信息的,欧洲证券与市场管理局可向所涉成员国的其他监管机构、财政部(如其掌握了审慎信息)、成员国中央银行或统计局提出有正当理由和经论证的信息请求。

6.未能获得信息或未能根据第1款或第5款及时获得信息的,欧洲证券与市场管理局可直接向相关的金融市场参与者提出有正当理由和经论证的信息请求。该等信息请求应说明需要各个相关金融市场参与者提供信息的原因。

欧洲证券与市场管理局应通知相关主管部门按照本款和第5款提出的请求。

经欧洲证券与市场管理局请求,主管部门应协助欧洲证券与市场管理局收集信息。

7.欧洲证券与市场管理局仅可以出于履行本条例赋予的职责的目的使用根据本条接收到的保密信息。

第36条　与欧洲系统性风险委员会的关系

1.欧洲证券与市场管理局应紧密并定期地与欧洲系统性风险委员会开展合作。

2.欧洲证券与市场管理局应定期并及时地向欧洲系统性风险委员会提供完成其职责所必要的信息。按第1092/2010号(欧盟)条例第15条的规定,经欧洲系统性风险委员会合理请求,任何为完成其职责所必要的且非摘要或汇总格式的数据均应立即提供给欧洲系统性风险委员会。欧洲证券与市场管理局应与欧洲系统性风险委员会合作,为保密信息特别是与具体金融市场参与者有关的信息的发送设置充分的内部程序。

3.欧洲证券与市场管理局应依照第4款和第5款确保对第1092/2010号(欧盟)条例第16条所述欧洲系统性风险委员会预警和建议进行恰当的跟进。

4.收到欧洲系统性风险委员会向欧洲证券与市场管理局提出的预警或建议后,欧洲证券与市场管理局应立即召开监管机构理事会会议,并对该预警或建议对于其充分履行职责的意义进行评估。

It shall decide, by the relevant decision-making procedure, on any actions to be taken in accordance with the powers conferred upon it by this Regulation for addressing the issues identified in the warnings and recommendations.

If the Authority does not act on a recommendation, it shall explain to the ESRB and the Council its reasons for not doing so.

5. On receipt of a warning or recommendation from the ESRB addressed to a competent national supervisory authority, the Authority shall, where relevant, use the powers conferred upon it by this Regulation to ensure a timely follow-up.

Where the addressee intends not to follow the recommendation of the ESRB, it shall inform and discuss with the Board of Supervisors its reasons for not acting.

The competent authority shall take due account of the views of the Board of Supervisors when informing the Council and the ESRB in accordance with Article 17 of Regulation (EU) No 1092/2010.

6. In discharging the tasks set out in this Regulation, the Authority shall take the utmost account of the warnings and recommendations of the ESRB.

Article 37 Securities and Markets Stakeholder Group

1. To help facilitate consultation with stakeholders in areas relevant to the tasks of the Authority, a Securities and Markets Stakeholder Group shall be established. The Securities and Markets Stakeholder Group shall be consulted on actions taken in accordance with Articles 10 to 15 concerning regulatory technical standards and implementing technical standards and, to the extent that these do not concern individual financial market participants, Article 16 concerning guidelines and recommendations. If actions must be taken urgently and consultation becomes impossible, the Securities and Markets Stakeholder Group shall be informed as soon as possible.

The Securities and Markets Stakeholder Group shall meet at least four times a year.

2. The Securities and Markets Stakeholder Group shall be composed of 30 members, representing in balanced proportions financial market participants operating in the Union, their employees' representatives as well as consumers, users of financial services and representatives of SMEs. At least five of its members shall be independent top-ranking academics. Ten of its members shall represent financial market participants.

3. The members of the Securities and Markets Stakeholder Group shall be appointed by the Board of Supervisors, following proposals from the relevant stakeholders. In making its decision, the Board of Supervisors shall, to the extent possible, ensure an appropriate geographical and gender balance and representation of stakeholders across the Union.

4. The Authority shall provide all necessary information, subject to professional secrecy, as set out in Article 70, and ensure adequate secretarial support for the Securities and Markets Stakeholder Group. Adequate compensation shall be provided to

欧洲证券与市场管理局依据本条例所授予的权力对预警和建议提出的问题采取任何行动的，应通过相关的决策程序作出决定。

欧洲证券与市场管理局不针对建议采取任何行动的，应向欧洲系统性风险委员会和欧盟理事会说明理由。

5.收到欧洲系统性风险委员会向国家级监管机构发出的预警或建议后，欧洲证券与市场管理局应在适当时运用本条例所授予的权力确保及时采取跟进行动。

被建议方无意遵循欧洲系统性风险委员会的建议的，应通知监管机构理事会并与其讨论其不采取行动的理由。

主管部门应在根据第1092/2010号（欧盟）条例第17条通知欧盟理事会和欧洲系统性风险委员会时，充分考虑监管机构理事会的意见。

6.欧洲证券与市场管理局在履行本条例所规定的职责时，应充分考虑欧洲系统性风险委员会的预警和建议。

第37条　证券与市场利益相关者小组

1.为了便于就欧洲证券与市场管理局职责相关领域征求利益相关者的意见，应设立一个证券与市场利益相关者小组。根据第10条至第15条的规定所采取的与监管性技术标准和实施性技术标准有关的行动，以及在不涉及具体金融市场参与者的范围内根据第16条的规定所采取的与指引和建议有关的行动，均应征求证券与市场利益相关者小组的意见。在必须采取紧急行动而不可能提前征求其意见的情况下，应尽早通知证券与市场利益相关者小组。

证券与市场利益相关者小组每年至少应召开4次会议。

2.证券与市场利益相关者小组应由30名成员组成，以平衡的比例代表在欧盟运营的金融市场参与者、其员工代表以及消费者、金融服务用户以及中小企业代表。其中至少应有5名成员是独立的一流学者；应有10名成员代表金融市场参与者。

3.证券与市场利益相关者小组成员的人选应由监管机构理事会根据相关的利益相关者的提议任命。作出决定时，监管机构理事会应尽可能确保该利益相关者小组成员在欧盟范围内适当的地理分布平衡和性别平衡。

4.欧洲证券与市场管理局应在遵循第70条规定的职业保密义务前提下为证券与市场利益相关者小组提供一切必要信息，并确保为其提供充分的秘书支持。对证券与市场利益相关者小组中代表非营利机构的成员（行业代表除外）提供充足的报酬。证

members of the Securities and Markets Stakeholder Group that are representing non-profit organisations, excluding industry representatives. The Securities and Markets Stakeholder Group may establish working groups on technical issues. Members of the Securities and Markets Stakeholder Group shall serve for a period of two-and-a-half years, following which a new selection procedure shall take place.

The members of the Securities and Markets Stakeholder Group may serve two successive terms.

5. The Securities and Markets Stakeholder Group may submit opinions and advice to the Authority on any issue related to the tasks of the Authority with particular focus on the tasks set out in Articles 10 to 16 and Articles 29, 30 and 32.

6. The Securities and Markets Stakeholder Group shall adopt its rules of procedure by a majority of two-thirds of its members.

7. The Authority shall make public the opinions and advice of the Securities and Markets Stakeholder Group and the results of its consultations.

Article 38 Safeguards

1. The Authority shall ensure that no decision adopted under Articles 18 or 19 impinges in any way on the fiscal responsibilities of Member States.

2. Where a Member State considers that a decision taken under Article 19(3) impinges on its fiscal responsibilities, it may notify the Authority and the Commission within 2 weeks after notification of the Authority's decision to the competent authority that the decision will not be implemented by the competent authority.

In its notification, the Member State shall clearly and specifically explain why and how the decision impinges on its fiscal responsibilities.

In the case of such notification, the decision of the Authority shall be suspended.

Within a period of 1 month from the notification by the Member State, the Authority shall inform the Member State as to whether it maintains its decision or whether it amends or revokes it. If the decision is maintained or amended, the Authority shall state that fiscal responsibilities are not affected.

Where the Authority maintains its decision, the Council shall take a decision, by a majority of the votes cast, at one of its meetings not later than 2 months after the Authority has informed the Member State as set out in the fourth subparagraph, as to whether the Authority's decision is maintained.

Where the Council, after having considered the matter, does not take a decision to maintain the Authority's decision in accordance with the fifth subparagraph, the Authority's decision shall be terminated.

3. Where a Member State considers that a decision taken under Article 18(3) impinges on its fiscal responsibilities, it may notify the Authority, the Commission and the

券与市场利益相关者小组可就技术性问题设立工作组。证券与市场利益相关者小组成员的任期为两年半,任期结束后进行新一轮的遴选。

证券与市场利益相关者小组的成员可连任2期。

5.证券与市场利益相关者小组可针对与欧洲证券与市场管理局职责(特别是第10条至第16条以及第29条、第30条和第32条所列职责)有关的任何问题向欧洲证券与市场管理局呈报意见和建议。

6.证券与市场利益相关者小组通过其程序规则时,应经2/3成员的同意。

7.欧洲证券与市场管理局应公布证券与市场利益相关者小组的意见和建议及其磋商结果。

第38条　保障措施

1.欧洲证券与市场管理局应确保根据第18条或第19条作出的任何决定不会以任何方式对成员国的财政责任造成影响。

2.如有成员国认为根据第19条第3款作出的决定影响了其财政责任,则在欧洲证券与市场管理局通知主管部门其决定后的2周内,该成员国可通知欧洲证券与市场管理局和欧盟委员会该成员国将不实施该项决定。

成员国应在其通知中清楚具体地说明该项决定为何以及如何会影响其财政责任。

在成员国作出上述通知的情况下,欧洲证券与市场管理局的决定应暂停执行。

欧洲证券与市场管理局应在成员国发出通知后1个月内通知成员国是否维持决定还是修改或撤销决定。在维持或修改其决定的情形下,欧洲证券与市场管理局应声明成员国的财政责任未受影响。

欧洲证券与市场管理局维持其决定的,欧盟理事会应在欧洲证券与市场管理局按第4项通知成员国之后2个月内召开的任何欧盟理事会会议中,通过多数票投票决定是否维持欧洲证券与市场管理局的决定。

欧盟理事会经审议后未根据第5项决定维持欧洲证券与市场管理局的决定的,应终止欧洲证券与市场管理局的决定。

3.如有成员国认为欧洲证券与市场管理局根据第18条第3款作出的决定影响了其财政责任,则在欧洲证券与市场管理局通知主管部门其决定后的3个工作日内,该成

Council within three working days after notification of the Authority's decision to the competent authority that the decision will not be implemented by the competent authority.

In its notification, the Member State shall clearly and specifically explain why and how the decision impinges on its fiscal responsibilities.

In the event of such notification, the decision of the Authority shall be suspended.

The Council shall, within ten working days, convene a meeting and take a decision, by a simple majority of its members, as to whether the Authority's decision is revoked.

Where the Council, after having considered the matter, does not take a decision to revoke the Authority's decision in accordance with the fourth subparagraph, the suspension of the Authority's decision shall be terminated.

4. Where the Council has taken a decision in accordance with paragraph 3 not to revoke a decision of the Authority relating to Article 18(3), and the Member State concerned still considers that the decision of the Authority impinges upon its fiscal responsibilities, that Member State may notify the Commission and the Authority and request the Council to re-examine the matter. The Member State concerned shall clearly set out the reasons for its disagreement with the decision of the Council.

Within a period of 4 weeks after the notification referred to in the first subparagraph, the Council shall confirm its original decision or take a new decision in accordance with paragraph 3.

The period of 4 weeks may be extended by four additional weeks by the Council, if the particular circumstances of the case so require.

5. Any abuse of this Article, in particular in relation to a decision by the Authority which does not have a significant or material fiscal impact, shall be prohibited as incompatible with the internal market.

Article 39 Decision-making procedures

1. Before taking the decisions provided for in this Regulation, the Authority shall inform any named addressee of its intention to adopt the decision, setting a time limit within which the addressee may express its views on the matter, taking full account of the urgency, complexity and potential consequences of the matter. This applies mutatis mutandis to recommendations as referred to in Article 17(3).

2. The decisions of the Authority shall state the reasons on which they are based.

3. The addressees of decisions of the Authority shall be informed of the legal remedies available under this Regulation.

4. Where the Authority has taken a decision pursuant to Article 18(3) or (4), it shall review that decision at appropriate intervals.

5. The decisions which the Authority takes pursuant to Articles 17, 18 or 19 shall be made public and shall state the identity of the competent authority or financial market

员国可通知欧洲证券与市场管理局、欧盟委员会和欧盟理事会该成员国将不实施该项决定。

成员国应在其通知中清楚具体地说明该项决定为何以及如何影响其财政责任。

在成员国作出上述通知的情况下,欧洲证券与市场管理局的决定应暂停执行。

欧盟理事会应在10个工作日内召开会议,以简单多数票决定是否撤销欧洲证券与市场管理局的决定。

欧盟理事会经审议该事宜后并未根据第4项决定撤销欧洲证券与市场管理局的决定的,应终止欧洲证券与市场管理局决定的暂停执行。

4.如果欧盟理事会根据第3款决定不撤销欧洲证券与市场管理局与第18条第3款有关的决定,而所涉成员国仍认为欧洲证券与市场管理局的决定影响了其财政责任,则该成员国可通知欧盟委员会和欧洲证券与市场管理局并要求欧盟理事会重新审查该事宜。所涉成员国应清楚说明其对欧盟理事会决定持异议的理由。

第1项所述的通知发出后4周内,欧盟理事会可重申其原决定或根据第3款作出新的决定。

案件有特殊情况的,欧盟理事会可将上述4周期限再延长4周。

5.任何滥用本条款的行为,特别是在欧洲证券与市场管理局的决定并不对成员国的财政责任造成任何重大或实质性影响的情况下滥用本条款,均应被视为与欧盟内部市场不相容而被禁止。

第39条　决策程序

1.在作出本条例所规定的决定前,欧洲证券与市场管理局应通知该等决定所针对的任何具名对象其有意作出该决定,并在充分考虑事宜的紧迫性、复杂性和潜在后果的情况下设定时限,允许决定所针对的对象就该事宜表达观点。第17条第3款所述的建议比照上述规定处理。

2.欧洲证券与市场管理局发布的决定应阐明作出决定所基于的理由。

3.应通知欧洲证券与市场管理局决定所针对的对象其可根据本条例获得的法律救济。

4.欧洲证券与市场管理局根据第18条第3款或第4款作出决定后,应以适当的频率审评该项决定。

5.欧洲证券与市场管理局应公布其根据第17条、第18条或第19条作出的决定并说明所涉主管部门或金融市场参与者的身份以及决定的主要内容,除非公布上述内容

participant concerned and the main content of the decision, unless such publication is in conflict with the legitimate interests of financial market participants in the protection of their business secrets or could seriously jeopardise the orderly functioning and integrity of financial markets or the stability of the whole or part of the financial system of the Union.

CHAPTER Ⅲ ORGANISATION

SECTION 1 Board of Supervisors

Article 40 Composition

1. The Board of Supervisors shall be composed of:

(a) the Chairperson, who shall be non-voting;

(b) the head of the national public authority competent for the supervision of financial market participants in each Member State, who shall meet in person at least twice a year;

(c) one representative of the Commission, who shall be non-voting;

(d) one representative of the ESRB, who shall be non-voting;

(e) one representative of each of the other two European Supervisory Authorities who shall be non-voting.

2. The Board of Supervisors shall convene meetings with the Securities and Markets Stakeholder Group regularly, at least twice a year.

3. Each competent authority shall be responsible for nominating a high-level alternate from its authority, who may replace the member of the Board of Supervisors referred to in paragraph 1(b), where that person is prevented from attending.

4. In Member States where more than one authority is responsible for the supervision according to this Regulation, those authorities shall agree on a common representative. Nevertheless, when an item to be discussed by the Board of Supervisors does not fall within the competence of the national authority being represented by the member referred to in paragraph 1(b), that member may bring a representative from the relevant national authority, who shall be non-voting.

5. For the purpose of acting within the scope of Directive 97/9/EC, the member of the Board of Supervisors referred to in paragraph 1(b) may, where appropriate, be accompanied by a representative from the relevant bodies which administer investor compensation schemes in each Member State, who shall be non-voting.

6. The Board of Supervisors may decide to admit observers.

与金融市场参与者保护其商业秘密的合法权益有冲突，或可能严重危害欧盟金融市场有序运行和诚信度或整个或部分金融系统的稳定。

第三章　组织结构

第1节　监管机构理事会

第40条　构成

1.监管机构理事会组成如下：

(a)主席，无表决权；

(b)每个成员国内主管金融市场参与者监管的国家级公共机构的负责人，该等负责人每年应至少亲自出席2次会议；

(c)欧盟委员会1名代表，无表决权；

(d)欧洲系统性风险委员会1名代表，无表决权；

(e)另外两个欧洲监管机构各自的1名代表，无表决权。

2.监管机构理事会应定期召开与证券与市场利益相关者小组的会议，每年至少2次。

3.各主管部门应负责从其部门中指定1名高级别的替补人员，以在第1款第b项所述的监管机构理事会理事不能参加会议时代替其出席。

4.某成员国如有多个部门负责本条例下的监管工作，则该等部门应指定1名共同的代表。然而，监管机构理事会讨论的事项不属于第1款第b项中的理事所代表的国家级监管机构的职权范围的，该成员可携1名来自相关国家级监管机构的代表与会，该代表无投票权。

5.为在第97/9/EC号指令的范围内行事，第1款第b项所述监管机构理事会的理事可在适当时由其所属成员国负责管理投资者补偿计划的相关机构的代表陪同，该代表无表决权。

6.监管机构理事会可决定设立观察员。

The Executive Director may participate in meetings of the Board of Supervisors without the right to vote.

Article 41 Internal committees and panels

1. The Board of Supervisors may establish internal committees or panels for specific tasks attributed to the Board of Supervisors, and may provide for the delegation of certain clearly defined tasks and decisions to internal committees or panels, to the Management Board or to the Chairperson.

2. For the purposes of Article 19, the Board of Supervisors shall convoke an independent panel to facilitate an impartial settlement of the disagreement, consisting of the Chairperson and two of its members, who are not representatives of the competent authorities which are party to the disagreement and who have neither any interest in the conflict nor direct links to the competent authorities concerned.

3. Subject to Article 19(2), the panel shall propose a decision for final adoption by the Board of Supervisors, in accordance with the procedure set out in the third subparagraph of Article 44(1).

4. The Board of Supervisors shall adopt rules of procedure for the panel referred to in paragraph 2.

Article 42 Independence

When carrying out the tasks conferred upon it by this Regulation, the Chairperson and the voting members of the Board of Supervisors shall act independently and objectively in the sole interest of the Union as a whole and shall neither seek nor take instructions from Union institutions or bodies, from any government of a Member State or from any other public or private body.

Neither Member States, the Union institutions or bodies, nor any other public or private body shall seek to influence the members of the Board of Supervisors in the performance of their tasks.

Article 43 Tasks

1. The Board of Supervisors shall give guidance to the work of the Authority and shall be in charge of taking the decisions referred to in Chapter Ⅱ.

2. The Board of Supervisors shall adopt the opinions, recommendations, and decisions, and issue the advice referred to in Chapter Ⅱ.

3. The Board of Supervisors shall appoint the Chairperson.

4. The Board of Supervisors shall adopt, before 30 September of each year, on the basis of a proposal by the Management Board, the work programme of the Authority for the coming year, and shall transmit it for information to the European Parliament, the Council and the Commission.

The work programme shall be adopted without prejudice to the annual budgetary

执行主任可参与监管机构理事会的会议，但无表决权。

第41条　内部委员会和专家小组

1.监管机构理事会可为其承担的特别职责设立内部委员会或专家小组，并可允许将某些清楚界定的职责和决定委托给内部委员会或专家小组、管理委员会或主席。

2.出于第19条之目的，监管机构理事会应召集独立的专家小组，促进分歧的公正解决，该专家小组由监管机构理事会主席和2名成员组成，他们应为非分歧一方主管部门的代表，在所涉主管部门的冲突中无利害关系，与所涉主管部门亦无直接关联。

3.在遵守第19条第2款的前提下，专家小组应向监管机构理事会提出决定建议，以供后者依照第44条第1款第3项规定的程序最终通过。

4.监管机构理事会应通过第2款所述专家小组的程序规则。

第42条　独立性

监管机构理事会主席以及有表决权的成员履行本条例所赋予的职责时，应仅代表欧盟整体利益独立客观地行事，不得寻求或听从欧盟机构或单位、任何成员国政府或任何其他公共或私人机构的指示。

各成员国、欧盟机构或单位以及任何其他公共或私人机构均不得试图影响监管机构理事会理事履行其职责。

第43条　职责

1.监管机构理事会应为欧洲证券与市场管理局的工作提供指导并负责作出第二章所述的决定。

2.监管机构理事会应制定第二章所述的意见、建议和决定，并发布第二章所述的建议。

3.监管机构理事会应任命1名主席。

4.监管机构理事会应于每年9月30日前根据管理委员会的提议通过欧洲证券与市场管理局下一年度的工作计划，并将其发送给欧洲议会、欧盟理事会和欧盟委员会供其参考。

工作计划的通过不得影响年度预算程序，并应予公布。

procedure and shall be made public.

5. The Board of Supervisors shall, on the basis of a proposal by the Management Board, adopt the annual report on the activities of the Authority, including on the performance of the Chairperson's duties, on the basis of the draft report referred to in Article 53(7) and shall transmit that report to the European Parliament, the Council, the Commission, the Court of Auditors and the European Economic and Social Committee by 15 June each year. The report shall be made public.

6. The Board of Supervisors shall adopt the multi-annual work programme of the Authority, and shall transmit it for information to the European Parliament, the Council and the Commission.

The multi-annual work programme shall be adopted without prejudice to the annual budgetary procedure and shall be made public.

7. The Board of Supervisors shall adopt the budget in accordance with Article 63.

8. The Board of Supervisors shall exercise disciplinary authority over the Chairperson and the Executive Director and may remove them from office in accordance with Article 48(5) or Article 51(5) respectively.

Article 44 Decision making

1. Decisions of the Board of Supervisors shall be taken by a simple majority of its members. Each member shall have one vote.

With regard to the acts specified in Articles 10 to 16 and measures and decisions adopted under the third subparagraph of Article 9(5) and Chapter VI and by way of derogation from the first subparagraph of this paragraph, the Board of Supervisors shall take decisions on the basis of a qualified majority of its members, as defined in Article 16(4) of the Treaty on European Union and in Article 3 of the Protocol (No 36) on transitional provisions.

With regard to decisions in accordance with Article 19(3), for decisions taken by the consolidating supervisor, the decision proposed by the panel shall be considered as adopted, if approved by a simple majority, unless it is rejected by members representing a blocking minority of the votes as defined in Article 16(4) of the Treaty on European Union and in Article 3 of the Protocol (No 36) on transitional provisions.

For all other decisions in accordance with Article 19(3), the decision proposed by the panel shall be adopted by a simple majority of the members of the Board of Supervisors. Each member shall have one vote.

2. Meetings of the Board of Supervisors shall be convened by the Chairperson at his own initiative or at the request of one third of its members, and shall be chaired by the Chairperson.

3. The Board of Supervisors shall adopt and make public its rules of procedure.

5.监管机构理事会应根据管理委员会的提议在第53条第7款所述的报告草案基础上通过关于欧洲证券与市场管理局活动,包括主席职责履行情况的年度报告,并于每年6月15日前将该报告发送给欧洲议会、欧盟理事会、欧盟委员会、欧盟审计院以及欧洲经济与社会委员会。该报告应予公布。

6.监管机构理事会应通过欧洲证券与市场管理局的跨年度工作计划,并将其发送给欧洲议会、欧盟理事会和欧盟委员会供其参考。

跨年度工作计划的通过不得影响年度预算程序并应予公布。

7.监管机构理事会按照第63条的规定通过预算。

8.监管机构理事会对主席和执行主任行使纪律处分权,并可根据第48条第5款或第51条第5款免除其职务。

第44条　决策

1.监管机构理事会应以简单多数票通过决定。每名理事均有一票表决权。

作为本款第1项的例外,对于第10条至第16条所指明的法律文件以及依据第9条第5款第3项和第六章所采取的措施和作出的决定,监管机构理事会应以特定多数票通过决定,该特定多数票的定义见《欧洲联盟条约》第16条第4款以及关于过渡条款的《议定书(第36号)》第3条。

就第19条第3款下的决定而言,对于由并表监管机构作出的决定,专家小组提议的决定经简单多数票同意应视为通过,但是,被起否决作用的少数票的成员否决的情况除外,起否决作用的少数票的定义见《欧洲联盟条约》第16条第4款以及关于过渡规定的《议定书(第36号)》第3条。

对于所有其他根据第19条第3款所作的决定,由专家小组提议的决定应由监管机构理事会按简单多数票通过,每名理事均有一票表决权。

2.监管机构理事会会议应由主席主动召集或经1/3理事请求召集,由主席主持。

3.监管机构理事会应通过并公布其程序规则。

4. The rules of procedure shall set out in detail the arrangements governing voting, including, where appropriate, the rules governing quorums. The non–voting members and the observers, with the exception of the Chairperson and the Executive Director, shall not attend any discussions within the Board of Supervisors relating to individual financial market participants, unless otherwise provided for in Article 75(3) or in the acts referred to in Article 1(2).

SECTION 2 Management Board

Article 45 Composition

1. The Management Board shall be composed of the Chairperson and six other members of the Board of Supervisors, elected by and from the voting members of the Board of Supervisors.

Other than the Chairperson, each member of the Management Board shall have an alternate, who may replace him if he is prevented from attending.

The term of office of the members elected by the Board of Supervisors shall be two–and–a–half years. That term may be extended once. The composition of the Management Board shall be balanced and proportionate and shall reflect the Union as a whole. Mandates shall be overlapping and an appropriate rotating arrangement shall apply.

2. Decisions by the Management Board shall be adopted on the basis of a majority of the members present. Each member shall have one vote.

The Executive Director and a representative of the Commission shall participate in meetings of the Management Board without the right to vote.

The representative of the Commission shall have the right to vote on matters referred to in Article 63.

The Management Board shall adopt and make public its rules of procedure.

3. Meetings of the Management Board shall be convened by the Chairperson at his own initiative or at the request of at least a third of its members, and shall be chaired by the Chairperson.

The Management Board shall meet prior to every meeting of the Board of Supervisors and as often as the Management Board deems necessary. It shall meet at least five times a year.

4. The members of the Management Board may, subject to the rules of procedure, be assisted by advisers or experts. The non–voting members, with the exception of the Executive Director, shall not attend any discussions within the Management Board relating to individual financial market participants.

Article 46 Independence

The members of the Management Board shall act independently and objectively in

4.程序规则应详细规定表决安排，在适当时应包括关于法定人数的规则。除主席和执行主任外，无表决权的成员和观察员不得参加监管机构理事会关于具体金融市场参与者的任何讨论，但是第75条第3款或者第1条第2款所述法律文件另有规定的情况除外。

第2节　管理委员会

第45条　构成

1.管理委员会应由监管机构理事会主席和其他6名委员组成，该6名委员从监管机构理事会有表决权的理事中选出。

除主席之外，管理委员会的每名委员均应有1名替补人员，在其无法出席会议时代替其出席。

监管机构理事会所选出的管理委员会委员任期为两年半。该任期可延长1次。管理委员会的构成应是平衡并且成比例的，并应反映欧盟整体情况。不同管理委员会委员的任期应当有所重叠，并应实行适当的轮换安排。

2.管理委员会的决定应由出席会议的委员多数同意后通过。每名委员均有一票表决权。

执行主任和欧盟委员会1名代表应出席管理委员会的会议，但无表决权。

欧盟委员会的代表应有权就第63条所述事项进行表决。

管理委员会应通过并公布其程序规则。

3.管理委员会的会议应由主席主动召集或经至少1/3成员请求召集，由主席主持。

管理委员会应在每次监管机构理事会会议前及其认为必要的其他时间召开会议，每年至少应召开5次会议。

4.管理委员会的委员可按程序规则获得顾问或专家的协助。除执行主任之外，无表决权的委员不得参与管理委员会内部关于具体金融市场参与者的讨论。

第46条　独立性

管理委员会委员应仅代表欧盟整体利益独立客观地行事，不得寻求或听从欧盟

the sole interest of the Union as a whole and shall neither seek nor take instructions from the Union institutions or bodies, from any government of a Member State or from any other public or private body.

Neither Member States, the Union institutions or bodies, nor any other public or private body shall seek to influence the members of the Management Board in the performance of their tasks.

Article 47 Tasks

1. The Management Board shall ensure that the Authority carries out its mission and performs the tasks assigned to it in accordance with this Regulation.

2. The Management Board shall propose, for adoption by the Board of Supervisors, an annual and multi-annual work programme.

3. The Management Board shall exercise its budgetary powers in accordance with Articles 63 and 64.

4. The Management Board shall adopt the Authority's staff policy plan and, pursuant to Article 68(2), the necessary implementing measures of the Staff Regulations of Officials of the European Communities (hereinafter the 'Staff Regulations').

5. The Management Board shall adopt the special provisions on right of access to the documents of the Authority, in accordance with Article 72.

6. The Management Board shall propose an annual report on the activities of the Authority, including on the Chairperson's duties, on the basis of the draft report referred to in Article 53(7) to the Board of Supervisors for approval.

7. The Management Board shall adopt and make public its rules of procedure.

8. The Management Board shall appoint and remove the members of the Board of Appeal in accordance with Article 58(3) and (5).

SECTION 3 Chairperson

Article 48 Appointment and tasks

1. The Authority shall be represented by a Chairperson, who shall be a full-time independent professional.

The Chairperson shall be responsible for preparing the work of the Board of Supervisors and shall chair the meetings of the Board of Supervisors and the Management Board.

2. The Chairperson shall be appointed by the Board of Supervisors on the basis of merit, skills, knowledge of financial market participants and markets, and of experience relevant to financial supervision and regulation, following an open selection procedure.

Before taking up his duties, and up to 1 month after the selection by the Board of Supervisors, the European Parliament may, after having heard the candidate selected by

机构或单位、任何成员国政府或任何其他公共或私人机构的指示。

各成员国、欧盟机构或单位以及任何其他公共或私人机构均不得试图影响管理委员会委员履行其职责。

第47条　职责

1.管理委员会应确保欧洲证券与市场管理局完成本条例所赋予的使命和职责。

2.管理委员会应提出年度和跨年度工作计划,交由监管机构理事会通过。

3.管理委员会应根据第63条和第64条行使预算权。

4.管理委员会应通过欧洲证券与市场管理局的人事政策计划,并根据第68条第2款制定实施《欧洲共同体官员的人事条例》(以下简称《人事条例》)的必要措施。

5.根据第72条的规定,管理委员会应通过关于欧洲证券与市场管理局文件查阅权的特殊规定。

6.在第53条第7款所述报告草案的基础上,管理委员会应将关于欧洲证券与市场管理局活动(包括主席职责)的年度报告呈报监管机构理事会审批。

7.管理委员会应通过并公布其程序规则。

8.管理委员会应根据第58条第3款和第5款任免行政复议委员会的成员。

第3节　主　　席

第48条　任命和职责

1.欧洲证券与市场管理局由主席代表。主席应为全职、独立的专业人士。

主席负责筹备监管机构理事会的工作,并主持监管机构理事会以及管理委员会的会议。

2.主席由监管机构理事会根据其成就、技能、对金融市场参与者和市场的认识、与金融监管和规制相关的经验,经过公开遴选程序任命。

在获选者到任前,直至其被监管机构理事会选出满1个月期间内,欧洲议会都有权在听取获选者意见后对其任命提出异议。

the Board of Supervisors, object to the designation of the selected person.

The Board of Supervisors shall also elect, from among its members, an alternate who shall carry out the functions of the Chairperson in his absence. That alternate shall not be elected from among the members of the Management Board.

3. The Chairperson's term of office shall be 5 years and may be extended once.

4. In the course of the 9 months preceding the end of the five-year term of office of the Chairperson, the Board of Supervisors shall evaluate:

(a) the results achieved in the first term of office and the way they were achieved;

(b) the Authority's duties and requirements in the coming years.

The Board of Supervisors, taking into account the evaluation may extend the term of office of the Chairperson once subject to confirmation by the European Parliament.

5. The Chairperson may be removed from office only by the European Parliament following a decision of the Board of Supervisors.

The Chairperson shall not prevent the Board of Supervisors from discussing matters relating to the Chairperson, in particular the need for his removal, and shall not be involved in deliberations concerning such a matter.

Article 49 Independence

Without prejudice to the role of the Board of Supervisors in relation to the tasks of the Chairperson, the Chairperson shall neither seek nor take instructions from the Union institutions or bodies, from any government of a Member State or from any other public or private body.

Neither Member States, the Union institutions or bodies, nor any other public or private body shall seek to influence the Chairperson in the performance of his tasks.

In accordance with the Staff Regulations referred to in Article 68, the Chairperson shall, after leaving service, continue to be bound by the duty to behave with integrity and discretion as regards the acceptance of certain appointments or benefits.

Article 50 Report

1. The European Parliament and the Council may invite the Chairperson or his alternate to make a statement, while fully respecting his independence. The Chairperson shall, make a statement before the European Parliament and answer any questions put by its members, whenever so requested.

2. The Chairperson shall report in writing on the main activities of the Authority to the European Parliament when requested and at least 15 days before making the statement referred to in paragraph 1.

3. In addition to the information referred to in Articles 11 to 18 and Articles 20 and 33, the report shall also include any relevant information requested by the European Parliament on an ad-hoc basis.

监管机构理事会还应从其理事中选出1名替补人员，在主席缺席的情况下代为行使其职能。该替补人员不得为管理委员会的委员。

3.主席的任期为5年，可延长1次。

4.在主席5年任期结束前的9个月期间内，监管机构理事会可对下列方面作出评价：

（a）主席在首期任期内取得的工作成果以及取得该成果的方式；

（b）未来几年欧洲证券与市场管理局的职责和要求。

在上述评价的基础上，监管机构理事会可经欧洲议会确认后将主席任期延长1次。

5.只有在监管机构理事会作出罢免决定后，欧洲议会方能免除主席职务。

主席不得妨碍监管机构理事会讨论与主席有关的事宜，特别是围绕罢免其职务所进行的必要讨论，并且不得参与涉及上述事宜的审议。

第49条　独立性

不影响监管机构理事会就主席的职责发挥作用的情况下，主席不得寻求或听从欧盟机构或单位、任何成员国政府或任何其他公共或私人机构的指示。

各成员国、欧盟机构或单位或任何其他公共或私人机构均不得试图影响主席履行其职责。

根据第68条所述的《人事条例》，主席离职后在接受某些任命或利益方面仍应受诚信和谨慎义务约束。

第50条　报告

1.欧洲议会和欧盟理事会可在充分尊重主席独立性的前提下要求主席或其替补人员作出陈述。任何时候经欧洲议会要求，主席均应向后者作出陈述并回答其议员所提出的任何问题。

2.经欧洲议会要求并至少在进行第1款提及的陈述的15日前，主席应就欧洲证券与市场管理局的主要活动向欧洲议会提交书面报告。

3.除了第11条至第18条以及第20条和第33条所述的信息外，报告还应包括欧洲议会专门要求提供的任何相关信息。

SECTION 4 Executive Director

Article 51 Appointment

1. The Authority shall be managed by an Executive Director, who shall be a full-time independent professional.

2. The Executive Director shall be appointed by the Board of Supervisors, after confirmation by the European Parliament, on the basis of merit, skills, knowledge of financial market participants and markets, and experience relevant to financial supervision and regulation and managerial experience, following an open selection procedure.

3. The Executive Director's term of office shall be 5 years and may be extended once.

4. In the course of the 9 months preceding the end of the Executive Director's term of office, the Board of Supervisors shall evaluate in particular:

(a) the results achieved in the first term of office and the way they were achieved;

(b) the Authority's duties and requirements in the coming years.

The Board of Supervisors, taking into account the evaluation referred to in the first subparagraph, may extend the term of office of the Executive Director once.

5. The Executive Director may be removed from office only upon a decision of the Board of Supervisors.

Article 52 Independence

Without prejudice to the respective roles of the Management Board and the Board of Supervisors in relation to the tasks of the Executive Director, the Executive Director shall neither seek nor take instructions from the Union institutions or bodies, from any government of a Member State or from any other public or private body.

Neither Member States, the Union institutions or bodies, nor any other public or private body shall seek to influence the Executive Director in the performance of his tasks.

In accordance with the Staff Regulations referred to in Article 68, the Executive Director shall, after leaving service, continue to be bound by the duty to behave with integrity and discretion as regards the acceptance of certain appointments or benefits.

Article 53 Tasks

1. The Executive Director shall be in charge of the management of the Authority and shall prepare the work of the Management Board.

2. The Executive Director shall be responsible for implementing the annual work programme of the Authority under the guidance of the Board of Supervisors and under the control of the Management Board.

3. The Executive Director shall take the necessary measures, notably the adoption of

第4节 执行主任

第51条 任命

1.欧洲证券与市场管理局应由一名执行主任负责管理,执行主任应为全职、独立的专业人士。

2.执行主任应由监管机构理事会根据其成就、技能、对金融市场参与者和市场的认识、与金融监管和规制相关的经验以及管理经验,经过公开遴选程序并经欧洲议会确认后任命。

3.执行主任的任期为5年,可延长1次。

4.执行主任任期结束前的9个月期间内,监管机构理事会尤其可对下列方面进行评价:

(a)执行主任在首期任期内取得的工作成果以及取得该成果的方式;

(b)未来几年欧洲证券与市场管理局的职责和要求。

在第1项所述评价的基础上,监管机构理事会可将执行主任的任期延长1次。

5.经监管机构理事会作出决定后方能免除执行主任职务。

第52条 独立性

不影响管理委员会和监管机构理事会就执行主任的职责发挥各自作用的情况下,执行主任不得寻求或听从欧盟机构或单位、任何成员国政府或任何其他公共或私人机构的指示。

各成员国、欧盟机构或单位以及任何其他公共或私人机构均不得试图影响执行主任履行其职责。

根据第68条提及的《人事条例》,执行主任离职后在接受某些任命或利益方面仍应受诚信和谨慎义务约束。

第53条 职责

1.执行主任应负责管理欧洲证券与市场管理局并布置管理委员会的工作。

2.执行主任应在监管机构理事会的指导以及管理委员会的管理下,负责实施欧洲证券与市场管理局的年度工作计划。

3.根据本条例,执行主任应采取必要的措施,特别是应通过内部行政指示和通知

internal administrative instructions and the publication of notices, to ensure the functioning of the Authority, in accordance with this Regulation.

4. The Executive Director shall prepare a multi-annual work programme, as referred to in Article 47(2).

5. Each year by 30 June, the Executive Director shall prepare a work programme for the following year, as referred to in Article 47(2).

6. The Executive Director shall draw up a preliminary draft budget of the Authority pursuant to Article 63 and shall implement the budget of the Authority pursuant to Article 64.

7. Each year the Executive Director shall prepare a draft report with a section on the regulatory and supervisory activities of the Authority and a section on financial and administrative matters.

8. The Executive Director shall exercise in respect to the Authority's staff the powers laid down in Article 68 and manage staff matters.

CHAPTER Ⅳ JOINT BODIES OF THE EUROPEAN SUPERVISORY AUTHORITIES

SECTION 1 Joint Committee of European Supervisory Authorities

Article 54 Establishment

1. The Joint Committee of the European Supervisory Authorities is here by established.

2. The Joint Committee shall serve as a forum in which the Authority shall cooperate regularly and closely and ensure cross-sectoral consistency with the European Supervisory Authority (European Banking Authority) and the European Supervisory Authority (European Insurance and Occupational Pensions Authority), in particular regarding:

— financial conglomerates,

— accounting and auditing,

— micro-prudential analyses of cross-sectoral developments, risks and vulnerabilities for financial stability,

— retail investment products,

— measures combating money laundering; and,

— information exchange with the ESRB and developing the relationship between the

来确保欧洲证券与市场管理局的有效运行。

4.执行主任应制订第47条第2款所述的跨年度工作计划。

5.每年6月30日前,执行主任应为下一年度制订第47条第2款所述的工作计划。

6.执行主任应根据第63条起草欧洲证券与市场管理局初步预算草案并根据第64条实施欧洲证券与市场管理局的预算。

7.执行主任每年均应起草一份报告草案,其中一节关于欧洲证券与市场管理局的规制和监管活动,另一节关于财务和行政管理事宜。

8.执行主任应对欧洲证券与市场管理局的工作人员行使第68条规定的权力,并负责管理人事。

第四章　欧洲监管机构的联合机构

第1节　欧洲监管机构联合委员会

第54条　设立

1.特此设立欧洲监管机构联合委员会。

2.联合委员会应充当欧洲证券与市场管理局与两个欧洲监管机构(欧洲银行业管理局和欧洲保险与职业养老金管理局)之间的平台,该等机构通过此一平台得以开展定期紧密合作并保持跨行业监管一致性,尤其是在下列几个方面:

——金融集团,
——会计和审计,
——对金融稳定的跨行业变化、风险和薄弱环节的微观审慎分析,

——零售投资产品,
——打击洗钱活动的措施,和
——与欧洲系统性风险委员会的信息交流以及欧洲系统性风险委员会和各欧洲

ESRB and the ESAs.

3. The Joint Committee shall have a dedicated staff provided by the ESAs that shall act as a secretariat. The Authority shall contribute adequate resources to administrative, infrastructure and operational expenses.

4. In the event that a financial market participant reaches across different sectors, the Joint Committee shall resolve disagreements in accordance with Article 56.

Article 55 Composition

1. The Joint Committee shall be composed of the Chairpersons of the ESAs, and, where applicable, the Chairperson of any Sub-Committee established under Article 57.

2. The Executive Director, a representative of the Commission and the ESRB shall be invited to the meetings of the Joint Committee, as well as of any Sub-Committees referred to in Article 57, as observers.

3. The Chairperson of the Joint Committee shall be appointed on an annual rotational basis from among the Chairpersons of the ESAs. The Chairperson of the Joint Committee shall be a Vice-Chair of the ESRB.

4. The Joint Committee shall adopt and publish its own rules of procedure. The rules may specify further participants in the meetings of the Joint Committee.

The Joint Committee shall meet at least once every 2 months.

Article 56 Joint positions and common acts

Within the scope of its tasks in Chapter Ⅱ, and, in particular with respect to the implementation of Directive 2002/87/EC, where relevant, the Authority shall reach joint positions with the European Supervisory Authority (European Insurance and Occupational Pensions Authority) and with the European Supervisory Authority (European Banking Authority), as appropriate.

Acts under Articles 10 to 15, 17, 18 or 19 of this Regulation in relation to the application of Directive 2002/87/EC and of any other Union acts referred to in Article 1(2) that also fall within the area of competence of the European Supervisory Authority (European Banking Authority) or the European Supervisory Authority (European Insurance and Occupational Pensions Authority) shall be adopted, in parallel, by the Authority, the European Supervisory Authority (European Banking Authority) and the European Supervisory Authority (European Insurance and Occupational Pensions Authority), as appropriate.

Article 57 Sub-Committees

1. For the purposes of Article 56, a Sub-Committee on Financial Conglomerates to the Joint Committee shall be established.

2. The Sub-Committee shall be composed of the individuals referred to in Article 55(1), and one high-level representative from the current staff of the relevant competent authority

监管机构之间关系的建立。

3.各欧洲监管机构应为联合委员会提供1名专职的工作人员作为秘书。欧洲证券与市场管理局应为行政、基础设施和运营开支提供充足的资源。

4.对于涉足多个行业的金融市场参与者，联合委员会应依照第56条的规定解决分歧。

第55条　构成

1.联合委员会应由各欧洲监管机构的主席以及依据第57条设立的任何分委员会的主席（如有）组成。

2.执行主任以及欧盟委员会和欧洲系统性风险委员会应各有1名代表被邀请作为观察员参加联合委员会以及第57条所述的任何分委员会的会议。

3.联合委员会的主席应每年由各欧洲监管机构的主席轮流担任。联合委员会的主席应兼任欧洲系统性风险委员会的副主席。

4.联合委员会应通过并公布其程序规则。除上述参会人员外，规则可具体规定其他可参加联合委员会会议的人选。

联合委员会应至少每2个月召开1次会议。

第56条　共同立场和通用法律文件

在第二章所述的欧洲证券与市场管理局职责范围内，特别是与实施第2002/87/EC号指令有关的职责（如适用）范围内，欧洲证券与市场管理局应与欧洲监督机构（欧洲保险与职业养老金管理局或欧洲证券与市场管理局）（视具体情况而定）达成共同立场。

本条例第10条至第15条、第17条、第18条或第19条中与第2002/87/EC指令以及第1条第2款所述欧盟立法的适用有关的，并且同时也属于欧洲监管机构（欧洲银行业管理局或欧洲保险与职业养老金管理局）职权管辖范围的立法，应同时由欧洲证券与市场管理局与欧洲监管机构（欧洲银行业管理局或欧洲保险与职业养老金管理局）（视具体情况而定）共同通过。

第57条　分委员会

1.为了第56条之目的，应在联合委员会下设立一个金融集团分委员会。

2.分委员会应由第55条第1款所述的个人以及各成员国相关主管部门现任工作人员中选派的高级别代表组成。

from each Member State.

3. The Sub-Committee shall elect a Chairperson from among its members, who shall also be a member of the Joint Committee.

4. The Joint Committee may establish further Sub Committees.

SECTION 2 Board of Appeal

Article 58 Composition and operation

1. The Board of Appeal shall be a joint body of the ESAs.

2. The Board of Appeal shall be composed of six members and six alternates, who shall be individuals of a high repute with a proven record of relevant knowledge and professional experience, including supervisory, experience to a sufficiently high level in the fields of banking, insurance, occupational pensions, securities markets or other financial services, excluding current staff of the competent authorities or other national or Union institutions involved in the activities of the Authority. The Board of Appeal shall have sufficient legal expertise to provide expert legal advice on the legality of the Authority's exercise of its powers.

The Board of Appeal shall designate its President.

3. Two members of the Board of Appeal and two alternates shall be appointed by the Management Board of the Authority from a short-list proposed by the Commission, following a public call for expressions of interest published in the Official Journal of the European Union, and after consultation of the Board of Supervisors.

The other members shall be appointed in accordance with Regulation (EU) No 1093/2010 and Regulation (EU) No 1094/2010.

4. The term of office of the members of the Board of Appeal shall be 5 years. That term may be extended once.

5. A member of the Board of Appeal appointed by the Management Board of the Authority shall not be removed during his term of office, unless he has been found guilty of serious misconduct and the Management Board takes a decision to that effect after consulting the Board of Supervisors.

6. The decisions of the Board of Appeal shall be adopted on the basis of a majority of at least four of its six members. Where the appealed decision falls within the scope of this Regulation, the deciding majority shall include at least one of the two members of the Board of Appeal appointed by the Authority.

7. The Board of Appeal shall be convened by its President when necessary.

8. The ESAs shall ensure adequate operational and secretarial support for the Board of Appeal through the Joint Committee.

3.分委员会应从其委员中选出1名主席，该主席应同时为联合委员会的委员。

4.联合委员会还可进一步设立其他分委员会。

第2节 行政复议委员会

第58条 构成和运作

1.行政复议委员会应为各个欧洲监管机构之间的一个联合机构。

2.行政复议委员会应由6名委员和6名替补委员组成，其应具有良好声誉，并且能证明其在银行业、保险、职业养老金、证券市场或其他金融服务领域有足够的相关知识和专业经验（包括监管经验），但其中不得有参与欧洲证券与市场管理局活动的主管部门或其他国家级或欧盟机构的现任工作人员。行政复议委员会应具备足够的法律专业知识就欧洲证券与市场管理局权力行使的合法性提供专业的法律意见。

行政复议委员会应指定1名主席。

3.在《欧盟公报》上发布征寻公告并咨询监管机构理事会的意见后，由欧洲证券与市场管理局的管理委员会从欧盟委员会提议的一份候选人短名单中任命行政复议委员会的2名委员以及2名替补委员。

其他委员应根据第1093/2010号（欧盟）条例以及第1094/2010号（欧盟）条例任命。

4.行政复议委员会委员的任期为5年。任期可延长1次。

5.由欧洲证券与市场管理局管理委员会任命的行政复议委员会委员不得在其任期内被免职，但是，被发现有严重不当行为并且管理委员会在咨询监管机构理事会的意见后决定免除其职务的除外。

6.行政复议委员会的决定应由其6名委员中的至少4名同意后方能通过。行政复议所涉欧洲证券与市场管理局决定属于本条例管辖范围的，同意行政复议决定的委员中应至少包括由欧洲证券与市场管理局任命的2名行政复议委员会委员其中的1名。

7.行政复议委员会应在必要时由其主席召集。

8.各欧洲监管机构应确保通过联合委员会对行政复议委员会提供充分的运作和秘书支持。

Article 59 Independence and impartiality

1. The members of the Board of Appeal shall be independent in making their decisions. They shall not be bound by any instructions. They shall not perform any other duties in relation to the Authority, its Management Board or its Board of Supervisors.

2. Members of the Board of Appeal shall not take part in any appeal proceedings in which they have any personal interest, if they have previously been involved as representatives of one of the parties to the proceedings, or if they have participated in the decision under appeal.

3. If, for one of the reasons referred to in paragraphs 1 and 2 or for any other reason, a member of a Board of Appeal considers that another member should not take part in any appeal proceedings, he shall inform the Board of Appeal accordingly.

4. Any party to the appeal proceedings may object to the participation of a member of the Board of Appeal on any of the grounds referred to in paragraphs 1 and 2, or if suspected of bias.

No objection may be based on the nationality of members nor shall it be admissible if, while being aware of a reason for objecting, the party to the appeal proceedings has nonetheless taken a procedural step other than objecting to the composition of the Board of Appeal.

5. The Board of Appeal shall decide on the action to be taken in the cases specified in paragraphs 1 and 2 without the participation of the member concerned.

For the purpose of taking that decision, the member concerned shall be replaced on the Board of Appeal by his alternate. Where the alternate is in a similar situation, the Chairperson shall designate a replacement from among the available alternates.

6. The members of the Board of Appeal shall undertake to act independently and in the public interest.

For that purpose, they shall make a declaration of commitments and a declaration of interests indicating either the absence of any interest which may be considered prejudicial to their independence or any direct or indirect interest which might be considered prejudicial to their independence.

Those declarations shall be made public, annually and in writing.

CHAPTER V REMEDIES

Article 60 Appeals

1. Any natural or legal person, including competent authorities, may appeal against a

第59条 独立性与公正性

1.行政复议委员会的委员应独立作出决定。他们不受任何指示的约束,不得履行与欧洲证券与市场管理局、其管理委员会或其监管机构理事会有关的任何其他职责。

2.如果行政复议程序涉及行政复议委员会某委员的个人利益,或其之前曾作为行政复议程序一方当事人的代表涉案或曾经参与作出被复议的欧洲证券与市场管理局决定,则其不得参与行政复议程序。

3.出于第1款和第2款所述的理由之一或任何其他理由,有行政复议委员会委员认为其他委员不应参与任何行政复议程序的,应将该情况通知行政复议委员会。

4.基于第1款和第2款所述的任何理由或在涉嫌有失公允的情况下,行政复议程序的任何一方均可申请行政复议委员会委员回避。

不能以委员的国籍为由申请回避;当行政复议程序的一方当事人明知有理由申请回避而不提出申请且继续行政复议程序的,之后不得再提出回避申请。

5.行政复议委员会应就第1款和第2款所指情况下所需采取的行动作出决定,作上述决定时所涉委员不得参与。

为作出该决定,所涉委员应由其替补委员代替其出席行政复议委员会。该名替补人员处于类似状况的,主席应从其他可供选择的替补人员当中指定1名出席。

6.行政复议委员会的委员应承诺独立地出于公众利益行事。

为此,行政复议委员会的委员应作出承诺声明和利害关系声明,说明其本人不存在可被视为对其独立性产生影响的任何利害关系或任何直接或间接利益。

该等声明应每年以书面形式公布。

第五章 救 济

第60条 行政复议

1.任何自然人或法人,包括主管部门,均可针对欧洲证券与市场管理局的下列决定

decision of the Authority referred to in Articles 17, 18 and 19 and any other decision taken by the Authority in accordance with the Union acts referred to in Article 1(2) which is addressed to that person, or against a decision which, although in the form of a decision addressed to another person, is of direct and individual concern to that person.

2. The appeal, together with a statement of grounds, shall be filed in writing at the Authority within 2 months of the date of notification of the decision to the person concerned, or, in the absence of a notification, of the day on which the Authority published its decision.

The Board of Appeal shall decide upon the appeal within 2 months after the appeal has been lodged.

3. An appeal lodged pursuant to paragraph 1 shall not have suspensive effect.

However, the Board of Appeal may, if it considers that circumstances so require, suspend the application of the contested decision.

4. If the appeal is admissible, the Board of Appeal shall examine whether it is well-founded. It shall invite the parties to the appeal proceedings to file observations on its own notifications or on communications from the other parties to the appeal proceedings, within specified time limits. Parties to the appeal proceedings shall be entitled to make oral representations.

5. The Board of Appeal may confirm the decision taken by the competent body of the Authority, or remit the case to the competent body of the Authority. That body shall be bound by the decision of the Board of Appeal and that body shall adopt an amended decision regarding the case concerned.

6. The Board of Appeal shall adopt and make public its rules of procedure.

7. The decisions taken by the Board of Appeal shall be reasoned and shall be made public by the Authority.

Article 61 Actions before the Court of Justice of the European Union

1. Proceedings may be brought before the Court of Justice of the European Union, in accordance with Article 263 TFEU, contesting a decision taken by the Board of Appeal or, in cases where there is no right of appeal before the Board of Appeal, by the Authority.

2. Member States and the Union institutions, as well as any natural or legal person, may institute proceedings before the Court of Justice of the European Union against decisions of the Authority, in accordance with Article 263 TFEU.

3. In the event that the Authority has an obligation to act and fails to take a decision, proceedings for failure to act may be brought before the Court of Justice of the European Union in accordance with Article 265 TFEU.

4. The Authority shall be required to take the necessary measures to comply with the judgment of the Court of Justice of the European Union.

提出行政复议申请:第17条、第18条以及第19条所述的决定;根据第1条第2款所述欧盟法律文件作出的针对上述主体的任何其他决定;对于尽管表面看来是针对其他人作出的,但实际上与上述主体本人有直接和个人关系的决定,也可提出行政复议申请。

2.所涉主体可在欧洲证券与市场管理局向其发出决定通知的2个月内,或者未作通知的,在其决定公布之日的2个月内,以书面形式向欧洲证券与市场管理局提出行政复议申请并附上一份行政复议申请理由说明。

行政复议委员会应在行政复议申请提交后2个月内作出行政复议决定。

3.根据第1款提交的行政复议申请对所涉决定无暂停效力。

然而,行政复议委员会可在其认为必要的情况下,暂停实施受到质疑的决定。

4.对于可受理的行政复议申请,行政复议委员会应审查是否有充足的理由。行政复议委员会应要求行政复议程序的各当事人在规定的时限内提交其对行政复议委员会所发通知的意见或者对从行政复议程序其他当事人收到的信函的意见。行政复议程序的各当事人均有权作口头陈述。

5.行政复议委员会可确认欧洲证券与市场管理局的主管机构的决定,或将案件退回欧洲证券与市场管理局的主管机构。该机构应受行政复议委员会的决定约束,并应就所涉案件修改其决定。

6.行政复议委员会应通过并公布其程序规则。

7.行政复议委员会的决定应有合理依据并应由欧洲证券与市场管理局予以公布。

第61条　在欧盟法院的行政诉讼

1.根据《欧洲联盟运行条约》第263条,如行政复议委员会的决定受到质疑,或者在相关方无权向行政复议委员会提出行政复议申请的情况下,欧洲证券与市场管理局可向欧盟法院提起行政诉讼。

2.各成员国和欧盟机构,以及任何自然人或法人,均可根据《欧洲联盟运行条约》第263条就欧洲证券与市场管理局的决定向欧盟法院提起行政诉讼。

3.欧洲证券与市场管理局有义务采取行动但未作决定的,相关方可根据《欧洲联盟运行条约》第265条就其不采取行动向欧盟法院提起行政诉讼。

4.欧洲证券与市场管理局应采取必要措施以执行欧盟法院的判决。

CHAPTER Ⅵ FINANCIAL PROVISIONS

Article 62 Budget of the Authority

1. The revenues of the Authority, a European body in accordance with Article 185 of Council Regulation (EC, Euratom) No 1605/2002 of 25 June 2002 on the Financial Regulation applicable to the general budget of the European Communities [1] (hereinafter the 'Financial Regulation'), shall consist, in particular, of any combination of the following:

(a) obligatory contributions from the national public authorities competent for the supervision of financial market participants which shall be made in accordance with a formula based on the weighting of votes set out in Article 3(3) of Protocol (No 36) on transitional provisions. For the purposes of this Article, Article 3(3) of Protocol (No 36) on transitional provisions shall continue to apply beyond the deadline of 31 October 2014 therein established;

(b) a subsidy from the Union, entered in the General Budget of the European Union (Commission Section);

(c) any fees paid to the Authority in the cases specified in the relevant instruments of Union law.

2. The expenditure of the Authority shall include, at least, staff, remuneration, administrative, infrastructure professional training and operational expenses.

3. Revenue and expenditure shall be in balance.

4. Estimates of all Authority revenue and expenditure shall be prepared for each financial year, corresponding to the calendar year, and shall be presented in the budget of the Authority.

Article 63 Establishment of the budget

1. By 15 February each year, the Executive Director shall draw up a draft statement of estimates of revenue and expenditure for the following financial year, and shall forward it to the Management Board and the Board of Supervisors, together with the establishment plan. Each year, the Board of Supervisors shall, on the basis of the draft statement drawn up by the Executive Director and approved by the Management Board, produce a statement of estimates of revenue and expenditure of the Authority for the following financial year. That statement of estimates, including a draft establishment plan, shall be

1 OJ L 248, 16.9.2002, p. 1.

第六章 财务规定

第62条 欧洲证券与市场管理局的预算

1.根据《欧盟理事会关于适用于欧洲共同体总预算的财务条例的第1605/2002号(欧共体和欧洲原子能共同体)条例》[1](2002年6月25日)(以下简称《财务条例》)的第185条,欧洲机构欧洲证券与市场管理局的收入应主要包括下列各项的任意组合:

(a)来自主管金融市场参与者监管的国家级公共机构的义务缴款,该等缴款的计算公式应以关于过渡条款的《议定书(第36号)》第3条第3款所规定的加权票数为基础。为本条之目的,关于过渡条款的《议定书(第36号)》第3条第3款应在其设定的到期日2014年10月31日之后继续适用;

(b)在欧盟总预算(欧盟委员会部分)中列支的欧盟补助;

(c)欧洲证券与市场管理局在欧盟法律相关法律文件所具体规定的情况下收取的任何费用。

2.欧洲证券与市场管理局的开支至少应包括人员、薪酬、行政管理、基础设施、专业培训和运营费用。

3.欧洲证券与市场管理局应保持收支平衡。

4.欧洲证券与市场管理局预算中应包含欧洲证券与市场管理局每个会计年度(与日历年度一致)所有收支的估算。

第63条 预算制定

1.每年2月15日前,执行主任应起草下个会计年度收支的估算报表草案,并和预算制订计划一起转发给管理委员会和监管机构理事会。监管机构理事会每年均应在执行主任起草并经管理委员会批准的报表草案的基础上,制定关于欧洲证券与市场管理局下个会计年度收支的估算报表。监管机构理事会应将该估算报表连同一份预算制订计划草案于3月31日前发送给欧盟委员会。在通过估算报表前,执行委员会制定的草案应先获得管理委员会批准。

1 2002年9月16日《欧盟公报》L 248,第1页。

transmitted by the Board of Supervisors to the Commission by 31 March. Prior to adoption of the statement of estimates, the draft prepared by the Executive Director shall be approved by the Management Board.

2. The statement of estimates shall be transmitted by the Commission to the European Parliament and to the Council (hereinafter referred to together as the 'budgetary authority'), together with the draft budget of the European Union.

3. On the basis of the statement of estimates, the Commission shall enter in the draft budget of the European Union the estimates it deems necessary in respect of the establishment plan and the amount of the subsidy to be charged to the General Budget of the European Union in accordance with Articles 313 and 314 TFEU.

4. The budgetary authority shall adopt the establishment plan for the Authority. The budgetary authority shall authorise the appropriations for the subsidy to the Authority.

5. The budget of the Authority shall be adopted by the Board of Supervisors. It shall become final after the final adoption of the General Budget of the European Union. Where necessary, it shall be adjusted accordingly.

6. The Management Board shall, without delay, notify the budgetary authority of its intention to implement any project which may have significant financial implications for the funding of its budget, in particular any project relating to property, such as the rental or purchase of buildings. It shall inform the Commission thereof. If either branch of the budgetary authority intends to issue an opinion, it shall, within 2 weeks of receipt of the information on the project, notify the Authority of its intention to issue such an opinion. In the absence of a reply, the Authority may proceed with the planned operation.

7. For the first year of operation of the Authority, ending on 31 December 2011, the financing of the Authority by the Union is subject to an agreement by the budgetary authority as provided for in Point 47 of the Interinstitutional Agreement on budgetary discipline and sound financial management.

Article 64 Implementation and control of the budget

1. The Executive Director shall act as authorising officer and shall implement the Authority's budget.

2. By 1 March following the completion of each financial year, the Authority's accounting officer shall forward to the Commission's accounting officer and to the Court of Auditors the provisional accounts, accompanied by the report on budgetary and financial management during the financial year. The Authority's accounting officer shall also send the report on budgetary and financial management to the members of the Board of Supervisors, the European Parliament and the Council by 31 March of the following year.

The Commission's accounting officer shall then consolidate the provisional accounts

2.欧盟委员会应将估算报表连同欧盟的预算草案一起发送给欧洲议会和欧盟理事会(以下统称预算部门)。

3.根据《欧洲联盟运行条约》第313条和第314条,欧盟委员会应在估算报表的基础上将其认为对预算制订计划属于必要的估算金额以及应在欧盟总预算中列支的补助额纳入欧盟的预算草案。

4.预算部门应通过欧洲证券与市场管理局的预算制订计划。预算部门应核准将补助划拨给欧洲证券与市场管理局。

5.欧洲证券与市场管理局的预算应由监管机构理事会通过。在欧盟总预算最终通过后,欧洲证券与市场管理局的预算也随之通过,必要时应根据欧盟总预算对其作相应调整。

6.管理委员会如有意实施任何可能会对其预算经费产生重大财务影响的项目,特别是与物业(如租用或购买建筑物)有关的任何项目,应立即通知预算部门。管理委员会应将上述意向如实通知欧盟委员会。任一预算部门有意就上述项目提出意见的,应在收到项目信息后2周内将该意向通知欧洲证券与市场管理局。如预算部门未针对管理委员会通知作出答复,则欧洲证券与市场管理局可按计划开展项目。

7.根据《关于预算纪律和健全的财务管理的机构间协议》的第47目,在欧洲证券与市场管理局运作的首年(即于2011年12月31日结束的年度),在向欧洲证券与市场管理局提供经费前,欧盟应先获得预算部门的同意。

第64条　预算的实施和控制

1.执行主任应作为欧洲证券与市场管理局的预算核准官员,并应负责实施欧洲证券与市场管理局的预算。

2.在每个会计年度结束后至下一年度的3月1日前,欧洲证券与市场管理局的会计官员应将该会计年度的临时财务报表连同关于该会计年度预算和财务管理的报告转发给欧盟委员会的会计官员以及欧盟审计院。欧洲证券与市场管理局的会计官员还应在次年3月31日前将预算和财务管理报告发送给监管机构理事会的理事、欧洲议会和欧盟理事会。

根据《财务条例》第128条,欧盟委员会的会计官员应对其所收到的各机构和派出

of the institutions and decentralised bodies in accordance with Article 128 of the Financial Regulation.

3. After receiving the observations of the Court of Auditors on the provisional accounts of the Authority in accordance with Article 129 of the Financial Regulation, the Executive Director, acting on his own responsibility, shall draw up the final accounts of the Authority and transmit them, for opinion, to the Management Board.

4. The Management Board shall deliver an opinion on the final accounts of the Authority.

5. The Executive Director shall transmit those final accounts, accompanied by the opinion of the Management Board, by 1 July following the completion of the financial year, to the Members of the Board of Supervisors, the European Parliament, the Council, the Commission and the Court of Auditors.

6. The final accounts shall be published.

7. The Executive Director shall send the Court of Auditors a reply to the latter's observations by 30 September. He shall also send a copy of that reply to the Management Board and the Commission.

8. The Executive Director shall submit to the European Parliament, at the latter's request and as provided for in Article 146(3) of the Financial Regulation, any information necessary for the smooth application of the discharge procedure for the financial year in question.

9. The European Parliament, following a recommendation from the Council acting by qualified majority, shall, before 15 May of the year N+2, grant a discharge to the Authority for the implementation of the budget comprising revenue from the General Budget of the European Union and competent authorities for the financial year N.

Article 65 Financial rules

The financial rules applicable to the Authority shall be adopted by the Management Board after consulting the Commission. Those rules may not depart from Commission Regulation (EC,Euratom) No 2343/2002 of 19 November 2002 on the framework Financial Regulation for the bodies referred to in Article 185 of Council Regulation (EC, Euratom) No 1605/2002 on the Financial Regulation applicable to the general budget of the European Communities [1] unless the specific operational needs for the functioning of the Authority so require and only with the prior agreement of the Commission.

Article 66 Anti-fraud measures

1. For the purposes of combating fraud, corruption and any other illegal activity, Regulation (EC) No 1073/1999 shall apply to the Authority without any restriction.

1 OJ L 357, 31.12.2002, p. 72.

单位的临时财务报表进行合并工作。

3.收到欧盟审计院根据《财务条例》第129条对欧洲证券与市场管理局临时财务报表作出的评述后，执行主任应自行负责起草欧洲证券与市场管理局的最终报表并将其发送给管理委员会以征求其意见。

4.管理委员会应提交关于欧洲证券与市场管理局最终报表的意见。

5.执行主任应在会计年度结束之后下一年度的7月1日前将该等最终报表连同管理委员会的意见发送给监管机构理事会理事、欧洲议会、欧盟理事会、欧盟委员会以及欧盟审计院。

6.最终报表应予公布。

7.执行主任应在9月30日前就欧盟审计院的评述向其作出答复。执行主任还应将一份该答复发送给管理委员会和欧盟委员会。

8.经欧洲议会要求，以及根据《财务条例》第146条第3款，执行主任应向其递交所涉会计年度的预算审批程序顺利实施所必要的任何信息。

9.欧洲议会应在第N+2年的5月15日前依照欧盟理事会经特定多数通过的建议，批准欧洲银行业管理局对第N个会计年度包括来自欧盟总预算和主管部门收入的预算的实施结果。

第65条　财务规则

欧洲证券与市场管理局所适用的财务规则应由管理委员会在咨询欧盟委员会意见后通过。该等规则不得偏离《欧盟委员会关于〈欧盟理事会关于适用于欧洲共同体总预算的财务条例的第1605/2002号（欧共体和欧洲原子能共同体）条例〉第185条所指机构的框架性〈财务条例〉的第2343/2002号（欧共体和欧洲原子能共同体）条例》[1]（2002年11月19日），但是，出于欧洲证券与市场管理局运行的特殊运营需要并且仅在经欧盟委员会事先同意的情况下除外。

第66条　反欺诈措施

1.为反欺诈、腐败以及其他非法活动之目的，第1073/1999号（欧共体）条例应不受限制地适用于欧洲证券与市场管理局。

1　2002年12月31日《欧盟公报》L 357，第72页。

2. The Authority shall accede to the Interinstitutional Agreement concerning internal investigations by OLAF and shall immediately adopt appropriate provisions for all staff of the Authority.

3. The funding decisions and the agreements and the implementing instruments resulting from them shall explicitly stipulate that the Court of Auditors and OLAF may, if need be, carry out on-the-spot checks on the beneficiaries of monies disbursed by the Authority as well as on the staff responsible for allocating these monies.

CHAPTER Ⅶ GENERAL PROVISIONS

Article 67 Privileges and immunities

The Protocol (No 7) on the privileges and immunities of the European Union annexed to the Treaty on European Union and to the TFEU shall apply to the Authority and its staff.

Article 68 Staff

1. The Staff Regulations, the Conditions of Employment of Other Servants and the rules adopted jointly by the Union institutions for the purpose of applying them shall apply to the staff of the Authority, including its Executive Director and its Chairperson.

2. The Management Board, in agreement with the Commission, shall adopt the necessary implementing measures, in accordance with the arrangements provided for in Article 110 of the Staff Regulations.

3. In respect of its staff, the Authority shall exercise the powers conferred on the appointing authority by the Staff Regulations and on the authority entitled to conclude contracts by the Conditions of Employment of Other Servants.

4. The Management Board shall adopt provisions to allow national experts from Member States to be seconded to the Authority.

Article 69 Liability of the Authority

1. In the case of non-contractual liability, the Authority shall, in accordance with the general principles common to the laws of the Member States, make good any damage caused by it or by its staff in the performance of their duties. The Court of Justice of the European Union shall have jurisdiction in any dispute over the remedying of such damage.

2. The personal financial liability and disciplinary liability of Authority staff towards the Authority shall be governed by the relevant provisions applying to the staff of the Authority.

Article 70 Obligation of professional secrecy

1. Members of the Board of Supervisors and the Management Board, the Executive

2.欧洲证券与市场管理局应加入《关于欧洲反欺诈办公室内部调查的机构间协议》,并应立即通过针对欧洲证券与市场管理局所有工作人员的适当规定。

3.经费筹措决定以及由此产生的协议和实施性法律文件应明确规定,欧盟审计院和欧洲反欺诈办公室可在必要时对欧洲证券与市场管理局支出款项的受益人以及负责分配该等款项的工作人员进行现场调查。

第七章　一般条款

第67条　特殊权利和豁免

《欧洲联盟条约》和《欧洲联盟运行条约》附录关于欧盟的特殊权利和豁免的《议定书(第7号)》应适用于欧洲证券与市场管理局及其工作人员。

第68条　工作人员

1.《人事条例》、《其他人员的聘用条件》以及欧盟机构为上述文件的适用联合通过的规则应适用于欧洲证券与市场管理局的工作人员,包括其执行主任和主席。

2.根据《人事条例》第110条所规定的安排,管理委员会与欧盟委员会达成一致后应制定必要的实施细则。

3.欧洲证券与市场管理局应对其工作人员行使《人事条例》授予的任命权以及《其他人员的聘用条件》授予的签订聘用合同的权力。

4.管理委员会应通过相关规定以允许从各成员国借调国内的专家到欧洲证券与市场管理局。

第69条　欧洲证券与市场管理局的责任

1.对于欧洲证券与市场管理局或其工作人员在履行职责时造成的不属于合同责任的任何损害,欧洲证券与市场管理局应根据各成员国国内法律通用的一般原则进行赔偿。欧盟法院应对上述损害赔偿引发的任何争议有司法管辖权。

2.欧洲证券与市场管理局工作人员对欧洲证券与市场管理局承担的个人财务责任和违纪责任应受适用于欧洲证券与市场管理局工作人员的相关规定管辖。

第70条　职业保密义务

1.监管机构理事会的理事和管理委员会的委员、执行主任、欧洲证券与市场管理

Director, and members of the staff of the Authority including officials seconded by Member States on a temporary basis and all other persons carrying out tasks for the Authority on a contractual basis shall be subject to the requirements of professional secrecy pursuant to Article 339 TFEU and the relevant provisions in Union legislation, even after their duties have ceased.

Article 16 of the Staff Regulations shall apply to them.

In accordance with the Staff Regulations, the staff shall, after leaving service, continue to be bound by the duty to behave with integrity and discretion as regards the acceptance of certain appointments or benefits.

Neither Member States, the Union institutions or bodies, nor any other public or private body shall seek to influence staff members of the Authority in the performance of their tasks.

2. Without prejudice to cases covered by criminal law, any confidential information received by persons referred to in paragraph 1 whilst performing their duties may not be divulged to any person or authority whatsoever, except in summary or aggregate form, such that individual financial market participants can not be identified.

Moreover, the obligation under paragraph 1 and the first subparagraph of this paragraph shall not prevent the Authority and the national supervisory authorities from using the information for the enforcement of the acts referred to in Article 1(2), and in particular for legal procedures for the adoption of decisions.

3. Paragraphs 1 and 2 shall not prevent the Authority from exchanging information with national supervisory authorities in accordance with this Regulation and other Union legislation applicable to financial market participants.

That information shall be subject to the conditions of professional secrecy referred to in paragraphs 1 and 2. The Authority shall lay down in its internal rules of procedure the practical arrangements for implementing the confidentiality rules referred to in paragraphs 1 and 2.

4. The Authority shall apply Commission Decision2001/844/EC/ECSC, Euratom of 29 November 2001 amending its internal Rules of Procedure [1].

Article 71 Data protection

This Regulation shall be without prejudice to the obligations of Member States relating to their processing of personal data under Directive 95/46/EC or the obligations of the Authority relating to its processing of personal data under Regulation (EC) No 45/2001 when fulfilling its responsibilities.

1 OJ L 317, 3.12.2001, p. 1.

局工作人员（包括成员国暂时借调的官员）以及所有其他按合同为欧洲证券与市场管理局履行职责的人员在欧洲证券与市场管理局任职期间以及任职结束后，均应遵守《欧洲联盟运行条约》第339条以及欧盟立法相关条款规定的职业保密要求。

《人事条例》第16条应适用于上述人员。

根据《人事条例》，工作人员离职后在接受特定任命和利益时应继续受诚信和谨慎义务约束。

各成员国、欧盟机构或单位或任何公共或私人机构均不得试图影响欧洲证券与市场管理局工作人员履行其职责。

2.第1款所指人员在履行职责时收到的任何保密信息均不得泄露给任何个人或部门，但是，以无法识别具体金融市场参与者的摘要或汇总的形式披露的除外。上述规定不影响相关情形下刑法的适用。

另外，第1款以及本款第1项中的义务应不妨碍欧洲证券与市场管理局和各国家级监管机构将信息用于执行第1条第2款所述立法，特别是用于通过决定的法律程序。

3.第1款和第2款应不妨碍欧洲证券与市场管理局根据本条例以及其他适用于金融市场参与者的欧盟立法与各国家级监管机构交换信息。

该等信息受第1款和第2款所述职业保密条件的约束。欧洲证券与市场管理局应在其内部程序规则中规定实施第1款和第2款所述保密规则的具体安排。

4.欧洲证券与市场管理局应适用修改其内部程序规则的欧盟委员会第2001/844/EC/ECSC号（欧洲原子能共同体）决定[1]（2001年11月29日）。

第71条　数据保护

本条例不影响成员国在第95/46/EC号指令下与个人数据处理有关的义务或欧洲证券与市场管理局在履行职责过程中应遵循的第45/2001号（欧共体）条例下与个人数据处理有关的义务。

1　2001年12月3日《欧盟公报》L 317，第1页。

Article 72 Access to documents

1. Regulation (EC) No 1049/2001 shall apply to documents held by the Authority.

2. The Management Board shall, by 31 May 2011, adopt practical measures for applying Regulation (EC) No 1049/2001.

3. Decisions taken by the Authority pursuant to Article 8 of Regulation (EC) No 1049/2001 may be the subject of a complaint to the Ombudsman or of proceedings before the Court of Justice of the European Union, following an appeal to the Board of Appeal, as appropriate, in accordance with the conditions laid down in Articles 228 and 263 TFEU respectively.

Article 73 Language arrangements

1. Council Regulation No 1 determining the languages to be used by the European Economic Community [1] shall apply to the Authority.

2. The Management Board shall decide on the internal language arrangements for the Authority.

3. The translation services required for the functioning of the Authority shall be provided by the Translation Centre for the Bodies of the European Union.

Article 74 Headquarters Agreement

The necessary arrangements concerning the accommodation to be provided for the Authority in the Member State where its seat is located and the facilities to be made available by that Member State, as well as the specific rules applicable in that Member State to the Executive Director, the members of the Management Board, the staff of the Authority and members of their families shall be laid down in a Headquarters Agreement between the Authority and that Member State concluded after obtaining the approval of the Management Board.

That Member State shall provide the best possible conditions to ensure the proper functioning of the Authority, including multilingual, European-oriented schooling and appropriate transport connections.

Article 75 Participation of third countries

1. Participation in the work of the Authority shall be open to third countries which have concluded agreements with the Union whereby they have adopted and are applying Union law in the areas of competence of the Authority as referred to in Article 1(2).

2. The Authority may cooperate with the countries referred to in paragraph 1, applying legislation which has been recognised as equivalent in the areas of competence of the Authority referred to in Article 1(2), as provided for in international agreements concluded by the Union in accordance with Article 216 TFEU.

3. Under the relevant provisions of the agreements referred to in paragraphs 1 and 2,

---

1 OJ 17, 6.10.1958, p. 385.

第72条　文件查阅权

1.第1049/2001号(欧共体)条例应适用于欧洲证券与市场管理局所持有的文件。

2.管理委员会应在2011年5月31日前制定适用第1049/2001号(欧共体)条例的具体措施。

3.针对欧洲证券与市场管理局根据第1049/2001号(欧共体)条例第8条作出的决定,在适当情况下所涉人员可首先向行政复议委员会提出行政复议申请,若对行政复议结果不服,可再分别依照《欧洲联盟运行条约》第228条和第263条所列条件向申诉官申诉或向欧盟法院提起行政诉讼。

第73条　语言安排

1.确定欧洲经济共同体所用语言的欧盟理事会第1号条例[1]应适用于欧洲证券与市场管理局。

2.管理委员会应就欧洲证券与市场管理局的内部语言安排作出决定。

3.欧洲证券与市场管理局运行所需的翻译服务应由欧盟翻译中心提供。

第74条　《总部协议》

获得管理委员会批准之后,欧洲证券与市场管理局与其总部所在的成员国之间应缔结一份《总部协议》,规定该成员国应向欧洲证券与市场管理局提供的住宿条件和供其使用的设施相关的必要安排,以及该成员国适用于执行主任、管理委员会委员、欧洲证券与市场管理局工作人员及其家属的具体规则。

该成员国应尽可能提供最好的条件以确保欧洲证券与市场管理局的稳健运行,包括多语的欧洲模式教育以及适当的交通便利。

第75条　第三国的参与

1.第三国与欧盟缔结了相关协议,因此已经采纳并正在适用第1条第2款所述欧洲证券与市场管理局职权管辖范围内的欧盟法律的,应能参与欧洲证券与市场管理局的工作。

2.根据欧盟依照《欧洲联盟运行条约》第216条缔结的国际协议,欧洲证券与市场管理局可与第1款所述的国家合作适用已被认定在欧洲证券与市场管理局第1条第2款所述职权管辖范围内与欧盟立法等效的立法。

3.根据第1款和第2款所述协议的相关规定,应作出相应安排,以特别指明第1款所

1　1958年10月6日《欧盟公报》17,第385页。

arrangements shall be made specifying, in particular, the nature, scope and procedural aspects of the involvement of the countries referred to in paragraph 1 in the work of the Authority, including provisions relating to financial contributions and to staff. They may provide for representation, as an observer, on the Board of Supervisors, but shall ensure that those countries do not attend any discussions relating to individual financial market participants, except where there is a direct interest.

CHAPTER Ⅷ TRANSITIONAL AND FINAL PROVISIONS

Article 76 Preparatory actions

1. Following the entry into force of this Regulation, and before the establishment of the Authority, CESR shall act in close cooperation with the Commission to prepare for the replacement of CESR by the Authority.

2. Once the Authority has been established, the Commission shall be responsible for the administrative establishment and initial administrative operation of the Authority until the Authority has appointed an Executive Director.

For that purpose, until such time as the Executive Director takes up his duties following his appointment by the Board of Supervisors in accordance with Article 51, the Commission may assign one official on an interim basis in order to fulfil the functions of the Executive Director. That period shall be limited to the time necessary for the appointment of an Executive Director of the Authority.

The interim Executive Director may authorise all payments covered by credits provided in the budget of the Authority, once approved by the Management Board and may conclude contracts, including staff contracts following the adoption of the Authority's establishment plan.

3. Paragraphs 1 and 2 are without prejudice to the powers of the Board of Supervisors and the Management Board.

4. The Authority shall be considered the legal successor of CESR. By the date of establishment of the Authority, all assets and liabilities and all pending operations of CESR shall be automatically transferred to the Authority. The CESR shall establish a statement showing its closing asset and liability situation as of the date of that transfer. That statement shall be audited and approved by CESR and by the Commission.

Article 77 Transitional staff provisions

1. By way of derogation from Article 68, all employment contracts and secondment

述国家涉入欧洲证券与市场管理局工作的性质、范围和程序，包括与费用分摊和工作人员有关的规定。根据该等安排，第三国可作为监管机构理事会的观察员，但应确保该等国家不参与任何与具体金融市场参与者有关的讨论，存在直接利害关系的除外。

第八章　过渡规定和最终条款

第76条　筹备活动

1.本条例生效后至欧洲证券与市场管理局成立前的期间内，欧洲证券监管机构委员会应与欧盟委员会紧密合作，为欧洲证券与市场管理局取代欧洲证券监管机构委员会做好筹备工作。

2.欧洲证券与市场管理局成立后，在欧洲证券与市场管理局任命执行主任之前，应由欧盟委员会负责欧洲证券与市场管理局的行政设立和初始行政运作。

为此，在监管机构理事会根据第51条任命执行主任之后，直至执行主任到任之前，欧盟委员会可临时委派一名官员履行执行主任的职能。该段时间应限于欧洲证券与市场管理局任命执行主任所必要的时期。

临时执行主任经管理委员会批准，可核准欧洲证券与市场管理局预算贷方项目所涵盖的所有支出，并可签订合同，包括在通过欧洲证券与市场管理局预算制订计划后签订的劳动合同。

3.第1款和第2款不影响监管机构理事会和管理委员会的权力。

4.欧洲证券与市场管理局应被视为欧洲证券监管机构委员会的合法继任机构。在欧洲证券与市场管理局成立之日，欧洲证券监管机构委员会的所有资产和债务以及所有待执行的运营事务将自动转移给欧洲证券与市场管理局。欧洲证券监管机构委员会应制定一份报表表明其截至转移当日期末资产和债务的情况。该报表应由欧洲证券监管机构委员会和欧盟委员会审计和批准。

第77条　过渡期人事规定

1.作为第68条的例外，欧洲证券监管机构委员会或其秘书处签订的并于2011年1

agreements concluded by CESR or its Secretariat and in force on 1 January 2011 shall be honoured until their expiry date. They may not be extended.

2. All members of staff under contracts referred to in paragraph 1 shall be offered the possibility of concluding temporary agent contracts under Article 2(a) of the Conditions of Employment of Other Servants at the various grades as set out in the Authority's establishment plan.

An internal selection limited to staff who have contracts with CESR or its Secretariat shall be carried out after the entry into force of this Regulation by the authority authorised to conclude contracts in order to check the ability, efficiency and integrity of those to be engaged. The internal selection procedure shall take full account of the skills and experience demonstrated by the individuals' performance prior to the engagement.

3. Depending on the type and level of functions to be performed, successful applicants shall be offered temporary agents' contracts of a duration corresponding at least to the time remaining under the prior contract.

4. The relevant national law relating to labour contracts and other relevant instruments shall continue to apply to staff members with prior contracts who choose not to apply for temporary agent's contracts or who are not offered temporary agents contracts in accordance with paragraph 2.

Article 78 National provisions

The Member States shall make such provision as is appropriate to ensure the effective application of this Regulation.

Article 79 Amendments

Decision No 716/2009/EC is hereby amended in so far as CESR is removed from the list of beneficiaries set out in Section B of the Annex to that Decision.

Article 80 Repeal

Commission Decision 2009/77/EC, establishing CESR, is hereby repealed with effect from 1 January 2011.

Article 81 Review

1. By 2 January 2014 and every 3 years thereafter, the Commission shall publish a general report on the experience acquired as a result of the operation of the Authority and the procedures laid down in this Regulation. That report shall evaluate, inter alia:

(a) the convergence in supervisory practices reached by competent authorities,

(i) the convergence in functional independence of the competent authorities and in standards equivalent to corporate governance;

(ii) the impartiality, objectivity and autonomy of the Authority;

(b) the functioning of the colleges of supervisors;

(c) the progress achieved towards convergence in the fields of crisis prevention,

月1日有效的所有劳动合同和借调协议,均应履行至到期日,不得延期。

2.第1款所述合同下的所有工作人员均应有机会按照欧洲证券与市场管理局的预算制订计划所列各种级别签订符合《其他人员的聘用条件》第2条第a款的临时劳动合同。

本条例生效后,获得授权签订合同的部门应开展内部遴选,遴选对象仅限于与欧洲证券监管机构委员会或其秘书处有合同关系的工作人员,以对拟聘用人员的能力、效率和诚信进行审查。内部遴选程序应充分考虑候选人聘用前在工作中所展现出的个人技能和经验。

3.根据待履行职能的类型和级别,被录用的申请人应获得临时劳动合同,该等合同的期限应至少相当于先前合同未履行的时间。

4.与劳动合同有关的国内法律以及其他相关法律文件应继续适用于之前签订过合同,但选择不申请临时劳动合同或未根据第2款获得临时劳动合同的工作人员。

第78条 成员国的规定

各成员国应制定适当的规定以确保本条例的有效适用。

第79条 修正

应对第716/2009/EC号决定作出修正,从附录第B节所列的受益者名单中删除欧洲证券监管机构委员会。

第80条 废止

设立欧洲证券监管机构委员会的欧盟委员会第2009/77/EC号决定特此于2011年1月1日废止。

第81条 审评

1.2014年1月2日前,欧盟委员会应发布一份综合报告,说明其在欧洲证券与市场管理局运营和本条例所列程序方面取得的经验,并于此后每3年发布一份该等综合报告。该报告应评价的问题包括但不限于:

(a)各主管部门所达到的监管实践的趋同:

(i)各主管部门职能上的独立性趋同以及与公司治理等效之标准的趋同;

(ii)欧洲证券与市场管理局的公正性、客观性和自主性;

(b)监管团的运作;

(c)在危机预防、管理和清盘领域(包括欧盟经费筹措机制)取得的趋同程度;

management and resolution, including Union funding mechanisms;

(d) the role of the Authority as regards systemic risk;

(e) the application of the safeguard clause established in Article 38;

(f) the application of the binding mediation role established in Article 19.

2. The report referred to in paragraph 1 shall also examine whether:

(a) it is appropriate to continue separate supervision of banking, insurance, occupational pensions, securities and financial markets;

(b) it is appropriate to undertake prudential supervision and supervise the conduct of business separately or by the same supervisor;

(c) it is appropriate to simplify and reinforce the architecture of the ESFS in order to increase the coherence between the macro and the micro levels and between the ESAs;

(d) the evolution of the ESFS is consistent with that of the global evolution;

(e) there is sufficient diversity and excellence within the ESFS;

(f) accountability and transparency in relation to publication requirements are adequate;

(g) the resources of the Authority are adequate to carry out its responsibilities;

(h) it is appropriate for the seat of the Authority to be maintained or to move the ESAs to a single seat to enhance better coordination between them.

3. Concerning the issue of direct supervision of institutions or infrastructures of pan-European reach and taking account of market developments, the Commission shall draw up an annual report on the appropriateness of entrusting the Authority with further supervisory responsibilities in this area.

4. The report and any accompanying proposals, as appropriate, shall be forwarded to the European Parliament and to the Council.

Article 82 Entry into force

This Regulation shall enter into force on the day following its publication in the Official Journal of the European Union.

It shall apply from 1 January 2011, with the exception of Article 76 and Article 77(1) and (2), which shall apply as from the date of its entry into force.

The Authority shall be established on 1 January 2011.

This Regulation shall be binding in its entirety and directly applicable in all Member States.

Done at Strasbourg, 24 November 2010.

For the European Parliament
The President
J. BUZEK

For the Council
The President
O. CHASTEL

(d)欧洲证券与市场管理局在系统性风险方面所起的作用；

(e)第38条所确立的保障条款的适用；

(f)第19条所设定的有约束力的调解角色的应用。

2.第1款所述的报告还应对下列事项进行审查：

(a)是否宜继续对银行业、保险、职业养老金、证券以及金融市场进行分业监管；

(b)是否宜分别开展审慎监管和业务活动监管或由一个监管机构同时进行上述两项监管；

(c)是否宜简化和加强欧洲金融监管机构体系的结构，以加强宏观和微观层面以及各欧洲监管机构之间的相互一致性；

(d)欧洲金融监管机构体系的发展是否与全球发展一致；

(e)欧洲金融监管机构体系内是否具有足够的多样性和卓越性；

(f)在公开相关要求方面是否有充分的问责制和透明度；

(g)欧洲证券与市场管理局的资源是否能保证其充分履行责任；

(h)欧洲证券与市场管理局的地点是否宜保持不变，还是应将各欧洲监管机构迁至同一地点以加强相互之间的协调。

3.对于泛欧范围内的机构或基础设施的直接监管问题，考虑到市场的发展，欧盟委员会应起草一份关于是否应在此领域赋予欧洲证券与市场管理局更多监管责任的年度报告。

4.报告及随附的任何提议（如有）均应转发给欧洲议会和欧盟理事会。

第82条　生效

本条例应于《欧盟公报》公布，公布的次日生效。

本条例应于2011年1月1日起适用，但第76条以及第77条第1款和第2款应从本条例生效之日起适用。

欧洲证券与市场管理局应于2011年1月1日成立。

本条例所有内容对各成员国均具有约束力，并可直接适用于所有成员国。

2010年11月24日于斯特拉斯堡通过。

欧洲议会议长　　　　　　　　欧盟理事会主席

J.布泽克　　　　　　　　　　O.查斯特尔

REGULATIONS COUNCIL REGULATION (EU) NO 1096/2010

欧盟理事会
第1096/2010号(欧盟)条例

REGULATIONS
COUNCIL REGULATION (EU) NO 1096/2010

of 17 November 2010 conferring specific tasks upon the European Central Bank concerning the functioning of the European Systemic Risk Board

THE COUNCIL OF THE EUROPEANUNION,

Having regard to the Treaty on the Functioning of the European Union, and in particular Article 127(6) thereof,

Having regard to the proposal from the European Commission,

Having regard to the opinion of the European Parliament [1],

Having regard to the opinion of the European Central Bank [2],

Whereas:

(1) The financial crisis has revealed important shortcomings in financial supervision, which has failed to anticipate adverse macro-prudential developments and prevent the accumulation of excessive risks in the financial sector, and has in particular highlighted the weaknesses of the existing macro-prudential oversight.

(2) In November 2008, the Commission mandated a High Level Group chaired by Mr Jacques de Larosière (the de Larosière Group) to make recommendations on how to strengthen European supervisory arrangements with a view to better protecting the citizen and rebuilding trust in the financial system.

(3) In its final report presented on 25 February 2009, the de Larosière Group recommended, among other things, the establishment of a body at the level of the Union charged with overseeing risk in the financial system as a whole.

1 Opinion of 22 September 2010 (not yet published in the Official Journal).

2 OJ C 270, 11.11.2009, p. 1.

欧盟理事会
第1096/2010号(欧盟)条例

(本条例于2010年11月17日通过,赋予欧洲中央银行
有关欧洲系统性风险委员会运行方面的特定职责)

欧盟理事会,

根据《欧盟运行条约》,特别是其中的第127条第6款,

根据欧盟委员会的提议,

根据欧洲议会的意见[1],

根据欧洲中央银行的意见[2],

鉴于下列情形,通过本指令:

(1)金融危机暴露出金融监管的若干重要缺陷——既无法预见不利的宏观审慎变化,也无法避免金融行业内过度风险的累积,尤其突出了现有宏观审慎监控方面的弱点。

(2)2008年11月,欧洲理事会委托一个由雅克·德·拉罗西埃先生领导的高级工作组德·拉罗西埃小组,就如何加强欧洲监管安排以更好地保护公众利益并重建公众对金融系统的信任提出建议。

(3)在其于2009年2月25日提交的最终报告中,德·拉罗西埃小组特别建议设立一个欧盟层级的机构,负责监管整体金融系统的风险。

1 2010年9月22日的意见(未曾在《欧盟公报》上公开)。

2 2009年11月11日《欧盟公报》C 270,第1页。

(4) In its Communication of 4 March 2009 entitled 'Driving European Recovery', the Commission welcomed and broadly supported the recommendations of the de Larosière Group. At its meeting of 19 and 20 March 2009, the European Council agreed on the need to improve the regulation and supervision of financial institutions within the Union and to use the de Larosière Group's report as a basis for action.

(5) In its Communication of 27 May 2009 entitled 'European Financial Supervision', the Commission set out a series of reforms to the current arrangements for safeguarding financial stability at the level of theUnion, notably including the creation of a European Systemic Risk Board (ESRB) responsible for macro-prudential oversight. The Council, on 9 June 2009, and the European Council, at its meeting of 18 and 19 June 2009, supported the view of the Commission and welcomed the Commission's intention to bring forward legislative proposals so that the new frame work could be fully established.

(6) Regulation (EU) No 1092/2010 of the European Parliament and of the Council [1] established macro-prudential oversight of the financial system at the level of the Union and a European Systemic Risk Board (ESRB).

(7) Given its expertise on macro-prudential issues, the European Central Bank (ECB) can make a significant contribution to the effective macro-prudential oversight of the Union's financial system.

(8) The Secretariat of the ESRB (the Secretariat) should be ensured by the ECB and, to this effect, the ECB should provide sufficient human and financial resources. The staff of the Secretariat should therefore be subject to the Conditions of Employment for Staff of the ECB. In particular, according to the preamble of the Decision of the ECB of 9 June 1998 on the adoption of the Conditions of Emploment for Staff of the European Central Bank as amended on 31 March 1999 (ECB/1998/4) [2], the staff of the ECB should be recruited on the broadest possible geographical basis from among nationals of the Member States.

(9) On 9 June 2009, the Council concluded that the ECB should provide analytical, statistical, administrative and logistical support to the ESRB. As it is the task of the ESRB to cover all aspects and areas of financial stability, the ECB should involve national central banks and supervisors to provide their specific expertise. The option to confer specific tasks concerning policies relating to prudential super vision upon the ECB provided for by the Treaty on the Functioning of the European Union should therefore be exercised, by conferring on the ECB the task of ensuring the Secretariat to the ESRB.

(10) The ECB should be entrusted with the task of providing statistical support to

1 See page 1 of this Official Journal.

2 OJ L 125, 19.5.1999, p. 32.

（4）在2009年3月4日名为《推动欧洲复苏》的通报中，欧盟委员会欣然接受并支持德·拉罗西埃小组提出的建议。欧盟理事会在2009年3月19日和20日的会议中同意，有必要改善对欧盟金融机构的规制和监管并以德·拉罗西埃小组的报告作为行动的基础。

（5）在2009年5月27日名为《欧洲金融监管》的通报中，欧盟委员会建议对目前欧盟层级保证金融稳定的安排进行一系列的改革，尤其包括设立一个负责宏观审慎监控的欧洲系统性风险委员会（ESRB）。欧盟理事会和欧洲理事会分别在2009年6月9日以及2009年6月18日和19日的会议中，对欧盟委员会的建议表示支持，并欢迎其提出立法提案以便新框架得以全面建立。

（6）欧洲议会与欧盟理事会第1092/2010号（欧盟）条例[1]确立了在欧盟层面对金融系统进行宏观审慎监控，并设立了欧洲系统性风险委员会（ESRB）。

（7）凭借其在宏观审慎问题上的专业知识，欧洲中央银行（ECB）能为欧盟金融系统的有效宏观审慎监控作出重大的贡献。

（8）欧洲中央银行应确保欧洲系统性风险委员会秘书处（以下简称秘书处）的运行，为此，欧洲中央银行应提供足够的人力和财力资源。秘书处的工作人员应适用《欧洲中央银行工作人员聘用条件》。特别是，根据《欧洲中央银行关于通过1999年3月31日修正的〈欧洲中央银行工作人员聘用条件〉的第ECB/1998/4号决定》[2]（1998年6月9日）的前言，应尽可能广泛地从成员国的公民中招聘欧洲中央银行的工作人员。

（9）2009年6月9日，欧盟理事会认定，欧洲中央银行应向欧洲系统性风险委员会提供分析、统计、行政和后勤支持。由于欧洲系统性风险委员会的职责涉及金融稳定的诸多方面，欧洲中央银行应要求各成员国中央银行和监管机构提供其特殊专长。因此，在选择根据《欧盟运行条约》赋予欧洲中央银行关于审慎监管政策的特定职责的同时，也应赋予欧洲中央银行承担欧洲系统性风险委员会秘书处运行的职责。

（10）欧洲中央银行应被委以向欧洲系统性风险委员会提供统计支持的职责。因

1 请见本《欧盟公报》，第1页。

2 1999年5月19日《欧盟公报》L 125，第32页。

the ESRB. The collection and processing of information as set out in this Regulation and as necessary for the performance of the tasks of the ESRB should therefore fall under Article 5 of the Statute of the European System of Central Banks and of the ECB, and under Council Regulation (EC) No 2533/98 of 23 November 1998 concerning the collection of statistical information by the European Central Bank [1]. Accordingly, confidential statistical information collected by the ECB or the European System of Central Banks should be shared with the ESRB. In addition, this Regulation should be without prejudice to Regulation (EC) No 223/2009 of the European Parliament and of the Council of 11 March 2009 on European statistics [2].

(11) The Secretariat should prepare the meetings of the ESRB and support the work of the General Board, the Steering Committee, the Advisory Technical Committee and the Advisory Scientific Committee of the ESRB. On behalf of the ESRB, the Secretariat should collect all information necessary for the achievement of the tasks of the ESRB.

HAS ADOPTED THIS REGULATION:

Article 1 Membership

The President and Vice-President of the European Central Bank (ECB) shall be Members of the General Board of the European Systemic Risk Board (ESRB) as set up by Regulation (EU) No 1092/2010.

Article 2 Support of the ESRB

The ECB shall ensure a Secretariat, and thereby provide analytical, statistical, logistical and administrative support to the ESRB. The mission of the Secretariat as defined in Article 4(4) of Regulation (EU) No 1092/2010, shall include in particular:

(a) the preparation of the ESRB meetings;

(b) in accordance with Article 5 of the Statute of the European System of Central Banks and the European Central Bank and Article 5 of this Regulation, the collection and processing of information, including statistical information, on behalf and for the benefit of the fulfilment of the tasks of the ESRB;

(c) the preparation of the analyses necessary to carry out the tasks of the ESRB, drawing on technical advice from national central banks and supervisors;

(d) the support to the ESRB in its international cooperation at administrative level with other relevant bodies on macro-prudential issues;

(e) the support to the work of the General Board, the Steering Committee, the Advisory Technical Committee and the Advisory Scientific Committee.

Article 3 Organisation of the Secretariat

1. The ECB shall provide sufficient human and financial resources for the fulfilment

1 OJ L 318, 27.11.1998, p. 8.

2 OJ L 87, 31.3.2009, p. 164.

此,本条例规定的为履行欧洲系统性风险委员会职责所必要的信息收集和处理工作,应受《欧洲中央银行体系及欧洲中央银行章程》第5条以及《欧盟理事会关于欧洲中央银行统计信息收集工作的第2533/98号(欧共体)条例》[1](1998年11月23日)管辖。因此,欧洲中央银行或欧洲中央银行体系所收集到的保密统计信息应与欧洲系统性风险委员会共享。此外,本条例不得违背《欧洲议会与欧盟理事会关于欧洲统计的第223/2009号(欧共体)条例》(2009年3月11日)[2]。

(11)秘书处应筹备欧洲系统性风险委员会的会议,并支持欧洲系统性风险委员会总委员会、指导委员会、技术咨询委员会以及科学咨询委员会的工作。秘书处应代表欧洲系统性风险委员会收集为完成后者职责所必要的一切信息。

兹通过本指令如下:

第1条 会员资格

欧洲中央银行(ECB)的行长和副行长应为依据第1092/2010号(欧盟)条例设立的欧洲系统性风险委员会(ESRB)的总委员会委员。

第2条 对欧洲系统性风险委员会的支持

欧洲中央银行应确保欧洲系统性风险委员会秘书处的运行,为此应向欧洲系统性风险委员会提供分析、统计、后勤和行政的支持。第1092/2010号(欧盟)条例第4条第4款所定义的秘书处的使命主要包括:

(a)筹备欧洲系统性风险委员会的会议;

(b)根据《欧洲中央银行体系及欧洲中央银行章程》第5条以及本条例第5条的规定,代表欧洲系统性风险委员会并为完成后者职责而收集和处理信息,其中包括统计信息;

(c)根据成员国中央银行和监管机构的技术性建议,向欧洲系统性风险委员会提供履行其职责所必要的分析;

(d)在管理层面上为欧洲系统性风险委员会与其他相关机构就宏观审慎事项的国际合作提供支持;

(e)支持总委员会、指导委员会、技术咨询委员会以及科学咨询委员会的工作。

第3条 秘书处的组织结构

1.欧洲中央银行应提供足够的人力和财力,以履行其确保秘书处运行的职责。

1 1998年11月27日《欧盟公报》L 318,第8页。

2 2009年3月31日《欧盟公报》L 87,第164页。

of its task of ensuring the Secretariat.

2. The head of the Secretariat shall be appointed by the ECB, in consultation with the General Board of the ESRB.

Article 4 Management

1. The ESRB's Chair and its Steering Committee shall give directions to the head of the Secretariat on behalf of the ESRB.

2. The head of the Secretariat or his representative shall attend the meetings of the General Board, the Steering Committee, the Advisory Technical Committee and the Advisory Scientific Committee of the ESRB.

Article 5 Collection of information on behalf of the ESRB

1. The ESRB shall determine the information necessary for the purposes of the performance of its tasks, as set out in Article 3 of Regulation (EU) No 1092/2010. In view thereof, the Secretariat shall collect all the necessary information on behalf of the ESRB on a regular and ad hoc basis, in accordance with Article 15 of Regulation (EU) No 1092/2010 and subject to Article 6 of this Regulation.

2. On behalf of the ESRB, the Secretariat shall make available to the European Supervisory Authorities the information on risks necessary for the performance of their tasks.

Article 6 Confidentiality of information and documents

1. Without prejudice to the application of criminal law, any confidential information received by the Secretariat while per forming its duties may not be divulged to any person or authority outside the ESRB whatsoever, except in summary or aggregate form, such that individual financial institutions cannot be identified.

2. The Secretariat shall ensure that documents are submitted to the ESRB in a manner which ensures their confidentiality.

3. The ECB shall ensure the confidentiality of the information received by the Secretariat for the performance of the tasks of the ECB under this Regulation. The ECB shall establish internal mechanisms and adopt internal rules to ensure the protection of information collected by the Secretariat on behalf of the ESRB. The ECB staff shall comply with the applicable rules relating to professional secrecy.

4. Information acquired by the ECB as a result of the application of this Regulation shall only be used for the purposes mentioned in Article 2.

Article 7 Access to documents

1. The Secretariat shall ensure the application of Decision of the European Central Bank of 4 March 2004 on public access to European Central Bank documents (ECB/2004/3) [1].

1 OJ L 80, 18.3.2004, p. 42.

2.秘书长应由欧洲中央银行在与欧洲系统性风险委员会总委员会磋商后任命。

第4条 管理

1.欧洲系统性风险委员会主席及其指导委员会应代表欧洲系统性风险委员会对秘书长作出指导。

2.秘书长或其代表应参加欧洲系统性风险委员会总委员会、指导委员会、技术咨询委员会以及科学咨询委员会的会议。

第5条 代表欧洲系统性风险委员会收集信息

1.欧洲系统性风险委员会应确定对履行其在第1092/2010号（欧盟）条例第3条中的职责所必要的信息。为此，秘书处应依照第1092/2010号（欧盟）条例第15条的规定并在满足本条例第6条的规定的前提下，代表欧洲系统性风险委员会定期和专门收集所有必需的信息。

2.秘书处应代表欧洲系统性风险委员会向欧洲监管机构提供履行其职责所必要的与风险有关的信息。

第6条 信息和文件的保密

1.在不影响刑法适用的情况下，秘书处在履行其职责时收到的任何保密信息均不得泄露给任何人或除欧洲系统性风险委员会外的任何部门，但是，以无法识别具体金融机构的摘要或汇总的形式披露的除外。

2.秘书处应确保能以保证文件保密性的方式向欧洲系统性风险委员会呈报文件。

3.欧洲中央银行应确保对秘书处为履行欧洲中央银行在本条例中的职责而收到的信息予以保密。欧洲中央银行应建立内部机制并通过内部规定，以确保对秘书处代表欧洲系统性风险委员会收集的信息进行保护。欧洲中央银行的工作人员应遵守与职业保密有关的适用规则。

4.欧洲中央银行由于本条例适用而获得的信息应仅用于本条例第2条所述之目的。

第7条 查阅文件

1.秘书处应确保适用《欧洲中央银行关于公众查阅欧洲中央银行文件的第ECB/2004/3号决定》[1]（2004年3月4日）。

1 2004年3月18日《欧盟公报》L 80，第42页。

2. The practical arrangements for the application of Decision ECB/2004/3 to documents relating to the ESRB, shall be adopted by 17 June 2011.

Article 8 Review

By 17 December 2013, the Council shall examine this Regulation, on the basis of a report from the Commission. After having received opinions from the ECB and from the European Supervisory Authorities, it shall determine whether this Regulation should be reviewed.

Article 9 Entry into force

This Regulation shall enter into force on the day following its publication in the Official Journal of the European Union.

It shall apply from 16 December 2010.

This Regulation shall be binding in its entirety and directly applicable in all Member States.

Done at Brussels, 17 November 2010.

For the Council
The President
D. REYNDERS

2.2001年6月17日前应采取对欧洲系统性风险委员会相关文件适用第ECB/2004/3号决定的具体安排。

第8条 审评

欧盟理事会应在2013年12月17日前，在欧盟委员会报告的基础上对本条例进行审查。收到欧洲中央银行和欧洲监管机构的意见后，欧盟理事会应决定是否应对本条例进行审评。

第9条 生效

本条例应于《欧盟公报》公布，公布的次日生效。

本条例于2010年12月16日起适用。

本条例所有内容对各成员国均具有约束力，并可直接适用于所有成员国。

2010年11月17日于布鲁塞尔通过。

欧盟理事会主席

D.雷恩德斯

Glossary 词汇表

Advanced measurement approach	高级计量法
Bank for International Settlements	国际清算银行
Banking stakeholder group	银行业利益相关者小组
Basic instruments	基本法律文件
Board of Appeal	行政复议委员会
Board of Supervisors	监管机构理事会
Branches	分支机构
Calendar year	日历年度
Capital adequacy	资本充足性
Central competent administrative authority	中央行政主管部门
Commission	欧盟委员会
Commission communication on implementing the framework for financial markets: Action Plan	《落实金融市场框架:行动计划》
Commission Regulation (EC, Euratom) No 2343/2002 of 19 November 2002 on the framework Financial Regulation for the bodies referred to in Article 185 of Council Regulation (EC, Euratom) No 1605/2002 on the Financial Regulation applicable to the general budget of the European Communities	《欧盟委员会关于〈欧盟理事会关于适用于欧洲共同体总预算的财务条例的第1605/2002号(欧共体和欧洲原子能共同体)条例〉第185条所指机构的框架性〈财务条例〉的第2343/2002号(欧共体和欧洲原子能共同体)条例》(2002年11月19日)
Commissioner	委员
Committee of European Banking Supervisors (CEBS)	欧洲银行业监管机构委员会
Committee of European Insurance and Occupational Pensions Supervisors	欧洲保险与职业养老金监管机构委员会
Committee of European Securities Regulators	欧洲证券监管机构委员会
Conditions of Employment of Other Servants of the European Communities	《欧洲共同体其他人员的聘用条件》
Consolidating supervisor	并表监管机构
Convergence	趋同
Cooperative bank	合作银行
Costs and benefits	成本和收益
Council (of The European Union)	欧盟理事会

续表

Council Directive 64/225/EEC of 25 February 1964 on the abolition of restrictions on freedom of establishment and freedom to provide services in respect of reinsurance and retrocession	《欧洲经济共同体理事会关于废止新设业务限制及提供再保险和转分保限制的第 64/225/EEC 号指令》(1964 年 2 月 25 日)
Council Directive 73/239/EEC of 24 July 1973 on the coordination of laws, regulations and administrative provisions relating to the taking up and pursuit of the business of direct insurance other than life assurance	《欧洲经济共同体理事会协调关于开办和经营直接保险(寿险除外)业务的法律、法规和规章的第 73/239/EEC 号指令》(1973 年 7 月 24 日)
Council Directive 73/240/EEC of 24 July 1973 abolishing restrictions on freedom of establishment in the business of direct insurance other than life assurance	《欧洲经济共同体理事会关于废止新设直接保险(寿险除外)业务限制的第 73/240/EEC 号指令》(1973 年 7 月 24 日)
Council Directive 76/580/EEC of 29 June 1976 amending Directive 73/239/EEC on the coordination of laws, regulations and administrative provisions relating to the taking up and pursuit of the business of direct insurance other than life assurance	《欧洲经济共同体理事会修正〈协调关于开办和经营直接保险(寿险除外)业务的法律、法规和规章的第 73/239/EEC 号指令〉的第 76/580/EEC 号指令》(1976 年 6 月 29 日)
Council Directive 78/473/EEC of 30 May 1978 on the coordination of laws, regulations and administrative provisions relating to Community co-insurance	《欧洲经济共同体理事会协调关于欧共体共同保险的法律、法规和规章的第 78/473/EEC 号指令》(1978 年 5 月 30 日)
Council Directive 84/641/EEC of 10 December 1984 amending, particularly as regards tourist assistance, the First Council Directive 73/239/EEC on the coordination of laws, regulations and administrative provisions relating to the taking-up and pursuit of the business of direct insurance other than life assurance	《欧洲经济共同体理事会特别针对旅游协助修正〈欧洲经济共同体理事会协调关于开办和经营直接保险(寿险除外)业务的法律、法规和规章的 73/239/EEC 第一号指令〉的第 84/641/EEC 号指令》(1984 年 12 月 10 日)
Council Directive 87/344/EEC of 22 June 1987 on the coordination of laws, regulations and administrative provisions relating to legal expenses insurance	《欧洲经济共同体理事会协调关于诉讼费用保险的法律、法规和规章的第 87/344/EEC 号指令》(1987 年 6 月 22 日)
Council Directive 88/357/EEC of 22 June 1988 on the coordination of laws, regulations and administrative provisions relating to direct insurance other than life assurance and laying down provisions to facilitate the effective exercise of freedom to provide services	《欧洲经济共同体理事会协调关于直接保险(寿险除外)的法律、法规和规章以及制定相关条款以便有效行使提供服务自由权的第 88/357/EEC 号指令》(1988 年 6 月 22 日)

续表

Council Directive 92/49/EEC of 18 June 1992 on the coordination of laws, regulations and administrative provisions relating to direct insurance other than life assurance (third non-life insurance Directive)	《欧洲经济共同体理事会协调关于直接保险(寿险除外)的法律、法规和规章的第 92/49/EEC 号指令》(1992 年 6 月 18 日)
Council Regulation (EC Euratom) No 1605/2002 of 25 June 2002 on the Financial Regulation applicable to the general budget of the European Communities	《欧盟理事会关于适用于欧洲共同体总预算的财务条例的第 1605/2002 号(欧共体和欧洲原子能共同体)条例》(2002 年 6 月 25 日)
Council Regulation (EC) No 2533/98 of 23 November 1998 concerning the collection of statistical information by the European Central Bank	《欧盟理事会关于欧洲中央银行统计信息收集工作的第 2533/98 号(欧共体)条例》(1998 年 11 月 23 日)
Court of Auditors	欧盟审计院
De Larosière Report	《德・拉罗西埃报告》
Decision No 716/2009/EC of the European Parliament and of the Council of 16 September 2009 establishing a Community programme to support specific activities in the field of financial services, financial reporting and auditing	《欧洲议会与欧盟理事会设立一项支持金融服务领域特定活动、财务报告和审计的欧共体计划的第 716/2009/EC 号决定》(2009 年 9 月 16 日)
Declaration (No 39) on Article 290 of the Treaty on the Functioning of the European Union (TFEU)	《关于〈欧洲联盟运行条约〉(TFEU)第 290 条的声明(第 39 号)》
Delegate	受托部门
Delegated acts	授权立法
Delegating authority	委托部门
Directive 2001/17/EC of the European Parliament and of the Council of 19 March 2001 on the reorganisation and winding-up of insurance undertakings	《欧洲议会与欧盟理事会关于保险公司的重组和停业清理的第 2001/17/EC 号指令》(2001 年 3 月 19 日)
Directive 2001/34/EC of the European Parliament and of the Council of 28 May 2001 on the admission of securities to official stock exchange listing and on information to be published on those securities	《欧洲议会与欧盟理事会关于证券获准在证券交易所正式上市以及应公布的与该等证券有关的信息的第 2001/34/EC 号指令》(2001 年 5 月 28 日)
Directive 2002/47/EC of the European Parliament and of the Council of 6 June 2002 on financial collateral arrangements	《欧洲议会与欧盟理事会关于金融抵押品安排的第 2002/47/EC 号指令》(2002 年 6 月 6 日)
Directive 2002/65/EC of the European Parliament and of the Council of 23 September 2002 concerning the distance marketing of consumer financial services	《欧洲议会与欧盟理事会关于远程营销消费者金融服务的第 2002/65/EC 号指令》(2002 年 9 月 23 日)

续表

Directive 2002/83/EC of the European Parliament and of the Council of 5 November 2002 concerning life assurance	《欧洲议会与欧盟理事会关于寿险的第 2002/83/EC 号指令》(2002 年 11 月 5 日)
Directive 2002/87/EC of the European Parliament and of the Council of 16 December 2002 on the supplementary supervision of credit institutions, insurance undertakings and investment firms in a financial conglomerate	《欧洲议会与欧盟理事会关于对金融集团下属信贷机构、保险公司以及投资公司实施补充监管的第 2002/87/EC 号指令》(2002 年 12 月 16 日)
Directive 2002/92/EC of the European Parliament and of the Council of 9 December 2002 on insurance mediation	《欧洲议会与欧盟理事会关于保险调解的第 2002/92/EC 号指令》(2002 年 12 月 9 日)
Directive 2003/41/EC of the European Parliament and of the Council of 3 June 2003 on the activities and supervision of institutions for occupational retirement provision	《欧洲议会与欧盟理事会关于职业退休金管理机构的活动和监管的第 2003/41/EC 号指令》(2003 年 6 月 3 日)
Directive 2003/6/EC of the European Parliament and of the Council of 28 January 2003 on insider dealing and market manipulation (market abuse)	《欧洲议会与欧盟理事会关于内幕交易和市场操纵(市场滥用)的第 2003/6/EC 号指令》(2003 年 1 月 28 日)
Directive 2003/71/EC of the European Parliament and of the Council of 4 November 2003 on the prospectus to be published when securities are offered to the public or admitted to trading	《欧洲议会与欧盟理事会关于向公众发行证券或证券获准交易时所应公布的招募说明书的第 2003/71/EC 号指令》(2003 年 11 月 4 日)
Directive 2004/109/EC of the European Parliament and of the Council of 15 December 2004 on the harmonisation of transparency requirements in relation to information about issuers whose securities are admitted to trading on a regulated market	《欧洲议会与欧盟理事会协调关于证券获准在受监管市场交易的发行人的信息透明度要求的第 2004/109/EC 号指令》(2004 年 12 月 15 日)
Directive 2004/39/EC of the European Parliament and of the Council of 21 April 2004 on markets in financial instruments	《欧洲议会与欧盟理事会关于金融工具市场的第 2004/39/EC 号指令》(2004 年 4 月 21 日)
Directive 2005/60/EC of the European Parliament and of the Council of 26 October 2005 on the prevention of the use of the financial system for the purpose of money laundering and terrorist financing	《欧洲议会与欧盟理事会关于防范利用金融系统从事洗钱和恐怖分子融资的第 2005/60/EC 号指令》(2005 年 10 月 26 日)
Directive 2005/68/EC of the European Parliament and of the Council of 16 November 2005 on reinsurance	《欧洲议会与欧盟理事会关于再保险的第 2005/68/EC 号指令》(2005 年 11 月 16 日)
Directive 2006/48/EC of the European Parliament and of the Council of 14 June 2006 relating to the taking up and pursuit of the business of credit institutions	《欧洲议会与欧盟理事会关于开办和经营信贷机构业务的第 2006/48/EC 号指令》(2006 年 6 月 14 日)

续表

Directive 2006/49/EC of the European Parliament and of the Council of 14 June 2006 on the capital adequacy of investment firms and credit institutions	《欧洲议会与欧盟理事会关于投资公司和信贷机构资本充足性的第 2006/49/EC 号指令》(2006 年 6 月 14 日)
Directive 2007/64/EC of the European Parliament and of the Council of 13 November 2007 on payment services in the internal market	《欧洲议会与欧盟理事会关于内部市场支付服务的第 2007/64/EC 号指令》(2007 年 11 月 13 日)
Directive 2009/110/EC of the European Parliament and of the Council of 16 September 2009 on the taking up, pursuit and prudential supervision of the business of electronic money institutions	《欧洲议会与欧盟理事会关于开办、经营和审慎监管电子货币机构业务的第 2009/110/EC 号指令》(2009 年 9 月 16 日)
Directive 2009/138/EC of the European Parliament and of the Council of 25 November 2009 on the taking-up and pursuit of the business of Insurance and Reinsurance (Solvency II)	《欧洲议会与欧盟理事会关于开办和经营保险与再保险业务的第 2009/138/EC 号指令》(保险偿付能力标准 II)(2009 年 11 月 25 日)
Directive 2009/65/EC of the European Parliament and of the Council of 13 July 2009 on the coordination of laws, regulations and administrative provisions relating to undertakings for collective investment in transferable securities (UCITS)	《欧洲议会与欧盟理事会协调关于可转让证券集合投资计划(UCITS)的法律、法规和规章的第 2009/65/EC 号指令》(2009 年 7 月 13 日)
Directive 94/19/EC of the European Parliament and of the Council of 30 May 1994 on deposit-guarantee schemes	《欧洲议会与欧盟理事会关于存款担保计划的第 94/19/EC 号指令》(1994 年 5 月 30 日)
Directive 95/46/EC of the European Parliament and of the Council of 24 October 1995 on the protection of individuals with regard to the processing of personal data and on the free movement of such data	《欧洲议会与欧盟理事会关于处理个人资料时对个人的保护以及该等资料自由流动的第 95/46/EC 号指令》(1995 年 10 月 24 日)
Directive 97/9/EC of the European Parliament and of the Council of 3 March 1997 on investor-compensation schemes	《欧洲议会与欧盟理事会关于投资者补偿计划的第 97/9/EC 号指令》(1997 年 3 月 3 日)
Directive 98/26/EC of the European Parliament and of the Council of 19 May 1998 on settlement finality in payment and securities settlement systems	《欧洲议会与欧盟理事会关于支付系统和证券结算系统的结算终结性的第 98/26/EC 号指令》(1998 年 5 月 19 日)
Directive 98/78/EC of the European Parliament and of the Council of 27 October 1998 on the supplementary supervision of insurance undertakings in an insurance group	《欧洲议会与欧盟理事会关于对保险集团下属保险公司实施补充监管的第 98/78/EC 号指令》(1998 年 10 月 27 日)
Directive of the European Parliament and of the Council on the taking-up and pursuit of the business of Insurance and Reinsurance (Solvency II)	《欧洲议会与欧盟理事会关于开办和经营保险与再保险业务的指令》(保险偿付能力标准 II)

续表

Discharge procedure	预算审批程序
Driving European Recovery	《推动欧洲复苏》
Durable medium	耐久媒介
E-money institutions	电子货币机构
Equivalence decisions	等效性决定
European Systemic Risk Board (ESRB)	欧洲系统性风险委员会
European Banking Authority	欧洲银行业管理局
European Banking Committee	欧洲银行业委员会
European Central Bank	欧洲中央银行
European Council	欧洲理事会
European Insurance and Occupational Pensions Authority	欧洲保险与职业养老金管理局
European Parliament	欧洲议会
European Securities and Markets Authority (ESMA)	欧洲证券与市场管理局
European statistical system and the european system of central banks	欧洲统计系统和欧洲中央银行体系
European Supervisory Authority (ESA)	欧洲监管机构
European System of Financial Supervision (ESFS)	欧洲金融监管体系
European System of Financial Supervisors (ESFS)	欧洲金融监管机构体系
European Systemic Risk Council	欧洲系统性风险理事会
Executive Director	执行主任
Extra-judicial mechanisms	司法外机制
Final Act of the Intergovernmental Conference	政府间会议《最后决议》
Financial Conglomerates Committee	金融集团委员会
Financial inclusion	金融融入
Financial infrastructure	金融基础设施
Financial intermediaries	金融中介机构
Financial services policy (2005 to 2010) White Paper	《2005 年至 2010 年金融服务政策白皮书》
Financial Stability Board	金融稳定委员会
Financial year	会计年度
Four-level 'lamfalussy' approach	"莱姆法路西"四级立法程序

续表

Fund of funds	组合基金
Guidance to Assess the Systemic Importance of Financial Institutions, Markets and Instruments: Initial Considerations	《金融机构、市场和工具之系统性重要性的评估指引:初步意见》
Head of the Secretariat	秘书长
Headquarters Agreement	《总部协议》
Hedge funds	对冲基金
High-level group	高级工作组
High-level representative	高级别代表
Implementing acts	实施性立法
Implementing technical standards	实施性技术标准
Interinstitutional Agreement between the European Parliament, the Council and the Commission of 17 May 2006 on budgetary discipline and sound financial management	《欧洲议会、欧盟理事会和欧盟委员会关于预算纪律和健全的财务管理的机构间协议》(2006 年 5 月 17 日)
Interinstitutional Agreement of 25 May 1999 between the European Parliament, the Council of the European Union and the Commission of the European Communities concerning internal investigations by the European Anti-Fraud Office (OLAF)	欧洲议会、欧盟理事会以及欧盟委员会于 1999 年 5 月 25 日签订的《关于欧洲反欺诈办公室(OLAF)内部调查的机构间协议》
Internal model for market risk approach	市场风险内部模型法
Internal Ratings Based approach	内部评级法
International Monetary Fund	国际货币基金组织
Joint Committee of the European Supervisory Authorities	欧洲监管机构联合委员会
Lamfalussy follow-up: future structure of supervision	《莱姆法路西的后续行动:未来监管结构》
Legislative act	框架立法
Mixed financial holding company	混合金融控股公司
Money laundering	洗钱
National competent authority	国家级主管部门
Non-complex financial instruments	非复杂金融工具
Occupational pension schemes	职业养老金计划
Ombudsman	申诉官
Peer reviews	同行审评

续表

President of the Economic and Financial Committee (EFC)	经济与金融委员会(EFC)的主席
Principal	本金
Principle of proportionality	比例原则
Principle of subsidiarity	辅助性原则
Qualified majority	特定多数
Recapitalisation	再注资
Recovery and resolution arrangements	恢复和清盘安排
Regulation (EC) No 1049/2001 of the European Parliament and of the Council of 30 May 2001 regarding public access to European Parliament, Council and Commission documents	《欧洲议会与欧盟理事会关于公众查阅欧洲议会、欧盟理事会和欧盟委员会文件的第1049/2001号(欧共体)条例》(2001年5月30日)
Regulation (EC) No 1073/1999 of the European Parliament and of the Council of 25 May 1999 concerning investigations conducted by the European Anti-Fraud Office (OLAF)	《欧洲议会与欧盟理事会关于欧洲反欺诈办公室(OLAF)所开展的调查的第1073/1999号(欧共体)条例》(1999年5月25日)
Regulation (EC) No 1781/2006 of the European Parliament and of the Council of 15 November 2006 on information on the payer accompanying transfers of funds	《欧洲议会与欧盟理事会关于汇款随附之付款人信息的第1781/2006号(欧共体)条例》(2006年11月15日)
Regulation (EC) No 223/2009 of the European Parliament and of the Council of 11 March 2009 on European statistics	《欧洲议会与欧盟理事会关于欧洲统计的第223/2009号(欧共体)条例》(2009年3月11日)
Regulation (EC) No 45/2001 of the European Parliament and of the Council of 18 December 2000 on the protection of individuals with regard to the processing of personal data by the Community institutions and bodies and on the free movement of such data	《欧洲议会与欧盟理事会关于欧共体机构和单位处理个人资料时对个人的保护以及该等资料自由流动的第45/2001号(欧共体)条例》(2000年12月18日)
Regulation (EU) No 1092/2010 of the European Parliament and of the Council of 24 November 2010 on European Union macro-prudential oversight of the financial system and establishing a European Systemic Risk Board	《欧洲议会与欧盟理事会关于欧盟对金融系统的宏观审慎监控以及设立欧洲系统性风险委员会的第1092/2010号(欧盟)条例》(2010年11月24日)
Regulation (EU) No 1093/2010 of the European Parliament and of the Council of 24 November 2010 establishing a European Supervisory Authority (European Banking Authority)	《欧洲议会与欧盟理事会设立欧洲监管机构欧洲银行业管理局的第1093/2010号(欧盟)条例》(2010年11月24日)

续表

Regulation (EU) No 1094/2010 of the European Parliament and of the Council of 24 November 2010 establishing a European Supervisory Authority (European Insurance and Occupational Pensions Authority)	《欧洲议会与欧盟理事会设立欧洲监管机构欧洲保险与职业养老金管理局的第 1094/2010 号(欧盟)条例》(2010 年 11 月 24 日)
Regulation (EU) No 1095/2010 of the European Parliament and of the Council of 24 November 2010 establishing a European Supervisory Authority (European Securities and Markets Authority)	《欧洲议会与欧盟理事会设立欧洲监管机构欧洲证券与市场管理局的第 1095/2010 号(欧盟)条例》(2010 年 11 月 24 日)
Regulation of the European Parliament and of the Council on Credit Rating Agencies	《欧洲议会与欧盟理事会关于信用评级机构的条例》
Regulatory arbitrage	监管套利
Regulatory technical standards	监管性技术标准
Resilience	抗冲击能力
Retail users	零售用户
Risk diversification	风险分散
Savers	储蓄者
Savings bank	储蓄银行
Secondment schemes	人员借调计划
Settlement finality	结算终结性
Short settlement cycle	短结算周期
Single rulebook	单一规则手册
Small and medium-sized enterprises	中小企业
Staff Regulations of Officials	《欧洲共同体官员的人事条例》
Stress tests	压力测试
Sub-Committee	分委员会
Sunset clause	日落条款
Supervisory college	监管团
Suspension or removal	停牌或摘牌

续表

Technical provisions	技术准备金
Tied agents	固定代理人
Treaty Establishing the European Community (EC Treaty)	《欧洲共同体条约》(《欧共体条约》)
Treaty of Lisbon	《里斯本条约》
Treaty on European Union	《欧洲联盟条约》
Treaty on the Functioning of the European Union (TFEU)	《欧洲联盟运行条约》

Postscript

China's capital market was established and has developed on the basis of the experience of major foreign capital markets. As a result China constantly is faced with issues for which it needs to acquire knowledge of, learn from and refer to examples set by foreign capital market systems. However, the current Chinese translations of foreign securities-and futures-related legislations are not sufficiently systematic, professional, authoritative and are often inaccurate. The acquisition of a comprehensive and precise knowledge of the operating systems and regulatory rules of major foreign capital markets is essential for China to benefit from the experience developed and lessons drawn by these markets and thus is objectively necessary for China to further improve the Chinese capital market system construction, promote a stable development of said system and enhance the participation of Chinese market entities in international competition. For the aforementioned purposes, the China Securities Regulatory Commission (CSRC) initiated the project to translate the most important foreign capital market legislations published as the Digest of Legislation Related to Foreign Capital Markets (hereinafter referred to as the "Digest"). The Shenzhen Stock Exchange (SZSE) has taken charge of the translation project of laws and regulations governing the capital markets in the European Union.

To facilitate the implementation of the project, at the SZSE we have established a mechanism in accordance with the general standards required by the CSRC, which consisted of entrusting the translation to a translation team through a selection process and the translation review to relevant experts to ensure the quality of the translation. One the one hand, the translation team was selected based on its competences in legal translation and the quality of its trial translation. On the other hand, the translation draft was reviewed and validated by individuals from relevant units and departments of the CSRC and prestigious universities deemed to be experts in the concerned foreign languages and the Chinese language, well versed in Chinese and relevant foreign laws and having an in-depth knowledge of both Chinese and foreign capital markets. Those experts whose work experience and educational background are the most relevant to the subject matters dealt with in specific sections of the translation draft were designated to revise the same. The translation draft underwent multiple rounds of revision and random quality check and was finalized after adequate communications with the translators.

后　记

中国资本市场是在学习、借鉴境外主要资本市场经验的基础上建立并发展起来的。在此过程中,仍不断遇到需要了解、借鉴、参考境外市场制度的问题。但是,现有的境外证券期货法律中文译本,存在系统性、专业性、权威性、准确性不足等问题。全面、准确掌握境外主要资本市场运行制度、监管规则,是科学借鉴成熟市场经验教训的必要基础,是进一步完善市场制度建设、推进市场稳定发展、推动市场主体参与国际竞争的客观要求。为此,中国证监会启动了打造介绍境外市场法律制度权威平台的项目,即组织翻译主要资本市场重要法律规则,并将翻译成果编辑成《境外资本市场重要法律文献译丛》(以下简称《译丛》)公开出版发行。在本次项目上,深圳证券交易所承担了欧盟证券市场重要法律文献翻译出版的有关工作。

为了做好此项工作,我们根据中国证监会的统一要求,建立了"择优确定翻译人员、专家评审保证翻译质量"的工作机制。一方面,以法律文献翻译实力和试译稿质量为标准,择优选定翻译单位;另一方面,从证监会系统相关单位、部门和知名高校院所等推荐的"三通"专家(即精通中外语言、精通中外法律、精通中外资本市场)中,抽选工作学习经历与具体项目最相关的专家对翻译稿进行多轮审校以及质量抽检,并在与翻译人员进行充分沟通的基础上定稿。

As the Laws on Reforms to the Supervisory Structure of the Financial Sector within the European Union, as part of the Digest, is about to come to the press, as the undertaker for the translation and publication of the book, we would like to express our earnest and profound gratitude to the many organizations and individuals as follows. First of all, we would like to thank the CSRC's Department of Legal Affairs and the staff members involved in this project for their great contribution to the wide-ranging and sophisticated overall planning and guidance for the translation and publication of this book. The very first volume of the Digest, *The Markets in Financial Instruments Directive of the European Union* (MiFID) translated and published under their direction, has been an excellent model for us to follow. Secondly, our thanks are due to the translation team from Ubica Translation Center Beijing led by Ms. Chu Naiming and the panel of review composed of experts, including Professor Zhou Zhongfei, Associate Professor Lou Jianbo and PhD Zhang Xin; together they completed the translation and the review work conscientiously and rigorously. In particular, our thanks go to Professor Shen Sibao from the School of Law, University of International Business and Economics who, amid his heavy schedule, took up the overall and final review of the work and contributed a preface for this book. Thirdly, we owe our gratitude to relevant departments and units of the CSRC and the SZSE for the valuable support they gave to our endeavor. Finally, we thank the staff members at Law Press·China, especially Ms. Shen Xiaoying and Ms. Wang Jinjing, who contributed enormously to the editing and publication of the book. Again, the SZSE addresses its most sincere thanks to all those who are mentioned above!

Due to time constraints pertaining to the translation and editing work, errors and inaccuracies in the book will be inevitable. Your comments, criticism and corrections will be welcome.

Shenzhen Stock Exchange

July 2013

在《译丛》之《欧盟金融监管体制改革法规汇编》即将付梓之际，作为本书翻译出版的承办单位，我们有许多发自肺腑的感谢之辞：首先，感谢中国证监会法律部及其相关工作人员，作为《译丛》的组织者，他们为本书的翻译和出版做了全面且细致的统筹和指导，其组织完成的《译丛》之《欧盟金融工具市场指令》为本书树立了榜样；其次，感谢瞿乃明女士带领的北京优笔客翻译中心的翻译团队，周仲飞教授、楼建波副教授、张昕博士等评审专家，他们以认真负责的态度和严谨务实的作风，完成了翻译和审校工作，其中特别要感谢对外经济贸易大学法学院沈四宝教授在百忙之中拨冗亲自承担总译校，并为本书作序；再次，感谢中国证监会其他相关会内部门及其工作人员，深圳证券交易所相关部门及其工作人员，对我们工作的支持；最后，感谢法律出版社及其相关工作人员，尤其是沈小英女士、王津京女士，为本书的编辑、出版做了大量工作。我们在此一并致以诚挚的谢意！

由于编译时间有限，书中难免有疏漏、不足之处，欢迎读者批评指正。

深圳证券交易所
2013年7月

图书在版编目(CIP)数据

欧盟金融监管体制改革法规汇编/中国证券监督管理委员会编译. —北京:法律出版社, 2013.7
ISBN 978-7-5118-5136-9

Ⅰ.①欧… Ⅱ.①中… Ⅲ.①欧洲国家联盟—金融监管—法规—汇编 Ⅳ.①D950.228

中国版本图书馆 CIP 数据核字(2013)第 153635 号

责任编辑/王津京　　**装帧设计**/贾丹丹

出版/法律出版社　　**编辑统筹**/财税出版分社
总发行/中国法律图书有限公司　　**经销**/新华书店
印刷/北京中科印刷有限公司　　**责任印制**/吕亚莉

开本/787 毫米×1092 毫米　1/16　　**印张**/42.25　**字数**/979 千
版本/2013 年 11 月第 1 版　　**印次**/2013 年 11 月第 1 次印刷

法律出版社/北京市丰台区莲花池西里 7 号(100073)
电子邮件/info@lawpress.com.cn　　**销售热线**/010-63939792/9779
网址/www.lawpress.com.cn　　**咨询电话**/010-63939796

中国法律图书有限公司/北京市丰台区莲花池西里 7 号(100073)
全国各地中法图分、子公司电话:
第一法律书店/010-63939781/9782　**西安分公司**/029-85388843　**重庆公司**/023-65382816/2908
上海公司/021-62071010/1636　**北京分公司**/010-62534456　**深圳公司**/0755-83072995

书号:ISBN 978-7-5118-5136-9　　**定价:**223.00 元

(如有缺页或倒装,中国法律图书有限公司负责退换)